SCRIPTURE STUDY

FOR LATTER-DAY SAINT FAMILIES

THE BOOK OF MORMON

SCRIPTURE STUDY

FOR LATTER-DAY SAINT FAMILIES

THE BOOK OF MORMON

Dennis H. Leavitt and Richard O. Christensen
with
Bruce L. Andreason, Randall C. Bird, John Bushman, Dean E. Garner, Lynn H. Hatch,
Nihla W. Judd, Todd A. Knowles, and Mark D. Ogletree

DESERET
BOOK
SALT LAKE CITY, UTAH

Library of Congress Cataloging-in-Publication Data

Scripture study for Latter-day Saint families : the book of Mormon / Dennis H. Leavitt . . . [et al.].
    p.   cm.
    Includes bibliographical references and index.
    ISBN-10 1-57008-983-3 (pbk.)
    ISBN-13 978-1-57008-983-1 (pbk.)
    1. Book of Mormon—Criticism, interpretation, etc.   2. Family—Religious life.   I. Leavitt, Dennis H.   II. Title.

BX8627.S37 2003
289.3'22'071—dc21   2003009154

Printed in the United States of America
LSC Communications, Harrisonburg, VA

40 39 38 37

CONTENTS

PREFACE: THE POWER OF THE WORD

"It was the best of times, it was the worst of times, it was the age of wisdom, it was the age of foolishness, it was the epoch of belief, it was the epoch of incredulity, it was the season of Light, it was the season of Darkness, it was the spring of hope, it was the winter of despair." (Charles Dickens, *A Tale of Two Cities,* p. 9.) This classic statement in many ways captures the spirit of the latter days. We suppose that never have young Latter-day Saints been so strong and vibrant. They stand for truth. They pray consistently, and they read their scriptures like no other generation before them.

Simultaneously, however, the world is filled with awful sin. President Ezra Taft Benson said it this way: "Never has the Church had a more choice group of young people than at present, and Satan is well aware of who they are. He is doing everything in his power to thwart them in their destiny. He knows that they have been sent to earth in this crucial period of the world's history to build the Kingdom of God and establish Zion in preparation for the second coming of the Lord Jesus Christ. Yes, our youth have an awesome challenge." (*Teachings of Ezra Taft Benson,* pp. 562–63.)

Similarly, Elder Boyd K. Packer declared, "It is a great challenge to raise a family in the darkening mists of our moral environment." ("Our Moral Environment," *Ensign,* May 1992, p. 68.) With all these negative and wicked influences, where do we turn for peace and safety to help keep our children protected and pure?

Despite the challenges that face Latter-day Saint parents, and irrespective of all the worldly interventions designed to save our young people, the solution for saving our youth lies in prevention, not redemption. And what better way to insulate or shield or protect our youth from Satan's fiery darts than by studying the word of God. Remember Alma's declaration: "As the preaching of the word had a great tendency to lead the people to do that which was just—yea, it had had more powerful effect upon the minds of the people than the sword, or anything else." (Alma 31:5.)

LACK OF SCRIPTURE USE

Unfortunately, too many families do not take advantage of the blessings promised to those who rely on the scriptures. President Harold B. Lee explained, "We need to teach our people to find their answers in the scriptures. . . . But the unfortunate thing is that so many of us are not reading the scriptures. We do not know what is in them, and therefore we speculate about the things that we ought to have found in the scriptures themselves. I think that therein is one of our biggest dangers of today." ("Find the Answers in the Scriptures," *Ensign,* December 1972, p. 3.)

In Dyer and Kunz's study of effective Mormon families (*Effective Mormon Families*), they found that only 28 percent of effective Mormon families read their scriptures regularly. Elder Gene R. Cook has estimated from traveling as a General Authority that only 10 to 15 percent of Church members read the scriptures together as families. (See *Raising Up a Family to the Lord,* p. 110.)

If parents fail to use the scriptures in their families, then their children will certainly be denied some of the great blessings that come from regular and consistent scripture use. In fact, if youth do not see their parents model scripture use, they will be less likely to use the scriptures when they become parents. Such trends have tragic consequences.

THE BLESSINGS OF SCRIPTURE USE

On the other hand, those who immerse themselves in the scriptures, and who subsequently learn and apply the saving truths, reap blessings not only for this life but also for all eternity. They come to understand that the word of God leads us to Christ, and they can testify of that truth. (See Alma 31:5; Helaman 3:29.)

Those who use the scriptures regularly know the truth of Elder Boyd K. Packer's statement: "True doctrine, understood, changes attitudes and behavior. The study of the doctrines of the gospel will improve behavior quicker than the study of behavior will improve behavior." (Conference Report, October 1986, p. 20.)

Those who study the scriptures learn to hear the voice of the Lord. Elder Gene R. Cook has written, *"One of the most important things learned in reading the scriptures is how to hear the voice of the Lord to us.* Instruction comes not only from reading the words; when we prayerfully ponder them, the Lord can speak 'between the lines' to us. In other words, he can speak to us about our current problems while we are reading the content of the scriptures. In fact, the very act of reading them (it almost doesn't matter where) seems to open the door to direction from the Lord if we approach our reading humbly. The scriptures are one of the greatest tools we have for communicating with the Lord." (*Raising Up a Family to the Lord,* p. 109; emphasis added.)

Those who study the scriptures will receive power in their lives. This power is real. You can feel it; you can sense it. Those who study the scriptures will be blessed to have their prayers

answered. Elder Boyd K. Packer promised, "There is no question—personal or social or political or occupational—that need go unanswered. Therein is contained the fullness of the everlasting gospel. Therein we find principles of truth that will resolve every confusion and every problem and every dilemma that will face the human family or any individual in it." ("Teach the Scriptures," Address to Religious Educators, 14 October 1977, p. 5.)

THE RESPONSIBILITIES OF PARENTS

We know that blessings come with gospel study. However, the question still remains, "Who will teach our children?" Elder Jeffrey R. Holland taught, "A recent study conducted by the Church has forcefully confirmed statistically what we have been told again and again. That is, if loving, inspired instruction and example are not provided at home, then our related efforts for success in and around Church programs are severely limited. It is increasingly clear that we must teach the gospel to our families personally, live those teachings in our homes, or run the risk of discovering too late that a Primary teacher or priesthood adviser or seminary instructor could not do for our children what we would not do for them." ("Within the Clasp of Your Arms," *Ensign,* May 1983, p. 36.)

Too often, we substitute the time we should devote to teaching our children with other pursuits. In fact, we may well spend more hours each week preparing lessons for other children in the ward than we do for our own. As it turns out, too many of us as parents are preparing a banquet for strangers while leaving the crumbs for those whom we will be with eternally, our own children!

Remember, when Alma the Younger was in the darkest abyss of sin, it wasn't the words of his seminary teacher that came to his mind but the teachings of his father. And when Enos's soul hungered, it wasn't the teachings from a Young Men's president that came to his mind; instead, it was the spiritual teachings of his father. And although the stripling warriors did not doubt, it was not because of what they learned from a Primary teacher; it was the words of their mothers that strengthened their faith.

At a recent General Conference, General Primary President Coleen K. Menlove reminded parents, "Casual, infrequent family prayers, scripture study, and family home evenings will not be enough to fortify our children. Where will children learn the gospel and standards such as chastity, integrity, and honesty if not at home? These values can be reinforced at church, but parents are the most capable and most effective in teaching them to their children." ("A Voice of Gladness for Our Children," *Ensign,* November 2002, p. 14.)

It is not the job of institutions, including the Church, to teach and raise our children. That job belongs primarily to parents. The purpose of the Church, as Sister Menlove taught, is to reinforce what parents are teaching at home.

The purpose of this book is to help parents with that responsibility. For many families, scripture study is a challenge at best. Some parents may feel that they do not have enough time to study the gospel with their families. Others may feel that their children do not get that much out of family scripture study because they are too tired, too bored, or too irritable early in the morning or late at night. Still others may feel that there is no variety in their scripture study—every day, the same old thing, which means quickly going around the room with each person reading a verse or two. This book is full of great ideas for family scripture study. Parents will thrill as they open up chapters and discover activities, object lessons, stories, quotations, and insights that will help them lead their families through the Book of Mormon.

INTRODUCTION

The most important teaching in the Church should take place within the home. In a letter dated 11 February 1999 and addressed to "Members of the Church Throughout the World," the First Presidency extended the following counsel: "We call upon parents to devote their best efforts to the teaching and rearing of their children in gospel principles which will keep them close to the Church. The home is the basis of a righteous life, and no other instrumentality can take its place or fulfill its essential functions in carrying forward this God-given responsibility."

Family scripture study provides a great opportunity for such teaching to occur. This book has been written to enhance those teaching moments when your family is studying the scriptures together. Just imagine a parent or child excitedly reviewing *Scripture Study for Latter-day Saint Families: The Book of Mormon* and in moments having ideas to lead family scripture study.

WHAT YOU WILL FIND IN THIS BOOK

Every effort has been made to make this book simple to use, even for children. As you thumb through it, you will notice that it follows the Book of Mormon sequentially. Creative teaching ideas have been provided for every chapter in the Book of Mormon. An effort has also been made to include nearly every verse. This will help you thoroughly study this important book of scripture.

You will find many helpful and exciting tools in this book: object lessons, activities, scripture insights, prophetic quotations, discussion questions, stories, and many other learning aids designed to help your family unlock the scriptures and deepen testimonies. You will find yourselves having enjoyable and inspirational experiences with the scriptures in your family.

HOW TO USE THIS BOOK

It is important to note that this is a resource book. Do not feel obligated to use every lesson. Think of the book as a small buffet of scripture teaching ideas you may pick and choose from as part of your daily scripture diet. Simply review the material for the chapter or verses you are studying and, with the aid of the Spirit, select those teaching ideas you think would be most helpful to your family. Help your children use this book so they will be encouraged to teach the family also.

Each chapter is divided into shorter scripture blocks that have a unifying message or theme. The scripture is listed first, followed by a simple question or statement. The question or statement gives you an idea of the topics discussed in that particular chapter. As you read these questions and statements, you can quickly find a topic your family might need to consider.

You will also see an icon or small picture. These icons are quick visual prompts to let you know what kind of teaching ideas you might use with that chapter. Though many lessons use more than one teaching approach, the icon identifies the major approach for that set of verses. The icons you will find are explained below:

 This is the activity icon. It lets you know your family will be actively involved during the lesson. The activity might be drawing pictures, creating posters, taking a quiz, or making a list. Some activities might be more involved than others and may require preparation in advance.

This is the insight icon. It lets you know that questions, cross-references, side-by-side comparisons, or other teaching devices will be used to lead your family to find insights in the scriptures.

This is the object lesson icon. Simple objects or experiments can draw the mind to see spiritual parallels in the scriptures. We have attempted to keep the object lessons simple so they can be used with children of various ages.

This is the quotation icon. It identifies teaching suggestions that rely on counsel from living prophets to help us understand a doctrine or scriptural concept or help us apply important principles in our lives.

This is the story icon. It points to a story used to help teach a block of scripture. Sometimes the story is a personal one told by a family member. Sometimes you will find a case study that develops a situation where answers can be found in the scriptures. You may even find a story told by a General Authority. Sometimes the story simply inspires you to do better.

This is the writing and scripture marking icon. It identifies activities that are designed to allow your family to write their impressions and feelings in a journal or other book. Pondering and expressing thoughts in writing is helpful in making gospel principles and doctrines part of our thinking and actions. And marking the scriptures personalizes them so that family members can remember what was important to them.

HELPING YOUR FAMILY BECOME STUDENTS OF THE SCRIPTURES

This book assumes each family member will have his or her own scriptures to study. The teaching ideas invite everyone to participate in scripture study. There will be a lot of searching in the pages of your scriptures. Often you will be asked to look for things in a block of scripture that you might mark, list, or discuss. As you study in this manner, your scriptures will become a handbook for life. On subsequent visits to these scripture pages, they will be marked or have marginal notes that will remind family members of principles learned before.

Whatever you do, don't read for mileage! In other words, don't read just to see how far you can get in the scriptures. Often families try to read a certain number of verses or chapters each time they read. Speaking about this, Howard W. Hunter said, "We should not be haphazard in our reading but rather develop a systematic plan for study. There are some who read to a schedule of a number of pages or a set number of chapters each day or week. This may be perfectly justifiable and may be enjoyable if one is reading for pleasure, but it does not constitute meaningful study. It is better to have a set amount of time to give scriptural study each day than to have a set amount of chapters to read. Sometimes we find that the study of a single verse will occupy the whole time." ("Reading the Scriptures," *Ensign*, November 1979, pp. 64–65.)

You might also find the following suggestions helpful:
- When possible have a set time for scripture study: each morning, at dinnertime, or each night.
- Make sure everyone has scriptures, marking pens or pencils, and maybe a journal.
- When you come across difficult words, be sure to stop and define them.
- Don't be afraid to slow down as you study. Study a few verses at a time. Study until you find a principle to incorporate into your daily living.

Scripture study invites questions and encourages the discussion of ideas. As we think about and discuss the scriptures, the Spirit will have an opportunity to teach and witness of important truths. Scripture study isn't just reading; it is searching for spiritual treasures. Elder Henry B. Eyring taught, "We treasure the word of God not only by reading the words of the scriptures but by studying them. We may be nourished more by pondering a few words, allowing the Holy Ghost to make them treasures to us, than to pass quickly and superficially over whole chapters of scripture." ("Feed My Lambs," *Ensign,* November 1997, p. 84.)

WHAT BLESSINGS MIGHT YOU REAP?

Imagine what might happen as a result of studying the scriptures together as a family. What value might there be in an increased understanding of the scriptures? What would it mean to young and old alike to be comfortable and conversant with the scriptures? Notice these promises given by President Ezra Taft Benson: "When individual members and families immerse themselves in the scriptures regularly and consistently . . . testimonies will increase. Commitment will be strengthened. Families will be fortified. Personal revelation will flow." ("The Power of the Word," *Ensign,* May 1986, p. 81.)

We hope you find this book useful. We hope it will help bless you and your family. It is our wish that you might find some keys to unlocking the scriptures and feasting upon the words of Christ. (See 2 Nephi 31:20.)

THE OPENING PAGES:
"THE MOST CORRECT OF ANY BOOK ON EARTH"

THE TITLE PAGE—AN INTRODUCTION TO THE BOOK OF MORMON

Have your family turn to the Book of Mormon's title page. Ask them if they know how the title page came to be. Share the following statement by the Prophet Joseph Smith: "I wish to mention here that the title-page of the Book of Mormon is a literal translation, taken from the very last leaf on the left hand side of the collection or book of plates, which contained the record which has been translated, the language of the whole running the same as all Hebrew writing in general; and that said title page is not by any means a modern composition, either of mine or of any other man who has lived or does live in this generation" (*History of the Church,* 1:71).

LDS scholar Sidney B. Sperry added, "The words at the top of the title page of the Nephite record immediately above the two main paragraphs state that the Book of Mormon is an account written by the hand of Mormon upon plates taken from the plates of Nephi. . . . One reading these words for the first time might get the impression that Mormon wrote the title page, but this impression would be quickly dispelled on reading the first paragraph, where it is explained that the record was sealed by the hand of Moroni, and hid up into the Lord. In other words, Moroni, son of Mormon, was the author of the title page and the last Nephite to possess the plates before they were hidden." (Sidney B. Sperry, *Book of Mormon Compendium,* p. 42.)

Study the title page and the statements given above with your family and look for answers to the following questions:

- Why is the book called the Book of Mormon? (Mormon wrote most of it.)
- Who wrote the title page? (Moroni.)
- Who was the book written to? (Lamanites, Jews, and Gentiles.)
- Who translated it?
- Who published it?

THE TITLE PAGE—WHY WAS THE BOOK OF MORMON WRITTEN?

Ask family members to write, in one sentence, a goal that is important for each of them to accomplish. Discuss different ways they could write that sentence to give it greater emphasis (for example, they might use an exclamation mark, use different colors, or make some of the words larger). Explain that one way we might highlight an important part is by capitalizing certain words.

Have your family read the second paragraph of the title page and find what sentence is emphasized. Why is that an important sentence? What does it tell us about the main purpose the Book of Mormon was written? Ask everyone to read this paragraph again and look for other reasons the Book of Mormon was written. Challenge your family to look for messages and teachings about

Jesus Christ as they continue to study the Book of Mormon.

Explain to your family that the title "The Book of Mormon" has been on all editions of the Book of Mormon since it was first published in 1830. In 1982 Elder Boyd K. Packer announced, "You should know also that by recent decision of the Brethren, the Book of Mormon will henceforth bear the title 'The Book of Mormon,' with the subtitle 'Another Testament of Jesus Christ.'" ("Scriptures," *Ensign,* November 1982, p. 53.)

Ask your family why the subtitle "Another Testament of Jesus Christ" is important. How can it be helpful to members of the Church? What benefit might it be to those of other faiths?

INTRODUCTION–WHAT DO YOU KNOW ABOUT THE BOOK OF MORMON?

Invite everyone to read the one-page introduction in the Book of Mormon to prepare for a small quiz to test his or her knowledge. After everyone has finished reading, give the following quiz:

- What was the name of the "prophet-historian" who compiled the Book of Mormon?
- During what biblical event did the Jaredites come to the Americas?
- What was the crowning event of the Book of Mormon?
- Joseph Smith taught that "the Book of Mormon was the most correct of any book on earth, and the _____ of our religion."
- How many total special witnesses were chosen to see the gold plates?
- Where in the book do we find the promise of how we can know the Book of Mormon is true?

Show the family what a keystone looks like and ask why the keystone is so important in holding up an arch. Read the following quotation from President Ezra Taft Benson to your family:

"Just as the arch crumbles if the keystone is removed, so does all the Church stand or fall with the truthfulness of the Book of Mormon. The enemies of the Church understand this clearly. This is why they go to such great lengths to try to disprove the Book of Mormon, for if it can be discredited, the Prophet Joseph Smith goes with it. So does our claim to priesthood keys, and revelation, and the restored Church. But in like manner, if the Book of Mormon be true—and millions have now testified that they have the witness of the Spirit that it is indeed true—then one must accept the claims of the Restoration and all that accompanies it.

"Yes, the Book of Mormon is the keystone of our religion—the keystone of our testimony, the keystone of our doctrine, and the keystone in the witness of our Lord and Savior." (*A Witness and a Warning,* p. 19.)

INTRODUCTION–"THE BOOK OF MORMON WILL CHANGE YOUR LIFE"

As a family, read the sixth paragraph of the Book of Mormon's introduction and identify blessings that come from studying the book. Read the following quotation by Ezra Taft Benson and ask each family member to listen for the blessings he mentions:

"May I admonish you to participate in a program of daily reading and pondering of the scriptures. . . . The Book of Mormon will change your life. It will fortify you against the evils of our day. It will bring a spirituality into your life that no other book will. It will be the most important book you will read in preparation for a mission and for life. A young man [or young woman] who knows and loves the Book of Mormon, who has read it several times, who has an abiding testimony of its truthfulness, and who applies its teachings will be able to stand against the wiles of

BOOK AND YEAR COMPARISON

| YEAR | 600 BC | 500 BC | 400 BC | 300 BC | 200 BC | 100 BC | BC AD BIRTH OF JESUS | 100 | 200 | 300 | 400 |

Book labels: 1st NEPHI · 2nd NEPHI · JACOB · ENOS · JAROM · OMNI · Time covered in Omni 1:27–30 & Mosiah 9–22 flashback · MOSIAH · ALMA · HELAMAN · 3rd NEPHI · 4th NEPHI · MORMON · MORONI

RECORD KEEPERS

Lehi · Nephi · Jacob · Enos · Jarom · Omni · Amaron · Chemish · Abinadom · Amaleki · Mosiah 1 · Benjamin · Mosiah 2 · Alma 1 · Alma 2 · Shiblon · Helaman 1 · Helaman 2 · Nephi 2 · Nephi 3 · Nephi 4 · Amos 1 · Amos 2 · Ammaron · Mormon · Moroni

KEY EVENTS (SEE LIST, NEXT PAGE)

1 2 3 4 5 6 7 8 9 10 11 12 13 14 15 16 17 18 19 20 21 22 23 24 25 26 27 28 29 30 31 32 33 34 35 36

BOOK AND PAGE COUNT COMPARISON

ETHER*

| PAGES | 0 | 50 | 100 | 150 | 200 | 250 | 300 | 350 | 400 | 450 | 500 |

KEY EVENTS

(See chart, previous page)

1. Lehi travels with his family to the Promised Land
2. Lehi dies
3. The Nephites separated from the Lamanites
4. Nephi quotes and explains the prophecies of Isaiah
5. Nephi dies
6. Jacob quotes Zenos' Allegory
7. Sherem contends with Jacob
8. Enos prays for forgiveness
9. Mosiah takes his people North and finds the people of Zarahemla
10. King Benjamin's address
11. Zeniff leads group of Nephites back to the land of Nephi
12. Noah rules in the land of Nephi
13. Abinadi prophesises and is slain
14. Limhi and his people return to the land of Zarahemla
15. Conversion of Alma the Younger
16. Reign of Judges begins
17. Sons of Mosiah serve 14-year mission to the Lamanites
18. Alma and Amulek preach the gospel
19. Korihor is an antichrist
20. Wars between the Lamanites and Nephites
21. Captain Moroni leads the Nephites
22. 2,000 stripling warriors fight for righteousness
23. Hagoth sails northward
24. Gadianton robbers
25. Nephi and Lehi miraculously saved
26. Samuel the Lamanite prophecies of Christ
27. Birth of Jesus Christ
28. Gadianton robbers destroyed
29. Great destructions in Americas
30. Jesus Christ appears and ministers to the Nephites
31. Years of righteousness and peace
32. Years of wickedness and wars
33. Mormon inserts the "Words of Mormon" after the book of Omni
34. Nephites destroyed
35. Moroni wanders alone
36. Moroni buries the gold plates in Cumorah

* Ether covers a time span somewhere between 2200 B.C. and 559 B.C.

the devil and will be a mighty tool in the hands of the Lord." ("To the 'Youth of the Noble Birthright,'" *Ensign,* May 1986, pp. 43–44, and "To the Young Women of the Church," *Ensign,* November 1986, p. 82.)

Show "The Challenge" (included at the end of this chapter) and ask each family member if he or she will take the challenge to participate in a program of daily reading and pondering of the scriptures and giving a full effort when studying the scriptures as a family. Invite family members to sign their names to the document. Read the promise President Benson gave to families who study the scriptures together: "When individual members and families immerse themselves in the scriptures regularly and consistently, these other areas of activity will automatically come. Testimonies will increase. Commitment will be strengthened. Families will be fortified. Personal revelation will flow" ("The Power of the Word," *Ensign,* May 1986, p. 81).

THE TESTIMONY OF THE WITNESSES— WHAT ELSE DID THE WITNESSES SEE?

Ask your family to imagine they are in a courtroom. Ask what the purpose is of bringing witnesses to the stand. What kinds of things might witnesses be asked to testify of? How strong a case would a lawyer have with only one witness? How many witnesses would be needed to make a stronger case? Read together the testimony of the three and eight witnesses and evaluate strength of their testimonies. Now read how Joseph Smith felt after other witnesses had seen the plates and he was not the only witness:

"On coming in, Joseph threw himself down beside me, and exclaimed, 'Father, mother, you do not know how happy I am: the Lord has now caused the plates to be shown to three more besides myself. They have seen an angel, who has testified to them, and they will have to bear wit-

ness to the truth of what I have said, for now they know for themselves, that I do not go about to deceive the people, and I feel as if I was relieved of a burden which was almost too heavy for me to bear, and it rejoices my soul, that I am not any longer to be entirely alone in the world.'" (Lucy Mack Smith, *History of Joseph Smith by His Mother,* pp. 152–53.)

Other than the plates and the angel, what else were the three witnesses privileged to see? (See D&C 17:1.) How was this different from what the eight witnesses saw?

TESTIMONY OF THE PROPHET JOSEPH SMITH— "STUMP OR BE STUMPED"

Play a game with the family called "Stump or Be Stumped." To play this game you will need some small candies, such as M&Ms. Give family members enough time to read the Testimony of the Prophet Joseph Smith in their copies of the Book of Mormon. Have them look for details they could be asked about. They can also look for a question to stump a parent. When they are finished reading, ask each family member, "Stump or be stumped?" If the person says "Stump," then he or she asks you a question about the story. If he or she says "Be stumped," then ask the person a question you have taken from the text. Those who give correct answers or are able to stump a parent receive a small candy.

A BRIEF EXPLANATION ABOUT THE BOOK OF MORMON—THE CONTENTS OF THE PLATES

Using the chart, point out how the books are grouped. Ask your family to take marking pens or pencils and bracket these groupings in their scriptures on the "Names and Order of Books in the Book of Mormon" page.

THE NAMES AND ORDER OF THE BOOKS IN THE BOOK OF MORMON— LEARNING THE BOOKS IN ORDER

Help your family learn the books of the Book of Mormon in order by singing "The Books of the Book of Mormon" from the *Children's Songbook,* p. 119. The tune is from "Ten Little Indians." After the family members think they know the books, have each person say them in order.

As a family you could try a more challenging quiz by randomly naming a book of the Book of Mormon and having a family member name the book that follows it in order.

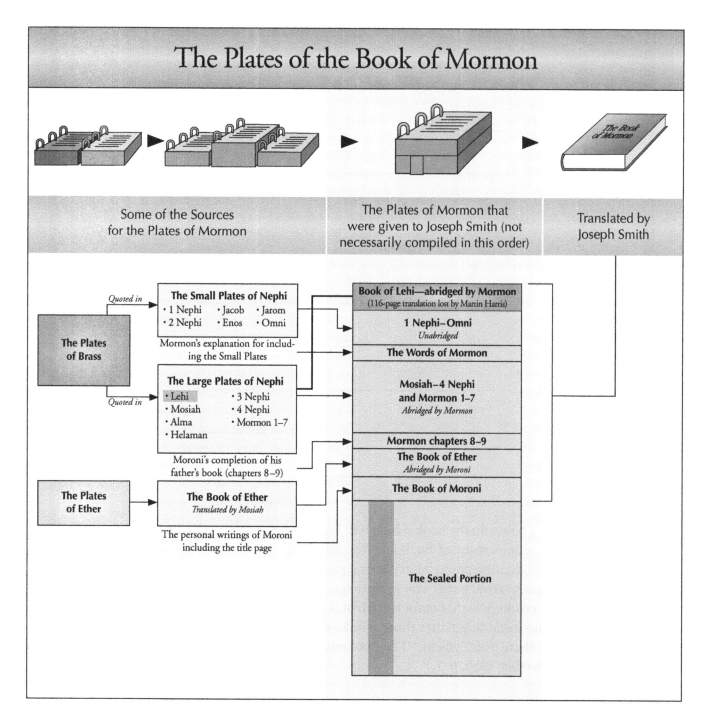

The Plates of the Book of Mormon

Some of the Sources for the Plates of Mormon

The Plates of Mormon that were given to Joseph Smith (not necessarily compiled in this order)

Translated by Joseph Smith

The Plates of Brass

Quoted in

The Small Plates of Nephi
- 1 Nephi
- 2 Nephi
- Jacob
- Enos
- Jarom
- Omni

Mormon's explanation for including the Small Plates

Quoted in

The Large Plates of Nephi
- Lehi
- Mosiah
- Alma
- Helaman
- 3 Nephi
- 4 Nephi
- Mormon 1–7

Moroni's completion of his father's book (chapters 8–9)

The Plates of Ether

The Book of Ether
Translated by Mosiah

The personal writings of Moroni including the title page

Book of Lehi—abridged by Mormon
(116-page translation lost by Martin Harris)

1 Nephi–Omni
Unabridged

The Words of Mormon

Mosiah–4 Nephi and Mormon 1–7
Abridged by Mormon

Mormon chapters 8–9

The Book of Ether
Abridged by Moroni

The Book of Moroni

The Sealed Portion

THE CHALLENGE

"The Book of Mormon will change your life."
—*Ezra Taft Benson*

I hereby agree to see if the Book of Mormon will change my life by participating with my family in a daily program of reading and pondering the scriptures.

_____

_____

_____

_____

_____

_____

_____

_____

"There is a power in the book which will begin to flow into your lives the moment you begin a serious study of the book. You will find greater power to resist temptation. You will find the power to avoid deception. You will find the power to stay on the strait and narrow path. The scriptures are called "the words of life." (D&C 84:85), and nowhere is that more true than it is of the Book of Mormon. When you begin to hunger and thirst after those words, you will find life in greater and greater abundance" (Ezra Taft Benson, "The Book of Mormon—Keystone of Our Religion," *Ensign,* November 1986, p. 7.)

1 NEPHI

Nephi, the son of Lehi and Sariah, wrote 1 Nephi because the Lord commanded him to do so. This book contains an account of Nephi's "proceedings" in his day and helps show that "the tender mercies of the Lord are over all those whom he hath chosen because of their faith." (See 1 Nephi 1:17, 20.) 1 Nephi is an account of Lehi's family leaving their home in Jerusalem, traveling through the wilderness across an ocean, and arriving in the promised land. Nephi's purpose in writing was to "persuade men to come unto the God of Abraham, and the God of Isaac, and the God of Jacob, and be saved." (1 Nephi 6:4.) The time period covered by 1 Nephi is 600–588 B.C., or about thirteen years.

1 NEPHI 1: THE CALLING OF A PROPHET

1 Nephi 1 Headnote
Who wrote the headnote, or introduction, to 1 Nephi?

Read the headnote to 1 Nephi 1 with your family and ask them if they can discover who wrote that paragraph. After they have had a chance to discuss it, explain that the headnotes, which introduce more than half of the books in the Book of Mormon, were all part of the original record given to the Prophet Joseph Smith. Notice that the headnote to 1 Nephi ends with Nephi's own words: "This is according to the account of Nephi; or in other words, I, Nephi, wrote this record."

1 Nephi 1:1
When did Nephi write his record?

Explain to your family that Nephi did not write this record until thirty years after his family left Jerusalem and arrived in the promised land. (See 2 Nephi 5:28–31.) Ask your family how knowing this could be an encouragement to those who may not yet have started their personal histories. Would it ever be too late to begin recording our life's experiences? What can we do as a family to begin work on our personal history?

1 Nephi 1:1
"Many afflictions" yet "highly favored"?

Have each family member draw a scale and number it from 1 to 10. Ask them to put a mark on the scale showing the amount of affliction they have experienced (1 would be little or no affliction, and 10 would be extreme affliction). Have them also mark where on the scale they think best describes how favored they are by the Lord. Read 1 Nephi 1:1 and talk about where Nephi may have marked his scale. As a family, discuss how a person can have "many afflictions" and still be "highly favored of the Lord." What does that teach us about Heavenly Father? What does it teach us about Nephi's attitude? Where do you think Nephi might have marked the scale for us?

1 Nephi 1:2
In what language did Nephi write on the plates?

Read 1 Nephi 1:2 with your family and point out that we are really not certain what Nephi meant when he referred to the "learning of the Jews and the language of the Egyptians." Near the end of the book, Moroni described their writing as "reformed Egyptian." (Mormon 9:32.)

Share the following statements with your family: "It is unknown whether Nephi, Mormon, or Moroni wrote Hebrew in modified Egyptian characters or inscribed their plates in both the Egyptian language and Egyptian characters or whether Nephi wrote in one language and Mormon and Moroni, who lived some nine hundred years later, in another." (*Encyclopedia of Mormonism,* "Book of Mormon Language".)

"The historians of the book reported that their original Hebrew language had been changed, and that the Egyptian characters had been altered and adapted for the writing of the Hebrew language for space-saving and taught specially, usually father to son. These characters were referred to as 'reformed Egyptian,' and for this reason the historians report it was harder to avoid mistakes, which they said were faults of the scribes and not of God. They also said that 'none other people knoweth our language'" (Franklin S. Harris, Jr., *Book of Mormon: Message and Evidences,* p. 115).

1 Nephi 1:4
Who was Zedekiah?

Have your family members mark the name *Zedekiah* as you read this verse and explain that the mention of this Jewish king helps us know when Lehi lived at Jerusalem. Point out the date at the bottom of that page in the Book of Mormon. Have them find the name *Zedekiah* in the Bible Dictionary and find one other connec-

tion he has with the Book of Mormon. (See Bible Dictionary, "Zedekiah," p. 792.) Explain that we will learn more about his son Mulek later in the Book of Mormon.

1 Nephi 1:5–20
How does the Lord call and prepare His prophets?

Tell your family that often when the Lord needs a person to serve, the person may be called to go through certain trials or other faith-promoting experiences. Read 1 Nephi 1:5–20 together and then ask the following questions. Write the answers where all can see them.

- What did Lehi do first? (Verse 5, pray.)
- What did he see? (Verses 6–10, God.)
- What was he given? (Verse 11, a book.)
- What did he learn? (Verses 13–14, the goodness of God.)
- What did he do with what he learned? (Verse 18, preached and warned the people.)
- How did the people respond to his message? (Verses 19–20, mocked him and wanted to kill him.)

Tell your family that the first three chapters of Ezekiel tell of Ezekiel's call to be a prophet. Have someone read aloud the chapter headings for Ezekiel chapters 1–3 and then ask your family what similarities they see between Ezekiel's call and Lehi's call.

Read or tell the account of Joseph Smith's calling as a prophet in Joseph Smith—History 1:8–25. Ask your family what they see in Joseph's experience that reminds them of Lehi and Ezekiel. Bear your testimony that Joseph Smith was a prophet of God just like Ezekiel and Lehi.

1 Nephi 1:5–20
An evidence that Joseph Smith did not write the Book of Mormon

Point out to your family that many of the verses in 1 Nephi 1:5–20 begin with the word "And." Some English teachers would say it is improper grammar to start a sentence with a conjunction like "And." In English it might be considered poor writing; however, in Semitic languages it is very common and is strong evidence that Joseph Smith translated the Book of Mormon and did not write it. You might want to look at Genesis 1 in the Old Testament for further evidence of this writing style.

1 Nephi 1:20
A promise to you from Nephi

Invite your family members to mark the last half of verse 20 where Nephi promises to show us how the "tender mercies of the Lord" make the faithful "mighty even unto the power of deliverance." Tell your family to look for examples of this principle as they read the rest of the Book of Mormon.

1 NEPHI 2: COMING TO KNOW FOR YOURSELF

1 Nephi 2:1
Does revelation sometimes come through dreams and visions?

Have family members compare 1 Nephi 1:8 and 1 Nephi 2:1 and find two ways the Lord communicated to Lehi. Visions and dreams are some of the ways the Lord communicates to His prophets. (See Numbers 12:6.) The Prophet Joseph Smith has written, "Where faith is, there will the knowledge of God be also, with all things which pertain thereto—revelations, visions, and dreams, as well as every necessary thing, in order that the possessors of faith may be perfected, and obtain salvation." (*Lectures on Faith*, Lecture 7, p. 69.)

1 Nephi 2:1–3
Is this an example of the Lord's "tender mercies"?

Review with your family what Nephi promised to show us in 1 Nephi 1:20. Then read 1 Nephi 2:1–3 and ask how these verses are an example of how the Lord delivers the faithful.

1 Nephi 2:4
How wealthy was Lehi?

Read 1 Nephi 2:4 and 1 Nephi 3:25 with your family and ask if there is any evidence in these verses about how much wealth Lehi was leaving behind. What does that teach us about Lehi's willingness to give up all for the gospel's sake? When Jesus was asked if it was possible for a rich man to enter the kingdom of heaven, He said that rich men could enter, "if they will forsake all things for my sake." (JST, Matthew 19:26.) Lehi was that kind of a man. What can we do to make heavenly things more important in our lives than earthly things?

1 Nephi 2:2–13
What would you take into the wilderness?

After reading 1 Nephi 2:2–4, show your family a suitcase or backpack. Pretend that, like Lehi's family, your family is going to leave civilization to live in the wilderness. Ask what two things each person would take with them other than the basic provisions like clothes, tents, and food. After they decide, ask why they would take those things. Discuss what items would be of greatest value to your family.

Next, read verses 11–13 and ask what Laman and Lemuel thought was the most important. Find the phrase in verse 12 that explains why the oldest brothers complained so much. How does understanding Heavenly Father's plan for us help us handle adversity and make choices that will bring us the greatest happiness?

1 Nephi 2:7
"An attitude of gratitude"

Have family members read 1 Nephi 2:7 and tell what is the first thing the prophet Lehi did when he was safely out of Jerusalem. What do you think most people would be feeling if they had just had to leave all their possessions behind and go into the wilderness?

Elder James E. Faust taught, "A grateful heart is a beginning of greatness. It is an expression of humility. It is a foundation for the development of such virtues as prayer, faith, courage, contentment, happiness, love, and well-being. But there is a truism associated with all types of human strength: 'Use it or lose it.' When not used, muscles weaken, skills deteriorate, and faith disappears. . . .

"Gratitude is not only an expression of faith; it is a saving principle. The Lord has said, 'And in nothing doth man offend God, or against none is his wrath kindled, save those who confess not his hand in all things, and obey not his commandments' (D&C 59:21). It is clear to me from this scripture that to 'thank the Lord thy God in all things' (D&C 59:7) is more than a social courtesy; it is a binding commandment." ("The Message: An Attitude of Gratitude," *New Era,* November 1993, p. 6.)

Ask family members to suggest ways your family could develop an "attitude of gratitude."

1 Nephi 2:10
Whoever heard of a steadfast valley?

Ask family members if Lehi's description of a "steadfast valley" in 1 Nephi 2:10 seemed a little odd to them. Hugh Nibley wrote, "As if to prove that no westerner could possibly have dreamed up Nephi's account, we are challenged by the remarkable expression, 'like unto this valley, firm and steadfast, and immovable' (1 Nephi 2:10). Who west of Suez would ever think of such an image? . . . For we, of course, know all about everlasting hills and immovable mountains, the moving of which is the best-known illustration of the infinite power of faith, but who ever heard of a steadfast valley? The Arabs, to be sure. For them the valley, and not the mountain, is the symbol of permanence. It is not the mountain of refuge to which they flee, but the valley of refuge. The great depressions that run for hundreds of miles across the Arabian peninsula pass for the most part through plains devoid of mountains. It is in these ancient riverbeds alone that water, vegetation, and animal life are to be found when all else is desolation. They alone offer men and animals escape from their enemies and deliverance from death by hunger and thirst. The qualities of firmness and steadfastness, of reliable protection, refreshment, and sure refuge when all else fails, which other nations attribute naturally to mountains, the Arabs attribute to valleys." (*Collected Works of Hugh Nibley,* 5:91–92.)

1 Nephi 2:12–16
Hard hearts vs. soft hearts: is there a formula for believing?

Write out the following questions and ask family members to think about them but don't discuss them just yet:

- Why did Nephi believe and obey his father while Laman and Lemuel murmured and rebelled?
- Did Nephi always know, or did something happen that gave Nephi a need to know?
- Does Heavenly Father make some people naturally more believing and others naturally less believing?
- Do we have some control over whether we believe or not?

Have family members search 1 Nephi 2:12 for the reason Laman and Lemuel murmured and rebelled ("they knew not the dealings of that God who had created them"). Next read verse 16 together and list the reasons Nephi did not rebel:

1. He had "great desires" to know if the things his father said were true.

2. He really prayed, "cried," unto the Lord.

3. The Lord visited him and softened his heart so he believed.

Review and discuss the questions shown previously. Bear testimony that we can use Nephi's formula for believing at any time about any principle of the gospel, and God will soften our hearts and help us to understand and believe just as He did for Nephi. Once Nephi knew for himself, he no longer had to wonder or rely on his father's testimony.

Share the following statement from Elder Heber C. Kimball: "To meet the difficulties that are coming, it will be necessary for you to have a knowledge of the truth of this work for yourselves. . . . The time will come when no man nor woman will be able to endure on borrowed light. Each will have to be guided by the light within himself. If you do not have it, how can you stand?" (In Orson F. Whitney, *Life of Heber C. Kimball,* p. 450.)

Share with your family how you found out the gospel was true and what caused you to want to find out for yourself. Invite them to write their testimony in their journal and describe how they came to know the gospel was true.

1 Nephi 2:16–19
What kind of person was Nephi?

Read 1 Nephi 2:16–19 together and look for the qualities young Nephi had. Responses might include:

- "Exceedingly young."
- "Large in stature."
- Desired to know the things of God.
- Prayerful.
- Believing.
- Not rebellious.
- Helpful and loving to siblings.
- Prayed for family.
- Humble.

Discuss how each of these qualities would help Nephi in his calling as a prophet of God. Which of these qualities reminds you of the Prophet Joseph Smith?

1 NEPHI 3: "I WILL GO AND DO . . . FOR I KNOW"

1 Nephi 3:1
Should we speak "to" or "with" the Lord?

Show a telephone and ask what a phone is used for. When you use the phone, do you talk "to" your friend or "with" them? What is the difference between talking "to" someone and "with" them? Read 1 Nephi 3:1 and discover how Nephi and the Lord communicated. What does this teach you about your own prayers? What can you do to ensure that your prayers are more of a conversation "with" God instead of just a way of talking "to" Him?

1 Nephi 3:1–6
Does God have favorites?

 Play the "favorites" game with your family. Choose a topic such as, food, movies, animals, colors, or friends. Ask family members to tell who or what their favorites are. Ask them why something or someone becomes a favorite. Next, ask if they think the Lord has favorites. Read 1 Nephi 3:1–6 and look for who might be "favored of the Lord." Why does Lehi say that Nephi would be so favored? Read 1 Nephi 17:35 and find who else is "favored" of the Lord. Why do you think the Lord favors the righteous? What can you do to be "favored of the Lord"?

1 Nephi 3:1–7
I will go and do . . . for I know

Introduce these verses by asking questions such as the following: What has been the most difficult challenge of your life? What made it so difficult? What helped you get through it? Then read together 1 Nephi 3:1–4 and look for the challenge Lehi's sons received from the Lord. Then read 1 Nephi 3:5–7 and compare how Laman and Lemuel reacted to this assignment with how Nephi reacted. Why did Laman and Lemuel murmur and complain and Nephi respond with faith? (See 1 Nephi 2:12–16 and the teaching idea for those verses.) Nephi said, "I will go and do . . . for I know!" How would you change that phrase to apply to Laman and Lemuel?

When you are asked to serve at home or at Church, is your attitude more like Nephi's or Laman's? What does 1 Nephi 3:6 teach us about how our attitude can affect our service?

1 Nephi 3:7–31; 4:1–26
How does the Lord prepare the way?

Review 1 Nephi 3:7–9 together as a family. Did Nephi know at that moment what "the way" was that the Lord would provide?

In 1 Nephi chapters 3–4, Nephi and his brothers made three different attempts to get the plates. Read 1 Nephi 3:10–14 and identify the first "way" the brothers tried to get the plates (Laman just asked for them). How well did it work?

Next read 1 Nephi 3:15–27. What was the second "way" the brothers tried to get the plates? (They tried to buy them.) How well did this way work?

Then read 1 Nephi 4:1–6. How did Nephi approach the problem differently on this third attempt? Continue reading 1 Nephi 4:7–26 with your family and ask why this attempt succeeded when the others failed.

Share the following explanation by Elder L. Tom Perry:

"Several decisions faced these young men as they approached Laban to ask for the records. It's most interesting to me to note the process by which they made those decisions. First, the decision was to leave it to chance. And they cast lots, and the lot fell to Laman. . . . Laban was not too pleased with this request. . . . He said, 'Behold thou art a robber, and I will slay thee' (1 Ne. 3:13). That was enough for Laman; he fled and came back and reported to his brothers that leaving the assignment to chance did not work.

"So they approached the house of Laban and displayed the gold and silver and offered to trade these precious things for the plates of brass. When Laban saw the property and that it was exceedingly great, he did lust after it. . . . He sent his servants after the boys to slay them, and they had to flee, leaving their property behind. Things of the world did not produce the records.

"So by night Nephi led his brothers outside the wall of Jerusalem. He crept inside towards the house of Laban, this time not leaving it to chance or to worldly things, but going by faith. He said, 'I was led by the Spirit, not knowing beforehand the things which I should do' (1 Ne. 4:6). . . .

"As he came to the house of Laban, he found a man fallen to the earth, drunken with wine. On coming closer, he discovered it was Laban. Laban had been delivered into his hands. The Lord had opened the way to obtain the record. Making the decision to place his trust in the Lord produced the results." ("Making the Right Decisions," *Ensign,* November 1979, p. 35.)

1 Nephi 3:9
How far from Jerusalem was Lehi's camp?

 Ask your family the following questions:

- Have you ever forgotten something when going on a trip?
- Did you go back to get what you forgot or did you just go on without it?
- How important would the item have to be to make you travel back to get it?

Explain that when Lehi and his family left Jerusalem, they also left something behind, but it wasn't something they forgot. Read 1 Nephi 3:1–4 with your family to help them find out what the Lord wanted them to go back to Jerusalem and get.

To help your family understand how important the plates of brass were, read 1 Nephi 2:2–6 and ask them where Lehi was when he received the command to send his sons back and get the plates. Have them turn to the maps in the back of their Bibles and find a map (such as Bible Map 3) that shows the area from Jerusalem down to the Red Sea. Using the scale shown on the Bible map, ask them to measure about how far Lehi's family had traveled from Jerusalem to the shores of the Red Sea. (About 175 miles or 282 km.) How long do you think it took them to walk that far? Read 1 Nephi 3:9

and find out what they took with them that indicates they thought they would be gone a while. What does that tell you about how important the Lord felt the plates of brass were?

1 Nephi 3:11
What does it mean to "cast lots"?

Have your family read 1 Nephi 3:11 and then ask: Have you ever tried to determine who should be first to choose or do something? Maybe to decide who makes the first choice in choosing teammates or who gets the first choice of treats. Did you choose different lengths of sticks or a number between 1 and 10? This is similar to what Laman, Lemuel, Sam, and Nephi did when they "cast lots" to see who would be the one to go into Jerusalem and ask Laban for the plates of brass. Although we do not know exactly how they cast lots in Lehi's day, it was the same idea as "drawing straws" in our day.

1 Nephi 3:19–20
Why would Lehi want a set of metal plates?

Would you choose to carry scriptures to church on Sunday if they were metal plates? Since the plates of brass were made of metal, why do you think the Lord wanted Lehi's sons to obtain them?

Tell your family that Nephi gave reasons for obtaining the plates of brass in 1 Nephi 3:19–20. Read these verses with your family and ask them to share reasons that they find. (The plates would help preserve their language and the teachings of prophets.) It's easy to see how valuable the plates were for preserving the teachings of prophets, but why were they important for preserving their language? Explain that the Book of Mormon tells of another group of Jews who came from Jerusalem without bringing any records with them. Have them find Omni 1:17 and tell what happened to that group. How might our lives be different if we didn't have the scriptures?

1 NEPHI 4: "I WAS LED BY THE SPIRIT . . ."

1 Nephi 4:1–3
The power of the scriptures

To obtain the plates, Nephi and his brothers had to face Laban again, a man who had tried to kill them. Have a family member read 1 Nephi 3:31 and explain why Laman and Lemuel were afraid of Laban. Then read 1 Nephi 4:1 and discuss why Nephi was not afraid. Then have family members search 1 Nephi 4:2 and find which Old Testament scripture story Nephi used as proof that the Lord was mightier than Laban. Discuss the following questions: What does that teach us about the faith Nephi had in the scriptures? What could we do to make the scriptures a more powerful part of our lives? Bear testimony to your family that the scriptures are not myths or fairy tales but true stories of how the Lord works in the lives of real people.

1 Nephi 4:6–18
Recognizing and following the voice of the Spirit

After studying 1 Nephi 4:6–18, ask your family to suppose it had been Nephi's brother Laman who had found Laban lying unconscious on the ground. Do you think Laman would have needed any promptings from the Spirit to slay the man who had stolen all his wealth and tried to kill him? Feelings of anger and revenge would have been natural in this situation. How did Nephi know it was the Spirit of the Lord that required him to slay Laban and not his own emotions? Do you think this was the first time Nephi had heard and followed the voice of the Spirit? (See 1 Nephi 1:1.)

Elder S. Dilworth Young said, "I can testify to you that there will be none of you have any adventure greater, more thrilling, and more joyful than finding out how to interpret the Spirit which comes unto you bearing testimony of the truth. Young folks have to learn how, so do we older folks. We have to find out the technique by which the Spirit whispers in our hearts. We have to learn to hear it and to understand it and to know when we have it, and that sometimes takes a long time.

"But no matter what your age, you do not need to wait until you are old to know. . . . As [a child] grows and has that imprint upon him, he will have joy and satisfaction and peace and happiness beyond anything that can be described with words.

"So I would say to the young folks of the Church, . . . if you will ask, not doubting that you can have an answer, the answer will come in the whispering. Then you must learn to interpret the whispering. At first it likely will come as something akin to a feeling, although not a feeling. There will finally come into your minds the words expressive of the feeling, and those words properly interpreted will be the whispering of the Spirit." (Conference Report, April 1959, p. 59–60.)

Elder Richard G. Scott explained why Nephi was able to follow the voice of the Spirit so successfully: "Nephi was willing to try time and again, using his best efforts. He expressed faith that he would be helped. He refused to be discouraged. But because he acted, had confidence in the Lord, was obedient, and properly used his agency, he received guidance. He was inspired step after step to success, and in his mother's words was 'given . . . power [to] accomplish the thing which the Lord hath commanded' (1 Nephi 5:8).

"Nephi knew he was required to confide in God, to exercise faith, and to act so that he could receive help, step by step. He did not murmur nor ask for a full explanation. But, observe particularly, he did not wait passively for help. He acted! By following spiritual law, he was inspired and given power to act." ("Learning to Recognize Answers to Prayer," *Ensign,* November 1989, p. 32.)

Share your testimony on the importance of following the Spirit.

1 Nephi 4:10–18
Would God really command Nephi to kill?

Read 1 Nephi 4:6–18 together and then explain that some people find it difficult to believe that the Spirit would command Nephi to kill. The Prophet Joseph Smith said, "God said, 'Thou shalt not kill;' and another time he said, 'thou shalt utterly destroy'—This is the principle on which the government of heaven is conducted—by revelation adapted to the circumstances in which the children of the kingdom are placed. Whatever God requires is right, no matter what it is, although we may not see the reason thereof till long after the events transpire." (*Teachings of the Prophet Joseph Smith,* p. 256.)

Perhaps there has been a time in your life when you found a commandment of the Lord difficult to understand. Discuss with your family what have you learned as you look back on these situations. Share your testimony that the Lord knows what He is doing and that being obedient is always right.

1 Nephi 4:13–16
What are the scriptures worth?

After studying 1 Nephi 4:13–16 with your family, ask them what powerful lesson they see in these verses about the value of the written words of God. Make sure they see that the Lord felt that the scriptures were worth more than Laban's life. Discuss how your family could gain a greater appreciation for the value of the scriptures.

1 Nephi 4:17–18
Why was Nephi required to kill Laban?

After reading 1 Nephi 4:17–18, ask family members to discuss the following: The Lord certainly could have caused the drunken Laban to hit his head on a rock and already be dead when Nephi found him. Why, then, was Nephi required to actually do such a difficult thing?

After some discussion, explain that what Nephi was required to do reminds us of when Abraham was required to offer up his only son. (See Genesis 22:1–12; D&C 101:4–5.) Speaking of Abraham's test, Elder George Q. Cannon said, "Why did the Lord ask such things of Abraham? . . . God did not do this for His own sake; for He knew by His foreknowledge what Abraham would do; but the purpose was to impress upon Abraham a lesson, and to enable him to attain unto knowledge that he could not obtain in any other way. That is why God tries all of us. It is not for His own knowledge for He knows all things beforehand. . . . But He tries us for our own good, that we may know ourselves, for it is most important that a man should know himself. He required Abraham to submit to this trial because he intended to give him glory, exaltation and honor; He intended to make him a king and a priest, to share with Himself the glory, power and dominion which He exercised (Conference Report, April 1899, pp. 66–67).

Discuss what Nephi knew after this experience that he did not know before. How would that knowledge change his relationship with his Heavenly Father forever?

1 Nephi 4:32–37
Our word should be enough

Have family members compare 1 Nephi 4:32 with 1 Nephi 3:15 and tell of any similarities they see. Explain that what happened between Nephi and Zoram is another example of the power of an oath in that culture. Swearing an oath on your own life or on the life of God was comparable to saying, "With God as my witness, I will do as I have promised or die trying." Read 1 Nephi 4:32–37 and discuss how Zoram's immediate trust in Nephi's words and his willingness to make an oath in return reveal how powerful the oath was.

Apply this principle to your own family by discussing the following questions. Consider the promises that you have made; how committed have you been to keeping your word? How do you feel about people who never keep their word?

How would our world be different if people kept their promises?

1 NEPHI 5: THE VALUE OF RECORDS

1 Nephi 5:1–3
Why did Sariah complain?

After reading 1 Nephi 5:1–3, share the following information with your family to help them understand Sariah's feelings. The distance from Jerusalem to the Red Sea is about 175 miles, a journey that could take weeks in Lehi's day. Sister Barbara B. Smith, former Relief Society general president, said, "Sariah, the wife of Lehi, had the wrenching experience of leaving their home and their possessions to travel in the wilderness. We are not told of the trials she may have experienced; but going on foot, living in tents, and cooking over an open fire could have been devastating after their comfortable life in Jerusalem." ("Application of Welfare Principles in the Home: A Key to Many Family Problems," *Ensign,* November 1982, p. 85.)

Despite all of this, it wasn't until her sons had been gone longer than she thought was right that the Book of Mormon gives the first indication of Sariah murmuring. To Sariah's credit, when she saw how the Lord protected her sons, she bore a powerful testimony (see 1 Nephi 5:8), and the Book of Mormon never mentions her complaining again. How do you think your mother would feel if you were long overdue from a dangerous assignment?

1 Nephi 5:4–6
How do you respond to criticism?

Ask family members to think back on a time when they felt they were criticized unfairly. How did it make them feel? How would most people in the world today respond to such criticism?

Then ask them to study 1 Nephi 5:1–6 and

notice how Lehi responded to his wife's criticism. What did Lehi know because he was a "visionary man"? (See verse 5.) Find the word in verse 6 that best describes how Lehi handled his wife's criticism.

1 Nephi 5:2–8
What are your reasons for believing?

 Read 1 Nephi 5:2–5 with your family and ask them why they think Sariah said "My sons are no more" (verse 2) and Lehi said, "The Lord will deliver my sons" (verse 5). Then read verses 7–8 and ask, "What happened to turn Sariah's worrying and doubt into a strong testimony that the Lord had "commanded [her] husband" and "protected [her] sons" in verse 8?

Share the following statement from Elder James E. Talmage: "From trustworthy evidence, rightly interpreted, true faith will spring." (James E. Talmage, *Articles of Faith,* p. 91.) Bear testimony to your family about some of the evidences you have received that have helped your faith grow. Invite other family members to do the same.

1 Nephi 5:10–14
Be a scripture detective

Ask your family to read 1 Nephi 5:10 and find the word that describes what Lehi did with the writings on the plates of brass. What is the difference between "reading" and "searching"?

Read verses 11–14 with your family and mark the valuable teachings Lehi found on the plates. The things you mark could include:

1. An account of the creation of the world. (Verse 11.)

2. An account of Adam and Eve. (Verse 11.)

3. A record of the Jews from the beginning to their present day. (Verse 12.)

4. Prophecies of the holy prophets from the beginning down to Jeremiah. (Verse 13.)

5. A genealogy of his fathers.

Why do you think it was important for Lehi's family to take this information with them to their promised land?

1 Nephi 5:11–16
How do the plates of brass compare to our Old Testament?

After reading 1 Nephi 5:11–16, share with your family the following information: "There was more on [the brass plates] than there is in the Old Testament as we now have it. (1 Nephi 13:23.) The prophecies of Zenock, Neum, Zenos, Joseph the son of Jacob, and probably many other prophets were preserved by them and many of these writings foretold matters pertaining to the Nephites. (1 Ne. 19:10, 21; 2 Ne. 4:2, 15; 3 Nephi 10:17.)

"The value of the Brass Plates to the Nephites cannot be overestimated. By means of them they were able to preserve the language (1 Ne. 3:19), most of the civilization, and the religious knowledge of the people from whence they came. (1 Ne. 22:30) (Bruce R. McConkie, *Mormon Doctrine,* p. 103).

1 Nephi 5:14–21
The importance of knowing who you are

Ask each family member to write from memory as much of their personal pedigree chart as they can. After each has had a chance to write it down, discuss what they know about the person furthest back on their list. This would be a great opportunity to spotlight one of your ancestors and share a story about one of their positive character traits.

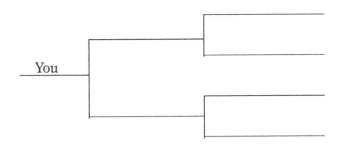

President Spencer W. Kimball said, "Over the years as my thoughts and heart have turned to the lives of my noble ancestors, my appreciation for them has increased. Learning about my ancestors has not only turned my heart to them, but has helped me see eternity more clearly. My own life is rooted not just in the present, but in the lives of my ancestors as well." ("The Things of Eternity—Stand We in Jeopardy?" *Ensign*, January 1977, p. 3.)

Have each family member read 1 Nephi 5:14–16 and look for what Lehi found out about his genealogy from the brass plates. Ask, "What was important about Lehi's knowing he was a descendant of Joseph, who was sold into Egypt?" If there are family members who have received their patriarchal blessings, ask from which son of Israel they descended.

Have family members circle or underline the word "preserved" or "preserve" each time it is used in verses 1 Nephi 5:14–15. Ask who was preserved and how they were preserved. Ask, "What insights does this give into what the Lord will do for us?"

Look for the word "preserve" again in verse 21. Ask, "Why were the brass plates of great worth to Lehi and his family? Why would it be important for us, today, to carry our scriptures with us as we journey through this life 'towards the land of promise'? What is the promised land you want most?"

1 Nephi 5:18–19
What is the future of the plates of brass?

Ask family members to read 1 Nephi 5:18–19 and tell what Lehi said would happen to the plates of brass. Then share the following statement: "From prophet to prophet and generation to generation the Brass Plates were handed down and preserved by the Nephites. (Mosiah 1:16; 28:30; 3 Ne. 1:2.) At some future date the Lord has promised to bring them forth, undimmed by time and retaining their original brightness, and the scriptural accounts recorded on them are to 'go forth unto every nation, kindred, tongue, and people.' (Alma 37:3–5; 1 Ne. 5:18–19.)." (Bruce R. McConkie, *Mormon Doctrine*, p. 103.)

1 NEPHI 6: NEPHI WRITES TO PLEASE GOD

1 Nephi 6:1–6
Why I choose to please God

 Write the following question on a piece of paper large enough for everyone to read: "Do you think Nephi expected that everyone would like his book?" Then have them search 1 Nephi 6:4–5 for an answer. Ask them to share what they found. Then ask, "Whom was Nephi trying to please with the things he was writing and why?" To help answer that question, share the following statement from Elder M. Russell Ballard: "We must know what we do is pleasing before God and understand that this knowledge comes to us through sacrifice and obedience. Those who come unto Christ in this way receive a confidence that whispers peace to their souls and that will eventually enable them to lay hold upon eternal life." ("The Law of Sacrifice," *Ensign*, October 1998, p. 7.)

Discuss the following questions: "What is our family doing to please the Lord?" "What more can we do?"

Take a piece of paper or poster board and draw a line on it, making two columns. Label column 1 "Things That Please God" and column 2 "Things That Please the World." Place the poster where everyone can see it. Throughout the coming week, as family members think of things that fit in either category, have them add them to the poster. Have a follow-up discussion about the things they discovered at the end of the week. Bear your testimony of the blessings that come from the things that please God.

1 NEPHI 7: ISHMAEL'S FAMILY JOINS LEHI'S FAMILY IN THE WILDERNESS

1 Nephi 7:1–2

How important is marriage in the eyes of the Lord?

 Have a family member read 1 Nephi 7:1–2 and find out why the Lord wanted the brothers to go back to Jerusalem a second time.

Explain that there are many people in the world today who seem to think that marriage and family are no longer important. Show family members pictures of your courtship or wedding day. Explain how you met each other and how the Lord directed your courtship and marriage. Then ask what reason the Lord gave in verse 1 for going back after Ishmael's family. (See also Genesis 1:27–28.) Imagine that you were one of Ishmael's daughters. What concerns might you have had about joining Lehi's family in the wilderness? What concerns would Ishmael have had? What role did the Lord play in convincing them to go into the wilderness?

The First Presidency solemnly proclaimed, "Marriage between a man and a woman is ordained of God and . . . the family is central to the Creator's plan for the eternal destiny of His children." ("The Family: A Proclamation to the World," *Ensign*, November 1995, p. 102.)

Elder Bruce R. McConkie declared, "The most important things that any member of the Church of Jesus Christ of Latter-day Saints ever does in this world are: 1. To marry the right person, in the right place, by the right authority; and 2. To keep the covenant made in connection with this holy and perfect order of matrimony—thus assuring the obedient persons of an inheritance of exaltation in the celestial kingdom." (*Mormon Doctrine*, p. 118.)

1 Nephi 7:2

Why was Ishmael's family chosen?

To help your family understand why the Lord chose Ishmael's family to go with Lehi's family, share the following information: "We know from one source that the families were not only acquainted but also related. Elder Erastus Snow explained in a sermon delivered in May 1882: 'The Prophet Joseph Smith informed us that the record of Lehi was contained on the 116 pages that were first translated and subsequently stolen, and of which an abridgement is given us in the first Book of Nephi, which is the record of Nephi individually, he himself being of the lineage of Manasseh; but that *Ishmael was of the lineage of Ephraim, and that his sons married into Lehi's family,* and Lehi's sons married Ishmael's daughters.' (*Journal of Discourses,* 23:184; italics added.) That is to say, it appears that Ishmael's sons were already married to Lehi's daughters before the journey began." (*Doctrinal Commentary on the Book of Mormon,* 1:53–54.)

1 Nephi 7:5–12

Scavenger Hunt

 Ask each family member to mark the words *heart* and *hearts* in verses 5 and 8. Ask whose hearts were being talked about. Invite everyone to read those verses and look for the difference between Ishmael's heart and the hearts of Laman and Lemuel. Ask each of your children to search your home and find three items: one that represents Ishmael's heart, one that represents Laman and Lemuel's hearts, and one that represents their own heart. Discuss which items they selected and why. Read together 1 Nephi 7:9–12 and find some reasons for Laman's and Lemuel's hard hearts. (Hearkened not unto the Lord, forgot their spiritual witnesses, forgot the great things the Lord did for them.) What should we do and what should we remember to help our hearts stay soft?

1 Nephi 7:13

Find the prophecy

Have family members search 1 Nephi 7:13 to find what the Lord prophesied about Jerusalem. The fulfillment of this prophecy can be found by reading the chapter heading for 2 Kings 25. (For the approximate years Jerusalem was under siege, see Bible Dictionary, "Chronology," p. 639). Even though this prophecy is sad, ask family members why it is comforting to know that "all things which the Lord hath spoken" must be fulfilled. (See also D&C 1:36–37.) What are some promises the Lord has made to your family that make you happy and hopeful?

1 Nephi 7:16–18
Discuss a miracle

Read 1 Nephi 7:16–18 with your family and ask what great miracle Nephi experienced because of his prayer of faith. Share the story of any miracles or answers to prayer your family or ancestors have received. Invite family members to tell of a time when they have received answers to their prayers. Why is it important to remember those miracles? (See 1 Nephi 7:11.)

1 Nephi 7:21
Why was Nephi so quick to forgive?

Read the story of Nephi forgiving his brothers in 1 Nephi 7:19–21. As you read these verses, number some of the essential steps to repentance. For example, we must:

1. Soften our hearts.
2. Stop doing the sin.
3. Ask others for their forgiveness.
4. Pray to the Lord for forgiveness.

Read aloud the following scriptures and prophetic statements, and then invite each family member to write in their journals a summary of why is it important to forgive others:

- Matthew 18:34–35.
- D&C 64:10–11.
- "He who will not forgive others breaks down the bridge over which he himself must travel." (Spencer W. Kimball, *The Miracle of Forgiveness*, p. 269.)
- "A common error is the idea that the offender must apologize and humble himself to the dust before forgiveness is required. Certainly, the one who does the injury should totally make his adjustment, but as for the offended one, he must forgive the offender regardless of the attitude of the other. . . .
- "Yes, to be in the right we must forgive, and we must do so without regard to whether or not our [enemy] repents, or how sincere is his transformation, or whether or not he asks our forgiveness." (Spencer W. Kimball, *The Miracle of Forgiveness,* pp. 282–83.)

1 Nephi 7:1–22
Treating each other with love, kindness, and forgiveness

Assign each member of your family to imagine they are one of the following people: Laman, Lemuel, or Nephi. Ask them to silently read 1 Nephi 7:1–22 from the perspective of the person they were assigned. As they read, have them make a list of the kind and the unkind things their person did to their family.

When all have finished, have them report what they discovered. Discuss the following questions:

- How would it make you feel if we treated our family members the way Laman and Lemuel treated theirs?
- What did Nephi do for his family that impressed you?
- What could we do as family members to follow Nephi's example?
- Why do you think it is important to treat our family members with love, kindness, respect, and forgiveness?

Read 1 Nephi 7:16, 20 and discuss how difficult it would be to forgive someone who did such hurtful things to us. Share a story from your own family of forgiveness and the healing that it brings. Invite family members to share experiences they have had.

1 NEPHI 8: THE TREE OF LIFE

1 Nephi 8:2
What are some ways Heavenly Father talks to His children?

Read 1 Nephi 8:1–2 with your family and ask what method the Lord used to talk to Lehi. Ask family members if they can think of any other ways the Lord talks to us. Elder Dallin H. Oaks said, "Revelation is communication from God to man. It can occur in many different ways. Some prophets, like Moses and Joseph Smith, have talked with God face to face. Some persons have had personal communication with angels. Other revelations have come, as Elder James E. Talmage described it, 'through the dreams of sleep or in waking visions of the mind' (James E. Talmage, *Articles of Faith,* p. 229).

"In its more familiar forms, revelation or inspiration comes by means of words or thoughts communicated to the mind (see D&C 8:2–3; Enos 1:10), by sudden enlightenment (see D&C 6:14–15), by positive or negative feelings about proposed courses of action, or even by inspiring performances, as in the performing arts. As Elder Boyd K. Packer has stated, 'Inspiration comes more as a feeling than as a sound' (Boyd K. Packer, "Prayers and Answers," *Ensign,* November 1979, pp. 19–20)." (Dallin H. Oaks, "Revelation," *New Era,* September 1982, p. 38.)

Share an experience you have had when you have felt the Lord communicating with you. Invite family members to share experiences they have had.

1 Nephi 8:1–36
What is the meaning of Lehi's dream of the tree?

After reading Lehi's dream with your family, share the following statement: "Seeing mortality as a wilderness fraught with darkness, dreariness, and moral hazards is essential to understanding Lehi's dream. (Lehi's own life experience made this imagery both natural and appropriate.) The central message of this dream is that there is 'a tree, whose fruit [is] desirable to make one happy'—'the love of God, which sheddeth itself abroad in the hearts of the children of men; wherefore, it is the most desirable above all things.' This love has as its ultimate statement 'the condescension of God' through the advent of Jesus Christ in the flesh to minister among men and then to be 'lifted up upon the cross and slain for the sins of the world.'

"The challenge of mortality is to find and remain close to this tree, with its divine fruit, in the midst of a vast moral and spiritual wilderness. Some means of direction is needed. In his dream, Lehi followed the man in the white robe, his compass bearer on a journey that lasted 'many hours' through a 'dark and dreary waste.' Eventually, Lehi's followership led him to his celestial destination. The dream then teaches that he who would follow in Lehi's path, which is 'strait and narrow,' will find a 'rod of iron' beside the path—'the word of God'—to which the wayfarer must hold fast in order to find the tree and partake of the fruit. The path and the rod of iron, though passing perilously by the precipice of spiritual death, nonetheless will safely guide the seeking traveler through mortality's wasteland." (Lance B. Wickman, "Of Compasses and Covenants," *Ensign,* June 1996, p. 39.)

Ask family members how the scriptures are like a rod of iron that leads us to the Savior.

1 Nephi 8:7–10
Prayer delivers us from darkness

Ask family members to search 1 Nephi 8:7–10 and find out how Lehi was delivered from the darkness he had walked in "for the space of many hours." Bear your testimony of how prayer can lift us from darkness and help us see the world more clearly.

1 Nephi 8:10–33
Can you find yourself in Lehi's dream?

After reading about Lehi's dream in 1 Nephi 8:1–36, assign each family member one or more of the following scripture passages: 1 Nephi 8:21–23; 1 Nephi 8:24–25,28; 1 Nephi 8:26–27; 1 Nephi 8:30; 1 Nephi 8:31–33. Ask them to look for what the people in those verses wanted, where they ended up, and why. After they have searched their verses, invite each family member to report what they found. If you have younger children, invite them to draw a picture of what they think Lehi saw. As a family, discuss some of the following questions:

- Why did Lehi want to get to the tree?
- What do you think the tree stands for?
- How did the rod of iron help them get to the tree?
- How we can get to the tree and stay there?
- Why did some become ashamed after they got to the tree?
- Why do you think Lehi wasn't ashamed?
- Which group would you want to be in?
- Why do some people make fun of those who are trying to keep God's commandments?
- What is the best thing to do when people make fun of you for trying to be good?

President Ezra Taft Benson declared, "Have good associates or don't associate at all. Be careful in the selection of your friends. If in the presence of certain persons you are lifted to nobler heights, you are in good company. But if your friends or associates encourage base thoughts, then you had best leave them." (*God, Family, Country,* p. 241.)

Consider sharing the following story with your family:

"Many years ago I used to play on a basketball team—in fact we went all the way to the state tournament. The night of the state tournament, just before the game started, one of the cheerleaders came onto the floor and asked the fellows if they would like to come over to her house for a party after the game. Thinking more about the game, the fellows did not give it a second thought—they did not even respond to her question. But after the game ended and we had won, one of the team members remembered the invitation. So the whole basketball team—all twelve of us—got together and went over to the girl's house.

"We found that the girl's parents were gone over the weekend, and that she had invited exactly twelve girls to her home as well as the team. She soon rolled the rug back and had the stereo going. They turned it up loud, and then the girl who was the hostess went into the kitchen and came out with a carton of cigarettes. She threw a package over to the fellow who was sitting on the end, and she said, 'Hey, training's all over. We can smoke tonight.'

"Well, we were from a Mormon community. I watched the first fellow—he took a cigarette. Then the girl next to him took one. So did the girl next to her. And as the cigarettes got closer and closer to me, it seemed that almost everyone there was taking a cigarette.

"It was an embarrassing moment and I did not know how to handle it. Finally I thought, 'Oh well, it's only one cigarette and I guess I can smoke with them.' Anyway, when the cigarettes went to the fellow right next to me, he said, 'No thanks, I don't smoke,' and passed them on.

"The strength of the friend on my left gave me the courage to do what I really wanted to do all along. I said, 'No thanks,' too.

"The thing I have wondered through all of these years is, what would have happened to me if I had been sitting on the other side of my friend?" (As cited in Vaughn J. Featherstone, *A Generation of Excellence,* pp. 169–70.)

As a family, list some good families and individuals in your community and Church that you could reach out to and include in your circle of good friends.

1 NEPHI 9: "FOR A WISE PURPOSE"

1 Nephi 9:2–4
The Plates of Nephi

Place a stack of dinner plates (about 4 or 5) on a table and a stack of smaller plates (2 or 3) next to it. Ask family members what plates are used for. Ask, "What is one of your favorite memories of using a plate? Did you know that Nephi also used two sets of plates but a very different kind?" Have them turn to "A Brief Explanation about the Book of Mormon" in the front of your Book of Mormon and ask someone to read item number 1: "The Plates of Nephi." Then ask what we call the two kinds of plates that Nephi used. (The large plates and the small plates.) Ask what was written on the large plates and the small plates.

Have your family turn to 1 Nephi 9:2–4 and look for the words "these plates" and "other plates" and underline them. Ask, "Which set of plates do you think the words 'these plates' refer to? What about the words 'other plates'?" Have family members write "small plates" next to the words "these plates" in their scriptures and "large plates" next to the words "other plates."

Bear your testimony that the Lord went to a lot of effort to bring these words to us, and encourage your family to make the study of the scriptures a lifelong practice.

1 Nephi 9:5–6
Why did the Lord tell Nephi to make another set of plates?

Ask your family, "Have you ever done something, just to be obedient, that didn't seem to make sense at the time, only to find out the reason later and then you were glad you obeyed?" Then explain, "Nephi had a similar experience. He had already made a set of plates to record the history of his family, which we call the 'large plates' of Nephi." (See 1 Nephi 9:2 footnote a.) Read 1 Nephi 9:5–6 with your family and

point out that Nephi didn't know why the Lord wanted him to make a second set of plates.

Elder James E. Talmage said, "The Plates of Nephi are so named from the fact that they were prepared and their record was begun by Nephi, son of Lehi. These plates were of two kinds, which may be distinguished as the larger plates and the smaller plates. . . .

"The object of this double line of history was unknown to Nephi; *it was enough for him that the Lord required the labor;* that it was for a wise purpose will be shown." (*Articles of Faith,* pp. 263–64; emphasis added.)

What does this teach us about Nephi and his trust in the Lord?

Explain to your family that Nephi did not know the reason for the second set of plates, but we do. Elder Jeffrey R. Holland taught:

"At least six times in the Book of Mormon, the phrase 'for a wise purpose' is used in reference to the making, writing, and preserving of the small plates of Nephi. (See 1 Ne. 9:5; W of M 1:7; Alma 37:2, 12, 14, 18.) We know one such wise purpose—the most obvious one—was to compensate for the future loss of 116 pages of manuscript translated by the Prophet Joseph Smith from the first part of the Book of Mormon. (See D&C 3, 10.)

"But it strikes me that there is a 'wiser purpose' than that, or perhaps more accurately, a 'wiser purpose' in that. The key to such a suggestion is in D&C 10:45. As the Lord instructs Joseph Smith on the procedure for translating and inserting the material from the small plates into what had been begun as the translation of the abridged large plates, he says, 'Behold, there are many things engraven upon the [small] plates of Nephi which do throw *greater views* upon my gospel' (emphasis added).

"So clearly this was not a *quid pro quo* in the development of the final Book of Mormon product. It was not tit for tat, this for that—116 pages of manuscript for 142 pages of printed text. Not so. We got back more than we lost. And it was known from the beginning that it would be so. We do not know exactly what we have missed in the lost 116 pages, but we do know that what we received on the small plates was the personal declarations of three great witnesses, three of the great doctrinal voices of the Book of Mormon, testifying that Jesus is the Christ." ("For a Wise Purpose," *Ensign,* January 1996, pp. 13–14.)

Ask, "What other events have occurred in scripture or your own life that let you know God sees all things from the beginning to the end?"

1 NEPHI 10: LEHI SEES THE FUTURE

1 Nephi 10:1
Nephi begins his own record

Tell your family that 1 Nephi 10:1 marks a significant beginning in the Book of Mormon record. Have them read that verse and see if they can tell what it is. Then share the following: "Up to now [1 Nephi chapters 1–9] Nephi had been summarizing the experiences of his father and abridging the record of Lehi. Now Nephi began an account of his own reign and ministry, which, of course, necessitated that a few more details of the teachings of Lehi and the doings of Laman and Lemuel be included." (Joseph Fielding McConkie and Robert L. Millet, *Doctrinal Commentary on the Book of Mormon,* 1:62.)

1 Nephi 10:1–14
The absolute reliability of prophecy

In 1 Nephi 10:1–14, Nephi records Lehi's prophecies about the Jews (verses 1–11) and the Gentiles and the rest of the house of Israel (verses 11–14). Have family members search these verses and together make a list of the things Lehi prophesied. Then discuss the list and show how they have all been, or are being, fulfilled. Bear your testimony about how reliable the Lord's promises are. (See also D&C 1:37–38.) Ask what promises the Lord has made to your family. Read

D&C 82:10 and discuss how you can make sure these promises come true.

1 Nephi 10:4–6
What does the title *Messiah* mean?

 Read 1 Nephi 10:4–6 with your family and have them mark three different titles for Jesus (*Messiah, Savior,* and *Redeemer*). Ask family members to turn to page 731 of the Bible Dictionary and find the entry for "Messiah." Have them search the first paragraph and find what *Messiah* means. What is the New Testament word that means the same thing? According to verses 4–6, what is Jesus "chosen" to do?

1 Nephi 10:4–6
Why do we need a Redeemer?

Ask each family member to draw the following scene: "Imagine you are walking through a forest by yourself. You take a step onto some loose brush only to find that it gives way, causing you to fall into a deep pit below. You are not hurt, but as you look around the pit, you realize there is no way for you to get out." Give everyone time to finish their drawing and then have them share what they drew. Ask them to tell what they would do in that situation.

Read 1 Nephi 10:4–6 with your family and ask them to find something in those verses that is like the pit that they drew. Then read following statement from President Joseph Fielding Smith: "This was precisely the condition that Adam placed himself and his posterity in, when he partook of the forbidden fruit. All being together in the pit, none could gain the surface and relieve the others. The pit was banishment from the presence of the Lord and temporal death, the dissolution of the body. And all being subject to death, none could provide the means of escape. Therefore, in his infinite mercy, the Father heard the cries of his children and sent his Only Begotten Son, who was not subject to death nor to sin, to provide the means of escape.

This he did through his infinite atonement and the everlasting gospel." (*Doctrines of Salvation,* 1:127.)

Elder Ted E. Brewerton of the Seventy explained what we must do to make the Atonement work for us:

"Imagine . . . that your sins have pulled you into the bottom of a deep pit. From a cliff high above, the Lord tosses a rope to you—the rope of mercy. In order for the rope to be of any help, you must tie it around you and fasten it with the knot of repentance. This is the only way to be pulled free of sin.

"In a very real way, repentance is one of the gifts we give to our Savior when we 'offer a sacrifice unto the Lord [our] God in righteousness, even that of a broken heart and a contrite spirit' (D&C 59:8). Through repentance, we may 'come boldly unto the throne of grace, that we may obtain mercy, and find grace to help in time of need' (Heb. 4:16). Nephi taught: 'For we know that it is by grace that we are saved, after all we can do' (2 Nephi 25:23).

"The grace of Jesus Christ makes up for our deficiencies when we are striving with all of our hearts to obey. Then we are promised that we will receive grace for grace unto salvation: 'For if you keep my commandments you shall receive of his fulness, and be glorified in me as I am in the Father; therefore, I say unto you, you shall receive grace for grace.' (D&C 93:20)." ("Rejoice in Christ," *Ensign,* December 1994, p. 8.)

Share with your family the following statement from President Ezra Taft Benson:

"Just as a man does not really desire food until he is hungry, so he does not desire the salvation of Christ until he knows why he needs Christ.

"No one adequately and properly knows why he needs Christ until he understands and accepts the doctrine of the Fall and its effect upon all mankind. And no other book in the world explains this vital doctrine nearly as well as the Book of Mormon." ("The Book of Mormon and the Doctrine and Covenants," *Ensign,* May 1987, p. 85.)

1 Nephi 10:12–14
What is the scattering and gathering of Israel?

Read 1 Nephi 10:12–14 with your family and ask if anyone can explain what it means when it says that the children of Israel would be "scattered" and "gathered." Use the following information to help with the explanation: Because of their unrighteousness and rebellion, the Lord scattered the twelve tribes of Israel. However, the Lord also used this scattering of his chosen people among the nations of the world to bless those nations. Lehi compared the house of Israel to an olive tree whose branches would be scattered all over the world because of their unbelief. He saw his own family as a part of that scattering. (See 1 Nephi 10:11–13.) He also prophesied that after the gospel had been taken to the Gentiles, the scattered branches of the house of Israel would be gathered again. Lehi then explained that to be "grafted in" to the tree, which represents the house of Israel, means to "come to the knowledge of the true Messiah" (verse 14). In other words, the way a person truly becomes a member of the house of Israel is to hear and accept the gospel of Jesus Christ.

Ask your family, "How are members of the Church helping to gather scattered Israel?"

1 Nephi 10:17
To listen requires more than hearing

Have a family member read 1 Nephi 10:17. Point out that Nephi had faith that he could "see" and "hear" and "know" the things his father saw "by the power of the Holy Ghost." There is a character in the Chinese language that is a good illustration of what Nephi knew. The Chinese character *Ting* means "to listen." It is made up of three characters, which individually are ear, eye, and heart.

To really listen to the Spirit, as Nephi was willing to do, we must do more than hear; we must see, hear, and know or feel with our heart. D&C 1:2 helps our understanding. Here the Lord tells us, "The voice of the Lord is unto all men . . . and there is no *eye* that shall not see, neither *ear* that shall not hear, neither *heart* that shall not be penetrated." (Italics added.) If we are to come to know what Nephi knew, perhaps we must *ting*.

Ask, "What can we do with our ears, our eyes, and our hearts to be able to see, to hear, and to feel messages from our Father in Heaven?"

1 Nephi 10:19
What are the mysteries of God?

"The term mysteries of God as used in the Book of Mormon denotes the saving principles of the gospel of Jesus Christ. They are termed mysteries because they are unavailable to the natural man, not because they are mysterious or difficult to understand. They must be revealed from God through faith and obedience. They are designed to lead God's children to eternal life. 'A mystery is a truth that cannot be known except through divine revelation—a sacred secret.'" (Hyrum M. Smith and Janne M. Sjodahl, *The Doctrine and Covenants Commentary,* p. 141).

1 NEPHI 11: NEPHI ALSO SEES THE TREE OF LIFE

1 Nephi 11
Illustrating the vision of Nephi

Before family scripture study begins, ask younger family members to draw the following pictures:

- Mary holding baby Jesus. (Verse 20.)
- John the Baptist baptizing Jesus. (Verse 27.)
- Jesus healing people. (Verse 31.)
- Jesus on the cross. (Verse 33.)

When you study about each event in Nephi's vision, have the children show what they drew. When they show each event, ask family members to share how that event shows the Lord's love for us.

1 Nephi 11:1
What does it take to receive personal revelation?

Ask a family member to read the chapter heading to 1 Nephi 11 and summarize what this chapter is about. Then read 1 Nephi 11:1 and have them look for three things Nephi did before he received this great revelation ("desired to know"; believed the Lord was able to show it; and "sat pondering in his heart"). Explain that pondering (which is thinking deeply) is an important but seldom used key to receiving personal revelation. Look in the following verses for how pondering played a part in some of the greatest revelations found in all scripture: D&C 138:1; D&C 76:19; Enos 1:3, Helaman 10:2, and Joseph Smith—History 1:8–12. Challenge your family to take time to ponder the things they read and improve their personal revelation.

1 Nephi 11:2–25
What is the meaning of the tree of life?

Write the following questions where your family can see them. Ask them to look for the answers to those questions as you read 1 Nephi 11:2–24, together as a family.

- What did Nephi want to see? (Verse 3.)
- What question did Nephi have after he saw the tree? (Verse 11.)
- What was Nephi shown when he asked what the tree meant? (Verses 13–20.) (Among other things your list should include Nazareth, the Virgin Mary, and the Christ child called the Lamb of God. You may want to have them mark these in their scriptures.)
- How is the birth and mission of Jesus Christ like the tree Lehi saw?
- What did the fruit of the tree do for Lehi? (See 1 Nephi 8:12.)

- What did Jesus do for Lehi, and all people, that would make Lehi that happy? (Cleanse him from his sins through the Atonement.)
- Why is the atonement of Jesus most desirable and joyous?
- What must we do to feel the joy that Lehi talked about?
- How is the word of God like a "rod of iron" (verse 25) as we travel through this world?

1 Nephi 11:26–36
What does the "great and spacious building" have to do with the crucifixion of Christ and the persecutions of His apostles?

Read 1 Nephi 11:36 with your family and have them mark what Nephi said was the meaning of the "great and spacious building." Then go back and read 1 Nephi 11:26–36 and have them look for what Nephi saw that taught him that.

President Ezra Taft Benson said, "It was through pride that Christ was crucified. The Pharisees were wroth because Jesus claimed to be the Son of God, which was a threat to their position, and so they plotted His death. (See John 11:53.)" ("Beware of Pride," *Ensign,* May 1989, p. 5.)

Ask your family to think of examples today of people who fight against or make fun of that which is good. Ask, "Why do you think they get so angry with those who are trying to keep God's commandments? What can our family do to be strong in the face of that kind of criticism?"

1 Nephi 11:16, 26
What does "condescension" mean?

After studying 1 Nephi 11:2–25, ask your family to look again at verse 16. Ask them if they understand what the "condescension of God" means. Elder Bruce R. McConkie said, "As I understand the definition of *condescension,* it is the act of descending to a lower and less dignified state; of waiving the privileges of one's rank and status; of bestowing honors and favors upon one of lesser stature or status."

("Behold the Condescension of God," *New Era,* December 1984, p. 35.)

Elder Marion D. Hanks said, "In 1 Nephi 11 there is recorded the sobering inquiry from an angel to Nephi as to whether he knows 'the condescension of God' (1 Ne. 11:16). In effect, the Lord seems to be asking if Nephi understands how close to man God is willing to come, how far he is willing to go to help us, how much he loves us, how much he does and is willing to do for us." ("An Attitude—The Weightier Matters," *Ensign,* July 1981, p. 69.)

Bear your testimony to your family of how much Heavenly Father and Jesus must love us to be willing to come down from their exalted station to be with us and lead us back to them.

1 NEPHI 12: AN OVERVIEW OF NEPHITE HISTORY

Show your family a map and ask them to pretend they are going on a journey together. Ask, "What are some reasons you might want to use a map? What value is there in seeing where you have been, where you are, and where you are going?" Explain to your family that just as a map overview helps us understand our journey better, an overview of Nephite history would help us understand the Book of Mormon better. First Nephi 12 provides just such a prophetic overview. In fact, 1 Nephi chapters 11–15 give us more than an overview of Nephite history; we also see a prophetic overview of what will happen to the Jews, the Gentiles, and the promised land after the Nephites.

Read the chapter headings for 1 Nephi 11–15 together as a family and list the events Nephi saw. Have your family write "Past" next to all the events on the list that have already come to pass or are happening now, and "Future" next to those events that we are still looking forward to. Ask your family how accurate Nephi's vision was of those things that have already happened. How accurate do you think his vision of future events will be?

Bear your testimony of what a blessing it is that the Lord still calls prophets to prepare us for what is coming in the future. Share the following statement:

"The Lord has blessed the lives of the Saints through the Presidents of the Church by enabling these prophets to see ahead of their times. Acting as seers (see Mosiah 8:15–16), they have been warned or made aware of future events or challenges long before these appeared on the horizon of human experience." (Richard Neitzel Holzapfel, "The Incomparable Blessings of the Priesthood," *Ensign,* October 1997, p. 46.)

Ask your family, "Do you believe that the prophet today sees ahead of his time? Can you think of any examples to share?" Read the following statement from President Gordon B. Hinckley:

"The time has now come to turn about and face the future. This is a season of a thousand opportunities. It is ours to grasp and move forward. What a wonderful time it is for each of us to do his or her small part in moving the work of the Lord on to its magnificent destiny.

"Now, what of the future? What of the years that lie ahead? It looks promising indeed.

"If we will go forward, never losing sight of our goal, speaking ill of no one, living the great principles we know to be true, this cause will roll on in majesty and power to fill the earth. Doors now closed to the preaching of the gospel will be opened. The Almighty, if necessary, may have to shake the nations to humble them and cause them to listen to the servants of the living God. Whatever is needed will come to pass.

"We have glimpsed the future, we know the way, we have the truth. God help us to move forward to become a great and mighty people spread over the earth, counted in the millions, but all of one faith and of one testimony and of one conviction, I humbly pray in the name of our great Redeemer and Savior, even Jesus Christ, amen." ("Look to the Future," *Ensign,* November 1997, pp. 67–68.)

Ask, "What is comforting about President Hinckley's view of the future? What have you seen happen since this statement was given in 1997 that shows he is right? What part do we need to play in the destiny of God's kingdom?"

1 Nephi 12:1–23
The burden of knowing the future

 Read 1 Nephi 12:1–23 as a family and discuss the events Nephi was shown would happen in the future. You may want to have family members label each event in the margins of their scriptures and write the reference where the fulfillment of these prophecies is found. Suggested labels are given in parentheses below:

- Verses 1–3: the growth of the Nephite and Lamanite nations in the new world, their wars and contentions (Nephite-Lamanite wars, 2 Nephi–3 Nephi 7).
- Verse 4: The great destruction experienced in the Americas at the time of Christ's death (Destruction at crucifixion, 3 Nephi 8).
- Verses 5–6: Jesus appears to the more righteous after His resurrection (Christ appears to the Nephites, 3 Nephi 9–11).
- Verses 7–10: Jesus chooses twelve Nephite disciples and gives them power (Twelve disciples chosen, 3 Nephi 12–30).
- Verses 11–12: The people enjoy two centuries of righteousness after Christ's visit (200 years of righteousness, 4 Nephi).
- Verses 13–19: The people return to wickedness, which eventually leads to the entire destruction of the Nephites (Return to wickedness—Nephites destroyed, Mormon and Moroni).
- Verses 20–23: the Lamanites divide and dwindle in unbelief (Lamanites dwindle in unbelief, Mormon 8:8).

Remind your family that Nephi received this revelation while his father's little colony was still camped by the Red Sea. They had not yet seen the promised land, and Nephi and his brothers were not even married. Ask your family what is exciting and what is sad about what Nephi saw. Ask them what that tells us about the burden of being a prophet.

1 Nephi 12:17–18
What is the meaning of the "mists of darkness" and the "spacious building?"

 Have a family member wear a blindfold for ten minutes before family scripture study. When you get to 1 Nephi 12:17, ask the blindfolded person what it was like being in the dark and what difficulties he or she encountered. Ask your family why they think the temptations of the devil are symbolized as mists of darkness that "blindeth the eyes." How is giving in to temptation like walking blind?

Tell your family that although Satan would have us think that sin will bring happiness, it never does. Read together 1 Nephi 12:18 and look for the meaning of the "large and spacious building." Explain that Satan would have us think that life in the large and spacious building is wonderful, but it is not. Share the following statement by Elder Glenn L. Pace:

"To those of you who are inching your way closer and closer to that great and spacious building, let me make it completely clear that the people in that building have absolutely nothing to offer except instant, short-term gratification inescapably connected to long-term sorrow and suffering. The commandments you observe were not given by a dispassionate God to prevent you from having fun, but by a loving Father in Heaven who wants you to be happy while you are living on this earth as well as in the hereafter." ("They're Not Really Happy," *Ensign,* November 1987, p. 40.)

Ask your family why they think a "great and spacious building" is a good symbol for the pride of the world.

1 NEPHI 13: NEPHI'S VISION OF LATTER-DAY AMERICA

1 Nephi 13:4
Who are the Gentiles?

After reading 1 Nephi 13:1–4 with your family, ask if anyone can explain who these "Gentile" nations were. Have them turn to page 679 in the Bible Dictionary and have someone read aloud the first paragraph of the entry for "Gentile." According to that paragraph, what are "Gentile" nations? (All nations that do not have the gospel.) Which "nations and kingdoms" did not have the gospel? (All nations were without the gospel until 1830 when it was restored through the Prophet Joseph Smith).

1 Nephi 13:4–9
What is the Great and Abominable Church?

As you read 1 Nephi 13:4–9, have your family look for the origin of the "great and abominable church" and for the things it desires. To help them understand what that church is, share the following statement from Elder Bruce R. McConkie:

"The titles *church of the devil* and *great and abominable church* are used to identify all churches or organizations of whatever name or nature—whether political, philosophical, educational, economic social, fraternal, civic, or religious—which are designed to take men on a course that leads away from God and his laws and thus from salvation in the kingdom of God. . . .

"Any church or organization of any kind whatever which satisfies the innate religious longings of man and keeps him from coming to the saving truths of Christ and his gospel is therefore not of God." (*Mormon Doctrine,* p. 138.)

Ask your family how they can avoid being deceived by people or organizations that would lead them away from Jesus Christ. (See 1 Nephi 8:33–34.)

1 Nephi 13:10–19

How well does the Lord know the future?

To help your family understand the wonderful prophecies the Lord gave to Nephi, play the following matching game. Write each of the following scriptural references on a separate small slip of paper: 1 Nephi 13:10; 1 Nephi 13:12; 1 Nephi 13:13; 1 Nephi 13:14–15; 1 Nephi 13:17–19; 1 Nephi 13:20–23.

On other slips of paper write the following: The Atlantic Ocean, Christopher Columbus, The Pilgrims, Other Colonists, The Revolutionary War, The Bible.

Lay the papers on the floor and as you read 1 Nephi 13:10–19, have your family match the scripture reference with the historical event. The correct matches are: 1 Nephi 13:10 = The Atlantic Ocean; 1 Nephi 13:12 = Christopher Columbus; 1 Nephi 10:13 = The Pilgrims; 1 Nephi 13:14–15 = Other Colonists; 1 Nephi 13:17–19 = The Revolutionary War; 1 Nephi 13:20–23 = The Bible.

Ask your family what they think is most remarkable about what Nephi saw. What does this teach us about how well the Lord knows our future?

1 Nephi 13:12

Who was the "man among the Gentiles"?

After reading 1 Nephi 13:12, ask your family who they think that man might be. Elder Mark E. Peterson said, "It was Christopher Columbus whom he saw, and he observed further that the discoverer was guided by divine power on his journey." (Mark E. Petersen, *The Great Prologue*, pp. 3, 26.)

In his own words Christopher Columbus recounted his feelings: "From my youth onward, I was a seaman and have so continued until this day. . . . The Lord was well disposed to my desire, and he bestowed upon me courage and understanding; knowledge of seafaring He gave me in abundance, of astronomy likewise. . . . I have studied all books—cosmographies, histories, chronicles, and philosophies, and other arts, for which our Lord unlocked my mind, sent me upon the sea, and gave me fire for the deed. Those who heard of my [enterprise] called it foolish, mocked me, and laughed. But who can doubt but that the Holy Ghost inspired me?" (Jacob Wassermann, *Columbus, Don Quixote of the Seas*, pp. 19–20.)

Ask your family what Columbus said that matches 1 Nephi 13:12. Tell your family that Columbus sailed in A.D. 1492. Have them look at the date at the bottom of the scripture page. Ask, "How many years before Columbus sailed did Nephi know about his voyage? What impresses you most about this prophecy?"

1 Nephi 13:14

How were the Lamanites "scattered before the Gentiles"?

After reading 1 Nephi 13:14, share the following statement by a historian: "From Columbus' landing in the West Indies, the driving began. At the turn of the twentieth century, there were an estimated 235,000 Indians living in North America. What happened to them all? Some scholars feel smallpox, bubonic plague, typhus, influenza, malaria, measles, yellow fever, were brought by the 'Gentiles.' . . . Slave labor took place in vast array. Thousands were shipped to Europe. In the West Indies the gentle people that met Columbus were worked to death. They were so bad off they were driven to mass suicide, the abstinence of having children so that their children would not be born into such conditions. In only fifty-six years, the population of Haiti and Santo Domingo went from an estimated two to three hundred thousand at the arrival of Columbus to less than five hundred surviving natives in 1548." (Kenneth Scott Latourette, *A History of the Expansions of Christianity, The Great Century*, 4:323.)

1 Nephi 13:24–29
What has been taken from the Bible and why?

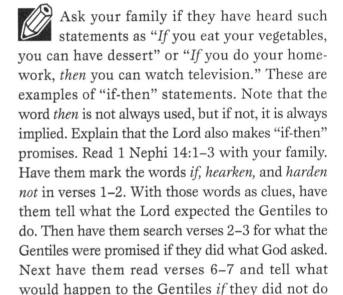 Read 1 Nephi 13:24–29 with your family and ask them if they can think of any "plain and precious" truths that are missing from the Bible. Have them turn to the Articles of Faith and pick out simple truths mentioned there that are not clear in the Bible. What does Articles of Faith 1:8 suggest is at least one reason truths are missing from the Bible?

The Prophet Joseph Smith said, "I believe the Bible as it read when it came from the pen of the original writers. Ignorant translators, careless transcribers, or designing and corrupt priests have committed many errors." (*Teachings of the Prophet Joseph Smith,* p. 327: see also *History of the Church,* 1:245.) Ask, "What does 1 Nephi 13:29 suggest as a reason Satan wanted truths taken from the Bible? Can you think of any examples of mistakes people make because the Bible is not clear enough?"

1 Nephi 13:31–42
What will the Lord do about the truths missing from the Bible?

As you read 1 Nephi 13:32–40, have your family look for two things the Lord promised to do about the mistakes in the Bible. To help them find what the Lord will do, ask the following questions when you come to these verses in your reading:

- Verse 35, What book was written by Nephi's seed and "hid up"? (The Book of Mormon).
- Verse 39, What "other books" have come forth that testify to the truth of Jesus Christ?

Share the following statement: "These other books are the Book of Mormon, The Doctrine and Covenants, and the revelations of the Lord to Joseph Smith." (Joseph Fielding Smith, *Man His Origin and Destiny,* pp. 411–12.)

Ask your family how much different we should be from the rest of the world because we have so many "plain and precious" truths restored to us. What if we do not study and apply them?

1 NEPHI 14: NEPHI'S VISION OF LATTER-DAY GENTILES

1 Nephi 14:1–7
Find the "if-then" promises

Ask your family if they have heard such statements as "*If* you eat your vegetables, you can have dessert" or "*If* you do your homework, *then* you can watch television." These are examples of "if-then" statements. Note that the word *then* is not always used, but if not, it is always implied. Explain that the Lord also makes "if-then" promises. Read 1 Nephi 14:1–3 with your family. Have them mark the words *if, hearken,* and *harden not* in verses 1–2. With those words as clues, have them tell what the Lord expected the Gentiles to do. Then have them search verses 2–3 for what the Gentiles were promised if they did what God asked. Next have them read verses 6–7 and tell what would happen to the Gentiles *if* they did not do what the Lord commanded.

Ask, "What additional meaning do these verses have for us when we realize that we, who have received the gospel in these last days, *are* the Gentiles referred to in these verses?"

1 Nephi 14:10
Why Are There "Two Churches Only"?

Read 1 Nephi 14:10 with your family and ask them why they think the Lord said there were really only two churches, even though we see many different churches all around us. To help answer that question, share the following statement from Elder Bruce R. McConkie: "The titles church of the devil and great and abominable church are used to identify all churches or organizations of whatever name or nature—whether political, philosophical, educational, economic, social, fraternal, civic, or religious—which are designed to take men on a course that leads away from God and his laws and thus from salvation in the kingdom of God." (*Mormon Doctrine,* pp. 137–38.)

Certainly truth and goodness can be found in many other churches, but the fulness of the gospel, that which provides salvation, is found only in The Church of Jesus Christ of Latter-day Saints.

1 Nephi 14:11–16
How the Saints Can Defeat the Great and Abominable Church

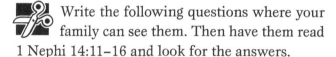 Write the following questions where your family can see them. Then have them read 1 Nephi 14:11–16 and look for the answers.

- What word is used to describe the number of Saints?
- How many would fight against them?
- Though their total numbers are small, where will the Saints be found? (Upon all the face of the earth.)
- How are the Saints able to survive this battle? (See especially verses 14–15.)
- What kind of weapons were the Saints armed with?

Bear your testimony to your family that no matter how numerous the wicked become, the Lord is more powerful still. Ask your family what these verses teach us about surviving in a wicked world. (Remember 1 Nephi 1:20.)

1 Nephi 14:18–30
Nephi sees the mission of John the Apostle

Assign your family to silently read 1 Nephi 14:18–30. Tell them they will have a quiz on what they have read. When they have finished, ask the following questions:

1. Who was the man Nephi saw in vision? (See verses 20, 27.3)

2. What was the book Nephi beheld proceeding out of the mouth of the Jew? (The Bible—verse 23.)

3. What did the angel say about the things that

were written in the book? (They were plain, pure, and precious and easy to understand—verse 23.)

4. Why was Nephi forbidden to write the all the things he saw? (See verse 25.)

5. Others have seen what Nephi saw. Where are their writings? (See verse 26.)

After the quiz, ask your family when they think we will get those purer accounts? Elder Bruce R. McConkie said, "We have not received, by any means, all of the word of the Lord. I think we have received most of the word of the Lord that is required until the Second Coming. The Lord has given all that people in the world have the spiritual capacity to receive at this time. There is going to be another great dispensation, that is, another great period of enlightenment, when he comes; and at that time he will reveal all things, such as the sealed portion of the Book of Mormon. But he will not reveal the sealed portion of the Book of Mormon now, and let us publish it to the world, because what it contains is so far beyond the spiritual capacity of men that it would drive people away from the truth rather than lead them to the truth. Actually, it is an act of mercy for the Lord to limit, to a particular people, the amount of revelation they receive." ("This Generation Shall Have My Word through You," *Ensign,* June 1980, p. 54.) (For more information about the sealed portion, see 2 Nephi 27:7; 3 Nephi 26:9–11; Ether 4:7.)

Ask family members why they think Nephi closed with what he said in verses 29–30. What can we do to make better use of the scriptures we have now and get ready for what is to come?

1 NEPHI 15: NEPHI TEACHES HIS BROTHERS

1 Nephi 15:2–11
How to get revelation from the Lord

Tell your family that 1 Nephi 15:1–11 uses the example of Laman and Lemuel to give us some wonderful insight into how we can receive personal revelation from the Lord. As you read verses 1–10 with your family, have them point out the reasons Nephi gives for why Laman and Lemuel did not understand what their father said to them about the dream he had in 1 Nephi 8. Then read together verse 11 and have them mark the three things Nephi said they must do to understand their father's dream. (Not harden their hearts, ask in faith, and be diligent in keeping the commandments.) Ask them how Nephi knew that this formula would help them receive their own revelation. (Remind them that 1 Nephi 11–14 contains the explanation of Lehi's dream that was revealed to Nephi that very same way.)

Bear testimony to your family of the importance of being worthy to receive personal revelation from the Lord. Share an experience you have had when the Lord has answered your prayers.

1 Nephi 15:21–29, 36
Label the objects

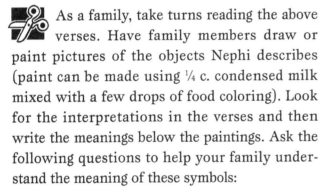 As a family, take turns reading the above verses. Have family members draw or paint pictures of the objects Nephi describes (paint can be made using ¼ c. condensed milk mixed with a few drops of food coloring). Look for the interpretations in the verses and then write the meanings below the paintings. Ask the following questions to help your family understand the meaning of these symbols:

- How is the word of God like an iron rod? (See verse 24; you may wish to sing "Hold to the Rod," *Hymns,* no. 274.)
- What promise does Nephi make to those who hold to the rod? (See verse 24.)
- How are temptations like fiery darts?
- How does filthiness separate us from God and the Saints? (See verses 26–30, 34.)

Display the pictures where your family will see them often during the coming week. Use them to remind your family of where they want to go and how they can get there.

1 Nephi 15:34
What does it mean to be clean?

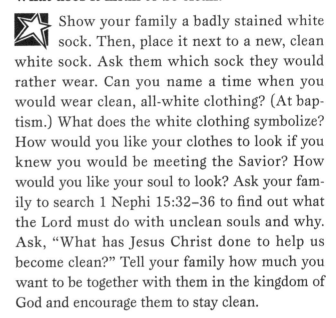 Show your family a badly stained white sock. Then, place it next to a new, clean white sock. Ask them which sock they would rather wear. Can you name a time when you would wear clean, all-white clothing? (At baptism.) What does the white clothing symbolize? How would you like your clothes to look if you knew you would be meeting the Savior? How would you like your soul to look? Ask your family to search 1 Nephi 15:32–36 to find out what the Lord must do with unclean souls and why. Ask, "What has Jesus Christ done to help us become clean?" Tell your family how much you want to be together with them in the kingdom of God and encourage them to stay clean.

1 NEPHI 16: DIRECTED BY THE LIAHONA

1 Nephi 16:1–39
Why were Laman and Lemuel so upset?

Show your family a school paper, test, or assignment that has been corrected. Look at the items that were marked wrong. Ask them why it is uncomfortable to have others correct our work, if showing our mistakes helps us to learn. What other corrections have you received besides on schoolwork?

Review with your family the message of 1 Nephi 15. (Use the chapter heading, and also pay special attention to verses 32–36.) Then read 1 Nephi 16:1–5 and ask why Nephi's brothers thought his message was hard? Why do the wicked take the "truth to be hard"? How could Nephi's counsel in verses 3–4 help us when we are corrected? According to verse 5, how did Nephi's brethren respond to his teaching?

Next read 1 Nephi 16:37–39 and ask how Nephi's correction of his brethren is similar to the correction described in these verses. The next time you are corrected, what might be the best way to respond?

1 Nephi 16:10–31
Do we have anything like a Liahona today?

Show your family a compass and teach them how it works. Have them find which direction is north. Give each member of your family a sheet of paper or perhaps a ball on which they can draw. Ask them to read 1 Nephi 16:10, 16, 26–30 and list as many descriptions of the Liahona as they can find. Have each person share what they found. Ask some of these questions:

- How did the Liahona help Lehi's family?
- Would you like to find a Liahona today? Why?
- What kind of guidance and direction would you seek?

Share the following statement with your family: "Wouldn't you like to have that kind of a ball, each one of you, so that you would always know when you were in error or in the wrong way? . . . That, my young brethren, you all have. The Lord gave to every boy, every man, every person, a conscience which tells him every time he starts to go on the wrong path. He is always told if he is listening; but people can, of course, become so used to hearing the messages that they ignore them until finally they do not register anymore." (Spencer W. Kimball, "Our Own Liahona," *Ensign*, November 1976, p. 77.)

Ask your family to list other blessings we have that give us direction like a Liahona. (Your list could include the scriptures, living prophets, prayer, and patriarchal blessings.) How do all these gifts give us guidance today? What do you think might happen if we ignore the messages and warnings we are given?

Tell your family of a time when the Spirit has guided you in one of those ways. Share your testimony of the importance of always giving heed to the promptings from the Lord.

1 Nephi 16:18–31
Lessons from a broken bow

Ask family members which of the following would be the most difficult for them to deal with:

1. Moving from your home because your parents lost their jobs.
2. Spending many weeks in a hospital because of illness.
3. Temporarily living in a shelter and relying on food storage because of a natural disaster.

Together, read 1 Nephi 16:13–21 and find out what challenges Lehi's family faced. Ask why this would be a difficult challenge. How does it compare to the three examples above?

Ask your family to look again at verse 20 and tell how most of the group, including Lehi, reacted to the lack of food. Murmuring may be a common reaction to hardship and hunger, but did complaining help solve their problem?

Compare the complaining of this group with what Nephi did in verses 22–30. How could Nephi's non-complaining and productive example help us in our difficult situations?

1 Nephi 16:23–27
Seek instruction from the proper leaders

After your family has read 1 Nephi 16:23–27, ask them why they think Nephi asked his father where to go to find food instead of simply asking God himself. What happened to Lehi after Nephi went to him for direction? To help illustrate why it was important for Nephi to look to Lehi for leadership, share the following story told by President Ezra Taft Benson:

"Some time ago, a young man came to my office requesting a blessing. He was about eighteen years of age and had some problems. There were no serious moral problems, but he was mixed up in his thinking and worried. He requested a blessing.

"I said to him, 'Have you ever asked your father to give you a blessing? Your father is a member of the Church, I assume?'

"He said, 'Yes, he is an elder, a rather inactive elder.'

"When I asked, 'Do you love your father?' he replied, 'Yes, Brother Benson, he is a good man. I love him.' He then said, 'He doesn't attend to his priesthood duties as he should. He doesn't go to church regularly, I don't know that he is a tithe payer, but he is a good man, a good provider, a kind man.'

"I said, 'How would you like to talk to him at an opportune time and ask him if he would be willing to give you a father's blessing?'

"'Oh,' he said, 'I think that would frighten him.'

"I then said, 'Are you willing to try it? I will be praying for you.'

"He said, 'All right; on that basis, I will.'

"A few days later he came back. He said, 'Brother Benson, that's the sweetest thing that has happened in our family.' He could hardly control his feelings as he told me what had happened. He said, 'When the opportunity was right, I mentioned it to Father, and he replied, "Son, do you really want me to give you a blessing?" I told him, "Yes, Dad, I would like you to."' Then he said, 'Brother Benson, he gave me one of the most beautiful blessings you could ever ask for. Mother sat there crying all during the blessing. When he got through there was a bond of appreciation and gratitude and love between us that we have never had in our home.'" ("A Message to the Rising Generation," *Ensign,* November 1977, pp. 31–32.)

1 NEPHI 17: NEPHI IS COMMANDED TO BUILD A SHIP

1 Nephi 17:1–6
Great blessings and raw meat

Ask your family to imagine that hot showers, warm meals, and clean clothes were suddenly no longer available. Would you consider that a blessing? Have your family read and com-

pare 1 Nephi 1:1 with 1 Nephi 17:1–2 and tell what Nephi's attitude was about the hardships he faced. Why do you think Nephi felt so blessed in spite of their sufferings?

To help answer that question, have your family read and compare 1 Nephi 17:3 with 1 Nephi 3:7. Ask them what Nephi is trying to teach us here about the relationship between obedience and the Lord's blessings. What do we need to do so the Lord will help us with the problems or trials that we face?

Tell your family that Joseph Smith's enemies once told him that the Latter-day Saints would be driven to hell. He responded, "And if we go to hell, we will turn the devils out of doors and make a heaven of it." (*History of the Church,* 5:517.) Bear your testimony that as long as we try our best to be obedient, the Lord will help us through all our trials.

1 Nephi 17:7–17
Whither shall I go that I may find ore?

Ask your family to suppose they were asked to do a difficult task like building a house or a highway bridge. Have them write down the first questions that come to mind. (It will probably be something like "How am I supposed to do that?") Then have them search 1 Nephi 17:7–10 and find the task Nephi was assigned. Write down the one question Nephi asked. What does it teach us about Nephi that he did not say, "How in the world am I supposed to build a ship?"

Then read 1 Nephi 17:15–22 together and compare Nephi's response to the way Laman and Lemuel reacted. What does their murmuring teach us about Laman and Lemuel? What would Laman and Lemuel have to do to have faith like Nephi's? (See 1 Nephi 2:16.)

President Harold B. Lee taught, "The trouble with us today, there are too many of us who put question marks instead of periods after what the Lord says. I want you to think about that. We shouldn't be concerned about why he said something, or whether or not it can be made so. Just trust the Lord." ("Admonitions for the Priesthood of God," *Ensign,* January 1973, p. 108.) Similarly, Elder Russell M. Nelson testified that "once you stop putting question marks behind the prophet's statements and put exclamation points instead, and do it, the blessings just pour." ("A Study in Obedience," *Ensign,* August 1982, p. 24.)

1 Nephi 17:23–43
How do you teach the hard of heart?

Tell your family that as they learned in 1 Nephi 17:20–22, Laman and Lemuel thought they would have been better off staying in Jerusalem. Explain that the rest of 1 Nephi 17 tells what Nephi did to convince his brothers to follow the Lord and their father, the prophet Lehi. Just before you read together each set of verses below, read or show the questions that go with that set of verses and have your family look for the answers as they read.

- 1 Nephi 17:23–27: What scripture story did Nephi tell? How is that story like what was happening to Lehi's family?

- 1 Nephi 17:28–30: How are these verses like what happened to Lehi's family?

- 1 Nephi 17:31–35: Why does the Lord bless one group of people and destroy another?

- 1 Nephi 17:36–43: What message do you think Nephi wanted Laman and Lemuel to get out of these verses?

- 1 Nephi 17:44–47: Nephi described two different "voices" the Lord can use to speak to us. Which one would you prefer and why?

- 1 Nephi 17:48–55: When Laman and Lemuel got angry and tried to kill Nephi, what finally convinced them to follow the Lord?

Ask each family member to say what part of this chapter impressed him or her the most and tell why.

1 Nephi 17:45
What is "the still small voice"?

 After reading 1 Nephi 17:45 with your family, tell them that listening to the voice of the Lord is a little like listening to the radio. Turn on a radio and tune it to a spot where all you can hear is static. Ask how this radio signal is like what Laman and Lemuel received from the Lord. Now tune the radio to a crystal-clear station. Ask how this signal is like what Nephi heard.

Share the following statement from Elder Boyd K. Packer: "The scriptures generally use the word *voice,* which does not exactly fit. These delicate, refined communications are not seen with our eyes, nor heard with our ears. And even though it is described as a voice, it is a voice that one feels, more than one hears." ("Candle of the Lord," *Ensign,* January 1983, p. 52.)

Ask your family why someone with a hard heart would have difficulty hearing the voice of the Spirit. Bear your testimony of how wonderful it is when you are able to feel communication from the Spirit.

1 NEPHI 18: SAILING TO THE PROMISED LAND

1 Nephi 18:1–4
How did Nephi know how to build a ship?

Ask your family how they would respond if someone asked them to do something beyond their ability (such as build a new home, perform surgery on someone, or write a new computer program). How would your response differ if the Lord did the asking? Read together 1 Nephi 17:8 and review what the Lord asked Nephi to do. Ask, "How did Nephi respond, even though he had never built a ship before? Why do you think Nephi responded the way he did?"

Have family members take turns reading aloud 1 Nephi 18:1–3. Then ask the following questions:

- How did Nephi know how to build a ship?
- What did Nephi do so the Lord could "show" him how to build a ship?
- According to verse 3, what did Nephi do to experience the power of prayer?
- What can you learn from Nephi about getting the Lord's help during challenging times?

1 Nephi 18:5–8
Be prepared

If there is a Boy Scout in the family, have him recite the scout motto ("Be prepared"). Ask your family to imagine that you're going on a long cruise together. Have each family member choose something they would want to take on the cruise and bring it to the kitchen table. After the family has gathered, discuss what each person brought to the table and how it would make them "prepared" for their cruise.

Explain that Lehi's family really did go on a long cruise. Have them scan 1 Nephi 18:5–8 and make a list of the things that they took with them. Discuss each item by asking why it was brought along and how it helped them to "be prepared." (Your list could include fruits, meat, honey, provisions, seeds, and family members.) You might ask the following questions:

- How do you think their preparations helped them when they arrived in the promised land?
- What can we learn from their physical journey to the promised land that might help us on our spiritual journey to the celestial kingdom? (See Alma 12:24.)
- According to D&C 38:30, what great blessing comes to those who are prepared physically and spiritually?

1 Nephi 18:9
Why do we forget the Lord?

Invite family members to share a funny experience when they forgot something or someone. Ask why they think it is sometimes easy to forget things. What are the most serious things

to forget about? Share the following quotation from Elder L. Tom Perry:

"Is the order of things right in our own lives? . . . Do we have an eternal perspective? Or have we fallen into the trap of investing in the things of this world first and then forgetting the Lord?" ("United in Building the Kingdom of God," *Ensign,* May 1987, p. 34.) Ask family members what it would mean to "forget the Lord."

Tell the family that they are going to search 1 Nephi 18 for examples of forgetting or remembering the Lord. On a piece of paper, draw three columns. Title the first column "Laman and Lemuel, the second "Ishmael's Sons," and the third "Nephi." Read together 1 Nephi 18:9–21 verse by verse. Under each column, write how those people either forgot or remembered the Lord. Ask the following questions:

- Why do you think Nephi's brothers so often forgot the Lord?
- How tempting would it have been for Nephi to have gone along with the others?
- What happens when a person sincerely remembers the Lord?

1 Nephi 18:11–20
Where do you go for help?

 Ask family members to whom they would go for help with the following problems:

- A math problem.
- Trouble with a friend.
- Lack of money.
- A serious disease.

Ask if it is possible to have a challenge that no one on earth can help with. What do you do then? Ask your family to search 1 Nephi 18:11–17 and tell how that is like what happened to Nephi. Have family members search verses 17–19 and find out who tried to help Nephi and how. Were they successful? Then read verse 20 together and find out how Nephi finally got free. What can we learn from Nephi's experience? Where can we always go for help? (See 1 Nephi 18:16.) Share the following quotation from President Gordon B. Hinckley:

"We have come to see how helpless man is when nature goes on a rampage. We're really helpless. There isn't much we can do. We come to realize that . . . when all is said and done we must put our trust in [God] and walk in obedience to His commandments. That is the only safety we have." ("News of the Church," *Ensign,* February 1999, p. 75.)

1 Nephi 18:21
What is a "type" of Christ?

Ask family members if they believe the following idea: "Every prophet is a type of Jesus." (Joseph Fielding McConkie and Donald W. Parry, *A Guide to Scriptural Symbols,* p. 91.) Explain that a "type" is a symbol, representation, or example of something else. Read together 1 Nephi 18:21 and look for what Nephi did that was a "type" of something similar that Jesus did. Compare what Nephi did with Mark 4:34–39. Invite your family to look for more ways that the lives of the prophets remind us of the Savior as you continue studying the Book of Mormon.

1 NEPHI 19: ALL SCRIPTURES ARE FOR OUR PROFIT AND LEARNING

1 Nephi 19:1–4
Two sets of plates

Remind your family that in 1 Nephi 9, they learned that when Nephi wrote about "these plates," he was referring to the small plates of Nephi; the phrase "first plates" or "other plates" refers to the large plates of Nephi. (See 1 Nephi 9:1–4.) Divide a piece of paper into two columns. Label the first column "The large plates of Nephi called 'first plates' or 'other plates.'" Label the second column "The small plates of Nephi called 'these plates.'" Read together 1 Nephi 19:1–4 and list in the appropriate column the

things Nephi said were on each set of plates. Ask which set of plates would be of the greatest benefit to us today?

Tell your family that when Joseph Smith began translating, he started with the material on the large plates. Have them read the section heading to D&C 10 and verse 1 and tell what happened to the first 116 pages of manuscript translated by the Prophet. Read D&C 10:10–14 to find out what Satan did to try to destroy the work of the translation of the Book of Mormon. Then read D&C 10:38–42 and see what the Lord told Joseph to do about Satan's plan. Ask your family what comfort they find in knowing that the Lord prepared two sets of plates to defeat Satan's plan more than 2,000 years in advance.

1 Nephi 19:7
How do people trample God under their feet?

Hold up a flag of a country for which you have great respect and love. Ask, "If people have a great love for their country, how do you think they might feel if another person burned their flag? What are some things that you consider special or sacred? How does it make you feel when someone makes fun of or mocks those things?"

Explain that the word "naught" means worthless, while the word "hearken" means to listen or obey. Have your family read 1 Nephi 19:7, substituting the definitions listed for the words "naught" and "hearken." Then ask how men "trample God under their feet."

1 Nephi 19:8–12
List the prophecies of Jesus Christ's life

Read 1 Nephi 19:8–10 and list on a piece of paper the prophecies of the Savior's life. Look in verse 9 for a phrase that is repeated three times and mark it ("he suffereth it"). One meaning of the word "suffereth" is "allowed." According to this verse, why would Jesus "allow" them to do those things to him. Ask, "Have there been times in your life when you chose not to retaliate after a wrong was done to you? How did you feel?"

1 Nephi 19:8–17
Who Were Zenock, Neum, and Zenos?

After reading 1 Nephi 19:8–12 with your family, ask them to look on the bottom of the page and find when Nephi wrote these prophecies. Remind them that Nephi was quoting the Old Testament prophets Zenock, Neum, and Zenos, whose writings were on the plates of brass. Therefore they must have lived before Lehi left Jerusalem in 600 B.C. Their testimonies and names are not found in our Old Testament and were apparently some of the "plain and most precious" truths removed from the Bible (1 Nephi 13:26). Without the Book of Mormon, we would know nothing about these three Old Testament prophets.

1 Nephi 19:13–16
Why were the Jews scattered, and when will they be gathered?

Tell your family that the scattering of Israel is often spoken in the Bible but the reasons for the scattering are often misunderstood. As you read 1 Nephi 19:13–14 with your family, have them find phrases that describe the reasons why the Israelites were hated and scattered.

Elder Bruce R. McConkie said, "Why was Israel scattered? The answer is clear. . . . Our Israelite forebears were scattered because they rejected the gospel, defiled the priesthood, forsook the church, and departed from the kingdom. They were scattered because they turned from the Lord, worshipped false gods, and walked in all the ways of the heathen nations. They were scattered because they forsook the Abrahamic covenant, trampled under their feet the holy ordinances, and rejected the Lord Jehovah, who is the Lord Jesus, of whom all their prophets testified." (*A New Witness for the Articles of Faith*, p. 515.)

Next have your family read 1 Nephi 19:15–16

and see what must happen before the Lord will gather scattered Israel home. Bear your testimony to your family that they are part of Israel that has accepted Jesus Christ and have been gathered out of the world to the Church of Jesus Christ.

1 Nephi 19:23
What does it mean to "liken" the scriptures to ourselves?

Many members of the Church wear a ring with the letters *CTR* on it. (If you have one, show it to your family.) Ask what these letters represent ("Choose the Right"). Invite a family member to tell of a time when he or she faced a difficult decision about keeping the standards of the gospel.

To see how the study of the scriptures can help us learn how to act in certain situations, read the following statement by Elder Carlos E. Asay: "How many times have parents heard a son or daughter complain, 'Let's not read the scriptures. They deal with people of an ancient day and are boring.' When complaints of this nature are voiced, it is likely that the parents have failed to do what Nephi did. Said he: 'I did liken all scriptures unto us, that it might be for our profit and learning' (1 Nephi 19:23)." (*Family Pecan Trees: Planting a Legacy of Faith at Home*, p. 39.)

To "liken" means "to compare; to represent as resembling or similar." (Noah Webster, *An American Dictionary of the English Language*.) So, to "liken" means to "apply." Tell your family that they may want to ask some of the following questions when reading scriptures for application:

- If I were in a similar situation, how would I act?
- Do I act like anyone in this story? (For example, am I more like Nephi or Laman?)
- Why did the Lord include this scripture or situation in the scriptures?
- What can I learn from these verses that can apply to my life? (For example: What can I learn about obedience from Nephi?)

Tell your family that another way to help

"liken the scriptures" unto us is to substitute our own name in the place of a name or pronoun in the scriptures. Have them pick one of your favorite scriptures and try it. (For example, 1 Nephi 3:7.)

Read the following statement by President Brigham Young: "Do you read the Scriptures, my brethren and sisters, as though you were writing them, a thousand, two thousand, or five thousand years ago? Do you read them as though you stood in the place of the men who wrote them? If you do not feel thus, it is your privilege to do so, that you may be as familiar with the spirit and meaning of the written word of God as you are with your daily walk and conversation, or as you are with your workmen or with your households." (*Discourses of Brigham Young,* p. 128.)

1 NEPHI 20–21: NEPHI SHARES ISAIAH 48–49

1 Nephi 20–21
What did Isaiah say that can be "likened" unto Lehi's people and to us?

Have your family turn to 3 Nephi 23:1–3 and find the name of a prophet Jesus specifically commanded us to read. Ask them what reasons Jesus gave for why Isaiah's words are so great. Review together 1 Nephi 19:23–24 and look for some reasons Nephi gave for sharing Isaiah's words with his people. (Answers might include: to persuade them to believe in Christ; for their "profit and learning"; so they might have the same hope as all the other children of Israel.) Tell your family that 1 Nephi 20 and 21 are the first of many chapters in the Book of Mormon that contain the words of Isaiah. Explain that we may not fully understand everything Isaiah said, but we can benefit from many things Isaiah said that can be applied or "likened" to our day. The ideas that follow are intended to help your family understand those applications.

1 Nephi 20:1–2
Why do we have the words of Isaiah in the Bible and again in the Book of Mormon?

 Tell your family to follow along in 1 Nephi 20:1 while you read the same verse from Isaiah 48:1. Have them look for words in their verse that are missing in the Isaiah verse. When they discover that 1 Nephi 20:1 explains that the "waters of Judah" are the "waters of baptism," tell them that the Book of Mormon version of Isaiah is often different from the version of Isaiah in our Bible. This change was added by Joseph Smith to help clarify what is meant by the "waters of Judah." Ask them what Isaiah said at the end of verse 1 that indicates why the Lord was unhappy with Israel. (They swear—which means to make a promise—in God's name but not honestly or righteously.)

Next, read 1 Nephi 20:2 together. Explain that to say you are of the "holy city" (which is Jerusalem) means to claim that you are righteous and chosen by God. Also explain that to "stay themselves" upon God means to stay close to or rely on God. Ask a family member to look at verse 2 again and explain in his or her own words what Isaiah said the children of Israel were doing wrong. (They claimed to be righteous but did not rely on God.) Tell your family to notice that both verses 1 and 2 of 1 Nephi 20 give that same message. Now have them read Isaiah 48:2 and look for what is missing from that verse that is preserved in 1 Nephi 20:2. Explain that the phrase "but they do not" that is missing from the Bible is preserved in the Nephite version of Isaiah. Tell your family that the Nephite version of Isaiah that came from the plates of brass is older and more accurate than the version of Isaiah in the Bible (for more information see Articles of Faith 1:8 and Bible Dictionary, "Preservation of the Text of the Old Testament," p. 623).

Help your family see that because of the missing parts, verses 1 and 2 of Isaiah 48 disagree and are confusing. Ask what this teaches us about the value of having the Book of Mormon version of

Isaiah. Invite your family to look for many such differences as they study the Isaiah chapters in the Book of Mormon.

1 Nephi 20:8–11
Why was the Lord so patient when the Israelites disobeyed over and over again?

 Show a ring or piece of jewelry made of gold. Ask how the gold in jewelry is different from gold when it comes out of the ground. Explain that gold ore is a mixture of gold and other rocks and that it has to be "refined" or heated in a blast furnace that melts the ore to separate the gold from the rock. Next have your family read 1 Nephi 20:8–11 and look for how people, such as the children of Israel, are like gold when it first comes out of the ground. Ask, "What sort of refining 'furnace' did the Lord use on Israel? How do afflictions help 'refine' a person? How does this help explain why the Lord did not destroy Israel when they were unrighteous? How is that like the Lord's dealings with Lehi's colony? Why does knowing this give comfort and hope to us today?"

1 Nephi 20:18–22
The gift of peace

 Read as a family D&C 135:4 and ask what Joseph Smith knew about what was going to happen to him. How could he be so calm, knowing what he knew?

Read together 1 Nephi 20:18–22 and ask your family how these verses help explain how Joseph Smith faced death. Ask them if they think the mobbers found peace even after they killed Joseph. Though the world may define peace as the absence of conflict, God can give a peace that remains constant even in the midst of conflict. Ask how that can help us be more at peace as we face our challenges.

1 Nephi 21:1–26
Understanding Isaiah's teaching style

Explain that Isaiah's writings can often be hard to understand because he uses objects as symbols and metaphors. While reading 1 Nephi 21, ask family members to mark or list each object that Isaiah uses. Stop every 5 verses or so and have them share the objects they found. Ask why Isaiah might have chosen that object and what he was trying to teach.

1 Nephi 21:8–16
The Gathering—an act of love

Ask your family to imagine that they or someone they know (or perhaps a favorite team) was in some kind of contest and was losing badly. Then at the last moment, as if by some miracle, they came back and won the contest. What feelings would they have experienced when all seemed lost? How would they have felt when the victory was won?

Tell your family that Isaiah placed the children of Israel in just such a situation. Have someone read aloud 1 Nephi 21:8–13 while the others pick out phrases that describe what the Lord will do for scattered Israel when He gathers them again in the last days. Then have someone read 1 Nephi 21:14 and tell how Israel (Zion) felt while they were still scattered before the gathering began.

Next read 1 Nephi 21:15–16 together. Ask how God's love is like the love of a mother. Do mothers love their children because they are always so easy to care for and they always do the right things? Do mothers love their children because children give back more than their mothers give to their children? It might be helpful to bring out baby books, scrapbooks, or photo albums and talk about what mothers do for their children.

Then ask your family what they think the Lord meant when he said, "I have graven [meaning carved or cut] thee upon the palms of my hands." (See 3 Nephi 11:13–15.) How might this suggest that there are some ways in which the Lord's love for us is greater than the love of a mother?

Show the family a wristwatch and ask them to pretend that the watch cost $10 or less. If the watch stopped working, would they pay to have it repaired at the jewelry store? Why not? On the other hand, if the watch were worth $400, would they be more likely to have it fixed? Why would they pay to fix the $400 watch but not the cheaper one? Ask them how that is like the Lord's love for us. Read together D&C 18:10–13 and share your testimony of how much the Savior loves, and wants to gather home, each one of us.

1 Nephi 21:20–23
Who can be children of Israel?

Show a picture of a poor child from a poor country and ask, "How could this child become a member of our family?" Could joining our family be a blessing to him or her? Could he or she be a blessing to our family?

Read 1 Nephi 21:20–23 with your family and explain that Isaiah is speaking as Israel who had lost her children when they were scattered among the Gentiles because of their disobedience. Ask, "When Israel is gathered again, where will her children come from?" (They will be gathered again from among the Gentiles.) According to verse 23, how will the Gentiles bless the children of Israel?

Next read Abraham 2:10 and ask what can happen to the Gentiles who "receive the gospel." Ask, "What does that teach us about the Lord's feelings for all His children? (See 2 Nephi 26:33.) What do you think the Lord expects us to do for those around us who do not have the gospel?"

1 NEPHI 22: NEPHI EXPLAINS ISAIAH

1 Nephi 22:1–9
"What meaneth these things which ye have read?"

Have a family member read aloud 1 Nephi 22:1 and find the first question Nephi's brothers asked. Tell your family that the rest of chapter 22 is Nephi's explanation of the words of Isaiah from 1 Nephi 20–21.

For example, read again 1 Nephi 21:21–23 with

your family and ask them if they understand how the Gentiles would be "nursing fathers" and "nursing mothers" to the children of Israel. Tell them Nephi helps explain that in 1 Nephi 22. Have them read 1 Nephi 22:7–8 and find what the Lord would do "among the Gentiles" that can be "likened unto [the Lamanites] being nourished by the Gentiles." (A marvelous work.) Next have them read 1 Nephi 22:9 and tell what that "marvelous work" would do for the Gentiles and all the house of Israel (Make known to them the covenants the Father made with Abraham).

Explain that Elder Joseph Fielding Smith said, "The marvelous work is the restoration of the church and the gospel with all the power and authority, keys and blessings which pertain to this great work for the salvation of the children of men." (*Church History and Modern Revelation,* 1:35.) To help your family understand what is so "nourishing" about understanding the covenants we make with Our Heavenly Father, share the following statement: "The fruit of keeping covenants is the companionship of the Holy Ghost and an increase in the power to love. That happens because of the power of the Atonement of Jesus Christ to change our very natures." (Henry B. Eyring, "Witnesses for God," *Ensign,* November 1996, p. 32.) Bear testimony to your family of the importance of making and keeping our covenants.

1 Nephi 22:10–12
Scattered Israel is to be gathered

Wear a shirt or sweater with long sleeves and then tell your family to imagine the following scene. You have all just finished dinner when they saw you stand up, walk over to the kitchen sink, and roll up your sleeves. Act out rolling up your sleeves as you ask, "What would you suppose I was about to do?" (Go to work doing the dishes.) Then have them read 1 Nephi 22:10–12 and find a similar phrase that indicates that the Lord was about to go to work ("Make bare his arm"). Ask them to find phrases that tell what the Lord was about to go to work to do

(Bring about his covenants and his gospel, gather scattered Israel).

To help your family understand our responsibilities in this great work of the Lord and its promised blessings, read to them the following statement from Elder M. Russell Ballard: "Sometimes we are tempted to let our lives be governed more by convenience than by covenant. It is not always convenient to live gospel standards and stand up for truth and testify of the Restoration. It usually is not convenient to share the gospel with others. It isn't always convenient to respond to a calling in the Church, especially one that stretches our abilities. Opportunities to serve others in meaningful ways, as we have covenanted to do, rarely come at convenient times. But there is no spiritual power in living by convenience. The power comes as we keep our covenants. As we look at the lives of these early Saints, we see that their covenants were the primary force in their lives. Their example and testimony were powerful enough to influence generation after generation of their children." ("Like a Flame Unquenchable," *Ensign,* May 1999, p. 86.)

1 Nephi 22:13–19
How can we survive the coming destructions?

 Read 1 Nephi 22:13–15 with your family and have them mark what is going to happen to the wicked in these last days. Then read together 1 Nephi 22:16–22 and have them mark all the phrases that describe what is going to happen to the righteous during this time of destruction. Ask your family how it is possible that fire can destroy the wicked and at the same time save the righteous. As an example consider sharing with your family the story of Shadrach, Meshach, and Abed-nego in Daniel 3:1–27. Ask your family to look again at what they marked in 1 Nephi 22:13–22 and tell why they think the righteous "need not fear."

1 Nephi 22:24–31
What will the Millennium be like?

 Read 1 Nephi 22:24–28 with your family and have them make a list of what Nephi says it will be like during the Millennium when Jesus comes again. Explain that the phrase "as calves of the stall" (verse 24) means that the righteous will be well cared for by Christ, who owns them, as opposed to wild calves who have to take care of themselves. Explain also that the Prophet Joseph Smith taught, "Christ and the resurrected saints will reign over the Earth during the 1000 years. They will not probably dwell upon the earth, but will visit when they please, or when it is necessary to govern it." (*Teachings of the Prophet Joseph Smith,* p. 268.)

Next have each family member share what they think would be the best part of being able to live during the Millennium and tell why. Share your testimony that the happiness of the Millennium is worth every effort we have to make to be worthy of that great blessing.

2 NEPHI

The book of Second Nephi comes from the small plates of Nephi and covers the time period between 588 and 545 B.C. In it you will find some of the greatest doctrinal teachings in the Book of Mormon. For example, 2 Nephi 2 and 9 are two of the greatest chapters on the plan of salvation in all of scripture. Second Nephi deals extensively with the scattering and gathering of the house of Israel. It also includes thirteen more chapters of Isaiah from the plates of brass. The central message, however, is the same as that of the Book of Mormon as a whole: it is "another testament of Jesus Christ."

2 NEPHI 1: LEHI COUNSELS HIS SONS

2 Nephi 1–4
What would your last words be?

 Ask your family to imagine they are parents and have found out that they have only a short time to live. Have them write down some things they would say to their family. Tell your family that 2 Nephi 1–4 are Father Lehi's final words of counsel to his family before he died. The words in chapter 1 are particularly directed toward Laman and Lemuel. As you study these chapters, compare what you might teach your children to what Lehi taught his.

2 Nephi 1:4
Fulfillment of prophecy

Ask your family if they can think of some way to tell a true prophet from a false one. After they have given some ideas, read them this statement from President Ezra Taft Benson: "The ultimate test of a true prophet is that when he speaks in the name of the Lord his words come to pass. That standard was explained by the Lord to Moses in these words: 'When a prophet speaketh in the name of the Lord, if the thing follow not, nor come to pass, that is the thing which the Lord hath not spoken, but the prophet hath spoken presumptuously' (Deut. 18:22)." ("Joseph Smith: Prophet to Our Generation," *Ensign,* March 1994, p. 2.)

Have someone read 2 Nephi 1:4 and tell which of Lehi's prophesies was now fulfilled (Jerusalem was destroyed). Ask your family if they remember Laman and Lemuel saying they would have been happy if they had stayed in Jerusalem. (See 1 Nephi 17:21.) Read with your family the account of the destruction of Jerusalem found in 2 Kings 25:1–10. Have them find verses that indicate that Laman and Lemuel would not have been happy if they had stayed in Jerusalem. Discuss what you can conclude about Lehi since his prophecy concerning Jerusalem came to pass. What would that mean for other prophecies Lehi made?

2 Nephi 1:5–12
Promises or warnings

Divide the family into two groups. Have both groups read 2 Nephi 1:5–12, with one group looking for promises to an obedient nation and the other group looking for warnings to a disobedient nation. Let them discuss as groups what they found. Then ask one member of each group to summarize for the family what they found.

2 Nephi 1:13–15
"Chains of hell" or "arms of love"?

 Have a family member sit in the center of the room, clap his hands once, and then hold his hands together. Take a thread or string that can break and wrap it once around the hands and tie it. Ask the family member to break the string. Then have them close their eyes and pretend to be asleep. While asleep, wrap the string around the hands many times so it can't be broken. Have someone else read 2 Nephi 1:13 out loud and tell the one whose hands are tied to try to do as the scripture says. When the family member cannot "shake off" the chain, ask your family:

- Why can't the chains be broken?
- What kind of chains do you think Lehi was referring to?
- What does Lehi say chains do to us?

Ask your family how this demonstration is like the following statement:

"The chains of habit are too small to be felt until they are too strong to be broken." (Samuel Johnson, *International Dictionary of Thoughts*, Chicago: J. G. Ferguson Publishing Co., 1969, p. 348; see also Elder Marvin J. Ashton, "'Shake Off the Chains with Which Ye Are Bound,'" *Ensign,* November 1986, p. 13.)

Next have someone read aloud 2 Nephi 1:15 and have your family imagine being held in the loving arms of the Savior. Ask them what they would rather be surrounded by, the "chains of hell" or the "arms of Christ's love." Have family members ponder these two questions:

- What bad habits or other things do I have in my life that bind me and keep me from becoming a better person?
- What must I *do* to break the chains that bind me?

2 Nephi 1:16–17
Hard hearts—soft hearts

 Read 2 Nephi 1:17 with your family and have them compare how Lehi describes his heart with how he describes Laman and Lemuel's hearts. Ask what caused Lehi's heavy heart ("The hardness of [his sons'] hearts"). Read again 1 Nephi 2:16 with your family and ask them what a person can do to soften a hard heart.

2 Nephi 1:21–28
What does it take to be a "real man"?

Read together 2 Nephi 1:21 and have your family look for what Lehi wanted his sons to be (Men). Ask your family how they think Laman and Lemuel felt about being told to "be men."

Next read together 2 Nephi 1:22–28 and have your family pick out the character traits that Lehi thought real men should have. Ask:

- How do you think Lehi's idea of what a real man was differed from what Laman thought?
- What character traits do you think "real men" should have?

Have family members turn to 3 Nephi 27:27 and see how Jesus answered the question: "What manner of men ought ye to be?" Bear your testimony of the power that comes to a person who patterns his life after the Savior.

2 Nephi 1:30
True friends

Ask your family to read 2 Nephi 1:30 and find the compliment Lehi gives to Zoram.

Give each family member a pencil and have them complete the following phrases in their journals:

- A true friend is . . .
- A true friend would . . .
- A true friend would not . . .

After everyone has had a chance to write, have them share what they wrote. Share the following insight from Elder Marvin J. Ashton:

"Someone has said, 'A friend is a person who is willing to take me the way I am.' Accepting this as one definition of the word, may I quickly suggest that we are something less than a real friend if we leave a person the same way we find him. . . . Acts of a friend should result in self-improvement, better attitudes, self-reliance, comfort, consolation, self-respect, and better welfare. Certainly the word *friend* is misused if it is identified with a person who contributes to our delinquency, misery, and heartaches. . . . It takes courage to be a real friend." ("What Is a Friend?" *Ensign,* January 1973, p. 41.)

Now have family members ponder these two questions:

- How important are my friends?
- Am I a "true friend"?

2 NEPHI 2: WE ARE FREE TO CHOOSE

2 Nephi 2:1–4

How can afflictions bless our lives?

 Have your family read 2 Nephi 2:1–4 and compare it to 1 Nephi 1:1. Ask them what relationship they see between adversity and blessings for Jacob and Nephi. What do you think the Lord meant when he told Jacob that He would "consecrate [bless] thine afflictions for thy gain"?

Next have them read D&C 121:7–8 and look for what the Lord told the Prophet Joseph Smith about adversity. Have them find and mark the phrase that explains what we must do to turn our afflictions into blessings ("Endure it well"). Tell your family about a difficult time you went through that later turned out to be a blessing.

2 Nephi 2:3–27

How are Jesus Christ, Adam, Eve, and the devil a part of God's plan?

Divide your family into groups and assign each group one or more of the following topics. Have them search the verses listed, write down the answers to the questions, and be prepared to report back on what role their person or principle plays in God's eternal plan.

Adam and Eve (2 Nephi 2:19–25)

- What did they choose? (See verse 19.)
- What are the good and bad consequences of their choice? (See verses 20–21, 25; see also Mormon 9:12, 14.)
- What would have happened if they had not chosen to partake of the fruit? (See verses 22–23; see also Moses 5:10–11.)

The Savior Jesus Christ (2 Nephi 2:3–10, 15–16, 21, 24–26)

- What does the Savior do for us? (See verses 3–10, 15–16, 21, 24–26; see also Mormon 9:13.)

Satan (2 Nephi 2:17–18, 27–29)

- How did Satan become a devil? (See verse 17.)
- Why is he miserable? (See verse 18.)
- Because of his misery, what does he desire for us? (See verse 18.)
- How can we avoid being miserable like him? (See verse 27.)
- What lie did he tell Eve? (See verse 18.)
- If we tell lies, whom will we be like?
- Why do you think living in the presence of Satan is called "eternal death"?

Law (2 Nephi 2:5–7, 26)

- What is the purpose and necessity of law? (See verses 5, 7, 26.)

Opposition and choice (2 Nephi 2:11–16, 23, 27–29)

- What is the role of opposition? (See verses 11–12.)
- Why do we need opposition to have a choice? (See verses 13, 16.)

After the groups have reported, read 2 Nephi 2:28–30 to your family and add your testimony to Lehi's of the importance of choosing eternal life through the plan of salvation given to us by a loving Heavenly Father and His Son Jesus Christ.

2 Nephi 2:5
How do we know good from evil?

Read 2 Nephi 2:5 with your family and ask if the first sentence applies to everyone. Do all people really know the difference between good and evil? To help answer that question, share the following statement:

"Parents and teachers need to know that a youngster can tell right from wrong. This knowledge may be distorted or perverted or covered up in unfortunate life experiences, but intuitively, as a part of the spiritual endowment of all humanity, there is a knowledge of right from wrong.

"That gives me great hope, for then I understand that every child of God, however reprobate [corrupt] he may have become . . . has hidden within him the spark of divinity and a sensitivity to that which is wrong as compared to that which is right." (Boyd K. Packer, *Teach Ye Diligently*, pp. 81–82.)

2 Nephi 2:11–27
What choice did Adam really have?

Invite a family member to participate in a demonstration. Hold out both of your hands, palms up, to show that they are empty. Ask the family member to choose which fruit he or she would like. When the person says there is no fruit to choose, place an actual piece of fruit in one hand and say, "Now choose which fruit you would like." Ask your family if they think the family member really had a choice. Make sure they understand that to have a choice there must be at least two possibilities.

Read 2 Nephi 2:11–12, 15–16 with your family and ask them to identify the two choices Adam and Eve had. Share the following statement from Elder Bruce R. McConkie:

"Thus we see why the Lord gave two conflicting commandments—one to become mortal and have children, the other to not eat of the tree of knowledge of good and evil out of which mortality and children and death would result. The issue is one of choosing between opposites. Adam must choose to become mortal so he could have children, on the one hand; on the other hand, he must choose to remain forever in the garden in a state of innocence. He chose to partake of the forbidden fruit so that the purposes of God might be accomplished by providing a probationary estate for his spirit children. Adam must needs fall so that he would know good from evil, virtue from vice, righteousness from wickedness. He could not have done this without breaking a law and becoming subject to sin. He chose the Lord's way; there was no other way whereby salvation might come unto the children of men." (*A New Witness for the Articles of Faith,* p. 91.)

2 Nephi 2:27–29
What are our two great choices?

Have your family search 2 Nephi 2:27–29 and find what Lehi says our two great choices are. (You may want to mark them.) Ask:

- Who wants us to choose eternal life?
- Who wants us to choose eternal death?
- What do we learn about Lehi's choice in verse 30?
- What does Lehi want his children to choose?

Testify to your family of your desires for each of them to choose righteousness.

2 NEPHI 3: LEHI BLESSES HIS SON JOSEPH

2 Nephi 3:1–25
Who are the four Josephs mentioned in this chapter?

Give each family member four different colored pencils. Explain that 2 Nephi 3 tells about four different "Josephs" (Joseph who was sold into Egypt; Joseph the son of Lehi; Joseph Smith Sr.; Joseph Smith Jr.). Look through the chapter and see how many times you can find the name *Joseph.* Using the following guide, select a color for each Joseph and have family members mark each reference to each Joseph in the selected color:

- Joseph who was sold into Egypt: 2 Nephi 3:4–22.
- Joseph the son of Lehi: 2 Nephi 3:1–3, 22–25.
- Joseph Smith Sr., the Prophet's father: 2 Nephi 3:15.
- Joseph Smith Jr., the prophet of the restoration: 2 Nephi 3:7–9, 11, 13–15, 17–19.

Ask family members to look for information about these four Josephs as they mark their scriptures. Take turns sharing important information your family found about each Joseph.

2 Nephi 3:2
Notice the "if"

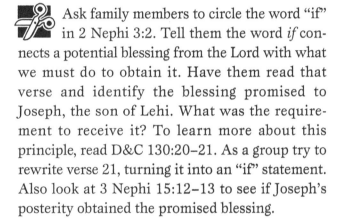 Ask family members to circle the word "if" in 2 Nephi 3:2. Tell them the word *if* connects a potential blessing from the Lord with what we must do to obtain it. Have them read that verse and identify the blessing promised to Joseph, the son of Lehi. What was the requirement to receive it? To learn more about this principle, read D&C 130:20–21. As a group try to rewrite verse 21, turning it into an "if" statement. Also look at 3 Nephi 15:12–13 to see if Joseph's posterity obtained the promised blessing.

2 Nephi 3:2–25
How is a family like a tree?

Gather your family around a tree, or show them a picture of a tree, or have them draw one. Ask them to identify the tree's different parts. (Roots, trunk, branches, leaves.) Talk about the phrase "family tree" and discuss why a family might be compared to a tree. Give the following four labels to a family member: parent, yourself, child, grandchild. Ask him or her to place each label on the part of the tree that best represents that role in a family (roots = parents; trunk = yourself; branches = child; leaves = grandchild).

In 2 Nephi 3, words similar to this tree analogy are used to talk about Joseph's family. To help your family better understand this chapter, have them look for the words and phrases listed below, identify their meaning, and then mark them.

Words or Phrases	Verses from 2 Nephi 3
"seed"	2, 3, 16, 23–24
"fruit of my (thy) loins"	4–7, 11–12, 14, 18–19, 21
"branch"	5
"seed of thy loins"	11

Interpretation or Meaning

These all refer to a person's future family. They have to do with a person's children, grandchildren, and so on, including their entire posterity.

2 Nephi 3:7–9
The Prophet Joseph Smith

Ask family members if they know why their parents chose their names, and what their name means or why it is important. Why is a person's name important?

Show a picture of the Prophet Joseph Smith and share your testimony of him and your love for him. (See D&C 135:3.) Read Joseph Smith—History 1:3–4 to learn how Joseph Smith received his name.

Read 2 Nephi 3:11, 14–15 with your family and explain that Lehi prophesied in 580 B.C. that Joseph Smith would be born and would be named Joseph. Explain further that Lehi was really quoting a prophecy made by Joseph in Egypt more than 1,000 years before Lehi. Ask your family if they are surprised that Joseph Smith was known by name 3,500 years before he was born. What does that teach us about prophecy and our Heavenly Father?

Share the following statement from Brigham Young:

"It was decreed in the counsels of eternity, long before the foundations of the earth were laid, that he, Joseph Smith, should be the man, in the last dispensation of this world, to bring forth the word of God to the people, and receive the fulness of the keys and power of the Priesthood of the Son of God. The Lord had his eyes upon him, and upon his father, and upon his father's father, and upon their progenitors clear back to Abraham, and from Abraham to the flood, from the flood to Enoch, and from Enoch to Adam. He has watched that family and that blood as it has circulated from its fountain to the birth of that man. He was fore-ordained in eternity to preside over this last dispensation." (*Discourses of Brigham Young,* p. 108.)

2 Nephi 3:12–13
The Bible and Book of Mormon

 Write the phrases "confounding false doctrines" and "knowledge of my covenants" on a small board and only a question mark on another. Read 2 Nephi 3:12 and have your family look for the phrases listed on the board. Ask them what needs to grow together in order for us to "confound false doctrines" and come to "know the covenants of the Lord" (That which was written by the fruit of the loins of Judah and that written by the fruit of Joseph's loins).

Teach your family that the phrase "fruit of the loins of Judah" refers to the Bible. Hold up a nail and say that it represents the Bible. Then using a hammer, nail the two boards together on one end. Show the family how the two boards can still be moved and twisted, even though a nail is holding them together. Discuss these questions:

- How does this show that doctrines can be misinterpreted, even though people have the teachings of the Bible?
- What does the eighth Article of Faith teach us about the Bible?
- Can you think of any evidence that the Bible can easily be misinterpreted? (For example, there are hundreds of different churches, and they all use the Bible).

Now hold up a second nail and say that this nail represents the Book of Mormon. Nail it into the two boards on the opposite end. Show your family how the boards will not twist around now. Ask the following questions:

- Why does the second nail make such a difference?

- How does the Book of Mormon, which is another testament of Jesus Christ, help us confound false doctrines and better understand our covenants?
- What is an example of a doctrine in the Bible, which is clarified by the Book of Mormon?
- What can you do to help the Bible and the Book of Mormon "grow together" in your life?

Read the following message from President Ezra Taft Benson:

"The Book of Mormon exposes the enemies of Christ. It confounds false doctrines and lays down contention. (See 2 Nephi 3:12.) It fortifies the humble followers of Christ against the evil designs, strategies, and doctrines of the devil in our day." ("The Book of Mormon Is the Word of God," *Ensign,* May 1975, p. 63.)

2 NEPHI 4: "MY SOUL DELIGHTETH IN THE SCRIPTURES"

2 Nephi 4:3–11
The eternal importance of the family

Read together Doctrine and Covenants 68:25 and ask your family what that verse teaches about the responsibility of being a father or a mother. Tell them that they will see an example of what the Lord meant by "the sin be upon the heads of the parents" in 2 Nephi 4.

Assign the following scripture blocks to different people. Have them study their verses and report what Lehi said to:

- Laman and his children. (2 Nephi 4:3–7.)
- Lemuel and his children. (2 Nephi 4:8–9.)
- Sam and his children. (2 Nephi 4:11.)

After each group has reported, ask them what the Lord said to Laman's children that was similar to what was said in Doctrine and Covenants 68:25. (See verse 6.) Ask:

- Why do you think Lehi was so harsh with Laman? (See verse 5.)
- How was the blessing Sam and his children received different?
- What does that tell you about the kind of parents Sam and his wife were?

Read aloud the following excerpt from "The Family: A Proclamation to the World." Have your family choose phrases that describe what the Lord expects from parents.

"Husband and wife have a solemn responsibility to love and care for each other and for their children. 'Children are an heritage of the Lord' (Psalms 127:3). Parents have a sacred duty to rear their children in love and righteousness, to provide for their physical and spiritual needs, to teach them to love and serve one another, to observe the commandments of God and to be law-abiding citizens wherever they live. Husbands and wives—mothers and fathers—will be held accountable before God for the discharge of these obligations." (*Ensign,* November 1995, p. 102.)

Discuss the phrases they picked out. Bear your testimony of how seriously you take your responsibility as a parent. Ask what children can do to help parents fulfill the great responsibility Heavenly Father has placed upon them.

2 Nephi 4:15–16
What value is there in daily scripture study?

Place items in front of your family that they would think are desirable (such as a soccer ball, a favorite video, a favorite food, and so on). Discuss how much they like those things and then place beside them a copy of the scriptures. Ask them to think about, but not answer out loud, how the scriptures compare in importance to those other items.

Then read 2 Nephi 4:15–16 together and ask your family how important they think Nephi would rate the scriptures in comparison to his favorite food or entertainment. Discuss the following:

- How do you think Nephi got to the point where he "delighted" in the scriptures?
- What do you think it means to ponder the scriptures?

Tell your family how much comfort, direction, and strength you receive from pondering the scriptures. Share the following statement from Elder Dallin H. Oaks:

"Just as continuing revelation enlarges and illuminates the scriptures, so also a study of the scriptures enables men and women to receive revelations. . . . This happens because scripture reading puts us in tune with the Spirit of the Lord.

"The idea that scripture reading can lead to inspiration and revelation opens the door to the truth that a scripture is not limited to what it meant when it was written but may also include what that scripture means to a reader today. Even more, scripture reading may also lead to current revelation on whatever else the Lord wishes to communicate to the reader at that time. We do not overstate the point when we say that the scriptures can be a Urim and Thummim to assist each of us to receive personal revelation." ("Scripture Reading and Revelation," *Ensign,* January 1995, p. 8.)

2 Nephi 4:15–35
The Psalm of Nephi

Tell your family about your favorite Church hymn. Read to them some of the verses that are especially meaningful to you and explain why they touch your soul. Ask them which hymns are their favorites and have them tell why.

Then tell them that 2 Nephi 4:15–35 is sometimes called the "Psalm of Nephi." A psalm is like a song or hymn. In these verses Nephi expresses the deep feelings of his soul. Invite your family to read verses 15–35 silently to themselves and prayerfully ponder their meaning. Have them pick out the verses that touch their hearts and speak to their souls. Then have each family member read aloud the verses they chose and tell what they learned and felt from those verses.

2 Nephi 4:27–35
How can I escape temptation?

Ask your family members to think of a temptation or weakness they struggle with (do not ask them to tell what it is; just have them identify it in their minds). Ask them what difference it would make in their lives if that temptation suddenly became disgusting and repulsive to them. Explain that Nephi gives us an example of how to make that happen.

Have someone read aloud 2 Nephi 4:27–29. Ask your family to pick out what seems to be Nephi's temptation. (To get angry when his brothers won't listen and repent [see 2 Nephi 4:13; 5:1–4].) Ask them what most people pray for when another person makes them angry. (They usually pray for God to change the other person.)

Then read together 2 Nephi 4:30–35 and have your family pick out phrases that describe what Nephi prayed for. Who did Nephi want the Lord to change? Bear your testimony of the power of the Lord to change our hearts so that instead of being tempted we "shake at the appearance of sin."

2 NEPHI 5: A HOUSE DIVIDED

2 Nephi 5:1–6
When the Lord sends a warning!

Place the following items (or similar ones) on a table: medicine bottle with a warning label, a book of scripture, a drawing of a warning sign, a picture of a skull and bones, and a picture of the Savior. Discuss how these items might serve similar purposes. Ask:

- How do the scriptures provide warnings?
- How does the Savior?

- Of all these sources of warnings, which is the most important?

Read together 2 Nephi 5:1–4 and ask your family to identify the dangers that lurked in the lives of Nephi and others. Ask them why it is most tragic to know that Nephi's greatest danger came from within his own family. Discuss which of the items of warning would have been the most useful to Nephi at this time in his life. Have family members identify a source of warning as you read 2 Nephi 5:6–7. Ask:

- What source warned Nephi of danger?
- What was he to do?
- Who went with him? (All those who "believed in the warnings and revelations of God.")

Ask your family how they can practice being people who "believe in the warnings and revelations of God." (Listen to and obey the prophet, Church leaders, parents, inspired scriptures, and the Spirit.)

2 Nephi 5:7–17
Moving to a new home

Invite a family member to share an experience (or have the family imagine one) where the family moved to a different community. Ask them what they think the hardest part of moving would be. What could you do to make it easier? Explain that Nephi, along with many other family members, had a similar experience.

Have someone read 2 Nephi 5:27 and tell what it was like for Nephi's people. ("They lived after the manner of happiness.") Tell your family they are going to find out what that means. Divide up the verses in 2 Nephi 5:7–17 and have family members search them for things that might lead to living in a "manner of happiness." Some important things might include:

- Keeping the commandments.
- Planting and harvesting crops.
- Raising animals.

- Having the scriptures and Liahona.
- Making swords for protection.
- Building homes, buildings, and a temple.
- Being skilled and industrious.

Discuss how each of these helped Nephi's colony to find happiness. How might similar things help us be happy in a new home?

As an alternative, read the following verses with your family and identify Nephi's formula for happiness:

- 2 Nephi 5:10: Nephi's people keep the commandments.
- 2 Nephi 5:11: They prosper.
- 2 Nephi 5:12: They enjoy the guidance of the Liahona (which represents the Holy Ghost).
- 2 Nephi 5:12: They have families.
- 2 Nephi 5:15–17: They work and learn to be industrious.

Share the following story from President Gordon B. Hinckley:

"My father had a horse and buggy when I was a boy. Then one summer day in 1916, a wonderful thing happened. It was an unforgettable thing. When he came home that evening he arrived in a shining black brand-new Model T Ford. . . . The most interesting thing was the lights. The car had no storage battery. The only electricity came from what was called a magneto. The output of the magneto was determined by the speed of the engine. If the engine was running fast, the lights were bright. If the engine slowed, the lights became a sickly yellow. I learned that if you wanted to see ahead as you were going down the road, you had to keep the engine running at a fast clip. So, just as I'd discovered, it is with our lives. Industry, enthusiasm, and hard work lead to enlightened progress. You have to stay on your feet and keep moving if you are going to have light in your life." ("Some Lessons I Learned as a Boy," *Ensign*, May 1993, p. 54.)

2 Nephi 5:20–25
What happened to Laman and Lemuel after Nephi left?

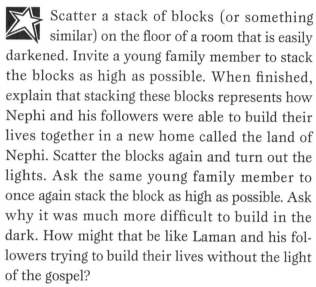 Scatter a stack of blocks (or something similar) on the floor of a room that is easily darkened. Invite a young family member to stack the blocks as high as possible. When finished, explain that stacking these blocks represents how Nephi and his followers were able to build their lives together in a new home called the land of Nephi. Scatter the blocks again and turn out the lights. Ask the same young family member to once again stack the block as high as possible. Ask why it was much more difficult to build in the dark. How might that be like Laman and his followers trying to build their lives without the light of the gospel?

Have the family scan 2 Nephi 5:20–25 and pick out words or phrases that show that the Lamanites were in the dark. Have everyone share something they found. Note how the Lamanites compare with the Nephites. (See 2 Nephi 5:10–17.) Ask your family why is it so important to have the light of the gospel in our lives. How might it bless us regardless of where we live?

2 Nephi 5:26
What priesthood did the Nephites hold?

Read together 2 Nephi 5:26 and ask what priesthood Jacob and Joseph held. Share the following statement by President Joseph Fielding Smith:

"The Nephites officiated by virtue of the Melchizedek Priesthood from the days of Lehi to the days of the appearance of our Savior among them. It is true that Nephi consecrated Jacob and Joseph that they should be priests and teachers over the land of the Nephites, but the fact that plural terms priests and teachers were used indicates that this was not a reference to the definite office in the priesthood in either case, but it was a general assignment to teach, direct, and admonish the people. Otherwise the terms priest and teacher would have been given, in the singular." (*Answers to Gospel Questions,* 1:124.)

Ask your family what holders of the Melchizedek Priesthood can do that those who hold the Aaronic Priesthood cannot. (Bless the sick, confirm people as Church members, receive their temple endowment, and so on.) How might these things have helped the Nephites live "after the manner of happiness" (2 Nephi 5:27)?

2 Nephi 5:29–34
Nephi is commanded to make the small plates of Nephi

 Read 2 Nephi 2:29–31 with your family and explain that Nephi reminds us that he is keeping his record on two sets of plates. (See also the ideas for 1 Nephi 9:5–6 and 1 Nephi 19:1–4 and the diagram of the plates of the Book of Mormon on p. 9.)

Write the following questions on separate sheets of paper large enough to be read by the family:

- What is written on the small plates?
- Who will be pleased with the small plates?
- What is written on the other plates?
- What is especially tragic about the "wars and contentions" Nephi wrote about? (Their wars were against their own family members whom they had recently separated from).

Show your family one question at a time and have them search 2 Nephi 5:31–34 to find the answer. Ask them how they think the Nephites might have felt having to fight against their brothers and cousins.

2 NEPHI 6: JACOB QUOTES THE PROPHET ISAIAH

2 Nephi 6:1–3
How would you describe an effective Church leader?

 Invite someone in your family to tell about a bishop or other church leader that had a positive influence on his or her life. Discuss what made this person so influential. Ask your family to read 2 Nephi 6:1–3 and pick out phrases that show what kind of a leader Jacob was. Ask family members what similarities they see between Jacob and the Church leader they thought of.

Have someone look up the word *anxiety* in the dictionary and read the definition to the family. Ask why they think Jacob felt great anxiety for the welfare of his people. Do you think the president of the Church today feels that way about us?

2 Nephi 6:6–11
Jacob explains Isaiah's prophecy

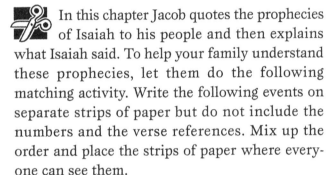 In this chapter Jacob quotes the prophecies of Isaiah to his people and then explains what Isaiah said. To help your family understand these prophecies, let them do the following matching activity. Write the following events on separate strips of paper but do not include the numbers and the verse references. Mix up the order and place the strips of paper where everyone can see them.

1. Jerusalem destroyed by Nebuchadnezzar, King of Babylon, the Jews taken captive. (Verse 8.)
2. Cyrus, King of Persia, allows the Jews to return to Jerusalem. (Verse 9.)
3. Jesus is born and ministers to the Jews. (Verse 9.)
4. Jesus is scourged and crucified. (Verse 9.)
5. Jerusalem is captured by the Romans and the Jews are afflicted and scattered to other lands because they rejected the Savior. (Verses 10–11.)
6. The Jews will be gathered again when their hearts turn again to their Redeemer, Jesus Christ. (Verse 11.)
7. The Gentiles who repent and help build Zion will be saved. (Verse 12.)

Read together 2 Nephi 6:8–11 and place the events in their proper order as your family discovers them. Next, go to Bible Dictionary, "Chronology," and have them search pages 639 through 645 and find the approximate dates for events 1–5. Remind your family that Isaiah prophesied about 750 B.C. and ask them what this teaches about the Lord's prophets. Explain that events 6 and 7 are now beginning to be fulfilled. Remind your family that they themselves are the Gentiles referred to in 2 Nephi 6:12 (event 7).

Read together 2 Nephi 6:14–15 and mark what the Lord promises to do for those who believe and for these who believe not. Bear your testimony to your family that just as everything Isaiah prophesied has come true up to this time, the things that are still future will also surely come to pass. Read the following statement from President Gordon B. Hinckley:

"We cannot say it frequently enough. Turn away from youthful lusts. Stay away from drugs. They can absolutely destroy you. Avoid them as you would a terrible disease, for that is what they become. Avoid foul and filthy talk. It can lead to destruction. Be absolutely honest. Dishonesty can corrupt and destroy. Observe the Word of Wisdom. You cannot smoke; you must not smoke. You must not chew tobacco. You cannot drink liquor. . . . You must rise above these things which beckon with a seductive call. Be prayerful. Call on the Lord in faith, and He will hear your prayers. He loves you. He wishes to bless you. He will do so if you live worthy of His blessing." ("Converts and Young Men," *Ensign,* May 1997, p. 49.)

Ask, "Through whom does the Lord frequently call us back to Him?" (Parents, prophets, priesthood leaders, advisers, friends).

2 NEPHI 7: NEPHI QUOTES ISAIAH 50

2 Nephi 7:1
God has not moved

To help your family understand the words of Isaiah in 2 Nephi 7, explain that Isaiah often uses the imagery of marriage to describe the relationship between the Lord (the husband), Israel (the wife), and the children of Israel (their children).

Read 2 Nephi 7:1 together and have your family find words or phrases that describe how the "marriage" between the Lord and Israel is going. (Put thee away, cast thee off, divorcement, sold.) Ask whom it seems the children are blaming for the divorce. (The Lord.) Who does the Lord say has caused Israel to be "put away"? (Her own sins.)

Tell your family that the relationship between the Lord and Israel is a little like the following story:

There once was an older retired couple driving down the road. Coming from the other direction was a young couple. The young lady was sitting very close to the young man with her head resting on his shoulder. It was easy to see that these two were in love. The older lady in the first car then said, "Don't you wish we were still close like those two?" The man replied, "I'm not the one who has moved."

Ask your family who is like the Lord in this story and who is like Israel. Discuss the following questions:

- If you are further away from the Lord today than you were yesterday, who moved?
- What causes us to be separated from the love of the Lord?
- What must we do to move closer to the Lord?

2 Nephi 7:6
Christ's willing gift for us

Ask someone to read the heading for 2 Nephi 7 (the words in italics just before verse 1). Ask your family if they know what the word *Messiah* means. To help explain, read the entry for "Messiah" in the Bible Dictionary on page 731. What do you think the words "Isaiah speaks Messianically" mean? (Isaiah is speaking of the Messiah.)

Read together 2 Nephi 7:2–4, 8–9 and have your family pick out those things that represent the Lord's powers. Then read 2 Nephi 7:5–7 and discuss with your family, what the Messiah will do when He is born on earth, even though he has such great power. Share with your family the following statement:

"The God who created everything was judged to be nothing! And yet he endured it with complete patience. Imagine the Being whose power, whose light, whose glory holds the universe in order, the Being who speaks and solar systems, galaxies, and stars come into existence—standing before wicked men and being judged by them as being of no worth or value! When we think of what he could have done to these men who took him to judgment, we have a new and different sense of his condescension. When Judas led the soldiers and the high priest to the Garden of Gethsemane and betrayed him with a kiss, Jesus could have spoken a single word and leveled the entire city of Jerusalem. When the servant of the high priest stepped forward and slapped his face, Jesus could have lifted a finger and sent that man back to his original elements. When another man stepped forward and spit in his face, Jesus had only to blink and our entire solar system could have been annihilated. But he stood there, he endured, he suffered, he condescended." (Gerald N. Lund, "'Knowest Thou the Condescensions of God?'" *Doctrines of the Book of Mormon,* 1991 Sperry Symposium, pp. 85–86.)

2 Nephi 7:10–11
Who walks in darkness and sorrow?

If available, get a camping flint and stone, which can produce sparks. Turn off the lights for a moment and show how the flint can produce bright sparks. Ask your family how they would like to try to read or walk by the light of those sparks. Then turn the lights on and have someone read 2 Nephi 7:10 and answer the question there. (No one who fears the Lord and follows His servants will have to walk in darkness.) Have someone read aloud John 8:12 and tell what light the obedient walk by.

Then have your family read verse 2 Nephi 7:11 and look for the kind of light the wicked walk by.

(Their own sparks.) Bear your testimony that refusing to follow the Lord, thinking that you can see well enough without him, is to walk in darkness.

2 NEPHI 8: GOD WILL GATHER HIS SAINTS AND COMFORT ZION

2 Nephi 8:1–16
What can we really depend on?

 Ask your family to list as many different things as they can think of that people rely on to make them happy and prosperous in this life. (Examples might include careers, money, friends, possessions, government, entertainment, fame, and advice columns.) Read 2 Nephi 8:1–16 to your family as they follow along in their scriptures. Tell them not to worry about understanding everything; they should just look for things the Lord said would bring happiness and prosperity. Make another list. (This list might include following after righteousness, verse 1; living in Zion, verses 3–4, 11, 16; trusting in the Lord's righteousness and salvation, verses 5–6, 9–15.)

Have your family compare the two lists. Ask them which list seems the most reliable. Have your family look again at verses 6–8, 12. Ask them what the Lord said would happen to the things of this world. Why do you think so many people put so much trust in the things of men instead of trying to get close to the Lord? Bear your testimony about the troubled times we are facing and the importance of relying on the Lord.

2 Nephi 8:17–20
Who are these two "sons" lying in the street?

 Have a family member read 2 Nephi 8:17–20 and ask the following questions:

- What has happened to most of the "sons" of Jerusalem? (The children of Israel have been scattered.)
- How are the two sons in verses 19 different?

- Where are they lying?
- What kind of animal are they likened to?
- Is a bull captured in a net still dangerous?
- Who are these two sons?

To help answer the last question, share the following quotation from Elder Bruce R. McConkie:

"These two shall be followers of that humble man, Joseph Smith, through whom the Lord of Heaven restored the fullness of his everlasting gospel in this final dispensation of grace. No doubt they will be members of the Council of the Twelve or the First Presidency of the Church." (*Doctrinal New Testament Commentary*, 1:509–10; see also Revelation 11:3, 8–12, especially footnote 19a.)

2 NEPHI 9: THE GREAT PLAN OF HAPPINESS

Chapter Heading
The power of the Atonement

 Tell your family that a prophet of the Lord said that 2 Nephi 9 "should be carefully read by every person seeking salvation." (Joseph Fielding Smith, *Answers to Gospel Questions,* 4:57.) Have them read the chapter heading and identify those topics that would make this chapter so important. What event is mentioned twice in the heading? Share the following quotation from President James E. Faust:

"I wish to speak about the greatest event in all history. That singular event was the incomparable Atonement of our Lord and Savior, Jesus the Christ. This was the most transcendent act that has ever taken place, yet it is the most difficult to understand. My reason for wanting to learn all I can about the Atonement is partly selfish: Our salvation depends on believing in and accepting the Atonement. Such acceptance requires a continual effort to understand it more fully." ("The Atonement: Our Greatest Hope," *Ensign,* November 2001, p. 18.)

Challenge your family to study and ponder this

chapter and look for how the atonement of Jesus Christ affects them personally.

2 Nephi 9:4–9
What if there were no resurrection?

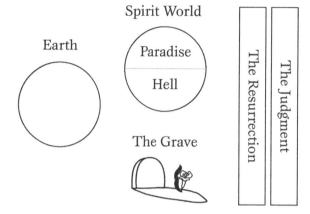 Draw or show the following illustration.

Put a glove on one hand and tell your family that the glove represents the physical body and the hand inside represents the spirit. As you remove the glove, explain that when someone dies the body and spirit separate. Ask them where the body goes. Read with your family 2 Nephi 9:4–6 and ask them what Jesus Christ has done for us because "all men" will die.

Next read together 2 Nephi 9:7 and ask what the word "infinite" means. To help with the definition, share the following from Elder Bruce R. McConkie:

"When the prophets speak of an *infinite* atonement, they mean just that. Its effects cover all men, the earth itself and all forms of life thereon, and reach out into the endless expanses of eternity." (*Mormon Doctrine,* p. 64.)

Discuss with your family what would happen to our bodies if Christ's infinite atonement had not brought about the "power of the resurrection." Then read 2 Nephi 8–9 and discuss what would have happened to our spirits if there was no resurrection. Share the following statement to help with the discussion:

"Why would it be that one would remain forever subject to Satan in the spirit world if there had been no resurrection? Would this also be true of a good man, one who had lived a life of morality and decency? Jacob's testimony was firm and his doctrine sound: had Christ not risen from the dead, we would all spend eternity in hell and eventually become servants of the father of lies.

"The Resurrection was the physical proof of our Lord's divine Sonship, the outward evidence that he was all he and his anointed servants said he was—the Messiah. If Jesus did not have the power to rise from the tomb—power to save the body—he did not have power to save the soul, the power to forgive sins" (Joseph Fielding McConkie and Robert L. Millet, *Doctrinal Commentary on the Book of Mormon,* 1:240.)

2 Nephi 9:10–13
How to escape the monster death and hell

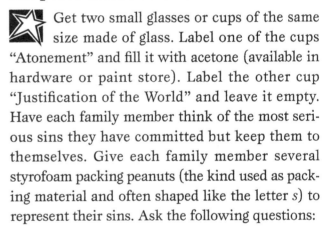 Ask your family what comes to mind when they hear the word *monster*. Have them read 2 Nephi 9:10 and see if their monster is anything like the monster mentioned there. Discuss how death is like a monster. What two kinds of death are mentioned there? Show the glove again (see the idea for 2 Nephi 9:4–9) and ask someone to explain what happens when the physical body dies.

Show the diagram you drew in the idea above and explain that spiritual death also involves a separation but of a different kind. Have them find what spiritual death is by searching 2 Nephi 9:6, 9. ("Cut off" or "shut out" of God's presence.) Read 2 Nephi 9:11–13 with your family and discuss the following questions:

- Where do spirits go when the body goes to the grave?
- Why do some spirits go to hell and some to paradise?
- What happens to our spirits and our bodies at the resurrection?
- How will your resurrected body be different from your mortal body?
- What do we learn in these verses that

explains why Jacob exclaimed, "O how great the goodness of our God"?

2 Nephi 9:13–18
What happens after the resurrection?

Show again the diagram from page 59 as you read 2 Nephi 9:13–15 with your family. Have them look for what happens after the resurrection that is the next step in Heavenly Fathers plan. (Judgment.) Ask them what will happen to our memory when we come before God for judgment. Discuss why that will be a joyful time for some and a frightening time for others.

2 Nephi 9:20–24
The power of the Atonement

Get two small glasses or cups of the same size made of glass. Label one of the cups "Atonement" and fill it with acetone (available in hardware or paint store). Label the other cup "Justification of the World" and leave it empty. Have each family member think of the most serious sins they have committed but keep them to themselves. Give each family member several styrofoam packing peanuts (the kind used as packing material and often shaped like the letter *s*) to represent their sins. Ask the following questions:

- What is the world's way of taking care of sin? (Justifying or rationalizing it.)
- How do we justify sin?
- What are some examples of things people sometimes say to justify their sins? (Everybody does it. It's not that bad. Just once won't matter.)

Hold up the cup labeled "Justification of the World" and ask how many sins we could fit into this small cup. Put several Styrofoam pieces in the cup and ask what happens to sins we try to rationalize away. (Nothing; they are still there).

Read together 2 Nephi 9:20–24 and ask what happens to sins that we allow the atonement of Jesus Christ to take care of. Have each family member put a styrofoam piece in the cup labeled

"Atonement" and watch as it is dissolved away. Discuss the following questions:

- What must we do so the Atonement will take care of our sins? (See verse 23.)
- What blessings await us if we do? (See verses 18–19, 23–24.)
- What did Jesus have to do to make this possible? (See verse 21.)
- How does that make you feel about your Savior?

2 Nephi 9:27–39
"The Ten Woes"

 Have your family scan 2 Nephi 9:27–38 and mark how many times Jacob uses the word *wo*. Explain that *wo* means sorrow, grief, or deep suffering. Read 2 Nephi 9:27 and explain that all these "woes" apply to those who know the commandments but refuse to repent and obey them.

Read 2 Nephi 9:30–38 with your family and discuss the following questions:

- What would the Lord have us do with our riches?
- What is the difference between a person who is deaf or blind and a person who "will not hear" or "will not see"?
- Who are the "uncircumcised of heart"? (Those who are proud and rebellious and do not take their covenants to heart.)
- What does it mean to "perish," "die," or "be thrust down to hell"? (See D&C 19:15–18.)
- What do you think it would feel like to "return to God, and behold His face, and remain in [your] sins"? Would "wo" be a good description of that feeling?

2 Nephi 9:28–29
When is wisdom foolishness?

Ask family members if they can remember President Gordon B. Hinckley's six "B's"? (Be grateful, Be smart, Be clean, Be true, Be humble, Be prayerful.) Tell them you want to talk about the second "B," Be Smart. Share the following quotation from President Hinckley:

"You are moving into the most competitive age the world has ever known. All around you is competition. You need all the education you can get. Sacrifice a car; sacrifice anything that is needed to be sacrificed to qualify yourselves to do the work of the world. That world will in large measure pay you what it thinks you are worth, and your worth will increase as you gain education and proficiency in your chosen field." ("A Prophet's Counsel and Prayer for Youth," *Ensign,* January 2001, p. 2.)

Now compare President Hinckley's counsel with what the prophet Jacob said in 2 Nephi 9:28–29 and discuss the following questions:

- According to President Hinckley, how will an education help us?
- According to Jacob, what danger is there in great learning?
- What do you think the difference is between learning and wisdom?
- How might our learning hinder us if we think we are wiser than our parents, our Church leaders, or even our Father in Heaven?
- What did Jacob say we must do to be wise instead of just learned?
- What are some ways we can include the "counsels of God" in our education? (Scripture reading, prayer, Church meetings, seminary, institute, Family Home Evening, and so on.)

2 Nephi 9:39
"Something to S.M.I.L.E. about"

Tell family members that an LDS stake used the word S.M.I.L.E. as an acronym for a phrase found in 2 Nephi 9:39. Ask your family to see if they can find it. Then have a family member read the following:

"The stake youth council of the Utah Hobble Creek Stake wanted to give the youth in the stake a reminder to be happy by living the commandments. They printed cards with the acronym

S.M.I.L.E. and distributed them throughout the stake. The letters are to remind the youth that 'to be Spiritually Minded Is Life Eternal.' 'You smile when you are happy, and there is no other way to eternal happiness than being spiritually minded,' says Chelsy Christensen, a Hobble Creek Stake youth representative." ("Bulletin Board," *New Era,* February 1998, p. 39.)

Discuss some or all of the following questions:

- What do you think it means to be "spiritually minded"?
- How does being "spiritually minded" lead to "life eternal"?
- What can we do to become more "spiritually minded"?
- What does it mean to be "carnally minded"? (Focused on the desires of the flesh.)
- How does being "carnally minded" lead to death?

Share the following statement by President Gordon B. Hinckley:

"Each of us, with discipline and effort, has the capacity to control his thoughts and his actions. This is part of the process of developing spiritual, physical, and emotional maturity. . . . We plead with people everywhere to live in accordance with the teachings of our Creator and rise above carnal attractions that often result in the tragedies that follow moral transgression." ("Reverence and Morality," *Ensign,* May 1987, p. 47.)

Discuss what your family can do to control thoughts and actions. Are there any television shows we shouldn't watch? How about our music? As a family, make a S.M.I.L.E. poster and display it where everyone will see it often.

2 Nephi 9:40–41
Who is the keeper of the gate?

Ask family members to read 2 Nephi 9:40–41 to themselves and insert their own name each time they find the words "my beloved brethren." Then discuss the following questions:

- What were your thoughts and feelings when you put your name in those verses?
- What is "the gate"?
- Who is the "keeper of the gate"?
- Why do you think it is important to know that Jesus is the "keeper of the gate"?

Read the following statement from Elder Neal A. Maxwell:

"Let us seek to become such true believers in Christ. Let us make our way, righteously and resolutely, notwithstanding our weaknesses, to the beckoning City of God. There, the sole and self-assigned gatekeeper is Jesus Christ. He awaits us not only to certify us, but because His deep, divine desire brings Him there to welcome us. If we acknowledge Him now, He will lovingly acknowledge us then." ("True Believers," *New Era,* April 1994, p. 24.)

2 Nephi 9:51
How do we spend our money and time?

Have family members make a list of how they have spent their money in the past week. Then have them make a list of how they have spent their time. Ask them to look in 2 Nephi 9:51 for counsel on how to spend money and time. Have them look at their lists and evaluate how they are doing. Ask them what they think Jacob meant when he said, "Let your soul delight in fatness"?

2 NEPHI 10: THE FATE OF THE HOUSE OF ISRAEL

2 Nephi 10:1–2
Can unbelieving children be restored?

Read 2 Nephi 10:1–2 with your family and have them tell what Jacob said would happen to the descendants of the Nephites. Why would many perish? (Unbelief.) Why would many be restored? (Because of the promises the Lord made to their righteous parents.)

Have someone read the following statement by

Elder Orson F. Whitney: "The Prophet Joseph Smith declared—and he never taught more comforting doctrine—that the eternal sealings of faithful parents and the divine promises made to them for valiant service in the Cause of Truth, would save not only themselves, but likewise their posterity. Though some of the sheep may wander, the eye of the Shepherd is upon them, and sooner or later they will feel the tentacles of Divine Providence reaching out after them and drawing them back to the fold. Either in this life or the life to come, they will return. They will have to pay their debt to justice; they will suffer for their sins; and may tread a thorny path; but if it leads them at last, like the penitent Prodigal, to a loving and forgiving father's heart and home, the painful experience will not have been in vain. Pray for your careless and disobedient children; hold on to them with your faith. Hope on, trust on, till you see the salvation of God." (Quoted by Elder Boyd K. Packer in "Our Moral Environment," *Ensign,* May 1992, p. 68.)

Discuss with your family ways that you can keep family members from straying from the Lord and the family. What can you do to help those that might be struggling with living gospel principles?

2 Nephi 10:2–22
Find the curses and blessings

 Take five pieces of paper and label each with one of the following titles and references:

- Nephites: 2 Nephi 10:2, 10, 19–20.
- Lamanites: 2 Nephi 10:10, 16, 18–19, 21.
- Jews: 2 Nephi 10:3, 5–8, 16.
- Gentiles: 2 Nephi 10:8–11, 13–14, 16, 18–19.
- Isles of the Sea: 2 Nephi 10:21–22.

Have family members choose one or more of the sheets of paper and then fold their papers in half. Have them label the left side of their paper "Blessings" and the right side of their paper "Curses." Explain that they are to read the verses and then list all blessings and curses that they find

there. Have each family member share what they have learned with the rest of the family. Discuss which blessings and curses would also apply to us.

2 Nephi 10:3–6
Why did the Jews reject their own God?

Read 2 Nephi 10:3–5 with your family and have them look for what caused the Jews to be to so wicked that they would crucify their Savior. Ask:

- According to 2 Nephi 26:29, what are priestcrafts?
- According to 2 Nephi 10:6, what consequences will the Jews suffer for their iniquity?
- How could priestcrafts become a problem for the Church today?

Bear your testimony of the importance of following the Lord's prophets who love us and seek only for our eternal happiness.

2 Nephi 10:23–25
What must I do to be saved?

Have your family silently read 2 Nephi 10:23–25 and pick out what impresses them most about Jacob's teachings in these verses. Have someone look up *reconcile* in the dictionary and then discuss what it means to "reconcile yourselves to the will of God." Read verse 24 and remind your family that even after they choose to obey God, something else is necessary to be saved and return to live with their Father in Heaven. Share your feelings about the grace and goodness of Jesus Christ in your life.

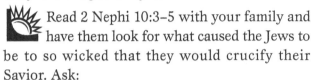

2 NEPHI 11: WITNESSES OF JESUS CHRIST

2 Nephi 11:1–4
Who are the three witnesses of Jesus Christ mentioned in this chapter?

 Read 2 Nephi 11:4 with your family and ask them to look for what Nephi said he

delighted in proving. Read Matthew 18:16 aloud and ask how more than one witness can help "prove" that a teaching is true. Have someone read the following quotation from Elder Jeffrey R. Holland:

"The Lord's manner of teaching and affirming, especially when it involves a covenant, has always provided more than one testimony." (*Christ and the New Covenant,* p. 33.)

Have family members silently read 2 Nephi 11:1–3 and mark the names of each person mentioned who was an eyewitness of Jesus Christ. Have them share what they found. You might like to read some of these additional insights from Elder Holland:

"In keeping with this same covenantal principle, it is interesting to note that there were three earlier witnesses—special witnesses—. . . of Divinity himself. . . . In declaring the special preparation these three had for receiving and teaching such 'greater views' of the gospel, Nephi revealed the most persuasive qualification of all. They all had seen the premortal Jesus Christ. . . . After reading these three witnesses from the small plates of Nephi, the reader knows two things in bold relief: that Jesus is the Christ, the Son of the Living God, and that God will keep his covenants and promises with the remnants of the house of Israel. Those two themes constitute the two principal purposes of the Book of Mormon, and they are precisely the introductory themes addressed by Nephi, Jacob, and Isaiah." (*Christ and the New Covenant,* pp. 34–35.)

2 Nephi 11:4–7
Make "happy" lists

Have each family member make a list in their journals titled "Three things that make me happy." Take turns sharing the lists. Ask your family why they enjoy these things.

Have everyone scan through 2 Nephi 11:4–7 and find the phrase that Nephi uses four times to express what makes him happy. Have family members write things in which Nephi delighted next to their "happy list" and discuss how Nephi's list compares with the lists made by family members. Ask why the doctrines on Nephi's list would help make a person happy. When have you experienced happiness because of one of Nephi's teachings?

2 Nephi 11:8
The Isaiah matching game

Explain to your family that Isaiah was an important Old Testament Prophet. His teachings would have been well-known to Saints living during the time of Lehi and Nephi. (See Bible Dictionary, "Isaiah," p. 707.) Read the last paragraph in the Bible Dictionary entry for "Isaiah" and discuss these questions:

• What are the best books available to help us understand the book of Isaiah?

• What will you better understand by learning more about Isaiah's teachings?

• How can having a greater understanding of the Savior's mission bless your life?

Have your family quickly look at the next thirteen chapter headings in the book of Mormon (2 Nephi 12–24). What do these chapters have in common? Read 2 Nephi 11:8 and mark why Nephi quoted so many of Isaiah's writings. As you study these chapters with your family, invite them to look for truths in Isaiah's teachings that bring them joy.

Give each family member a copy of the following matching game so they can familiarize themselves with the writings of Isaiah and become excited to study 2 Nephi 12–24. When they have finished, identify the correct answers.

____ 1. Isaiah's father

____ 2. A king in Isaiah's day

____ 3. Jesus Christ

____ 4. 740–701 B.C.

____ 5. What Jesus said

____ 6. What Nephi said

A. The subject of most of Isaiah's prophecies

B. "My soul delighteth in his [Isaiah's] words"

C. Uzziah

D. "Great are the words of Isaiah"

E. Amoz

F. The years Isaiah lived

correct answers:
1. E. See 2 Nephi 12:1.
2. C. See 2 Nephi 16:1.
3. A. See Bible Dictionary, "Isaiah."
4. F. See Bible Dictionary, "Isaiah."
5. D. See 3 Nephi 23:1–3.
6. B. See 2 Nephi 11:2.

2 NEPHI 12: ISAIAH SEES OUR DAY

2 Nephi 12:1–4
What is the "mountain of the Lord's house"?

Remind your family that the reason Nephi includes in his record the words of Isaiah is to give us reason to rejoice. (See 2 Nephi 11:8.) Read together 2 Nephi 12:1–4 and mark the things Isaiah said would happen in the "last days" that are a cause for rejoicing. Point out to your family that the chapter heading identifies the "mountain of the Lord's house" as the temple. Discuss what it would be like to live in a world where everyone followed the Lord and there was no war.

2 Nephi 12:5–22
What sins did Isaiah see in the last days?

Explain to your family that one of the interesting characteristics of Isaiah's prophecies is "dualism." That means that what he

prophesied would come true in more than one time period. For example, what Isaiah described in 2 Nephi 12 was true for his day but is also true for our day. Have a family member read 2 Nephi 12:5 and tell what Isaiah said about the house of Jacob.

Read 2 Nephi 12:6–22 together and mark all the things Isaiah said that apply to our day. Tell your family not to worry if they do not understand everything in every verse; they should just mark the things they do understand. Share the following explanations as needed to help them understand Isaiah's prophecies.

- Verse 6: The "east" and the "Philistines" and the "children of strangers" refer to those idolatrous nations all around Israel. Israel often turned to their wicked neighbors for revelation rather than to the prophets of God in their own land. Who are the wise men and experts people turn to today instead of the prophets?
- Verses 20–21: When the Savior comes again, what do you think the wicked will want to do with the material things they worshipped instead of the Lord?

2 NEPHI 13: THE TRAGEDY OF WORLDLINESS

2 Nephi 13:1–15
What if your world crumbled?

Write the following words or phrases on separate pieces of paper: food and water; president and congress; judges; prophets; soldiers and police; wise men and women; scientists and skilled workers. Hold up each piece of paper, one at a time. As you do, ask your family what would happen to our country if what is written on the paper was taken away. Explain that anciently Isaiah warned the children of Israel that they would lose these kinds of things. Read together 2 Nephi 13:1–3 and note the similarities. Then read 2 Nephi 13:4–5 to see what Isaiah said would happen if God took these things away. Ask:

- Who would rule over them? (Note that "children" and "babes" refer to learning and experience more than actual age.)
- How will the young treat those who are older?
- How will the unrespectable treat the respectable?
- Have you noticed any of these attitudes among your friends and others?

To understand why God would bring these things upon the children of Israel, read the chapter heading and 2 Nephi 13:8–9, 11, 15. Ask your family to list the evil things the children of Israel needed to repent of. According to verse 10, what hope was given to the righteous in the midst of all of this turmoil? Discuss with your family what you can do to avoid this awful fate in your community, church, and nation.

2 Nephi 13:16–24
Latter-day sins of the daughters of Zion

 Play a matching game. Copy the "Modern Meaning" list below onto a separate sheet of paper and then cut out each word. Place the pieces in the middle of a table. Tell your family to match some of Isaiah's difficult words (from 2 Nephi 13:16–26) with modern meanings.

Isaiah's Words	Modern Meaning
Haughty	Proud
Wanton	Flirting
Discover their secret parts	Reveal their secret sins
Cauls	Headbands
Round tires like the moon	Crescent necklaces
Mufflers	Veils
Tablets	Perfume boxes
Mantles	Capes
Wimples	Cloaks
Crisping-pins	Purses
Glasses	Mirrors
Rent	Rags
Stomacher	Fine robes
Sackcloth	Clothing made of course material
Burning	Branding (to identify a slave)

Once the family has matched all they can, help them with the other answers. Divide the matches among family members and read together 2 Nephi 13:16–24. Have them insert the modern word for the difficult one as they find them. Discuss the following questions:

- Who are the daughters of Zion? (Young women and women in the Church.)
- What does this teach us about some of the daughters of Zion in the last days?
- How can following after worldly fashions cause spiritual problems?
- What has the Lord said through his prophet that can help keep us safe?

Share the following statement by the First Presidency (if available, read the entire section titled "Dress and Appearance" in the "For the Strength of Youth" pamphlet) and discuss how its counsel might help you be safe in the last days:

"Prophets of God have always counseled His children to dress modestly. The way you dress is a reflection of what you are on the inside. Your dress and grooming send messages about you to others and influence the way you and others act. When you are well groomed and modestly dressed, you invite the companionship of the Spirit and can exercise a good influence on those around you." (*For the Strength of Youth*, pp. 14–15.)

2 NEPHI 14: A REFUGE FROM THE STORM

2 Nephi 14:2–4
Who will escape the Lord's coming?

Light a match; then have a family member read 2 Nephi 14:4 and tell how the match relates to the Lord's Second Coming. (See also Malachi 4:1; 1 Nephi 22:15; D&C 38:12.) What will this "spirit of burning" do to those in Zion and Jerusalem? (Wash and purge them by destroying those that are wicked.) Read together 2 Nephi 14:2–3 and ask:

- After the Lord comes again what will happen to "the branch of the Lord," meaning His righteous children?
- What will happen to the earth?
- Of those who are left, what kind of people will they be?
- How would you like to live then?
- What are you willing to do to live then?

2 Nephi 14:5–6
How can we survive life's storms?

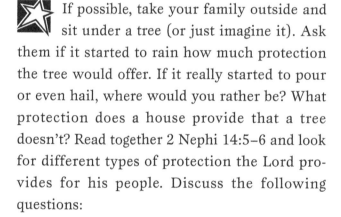 If possible, take your family outside and sit under a tree (or just imagine it). Ask them if it started to rain how much protection the tree would offer. If it really started to pour or even hail, where would you rather be? What protection does a house provide that a tree doesn't? Read together 2 Nephi 14:5–6 and look for different types of protection the Lord provides for his people. Discuss the following questions:

- What help or "defense" would a pillar of fire or cloud provide? (See also Exodus 13:19–21; 14:19–20.)
- What will provide safety from "heat," "storm," and "rain"? (A tabernacle.)
- What other kinds of storms do we need protection from? (Spiritual weakness, trials, temptations, and so on.)
- How would living with the righteous in Zion help with all of life's storms? (To help answer this question, read also D&C 115:5–6.)

2 NEPHI 15: ISRAEL LIKENED TO A VINEYARD

2 Nephi 15:1–7
What does the parable of the vineyard mean?

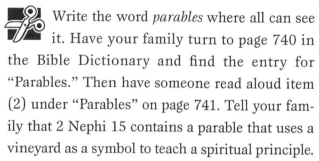 Write the word *parables* where all can see it. Have your family turn to page 740 in the Bible Dictionary and find the entry for "Parables." Then have someone read aloud item (2) under "Parables" on page 741. Tell your family that 2 Nephi 15 contains a parable that uses a vineyard as a symbol to teach a spiritual principle.

List the following items under the word "parables" on your paper: "vineyard," "the choicest vine" (also called "pleasant plant"), "grapes," "wild grapes," "the hedge," and "the wall." Then read 2 Nephi 15:1–7 with your family and have them mark those symbols as they find them in the parable. Ask the following questions:

- Which symbols do the verses tell us the meaning of? (See verse 7.)
- According to verse 2, what had God done to ensure that his people (choicest vine) would flourish and bring forth good grapes? (Fenced it; gathered out stones; built a tower.)
- What would the "grapes" and "wild grapes" represent? (Righteousness and unrighteousness.)
- What do a hedge and wall do for a vineyard? (Protect it from intruders.)
- What do verses 5–6 say will happen to Israel because of their unrighteousness?
- What do you think Isaiah is trying to teach in this parable?
- Why do some people choose wickedness over righteousness?

Next to each symbol on your paper, write its meaning. You also may want to have your family write the meanings in their scriptures.

2 Nephi 15:8–25
What sins in ancient Israel are found with us today?

Read 2 Nephi 15:8–25 with your family and list the sins Isaiah mentions. As you list each sin, discuss any current conditions in your community that may be similar. Use the following insights and questions as needed to help your family understand these verses.

- Verses 8–10: "Joining one house to another refers to building up great landed estates by oppressive means" (Donald W. Parry, Jay A. Parry, and Tina M. Peterson, *Understanding Isaiah*, p. 56.) Ask if there are people today who use dishonest or unfair means to gain wealth. Have your family find "bath," "homer," and "ephah" in the Bible Dictionary, "Weights and Measures," 788–89. What has happened to the productivity of the land because of these sins?
- Verses 11–17: Are there people today who are interested only in parties and entertainment? How does a lack of knowledge lead to captivity and bondage?
- Verses 18–19: Do you know people who are tied to their sins like a donkey to a cart because they are too proud to admit that their sinful behavior is wrong? Do you know others who will not believe unless they see some sign or proof that the gospel is true?
- Verse 20: Can you think of people today who "call evil good and good evil"? "Elder Spencer W. Kimball once said that the infidelity of our day, and the movies, books, and magazines that glamorize the unfaithful husbands and wives and make them heroes and heroines, reminded him of this verse in Isaiah (see Conference Report, October 1962, p. 56)." (Monte S. Nyman, *Great Are the Words of Isaiah*, p. 45.)
- Verses 21–23: Are the poor ever treated unfairly today because they are poor? Do the wicked ever go free because they are wealthy?
- Verses 24–25: What did Isaiah say would happen to the Jews because of these sins? Were the Jews smitten and scattered as Isaiah prophesied? What do you suppose will happen to those who are guilty of those same sins in our day?

2 Nephi 15:26
What does it mean to "hiss" to the nations?

Ask your family how they are usually summoned or called to dinner or other family events (for example, called to, whistled, or a phone call). When a person whistles at or to another person, what are they hoping the results will be?

Read together 2 Nephi 15:26 and look for the word Isaiah used to describe how the nations would be called. Explain that the word "hiss" seems strange today. Show your family Isaiah 5:26 and the meaning of the word "hiss" in footnote b. (Whistle.) Ask your family what it might mean then to "hiss" to the family. What will the Lord raise up in the last days that will get Israel's attention and cause them to speedily return? (2 Nephi 15:26.)

2 Nephi 15:26–30
Is it possible Isaiah saw trains and planes?

Tell your family that Isaiah was privileged to see the future. Read verse 26 and ask what the word *ensign* means. (A standard, flag, or banner.) Hold up the *Ensign* magazine and ask why the Church named its magazine the *Ensign*. What is the ensign to the nations spoken of in verse 30?

Elder Marion G. Romney declared, "[The Church of Jesus Christ of Latter-day Saints] is the standard which Isaiah said the Lord would set up for the people in the latter-days. . . . This Church is the ensign on the mountain spoken of by the Old Testament prophets." (Conference Report, April 1961, p. 119.)

Have someone read 2 Nephi 15:26–27. Explain that to "hiss" means to call. Ask them what purpose the ensign serves. (It is a call to gather quickly.) How has the Church become a gathering place for the nations? How can we, in our own wards and stakes, be an ensign to those around us?

Read together 2 Nephi 15:28–29. Explain that Isaiah also saw means of traveling quickly that were not familiar to him. To help your family see how difficult it is to describe something you've never seen before, place an object they are not familiar with in a bag. Invite a family member to look in the bag and then describe the object to the family. Ask family members to draw on a piece of paper what they think is being described.

Read the following statement by Elder LeGrand Richards: "Since there were neither trains nor airplanes in that day, Isaiah could hardly have mentioned them by name. However, he seems to have described them in unmistakable words. How better could 'their horses' hoofs be counted like flint, and their wheels like a whirlwind' than in the modern train? How better could 'their roaring . . . be like a lion' than in the roar of the airplane? Trains and airplanes do not stop for night. Therefore, was not Isaiah justified in saying: 'none shall slumber nor sleep; neither shall the girdle of their loins be loosed, nor the latchet of their shoes be broken'? With this manner of transportation the Lord can really 'hiss unto them from the end of the earth,' that 'they shall come with speed swiftly.' Indicating that Isaiah must have foreseen the airplane, he stated: 'Who are these that fly as a cloud, and as the doves to their windows?' (Isaiah 60:8.)." (*Israel! Do You Know?* p. 182.)

2 NEPHI 16: ISAIAH'S CALLING AS A PROPHET—NEPHI QUOTES ISAIAH 6

2 Nephi 16:1–3
What is a "train" and what are "seraphim"?

Read together 2 Nephi 16:1–3 and ask family members if they know what a "train" is or what "seraphim" are. Have someone look in a dictionary for a definition of the word *train* that has something to do with clothing. As they read aloud that definition, show them a picture of a wedding dress with a long train. To explain what seraphim are, have them turn to their Bible Dictionary under the heading "Seraphim." (See page 771.) Ask someone to read that definition.

Ask your family to imagine what this vision of the Lord might have been like. What similarities and differences do you see between Isaiah's vision and the visions of Lehi (see 1 Nephi 1:5–12) and Joseph Smith (see Joseph Smith—History 1:15–17)?

2 Nephi 16:4
Why is the temple full of smoke?

Light a stick of incense if you have some or a scented candle. Tell your family that in ancient times, the priests were commanded to burn incense in the temple, which produced a smoke having a pleasant scent. (See Exodus 30:1–8.) Read Revelation 8:3–4 and have them look for what the smoke of the incense represents. What does this symbol of the smoke in the temple teach us about the Lord and our prayers?

2 Nephi 16:5–8
Isaiah's mission call

Show your family a picture of a missionary and a picture of a nearby temple. Ask them why they think missionaries go to the temple before they go on a mission. What does a person have to do to be worthy to enter the temple? How would that help prepare them for a mission? Explain that in 2 Nephi 16 Isaiah sees in vision the Lord's heavenly temple before he is called to serve.

Have one family member read along in Isaiah 6:5–8 while the rest of the family reads together 2 Nephi 16:5–8. As you read, discuss the following questions:

- Why do you think Isaiah felt "undone" when he saw the Lord? (See footnote 5a for Isaiah 6:5 in your LDS edition of the Bible.)

- Do you ever feel unworthy to be in the Lord's presence? What can you do to change that?
- What did the Lord do about Isaiah's sins?
- What did the "live coal" represent? (See footnote 6a for Isaiah 6:6.)
- Now that Isaiah was cleansed from sin, how did he answer when the Lord said: "Whom shall I send?"
- Who else answered a call with these same words? (See Abraham 3:24–27.)

Explain that when Isaiah was called to serve, it involved becoming a witness that God lives. The apostles and prophets in our day are also called to be "special witnesses of the name of Christ in all the world." (D&C 107:23.) Rarely are such sacred experiences spoken of openly, but on occasion some witnesses have shared such experiences. Share the following account by Elder Melvin J. Ballard, a former member of the Quorum of the Twelve:

"That night I received a wonderful manifestation and impression which has never left me. I was carried to this place—into this room [in the temple]. . . . I was told there was another privilege that was to be mine; and I was led into a room where I was informed I was to meet someone. As I entered the room I saw, seated on a raised platform, the most glorious being I have ever conceived of, and was taken forward to be introduced to Him. As I approached He smiled, called my name, and stretched out His hands towards me. . . . He put His arms around me and kissed me, as He took me into His bosom, and He blessed me until my whole being was thrilled. As He finished I fell at His feet, and there saw the marks of the nails; and as I kissed them, with deep joy swelling through my whole being, I felt that I was in heaven indeed. The feeling that came to my heart then was: Oh! If I could live worthy . . . so that in the end when I have finished I could go into His presence and receive the feeling that I then had in His presence, I would give everything that I am and ever hope to be!"

(*Melvin J. Ballard: Crusader for Righteousness*, pp. 65–66.)

Ask, "How does this experience help you want to see the Lord one day?"

2 NEPHI 17: ISAIAH TEACHES ABOUT CHRIST THROUGH IMAGES OF WAR

2 Nephi 17:1–9
Ephraim and Syria conspire against Judah

 To help your family understand these verses, make a simple map showing Syria, Israel, and Judah (see Bible map "The Kingdoms of Israel and Judah"). Make it large enough for all to see. Read 2 Nephi 17:1–2 with your family. Explain that *Ephraim* is another name for the kingdom of Israel and that *house of David* is another name for the kingdom of Judah. Add the following labels to your map as you come to them in the verses:

- "King Ahaz" by Judah.
- "King Rezin" by Syria.
- "King Pekah, Remaliah's son" by Israel.

Using the map as a guide, have someone tell what is happening in 2 Nephi 17:1–2.

Read 2 Nephi 17:3–9 together as a family and answer the following questions:

- What did Isaiah tell King Ahaz to do about the attack from Ephraim and Syria? (Verse 4.)
- What did Isaiah say would happen to Ephraim? (Verse 8.)
- What reasons can you think of why Ahaz should want to listen to Isaiah?
- What did Isaiah say would happen if Ahaz refused to have faith in the Lord's promises? (See verse 9.)
- What have you experienced that causes you to have faith in the Lord's promises?

2 Nephi 17:10–16
One prophecy—two fulfillments! A sign to Ahaz and to Us

Have a family member read 2 Nephi 17:10–11 and explain what the Lord tells Ahaz to do. Then read 2 Nephi 17:12–17 and ask what the Lord did when King Ahaz refused to ask for proof of Isaiah's words. What sign was Ahaz given to show that both Ephraim and Syria would be defeated by Assyria?

Tell your family that Isaiah's prophecies were fulfilled when the Assyrians conquered both Syria and Ephraim. (See 2 Kings 15–17.) What does that teach us about the Lord's foreknowledge and the role of prophets? Bear testimony to your family of how vital it will be to listen to our modern prophets if we want to be prepared for the difficult times prophesied for our future.

Explain that it is unclear how the prophecy was fulfilled in Isaiah's day (see 2 Nephi 18:3–4), but we have a great deal of evidence of a far greater fulfillment many years later. Read together Matthew 1:20–25 and ask how Jesus fulfills the meaning of the name "Emmanuel."

2 NEPHI 18: ISAIAH INVITES US TO SEEK THE LORD

2 Nephi 18:1–4
What's in a Name?

Ask your family if they know why they were given the names they have. Then have them read 2 Nephi 18:1–4 and find the name Isaiah gave one of his sons. What does that name mean? (See footnote 1b.) Then read 2 Nephi 18:18 and have them look for the reason the Lord told Isaiah to give his son that name. Share the following insight to help them understand how the Lord used Isaiah and his children as "signs and wonders":

"Isaiah had told King Ahaz that the threat from Syria and Ephraim (Israel) would pass and the child Immanuel would be born in Judah as part of

the country's future destiny (Isa. 7:14–16) [2 Nephi 17:14–16]. Then the promise of relief from attack was made more immediate by the Lord's assurance that before a son yet to be born to Isaiah and his wife could learn to say *avi* (daddy) and *immi* (mommy), both Damascus of Syria and Samaria of Israel would be conquered by Assyria. The name of this baby was a token of Assyria's attack on northern Israel (Isa. 8:1*d*) [2 Nephi 18:1:*b*]." (Ellis T. Rasmussen, *A Latter-day Saint Commentary on the Old Testament,* p. 509.)

2 Nephi 18:5–18
What are the "Waters of Shiloah"?

Have your family turn to the maps in the back of their Bibles and find the map labeled "The Assyrian Empire" (old map set #10; new map set #5). Compare that map to the one referred to in 2 Nephi 17 in this book. Explain that this is the Assyrian Empire that Isaiah prophesied about in 2 Nephi 17–18.

Write the following questions where your family can see them:

- What are the "waters of Shiloah"?
- Who is like "the waters of the river, strong and many"?
- Who is both a "sanctuary" and "a stone of stumbling and for a rock of offense"?

Read 2 Nephi 18:5–18 with your family and look for answers to those questions. Share the following explanation if needed:

"The 'waters of Shiloah' had long been Jerusalem's water supply. . . . Water flowed to Shiloah from the spring Gihon, which represented the Lord's providence, whereas the 'waters of the river,' the Euphrates, represented the forces of Assyria. King Ahaz did not follow the prophet's advice, so Judah was invaded and Jerusalem besieged. It was not conquered, however, thanks to the stronger faith and better behavior of the next king, Hezekiah, son of Ahaz. Jerusalem was saved by the Lord, as promised by the 'stretching out of his wings' over the land of *Immanuel.* Nevertheless, the country was almost overwhelmed by Assyrian forces, reaching nearly to 'the neck' (Isa. 8:8, 10; Isa. 36–37).

"Because the Lord would save Judah, the prophet advised against a confederacy with other nations for security; the king and people should make the Lord their 'sanctuary.' Isaiah knew, however, that the Lord as Savior in those times, as also later during the Lord's life on earth, would be 'a stone of stumbling,' upon whom many unbelievers would 'stumble, and fall, and be broken, and be snared, and be taken' (Isa. 8:14–15).

"Neither the king nor the people would accept the testimony given to the Lord's disciples, nor would they understand the 'signs' and wonders provided through Isaiah. The names of Isaiah and his sons symbolize the scattering and gathering of Israel and the salvation of the Lord (Isa. 8:18*a*)." (Ellis T. Rasmussen, *A Latter-day Saint Commentary on the Old Testament*, p. 510.)

2 NEPHI 19: "UNTO US A CHILD IS BORN"

2 Nephi 19:1–7
Isaiah prophesies of the birth of the Savior

Bring a recording of Handel's "Messiah" and play the two selections that use the words from Isaiah 9:2 and Isaiah 9:6. (On the Mormon Tabernacle Choir's performance of Handel's *Messiah* published by NightPro, it is disc 1, tracks 10 and 11.) As you play the selections, have your family search 2 Nephi 19:1–7 and find the verses that that those words came from. Explain that Handel used many verses from Isaiah that prophesy of the life of the Savior.

Read 2 Nephi 19:1–2 with your family and have them find the map in the back of their Bibles that shows where the tribes of Zebulun and Naphtali settled (old map set #5; new map set #3). Then have them find another map of Palestine in New Testament times and find what that same

area was called then (old map set #14; new map set #11). (Galilee.) Ask them what they think the "great light" is that Isaiah said would shine in the land of Galilee? (Jesus Christ, the light of the world, was born in Nazareth of Galilee.)

Next read 2 Nephi 9:6–7 together and mark the other names Isaiah uses to describe Jesus. What do each of those names teach us about the character and mission of the Savior.

2 Nephi 19:12–21
What does the Lord do when He gets angry?

Ask your family what often happens in the world when one person gets really angry with another. (Perhaps you could think of an example of anger, hatred, or desire to hurt or get revenge.) Ask why it is so hard to forgive when we are hurt or wronged by another.

Read 2 Nephi 19:12–21 with your family and have them look for reasons why the Lord is angry with Israel. Then have them search those verses again to find a sentence that appears three times in these verses that describes what the Lord did about His anger over the wickedness of Israel. Share your testimony of how comforting it is that even when we have offended the Lord or made Him angry, His "hand is stretched out still" to help us.

2 NEPHI 20: THE DESTRUCTION OF ASSYRIA— A TYPE FOR THE SECOND COMING?

2 Nephi 20:1–2
What is our responsibility to the poor and the needy?

Have family members read 2 Nephi 20:1–2 and find one of the evil practices the Lord condemns. (Unfair treatment of the poor.) Now read D&C 104:15–18 to see the modern teachings of the Lord concerning this doctrine. Ask how the Church helps us fulfill this responsibility. (Fast offerings, welfare projects, home teaching, humanitarian aid, perpetual education fund, and so on.) Share the following story:

"Recently, while in my car leaving my office I was stopped two blocks away at a stoplight. A man who appeared to be homeless walked across the crosswalk in front of me. I couldn't help but notice his shoes. Actually, the shoes were only a façade. As he approached, his toes were visible where the top of the shoe should have connected with the sole. As he walked away, even more visible were the bare bottoms of his feet as he tried to walk swiftly away, obviously struggling not to limp as he tried to walk as normal as possible. . . .

"I drove away but could not get the scene out of my mind. While turning on to the freeway, I thought of my closet full of shoes and about trying to decide which pair to wear. I looked down at my new walking shoes that were so comfortable. The next exit was more than a mile away, but I took it and drove back to try and see if I could help this man in some way.

"A few minutes later I was back on the same street, and sure enough he was still walking. I looked again at his feet and in a quick glance determined that his shoe size would be very close to my own. I turned into a parking lot and stopped near the sidewalk, where he would have to walk right past me, untied my shoes, held them inside the car and as he walked past called to him, 'Sir, may I see you for a minute?' He hesitated briefly, not sure that I was calling to him. When he came over to the window of the car I said, 'I couldn't help but notice your shoes.' He said, 'Yeah, I've been doing a lot of walking lately.' I handed him my shoes through the car window. He asked, 'What size are they?' 'Size 9,' I said. 'That's my size,' he said, and then offered a very sincere, 'Mister, thanks a lot.'

"I don't think I will ever forget his face. As he walked away and as I drove away in my stocking feet, I felt a calm, peaceful feeling." (Guy A. Irwin, *Church News,* November 24, 1990, p. 11.)

Ask family members what they could do

personally to help the needy. Then ask what you could do as a family.

2 Nephi 20:5–19
Look who's working for the Lord!

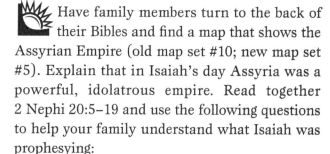 Have family members turn to the back of their Bibles and find a map that shows the Assyrian Empire (old map set #10; new map set #5). Explain that in Isaiah's day Assyria was a powerful, idolatrous empire. Read together 2 Nephi 20:5–19 and use the following questions to help your family understand what Isaiah was prophesying:

- What did the Lord mean by "O Assyrian the rod of mine anger"? (Verses 5–6.)
- Who is the "hypocritical nation"? (See footnote 6a.)
- Did the Assyrians know that when they conquered Israel they were working for the God of Israel? (Verses 7–11.)
- Why did the Assyrians think they had successfully conquered so many other nations? (Verses 13–14.)
- What did God say would happen to Assyria because they boasted in their own strength? (Verses 12, 15–19.)
- In what way was the king of Assyria just a tool in the Lord's hand?
- How is the Assyrian conquest of Israel an example of the principle taught in Mormon 4:5? (The Lord used wicked Assyria to punish wicked Israel.)
- What modern situations can you think of that are examples of this same principle?

2 Nephi 20:20–27
The destruction of Assyria—a twice-fulfilled prophecy

Have someone read aloud the chapter heading to 2 Nephi 20 and explain what two messages the Lord was giving when Isaiah prophesied of the destruction of Assyria. Show your family a piece of cloth, an old shirt or something similar, and tear it into two pieces (one large and one small). Throw the larger piece away and keep the smaller piece. Invite your family to read 2 Nephi 20:20–22. Then ask, "What does this small piece or 'remnant' of the cloth represent? What has changed with this latter-day remnant of the house of Israel?" (They have forsaken wickedness and turned to the Lord.)

Read 2 Nephi 20:24–27 with your family and remind them that the Assyrians are used here as a symbol for latter-day wickedness. Discuss the following questions:

- What phrases can you find that explain what will happen to the wicked in the last days?
- What promises does the Lord make to his "people that dwellest in Zion"?
- How long will the Saints be oppressed by the wicked? (Verses 24–25.)
- By what power will the righteous be freed from the burden of the wicked? (Verse 27.)
- What does "the anointing" mean? (See footnote 27b.) Explain that "Christ" means "the anointed one."

Bear testimony to your family of the power of the atonement of Jesus Christ to lift our burdens, whatever they may be.

2 NEPHI 21–22: WE WILL PRAISE THE LORD DURING THE MILLENNIUM

2 Nephi 21:1–9
Is the thought of being judged by Jesus Christ a frightening idea or a comforting one?

 Remind your family that Isaiah often used symbols to teach important principles. Often the best help for understanding Isaiah comes from modern scripture. Have your family follow along while you read 2 Nephi 21:1. Have them mark the words "stem" and "branch." Explain that some early members of the Church wanted to know what those symbols meant. Have your family read D&C 113:1–2 and find out who

the "stem" is. Have them write "Jesus Christ" in the margin of their scriptures next to 2 Nephi 21:1 and draw a line to the word "stem" in the verse. To find out who the "branch" is, read 2 Nephi 21:2–5 together and pick out phrases that describe him. Ask them who is the only righteous judge they know of that can do all those things. (Jesus Christ; see also Jeremiah 23:5–6.) Have them draw another line from the words "Jesus Christ" in their margin to "branch" in 2 Nephi 21:1.

Read 2 Nephi 21:3–4 again to your family and ask them what sort of person should be afraid of being judged by Jesus Christ. To help your family understand how Jesus will judge those who believe and follow Him, read D&C 45:3–5. Would it be worth it to keep the commandments to have that kind of experience at the final judgment?

2 Nephi 21:1, 10
Who is the "rod" and the "root"?

 Read 2 Nephi 21:1, 10 with your family and have them mark the words "rod" and "root." Then read D&C 113:3–6 and pick out the phrases that describe the "rod" and the "root." Ask your family who they think fits that description. Ask, "What latter-day servant of Christ do you know of that was given the 'keys of the kingdom'?" For help see D&C 110:11–16 and share the following insight:

"Certainly the priesthood power bestowed on Joseph Smith, the Prophet of the Restoration, qualifies him to be this servant. Consider also the Angel Moroni's proclamation, following a recitation of the eleventh chapter of Isaiah to young Joseph, that 'it was about to be fulfilled.' (JS H 1:40.) Furthermore, the ancient seer Joseph, he who rose to such power in ancient Egypt, prophesied that one of his descendants bearing the name of Joseph would be raised up to do a great work for the Lord. (2 Nephi 3:6–15; JST, Genesis 50:26–33.)" (Hoyt W. Brewster, Jr., *Isaiah Plain and Simple*, p. 109.) Write "Joseph Smith" in the margin next to 2 Nephi 21:1, 10 and draw a line to the words "rod" and "root." What do these verses teach us about the importance of the mission of the Prophet Joseph Smith?

2 Nephi 21:6–9
What will the Millennium be like?

 Have a family member print the following phrases on separate sheets of paper:

1. shall dwell with
2. shall lie down with
3. together
4. feed
5. their young ones shall lie down together
6. eat straw like
7. play on the hole of
8. put his hand on

Gather stuffed animals or pictures of the animals mentioned in 2 Nephi 21:6–8. (An "asp" and a "cockatrice" are names for poisonous snakes. See Bible Dictionary, "Asp," p. 615, and "Cockatrice," p. 647.) You will also need a picture of an infant and a toddler. Read 2 Nephi 21:6–9 with your family and play a matching game by asking family members to find the animals or children that belong to the above phrases. Discuss how the behavior of animals will change during the Millennium.

Share the following statements from Elder Bruce R. McConkie: "On the paradisiacal earth 'the enmity of beasts, yea, the enmity of all flesh, shall cease.' (D&C 101:26.) All animals shall mingle together in peace, and the appetites of the carnivorous beast shall be changed so that the grass of the field becomes the common diet of the animal world. (Isa 11:6–9; 65:25)." (*Mormon Doctrine,* p. 496.)

"Man and all forms of life will be vegetarians in the coming day; the eating of meat will cease, because, for one thing, death as we know it ceases. There will be no shedding of blood, because man and animals are changed (quickened) and blood no longer flows in their veins." (*Mormon Doctrine,* p. 658.)

Ask your family what they look forward to the most about the Millennium.

2 Nephi 21:10–16
The gathering of Israel

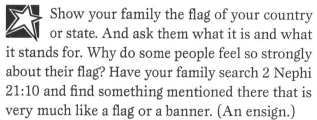 Show your family the flag of your country or state. And ask them what it is and what it stands for. Why do some people feel so strongly about their flag? Have your family search 2 Nephi 21:10 and find something mentioned there that is very much like a flag or a banner. (An ensign.)

Read together 2 Nephi 21:11–12 and ask what the purpose is for this ensign. (It indicates the gathering place.) Hold up the Church's *Ensign* magazine and ask if they can see why the Church named its magazine the *Ensign.*

As a fun family project you could plan and then draw a family ensign that represents your family values. (If you like, your ensign could be made of fabric and mounted on a flagpole. Such family ensigns are fun to mount at campouts or to display in your yard on special family occasions.)

Have your family individually search 2 Nephi 21:11–16 and report what they consider to be the most remarkable thing God will do in the gathering of His people in the last days. Discuss the following questions:

- How is the gathering a demonstration of the Lord's love for His people?
- How was your family gathered; in other words, where and when did your ancestors join the Church?
- What can your family do to serve the Lord by assisting in the gathering of Israel?

2 Nephi 22:1–6
Praise the Lord

 Have your family take turns reading verses in 2 Nephi 22:1–6. Encourage the family to mark the different ways that these verses give praise to the Lord. Ask them to put a star by all the things they already do to praise the Lord. Ask them what they think is the most important way we can give the Lord our praise and love. (See John 14:15.) Encourage them to write a goal in their journal regarding a specific thing they can do to praise the Lord.

Chapter 22 of 2 Nephi is very poetic. Let each family member pick a verse from chapter 22 and try to write it in poetic form. When all are finished, have them share what they wrote.

Choose a favorite hymn of praise out of the hymnbook and sing it together.

2 NEPHI 23–24: PROPHECIES OF THE SECOND COMING AND MILLENNIUM

2 Nephi 23:1
Why did Isaiah teach about Babylon?

Give each family member some blocks that they can stack (you may use other items such as paper cups, books, or boxes). Have a contest to see who can make the highest stack. With the highest stack left standing, read together 2 Nephi 23:1 and ask what city Isaiah saw in vision. How do you think Babylon could be compared to the highest stack of blocks?

Teach your family that Babylon was the most powerful and richest nation in Isaiah's day. Have them find Babylon in the maps in the back of their Bibles (old map set #11; new map set #9). Tell them that Babylon was the place where the Tower of Babel once stood. (For more information concerning Babylon, see Bible Dictionary, "Babylon," p. 618, and "Assyria and Babylonia," pp. 615–16.)

Ask family members to read the chapter heading for 2 Nephi 23 and look for what Babylon could be compared to and what Isaiah prophesied would eventually happen to Babylon. Read together 1 Nephi 11:36, 2 Nephi 12:12, and Proverbs 16:18 and find the common reason given there for why societies fall. (The sin of pride.)

Point out that the Nephite nation also fell because of pride (see Moroni 8:27), and the Lord proclaimed that in the last days the wicked, whom he compared to Babylon, will also fall (see D&C 1:16). Ask, "How can we avoid being part of Babylon (wickedness, worldliness, and pride) today?"

2 Nephi 23:2–21; 24:1–8
The great and dreadful day of the Lord

Tell your family that the prophet Malachi taught that the second coming of Jesus Christ would be both "great" and "dreadful." (Malachi 4:5.) Other prophets, including Isaiah, also wrote many prophecies about the Second Coming to help us understand it. To help your family understand this idea, show them an advertisement for the movies now playing at a local theater. Discuss which movie each person would most like to see and why. Ask some of the following questions:

- Would it be possible that in the same movie theater complex, two entirely different kinds of movies could be playing (such as a scary movie in one theater and a comedy in another; or a romance in one theater and a murder mystery in another)?
- Would your experience of watching one type of movie be changed, even though a different type of movie was playing at the same time in an adjoining theater? Why not?
- How much would you know about the experience others are having while watching another movie?

Explain that the experience people have as the Savior prepares the world for the second coming, and as He returns to the earth, could be compared to a movie theater. Even though the Savior will appear to the entire world, the experiences the righteous have will be very different from the experiences of the wicked. Often in scripture the wicked are compared to Babylon, while the righteous are compared to Israel. What the Lord teaches about each is completely opposite.

Make two columns on a large sheet of paper. Label one column "The Righteous" and the other "The Wicked." Read 2 Nephi 23:22 and find the phrases the Lord uses to explain what will happen to the righteous and the wicked. Write those phrases under the appropriate columns on your chart.

Divide your family into two groups. Ask half to read 2 Nephi 23:2—24:8 looking for things Isaiah prophesied would happen to the righteous. Have them add what they discover to the chart under the appropriate column.

Ask the other half of your family to read the same verses but to look for what Isaiah prophesied would happen to the wicked. Discuss your findings and share your testimony that while the wicked will be punished in the last days, the Lord will watch over and protect His people. As an additional testimony you may want to refer to D&C 1:12–16 and 109:24–26.

2 Nephi 24:12–23
How did Lucifer fall from heaven?

Ask your family to guess how many times the name *Lucifer* appears in the Bible. (Only once, in Isaiah 14:12. This is the chapter from which Nephi quotes in 2 Nephi 24.) Tell your family that Lucifer is the premortal name of Satan and that his name means "the shining one," "lightbringer," or "Son of the Morning." (Bible Dictionary, "Lucifer," p. 726.)

Read together 2 Nephi 24:12–23 and then share the following statements:

"The fall of the king of Babylon is compared to the fall of Lucifer. When the king of Babylon fell, the children of God on earth rejoiced; but when Lucifer, 'a son of the morning,' fell, the 'heavens wept over him' (D&C 76:26)." (*The Book of Mormon for Latter-day Saint Families,* p. 126.)

"Because our Heavenly Father chose Jesus Christ to be our Savior, Satan became angry and rebelled. There was war in heaven. Satan and his followers fought against Jesus and his followers. In this great rebellion, Satan and all the spirits who followed him were sent away from the presence of God and cast down from heaven. One-third of the spirits in heaven were

punished for following Satan: They were denied the right to receive mortal bodies." (*Gospel Principles,* pp. 18–19; see also Moses 3:4; Revelation 12:3–4, 7–9.)

Ask your family if Heavenly Father was powerful enough to stop Lucifer from rebelling and becoming the devil. What does it teach us about the importance of agency (our freedom to choose) that God let Lucifer and a third part of His spirit children choose to rebel? How well are we doing as a family in using our sacred agency wisely?

2 NEPHI 25: "MY SOUL DELIGHTS IN PLAINNESS"

2 Nephi 25:1–8
Why is Nephi easier to understand than Isaiah?

Read 2 Nephi 25:1–2, 5–6 with your family and have them pick out the things Nephi knew, that his children did not know, that made it easier for him to understand the words of Isaiah. (For example, he understood the way the Jews prophesied [verse 1], their culture and customs [verse 5], and their lands and people [verse 6].) Ask what your family could do to understand Isaiah better. (For example, they could learn more about Jewish religion, customs, and geography.)

Next read 2 Nephi 25:3–4, 7–8 and ask how Nephi said his writing was different from Isaiah's. What other suggestions did Nephi give in those verses for how we might understand Isaiah better? (Gain the "spirit of prophecy" and wait until you see them fulfilled.)

Ask someone to read Revelation 19:10 and tell what the "spirit of prophecy" is. Discuss how a testimony of who Jesus Christ is could help us understand Bible prophecy. Bear your testimony that the scriptures are like a gold mine: the more you dig, the more treasure you get.

2 Nephi 25:9–20
How accurate are the Lord's prophecies?

 These verses can be a quick review of Bible history for your family. Write the following events on a piece of paper large enough to be seen by everyone. This list is in the correct order; be sure to mix up the order on the paper you will show your family.

- Babylon destroys Jerusalem.
- The Jews are carried captive into Babylon.
- The Jews are freed from captivity and return to Jerusalem.
- Jesus Christ is born and teaches the Jews.
- The Jews reject and crucify Jesus.
- Jesus is resurrected.
- Jerusalem as destroyed by the Romans.
- The Jews are scattered among all nations.
- The Jews are persuaded to believe in Jesus Christ.
- The Lord will gather His people a second time.

Show your family the mixed-up list and together read 2 Nephi 25:10–20. Have them number each event on the list (1, 2, 3, and so on) as they discover them in the verses. Point out that every event up to the last two have occurred just as the Lord prophesied and that the last two are beginning to be fulfilled. Have your family look at 2 Nephi 25:9 and tell what the Lord promised to do before he sent destruction on His people. What warnings has the Lord sent us in our day about coming destructions? (See for example, D&C 29:14–21; D&C 45:65–71, or D&C 87:1–8.) Considering how accurate the Lord has been with all the other prophecies, what do you think our family should do to prepare for things that are prepared for our future?

2 Nephi 25:23–30
"The purpose of the law of Moses"

 Draw the accompanying diagram on a sheet of paper for your family to see.

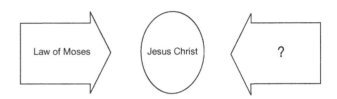

Read 2 Nephi 25:23–27 with your family and ask them how this diagram illustrates what Nephi said was the purpose of the law of Moses. If the purpose of the sacrifices of the law of Moses was to help them have faith in the future atonement of Jesus Christ, why does Nephi say that the law had become dead to them? (They understood and had faith in the coming of Christ, so, for them, it had accomplished its purpose.)

Have someone read aloud 2 Nephi 25:28–30. Ask your family what we do now, instead of the sacrifices of the law of Moses, to help us "believe in Christ and deny him not" and worship him each week? Have someone write "The sacrament" in place of the "?" on the diagram. Ask how the sacrament helps us remember the sacrifice of Jesus Christ.

2 NEPHI 26: NEPHI FORESEES THE DESTRUCTION OF HIS PEOPLE

2 Nephi 26:1–11
Would you like to know the end of the story from the beginning?

 Ask your family what they think is better: knowing the end of a book before you read it or not knowing the end before your read it. Write on a sheet of paper (or poster board) the following book names: 3 Nephi; Alma; Helaman; 4 Nephi; Mormon. Explain that Nephi saw the future of his people and wrote about it. As you read the verses from 2 Nephi 26 listed below, have your family locate the book that event is found in and let them search the chapter headings to find the right chapter.

- 2 Nephi 26:1 (3 Nephi 11).
- 2 Nephi 26:2 (Alma 48–62).
- 2 Nephi 26:3–4 (Helaman; especially chapters 13–14).
- 2 Nephi 26:5–6 (3 Nephi 8–9).
- 2 Nephi 26:9 (3 Nephi 10–11; 4 Nephi).
- 2 Nephi 26:10 (Mormon 6).

Ask your family how they think Nephi felt about seeing the destruction of his people. How would you feel if you were in Nephi's position? Read together 2 Nephi 26:7 and discuss how Nephi's words might be similar to theirs. Have different family members read 2 Nephi 26:8 and 2 Nephi 26:11 and discuss what Nephi learned from his experience that might help us as we live out our own stories on earth. Ask, "What kinds of things will cause the Spirit to stop striving with man? Now, how many of you would like to know the end of your story from the beginning?"

2 Nephi 26:12–13
How can you invite Jesus into your life?

Show the picture of Jesus standing at a door with no knob and knocking. (See *Gospel Art Picture Kit,* no. 237.) Ask, "Why is Jesus knocking? Why doesn't he just walk in?" (Make sure you note the missing doorknob.) What does this door represent? (The door to our hearts.) How is your heart like a door with no knob on the outside? What can we do to open the door and let Jesus into our lives? Read together 2 Nephi 26:12–13 and list Nephi's ideas on how we can invite Jesus into our lives and different ways he can bless us.

2 Nephi 26:14–17
Hearing voices

Have your family imagine standing in a cemetery where many of your ancestors are buried. If they could speak from their graves, what kinds of things might they say? How valuable would their messages be? Ask family members to think of this situation as you read 2 Nephi

© Intellectual Reserve, Inc.

26:14–17. Discuss the following questions as you read these verses:

- Who did Nephi say would "whisper out of the dust"?
- Why would they not be forgotten?
- Where are their voices recorded?
- What value is there in hearing their voices and listening to their messages?

2 Nephi 26:20–28
Whose invitation will you accept?

Ask family members if they have ever been invited to a party. How did they know if it was something they should attend? Explain that Nephi foresaw invitations the Gentiles would be given in the last days. Have one half of the family read 2 Nephi 26:20–22 and the other half read 2 Nephi 26:23–28. When they have finished reading, ask the following questions:

- Who "invited" the Gentiles to do the things prophesied in verses 20–22?
- Who sent the invitations in verses 23–28?
- What kinds of things did the devil invite the

Gentiles to do? (To be prideful, build false churches, get gain at all costs, not care for the poor, join secret combinations, and do other works of darkness.)

- "Flax" is a plant that yields a soft fiber used to make linen. What then does verse 22 teach us about how the devil binds us with "strong cords forever"?
- In contrast to the devil's dark works, what did Nephi teach us about the Savior? (See verse 23.)
- What kinds of things will the Savior invite the Gentiles to enjoy? (To come unto him, receive "milk and honey" or his blessings, worship in his church, and partake of his salvation freely.)
- The devil uses soft cords that combine to form strong cords to bind people to him. How does the Savior draw people to Him? (See verse 24.)

Discuss the kinds of invitations the devil sends and the kinds of invitations the Savior extends to us today. How does the Church help the Lord send invitations? Read together 2 Nephi 26:33 and discuss who the Savior sends invitations to. What can we do to make sure we accept the right invitations?

2 Nephi 26:29–31
What would you do for the love of money?

If possible, write out a check for a large amount of money (be sure to void it after the lesson). Show it to the family and ask what they would be willing to do for this check. (You might need to prompt them with ideas, such as take out the trash, do the dishes, run a marathon, exclude television watching for a year, get straight A's, go on a mission, get married in the temple, and so on.) What wouldn't you be willing to do for any amount of money?

Read together 2 Nephi 26:29–31 and look for those things Nephi saw that some people would do for money in the last days. You might ask:

- What is priestcraft? (Preaching for money or the world's praise without caring for Zion.)
- Why do you think the Lord forbids priestcraft?
- Why is it so dangerous?
- How can charity be an antidote for the sin of priestcraft?
- Why do your bishop and other ward leaders serve?
- What does this teach you about what should motivate you to serve in the Church?

2 NEPHI 27: A MARVELOUS WORK AND A WONDER

2 Nephi 27:1–5
How are the wicked like the blind and starving?

Have your family read 2 Nephi 27:1 and tell what the spiritual condition of the Gentiles and the Jews will be in the last days. Discuss how being lost in sin is like being drunk. Why don't the wicked see the results of their wrong choices?

Then read 2 Nephi 27:2–5 together and make a list of what will happen to the wicked in the last days. How are those who fight against the truth like a starving man who dreams about eating?

Ask your family if they are concerned about living in the last days when all these troubles are happening. Read together D&C 38:29–30 and have them pick out what the Lord said in our day about our fears. Why would unprepared people need to fear? What kind of preparation would help us not to be afraid?

2 Nephi 27:6–11
Why weren't all the gold plates translated?

Ask each family member to draw a picture of what they think the gold plates looked like that Joseph Smith received from Moroni. If some of them draw a seal around a portion of the plates, ask them to explain why they drew it that way. If no one does, explain that a portion of the gold plates were sealed. (See the illustration below.)

Invite your family to search Ether 4:4–7 and 2 Nephi 27:8–10 and list the contents of the sealed portion. According to those verses, why don't we have the sealed portion of the book now? Read the following statement by Elder Bruce R. McConkie: "He has withheld the sealed portion of the Book of Mormon from us because it is beyond our present ability to comprehend. We have not made that spiritual progression which qualifies us to understand its doctrines." ("Understanding the Book of Revelation," *Ensign,* September 1975, p. 87.) Read 2 Nephi 27:21–22 and ask when we will receive the sealed portion of the plates.

2 Nephi 27:12–14
How do we know Joseph Smith really had the gold plates?

 To help your family understand the Lord's promises in 2 Nephi 27:12–14, do the following demonstration. Place an egg and any two other items (for example, a key and a ball) into a box without letting your family see them. Without showing what is in the box, tell your family that you have a key, a ball, and "an item that has not been seen by human eyes or touched by human hands" (which is true if you are referring to the egg's yolk).

Ask your family if they believe your claim. Tell them that you wouldn't be surprised if they had a hard time believing it. Invite one family member to come up and look in the box. Have the person tell the rest of the family if what you said was true (but not reveal what the objects are). Ask how many now believe your claim as to what is in the box. Invite a second family member to come up and be a witness to what is in the box. Ask that person if what you told the family is true. Again ask your family if they believe your claim. Discuss why having more than one witness makes something more believable.

Read 2 Nephi 27:12–14 with your family and ask them how those verses are like your demonstration. Have them turn to the "Testimony of Three Witnesses" in the beginning of the Book of Mormon find out who these witnesses were and what they testified that they saw.

Explain that when we left our Father in Heaven's presence, we came to earth to see if we would walk by faith. This life is a test to see if we will believe in and follow God while being out of his presence. (See Abraham 3:24–25.) To help us during this test, God "ordained the law of witnesses, the law whereby he reveals himself to prophets and righteous men and sends them forth to teach his laws and bear testimony of their truth and divinity." (Bruce R. McConkie, *Promised Messiah,* p. 84.)

2 Nephi 27:9–20
The Lord's prophecies come to pass

 As your family studies 2 Nephi 27:9–18, have them mark the following six words or phrases:

1. A Man. (2 Nephi 27:9.)
2. Another. (2 Nephi 27:9, 15.)
3. Three Witnesses. (2 Nephi 27:12.)
4. A few. (2 Nephi 27:13.)
5. The learned. (2 Nephi 27:15,18.)
6. Him that is not learned. (2 Nephi 27:19–20.)

Then write the following names where your family can see them. Ask your family to match the names to the correct phrases in the scriptures. Use the references provided for help as needed.

a. Joseph Smith Jr.
b. Eight witnesses. (See "Testimony of the Eight Witnesses.")
c. Martin Harris, Oliver Cowdery, David Whitmer. (D&C 17:1; chapter heading.)
d. Charles Anthon, Samuel Mitchell. (JS—H 1:64–65.)
e. Martin Harris. (JS—H 1:63.)

(Answers: 1-a; 2-e; 3-c; 4-b; 5-d; 6-a. Note: Joseph Smith Jr. will be used twice.)

Read Isaiah 29:11–12 with your family and ask what Old Testament prophet also prophesied of the witnesses who would see the Book of Mormon. How does the matching exercise testify that Isaiah was a prophet?

2 Nephi 27:25–35
What is the "marvelous work and a wonder"?

Ask your family to describe some of the most marvelous things that they have witnessed during their lifetime. What made them stick out in their minds as marvelous or miraculous? Explain that Isaiah prophesied of a marvelous work Heavenly Father would perform in the last days. Read 2 Nephi 27:25–26 (which quotes Isaiah 29:13–14) together with your family. Ask them if they remember verse 25 from anywhere else in scripture. (See JS—H 1:19.) Ask, "Since the Lord quoted Isaiah's words in 2 Nephi 27:25 to the boy prophet Joseph Smith, what clue does that give you about what the 'marvelous work and a wonder' might be that Isaiah spoke of in 2 Nephi 27:26?"

To help answer this question, read 2 Nephi 27:27–35 with your family and have them pick out phrases that describe some of the marvelous things Heavenly Father will do in the last days.

Ask, "How could the restoration of this gospel and the translation of the Book of Mormon qualify as a marvelous work and a wonder? How does it make you feel to know you live in a day that the prophets testified of and looked forward to?"

2 NEPHI 28: THE POWER OF SATAN IN THE LATTER DAYS

2 Nephi 28
What are some of Satan's tricks?

Show a tool chest and ask why a family would have so many tools. (Different tasks require different tools.) Explain that Satan also has many different tools he uses on people. Not every tool will work on every person. Chapter 28 shows many of the tools and tricks Satan tries to use on us. President Ezra Taft Benson taught, "The Book of Mormon exposes the enemies of Christ. It confounds false doctrines and lays down contention. (See 2 Ne. 3:12.) It fortifies the humble followers of Christ against the evil designs, strategies, and doctrines of the devil in our day." ("The Book of Mormon Is the Word of God," *Ensign,* May 1975, p. 64.)

In this chapter Nephi describes ways in which Satan tries to trick us and lead us into sin. As you read 2 Nephi 28 with your family have them paraphrase the tricks or tools that they find. Below is a list of some of the tools Satan uses (an * is placed by verses that have other teaching ideas for them that you might want to use).

Verses 3–4. (Many contending churches that teach according to their own learning.)

Verses 5–6. (There is no God, or God no longer works with men on earth.)

Verse 7.* (There is no sin.)

Verses 8–10. (There may be sin, but it is no big deal. Compare D&C 1:31–32.)

Verses 11–15.* (Pride causes churches to care

more about their learning, their riches, and their buildings than their people.)

Verse 16. (Good is bad or not important.)

Verse 20. (Satan gets people angry against good.)

Verse 21–25.* (Everything is fine; we are in no danger.)

Verse 22. (There is no such thing as a devil.)

Verses 27–30. (We don't need any more scripture.)

Verse 31. (Man's advice is better then God's.)

After you have made your list ask your family to give examples of these deceptions that they have seen in the world today.

2 Nephi 28:7–8
"Eat, drink, and be merry"—right or wrong?

Have someone read 2 Nephi 28:7–8 and tell if the verses mean that we should never "eat, drink, and be merry." Ask, "If eating and drinking and being merry in itself is not bad, what do people do that would make it bad?" Give each person a sheet of paper and fold it in half. On one side, draw what the world and Satan would have us eat and drink and how Satan would have us be merry. On the other side of the paper, draw the things Heavenly Father would have us eat and drink, and the ways God has shown us to be happy. Have family members share what they drew on the papers. For a more complete discussion of what we should or shouldn't eat and drink, consider reading the Word of Wisdom in D&C 89. Discuss as a family the following questions:

- How does Satan try to make us think that the things on his side will bring us happiness?
- How does Satan tempt us with those things on his side? (Advertising, media, bad friends.)
- How does Satan want us to feel? (See 2 Nephi 2:27.)
- How does the Lord promote those things on His side? (Scriptures, prophets, Church leaders, family, good friends.)

- How does the Lord want us to feel? (See 2 Nephi 2:25.)
- What differences do you see between the "fun" that Satan offers and the joy that Heavenly Fathers has promised?

2 Nephi 28:8–9
How much punishment is "a few stripes"?

Have a family member read aloud 2 Nephi 28:8. Ask him or her what "a few stripes" means. (If no one knows, have someone find the appropriate definition for "stripe" in the dictionary.) Then read D&C 19:16–20 with your family and ask if they think "a few stripes" is an accurate description of what our punishments will be like if we do not repent. Read also D&C 76:101–6 and ask what more we can learn from these verses about those who "receive not the gospel, neither the testimony of Jesus"?

Next, have them read D&C 76:109–12 and tell what kingdom those people will go to even after they have paid for their own sins. Ask someone to read aloud 2 Nephi 28:9 again and explain why they think Nephi said that the idea of paying for your own sins was a "false, vain, and foolish" doctrine.

2 Nephi 28:15
The dreaded triple "wo"

Read 2 Nephi 28:15 and ask your family what they think "wo, wo, wo" means. ("Wo" means sorrow or grief.) Explain that the dreaded triple wo that is found in this verse only appears three other places in scripture: once in the Bible (Revelation 8:13), one other time in the Book of Mormon (3 Nephi 9:2), and once in the Doctrine and Covenants (D&C 38:6). Ask what behaviors Nephi lists in 2 Nephi 28:15 that would cause God to pronounce this triple wo.

Have your family find the eight other times the word *wo* is used 2 Nephi 28 and mark the kind of behavior the Lord is saying wo to. As a family, think of modern examples of each of those behaviors and discuss what you can do to avoid them.

2 Nephi 28:18
What is the "great and abominable church"?

See the teaching idea for 1 Nephi 13:4–9 on p. 32.

2 Nephi 28:20–25
Do you let Satan treat you like a baby?

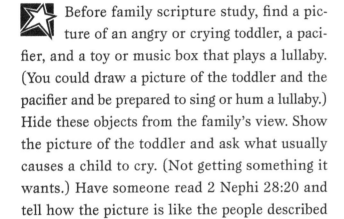 Before family scripture study, find a picture of an angry or crying toddler, a pacifier, and a toy or music box that plays a lullaby. (You could draw a picture of the toddler and the pacifier and be prepared to sing or hum a lullaby.) Hide these objects from the family's view. Show the picture of the toddler and ask what usually causes a child to cry. (Not getting something it wants.) Have someone read 2 Nephi 28:20 and tell how the picture is like the people described there. Why do the wicked get angry at the Lord, his servants, and his commandments?

Next read 2 Nephi 28:21–23 together and ask your family to think of nouns that come from "pacify" and "lull." Use the pacifier and the song for hints as needed. With those ideas in mind, discuss the following questions:

- What is a pacifier used for?
- How much nourishment does a baby get from a pacifier?
- How is that like people who think they are as good as they need to be and "all is well" in their life?
- What is a lullaby used for?
- How is that like the person who thinks there is no devil, no hell, and no consequences for sin?

Read 2 Nephi 28:24–25 and discuss why wo or sorrow will come to those who are at ease in Zion.

2 NEPHI 29: WE REALLY DO NEED MORE THAN THE BIBLE

2 Nephi 29:1–2
What is the "marvelous work"?

Read 2 Nephi 29:1 and ask your family if they remember what that "marvelous work" is that the Lord promised to do in the last days. (See also 2 Nephi 27:25–26.) Have a family member read the following: "This marvelous work is the restoration of the church and the gospel with all its power and authority, keys and blessings which pertain to this great work of salvation of the children of men." (Joseph Fielding Smith, *Church History and Modern Revelation*, 1:35.)

Read 2 Nephi 29:1–2 with your family and have them look for six blessings the Lord would extend through this marvelous work. If they need help, you can use the list below:

1. "That I may remember my covenants."
2. "That I may set my hand again the second time to recover my people."
3. "That I may remember the promises which I have made unto thee, Nephi."
4. "That I would remember your [Nephi's] seed."
5. "That the words of your [Nephi's] seed should proceed forth out of my mouth unto your seed."
6. "My words shall hiss forth unto the ends of the earth, for a standard unto my people, which are of the house of Israel."

Ask your family if any of those promises apply to them (specifically 1, 2, and 6). Share with them the following statement that helps explain our responsibility because of the covenants we have made with the Lord:

"The Book of Mormon is to be used 'for a standard unto my people, which are of the house of Israel,' the Lord says, and its words 'shall hiss forth unto the ends of the earth.' (2 Nephi. 29:2.)

We, the members of the Church, and particularly the missionaries, have to be the 'hissers,' or the tellers and testifiers, of the Book of Mormon unto the ends of the earth." (Ezra Taft Benson, "The Book of Mormon Is the Word of God," *Ensign,* May 1975, p. 65.)

2 Nephi 29:3–6
What can the Bible do for me?

Tell your family that the prime minster of Israel, David Ben Gurion, spoke of the Old Testament, saying, "We have preserved the book, and the book has preserved us." Discuss with your family what they think he meant. How might we say something similar about the Book of Mormon? The Doctrine and Covenants? The Pearl of Great Price?

Read together 2 Nephi 29:3–6 and discuss the following questions:

- What will people say when the Book of Mormon "hisses forth"?
- What group of people wrote the Bible?
- What thanks have the Jews been given for preserving this important book?
- How can we show our gratitude for all those who have helped preserve scripture?

2 Nephi 29:6–14
A Bible! A Bible! We have got a Bible

Assign a family member to stand and represent the Bible, another to represent the Book of Mormon, and another to represent God's children. Have the "Bible" and "Book of Mormon" lock their hands tightly and pick up "God's children" between them. What blessings come to God's children when they have both the Bible and the Book of Mormon? What would happen if we took one away? Read 2 Nephi 29:6–14 with your family and discuss the following questions:

- When the Book of Mormon comes forth, what will many people say? (Verse 6.)
- How do you suppose it makes the Lord feel

when people reject a sacred book he has sent to them?
- How is having the testimony of both the Bible and the Book of Mormon (and other scripture) a blessing in these last days? (You'll be judged by what it written there; see verse 11.)
- What is going to happen to all these records in the last days? (Verses 13–14.)

Bear your testimony of what a blessing it is to have all the scriptures to teach us what Heavenly Father would have us do to be happy. What advantage will we have if we study from the scriptures daily?

2 NEPHI 30: BECOMING COVENANT PEOPLE

2 Nephi 30:1–2
Who are God's covenant people?

Have your family review 2 Nephi 29:5 and tell who the Lord's covenant people were anciently. Ask if that means you have to have a certain family line or be born in a certain country to be part of the covenant people. Then read together 2 Nephi 30:1–2. Ask, "According to these verses, who are the Lord's covenant people? Can a Gentile be covenant? How? Can a Jew be not of the covenant? How? Who are the Lord's covenant people today?" President Gordon B. Hinckley observed, "We are a covenant people. . . . We make that covenant when we are baptized. . . . and great are the obligations that go with that covenant." (*Friend,* January 2000, inside front cover.) Ask family members what they think some of those obligations are. Have them look again at 2 Nephi 30:1–2 and the phrases that describe what the Lord expects of his covenant people

2 Nephi 30:3–8
The power of the Book of Mormon

Write the following question where all your family can see it: "Besides the Spirit, what is the greatest single tool available to every missionary?" After several responses, share this statement: "Combined with the Spirit of the Lord, the Book of Mormon is the greatest single tool which God has given us to convert the world. If we are to have the harvest of souls that President Kimball envisions, then we must use the instrument which God has designed for that task—the Book of Mormon." (Ezra Taft Benson, "A New Witness for Christ," *Ensign,* November 1984, p. 7.)

Read 2 Nephi 30:3–8 with your family and have them look for three groups of people that will be touched by the Book of Mormon. (The Gentiles, the remnant of Lehi's seed, and the Jews.) Discuss the following questions:

- Which group will get the Book of Mormon first?
- How will Lehi's descendants (the Lamanites) get the book?
- How will the Lamanites change because of that book?
- How will the Jews begin to change because of the Book of Mormon?
- Which group do we belong to?
- Why, then, is it important that we share our testimony of the Book of Mormon with others?
- Where will the testimony of the Book of Mormon need to go before the Lord will be finished gathering his people?
- What can we do as a family to make sure we fulfill our responsibility in this great effort?

2 Nephi 30:9–18
Millennial prophecies

In 2 Nephi 30:9–18 Nephi describes conditions that will exist at the Second Coming and during the Millennium. On a sheet of paper, make two columns and write references in one column. Then scramble the order of the prophecies and write them in the second column. Have family members search the references and match them with the correct prophecy by drawing lines from one to the other.

2 Nephi 30:9–10: Destruction of the wicked.
2 Nephi 30:12–14: Animals changed.
2 Nephi 30:16–17: All things revealed.
2 Nephi 30:18: Satan bound.

After they have matched the prophecies, discuss the meaning of each one as a family. You may want to use some of these additional references to help in your discussion: Destruction of the wicked: D&C 101:24–25. Animals changed: D&C 101:26; Isaiah 65:25. All things revealed: D&C 101:32–34. Satan bound: Revelation 20:1–3; 1 Nephi 22:26; D&C 101:28.

Ask your family how a knowledge of the Millennium can be a blessing to them today. Share the following insight: "Each day the forces of evil and the forces of good enlist new recruits. Each day we personally make many decisions showing the cause we support. The final outcome is certain—the forces of righteousness will win. But what remains to be seen is *where* each of us personally, now and in the future, will stand in this battle—and *how tall* we will stand. Will we be true to our last days and fulfill our foreordained missions?" (Ezra Taft Benson, "In His Steps," *Ensign,* September 1988, p. 2.) What can we do to limit the power of Satan in our lives right now?

2 NEPHI 31: THE DOCTRINE OF CHRIST

2 Nephi 31:1–2, 21
What is the doctrine of Christ?

Have a family member read aloud 2 Nephi 31:1–2 and tell what Nephi says he is going to speak about. Then have someone else read 2 Nephi 31:21 and find what Nephi said he just told us about. Explain to your family that this chapter is all about the "Doctrine of Christ." In a conference in 1889, Elder George Q. Cannon read 2 Nephi 31 to the Saints and declared, "I have read to you this afternoon the words of an inspired Prophet of God, telling us what the Gospel of the Lord Jesus Christ is. I do not recall for the moment any chapter that has been written either in the Old or New Testament, in the Book of Mormon or in the Book of Doctrine and Covenants, which more plainly and pointedly describes the Gospel of Jesus Christ and the first principles thereof than this chapter." (*Collected Discourses,* Vol. 1, May 26, 1889.)

2 Nephi 31:5–12
Since Jesus Christ is perfect, why was he baptized?

Ask your family what the purpose is for the ordinance of baptism. (See Articles of Faith 1:4 if needed.) Show a picture of Jesus being baptized by John, if one is available, and ask, "Since Jesus had no sins, why did he need to be baptized?" Have your family read 2 Nephi 31:5 and find the reason Nephi gives. ("To fulfil all righteousness.") Next have them mark the question Nephi asks in verse 6 and explain that Nephi answers that question in the next several verses. Have them scan 2 Nephi 31:7–12 and list all the ways they can find in which Jesus "did fulfil all righteousness in being baptized by water." (For example, he showed humility, was obedient, received the Holy Ghost, and gave us an example to follow.) Ask, "What does this teach us about our need to be baptized? Why would it be important to teach these things to our friends and neighbors who have not heard the truth?"

2 Nephi 31:8
What is the "form of a dove"?

Have a family member read 2 Nephi 31:8 aloud and tell what the phrase "the form of a dove" means. What characteristics does a dove have that are like the Holy Ghost? Share the following statement by the Prophet Joseph Smith: "The sign of the dove was instituted before the creation of the world, a witness for the Holy Ghost, and the devil cannot come in the sign of a dove. The Holy Ghost is a personage, and is in the form of a personage. It does not confine itself to the *form* of the dove, but in *sign* of the dove. The

Holy Ghost cannot be transformed into a dove; but the sign of a dove was given to John to signify the truth of the deed, as the dove is an emblem or token of truth and innocence." (*Teachings of the Prophet Joseph Smith,* p. 275.)

2 Nephi 31:12–13
The incomparable gift of the Holy Ghost

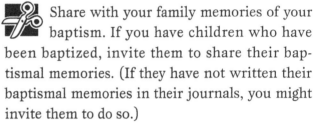 Share with your family memories of your baptism. If you have children who have been baptized, invite them to share their baptismal memories. (If they have not written their baptismal memories in their journals, you might invite them to do so.)

Read together 2 Nephi 31:12 and find the blessing the Lord promises to those who repent and are baptized. Draw or collect the following things and ask family members how these objects are like the Holy Ghost:

- Mouth. (The Holy Ghost speaks with a still, small voice.)
- Ear. (If we listen, we can hear his promptings.)
- Comforter, blanket, or quilt. (The Holy Ghost will comfort us.)
- Graduation cap, scroll, or school backpack. (The Holy Ghost teaches us the truth.)
- Flashlight or candle. (The Holy Ghost helps us see in dark world.)

Draw a line down the middle of a piece of paper and write "If" on one side and "Then" on the other. Have your family read 2 Nephi 31:13 and find the "If-Then" formula Nephi gives there. Write the phrases that describe what we must do in the "If" column on your paper. Then write what the Lord will do for us in the "Then" column. Ask if they know what it means to "speak with the tongue of angels"? (See 2 Nephi 32:3 for help if needed.) Tell your family how the gift of the Holy Ghost has helped direct your life. Encourage them to do the "Ifs" so that they also might receive the "Thens."

2 Nephi 31:17–21
The gate and the straight and narrow path

 Ask a child to use blocks to make a gate and a path. Read together 2 Nephi 31:17–21 and discuss the following questions:

- What is the gate?
- What is the path?
- Where does this path lead?
- How do we get on the path? (See verse 19.)
- What must we do to continue on the path?
- How is feasting upon the word different from just reading it?
- How can feasting upon the word help us love God and our fellowman more?
- Why is it so critical that we walk this path? (See verse 21.)

2 Nephi 31:20
Memorize the scripture

Take time as a family to memorize the beautiful passage found in verse 20. It might be helpful to write the verse on a chalkboard and then gradually erase the easiest words until all words have been erased. Another helpful way to memorize is to list the first letter of each word. Read the scripture together out loud from the scriptures two or three times, close the book, and then read it using just the letters. When all family members have successfully memorized this verse, ask them what steps they have discovered in this verse that will help them on their path to eternal life. Review this verse often; for example, during family scripture study or prayer time.

2 NEPHI 32: KNOW FOR YOURSELF THROUGH STUDY AND PRAYER

2 Nephi 32:1–9
A family feast

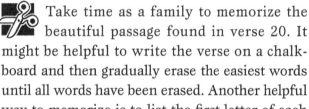 Consider reserving the study of this chapter for a time when your entire family can be together and you can prepare for and serve them a special dinner or feast.

Prepare a feast for your family. Make some of their favorite foods, and make special efforts to have a fancy table setting. As part of the preparation, make a copy of 2 Nephi 32:1–9 for each of them that could be read later at the dinner table.

Tell your family that this is a special occasion and that during the course of dinner you would like to have an important discussion. As you eat, discuss some of the following questions:

- What are some of the most important spiritual experiences you have had?
- How have you come to know the Church is true?
- What are you doing to stay on the right course?
- How can you know what path in life God would have you follow?
- If an angel were to come to you, what message do you think he would bring you from God?

When the meal is completed, give everyone a copy of 2 Nephi 32:1–9. Take turns reading until you have finished all nine verses. Ask:

- What did Nephi teach to those with questions concerning "what ye should do"?
- How would the words of angels help people know what direction to follow in life?
- How can we find the words of angels? (Be worthy of the Holy Ghost and feast upon the scriptures.)

Have family members describe how this dinner was a "feast" and how "feasting" is different from just eating. How would feasting on our scriptures be different from just reading them? Ask each member of your family to make a commitment that he or she will make a special effort to feast upon their scriptures each day of the coming week. Explain that you would like them each to give a report of their experience in an upcoming family home evening.

To end the meal, invite your family to join with you in a family prayer. Before you begin, ask these questions:

- What did Nephi teach us about prayer in 2 Nephi 32:8–9?
- Why do you think it is important to pray always?

At the conclusion of your prayer, share your love for your family and your testimony of scripture study and prayer. Invite each family member to discover the Lord's will for them through personal prayer. Invite them all to make prayer a part of their daily lives.

Share the following statements about the power of daily prayer and scripture study:

"The acquisition of understanding and enthusiasm for the Lord comes from following simple rules.

"One of those rules is to read the word of the Lord. I know that with the demands of your studies there is little time to read anything else. But I promise you that if you will read the words of that writing which we call scripture, there will come into your heart an understanding and a warmth that will be pleasing to experience. Let the Lord speak for Himself to you, and His words will come with a quiet conviction that will make the words of His critics meaningless." (Gordon B. Hinckley, "The Miracle That Is Jesus," *Improvement Era,* June 1966, p. 531.)

"Let us not treat lightly [His word]. . . . [It is] one of the most valuable gifts He has given us. . . . Recommit . . . immerse yourselves in them daily. . . . Read them in your families and teach your children to love and treasure them. Then prayerfully and in counsel with others, seek every way possible to encourage the members of the Church to follow your example." (Ezra Taft Benson, "The Power of the Word," *Ensign,* May 1986, p. 82.)

"I promise you that daily family prayer and scripture study will build within the walls of your home a security and bonding that will enrich your lives and prepare your families to meet the challenges of today and the eternities to come.

"God grant unto us the desire to seek Him reverently and humbly in prayer and the sincere desire to study His word, as contained in His holy scriptures." (L. Tom Perry, "Back to Gospel Basics," *Ensign,* May 1993, p. 90.)

2 Nephi 32:1, 8
Should we ponder the scriptures?

Have your family read 2 Nephi 32:1, 8, looking for the word Nephi uses to describe how Laman and Lemuel are dealing with the message they have received. Ask if it is wrong to "ponder" over the scriptures? What does it mean to ponder? To help your family understand the necessity of pondering, share the following statement:

"Surely the best of the 'best books' are the scriptures, and it is not simply linguistic chance that the divine injunction is to 'ponder' them. That word, in its English form, comes from a Latin root meaning weight—and the scriptures are the weightiest books we have. To ponder them suggests a slow and deliberate examination; indeed, there is no way to read the scriptures whimsically or superficially or quickly. They demand time, prayer, and honest meditation." (Jeffrey R. Holland, "Daddy, Donna, and Nephi," *Ensign,* September 1976, pp. 7–8.)

2 NEPHI 33: NEPHI'S FAREWELL

2 Nephi 33:1–6
The power of Nephi's words

Ask your family if they would rather speak in Church or just write a letter that could be sent to all the ward members. According to 2 Nephi 33:1–2, which would Nephi prefer to do? Why did Nephi prefer speaking to writing? What do many people do with the scriptures that is more difficult to do if the prophet were speaking to them in person? (See verse 2.)

Have family members take turns reading 2 Nephi 33:3–6. Ask them how Nephi felt about what he had written. Have them make a list of phrases that tell what he prayed his words would do for his people. Have your family think of one or two of their favorite passages from 1 and 2 Nephi and compare them to the list they just made. Which of Nephi's purposes do those passages fulfill for you? Invite family members to tell how they feel about the worth of Nephi's writings.

2 Nephi 33:11–15
Nephi's last farewell

Ask your family if they have ever seen a show or read a book where one of the characters gives a dying farewell speech. What is it about a persons last words that make them so important or meaningful? Tell your family that Nephi is about to give us his last words. Have your family take turns reading 2 Nephi 33:10–15. As you read, discuss some of following questions:

- If people really believe in Jesus Christ, how will they feel about the Book of Mormon?
- Why do some people who seem to believe in Jesus Christ reject the Book of Mormon?
- How can a person find out if the Book of Mormon is true?
- How will the unbelievers feel when they meet Nephi face to face at the judgment?
- What would you say to Nephi when you get the chance to meet him in the next life?

Conclude by bearing testimony of the power of Nephi's words and the influence of Nephi in your life.

2 Nephi 33
A final thought

Ask your family to suppose that there was a fire in your home. Would their first concern be to rescue their possessions or other family members? Once the family was safe, what would be some of the most important things they would grab on their way out the door? Have someone read 2 Nephi 33:3 and tell what seems to be Nephi's greatest concern. Because he was worried about his people, what did he want them to have that would be of great worth to them?

Ask your family why the scriptures might be of greater worth to the eternal welfare of the family

than some of the other things we are sometimes so concerned about. How much do we as a family appreciate our scriptures? Do we read them as often as we should?

Have a family member read the following poem:

The Family Bible
Old Brother Higgins built a shelf
   for the family Bible to rest itself
lest a sticky finger or grimy thumb
   might injure the delicate pages some.
He cautioned his children to touch it not
   and it rested there with never a blot
though the Higgins tribe were a troublesome lot.

His neighbor, Miggins, built a shelf
   "Come children," he said, "and help yourself."
His book is old and ragged and worn,
   with some of the choicest pages torn,
where children have fingered and thumbed and read.

But of the Miggins tribe I've heard it said,
each carries a Bible in his head.

Ask a family member what the difference was between the Higgins and the Miggins families? What does the poem teach about the effect of the word of God?

Share the following statement from President Marion G. Romney:

"I feel certain that if, in our homes, parents will read from the Book of Mormon prayerfully and regularly, both by themselves and with their children, the spirit of that great book will come to permeate our homes and all who dwell therein. The spirit of reverence will increase, mutual respect and consideration for each other will grow, the spirit of contention will depart, parents will counsel their children in greater love and wisdom, children will be more responsive and submissive to that counsel, righteousness will increase, faith, hope, and charity, the pure love of Christ will abound in our homes and lives bringing in their wake peace, joy, and happiness." (Conference Report, April 1960, pp. 112–13.)

JACOB

Jacob was the oldest of two sons born to Lehi in the wilderness. (See 1 Nephi 18:7.) Sometime before his death, Nephi gave Jacob the sacred responsibility to keep the small plates of Nephi. (See Jacob 1:1.) Jacob was an excellent choice to care for these sacred records because he took seriously his responsibility as a spiritual leader among the Nephites (see Jacob 1:18–19), and, most important to Nephi, he had also seen the Savior (see 2 Nephi 11:3). Jacob's record includes several sermons and warnings he gave to his people. You feel his anxious concern over the sins growing among the Nephites (see Jacob 2:4–6) but also his tender love for the innocent hurt by the insensitivity of the wicked (see Jacob 2:34–35). One critical event in his life was his encounter with Sherem, the first antichrist mentioned among the Nephites. (See Jacob 7.)

JACOB 1: "THAT WE MIGHT PERSUADE THEM TO COME UNTO CHRIST"

Jacob 1:1–4
Can you write a scripture?

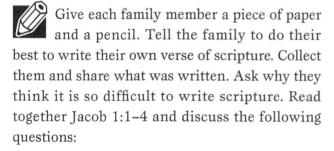 Give each family member a piece of paper and a pencil. Tell the family to do their best to write their own verse of scripture. Collect them and share what was written. Ask why they think it is so difficult to write scripture. Read together Jacob 1:1–4 and discuss the following questions:

- What did Nephi want Jacob to do?
- If you had been Jacob, how would you have responded to the assignment?
- What was to be written on the small plates?
- What does "engraven the heads of them" mean? (See Jacob 1:4 footnote b.)
- For whose sake was this record to be kept?

Have your family members share why they are grateful that Jacob and others felt impressed to write sacred things.

Jacob 1:5–16
What did the Nephites know about Jesus Christ?

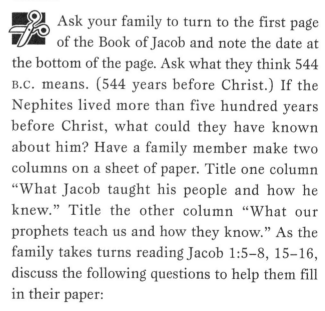 Ask your family to turn to the first page of the Book of Jacob and note the date at the bottom of the page. Ask what they think 544 B.C. means. (544 years before Christ.) If the Nephites lived more than five hundred years before Christ, what could they have known about him? Have a family member make two columns on a sheet of paper. Title one column "What Jacob taught his people and how he knew." Title the other column "What our prophets teach us and how they know." As the family takes turns reading Jacob 1:5–8, 15–16, discuss the following questions to help them fill in their paper:

- How did Jacob say the Nephites received information about the future? (See verse 6.)
- What two reasons did Jacob give for the revelations they received? (See verse 5.)
- What did Jacob want his people to do? (See verses 7–8.)

- What did he want them not to do? (See verses 15–16.)

Show your family the most recent conference edition of the *Ensign*. As you look together at the titles of the conference addresses, discuss the following questions:

- What do the prophets today seem to be anxious about?
- How do they know what they should talk about in conference?
- What do they want us to do?
- What do they want us not to do?
- In what ways is their message about the Savior similar to Jacob's?

Jacob 1:9–12
How many Nephis were there?

Ask your family how many Nephis they can think of in the Book of Mormon and then name them. (Nephi, Lehi's son; Nephi who welcomed the Savior in the Land Bountiful; Nephi who served a mission among the Lamanites in the book of Helaman). Why were so many individuals named Nephi? Read together Jacob 1:11 and look for another possible answer. (Many of the first kings of the Nephites were called by that name.) Read Jacob 1:9–12 and discuss the following questions:

- How did the Nephites feel about Nephi?
- What had he done for them that won their love?
- Why would it be difficult to be the leader succeeding Nephi?
- Who are the "Nephis" we can follow today?

Jacob 1:13–14
Who's the Nephite; who's the Lamanite?

Collect several pictures of Americans who come from different cultures or nations (China, Japan, Africa, South America, Europe, India, and so on). It would be important for the picture to give hints that they are Americans. Show the pictures to your family and ask what they all have in common. (They are all Americans.) Have family members read Jacob 1:13–14 and look for similarities to this object lesson. What did Jacob say the difference was between the Lamanites and the Nephites?

Jacob 1:15–19
"I . . . obtained my errand from the Lord"

Ask your family what an "errand" is. Who usually gives us errands to do? Why shouldn't a brother or sister ask you to do something pretending that the request came from your parents? Ask someone to read Jacob 1:17–18 and then ask your family who gave Jacob and Joseph their errand.

Read Jacob 1:15–16 together and look for and circle the word "began." What were the Nephites beginning to do? How does this explain why Jacob and Joseph received their errand from the Lord? Then read Jacob 1:19 and list what Jacob did to "magnify" his office as he fulfilled his errand from the Lord. Share the following quotation from President Gordon B. Hinckley:

"I am convinced that there are many, many thousands . . . who, with warmth and welcome, can be led to the eternal truths of the restored gospel of Jesus Christ. They are looking for something better than they have. They must be friendshipped. They must be fellowshipped. They must be made to feel comfortable and at home, so they can observe in the lives of the members of the Church those virtues they wish for themselves. . . .

"The world is our responsibility. We cannot evade it. I think of the words of Jacob in the Book of Mormon, who with his brother Joseph had been consecrated a priest and teacher unto the people: [he then read Jacob 1:19.]" (*Teachings of Gordon B. Hinckley,* p. 369.)

Ask what errands and responsibilities we have been given that make us similar to Jacob.

JACOB 2: JACOB WARNS OF TWO SERIOUS SINS

Jacob 2:1–11

Why must prophets always declare the truth, even when it is difficult?

Ask your family why it is difficult to tell people what they need to hear. Invite a family member to share a time when he or she asked someone to stop doing something wrong or to change a bad habit. Ask:

- How did the person respond?
- Was it difficult? Why or why not?
- What other circumstances could make it hard to call people to repentance? (During a bad movie, in front of a large crowd, and so on.)

Read Jacob 2:2–5 together and identify the reasons why Jacob felt the Nephites needed to change. According to Jacob 2:6–7, why was this difficult for Jacob? Read Jacob 2:10–11 and mark the reasons why Jacob had to tell the people to repent even though it was difficult. Have your family review Jacob 1:19 and tell what other reason Jacob had for calling his people to repentance. What implications do these verses have for us in our Church callings?

Jacob 2:12–19

Is being wealthy bad?

Place a large amount of money in front of your family, or ask them to imagine receiving a large sum of money (you could use play money). Make a list of some good things and bad things that could be done with it. Then study Jacob 2:12–19 to find answers to the following questions:

- Who blesses us with the wealth of this world? (See verse 13.)
- What are we counseled to seek before we seek for riches? (See verse 18.)
- What are we asked to do when the Lord blesses us with wealth? (See verse 19.)
- According to Jacob 2:13, what serious prob-

lem can come to those who misunderstand the purposes of wealth?

- What happens to those who refuse to share their wealth? (See D&C 56:16.)
- Why do you think Jacob put the word "if" in verse 19? Why might a person who has found the gospel *not* seek for riches?

Share the following statement from President David O. McKay: "If you work for wealth, you can get it; but before you make it an end in itself, take a look at those men who have sacrificed all to the accomplishment of this purpose, at those who have desired wealth for the sake of wealth itself. Gold does not corrupt man; it is in the motive of acquiring that gold that corruption occurs." (*Home Memories of President David O. McKay,* p. 242.)

Have family members imagine giving a talk about riches in church. Invite them to explain an important lesson about wealth based on what they learned from Jacob 2.

Jacob 2:20–22

What is so wrong with being proud?

Read together D&C 38:39 and look for the Lord's warning against becoming "like the Nephites of old." Ask your family if we need to "beware of pride," how they would define what it is. Allow them to make several suggestions and then read the following statement to your family:

"Most of us think of pride as self-centeredness, conceit, boastfulness, arrogance, or haughtiness. All of these are elements of the sin, but the heart, or core, is still missing.

"The central feature of pride is enmity—enmity toward God and enmity toward our fellowmen. Enmity means 'hatred toward, hostility to, or a state of opposition.' It is the power by which Satan wishes to reign over us.

"Pride is essentially competitive in nature. We pit our will against God's. When we direct our pride toward God, it is in the spirit of 'my will and not thine be done.' As Paul said, they 'seek their own, not the things which are Jesus Christ's.'

(Philip. 2:21.)." (Ezra Taft Benson, "Beware of Pride," *Ensign,* May 1989, p. 4.)

Remind your family that Jacob had just finished teaching the people to take care of the poor. Read together Jacob 2:20–21 to find out one reason they didn't give to the poor. What word does the Lord use to describe this sin? (See Jacob 2:21.) Tell your family that the word "abominable" means terrible or evil. How does this word help us understand how the Lord feels about pride?

Ask your family what can be done to overcome pride. Read together Alma 7:23 and ask:

- What is the cure for pride?
- How can our family become more humble?

Jacob 2:23–33
Why stay morally clean?

 With your family, take turns reading Jacob 2:23–27 and identify the "grosser crime" Jacob was concerned about. Continue reading Jacob 2:28–33 and list all the negative consequences of the Nephites' immorality. To help you with your list, discuss the following questions:

- How is what the Lord delights in different from what the world seems to delight in?
- What curse will the Nephites bring upon themselves by their disobedience?
- What suffering had the Nephites' sins caused already?

Read the following statement to your family: "The plaguing sin of this generation is sexual immorality. This, the Prophet Joseph said, would be the source of more temptations, more buffetings, and more difficulties for the elders of Israel than any other. (See *Journal of Discourses,* 8:55.)" (*The Teachings of Ezra Taft Benson,* p. 277.)

Show your family a picture of a temple. Ask them how they would feel if someone painted graffiti on it. Have a family member read 1 Corinthians 6:19 and tell what Paul said our bodies were like. Read the following statement by President Gordon B. Hinckley to your family:

"The Lord has made us attractive one to each

other for a great purpose. But this very attraction becomes a powder keg unless it is kept under control. It is beautiful when handled in the right way. It is deadly if it gets out of hand.

"Those who indulge in sexual activity outside the bonds of marriage do irreparable damage to themselves and rob the one with whom they are involved of that which can never by restored. . . .

"I plead with you to be careful, to stand safely back from the cliff of sin over which it is so easy to fall. Keep yourselves clean from the dark and disappointing evil of sexual transgression. Walk in the sunlight of that peace which comes from virtue." (*Way to Be,* pp. 58–60.)

Ask your family what they have learned from the scriptures and the statements from the prophets about the importance of being morally clean. Tell your family about the joy that comes from being obedient to the Lord's commandments.

JACOB 3: OBEDIENCE IS THE MEASURE OF RIGHTEOUSNESS

Jacob 3:1–2
The blessings of being "pure in heart"?

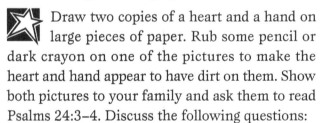 Draw two copies of a heart and a hand on large pieces of paper. Rub some pencil or dark crayon on one of the pictures to make the heart and hand appear to have dirt on them. Show both pictures to your family and ask them to read Psalms 24:3–4. Discuss the following questions:

- How do the pictures illustrate those verses?
- What would cause our hands to be unclean to the Lord? (Our actions.)
- What would cause our hearts to be impure to the Lord? (Our thoughts and feelings.)
- Which comes first, bad thoughts or bad actions?
- What blessing does the Lord promise to those with clean hands and pure hearts?

Have someone read Jacob 3:1–2 and tell what

additional blessings Jacob promised the pure in heart. Have them suggest some specific thing your family can do together to help them have clean hands and pure hearts. Read the following to your family:

"To become pure in heart—to achieve exaltation—we must alter our attitudes and priorities to a condition of spirituality, we must control our thoughts, we must reform our motives, and we must perfect our desires (Dallin H. Oaks, *Pure in Heart*, p. 140).

Jacob 3:2
The greatest feast ever

 Ask your family to describe the difference between a feast and a meal. Have each person tell what his or her favorite food is at a feast. Have someone read aloud Jacob 3:2. Ask your family what Jacob is inviting us to feast upon. Show your family a picture of Jesus (such as *Gospel Art Picture Kit,* no. 216, Jesus with little children) and ask them to imagine how it would feel to have the Savior put his loving arms around them. Ask, "What would you be willing to do to have that experience? What must we do before we can feast upon Christ's love?" (See the teaching idea for Jacob 3:1–2 above.)

Jacob 3:5–10
The importance of families

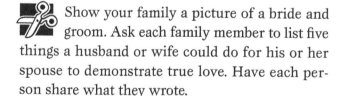 Show your family a picture of a bride and groom. Ask each family member to list five things a husband or wife could do for his or her spouse to demonstrate true love. Have each person share what they wrote.

As a family study Jacob 3:5–10 and look for answers to the following questions:

- Who did the Nephites think the "filthy" people were?
- Who did Jacob say was the most filthy?
- What commandment did the Lamanites keep better than the Nephites?
- What did Jacob say would happen to parents who set a bad example for their children?

Share the following statement from President David O. McKay: "The best thing a father can do for his children is to love their mother." (William G. Dyer and Phillip R. Kunz, *Effective Mormon Families,* p. 104.)

Share your love for your family and spouse and your gratitude for the blessings that come with having a loving family.

Jacob 3:9–12
How does the prophet help us repent?

Have your family take turns reading Jacob 3:9–12 and have them mark the sins Jacob said the Nephites were guilty of. Ask them why a prophet would clearly identify the sins of the people. How can pointing out a person's sins help him or her to change?

Read the following statements from President Harold B. Lee: "The more I see of life, the more I am convinced that we must impress you young people with the awfulness of sin rather than to content ourselves with merely teaching the way of repentance." (*Youth and the Church,* pp. 87–88.) "The heaviest burden that one has to bear in this life is the burden of sin." ("'Stand Ye in Holy Places,'" *Ensign,* July 1973, p. 123.)

Ask your family what counsel the prophet has given us about changes we need to make in our lives. Invite your family members to write in their personal journals the kind of changes they want to make. Encourage them to pray for the strength to do so.

JACOB 4: WE MUST FOCUS ON CHRIST

Jacob 4:1–3
Why should you keep a journal?

 Have a family member display a personal journal and ask why he or she keeps the journal. Ask your family, "What should we write about? What has the prophet asked us to do regarding journals?" Read the following thought by President Spencer W. Kimball:

"We hope you will begin [keeping a journal] as of this date. If you have not already commenced this important duty in your lives, get a good notebook, a good book that will last through time and into eternity for the angels to look upon. Begin today and write in it your goings and your comings, your deeper thoughts, your achievements, and your failures, your associations and your triumphs, your impressions and your testimonies. We hope you will do this, our brothers and sisters, for this is what the Lord has commanded, and those who keep a personal journal are more likely to keep the Lord in remembrance in their daily lives." ("President Kimball Speaks Out on Personal Journals," *Ensign,* December 1980, p. 61.)

Have someone read Jacob 4:1–3 and tell why it was so difficult for the Nephites to keep a journal. Ask, "Why did Jacob feel the need to keep a journal? How important has Nephi and Jacob's journal become to us?" Take turns reading the following ideas for keeping a journal and commit your family to choose one or two they think will help them keep better journals:

1. Get up half an hour earlier than you have been waking up. Spend fifteen minutes studying the scriptures and fifteen minutes writing in your journal.

2. Write while you are waiting in different places, like dentist's office, the car, or soccer practice.

3. Write while you commute on the bus or train to work.

4. Pack your journal in your lunchbox. Write while you eat.

5. Write while the baby takes a nap or your children are doing their homework.

6. Set aside half an hour each Sunday for "family journal time." Small children can draw pictures to illustrate the things they have done that week; school-age children and adults can write in their journals.

7. Make "family journal time" a regular part of family home evening. Have a special lesson on keeping journals to inaugurate the practice. Have a designated journal keeper each week in family home evening. (See Family Home Evening Resource Book, pp. 199–200, for lesson ideas.)

8. Jot a few ideas or key phrases on the calendar each day. At least once a week, use the calendar to bring your journal up to date.

9. Use a cassette tape recorder to keep an oral journal. Be sure to have your tapes transcribed, since audiotape will deteriorate with time.

10. Use a word processor or home computer to keep your journal on disk or tape. Be sure to keep a backup file or print a paper copy occasionally; when magnetic tapes and disks deteriorate, important files can be lost.

11. Keep copies of the letters you write to family and friends in a loose-leaf binder. Add an occasional page to tell about things you don't include in the letters. (Adapted from, Mary Lynn Hutchison, "24 Ways to Find Time for a Journal," *Ensign,* July 1986, pp. 64–65.)

Jacob 4:3–7
How to gain unshakable faith

Show your family a picture of Jesus calming the storm (such as *Gospel Art Picture Kit,* no. 214). Ask if they think they would be able to perform such a miracle. Tell your family that Jacob 4 explains how a person could do such miracles. Take turns reading Jacob 4:3–7 aloud and as you read discuss the following questions:

- Verses 3–4: What do these verses tell us Jacob wanted his children to know about him?
- Verse 5: Why did the Nephites keep the law of Moses?
- What law do we live in our day that replaced the law of Moses for us? (The gospel.)
- Verse 6: What else does Jacob say his people did so that their faith became unshaken?
- Besides the same witnesses Jacob had, what kinds of witnesses do we have today that the Lord lives and the gospel is true?

- How would searching the words of the prophets help your faith grow stronger?
- What did Jacob say he was able to do with his unshakeable faith?
- If you truly worshipped God in the name of Christ, kept his commandments, and did all the other things Jacob mentions here, what do you think you could do with your unshakeable faith?

Jacob 4:7–10
What does it mean to counsel the Lord?

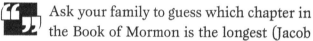 Read together Jacob 4:10 and ask your family what they think it means to counsel the Lord. Share the following statement by President Marion G. Romney: "In my view, seeking to counsel the Lord generally means disregarding the Lord's counsel, either knowingly or unknowingly, and in place thereof substituting our own counsel or the persuasion of men." ("'Seek Not to Counsel the Lord,'" *Ensign*, August 1985, p. 2.)

- Ask your family what they know about the Lord that would make his counsel more trustworthy than the advice of other people. Have them search Jacob 4:7–9 and list all the reasons they can find why we should trust the Lord's counsel to us instead of trying to get the Lord to agree with us.

Jacob 4:13–17
Where did the actions of the Jews lead them?

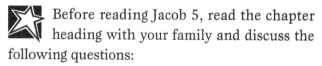 Ask your family what they think the scriptural phrase "looking beyond the mark" means. Tape a picture on the wall behind you of a famous person (movie star, political leader, athlete, and so on). Hold up a small picture of the Savior so your family can see both pictures. Ask again what it means to look beyond the mark. How do we sometimes look beyond the Savior?

Read together Jacob 4:14 and discuss how the Jews looked beyond the Savior and what happened to them because of it. Have your family study Jacob 4:15–17 and ask:

- What was the stone that the Jews rejected? (See Jacob 4:15d.)
- What blessings come to those who build upon Christ as a "sure foundation"? (See Helaman 5:12.)
- What did the Jews do instead of building upon the "sure foundation"?
- What can we do to build upon the Savior and escape the fate of the Jews?

JACOB 5–6: THE ALLEGORY OF THE OLIVE TREES

Jacob 5:1
Who was Zenos?

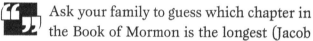 Ask your family to guess which chapter in the Book of Mormon is the longest (Jacob 5). Have them read Jacob 5:1 and find which prophet Jacob quoted in this chapter. Ask them to read Helaman 8:19 and find the only thing we know about Zenos' life.

Share the following statement by Elder Bruce R. McConkie: "I do not think I overstate the matter when I say that next to Isaiah himself—who is the prototype, pattern, and model of all the prophets—there was not a greater prophet in all Israel than Zenos." (Monte S. Nyman and Robert L. Millet, *The Joseph Smith Translation—The Restoration of Plain and Precious Things*, p. 17.)

Jacob 5:2–14
What do the symbols represent?

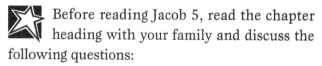 Before reading Jacob 5, read the chapter heading with your family and discuss the following questions:

- What is an allegory? (An allegory is like a parable. See *Bible Dictionary*, "Parables (2)," p. 741.)
- What two trees are used as symbols in this allegory?
- What four groups of people are mentioned in the heading?

- What events in the history of Israel will Jacob 5 deal with?

Explain that to understand an allegory, it is helpful to identify what the different symbols represent. Make a blank chart like the one below. Read Jacob 5:2–12 with your family and list the main symbols Zenos used in this allegory in the first column and their meaning in the second. You will find help for some of the symbols in the scripture footnotes. Your completed chart should look like this:

Symbol	Meaning
Tame olive tree	House of Israel
Vineyard	World
Master of the vineyard	Jesus Christ
Branches	Groups of people
Servants (footnote 4a)	Prophets
Wild olive tree (footnote 10a)	Gentiles
Fruit	Works of men
Decay (footnote 3d)	Wickedness or apostasy

Show your family a lamp and turn it on. Then unplug it from the power source and ask them why the light will not shine now. Ask why a light bulb needs electricity to work. If we were to compare our spirituality to this light, what would the electricity represent? What would the outlet represent? Why do we need to be connected to Jesus Christ to have spiritual life?

Show your family a living tree or plant. Cut off one of the branches or stems and ask your family what will happen to the cut-off branch. (It will wither and die.) Ask if there is a way to reattach the branch so that it would become part of the tree again and live? (Yes, grafting.)

Show your family the following pictures. Discuss the following questions:

- If the tree represents the house of Israel and the branches represent groups of people, what does the "pruning" of decaying branches symbolize? (The destruction of wicked groups of Israelites.)
- What would the "young and tender branches" represent? (Groups that were more righteous).
- What does the grafting of branches represent? (Moving groups of people from one place to another.)
- What might the roots of the olive tree represent? What is our source of life and nourishment? (Jesus Christ and the covenants we make with Him.)

Tell your family that pruning and grafting, which occur throughout the allegory, remind us that if we are not worthy of the gospel covenant, we will be cut off. It also reminds us that we can repent and return to the Lord and enjoy all the blessings of the house of Israel.

Jacob 5:3–77
Zenos' allegory

 Explain that Jacob 5 describes the workings of the Lord with the house of Israel from Old Testament times through the Millennium. It is best understood by identifying the four visits the master makes to his vineyard. You might want to have family members write the following labels in the margins of their scriptures next to the verses listed: "1st visit, before Christ, verses 3–14"; "2nd visit, at the time of Christ, verses 15–28"; "3rd visit, the great apostasy, verses 29–60"; "4th visit, the last days, verses 61–77."

You might consider doing this chapter as a

reader's theater. Have one family member be the narrator (doing the most reading), another be master or Lord of the vineyard (doing the next most reading), and one be the servant. (Your family could choose to act out their parts as well as read them. Also consider having family members move to different parts of the room as indicated in the allegory.) Have the narrator begin reading in Jacob 5:3 and ask the others to read as their parts come up in the verses.

As you read this allegory with your family use the following questions to help them understand it.

The First Visit, Jacob 5:3–14 (Before the time of Christ):

- What does the master of the vineyard see happening to his tame olive tree? (Verses 3–4.)
- What does the master do about the decay? (Prunes, nourishes, and grafts—see verses 4–14.)
- What does the grafting in of the branches of the wild olive tree represent? (Gentiles brought into the house of Israel.)
- What does the planting of the tame branches in the nethermost parts of the vineyard represent? (Scattering of Israel—see verses 8, 13–14 and footnotes 8a and 14a.)

The Second Visit, Jacob 5:15–28 (The time of Christ):

- When the master of the vineyard visits the second time, what does he discover about the wild branches that were grafted into the tame olive tree? (They were producing good fruit—see verse 17.)
- What has happened to the natural branches that had been planted in the nethermost parts of the vineyard? (They were producing fruit also, most good and some wild—see verses 20–25.)
- What branch of the house of Israel do you know that was taken to a choice land and at the time of Christ were partly righteous and partly wicked? (The Nephites and Lamanites.)

The Third Visit, Jacob 5:29–60 (The Great Apostasy):

- What did the master of the vineyard discover about the tame olive tree during his third visit? (It brought forth much fruit, but none of it was good—see verse 32.)
- What about the roots? (Still good—see verses 34–37.)
- What has happened to the branches planted throughout the vineyard? (All have become corrupt—see verses 38–39.)
- How does the master of the vineyard respond when he finds all the fruit corrupt? (He weeps—see verse 41.)
- What does the master decide to do to try to save his vineyard? (Graft some of the transplanted branches back into the original tame olive tree and vice versa, prune and destroy the most bitter branches, nourish the trees—see verses 52–60.)

The Fourth Visit, Jacob 5:61–77 (The Gathering of Israel and the Last Days):

- As the master makes a final effort to save his vineyard, whom does he enlist for help? (Other servants—see verses 61 and 70.)
- Who are these "other servants"? (Missionaries and others willing to help do the Lord's work.)
- What are they striving to "prepare the way" for in verse 61? (The Millennium—see footnote 61c.)
- What eventually happens to the bad branches? (They are cast into the fire as the good overcomes the bad—see verses 65–66.)
- What happens to the good fruit? (It is preserved with the Lord—see verse 77.)
- What does the master of the vineyard say about the servants who labored with him this last time? ("Blessed art thou" . . . for your diligence. . . . Ye shall have joy with me"—see verse 75.)

Ask family members if they noticed an over-riding phrase telling the master's feelings about the trees in his vineyard. (Have them look in Jacob 5:7, 11, 32, 46, 51, 66.) Ask if they can think of things they sometimes do that cause the Lord to grieve.

Jacob 6:1–6
Jacob's testimony

Tell your family that Jacob 6 summarizes Zenos' allegory of the olive tree. Read aloud to your family Jacob 6:1–6 and ask them what Jacob wanted his people to do because of what Zenos prophesied. What part should we play in helping scattered Israel to come home? What must we do to be able to do our part?

Jacob 6:1–13
Can you feel your Savior's love?

Place a reward or prize just out of arm's reach for your family. Have a contest and see which family member can stretch his or her arm the furthest to reach the prize. Read Jacob 6:4–5 together and ask:

- How do these verses relate to the object lesson?
- Why would the Savior stretch forth his hands to redeem or rescue you? (He loves you.)
- What invitation is given to those for whom he reaches? (Repent, cleave unto God, and harden not your hearts.)
- What does the word "cleave" mean, and what should we do to cleave to God?

Bear testimony that Zenos' allegory of the tame and wild olive trees is not so much a story about trees, branches, grafting, and fruit as it is a story of our Savior's love and his efforts to save all mankind. Invite family members to share their testimony about what they have learned from the allegory. You could conclude by reading the words of the song "I Feel My Savior's Love" (*Children's Songbook*, p. 74).

JACOB 7: SHEREM, THE FIRST RECORDED ANTICHRIST IN THE BOOK OF MORMON

Jacob 7:1–5
What is an antichrist?

Tell your family that in Jacob 7 they will read about an antichrist named Sherem. Ask your family what they think an antichrist might be. Share the following statement by Elder Bruce R. McConkie: "An antichrist is an opponent of Christ; he is one who is in opposition to the true gospel, the true Church, and the true plan of salvation. (1 John 2:19; 4:4–6.) He is one who offers salvation to men on some other terms than those laid down by Christ. Sherem (Jac. 7:1–23), Nehor (Alma 1:2–16), and Korihor (Alma 30:6–60) were antichrists who spread their delusions among the Nephites." (*Mormon Doctrine*, pp. 39–40.)

Read together Jacob 7:1–5 and compare Sherem with the prophet Jacob by asking some of the questions below:

- What talents or abilities did Sherem possess?
- What was the source of Sherem's power?
- What were Jacob's strengths?
- What was the source of Jacob's power?
- What kind of people would have been most influenced by Sherem?
- What kind of people would have rejected Sherem and followed Jacob?
- Why do you think so many people today follow those who tell them flattering falsehoods?

Jacob 7:5–21
The power of truth vs. the power of falsehood

Invite your best reader to read Jacob 7:6–21 aloud (or have three family members read the parts of Jacob, Sherem, and narrator). As you read, stop periodically to discuss some or all of the following questions:

- Why was Sherem unable to shake Jacob from the truth? (Verse 5.)
- What did Sherem want the people to believe? (Verse 7.)
- What was wrong with Sherem's contention that the "doctrine of Christ" was against the law of Moses? (Verse 7, 11; See also Jacob 4:4–5.)
- What did Sherem say in verse 9 that contradicts what he said in verse 7?
- What does that teach us about telling lies?
- What did Jacob say about Jesus Christ, and how did he know it? (Verses 11–12.)
- What did Sherem demand that Jacob show him? (Verse 13.)
- Why was that not a good idea? (Verses 15–20.)
- What do you find to be the most interesting about Sherem's confession?
- What was Sherem's greatest fear in the end? (Verse 19.)

Ask your family how differences between Sherem and Jacob are like the differences between those who teach against Christ today and young LDS missionaries. Share the following statement from Brigham Young: "When a false theory has to be maintained, it requires to be set forth with much care; it requires study, and learning, and cunning sophistry to gild over a falsehood and give it the semblance of truth, and make it plausible and congenial to the feelings of the people; but the most simple and unlearned person can tell you the truth. A child can tell you the truth, in child-like language, while falsehood requires the lawyer and the priest to tell it to make it at all plausible; it requires a scholastic education to make falsehood pass for truth." (*Journal of Discourses,* 11:214.)

Jacob 7:10–20
What's wrong with asking for a sign?

After studying the confrontation between Jacob and Sherem, ask family members if they have ever used the phrase "Prove it!"

When you use that phrase, what are you usually asking for? What phrase did Sherem use that was his way of saying "Prove it"? (See verse 13.) What happened in the story that shows that the Lord was not pleased that Sherem demanded a sign?

Read together D&C 63:8–12 and discuss what the Lord taught there about seeking for signs. What can we do to be more like Jacob and less like Sherem?

Jacob 7:21–25
How did the Nephites respond to Sherem's experience?

 Invite a family member to summarize the story of Sherem, the antichrist. Ask your family how successful Sherem was at first. (See Jacob 7:3.) If you were among his followers, what would you have thought when Sherem admitted on his deathbed that he lied? Have your family read Jacob 7:21–25 and look for how the Nephites reacted. Ask:

- Why did they fall to the earth?
- Why was Jacob pleased with this?
- What blessings came as a result of this spiritual crisis?
- What evidence is there that this experience increased their trust in God?
- How did they overcome Sherem's teachings? (See verse 23.)
- What can you do to avoid the deceptions in the world today?

Jacob 7:26
What was Jacob's life like?

Have your family silently read Jacob 7:26 and underline words that describe the Nephites during Jacob's day. Using the underlined words, have them write a brief paragraph (or draw a picture) of how they feel Jacob's people might appear to others. Ask:

- Have you ever felt feelings like those of these Nephites?
- What did you do about it?

- What can we learn from Ammon's attitude expressed in Alma 26:36?
- Although Jacob's life was difficult and challenging, why did he not shrink from his mission? (See Jacob 7:5, 12.)

Bear your testimony to your family that even though life is sometimes difficult, we, like Jacob, can find great strength in our relationship with the Lord.

ENOS

Enos was the son of Jacob (see Jacob 7:27) and the grandson of Lehi. His record was written on the small plates of Nephi about 420 B.C. (see Enos 1:25). Enos writes of his prayerful "wrestle" before the Lord to receive forgiveness of his sins. Once forgiven, Enos prayed for his brethren, the Nephites, and then for his enemies, the Lamanites.

ENOS 1: A MIGHTY PRAYER

Enos 1:1

How can righteous fathers bless and strengthen their children?

Read Enos 1:1 and ask your family to identify a phrase that describes how Enos was taught ("in the nurture and admonition of the Lord"). Explain that to *nurture* is to educate, train, or instruct. *Admonition* implies a mild rebuke or warning. The only other place in scripture where these two words are used together is in Ephesians 6:4, where Paul instructed the fathers in Ephesus. Share the following statements and have your family listen for clues about how they relate to Enos 1:1:

"In the divine scheme every soul has been given a father whose responsibility is not only to sire and provide the necessities of life, but also to train for mortality and life eternal . . . The teaching of the children by the father is basic from the beginning. The Lord ordained it so. Though Enos had strayed for a time, the teachings of his father prevailed, and he returned to worthiness." (Spencer W. Kimball, Conference Report, April 1965, pp. 61–62.)

"Twice blessed is the child who, while he or she is so young as perhaps to be unable to com-prehend the words, can nevertheless feel the spirit of prayer as a loving mother or a kind father helps with a few words of prayer at bedtime. Fortunate, indeed, are the boys and girls, including those in their teens, in whose homes there is the practice of morning and evening family prayer." (Gordon B. Hinckley, "The Environment of Our Homes," *Ensign,* June 1985, p. 6.)

Read 1 Nephi 1:1 together and look for similarities between Nephi's and Enos' fathers. What did they have in common? Read the following scriptures together and discuss what is taught there about the importance of parents' teachings in the conversion of their children: Enos 1:1–2, Alma 36:17, Alma 56:47–48, 2 Timothy 1:5, and 1 Nephi 2:16.

Enos 1:2

What does it mean to "wrestle" in prayer?

Ask your family what the word *wrestle* means. Read Enos 1:2 and ask why "wrestle" may have been used as a description for the prayer Enos offered. Share the following with your family:

"Some prayers are expressions of gratitude. Others are simple requests like those asking for a blessing on the food. Still others are heartfelt cries for help. Of these kinds of prayers, Jesus commanded us to pray having 'a sincere heart, with real intent, having faith in Christ.' (Moroni 10:4.) Patricia T. Holland observes: 'We are women now, not children, and we are expected to pray with maturity. The words most often used to describe urgent, prayerful labor are *wrestle, plead, cry,* and *hunger.* In some sense, prayer may be the hardest work we ever will engage in, and perhaps it should be.' (*Ensign,* Oct. 1987, p. 31.)." (Cited in the Visiting Teaching Message "Remember Him through Prayer," *Ensign,* July 1990, p. 62.)

Have family members tell about a time when their prayers were very earnest.

Enos 1:2–17
What can we learn from the mighty prayer Enos offered?

Ask each member of your family to share a difficult challenge he or she faced this week.

Discuss some of these questions:

- How often do you face these kinds of struggles?
- What do you do to deal with them?
- How could prayer help with that struggle?

Take turns reading Enos 1:2–17 and ask what problem Enos was facing. How did prayer help him? Have family members silently search the verses again and mark each word that shows how hard Enos prayed (for example: "wrestle" [verse 2], "hungered" [verse 4], "labored" [verse 12]). Invite each person to share what he or she found. Ask how those words show the sincerity of Enos' prayers.

Read Enos 1:16–17 aloud and emphasize the phrase "my soul did rest." Why was Enos finally able to rest? Have your family search the verses again and mark the word "faith" each time it appears. Ask:

- What part does faith have in prayer?
- What could you do to pray with greater faith?
- What word in verse 17 shows the blessing that came to Enos through his faith? ("Knew").

- Why was Enos able to go from believing to knowing?
- How would an answer from God help you while facing your difficult challenges?

Enos 1:4–13
Besides ourselves, who should we pray for?

 Invite family members to read Enos 1:4, 9, 11, and 13 and make a list of the people Enos prayed for. (Himself [see verse 4]; his "brethren" the Nephites [see verse 9]; the Lamanites, who were rivals and enemies to the Nephites [see verse 11]; and eventually those yet unborn who would benefit from the Book of Mormon [see verse 13]). Discuss the following questions:

- Why would it be important to pray for our own needs?
- Is it easy or difficult for you to pray for others? Why?
- Is it easy or difficult for you to pray for your enemies? Why?

Invite each family member to draw a picture that includes a family member, a friend, and someone who may be considered an enemy. Discuss why it would be important to pray for each of these people. Challenge them to pray for them today. Share this quotation from President Harold B. Lee: "You cannot lift another soul until you are standing on higher ground than he is . . . You cannot light a fire in another soul unless it is burning in your own soul." (*Stand Ye in Holy Places,* p. 187.)

Enos 1:5–8
Should we expect miraculous spiritual conversions like that of Enos?

Invite someone to read Enos 1:5–8 and then ask your family if they think Enos' experience is common or unusual. Does everyone have to have an experience like that to be saved? To help answer that question, share the following statement by President Ezra Taft Benson: "The scriptures record remarkable accounts of men whose lives changed dramatically, in an instant, as it were: Alma the Younger, Paul on the road to

Damascus, Enos praying far into the night, King Lamoni. Such astonishing examples of the power to change even those steeped in sin give confidence that the Atonement can reach even those deepest in despair.

"But we must be cautious as we discuss these remarkable examples. Though they are real and powerful, they are the exception more than the rule. For every Paul, for every Enos, and for every King Lamoni, there are hundreds and thousands of people who find the process of repentance much more subtle, much more imperceptible. Day by day they move closer to the Lord, little realizing they are building a godlike life." ("A Mighty Change of Heart," *Ensign,* October 1989, p. 5.)

Ask your family what they feel is comforting about what President Benson taught.

Enos 1:19–27
Make a prayer rock

Ask your family what they thought Enos did for the rest of his life after his conversion through mighty prayer. Do you think prayer was a part of his life from then on? Why do you think so? Take turns reading Enos 1:19–27 to see how his life ended.

Explain to your family that little reminders can help us pray more consistently. A rock painted with the word "prayer," for example, if left on a pillow could serve as a reminder to pray each night. Have each family member design and paint a prayer rock. Ask your family to use their rocks as a nightly reminder to say their personal prayers.

JAROM

Jarom, Enos' son, was given responsibility for the small plates of Nephi by his father. (See Jarom 1:1.) The fifteen verses written by Jarom span nearly sixty years and records how spiritual leaders "did threaten the people of Nephi according to the word of God" (Jarom 1:10) to keep them from destruction. They were "mighty men in the faith of the Lord" (Jarom 1:7) who testified of the plan of salvation (Jarom 1:2) to persuade their people to "look forward unto the Messiah and believe in him to come as though he already was" (Jarom 1:11).

JAROM 1: KEEP THE COMMANDMENTS AND PROSPER

Jarom 1:1–4
What were the spiritual problems of the Nephites?

Have your family read Jarom 1:3 and find four problems Jarom mentions. Discuss how each of these things represents spiritual sickness (for example, being hard-hearted is being rebellious; being spiritually deaf means refusing to hear the word of the Lord; the spiritually blind will not see the Lord's goodness in their lives; and those who have stiff necks are prideful).

Have a family member put on a pair of earmuffs, a blindfold, and a scarf around his or her neck. Once the person is dressed, have another family member read verse 3 out loud. Have the bundled-up family member take off the earmuffs, blindfold, and scarf. Ask the person how those coverings helped him or her hear, see, or read the verse with the family.

Have your family give examples of people being hard-hearted, spiritually deaf and blind, and stiff-necked. Read together Jarom 1:4 and ask how this verse is different from verse 3. How does becoming "unbundled" allow us to have "communion

with the Holy Spirit"? How can having the Spirit as a constant companion help keep us from all spiritual diseases?

Ask your family what they can do to hear the voice of the Lord. How can we see and recognize the Lord's mercy in our lives? Bear testimony about the Lord's goodness in your life.

Jarom 1:5–10
Why did the Nephites prosper?

Write on a sheet of paper the title "Top Ten." Have your family read Jarom 1:5–10 and look for the "top ten" reasons why the Nephites prospered. Have your family take turns listing the Nephites' successes as they find them. Discuss why the Nephites prospered and how each reason listed might also help your family to prosper and be successful.

Invite a family member to bear testimony of a blessing received or a success he or she had because of obedience to a gospel principle.

Jarom 1:10–12
How did the prophets keep the Nephites from being destroyed?

Have someone read Jarom 1:10–12 and look for *what* the Nephite prophets taught (to keep the commandments and to believe in

Christ as if he had already come) and *how* they taught it (they threatened, exhorted, and persuaded their people to prick their hearts continually). Ask your family what *would have been* the result of not following the prophets. What *was* the result for obedience? (See Mosiah 2:41.)

Share the following statement about the book of Mormon by President Gordon B. Hinckley: "I know of no other writing that sets forth with such clarity the tragic consequences to societies that follow courses contrary to the commandments of God. Its pages trace the stories of two distinct civilizations that flourished on the Western Hemisphere. Each began as a small nation, its people walking in the fear of the Lord. Each prospered, but with prosperity came growing evils. The people succumbed to the wiles of ambitious and scheming leaders who oppressed them with burdensome taxes, who lulled them with hollow promises, who countenanced and even encouraged loose and lascivious living, who led them into terrible wars that resulted in the death of millions and the final extinction of two great civilizations in two different eras.

"No other written testament so clearly illustrates the fact that when men and nations walk in the fear of God and in obedience to his commandments, they prosper and grow, but when they disregard him and his word, there comes a decay which, unless arrested by righteousness, leads to impotence and death." ("The Power of the Book of Mormon," *Ensign,* June 1988, p. 5.)

Choose as a family a commandment you could work on to better show your obedience and love to your Heavenly Father.

Jarom 1:11–12
Tell your own story of following the prophets and priesthood leaders

Read together Jarom 1:11–12 and look for words and phrases that show what prophets and church leaders do for their people. Ask your family why they think we need prophets and priesthood leaders today.

Have family members share a favorite story about a prophet or a local priesthood leader. They could tell why they love this leader and how they want to be like the leader, or or they could share how this leader inspires them to be more like the Savior.

OMNI

Although the Book of Omni is one of the shortest books from the small plates of Nephi, it has the most writers. It is also the last book translated from the small plates. Amaleki, the last writer, simply states, "These plates are full." (Omni 1:30.) The book of Omni provides insights not found anywhere else in the Book of Mormon. For example, here we learn of the inspired escape of Mosiah I (King Benjamin's father) with faithful Nephites to Zarahemla, how Zarahemla was inhabited by another colony who left Jerusalem soon after Lehi, and how the people of Zarahemla learned of the destruction of the Jaredites. Perhaps most important, Amaleki ends the record with an invitation for all to "come unto Christ" by offering their "whole souls." (Omni 1:26.)

OMNI 1: RECORDS AND PEOPLES

Omni 1:1–11
Do you keep a journal?

 Invite family members to bring their journals. Discuss how often they write in them and what they like to write about. Divide the following scriptures among family members: Omni 1:1–3; Omni 1:4–8; Omni 1:9; and Omni 1:10–11. Have them read the reference and be prepared to answer these questions:

- What was the name of your record keeper?
- About how often did he write in this book?
- What did he write about?

Read Jacob 1:1–4 to your family and discuss what was supposed to be written upon these plates. Ask them how true Omni, Amaron, Chemish, and Abinadom were to Nephi's instructions. Give your family a few minutes to write a journal entry according to the description given by Nephi.

Omni 1:12–19
Two groups of people, one nation

Ask your family if 1 + 1 = 1 is a true statement. After some suggestions are given, tell your family that today, in the scriptures, they will see at least one way for that to be true. Have them read Omni 1:12–18 and identify (1) two groups of people, and (2) all they can learn about each. Have them share insights as they find them. Their answers might include:

- The People of Mosiah: Mosiah was warned by God to lead faithful Nephites out of the land of Nephi. They found the people of Zarahemla. Mosiah and the Nephites taught them their language because they had "the word of God." As the peoples united, Mosiah was appointed king.
- The People of Zarahemla: They rejoiced when they met Mosiah's people because Mosiah's people had the brass plates. They had come out of Jerusalem at the time of Zedekiah and crossed "the great waters" (similar to Lehi's family). They were numerous and had

contentions and wars. Their language and religion was lost to them because they failed to bring any records.

Read Omni 1:19 and look for what happened to these two groups. Tell your family this is the only place this story is recorded in the Book of Mormon. Talk about why understanding this story would be important in helping you understand the rest of the Book of Mormon.

Omni 1:20–22
Who am I?

Tell your family you are going to describe a famous person in the Book or Mormon and you want them to guess who it is. Give the following clues:

- I was the last king of my people.
- I witnessed the total destruction of my people.
- The history of my people can be traced to the Tower of Babel.
- I slew Shiz and was the only one who survived a civil war.

Whether or not your family guesses that this is Coriantumr, have them read together Omni 1:20–22. Ask them to tell how Mosiah and his people were able to learn so much about Coriantumr. Tell your family that they can learn more about Coriantumr by reading Ether 12:1–2; 15:18–34.

Omni 1:23–25
King Benjamin: soldier-king or prophet-king?

Ask your family to think about kings they have read about in stories and describe the kinds of things kings do. (Answers might include make laws, lead armies in battle, and so on.) Then ask them to describe the kinds of things a prophet does. (Teach the people, prophesy, write scripture, and so on.)

Have your family read Omni 1:23–25 and tell whether King Benjamin seem to be more of a soldier-king or prophet-king? Tell them to keep

this question in mind as they learn more about King Benjamin in the Words of Mormon and the Book of Mosiah.

Omni 1:26
How can we give our whole soul?

Give family members some paper and have them draw what they think an altar looks like. Ask a family member to read the first paragraph from the Bible Dictionary under the heading "Altar" (see Bible Dictionary, "Altar," p. 606) to identify why altars were used anciently. Read together Omni 1:26 and look for Amaleki's teachings on how to "come unto Christ." Explain that anciently when people "offered" sacrifices, often the whole animal was given. What does Amaleki say we must give? (Our whole souls.) Ask your family what that means to them.

Share the following statement: "Only through sacrifice can we become worthy to live in the presence of God. Only through sacrifice can we enjoy eternal life. Many who have lived before us have sacrificed all they had. We must be willing to do the same if we would earn the rich reward they enjoy." (*Gospel Principles,* p. 175.)

Omni 1:27–30
Help find Amaleki's brother

Ask family members to tell what a "missing persons bulletin" is. Why is it important to spread the word about a missing person as quickly as possible? Read Omni 1:27–30 with your family and discuss the following questions:

- Who was reported missing? (Amaleki's brother.)
- Where was this brother headed when he was last seen? (The land of Nephi, also called Lehi-Nephi; see the map on the next page.)
- Why did he leave Zarahemla?

Tell your family that the account of what happened to this group is found in Mosiah chapters 9–22. Have them read the chapter heading for Mosiah 9 and answer the following questions:

- Who was the leader of the group?
- What did they do when they got to the land of Lehi-Nephi?

From what you have learned so far, what could you tell Amaleki about his brother?

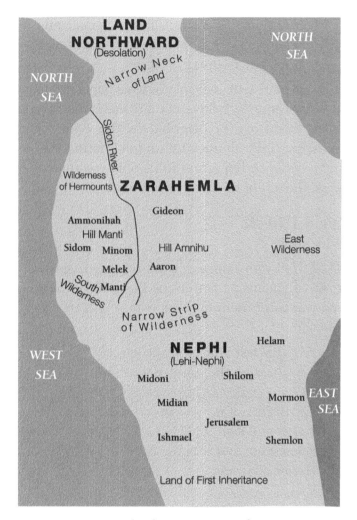

Book of Mormon Lands

WORDS OF MORMON

Near the end of Nephite history (about A.D. 385), the prophet Mormon made an abridgment (a shorter account) of the records of his people. He called his record the plates of Mormon. (See the diagram of the Book of Mormon plates on p. 9.) While he was making his abridgment, he came across another set of plates. The Spirit told him to include them in his writings even though he had already covered that part of Nephite history in his abridgment. This other set of plates, which include the first six books in the Book of Mormon, are known as the small plates of Nephi. Mormon wrote the Words of Mormon to help us understand that the small plates were not part of his abridgment of the large plates of Nephi. The Words of Mormon marks a transition from the small plates of Nephi to Mormon's abridgment of the large plates of Nephi.

WORDS OF MORMON 1: THE LORD KNOWS ALL THINGS

Words of Mormon 1:1–2
Why is this book out of place chronologically?

Ask your family to look for the date at the bottom of the last page of the Book of Omni (between 279 and 130 B.C.). Next have them find the date at the bottom of the first page of the Book of Mosiah (about 130 B.C.). Then have them read Words of Mormon 1:1–2 and tell what is happening in those verses and when. Ask your family if they can explain why the Words of Mormon are placed here when it was written so much later. To help with that explanation, have someone read aloud the introduction to the Words of Mormon above.

Words of Mormon 1:3–7
Why did Mormon include a second set of plates?

Tell your family that near the end of each calendar year, a group of people who claim to be able to predict the future attempt to do so. How often do you think they are right? Ask your family to tell the definition of the word *seer*. (See Bible Dictionary, "Seer," p. 771.) Discuss why it would be important to have a seer give us direction. Whom do we sustain today as prophets, seers, and revelators?

Take turns reading Words of Mormon 1:3–7 and list the reasons Mormon added the small plates of Nephi ("these plates") to his abridgment of the plates of Nephi. What words in verse 7 might indicate that Mormon was a seer?

To see the fulfillment of Mormon's inspiration, tell your family that while Joseph Smith translated the Book of Mormon plates, his scribe, Martin Harris, borrowed and lost 116 pages of the manuscript. The Lord told Joseph not to retranslate what he had already done but to translate from the small plates instead. Read the section heading to D&C 10 and verses 38–41 to find the "wise purpose" (Words of Mormon 1:7) the Lord had when He asked Mormon to include the small plates with his abridgment. Ask:

• What did the Lord know would happen?

• How does this insight into God's foreknowledge help you trust him?

Words of Mormon 1:8
For what do you pray?

Ask your family to read Words of Mormon 1:8 and discover the things for which Mormon prayed. Ask:

- Were Mormon's prayers centered on himself or on others?
- Why did Mormon pray for his enemies the Lamanites?
- What was Mormon's hope for them?
- What can this teach you about your own prayers?

Words of Mormon 1:12–18
How did Mormon feel about King Benjamin?

 Invite your family to list some people who have impressed them in their lives. What was it about those people that caused you to list them? Read Words of Mormon 1:12–17 with your family and have them list the things about King Benjamin that impress them.

Remind your family of the question that was asked in the teaching idea for Omni 1:23–25. (Was King Benjamin more a soldier-king or prophet-king?) Ask them how they would answer that question now.

MOSIAH

The Book of Mosiah covers approximately 109 years of history (from about 200 to 91 B.C.). This history was included on the large plates of Nephi and was later abridged by the prophet Mormon. The story in Mosiah is complex. It gives an account of the Nephite kings in the Land of Zarahemla (King Benjamin and King Mosiah II), as well as an account of the Nephite people living among the Lamanites in the land of Nephi. These Nephites were led by three kings, Zeniff, Noah, and Limhi. The book of Mosiah repeatedly illustrates the promise the Lord made to Nephi that those who keep the commandments will prosper in the land. (See 1 Nephi 2:20.)

MOSIAH 1: THE POWER OF GOD'S WORD

Mosiah 1:1
An abridgment

Select a short story or fairy tale that your entire family is familiar with. Have a contest retelling the story, seeing who can tell the story in the fewest words without leaving out essential elements. Explain that retelling a story in a shorter form is called *abridging*. Abridging is summarizing or abbreviating. Have your family study the diagram of the plates of the Book of Mormon on p. 9 and discuss the following questions:

- What books were written on the small plates of Nephi?
- What books were contained on the large plates of Nephi?
- Which of those, the small or large plates, were abridged?
- Who abridged the record found on the large plates of Nephi?
- According to Words of Mormon 1:5, how long could the Book of Mormon be if it were not abridged?

Have your family compare Mosiah 1:1 with 1 Nephi 1:1. Point out that Nephi wrote in "first person" (meaning he used the pronoun "I" to tell the story, because it was his own account). What "tense" is used in Mosiah 1:1? ("Third person"; Mormon used the pronoun "his" because he was telling the story about King Benjamin.) Explain that this is one evidence that the books of Mosiah through 4 Nephi are an abridgment by Mormon from the large plates of Nephi.

Mosiah 1:1–8
Was Benjamin a good parent?

Ask your family members to list something they have learned from their mother or father. Also ask them to tell of one additional thing they would love their mother or father to teach them.

Ask your family to read D&C 68:25–28 and find what the Lord expects parents to teach. (See also 1 Nephi 1:1.) Why do you think the Lord expects that of parents? Read Mosiah 1:1–8 and ask:

- What were the names of Benjamin's sons?
- What are several of the things he taught them?

- What verse best shows him sharing his testimony with his children?
- Why would it be important to hear the testimony of your parents?
- What do these verses teach you about King Benjamin as a father?

Read the following statement from the First Presidency and share your testimony with your family: "Husband and wife have a solemn responsibility to love and care for each other and for their children. . . . Parents have a sacred duty to rear their children in love and righteousness, to provide for their physical and spiritual needs, to teach them to love and serve one another, [and] to observe the commandments of God." ("The Family: A Proclamation to the World," *Ensign,* November 1995, p. 102.)

Mosiah 1:5–7
We "profit" from scripture study

Have one member of your family pretend that he or she owns a grocery store. Have them "sell" some food items to other family members, who buy the items with either real or play money. Discuss what it means to make a profit. Explain that profit is not just what people pay the owner for a product. The profit is what is left after paying for expenses (including the cost of products to sell, rent, and wages). Profit can be thought of as income minus expenses.

Now read Mosiah 1:5–7 together and ask what King Benjamin says we can "profit" from. Explain that to profit from the scriptures means we can gain more benefits out of study than we will expend in effort. Discuss the following:

- What "expenses" are there for scripture study? (Time and effort that could be spent on other activities.)
- What are some benefits of scripture study? (Increased testimony, understanding of the gospel, and so on.)
- How have you "profited" from scripture study?

Ask your family to read Mosiah 1:5 again and look for what King Benjamin said would happen to a society if they did not have scriptures. Have them look again at Omni 1:15–17 and tell how those verses prove that King Benjamin was right. What do you think would happen to our family if we neglected to study the scriptures we have?

Read the following statements: "One would not forgo partaking of the sacrament because he is trying to lose weight, yet some neglect the scriptures because they are too busy minding the pressing cares of the world." (Neal A. Maxwell, *Things As They Really Are,* p. 97.)

"No father, no son, no mother, no daughter should get so busy that he or she does not have time to study the scriptures and the words of modern prophets." (Spencer W. Kimball, "Boys Need Heroes Close By," *Ensign,* May 1976, p. 47.)

As a family, discuss how successful your family scriptures studies have been. Ask for suggestions on how to make them better. Recommit as a family to read each day.

Mosiah 1:11
What was the name given to the people?

Have someone read aloud Mosiah 1:11 and tell what King Benjamin wanted to give his people. Read Mosiah 5:8 together to discover what name was chosen. Discuss what it means to take upon us the name of Jesus Christ. Then share the following statements:

"Please remember this one thing. If our lives and our faith are centered upon Jesus Christ and his restored gospel, nothing can ever go permanently wrong. On the other hand, if our lives are not centered on the Savior and his teachings, no other success can ever be permanently right." (Howard W. Hunter, "Fear Not, Little Flock," *1988–89 Devotional and Fireside Speeches,* p. 112.)

"As his followers, we cannot do a mean or shoddy or ungracious thing without tarnishing his image. Nor can we do a good and gracious and generous act without burnishing more brightly the symbol of him whose name we have taken upon ourselves." (Gordon B. Hinckley, *Be Thou An Example,* p. 90.)

Mosiah 1:17
What are the consequences of unfaithfulness?

Read Mosiah 1:17 and list the consequences of unfaithfulness. Do you think these same consequences exist today for the unfaithful? Why or why not?

If it is appropriate, share a story about someone you know who suffered the consequences of being unfaithful. Talk about what we can do to help those who have left the Church to come back. Share your testimony about the need to be faithful and committed to the Lord Jesus Christ.

MOSIAH 2: KING BENJAMIN BEGINS HIS ADDRESS

Mosiah 2:1–4, 31
Why should we gather and listen to general conference?

Stand on a chair and have your family sit on the floor. Read Mosiah 2:1–2 and determine who was gathered. Discuss some of these questions:

* Why were the people gathering?
* Why do you think they would want to listen to King Benjamin?
* When do Church members gather together to listen to the prophet today?
* How have the words of the prophets in general conference helped you?

Have a family member read the following statement: "If you want to know what the Lord has for this people at the present time, I would admonish you to get and read the discourses that have been delivered at this conference, for what these brethren have spoken by the power of the Holy Ghost is the mind of the Lord, the will of the

Lord, the voice of the Lord, and the power of God unto Salvation." (Harold B. Lee, "To Ease the Aching Heart," *Ensign,* April 1973, p. 121.)

Ask your family to read Mosiah 2:4, 31 and look for blessings that would come from gathering to hear King Benjamin. What similar blessings do we obtain from general conference? Invite your family to make a list of ways that they can learn more while watching or listening to general conference.

Mosiah 2:5–8
Why was King Benjamin's sermon written down?

Have one family member go into another room so he or she cannot hear your discussion. Ask another family member to write down what is discussed as you read Mosiah 2:5–8. Discuss the following questions:

* Why did King Benjamin cause his words to be written down?
* Why couldn't all the people hear him?
* How is that similar to our discussion with one person in another room?

Bring back the person who was in the other room. Let the person read the notes that were kept. Ask the person:

* How do the written notes help you know what we talked about while you were out?
* How valuable would the notes be if your life somehow depended on that information?
* What if your eternal life depended on that information?
* When we cannot be at general conference when the prophet is speaking, what are some ways we can still receive his message?
* Why are the messages of general conference important to our family?

Read and discuss the following statement with your family: "For the next six months, your conference edition of the *Ensign* should stand next to your standard works and be referred to frequently. As my dear friend and brother Harold B.

Lee said, we should let these conference addresses 'be the guide to [our] walk and talk during the next six months. These are the important matters the Lord sees fit to reveal to this people in this day.'" (Ezra Taft Benson, "'Come unto Christ, and Be Perfected in Him,'" *Ensign,* May 1988, p. 84.)

Mosiah 2:10–18
How should a king rule his people?

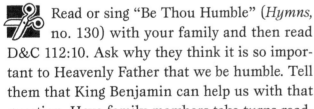 Read together Mosiah 2:10–18 and have your family underline the words "serve" or "service" each time they find them. Ask them how many times these words appear. How did Benjamin's attitude about service make him a good king?

As a family, make a list of the ways King Benjamin was different from political leaders today. Ask them how they would like King Benjamin to be the leader of their country. How might life be different if he were? If we can't have a King Benjamin to lead our country, what can we do to make the kind of difference in our neighborhood that he made in his?

Mosiah 2:19–26
What kind of attitude must we have if we are to serve God?

Read or sing "Be Thou Humble" (*Hymns,* no. 130) with your family and then read D&C 112:10. Ask why they think it is so important to Heavenly Father that we be humble. Tell them that King Benjamin can help us with that question. Have family members take turns reading Mosiah 2:19–26. As you read, mark the reasons he gave for why we should be humble.

Ask your family what they think Benjamin meant when he said we are less than the dust of the earth. Have them mark the reference to Helaman 12:7–8 in footnote b in Mosiah 2:25. Have someone read that reference aloud and tell what we do that the dust never does. (The dust never disobeys God.) On the other hand, what can we become that the dust never will? (We can become like God.) Ask, "What have we learned here about the

principle of humility that can help us achieve our great potential?" Read D&C 136:32–33 to your family and share your testimony of the importance of being humble before the Lord.

Mosiah 2:32–41
What is in a LIST?

Share with your family the following definition for the word *list:* To enroll; to register in a list or catalogue; to enlist. (*Webster's 1828 Dictionary,* "List.") Ask which definition reminds them of joining the army. When someone "enlists," whose choice is it?

Invite someone to read aloud Mosiah 2:32–37, replacing the words "list" and "listeth" with "enlist" and "enlisteth." Discuss with your family what additional meaning this gives to the verses. Ask, "Who leads the army referred to in these verses? Why is it such a serious sin to join the devil's army when you know better?"

Read together Mosiah 2:38–41 and discuss these questions:

- What warning is given to those who refuse to repent?
- How will the unrepentant feel at death?
- Why will mercy be unavailable to them?
- On the other hand, what will become of those who keep the commandments of God?

Have your family mark the phrases "never-ending torment" in verse 39 and "never-ending happiness" in verse 41. Ask someone to summarize what King Benjamin said we must do to avoid the torment and obtain the happiness.

MOSIAH 3: AN ANGELIC WITNESS OF JESUS CHRIST

Mosiah 3:1–4
An angel teaches a king

 Have family members read Mosiah 3:1–4 and find how King Benjamin learned about the things written in this chapter. What do you think it would be like to be taught by an angel? In verse 3, what did the angel say he had come to declare?

Have your family cross-reference Mosiah 3:3 with Luke 2:10–11. After reading in Luke, ask, "What do these scriptures have in common? What message was each angel declaring that could have been called a 'tiding of great joy'? Why do you think the birth of Jesus Christ would be a cause for such great joy?" Tell your family that studying Mosiah 3 will help them learn more about Jesus Christ's life and mission. It will give them a greater appreciation for the joy we can receive through his sacrifice.

Mosiah 3:5–10, 17
What service did the Savior give?

Ask each family member to make a list of the things they have done for other people in the past twenty-four hours. Ask them how it makes them feel when they serve others. Have each family member silently read Mosiah 3:5–10 and list some things the Savior did to serve others. Ask:

• Which of the Savior's gifts of service is the most impressive to you and why?
• According to Mosiah 3:17, what did the Savior provide for you that no one else could?
• Why is the Savior the only one who can offer salvation?

To help your family understand why Christ alone can offer salvation, share the following explanation from Elder James E. Talmage: "It was within His power to lay down His life voluntarily. He struggled and groaned under a burden such as no other being who has lived on earth might even conceive as possible. It was not physical pain, nor mental anguish alone, that caused Him to suffer such torture as to produce an extrusion of blood from every pore; but a spiritual agony of soul such as only God was capable of experiencing. No other man, however great his powers of physical

or mental endurance, could have suffered so." (*Jesus the Christ,* p. 613.)

Read D&C 18:10–13 with your family and discuss why Jesus Christ was willing to suffer to serve us.

Mosiah 3:11–18
Who enjoys the cleansing benefits of the Atonement?

Tell family members that in Mosiah 3:11–18, the angel describes three different kinds of people who will be covered by the atoning blood of Jesus Christ. Have them search those verses and find the three places where the atoning blood of Christ is mentioned. (Verses 11, 16, and 18.)

Have one person read Mosiah 3:11 aloud and tell who there will be covered by the Atonement. (Those who sin ignorantly.) Ask your family if any of them could be saved with that group.

Have another person read Mosiah 3:16 and tell who else will be covered by the Atonement (little children). Ask them why little children are automatically covered. (See D&C 29:46–47.) Can anyone in your family be included in that group? (Anyone under the age of eight would be; see D&C 68:25–27.)

Have another person read Mosiah 3:18 and describe who else can be saved by Christ's blood. (Those who repent and become as little children.) Ask your family which is the only group most of us could be saved in. (Only the last group.) Tell your family that the rest of Mosiah 3 helps us understand how to "become as a little child."

Mosiah 3:19–27
Putting off the natural man and why you might want to

Draw two blue lines on a piece of paper, one squiggly and the other straight. Ask your family to imagine that one of the lines represents a river and one represents a canal. Which blue line do you think represents the river? Why? Explain that a river is always crooked because water flows or follows a course of least resistance. If water's natural flow is altered by man's efforts, it can be channeled into a straight canal.

Have a family member read aloud Mosiah 3:19; then discuss the following questions:

- How could a "natural man" be compared to a river?
- Is it the natural man or the Saint that follows in the course of least resistance?
- How is a Saint like the canal?
- What are some things we choose to do, because it takes less effort, instead of what we should do? (Go to bed without prayer or scripture study, procrastinate doing home-work, not cleaning our bedroom, and so on.)
- Why would following a "course of least resist-ance" make us an enemy to God?

Have your family re-read Mosiah 3:19 and mark phrases that describe how we can put off the natural man. Ask them what it means to yield to "the enticings of the Holy Spirit." Ask, "How does the Atonement help us become Saints? What is it about children that we should try to emu-late?"

Have family members share examples of people they know who have "put off the natural man." What can we do as individuals to follow their example? Have each family member choose one characteristic from Mosiah 3:19 that they will work hardest on improving in the upcoming week.

MOSIAH 4: "SALVATION, THROUGH THE ATONEMENT"

Mosiah 4:1–3
The Atonement does more than cleanse us from sin

Show your family a container of mud and allow one person to get his or her hands muddy. Then hold up that person's favorite shirt or stuffed animal or other toy and ask if the person

would like to hold it now. Talk about how being dirty affects how you feel and what you can do.

Have another person read Mosiah 4:1–2 aloud and tell what happened to the people because of King Benjamin's words. Explain that carnal means "relating to the desires of the flesh; sensual; not spiritual." (*Webster's New Dictionary,* "Carnal.") Have them look again at the dirty hands and the container of mud and ask why they think Benjamin's people felt "less than the dust of the earth."

Now have the one with the dirty hands wash them with soap and water. Ask your family how that is like what the people asked the Lord to do for them in Mosiah 4:2. Read Mosiah 4:3 to your family and have them pick out phrases that describe the feelings associated with repentance. By what power were the people cleansed from sin and purified? Have them mark the word "fear" in verse 1 and the word "joy" in verse 3. Bear your testimony of the power of the Atonement to turn all our fears into joy.

Mosiah 4:6–8
Steps leading to repentance

(Note: for this idea, teach from a staircase if you have one in your home. If not, you may wish to draw a staircase, or show a picture of one.)

Ask your family to imagine the Savior standing at the top of a staircase. Read Moses 6:57 together and ask what we must do to return to the Saviors' presence. How is repentance like a staircase? What steps do you think are necessary to repent?

Have your family search Mosiah 4:6–11 and look for steps that lead to repentance. Discuss those they find and talk about how each of those steps can help us come unto Christ.

Mosiah 4:9–10
I believe so I will do!

Have family members read Mosiah 4:9–10 and mark each time the word "believe" is mentioned. Have each family member make a list of the items King Benjamin asked us to believe. Have them put a star by those things that are also something we should do. Invite them to hang their list in their rooms as a reminder. Challenge family members to "see that they do" those things during the upcoming week.

Mosiah 4:11–16, 26
How do we "retain" a remission of our sins?

Ask your family what they think it means to receive a "remission of your sins"? (It means to be released from guilt or penalty.) Who releases us from this guilt? How would you like to feel that way every day? Explain that the scriptures tell us how we can "retain" or keep this feeling every day.

Read as a family Mosiah 4:11–15, 26 and underline those things you should and shouldn't do each day to "retain a remission of your sins." Have family members privately choose one thing from the list they will work on each day this week to retain a remission of their sins.

Mosiah 4:16–23
"Are we not all beggars?"

Ask your family if they have ever encountered a beggar. Ask how they handled the situation. Have them read Mosiah 4:16–17 and tell how their experience was similar to or different from King Benjamin's instructions. Invite your family to read Mosiah 4:19–22 and discuss the following questions:

- In what ways are we all beggars?
- To whom do we beg or pray for blessings?
- How does God respond to our petitions?
- What would our lives be like if God withheld his blessings?
- How might King Benjamin's teachings change the way we deal with those in need in the future?

Show your family a "Tithing and Other Offerings" receipt. Discuss the different categories on the receipt. Talk about what donations we can give that will bless the poor and needy. Encourage your family to pay a generous fast offering. Sing together "Because I Have Been Given Much" (*Hymns,* no. 219).

Mosiah 4:24–25
"I give not because I have not"

Have a family member read aloud Mosiah 4:24–25 and find a situation when God does not expect us to give to the poor. Share the following statement by Elder Dallin H. Oaks and talk about how it relates to Mosiah 4:24–25: "Just as we will be accountable for our evil desires, we will also be rewarded for our righteous ones. Our Father in Heaven will receive a truly righteous desire as a substitute for actions that are genuinely impossible. My father-in-law was fond of expressing his version of this principle. When someone wanted to do something for him but was prevented by circumstances, he would say: 'Thank you. I will take the good will for the deed.'" (*Pure in Heart,* p. 59; see also 2 Corinthians 8:12.)

Mosiah 4:27
What is the prize and how can we win it?

Ask your family what would happen if they were in a race and tried to run faster than they had strength. Would you finish first? Would you even finish? Read together Mosiah 4:27 and notice how it relates to running a race. When it comes to caring for the poor and other service in the Church, why is it important that we not "run faster than we have strength"?

Mosiah 4:28
How do you feel about the neighbor who borrows but never returns?

Ask your family if they have ever loaned something and never got it back. How did you feel toward the borrower? Have someone read Mosiah 4:28 and tell how borrowing without returning is like not paying your debts. How can borrowing from a neighbor without returning cause him to sin?

Mosiah 4:29–30
What should we be watching?

 Display a magnifying glass, a pair of glasses, a microscope, or a telescope and ask family members how these objects relate to Mosiah 4:30. Have family members underline in their scriptures everything King Benjamin encourages us to "watch."

Make three posters with the following labels from Mosiah 5:30:

Watch your thoughts
Watch your words
Watch your deeds

Have family members write or draw on each poster ways to accomplish what the title suggests. Display the posters somewhere in the home to be a reminder of ways to avoid sin.

MOSIAH 5: BECOMING SONS AND DAUGHTERS OF CHRIST

Mosiah 5:1–2
What is the "mighty change" and how can I obtain it?

Show a picture of each family member from several years before. Ask in what ways they think they have changed the most. Ask them what kinds of changes they have experienced that are not so visible? Have them share their thoughts about the following questions:

- What does it mean to say a person has changed for the better?
- What might cause a person to change?
- How can you tell if a person has really changed?
- Do you think it would be easier to notice a change in another person or in yourself? Why?

Read Mosiah 5:1–2 together and look for the "mighty change" that came upon King Benjamin's people. Tell your family that such a "mighty change" is what Benjamin meant when he said we

must "put off the natural man and become a saint." (Mosiah 3:19). Share the following descriptions with your family:

"Christ says, Give me All. I don't want so much of your time and so much of your money and so much of your work: I want You. I have not come to torment your natural self, but to kill it. No half measures are any good. I don't want to cut off a branch here and a branch there, I want to have the whole tree down. . . . Hand over the whole natural self, all the desires which you think innocent as well as the ones you think wicked, the whole outfit. I will give you a new self instead. In fact, I will give you Myself: my own will shall become yours." (C. S. Lewis, *Mere Christianity*, p. 167.)

"God has created man with a mind capable of instruction, and a faculty which may be enlarged in proportion to the heed and diligence given to the light communicated from heaven to the intellect. . . . The nearer man approaches perfection, the clearer are his views, and the greater his enjoyments, till he has overcome the evils of his life and lost every desire for sin." (Joseph Smith, *History of the Church*, 2:8.)

Ask your family if they would like to be so converted that they have no desire to sin. How much easier would it be to live the commandments if you had "no more disposition to do evil but to do good continually"?

Ask your family if they remember what the people of King Benjamin did so that the Spirit could make this "mighty change" in their hearts. (See Mosiah 4:2–3; they asked to be forgiven and purified, and they had faith in Christ.) What did Benjamin say they must do to "retain a remission of their sins"? (See Mosiah 4:11–16.)

Bear your testimony of the power of the Lord to change us so that the things we are commanded to do are also the things we love to do. Share the following testimony from Elder Henry B. Eyring: "Heavenly Father . . . has provided a way to rise higher—almost beyond our limits of imagination—not by our own powers alone, which would not be nearly enough, but through the power of the

Atonement of his Son, Jesus Christ." ("Covenants," CES Fireside for College-Age Young Adults, 6 September 1996, p. 1.)

Mosiah 5:5–12
Are you willing to enter into a covenant with God?

 Have a family member read Mosiah 5:5 and tell what King Benjamin's people were willing to do because of their faith. Read together what a covenant is in the Bible Dictionary ("Covenant," p. 651). Ask how a covenant is similar to and different from a contract between people here on earth.

Read Mosiah 5:5–12 together and discuss these questions:

- What promises did King Benjamin's people make as they entered into a covenant? (Verse 5.)
- What blessing did they obtain because of their covenant? (Verse 7.)
- Whose name did they take upon them as part of their covenant? (Verse 8.)
- What promises are made to covenant keepers? (Verses 8–11.)
- According to Mosiah 6:1–2, how many of these people entered into a covenant?

To illustrate the value of making covenants with the Lord, invite the strongest and smallest members of your family to stand. Ask the person to imagine that the strongest family member represents Christ while the smallest represents each of us. Using a rope, handcuffs, or other material, tie the hands of these two people together. Ask them how the weaker person would be helped by uniting with the strongest. How is a covenant with Christ similar to being tied to or bound to Him?

Show your family this picture of a yoke and ask someone to read Matthew 11:29. Discuss the following questions:

- What is a yoke used for? (A yoke harnesses two animals together so that they can pull a heavier load than either could carry alone.)
- How is the covenant that binds us to the

Savior more like a yoke than ropes or handcuffs?
- What would be the value of being bound to or yoked to Jesus Christ?
- What kinds of burdens does Christ help us carry that are too much for us to bear alone?
- What advantages might this covenant relationship bring, if we began to stray away from Christ?
- According to Mosiah 5:15, what is the ultimate blessing to those who choose to be bound to Jesus Christ?

Share the following statement from President Howard W. Hunter: "Why face life's burdens alone, Christ asks, or why face them with temporal support that will quickly falter? To the heavy laden, Christ's yoke gives the power and peace of standing side by side with a God who will provide the support, balance, and the strength to meet our challenges and endure our tasks here in the hardpan field of mortality." (*That We Might Have Joy,* pp. 13–14.)

MOSIAH 6: MOSIAH II FOLLOWS HIS FATHER'S EXAMPLE

Mosiah 6:4–7
Was King Mosiah II as good as King Benjamin?

For the younger members of your family, write the following sentences on a piece of paper:

- King Mosiah "did walk in the ways of the _____."

- King Mosiah observed the Lord's judgments and _____.
- He also "did _____ his commandments."
- Along with his people, King Mosiah did also "_____ the earth."
- "There was no contention among all his people for the space of _____ years."

Ask your family what these verses teach us about the kind of king Mosiah II was. What are some traits that Mosiah possessed that we should try to emulate in our family? How would these traits help us have more peace in our family?

MOSIAH 7: AMMON DISCOVERS THE DESCENDANTS OF ZENIFF'S COLONY

Mosiah 7:1–15
What happened to the Colony of Zeniff?

 Mosiah 7 marks a change in the story line in the Book of Mormon. To understand this change show your family the map of Book of Mormon lands and review with them Omni 1:27–30. (See the teaching idea for Omni 1:27–30, "Help find Amaleki's brother," for more help if needed.) Have them draw their own simple outline map of the Book of Mormon lands using the map as a pattern. Have them label the Land of Lehi-Nephi and the Land of Zarahemla. Then have them draw a line indicating where Zeniff and his people started and where they were going when we last heard of them.

Next, read Mosiah 7:1–15 with your family and look for answers to these questions:

- Who did Mosiah send to look for Zeniff's colony? (Verses 2–3.)
- How many days did they wander in the wilderness and why? (Verse 4.)
- Who did they learn was now the king of Zeniff's people? (Verse 9.)
- Why was the king "exceedingly glad" to learn that Ammon and his men were from Zarahemla? (Verses 14–15.)

Have your family look again at the maps they made of the Book of Mormon lands. On the land of Zarahemla, have them write the names of the three Nephite kings who ruled there so far. (Mosiah I, Benjamin, Mosiah II; see Omni 1:23 and Mosiah 6:4–6.) Then have them read Mosiah 7:9 to find the names of the three Nephite kings in the Land of Lehi-Nephi during that same time. (Zeniff, Noah, Limhi.) Have them write those names on their maps also.

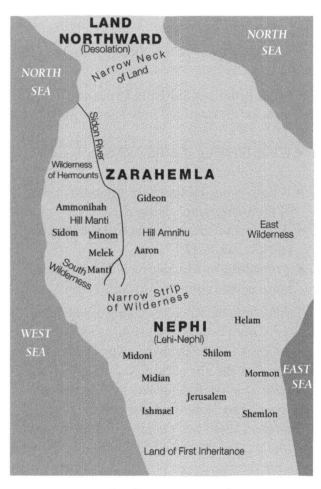

Book of Mormon Lands

Mosiah 7:20–33
Why were the people of Limhi in bondage to the Lamanites?

Have your family silently study Mosiah 7:20–28 and list as many reasons as they can find why Limhi and his people were in bondage to the Lamanites. Encourage them to look beyond the obvious reason of "iniquity." When they have finished, let each person share what he or she found. Encourage your family to mark those reasons in their books.

Discuss the following questions:

- How are Limhi's people like people today who are in bondage to sin?
- What kinds of things are people "over-zealous" for today that leads them to be deceived by Satan?
- Although they may not seek to kill them, how do those who want to sin treat modern prophets?
- How does the cost of sin today compare to the price of bondage for Limhi's people?

Read Mosiah 7:29–33 out loud to your family and bear your testimony of the power of the Lord to deliver us from bondage, both physical and spiritual. Testify also that the Lord can keep us from bondage if we will just follow the prophets and keep the commandments.

MOSIAH 8: PROPHET, SEER, AND REVELATOR

Mosiah 8:1–5
How well do you know your family history?

Display your family pedigree chart, a family Bible, a journal, or some other family record. Ask your family why they think we have been asked to keep family records. Have someone share an inspiring story from the life of a relative. Ask them how keeping better family records could bless us. Read together Mosiah 8:1–4 and ask the following questions:

- What did Ammon and King Limhi share with each other and Limhi's people? (The stories since Zeniff left Zarahemla.)
- What evidence do you find that Limhi's

people knew of the importance of keeping records?
- What was particularly inspiring about the account given by Ammon? (He shared King Benjamin's last words. You might want to review some of Benjamin's teachings by reading the chapter headings for Mosiah 2–5.)

Challenge your family to keep more complete and inspiring records of their own lives so that one day their relatives might be helped and inspired.

Mosiah 8:6–12
Name that book

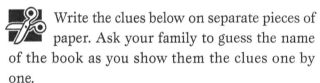 Write the clues below on separate pieces of paper. Ask your family to guess the name of the book as you show them the clues one by one.

- This book was written on twenty-four gold plates.
- These plates were written in a strange language.
- They were discovered in a land filled with bones and ruins.
- They were discovered by King Limhi's men who were sent to find Zarahemla.

If no one guesses the answer, read together Ether 15:33–34. (Ether wrote the record and left them so Limhi's people could find them.) Have family members take turns reading Mosiah 8:6–11 to learn more about the finding of Ether's record. Use the following questions to help them understand the verses:

- Why did Limhi send forty-three men on a journey? (To find Zarahemla and get help to be delivered out of bondage.)
- What happened to them instead of finding Zarahemla?
- What evidence was there to show that an awful tragedy had occurred in this land?
- What can we learn from the fact that Limhi's men went in search of Zarahemla to get help

from bondage to the Lamanites but the Lord led them to find a book of scripture instead?

Mosiah 8:12–19
The one who sees

If available, show your family several pictures of latter-day prophets (especially the current prophet). Ask them why they think the prophets mean so much to Latter-day Saints. Invite someone to read Mosiah 8:12 and find the question King Limhi asked Ammon. Why did he need someone to translate? Have another family member read Mosiah 8:13–14 and find Ammon's answer. What is a seer? Share the following statement by Elder John A. Widtsoe: "A seer is one who sees with spiritual eyes. He perceives the meaning of that which seems obscure to others; therefore he is an interpreter and clarifier of eternal truth. He foresees the future from the past and the present. This he does by the power of the Lord operating through him directly, or indirectly with the aid of divine instruments such as the Urim and Thummim. In short, he is one who sees, who walks in the Lord's light with open eyes." (*Evidences and Reconciliations,* p. 258.)

On a piece of paper that everyone can see, write, "A seer is a see-er." Ask what a seer "sees" that others might not. Display the pictures of latter-day prophets once again and ask your family to share examples of how these prophets "see." Read together Mosiah 8:15–19 and discuss the following questions:

- How did Ammon respond to Limhi's thought that "a seer is greater than a prophet"? ("A seer is a revelator *and* a prophet.")
- How might this explain why we sustain the president of the Church as a prophet, seer, and revelator?
- Where do the prophets get this power?
- What does it allow them to know?
- How did King Limhi respond to this knowledge?
- Why should we "rejoice exceedingly" and

give "thanks to God" for living in a day when prophets, seers, and revelators guide us?

Cross-reference Mosiah 8:15–19 with D&C 1:14, 29, 38. Read those verses and ask:

- Who was a prophet and seer in our day who was able to translate an ancient record by the gift and power of God?
- What will happen to those who reject the words and teachings of the Lord's seers?
- What do we know about how the prophet's words compare to the Lord's words?

Share your love and testimony of our current prophets, seers, and revelators. Invite your family to study and apply their words. Maybe you could share some of your favorite teachings from a recent general conference with your family.

MOSIAH 9: ZENIFF AND HIS PEOPLE RETURN TO THE LAND OF NEPHI

Mosiah 9:1–18
"Doing our own thing" can lead to trouble

Tell your family that Mosiah chapters 9–22 record the story of how Zeniff and his descendants attempted to establish a Nephite colony among the Lamanites in the land of Nephi (also called the land of Lehi-Nephi). Show your family the map on p. 122 and have them locate Zarahemla and the land of Lehi-Nephi. Read together Mosiah 9:1–3 and ask:

- What assignment did Zeniff have that brought him in contact with the Lamanites? (He was a spy.)
- What did Zeniff see in the Lamanites that led to a serious struggle?
- Why did Zeniff want to live among the Lamanites?
- How did Zeniff's over-eagerness to dwell in the land of Nephi lead his people into trouble?

- How were Zeniff's people different from the Lamanites?

To show your family just how much trouble Zeniff led his people into, take turns reading Mosiah 9:4–12. Ask them to look for how Zeniff got permission to settle in the land of Lehi-Nephi again. What were King Laman's motives for allowing Zeniff's people to settle in their land? (See verses 10–12.)

Ask your family if they think the Lord hates his children when they make mistakes. Tell them that Zeniff and his people illustrate how the Lord feels about us even when we make bad choices. Read aloud Mosiah 9:16–18 and ask:

- What did the Lamanites do that broke the promise they made in Mosiah 9:6?
- How were Zeniff's people able to defeat the more numerous Lamanite army?
- What does this tell us about the Lord's feelings toward his children?
- Where could you go for help even when your troubles were caused because of your own bad choices?

Testify of the Lord's love and tell about a time he helped you through a difficult situation that you got yourself into.

MOSIAH 10: THE LAMANITES BEGIN A WAR AGAINST ZENIFF'S PEOPLE

Mosiah 10:1–21
"In the strength of the Lord"

Read with your family Mosiah 9:17; 10:10, 19 and have them tell what these verses have in common. Then read together Mosiah 9:18; 10:3–5, 20–21 and discuss the following questions:

- How were Zeniff's people blessed because they relied on the strength of the Lord?
- Do you ever get into troubles or trials where you could use the Lord's strength?

- Does the Lord love us as much as he loved Zeniff's people?
- How can you get the Lord to help you in your struggles? (See Mosiah 10:17.)
- What can we do to show the Lord we trust him?

Invite each family member to recall a time when they enjoyed the Lord's strength and to record it in their journal.

Mosiah 10:11–18
What are the curses of false traditions?

Ask your family to name some of the traditions of your family or other families they know. Have them tell about who started these traditions and how long they have been going on. Discuss as a family why traditions can either be good or bad.

As a family, scan Mosiah 10:11–18 and list the traditions of the Lamanites mentioned there. Ask:

- How would you characterize the traditions of the Lamanites?
- What happens if traditions are based on things that aren't true?
- What are some religious, national, or ethnic traditions that people have today that are not true?
- What can we do to avoid this same trap?

Read the following statement by Elder Richard G. Scott: "Carefully study the scriptures and counsel of the prophets to understand how the Lord wants you to live. Then evaluate each part of your life and make any adjustments needed. Seek help from another you respect who has been able to set aside some deeply held convictions or traditions that are not in harmony with the Lord's plan. When in doubt, ask yourself, 'Is this what the Savior would want me to do?' . . .

"I testify that you will remove barriers to happiness and find greater peace as you make your first allegiance your membership in the Church of Jesus Christ, and His teachings the foundation of your life. Where family or national traditions or customs conflict with the teachings of God, set them aside. Where traditions and customs are in harmony with His teachings, they should be cherished and followed to preserve your culture and heritage. There is one heritage that you need never change. It is that heritage that comes from your being a daughter or son of Father in Heaven. For happiness, control your life by that heritage." ("Removing Barriers of Happiness," *Ensign,* May 1998, pp. 86–87.)

After reading Elder Scott's testimony, discuss any personal or family traditions that need to be set aside. Use any of the following that apply and add any of your own.

- How do we traditionally respond when someone offends or mistreats us?
- What is our traditional reaction when someone asks for our help?
- When it is time for personal or family prayer, scripture study, or family home evening, are we as supportive and pleasant as the Savior would want us to be?
- What do we usually do when we see someone who is sad or needs a friend?

Commit as a family to end bad traditions and start good ones.

MOSIAH 11: WICKED KING NOAH

Mosiah 11:1–15
Compare King Noah with King Benjamin

After reading about wicked King Noah in Mosiah 11:1–15, ask your family if they can think of a king that was the opposite of King Noah in many ways (King Benjamin). In the activity below, read the statement describing King Benjamin from the left-hand column. Ask your family to find a verse that explains how King Noah was opposite from King Benjamin's description.

King Benjamin	King Noah
Encouraged his people to keep the commandments. (Mosiah 1:11; 2:13.)	"Caused his people to commit sin." (Mosiah 11:2.)
Did not grievously tax the people. (Mosiah 2:14.)	Heavily taxed their riches. (Mosiah 11:3.)
Appointed righteous priests. (Mosiah 6:3.)	Removed the old righteous priests. (Mosiah 11:5.)
Served the people (Mosiah 2:12) and worked to support himself (Mosiah 2:14).	Had the people serve him so he could be a lazy wine-bibber. (Mosiah 11:6, 15.)

Later in this story your family will find more examples of how the two kings were opposites. Share with them items in the left column below and see if they already know how King Noah was opposite. If they do not know the rest of the story, tell them to look for these things as they read.

King Benjamin	King Noah
Taught the scriptures to his people. (Mosiah 1:3–5.)	Did not teach the scriptures. (Mosiah 12:26.)
Was himself a prophet and supported the prophets in their work. (Words of Mormon 1:16–18)	Put the prophet Abinadi to death. (Mosiah 17:12, 20.)
Fought with the sword of Laban to protect his people. (Words of Mormon 1:13.)	Abandoned his people to save his own life and sent his men to protect himself. (Mosiah 19:11, 20.)

Discuss with your family how they can develop the character traits of King Benjamin.

Mosiah 11:1–19
What do you know about King Noah?

 To play this game, you will need some small candy or other treat to reward correct answers. Explain that each family member will need to read Mosiah 11:1–19 in about five or six minutes. Then they will each get a chance to answer a question about their reading to win a treat. Younger family members could be assigned an older partner to read with them. Use some of these questions or make up some of your own. Adjust the questions according to the age of family members.

- Name two things wrong with King Noah's personal and social life. (See verse 2.)
- What percent tax did King Noah impose? (See verse 3.)
- What is *ziff* or what does it mean? (See verse 3 with footnote 3b.)
- How did Noah change the church? (See verse 5.)
- How did Noah get the people to support him? (See verse 7.)
- How many towers did Noah build? (See verses 12–13.)
- How did Noah and the priests spend their time? (See verse 14.)
- What fruit or crop did Noah have a special interest in? (See verse 15.)
- Noah's soldiers said fifty of them could stand against how many Lamanites? (See verse 19.)

Mosiah 11:18–29
Abinadi's first warning is conditional— "Except they repent . . ."

Ask your family if people are more likely to repent when life is going well or when life is difficult. Why? After they have had time to think about that question, have someone read aloud Mosiah 11:18–20. Discuss the following questions:

- Were King Noah's people doing well or not very well at this time?
- How did the Lord think they were doing?
- Who told the Nephites they needed to repent?
- How do you think they felt about the need to repent?

Have your family read Mosiah 11:21–25 and mark the things Abinadi said would happen if the people did not repent. Then have them scan Mosiah 11:26–29 and find how Noah and his people reacted to Abinadi's message. Have them find and mark the verse that tells how Abinadi escaped.

Have your family look again at the list of things Abinadi said would happen if the people did not repent. Ask them what they think the future will be like for those people? (Tell your family they will see what happens to these people in the next few chapters of Mosiah.) Has the prophet today given us any warnings about our future? (You can get some ideas from the latest conference edition of the *Ensign* or from the First Presidency Message at the front of every *Ensign.*) What would you predict for our future if we do not heed the words of our prophets? How will life be better if we do follow the prophet? Share with your family some personal examples of how following the counsel of the living prophets has kept people out of trouble.

MOSIAH 12: ABINADI TESTIFIES BEFORE KING NOAH AND HIS PRIESTS

Mosiah 12:1–8
Abinadi's second warning is unconditional— "It shall come to pass . . ."

Tell your family to suppose that late one night the house catches on fire. Have each person tell what he or she should do to get out safely. (You might choose to have them actually practice their escape route.) Ask the family what the consequences would be if they did not heed the warning to get out of the house. Ask if they can remember a time when they were warned not to do something but they disobeyed and did it anyway. What happened when they ignored the warning? Tell them that Mosiah 12 illustrates how foolish it is to ignore the Lord's warnings.

Ask your family to remember Abinadi's first warning and what he said would happen to Noah and his people "except they repent." (See Mosiah 11:21–25.) Have your family take turns reading Mosiah 12:1–7 and count how many times Abinadi says "will" or "shall." Ask them what the difference is between a warning that says "except they repent" and one that says "shall be brought into bondage"? (The first is conditional—they could escape bondage. The second is unconditional—bondage is certain.) What reason does Abinadi give in Mosiah 12:1 for this change?

Have someone read aloud Mosiah 12:8 and tell what additional warning Abinadi gave that is still conditional and could be avoided if they repent. Ask your family what principle about the Lord's warnings to His children they learn from this story. What should we do when the Lord warns us to repent? Read D&C 19:15–19 to your family and discuss what kind of suffering repentance can save us from.

Mosiah 12:1–37
Abinadi as a type of Christ

Read Moses 6:63 to your family and ask, "According to that verse, where should we see things that typify or remind us of Jesus Christ?" (Everywhere.) Explain that this is particularly true of the lives of the prophets. Have your family compare the verses below about

Abinadi with the verses from the New Testament that describe the life of the Savior. Discuss how these examples fulfill the promise of Moses 6:63.

Encourage your family to look for reminders of the Savior in everything they see and do. Close by reading or singing "I Believe in Christ" (*Hymns*, no. 134). Share your testimony of Christ.

Mosiah 12:27–37
How do you "apply your heart to understanding"?

Ask your family members if they have ever learned something about the gospel that was new to them but didn't *feel* new. Have you ever learned something new that made such perfect sense that it seemed as if you had always known it? Have someone read Mosiah 12:27 and find the reason Abinadi gave for why the wicked priests couldn't understand what he was teaching. Why do you think Abinadi used the word "hearts" instead of "minds' in that verse? Share the following quotation from Harold B. Lee: "When your heart tells you things that your mind does not know, then the Spirit is guiding you." (*The Teachings of Harold B. Lee*, p. 509.)

Ask your family what they think President Lee was teaching. What kind of learning takes place more through the heart or spirit than the mind? Why is it important to have the Spirit guide us as we try to understand the gospel?

Mosiah 12	Abinadi	Jesus Christ
Verse 1.	He came to the people in disguise.	Luke 2:4–7 (Jesus was born as an infant).
Verses 2–8.	He called people to repentance.	Revelation 2:16.
Verses 2–8.	The people rejected his message.	Luke 4:28–29.
Verse 9.	People were angry, bound him, and carried him before a king.	Matthew 26:47–57.
Verse 17.	He was cast into prison.	Matthew 27:26–28.
Verses 19–24.	Religious leaders tried to trap him in his own words.	Mark 11:27–33.
Verses 25–37.	Abinadi answered the priest's questions with a question.	Matthew 19:4.

As you study Mosiah 12:27–37 as a family, find each question Abinadi asked Noah's priests, note their answers, and underline Abinadi's accusations. What do the accusations have in common? (In each case Noah's priests had taught but not lived their religion.) Why is obedience to gospel principles a key to understanding them? (See John 7:17.) Bear your testimony to your family about the importance of learning spiritual things in the Lord's way.

MOSIAH 13: ABINADI CHALLENGES KING NOAH AND HIS PRIESTS

Mosiah 13:1–10
"Touch me not!"

Show your family the picture of Abinadi before King Noah found in a paperback copy of the Book of Mormon (or, if available, use *Gospel Art Picture Kit,* no. 308). Allow each family member to look carefully at the picture and then read together Mosiah 13:1–9. Ask the following questions:

- Why was Abinadi sure he would not be "destroyed at this time"? (See verse 3.)
- How was Abinadi protected from King Noah's men? (See verse 5.)
- Why were King Noah and his priests angry with Abinadi? (See verses 6–8.)
- How might this story give you courage when you face difficult tasks?

Have someone read the following statement: "When we know who we are and what God expects of us—when his 'law [is] written in [our] hearts'—we are spiritually protected." (Russell M. Nelson, "Children of the Covenant," *Ensign,* May 1995, p. 34.)

Ask, "How does the story of Abinadi help you to have courage in the callings you receive from the Lord?"

Mosiah 13:11–24
Writing the Ten Commandments in our hearts

As a family, see if you can list all the Ten Commandments from memory. To see how well you did, review Mosiah 12:35–36 and then read together Mosiah 13:12–24. Have your family underline the Ten Commandments to see how many they got right. Discuss the following questions:

- Why did Abinadi need to teach King Noah and his priests the Ten Commandments? (See Mosiah 13:11.)
- What do you think it means to have the commandments "written in your hearts"?
- How can we "write" the teachings of the scriptures in our hearts? (For example, see 1 Nephi 2:16.)
- How might that change who we are? (For example, see Mosiah 5:1–2.)

Share the following explanation by President Harold B. Lee: "The most important of all the commandments of God is that one that you are having the most difficulty keeping today. If it is one of dishonesty, if it is one of unchastity, if it is one of falsifying, not telling the truth, today is the day for you to work on that until you have been able to conquer that weakness. Put that aright and then you start on the next one that is most difficult for you to keep. That's the way to sanctify yourself by keeping the commandments of God." (*Teachings of Harold B. Lee,* p. 82.)

Discuss with your family how President Lee's plan might help us write the commandments in our hearts. Challenge family members to choose one of the commandments and try to completely obey that law for one week.

Mosiah 13:27–35
How is anyone saved?

Write the following phrases in large letters on a sheet of paper: The Gospel; The Scriptures; The Church; The Priesthood. Ask family members to select the one they think will save them in the celestial kingdom and explain why. Have your family study Mosiah 13:27–30 and look for what Abinadi said would save us. Ask them what the wicked priests said would save people. (The Law of Moses, see Mosiah 12:11; 13:27. For an explanation of what the law of Moses was, see *Bible Dictionary,* "Law of Moses," p. 722.) What was the purpose of the law of Moses?

Read Mosiah 13:31–35 with your family and have them find what was needed besides the law of Moses to be saved. (The atonement of Jesus Christ.)

Read the following statement by Elder Bruce R. McConkie: "Suppose we have the scriptures, the gospel, the priesthood, the Church, the ordinances, the organization, even the keys of the kingdom . . . and yet there is no atonement of Christ. What then? Can we be saved? Will all our good works save us? Will we be rewarded for all our righteousness?

"Most assuredly we will not. We are not saved by works alone, no matter how good; we are saved because God sent his Son to shed his blood in Gethsemane and on Calvary that all through him might ransomed be. We are saved by the blood of Christ (Acts 20:28; 1 Cor. 6:20)." (*Doctrines of the Restoration,* p. 76.)

MOSIAH 14: ABINADI QUOTES ISAIAH TO KING NOAH

Mosiah 14:2
What did the Savior look like?

Tell your family that in Mosiah 14 Abinadi quotes Isaiah to show that the prophets testified of the coming of the Messiah. Read together Isaiah 14:2 and discuss how Isaiah described the mortal Jesus Christ. Ask how the coming of the Savior as a baby was like a "tender plant." How was the spiritual condition of the Jews at the time of Christ's birth like "dry ground"?

Share the following statement to help explain why Isaiah said the Savior had "no . . . comeliness" and "no beauty": "There is no mystique, no dynamic appearance, no halo around his head, thunders do not roll and lightnings do not flash at his appearance. He is the Son of the Highest, but he walks and appears as the offspring of the lowest. He is a man among men, appearing, speaking, dressing, seeming in all outward respects as they are." (Bruce R. McConkie, *The Promised Messiah,* pp. 478–79.)

Discuss with your family why God had his Only Begotten Son appear this way. How was that a test of faith for the Jews of that day? How was the Savior's appearance in mortality different from how he will appear when he comes again? Conclude by singing "O God, the Eternal Father" (*Hymns,* no. 175), especially noting verse 3.

Mosiah 14:3–12
How do you feel about the Savior?

Divide your family into two groups and ask both to search Mosiah 14:3–5, 7–8, 10–12. Have one group make a list of how people would treat the Savior and the other a list of how the Savior would respond. Have them share their lists and discuss why they think people treated the Savior so badly. Why do you think God allowed his Son to be treated this way?

Explain that we know how people felt about the Savior in his day, but the real question is how we feel about him in our day. Discuss as a family how people today despise, reject, hide their face from, or fail to esteem the Savior. Ask family members to think of a time when they may have treated the Savior similarly and how it made them feel. Invite them to write in their journal how they can show their love for the Savior in the future.

Mosiah 14:3–9
Can you see what it means?

⭐ Display pictures of Jesus Christ in the garden of Gethsemane, on the cross, and at his burial (if available, use the *Gospel Art Picture Kit,* nos. 227, 230, 231, 232.) Read as a family Mosiah 14:3–6 one verse at a time. After each verse, look at the pictures and discuss how they help explain Isaiah's descriptions of the Savior. Then ask:

- How has the Savior borne our griefs and sorrows?
- How can we be healed by his stripes?
- How are we like sheep that have gone astray?
- Why do we do things our "own way"?

Read together Mosiah 14:7–9 and ask:

- Who were the wicked that Jesus made his grave with? (The thieves crucified next to him.)
- Who might the "rich" be that Isaiah refers to? (Joseph of Arimethea; see Matthew 27:57–59.)

Discuss with your family what this chapter teaches us about how well prophets can know the future. Ask what impresses them most about Isaiah's prophecies of the life of Jesus Christ.

MOSIAH 15: ABINADI TEACHES OF CHRIST

Mosiah 15:1
Who is the God that is being referred to in Mosiah 15?

Invite your family to list the three members of the Godhead. Then talk about whether the members of the Godhead are three separate beings or one person. (See D&C 130:22.) Read Mosiah 15:1 and ask:

- Which member of the Godhead came to earth and was born of a virgin? (Jesus.)
- What name was Jesus known by in the Old Testament? (See D&C 110:1–4.)

- From what you've just learned, who was Abinadi referring to when he said, "God himself shall come down among the children of men"?

Mosiah 15:1–5
How is Jesus Christ both the Father and the Son?

Write the following statement on a piece of paper and show it to your family: "All fathers are sons, but not all sons are fathers." Discuss whether or not your family thinks that statement is true, and help them understand what it means.

Read Mosiah 15:1–4 and Alma 11:38–39 as a family and talk about some ways Jesus Christ is both a son and a father. Tell your family that in his book *Christ and the New Covenant,* pp. 179–93, Elder Jeffrey R. Holland gave the following examples of how Christ is the Father:

1. Christ is the heir of all that the Father has.
2. Christ created the earth and is thus the Father of creation.
3. Christ atoned for our sins and thus becomes the spiritual Father of the redeemed.
4. Christ was the first resurrected and thus becomes the Father of the resurrection.

Elder Holland further explained, "There are ways in which Christ is so united with his Father that in some assignments he rightfully plays a fatherly role and rightfully bears the title of Father in doing so." (*Christ and the New Covenant,* p. 183.) To help more fully explain this difficult doctrine, you may wish to review the following scriptures with your family: Hebrews 1:2; Moses 1:33; D&C 19:16.

Mosiah 15:6–13
What does it mean to be the seed of Christ?

✂️ Have a family member briefly tell about his or her baptism. Next show a piece of bread and some water and ask what these two items have to do with our baptisms. (They are the emblems used in the sacrament, which is the sacred ordinance in which we renew our baptismal covenants. The bread and water represent the body and blood of our Savior.) Review the sacrament prayers with your family (see Moroni 4:3) and make a list of the covenants we make at baptism. Emphasize that at baptism we take upon ourselves the name of Christ.

Have your family read Mosiah 15:6–12 and make a list of the things Christ will do for those who take upon themselves his name. Have them find the last question asked in verse 10. (Who are Christ's seed or his children?) Then have them search verses 11–13 and find the two groups of people Abinadi says are Christ's seed.

Share the following statement from Elder Russell M. Nelson: "When we embrace the gospel and are baptized, we are born again. We take upon ourselves the sacred name of Jesus Christ. We become as his sons and daughters and are known as brothers and sisters. We become members of his family; he is the Father of our new life." ("A More Excellent Hope," *Ensign*, February 1997, p. 62.) You could sing "I Am a Child of God." (*Children's Songbook,* p. 2.)

Mosiah 15:13–19
What does "How beautiful . . . are the feet of those who shall hereafter publish peace" mean?

Have your family turn to Mosiah 12:20–21 and find the question the wicked priests asked Abinadi. Read together Mosiah 15:13–19 and look for Abinadi's explanation of what Isaiah meant by this phrase. Discuss the following questions to help your family discover what Isaiah meant:

- Who are those who have "published peace" in verses 13–14? (All past prophets.)
- How is teaching the gospel like publishing peace?
- Who are those who are publishing peace now (verse 16) and in the future (verse 17)? (Modern prophets, missionaries, us.)

- What would have happened if this message had not been published? (See Mosiah 15:19.)
- How do new converts feel about the missionaries who taught them the gospel?
- How do you feel about our current prophet?
- How are the feelings we have for those who teach us the gospel like Isaiah saying, "How beautiful upon the mountains are their feet"?
- How would you like someone to feel that way about you?

Mosiah 15:21–26
Who will come forth in the first resurrection?

 Have each family member draw a picture that they think best represents springtime. Have them show their pictures and talk about why they chose to draw what they did. Ask:

- What happens to the trees and plants in the spring?
- How do flower gardens change when spring arrives?
- What happens with many animals in the spring?
- What is your favorite part of spring?

Ask your family what similarities they see between the change from winter to spring and the death of Jesus Christ and his resurrection. As you read together Mosiah 15:21–26, have your family look for things that make the promise of a glorious resurrection even greater than the promise of spring.

Read Mosiah 15:21–25 and list with your family three different groups of people that will be part of the "first resurrection." (Believers, verse 22; those who died in ignorance of the gospel, verse 24; and little children, verse 25.) Have them mark footnote a in Mosiah 15:24 and read D&C 137:7. Ask them how modern revelation helps us understand Mosiah 15:24. Have them mark footnote a in Mosiah 15:25 and read D&C 137:10. How does that verse help clarify Mosiah 15:25?

Read the following clarification from Elder Bruce R. McConkie about the meaning of the "first resurrection": "To those who lived before the resurrection of Christ, the day of his coming forth from the dead was known as the first resurrection. Abinadi and Alma, for instance, so considered it. (Mosiah 15:21–25; Alma 40.) To those who have lived since that day, the first resurrection is yet future and will take place at the time of the Second Coming. (D&C 88:96–102.) We have no knowledge that the resurrection is going on now or that any persons have been resurrected since the day in which Christ came forth excepting Peter, James, and Moroni, all of whom had special labors to perform in this day which necessitated tangible resurrected bodies." (*Mormon Doctrine,* p. 639.)

MOSIAH 16: JESUS CHRIST IS THE LIGHT AND LIFE OF THE WORLD

Mosiah 16:1–5
Who will be excluded from the redemption?

Ask your family what they think it will be like when the Lord comes again. Invite them to share how they would feel if the Savior were to come tomorrow. What are some things you might want to do before he came? Take turns reading Mosiah 16:1–5 and discuss some of the following questions:

- Who will "see the salvation of the Lord"? (Verse 1.)
- What will happen to the wicked when Jesus comes again? (Verse 2.)
- Why can't they be redeemed? (Verses 2, 5.)
- How will they feel about that? (Verse 2.)
- If they refuse to "hearken" (listen to and obey) the Lord, who will have control over them? (Verses 3, 5.)
- Who else is "lost" besides the wicked? (All mankind, verse 4.)
- What must we do to be redeemed from the Fall? (Hearken unto the voice of the Lord, verse 2.)

Have your family list all the ways they can think of that the voice of the Lord is heard today. (The Holy Ghost, the scriptures, the words of the prophets, our local Church leaders, and our parents.) What will be the consequences if we are taught the truth but we refuse to hearken? Bear your testimony about the importance of being able to hear the Lord's voice and then obey what he asks us to do.

Mosiah 16:1–9
How can we see in the dark?

For this activity, you will need a flashlight. Turn off all the lights in the room so that it is very dark. Ask your family what the world would be like without the sun. How does it feel to be in total darkness? Turn on the flashlight and have a family member read Mosiah 16:9. Then ask:

- What light is this verse talking about? (Jesus is the light and life of the world.)
- In what way does the flashlight represent what is taught in this verse?

Keep the lights off as you read Mosiah 16:1–8, passing the flashlight to each person as he or she reads a verse. Once this activity is completed, ask your family:

- What kinds of things in these verses symbolize the darkness?
- In what ways are people living in darkness today?
- How does Jesus bring light into a darkened world?
- How did you feel when it was your turn to hold the light?

Bear testimony that Jesus is the light and life of the world. If we believe in him and live his teachings, we will never be in the darkness.

Mosiah 16:6–8
What if Christ had not come?

Ask your family to think about what would be different in our lives if Jesus

Christ had not come. Give each person a chance to suggest a difference and write them all in a list. (Suggestions may range from no church to no Christmas.) Read together Mosiah 16:6–7 and look for two things Abinadi said would be different if Christ had not come. Discuss with your family what the terms *redemption* and *resurrection* mean. (See Bible Dictionary, "Redemption," p. 760, and "Resurrection," p. 761, for help, if needed.) Ask your family what difference it would make for us in eternity if there were no redemption and no resurrection. Read together 2 Nephi 9:8–9 and ask what we would have become in the end if it were not for Jesus. How does this help you appreciate more fully what Jesus did? Read to your family Mosiah 16:8 and testify that Christ did come to bring us redemption and resurrection.

Mosiah 16:4, 13–15
Why do we need to be saved from our sins?

Ask your family to tell about a time when they were lost. Discuss how it feels to be lost and what it took to find your way home again. Read together Mosiah 16:4 and have them look for another way to be lost. What did the Savior do so that we do not have to be "endlessly lost"? Share the following statement by President Ezra Taft Benson: "Just as a man does not really desire food until he is hungry, so he does not desire the salvation of Christ until he knows why he needs Christ. No one adequately and properly knows why he needs Christ until he understands and accepts the doctrine of the Fall and its effect upon mankind" ("The Book of Mormon and the Doctrine and Covenants," *Ensign,* May 1987, p. 85).

Ask someone to explain why, according to President Benson, coming to understand the doctrine of the Fall is so important to our salvation. How does Jesus Christ help us when we are spiritually lost? Read Mosiah 16:13–15 to your family and testify that it is only through Jesus Christ that we can be redeemed from our sins.

MOSIAH 17–18: ALMA IS CONVERTED BY ABINADI AND LEADS THE CHURCH

Mosiah 17:1–4
Only one convert?

Ask your family to describe the feelings a missionary might have if during his whole mission he only found one person who believed his message. Read together Mosiah 17:1–4 and ask:

- Who believed in Abinadi's words?
- What courageous thing did he try to do for Abinadi?
- What was Alma forced to do?
- Why was it important that he "write all the words that Abinadi had spoken"?
- What might Abinadi have thought when King Noah sent servants to kill Alma? (His only convert would be killed.)

Write the following names on a sheet of paper: Nephi 2, Alma 2, Helaman 2, Nephi 3, Helaman 3, Alma 1. Assign each family member one or more of those names. Have them turn to the index in the back of their Book of Mormon and find that person. Have them prepare to report one important fact about the person's life and also who the person's father was. After each family member has reported, have them help you put the names in chronological order

Alma 1
Alma 2
Helaman 2
Helaman 3
Nephi 2
Nephi 3

and then ask them what all these men had in common. (They were all descended from Alma 1, also called Alma the Elder.) Ask, "Even though Abinadi only had one convert, how many lives were changed because of his missionary service?" Discuss with your family what that teaches us about the importance of missionary work and the success of Abinadi's mission to King Noah's people. Consider reading D&C 18:15 to help answer this question.

Mosiah 17:5–13
Counting the cost

 Gather together some money, a checkbook, or something else of value and show it to your family. Ask them what it might cost for each of the following: buy a candy bar, go to a movie, eat at a restaurant, buy a car, share the gospel.

Have your family take turns reading Mosiah 17:5–13 and then discuss the following questions:

- What did it cost Abinadi to take the Lord's message to King Noah?
- What could Abinadi have done to save his life and why didn't he do it?
- Do you think that today Abinadi wishes he had never gone on that mission?
- What does it cost most members of the Church today to share the gospel?
- Do you think that when you see Jesus Christ again you will be glad you took the time, and paid the price, to share the gospel with others?

Mosiah 17:14–20
Trusting the prophet's word

Ask a family member to tell how Abinadi lost his life. (See Mosiah 17:13.) Explain that before Abinadi died, he prophesied several things to Noah and his priests. Make a chart like the one below. As you read the verses with your family, have someone fill in the chart.

What Abinadi Said	What Happened
Mosiah 12:3	Mosiah 19:20
Mosiah 17:14–15	Alma 25:5–7
Mosiah 17:16–18	Alma 25:7–12

Ask your family what this teaches about prophets. Discuss what the living prophet has recently declared to us and what we ought to do about his counsel.

Mosiah 18:1–11
How important is baptism?

Ask your family to share some reasons why their baptismal covenants are important to them. If you have a paperback copy of the Book of Mormon, show your family the picture of Alma baptizing at the Waters of Mormon (or use *Gospel Art Picture Kit,* no. 309). If the picture is not available, you may consider having your family read Mosiah 18:1–7 and draw a picture of what they think this scene would have looked like. Discuss ways this picture shows the importance of baptism to these people. Read together Mosiah 18:1–7 and discuss the following:

- Whose words did Alma teach?
- Where did he teach them and why?
- How does this show the level of the people's faith and belief?

Alma explained the covenant of baptism just before he baptized the people. On a sheet of paper make two columns. Label one column "I Covenant," and the other "That I May." As you read Mosiah 18:8–10, have a family member list what we covenant to do at baptism and what we will receive of the Lord if we keep our covenants. Your chart may look like the following:

I covenant to:	That I may:
"come into the fold of God"	"be redeemed of God"
be "willing to mourn with those that mourn"	"be numbered with those of the first resurrection"
"be called his people"	"have eternal life"
"comfort those . . . in need of comfort"	have "his spirit more abundantly"
"stand as a witness of God at all times and in all things, and in all places . . . even unto death"	
"serve him and keep his commandments"	

Ask how Alma's people felt about the covenants they made with the Lord. (See Mosiah 18:11.) How will keeping our covenants show the Lord how we feel about our baptism? Discuss as a family ways they can mourn with, comfort, share a witness with, or bear the burdens of another person, especially other family members. Challenge them to do a specific service this week and then later report how it made them feel.

Mosiah 18:8
Bearing one another's burdens

Ask your family if they know what the word *synergy* means. Share the following definition by Elder M. Russell Ballard. You might choose to demonstrate synergy with some sticks instead of reading the example below.

"Synergism is defined as a 'united action of different agents or organisms producing a greater effect than the sum of the various individual actions' (Thorndike Barnhardt Dictionary, "Synergism"). The ancient moralist Aesop used to illustrate the concept by holding up a stick and asking for a volunteer among his listeners who thought he could break it. Of course the volunteer was able to break the stick easily. Then Aesop would put two sticks of the same size together and would ask the same volunteer to break them both at the same time. It was more difficult, but usually it could be done without too much trouble. The process was repeated, with another stick being added to the bundle each time, until the volunteer was unable to break the bundle of sticks. The moral to Aesop's illustration was simple: individually we are weak, but together we are strong." (*Counseling with our Councils,* pp. 10–11.)

Have someone read Mosiah 18:8 and explain what this object lesson has to do with our church membership. What are some things you have done to bear another person's burdens? Why do you think Heavenly Father wants us to help each other like that? Why is it important to work together in the Church? What does Moses 7:18 teach about this principle?

Mosiah 18:13–14
Did Alma baptize himself?

Have a family member read aloud Mosiah 18:13–14. Ask them why they think Alma and Helam both went under the water. Explain that some have thought that Alma was baptizing himself and Helam at the same time. Share the following statement to help explain what happened.

"There is no question but that Alma held the priesthood and was one ordained after the holy order of God. Thus he would have been baptized previously. Therefore, when Alma baptized himself with Helam that was not a case of Alma baptizing himself, but merely as a token to the Lord of his humility and full repentance." (Joseph Fielding McConkie and Robert L. Millet, *Doctrinal Commentary on the Book of Mormon,* 2:258.)

Mosiah 18:17–30
How do we become the children of God?

Share the following quotation from Elder Russell M. Nelson: "While children re-enacted the Christmas story, one child held high a star wrapped in aluminum foil, mounted on a broomstick. Later, someone commended the child for his stamina in holding that star so high for such a long period of time. The child, who had spoken no lines, joyfully replied, 'I had the most important part in the play. I showed people how to find Jesus.'

"We are to help the honest in heart to find Jesus. . . . We willingly and gratefully take His sacred name upon us. We enlist in His cause by covenant." ("Standards of the Lord's Standard-Bearers," *Ensign,* August 1991, p. 7.)

Ask your family what they can do to help others find Jesus. As you read Mosiah 18:17–30, have your family find and mark the ways Alma's people showed each other how to find Jesus and become the children of God.

Mosiah 18:31–35
Alma once again escapes King Noah

 Have family members read Mosiah 18:31–35 and discuss the following questions:

- How did King Noah finally discover Alma and his people?
- What was he going to do about them?
- How did Alma and his people escape?

Have your family mark the reference to Mosiah 23:1 in footnote a in Mosiah 18:34. Then have them turn to Mosiah 23:1 and look for who "apprised" Alma about the coming of Noah's army. What does this teach us about the concern the Lord has for his people? If possible, share an experience your family has had where the Lord guided you or warned you to keep you from harm or danger.

MOSIAH 19: WICKED KING NOAH IS DESTROYED BY FIRE

Mosiah 19:1–8
What do you do with a wicked king?

Read to your family Proverbs 29:2 and ask them to give reasons why this proverb is true. Review with your family Mosiah 11 and list examples from the reign of King Noah that illustrate that proverb. Ask them how a people can get rid of a wicked king. Then read together Mosiah 19:1–8 to see what happened to King Noah. Ask:

- What more do we learn about King Noah from these verses?
- What do you think led Gideon to want to kill his king?
- What was the only reason Gideon spared the King?
- How does this story relate to the proverb?
- What does this teach us about the importance of choosing good people to lead us?

Mosiah 19:9–13
Why is it best to think less of self and more of others?

Ask your family what they would choose to take with them if they had to leave home for the last time tomorrow. Have them share what they chose and explain why. Did any of them choose a family member? Discuss why we sometimes forget those we love the most. Read Mosiah 19:9–13 with your family and ask:

- What do we learn about King Noah's feelings for his people in these verses?
- What is it called when we think more of ourselves and less of others? (Selfishness.)
- What affect did King Noah have on other men? On their families?
- How does selfishness affect us?

Share the following statement by President Gordon B. Hinckley: "The family is falling apart all over the world. The old ties that bound together father and mother and children are breaking everywhere. We must face this in our own midst. There are too many broken homes among our own. The love that led to marriage somehow evaporates, and hatred fills its place. Hearts are broken, children weep. Can we not do better? Of course, we can. It is selfishness that brings about most of these tragedies." ("Look to the Future," *Ensign,* November 1997, p. 69.)

With your family discuss some ways to overcome selfishness in your family.

Mosiah 19:16–17
Why do we react to the world around us the way we do?

Ask your family if they have ever seen righteous children come from a home where the parents were not righteous. Ask them how that is possible. Read with your family Mosiah 19:16–17 and ask:

- Since most men followed King Noah into the wilderness to save their own lives, what do we learn about Limhi? (He stayed behind to help protect his family.)

- What does verse 17 call Limhi?
- Even though Limhi's father (King Noah) was wicked, what did he desire for him?
- How was Limhi different from his father?

Discuss with your family how Limhi could become a "just man" even though raised by a wicked father. Read the following from the *Church News:* "Anytime a child lives righteously he brings honor to his parents, whether those parents are themselves righteous or wicked. . . . So, honoring parents does not always imply obeying them. In those relatively few cases where parents may ask for or encourage unrighteous behavior in their children, the individual brings dishonor to his parents if he obeys them." ("Unrighteous Parents Honored by Child's Righteous Life," *Church News,* 9 June 1990.)

Discuss with your family the hopes and dreams you have for them. Ask them what kind of lives would bring honor to their earthly and heavenly parents.

Mosiah 19:18–24
The importance of following the prophet

 Assign family members to be one of the following: Gideon's men, people in the wilderness, King Noah, and Noah's priests. Have them silently read Mosiah 19:18–24 and look for information about their assigned name. Discuss what they learned.

Ask if anyone noticed that a prophecy was fulfilled in this story. Read together Mosiah 12:3 and identify the prophecy given by Abinadi. Discuss with your family how literally it was fulfilled. What does this teach us about the importance of prophets in our lives? Share the following statement by Elder Robert D. Hales: "I give my testimony that the prophets of this day have the qualities of the prophets of old and the other prophets of this dispensation. . . .

"We declare with soberness, and yet with the authority of God in us vested, that we have a prophet today. The President of the Church, as a prophet, is God's representative on earth and is appointed to lead His church. . . .

"Our spiritual safety lies in turning to the clear voice of our living prophet. If we listen to his voice and obey his counsel, we will be able to live as Christ would have us live and endure to the end so that one day we, along with our families, will return back into the presence of our Heavenly Father and our Savior, Jesus Christ." ("Hear the Prophet's Voice and Obey," *Ensign,* May 1995, p. 17.)

Mosiah 19:25–29
What is the price of wickedness?

 Show your family a check stub or tax form that shows the amount of taxes you pay. Discuss what taxes pay for. Then take turns reading the verses in Mosiah 19:25–29 and discuss the following questions:

- How much did Limhi's people have to pay in taxes?
- What did the taxes of Limhi's people pay for?
- What did the Lamanites do to make sure Limhi's people didn't leave the area?
- Why did the Lord let Limhi's people end up in bondage? (See Mosiah 12:1–2.)
- What word indicates that Limhi's people were receiving blessings from God, despite their difficult circumstance? (Peace.)

Bear your testimony to your family about the importance of following the prophet and the foolishness of thinking that breaking the commandments ever pays.

MOSIAH 20: THE LAMANITE DAUGHTERS ARE MISSING

Mosiah 20:1–26
Game time

 Have your family read the chapter out loud together and listen carefully for details that could be asked as game questions later. Encourage family members to mark key points and ideas in the chapter to help them remember the information for later.

After the reading, give each family member a piece of paper and have them number from 1–12. Read each question and have them write the letter they think provides the best answer. At the end of the game, ask each question again and have them identify the verses that contain the answer.

1. Why did the daughters of the Lamanites gather together? (Verses 1–2.)
    A. To bathe in the river.
    B. To gossip.
    C. To sing and dance.
    D. To do their nails.

2. Why did the priests of King Noah stay in the wilderness? (Verse 3.)
    A. They were afraid that Limhi's people would try to kill them.
    B. They liked camping.
    C. They were preparing to attack Limhi's people.
    D. They found a herd of llamas they liked.

3. How many Lamanite daughters did the priests of Noah kidnap? (Verse 5.)
    A. 12.
    B. 27.
    C. 24.
    D. Too many.

4. Who got blamed for the missing daughters? (Verses 6–7.)
    A. Limhi's people.
    B. The missing sons.
    C. The missing priests of Noah.
    D. The missing llamas.

5. How did King Limhi know the Lamanites were going to attack them? (Verse 8.)
    A. A vision.
    B. Spies.
    C. He saw from the tower.
    D. A little birdie told him.

6. What beasts did it seem the people of Limhi fought like? (Verses 10–11.)
    A. Tigers and bears.
    B. Two angry llamas.
    C. Lions and dragons.
    D. "Lions and tigers and bears—oh, my!"

7. Why did they fight so hard? (Verse 11.)
    A. There was a prize for the best fighter.
    B. To save their own lives and the lives of their families.
    C. So the daughters of the Lamanites would be impressed.
    D. Because dragons are scary!

8. What did the people of Limhi do with the captured king of the Lamanites? (Verses 13–14.)
    A. Fixed up his wounds.
    B. Let him die.
    C. Put him to death.
    D. Let the dragons eat him.

9. Who told King Limhi that the wicked priests probably took the daughters? (Verses 17–18.)
    A. Alma.
    B. The Lamanite king.
    C. A little birdie again.
    D. Gideon.

10. Who pleaded with the Lamanite army not to destroy Limhi's people? (Verse 25.)
    A. Gideon.
    B. Limhi.
    C. Noah.
    D. The king of the Lamanites.

11. What didn't the Nephites have when they met the Lamanites? (Verses 24–26.)
    A. Arms.
    B. Legs.
    C. A positive attitude.
    D. Tents.

12. What happened the second time the Lamanites went to attack them? (Verse 26.)
    A. The Lamanites won.
    B. The Nephites won again.
    C. It was a tie game.
    D. They all went home in peace.

Ask your family what this teaches us about the power of fighting for a righteous cause.

Mosiah 20:21
The consequences of not listening to the prophet

Have someone read Mosiah 20:21 aloud and tell the main reason Limhi's people faced so many problems. (You might choose to review Mosiah 12:1–8 for what Abinadi prophesied.) Ask family members what the leaders of the Church today have advised us to do or not to do. What advantages can you see in following their counsel? Could there be benefits and blessings for obedience that we do not yet see? Share the following statement from "The Family: A Proclamation to the World": "We warn that individuals who violate covenants of chastity, who abuse spouse or offspring, or who fail to fulfill family responsibilities will one day stand accountable before God. Further, we warn that the disintegration of the family will bring upon individuals, communities, and nations the calamities foretold by ancient and modern prophets." ("The Family: A Proclamation to the World," *Ensign,* November 1995, p. 102.)

Encourage your family to follow the counsel of the prophet. Discuss what some consequences might be if we don't.

MOSIAH 21: LIMHI'S PEOPLE TRY TO ESCAPE FROM THE LAMANITES

Mosiah 21:1–4
Promises, oaths, and covenants

Ask your family to think of a time when someone made a promise to them but never kept it. Ask, "How did it make you feel? Can you remember a time when you made a promise and didn't keep it? How did that make you feel?" Tell your family that there is an interesting example of the power of a promise in Mosiah 21. Have them

search Mosiah 21:1–4 and look for why the Lamanites did not kill Limhi's people. Even though the Lamanites were cruel and hated the Nephites, how did they feel about their promises or oaths?

Ask your family what we call the promises we make with God. (Covenants.) What are some covenants we have made with our Heavenly Father? (See Mosiah 18:8–10.) Are we as careful about the promises we make with God, whom we love, as the Lamanites were about the promises they made to the Nephites, whom they hated? Discuss as a family what you could do to be more faithful in keeping your sacred covenants.

Mosiah 21:5–16
Why would we want to be humble?

Take turns reading the story in Mosiah 21:5–12 and have your family count the number of times Limhi's people tried to fight their way to freedom. Ask them why they think Limhi's people kept losing wars with the Lamanites. Have your family search Abinadi's prophecy in Mosiah 11:23–25 for answers to the following questions:

- What did Abinadi say would happen to these people if they did not repent?
- Who was the only one who could deliver them?
- What did they need to do before the Lord would hear their prayers?

Next read together Mosiah 21:13–16 and ask:

- What did Limhi's people do when fighting failed to deliver them?
- How did humbling themselves bring about more change than going to war?
- What was the Lord able to do for them that they were unable to do for themselves?

Ask your family what kinds of problems people have today that are like bondage? (For example, bad habits of all kinds, fear, pride, anger, addictions, and so on.) How could humbly pleading with the Lord help deliver us from bondage? (See

Ether 12:27.) Share some or all of the following insights from President Ezra Taft Benson and discuss how your family could use them to increase humility:

"God will have a humble people. Either we can choose to be humble or we can be compelled to be humble. Let us choose to be humble. . . .

"We can choose to humble ourselves by conquering enmity [hatred] toward our brothers and sisters, esteeming them as ourselves, and lifting them as high or higher than we are. . . .

"We can choose to humble ourselves by receiving counsel and chastisement. . . .

"We can choose to humble ourselves by forgiving those who have offended us. . . .

"We can choose to humble ourselves by rendering selfless service. . . .

"We can choose to humble ourselves by going on missions and preaching the word that can humble others. . . .

"We can choose to humble ourselves by getting to the temple more frequently. . . .

"We can choose to humble ourselves by confessing and forsaking our sins and being born of God. . . .

"We can choose to humble ourselves by loving God, submitting our will to His, and putting Him first in our lives." (Adapted from "Beware of Pride," *Ensign,* May 1989, pp. 6–7.)

Mosiah 21:18–24
The Lord sends Ammon to help rescue Limhi's people

Tie a family member's hands behind his or her back. Give every other family member a favorite snack to eat. While eating, ask the one tied up how his or her situation is like being in bondage. What would the person be willing to do to get out of it? Untie the family member and then read together and compare Mosiah 8:7 with Mosiah 21:14. Ask your family what Limhi's people wanted more than anything else. What did they try to get free? Then take turns reading Mosiah 21:18–24. Ask:

- How can you tell that Limhi's people were in bondage and lived in fear?
- Why did they want to find King Noah's priests?
- Whom did Limhi mistake "Ammon and his brethren" for?
- Why do you think Limhi had such great joy when he found out who they were?
- How might Ammon be an answer to Limhi's people's prayers? (See verse 36.)

Mosiah 21:25–28
What was discovered by Limhi's search party?

 Show your family the map of Book of Mormon Lands on p. 122 and have them locate the Land of Nephi (also called the Land of Lehi-Nephi), the Land of Zarahemla, and the Land of Desolation. Then take turns reading Mosiah 21:25–28. Ask the following questions:

- What did Limhi's search party finally discover?
- What did they think they had found? (Zarahemla.)
- Why was meeting Ammon a relief to Limhi?
- What did the search party bring back with them?

Review what this important record was by assigning the following scripture references to different family members: Mosiah 8:7; Mosiah 8:9; Mosiah 8:8, 10–11; and Mosiah 21:26. Have them study their references and be prepared to give the answers that are found in their verses.

- How large was the search party sent out by King Limhi? (See Mosiah 8:7.)
- How many plates made up the record Limhi's people found while searching for Zarahemla? (See Mosiah 8:9.)
- What were the plates made of? (See Mosiah 8:9.)
- Name some other things the search party found. (See Mosiah 8:8, 10–11.)

• What land did the search party think they had discovered? (See Mosiah 21:26.)

Mosiah 21:32–35
Why is it important to always be worthy?

Share the following story: While a young man was preparing for a mission, he was seriously hurt at work. He was taken to a hospital and prepared for surgery. While the young man was lying on a hospital gurney, his father, a worthy priesthood holder, asked the male nurse standing next to him if he was a member of the LDS church. "Yes," came the response, "Will you help me give my son a blessing?" The reply was never to be forgotten: "I can't. I'm not worthy." While the young man was lying there in pain listening to the conversation, he vowed to himself never to be in a position where his faith or priesthood could not be used to bless the life of another.

Discuss with your family why it is important to always be worthy. Then read together Mosiah 21:32–35. Ask the following questions:

• Who declined an opportunity to baptize Limhi and some of his people?
• Why did Ammon decline?
• How would you feel if you were in Ammon's position?
• What do we learn about Ammon's truthfulness?
• What can we do to make sure we are always worthy to exercise our faith or priesthood to benefit the life of another?

MOSIAH 22: THE LORD DELIVERS LIMHI'S PEOPLE

Mosiah 22:1–16
What is the advantage of counseling together?

Assign members of your family to play the following roles: a narrator, the Lamanites, the people of Limhi, Gideon, Ammon, and King Limhi. Depending on the size and age of your family, you might include animals and other characters in the story.

As the narrator reads Mosiah 21:1–16, have family members act out their role in the escape of Limhi's people. If there is a speaking part (such as Gideon), have that person read his or her lines from the scriptures. After the activity, discuss the following questions:

• Who came up with the idea for the people to escape? (See verses 3–6.)
• How did they escape? (See verses 11–14.)
• How did counseling together as a people help them come up with an escape plan? (See verses 1–3.)
• What is the advantage of counseling with those you trust before getting involved with something?
• Why would counseling with your parents, bishop, or other Church leaders be important?

Read Alma 37:35–37 with your family and bear your testimony of the importance of counseling most of all with your Heavenly Father.

Mosiah 22:10–14
Ammon leads Limhi's people out of bondage

 Before family scripture study, invite a family member to play the part of a prophet and prepare to read D&C 101:8–9 and Moroni 7:3. Review as a family Mosiah 21:13–15 and ask someone to summarize the situation of Limhi's people. Invite your family to imagine being Limhi's people. Tell them that the prophet (insert family member's name) has a message for us; then have the person read D&C 101:8–9. Ask your family if that message means the Lord does not love us. Why is the Lord sometimes slow to come to our rescue?

Read together Mosiah 22:10–14. Ask:

• How did the Lord finally rescue Limhi's people?

- Who did the Lord provide to lead them to safety?
- How did King Mosiah greet them?

Ask your family how this story is like their own escape from this world and into the arms of the Savior. Have your "prophet" read aloud Moroni 7:3.

MOSIAH 23–24: THE BONDAGE AND DELIVERANCE OF ALMA AND HIS PEOPLE

Mosiah 23:1–14
Is it good to have a king?

Tell your family that Mosiah 23–24 marks a switch from the story of King Limhi and his people to the story of Alma and his people. Ask for a volunteer to give a brief summary of what has happened to Alma and his people to this point. (If they need help, have them read the chapter heading for Mosiah 18.) Explain that Mosiah 23 picks up the account where Mosiah 18 ends.

Have a family member read Mosiah 23:6–7 and find what the people wanted Alma to be and how he responded to their desire. Make two columns on a sheet of paper. Label one column "Pros" and the other "Cons." Have your family search Mosiah 23:7–14 for the pros and cons of having a king. List their responses in the appropriate column.

Ask, "According to Alma, what kind of men make good kings, and who should be trusted to be a teacher or minister?" (See verses 8 and 14.) Then ask your family if they can think of an example of a good king and a bad king they have studied about recently in the Book of Mormon (for example, King Benjamin and King Noah). Ask them to contrast the qualities of the two kings.

Ask your family if they know what sort of government we will have when Jesus Christ comes

again. Read Alma 5:50 and D&C 38:21–22 and discuss what it will be like to live in that kingdom.

Mosiah 23:15–29
Why did Alma's people end up in bondage?

Have your family search Mosiah 23:15–20 and pick out phrases that describe what kind of people Alma's followers were. Allow each person to share a phrase he or she found. Then read together Mosiah 23:21–24 and ask what was going to happen to Alma's people. Ask what reasons are given in the verses why the Lord let Alma's righteous people be put in bondage.

Ask someone to read aloud Mosiah 11:23 and tell if Alma and his people repented when Abinadi first warned them to. Read together Mosiah 12:1–2 and discuss what other reason the Lord had for allowing Alma's people to be put in bondage. What does this teach us about the Lord's warnings and promises?

Take turns reading the rest of the story in Mosiah 23:25–39. Ask what happened to Alma's people even after they were honest and kind to the Lamanites. Discuss the following explanation by Elder Neal A. Maxwell of three reasons why affliction or suffering may come into our lives:

1. "Some things happen to us because of our own mistakes and our own sins. . . .

2. "Still other trials and tribulations come to us merely as a part of living. . . . We are not immunized against all inconvenience and difficulties nor against aging. . . .

3. "There is another dimension of suffering, and other challenges that come to us even though we seem to be innocent. These come to us because an omniscient Lord deliberately chooses to school us: 'Nevertheless the Lord seeth fit to chasten his people; yea he trieth their patience and their faith' (Mosiah 23:21)." (*All These Things Shall Give Thee Experience*, pp. 29–30.)

Ask, "Which of those reasons helps explain why Alma's people were placed in bondage?"

Ask your family to think of some of the trials and afflictions they have had or are having in their lives and decide if the cause is number 1, 2, or 3. What promise has the Lord made to those who put their trust and faith in him when faced with trials and challenges? (See Mosiah 23:22.)

Mosiah 24:8–25
Compare the escapes

Divide the family into two groups. Tell one group that they will be studying the escape of Limhi's people and the other group that they will be studying the escape of Alma's people. Using the chart below, have each group study their assigned verses and the associated questions.

Ask family members why they think the Lord blessed Alma and his people more quickly and abundantly than he blessed Limhi's people. What important lessons can we learn from their experience?

Mosiah 24:21–22
Do you remember to give thanks?

Ask your family if they have ever done something nice for someone and never received any thanks. How did they feel? Have family members read Mosiah 24:21–22 and find what Alma and his people remembered to do after they had been delivered from bondage. Ask why it is important to show gratitude. (See D&C 59:21.) Ask each family member to suggest a way to show more gratitude in your family and to Heavenly Father for your blessings.

MOSIAH 25: ALMA ORGANIZES THE CHURCH OF GOD

Mosiah 25:1–11
What did King Mosiah want his people to learn?

Have your family search Mosiah 25:1–6 and look for why Mosiah gathered his people together. Ask how long they think that might have taken to gather everyone into groups and then read all those records to them. Remind your family that our abridged (shorter) version of those records consists of sixteen chapters (Mosiah 9–24). What do you suppose King Mosiah wanted his people to gain from hearing those accounts?

To help answer that question, read Mosiah 25:7–11 together as a family and mark the words that describe how Mosiah's people reacted to those stories (such as amazement, joy, or sorrow). Discuss the following questions:

- What caused them to have "exceeding great joy"?
- What caused them to be "filled with sorrow"?
- What caused them to "give thanks to God"?
- Why were they filled with "pain and anguish"?

Review with your family the stories in Mosiah chapters 9–24 using the chapter headings and any other details you wish to add. As you review each chapter, ask your family to make a list of principles or truths that Mosiah would want his people to remember. Here are just a few examples:

- Zeniff's story illustrates how obedience and faith can preserve freedom.

Limhi's People	Question	Alma's People
Mosiah 21:10–14.	When did each group decide to turn to the Lord in prayer for help?	Mosiah 23:27–28; 24:9–12.
Mosiah 21:15.	How did the Lord respond to their pleadings?	Mosiah 24:13–15.
Mosiah 22:1–13.	How were they able to escape?	Mosiah 24:16–20.

- Noah shows that wickedness leads to bondage.
- Limhi demonstrates how repentance and humility bring deliverance.
- Abinadi proves that the words of the prophets are true.
- Alma illustrates the power of patience and faith.

Add to your list the principles that your family members suggest and then discuss with your family how those truths would be valuable to Mosiah's people and could be used to guide our choices today.

Mosiah 25:12
What's in a name?

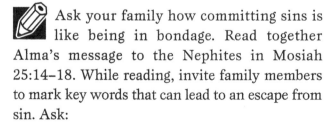 Ask your family if they know of anyone who has been adopted. Explain that it would be nice if everyone could grow up with their birth parents in happy families, but how can being adopted be a blessing in someone's life? Have your family read Mosiah 25:12 and tell who did not want to be called by the name of their fathers and why. What name did they want instead? What does that name tell us about what they believed and how they wanted to live?

Ask your family what other name we, as members of the Church, take upon ourselves. (See D&C 20:77.) What does that name say about what we believe and how we want to live?

Mosiah 25:14–18
Jesus Christ the Deliverer

Ask your family how committing sins is like being in bondage. Read together Alma's message to the Nephites in Mosiah 25:14–18. While reading, invite family members to mark key words that can lead to an escape from sin. Ask:

- What did Alma teach the people to do? (Verse 15.)
- What did he teach them to remember? (Verse 16.)

- Why is it important to remember who delivers us from bondage?
- What did the people then want to do? (Verses 17–18.)

Ask your family to look at the words they marked in those verses. Ask them to tell how those things can help deliver us from the bondage of sin. What is one thing we do each week to help us remember the Savior that they did not do in the days of Alma? How does taking the sacrament help us to remember our baptism and escape sin?

Mosiah 25:19–23
How were the Churches Alma established similar to our wards?

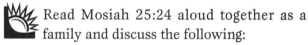 Have a family member read Mosiah 25:19–23. Ask family members to point out similarities between the churches Alma established and the wards in our stake. Ask your family how many churches there were in the land of Zarahemla. How was this like organizing a stake? What might they have called this stake?

Mosiah 25:24
What does it take to be the "people of God"?

Read Mosiah 25:24 aloud together as a family and discuss the following:

- What were Mosiah's people called?
- What did the Lord bless them with?
- What did the people do to receive those great blessings? (See Mosiah 25:15–18.)

Ask your family to read D&C 41:1 and tell what the Lord calls members of the Church today. Ask:

- What does the Lord want to give us?
- What does he say we must do to receive those blessings?
- Why will some people be cursed instead?
- What do you think it means to "hear" him? (Compare Mosiah 25:15–18.)

This may be a good time to express your gratitude for all of Heavenly Father's blessings to your family.

MOSIAH 26: TROUBLE WITH THE "RISING GENERATION"

Mosiah 26:1–6
Hard hearts vs. soft hearts

 Read Alma 26:1–6 as a family and find the phrases "did not," "could not," and "would not" every time they appear. Make a list of the things the "rising generation" *did not, could not,* and *would not* do.

Show your family a rock and a pillow and ask which of these best represents the hearts of that rising generation. Ask them if they remember when Laman and Lemuel had this same problem. Have them read 1 Nephi 2:12, 16 and compare Nephi's heart with Laman's and Lemuel's. Why was Nephi's heart soft? (He cried unto the Lord, the Lord softened his heart, and he believed.)

Now have your family look again at the list they made from Mosiah 26:1–6. Ask them which of the "nots" was the cause of the people's hard hearts (would not pray or call upon God) and which were the result of having a hard heart (all the others). What else happened because of their hard hearts? (See verse 6.)

Discuss with your family what people should do if they feel their hearts getting hard and their understanding and faith wavering. (See 1 Nephi 2:16.)

Mosiah 26:7–14
What can prayer do for you?

 As a family read Mosiah 26:7–14. Ask:

- What was the problem brought to Alma?
- Who did Alma try to delegate the problem to? (Verse 12.)
- Why did King Mosiah return the problem to Alma? (Verse 12.)
- What did Alma do to find the solution to his problem? (Verse 13.)

- Why is it so important to inquire of the Lord when we are faced with problems?
- Has there been a time in your life that you have asked the Lord to help you with a problem?
- How did the Lord help you with your problem?

Tell your family how you feel about prayer and the blessings that have come to your family through prayer. Sing or read the words to "Secret Prayer" (*Hymns,* no. 144).

Mosiah 26:15–20
What blessings came to Alma that can come to you?

 Have a member of your family move out of sight and read Alma 26:15–19 as if using the voice of the Lord. Have your family mark the seven times the Lord told Alma that he was blessed. Ask your family which of Alma's blessings they think is the most wonderful. (See verse 20.) What did Alma do that caused the Lord to promise him such a great blessing? Did this mean that Alma was now perfect?

Tell your family that we can also do what Alma did and receive the same blessing. Share the following statement from Elder Bruce R. McConkie: "When the Saints of God chart a course of righteousness, when they gain sure testimonies of the truth and divinity of the Lord's work, when they keep the commandments, when they overcome the world, when they put first in their lives the things of God's kingdom: when they do all these things, and then depart this life—though they have not yet become perfect—they shall nonetheless gain eternal life in our Father's kingdom; and eventually they shall be perfect as God their Father and Christ His Son are perfect." ("The Dead Who Die in the Lord," *Ensign,* November 1976, p. 107.)

Mosiah 26:21–24
Do we want to be sheep?

 Ask your family to imagine that they could choose to be any kind of animal in the world. Have each person share what he or she would choose and explain why. Have your family follow along as you read Mosiah 26:21. Ask, "Does anybody want to be a sheep?" Then read together Mosiah 26:22–24 and John 10:14–15, 27–28. Have your family mark all the reasons they find why we all want to be Christ's sheep.

Mosiah 26:25–28
What if your whole family got amnesia except you?

Invite one of the children in your family to imagine the following situation: One day you walk home from school and find the house locked when you get home. You try your key and it doesn't work. You then ring the doorbell and your mom answers, but instead of welcoming you in she says, "Who are you?" Your brothers and sisters are all there, but no one seems to know you. You try to explain that you live there, but they just look at you as if you are crazy. It seems as though your whole family has got amnesia. They finally tell you to stop playing silly games and just go find your own house.

Give the child a minute to really think about that situation and then ask how he or she would feel.

Read together Alma 26:25–28 and ask your family what will happen at the judgment that is like the story above. Who did Jesus say will not get to go home anymore? Where will they have to go instead? What would you be willing to do to make sure Jesus welcomed you home?

Mosiah 26:29–32
Who are we to forgive?

If possible, remind your family of a time recently when one family member did something accidentally to upset another family member. How did each person handle the situation? Read together Mosiah 26:29–31 and discuss the following questions:

- What does the Lord do about our sins when we repent?

- How often will he forgive us?
- What are we to do with those who trespass against us and then repent?
- What will become of us if we choose not to forgive?

Ask your family to suppose someone sins against them and they are not sorry and they do not repent. What are we supposed to do then? To help answer that question, read together D&C 64:9–11 and ask:

- What did the Lord say about those who refuse to forgive?
- Whom did the Lord say we must forgive?
- How would this apply to those who are not sorry for their sins?
- Why would it be better to forgive even those who are glad they harmed us than to continue to be angry about it?
- What will anger and contention do to our spiritual progression?

Share the following statement by Elder Marion D. Hanks: "It is reported that President Brigham Young once said that he who takes offense when no offense was intended is a fool, and he who takes offense when offense *was* intended is usually a fool. It was then explained that there are two courses of action to follow when one is bitten by a rattlesnake. One may, in anger, fear, or vengefulness, pursue the creature and kill it. Or he may make full haste to get the venom out of his system. If we pursue the latter course, we will likely survive, but if we attempt to follow the former, we may not be around long enough to finish what we started." (*Love*, pp. 95–96.)

Mosiah 26:32–39
Why were the names of some "blotted out"?

Ask your family if they know what it means to be excommunicated from the Church. Tell them that Mosiah 26:32–36 explains what that means, but in these verses it is called something else. Take turns reading those verses and ask:

- What did the Lord tell Alma to do with Church members who would not repent?
- What did he do with those who did repent?
- What do we call it today when someone's name is "blotted out"? (Excommunicated.)

Have your family search Mosiah 26:37–39 and pick out words or phrases that describe what happened to the Church after Alma "did regulate all the affairs of the church" according to the Lord's instructions. How does that help explain why sometimes people are excommunicated from the Church today?

MOSIAH 27: THE CONVERSION OF ALMA AND THE FOUR SONS OF KING MOSIAH

Mosiah 27:1–7
The relationship among unity, equality, and peace

Ask your family if they would like to have the Lord visit your home tomorrow. What kinds of things would they do to prepare? Have them read Mosiah 27:7 and find out who did get that opportunity. Read as a family Mosiah 27:1–5 and make a list of what the Nephites did that made it possible for the Lord to "visit them and prosper them." Ask how many things on their list have to do with equality. Have someone read aloud D&C 38:27; 70:14 and explain why he or she thinks unity and equality are essential to having Jesus Christ visit us.

Have someone read Mosiah 27:6 aloud and find what additional blessing came a result of their obedience. What can we do in our home to bring this peace so we can be prepared for the Lord to "visit" us?

Mosiah 27:8–10
What was the mission of Alma the Younger and the sons of Mosiah?

 Sing as a family "I Hope They Call Me on a Mission" (*Children's Songbook*, p. 169).

Discuss different missions that family members have served and ask younger family members to tell where they would like to serve. Ask how missions can bless the missionary. How can a mission bless the Church?

Then read Mosiah 27:8–10 as a family and find the kind of mission Alma and the sons of Mosiah went on. As you read, look for words and phrases that show the serious mistakes Alma and his friends were committing. You may want to have your family put a number next to each sin listed. Ask your family to share how this "mission" affected Alma and his friends. How did it influence other people? How did it influence the Church? Why do you think some people rebel against that which is good?

Mosiah 27:11–24
Do I need a conversion experience like Alma the Younger's?

Write the following names where all can see them: Paul the Apostle, Enos, and Alma the Younger. Ask your family what these names have in common. Tell a little about each one so your family can see that they all had remarkable conversion experiences. Take turns reading Mosiah 27:11–24. Use the following questions to help you discuss what you read:

- Why did the Lord send an angel to deal with Alma and the sons of Mosiah? (See verses 14, 16.)
- What did Alma and the four sons of Mosiah hear and feel?
- What happened to Alma when the angel left?
- How did Alma's father feel when his son was carried in unconscious and helpless?
- How long did they fast and pray for the unconscious Alma the Younger?
- How had Alma the Younger changed after he "received his strength"?

Ask your family if any of them have had an experience like Alma's. If someone hasn't had such an experience does that mean he or she is not converted? To help answer that question, share the following statement from President Ezra Taft Benson:

"We must be careful, as we seek to become more and more godlike, that we do not become discouraged and lose hope. Becoming Christlike is a lifetime pursuit and very often involves growth and change that is slow, almost imperceptible. The scriptures record remarkable accounts of men whose lives changed dramatically, in an instant, as it were: Alma the Younger, Paul on the road to Damascus, Enos praying far into the night, King Lamoni. Such astonishing examples of the power to change even those steeped in sin give confidence that the Atonement can reach even those deepest in despair.

"But we must be cautious as we discuss these remarkable examples. Though they are real and powerful, they are the exception more than the rule. For every Paul, for every Enos, and for every King Lamoni, there are hundreds and thousands of people who find the process of repentance much more subtle, much more imperceptible. Day by day they move closer to the Lord, little realizing they are building a godlike life. They live quiet lives of goodness, service, and commitment. They are like the Lamanites, who the Lord said 'were baptized with fire and with the Holy Ghost, and they *knew it not*' (3 Ne. 9:20; italics added)." ("A Mighty Change of Heart," *Ensign,* October 1989, p. 5.)

Have family members write their testimonies in their journal. Make sure they date the entry so they can review it in a year. Help your children read their entry from time to time and notice the change in their testimony and level of conversion.

Mosiah 27:25–27
What is a "new creature"?

Make available a small board, a hammer, and a nail. Have a family member drive the nail slightly into the board. Explain that driving the nail into the wood is like committing sin. Have another family member pull the nail out of the board with the claw of the hammer. Explain

that pulling the nail out of the board is like repentance. Invite another family member to touch the small hole on the board where the nail was. Tell the family that the hole reminds us of our sin so that we will never repeat it.

Ask your family how they feel about this lesson on repentance. Is it true doctrine? After several responses, have the family read Mosiah 27:25–27. Ask your family if a board with holes in it is a good symbol for being "changed . . . to a state of righteousness" and becoming "new creatures"? Why or why not? Share the following statement from Elder Jeffrey R. Holland:

"We learn that when repentance is complete we are born again and leave behind forever the self we once were. To me, none of the many approaches to teaching repentance falls more short than the well-intentioned suggestion that 'although a nail may be removed from a wooden post, there will forever be a hole in that post.' We know that repentance (the removal of that nail, if you will) can be a very long and painful and difficult task. . . . But where repentance is possible and its requirements are faithfully pursued and completed, there is no 'hole left in the post' for the bold reason that it is no longer the same post. It is a new post. We can start again, utterly clean, with a new will and a new way of life. Through repentance we are changed to what Alma calls 'new creatures' (Mosiah 27:26). . . . Repentance and baptism allow Christ to purify our lives in the blood of the Lamb and we are clean again. What we were, we never have to be again. . . . Christ is the power behind all repentance." ("Alma, Son of Alma," *Ensign,* March 1977, pp. 82–83.)

Hold up a new board with no holes in it. Ask your family what happens when we truly repent. (We become a "new creature" or a "new person.") How do we become "new"? (We are changed by the power of the Savior.) Testify to your family that it really is possible to become "new creatures."

Mosiah 27:28–31
Sorrowing sin vs. freeing forgiveness

Give each family member a sheet of paper. Have them fold it in thirds and label each column with one of the following headings:

Feelings that come with the recognition of sin.

Feelings that come with forgiveness.

What we will do when the Savior comes.

Read together Mosiah 27:28–31 and have your family look for words or phrases that fit in each column. Have them write what they find in the proper column. Ask your family what advantages they see in repenting and being forgiven before Christ comes. What does forgiveness free us from? Can you think of any commandments that you would not be willing to live to have that freedom?

Mosiah 27:32–37
How can you tell when someone has become a "new creature"?

Quickly review Mosiah 27:8–10 and summarize what Alma and the sons of Mosiah were like in those verses. Then read together Mosiah 27:32–37 with your family and note the changes that had come into their lives. Make a list of things Alma and the sons of Mosiah did that showed how deep their conversion was. Your list might include the following:

- They told everyone their conversion story.
- They taught Church members the importance of keeping the commandments.
- They tried to repair the damage they had done by confessing their sins to all they may have harmed.

Discuss with your family how they can tell that Alma, Ammon, Aaron, Omner, and Himni had become "new creatures." What blessings came to these young men and to others because of their deep conversion?

MOSIAH 28: MISSIONARIES INSTEAD OF KINGS

Mosiah 28:1–7
What are the attitudes of great missionaries?

Invite your family to list reasons why people go on missions. Have family members who have served a mission tell their reasons for going. Ask one of them if his or her reasons changed between the beginning and end of the mission. How do our feelings about *why* we do missionary work affect the way we do it?

Read together Mosiah 28:1–9 and have your family mark the reasons the sons of Mosiah desired to serve a mission. These reasons may include:

- To "bring [the Lamanites] to a knowledge of . . . God." (Verse 2.)
- To "convince them of the iniquity of their fathers" and thus "cure them of their hatred towards the Nephites." (Verse 2.)
- To help Lamanites "rejoice in the Lord their God." (Verse 2.)
- Help bring about friendly relations between Nephites and Lamanites, curing contentions in the land. (See verse 2.)
- To declare salvation to "every creature." (Verse 3.)
- Because the thought of anyone enduring endless torment made them "quake and tremble." (Verse 3.)
- Because the Spirit of the Lord had cleansed their souls and they wanted others to have the same opportunity. (See verse 4.)

Discuss the impact each reason listed would likely have on their efforts. Ask:

- What and how would they teach?
- What types of people would they teach and how would they treat them?
- How might these attitudes help us better share the gospel as member missionaries?

Elder Dallin H. Oaks counseled, "I hope no person we approach with an invitation to hear the message of the restored gospel feels that we are acting out of any reason other than a genuine love for them and an unselfish desire to share something we know to be precious. If we lack this love for others, we should pray for it." ("Sharing the Gospel," *Ensign,* November 2001, p. 8.)

Encourage family members to pray for "the Spirit of the Lord [to] work upon them" (Mosiah 28:4) and help them have the attitudes of Mosiah's sons toward sharing the gospel with other people.

Mosiah 28:10–16
Name those plates

Cut out six strips of paper. Write on three strips the following: Plates of brass, Plates of Nephi, Plates of Gold. Then write these phrases on the three remaining strips: Plates obtained by Nephi and brothers; Sacred writings of the Nephites; Record found by Limhi's people. Have your family read Mosiah 28:10–11 and identify all the different records Mosiah possessed. As they name the records, place that strip of paper on the floor in front of you. Lay the rest of the strips on the floor in random order and ask your family to match them. (The most unfamiliar records are the plates of gold found by Limhi's people. You may need to review Mosiah 8:7–9 to recall how that record was found and how it ended up in the hands of Mosiah.)

Read together Mosiah 28:13–16 and ask the following questions:

- How was Mosiah able to translate the "plates of gold" found by Limhi's people?
- Why does the Lord sometimes preserve records like this?
- What do we call a person with the gift to translate?
- In what ways are Mosiah and Joseph Smith similar? (See Joseph Smith—History 1:34–35.)

Discuss how this story can help increase testimonies of prophets, seers, and revelators living today.

Mosiah 28:17–20
Why is it necessary for me to know about the book of Ether?

Ask your family if they have ever read a book that was so good it made them laugh and cry. Invite them to tell about it. Explain that Mosiah's people had a similar experience with a book Mosiah translated from gold plates. Read together Mosiah 28:17–19 and discuss the following questions:

- What is the name of this book today? (The book of Ether. See the heading to that book.)
- How did this record affect Mosiah's people? (They mourned, but they also rejoiced.)
- What was "expedient" (necessary) for "all people" to know?

To learn more about this book and to see why Mormon considered it to be so important, take turns reading some of the chapter headings of the book of Ether. As you read, have family members look for (1) things that might cause people to mourn, (2) things that might cause people to rejoice, and (3) things that are so important that everyone needs to know about them.

MOSIAH 29: A NEW FORM OF GOVERNMENT

Mosiah 29:1–24
What makes one form of government better than another?

Remind your family that on September 11, 2001, a terrible tragedy occurred in the United States of America. Ask:

- What happened on that date?
- Where were you when you heard the news?
- What effect did this tragedy have on American patriotism?
- What feelings went through you as you heard the news?

Read together Article of Faith 1:12 or have a

family member recite it. Talk about what is required of the citizens of the United States.

Next take turns reading Mosiah 29:5–9 and list some concerns Mosiah had about his country being ruled by a king. Read Mosiah 29:11 and ask what solution King Mosiah proposed. Ask, "According to Mosiah 29:12 what are the advantages of having judges who are men of God in office?" Tell your family to look at Mosiah 29:13 and mark what Mosiah said about when it is best to have a king in leadership.

Read Mosiah 29:14–18 and ask:

- What traits does a good king possess? (Verses 14–15.)
- What can occur when a wicked king comes to power? (Verse 17–18.)
- What great leader led the children of Israel through the Red Sea on dry ground? (Moses.)
- Who led the pioneers from Nauvoo to the Salt Lake Valley? (Brigham Young.)
- What made Mosiah, Moses, and Brigham Young great leaders? (See Mosiah 29:40.)

Tell your family that one of the great keys to successful leadership is found in being righteous. Read D&C 121:41–46 and find the traits that make a good leader in the Church or in the world. Ask your family to name a few of their favorites from these verses.

Mosiah 29:13
Will we ever have a king again?

Ask your family which of the following they think is the ideal form of government:

- Monarchy (government ruled by a king or queen).
- Anarchy (no government or law and order).
- Theocracy (government ruled by officials regarded as divinely inspired).
- Democracy (a government in which the supreme power is held by the people).
- Republic (a government in which elected officials represent the will of the people).

- Dictatorship (a government or country in which absolute power is held by a dictator).

Ask which form of government exists in the United States of America. If they are not sure, ask them to say the Pledge of Allegiance, which has the answer. After they come to a conclusion of the best form of government, ask them to read Mosiah 29:13 and look for what form of government could be the best. Have someone read Revelation 17:14 and tell who that king will be. Which form of government will be on the earth during the Millennium?

Read the following statement: "In the Church of Christ where the government is that of the Kingdom of Heaven, neither autocracy nor democracy obtains, but government by Common Consent. That is to say, the initiative in all that pertains to the government of the Church rests with the Head of the Church, even our Lord Jesus Christ, and He exercises this sovereign function through his authorized servants, upon whom He has bestowed the Holy Priesthood; but it is the privilege of the people to accept, or reject, His laws and ordinances, for God has given every individual free agency. Obedience must be voluntary. The government of the Church has been called a *Theodemocracy*. It is the form of government that will be general during the Millennium." (Hyrum M. Smith and Janne M. Sjodahl, *The Doctrine and Covenants Commentary*, pp. 131–32.)

Mosiah 29:25–27
"By the voice of the people"

Have your family take a vote on any issue you decide (for example, what to have for dinner, who is to teach family home evening, or where to go for a family activity). Discuss these questions:

- Is it important for every family member to vote? Why?
- Should each family member's vote count the same? Why?
- Why is it important to express your opinion?

Ask your family if they have any idea of what percentage of people vote in a national election? (It ranges between 20 and 30 percent.) Ask:

- What are some possible reasons a person might not vote in an election?
- Who is responsible to elect righteous leaders?
- How do we get righteous people to run for political office?
- If we have only 30 percent of people voting in an election, who might be to blame when government leaders don't live up to people's expectations?

Invite your family to read Mosiah 29:27 and mark the words *if* and *then* in that verse. Ask, "What would happen if most of the people chose evil?" Tell your family that an *Ensign* article identified four governmental principles stated in Mosiah 29 that guided the reign of the judges. They are listed below. Read Mosiah 29:25–27 to your family and have them mark those four principles.

- The concept that law, not force, authority, or personality, rules in society. (Verse 25.)
- The procedure that law will be determined by the voice of the people, supporting and preserving their freedom. (Verse 25.)
- The recognition that correct principles of law are given to man by God through the prophets. (Verse 25.)
- A commitment to the necessity for a spiritual foundation of that law in society. (Verse 27.)

(See James R. Moss, "Six Nephite Judges: A Study in Integrity," *Ensign,* September 1977, pp. 61–62.)

Read the following statement by Elder Royden G. Derrick, a member of the presidency of the Seventy: "The history of the people of ancient America, recorded in the Book of Mormon, teaches that civilizations are built on moral foundations; that when people are morally strong, they do well; that when they are morally weak, they suffer. It teaches us that freedom cannot outlive morality and that freedom is not free—it must be earned." ("Moral Values and Rewards," *Ensign,* May 1981, p. 66.)

Ask how "the voice of the people" helps us and our leaders remain responsible. What "checks and balances" do we have in our government today to make sure our leaders don't overstep their bounds? (The three branches of government.) Read Mosiah 29:28–29 and ask what system of checks and balances the Nephites had?

Mosiah 29:40–43
Qualities of a great leader

Invite your family to name some of the wicked leaders in the history of the world. Ask, "In what different ways did these leaders come to power?" (Vote, murder, overthrow, and so on.) Ask your family to name some righteous leaders of the world. Invite your family to name some leadership differences between the two groups of leaders.

Read Mosiah 29:40–43 with your family to find what traits Mosiah had that caused the people to love him. Tell your family that one trait of a great leader is to train someone to take his or her place. Ask your family who presided and became the first chief judge after the death of Mosiah. What qualities did he possess that allowed people to trust him? (Verse 43.)

ALMA

The book of Alma covers from 91 to 53 B.C., a total of thirty-nine years in 161 pages of history. The Book of Alma is named after Alma the Younger and was translated from the large plates of Nephi, which were abridged by the prophet-historian Mormon. The book tells of the struggles of the Nephites in both the Land of Zarahemla and the Land of Nephi. In these chapters are recorded some of the greatest spiritual blessings, as well as some of the most terrible wickedness and wars in the book of Mormon.

ALMA 1: PRIESTCRAFT IS INTRODUCED

Alma 1:1–5
What is priestcraft?

Share a favorite story about the service given by your bishop, home teacher, or other priesthood or auxiliary leader. Have your family list some of the many ways Church leaders serve your family. Ask them how much money the Church pays the leaders to do their job? Why do you think they do so much service for free?

Read Alma 1:1–5 together. Ask:

- Who was the wicked man who came among the Nephites at this time? (You will find his name in verse 15.)
- According to verse 3, what did he want to change about the leaders of the Church?
- What dangers are there when the church leader is paid to preach? (He will preach what the people want to hear and not what God would have them hear.)
- According to verse 4, what did he want to change about the doctrine of the Church?
- Why would some people want to believe that doctrine?
- Do people today teach similar doctrines?

Have someone read Alma 1:12 aloud and tell what preaching for popularity and money is called. Next read 2 Nephi 26:29 together and ask your family why Nehor's teachings are a good example of priestcraft. Compare Nehor's priestcraft with the descriptions of the righteous priests in Alma 1:26–28. What did the righteous priests do to combat priestcraft? How does your bishop or other priesthood leader compare with the righteous leaders discussed in Alma 1? Invite a family member to tell why they are glad that our prophet does not just teach us what the world wants to hear.

Alma 1:7–17
Compare Gideon's death with Nehor's

Read Alma 1:7–9 with your family and ask them if they remember the role Gideon played when Limhi's people were in bondage to the Lamanites in the Book of Mosiah. As a family, go to the index under the heading of "Gideon" on page 124 and read about Gideon. Ask, "What were some of the good things Gideon did? Why do you think Gideon was willing to defend the Church, even though it meant he might be killed?"

Read about Nehor's death in Alma 1:10–17. Ask your family to describe the differences between his death and Gideon's death. Which of those two men do you think Heavenly Father was pleased with and why?

Alma 1:19–31
How should we deal with persecution?

 Ask your family if they have ever felt persecuted for choosing the right. Share with them any personal experiences you have had with persecution. You may want to share some Church history stories about the early Saints being persecuted in Missouri or Nauvoo.

Take turns reading Alma 1:19–28 and look for the persecutions the Saints were suffering about 90 b.c. Discuss the following questions:

- What two ways did the Church members deal with the persecution? (Verses 22, 25.)
- Why did some fight with those who persecuted them? (Verse 22.)
- What happened to those who turned to violence? (Verse 24.)
- What could you learn from their example?
- What happened to those who were patient in persecution? (Verses 25–28.)

Read Matthew 5:11–12 and look for what the Savior said about those who were persecuted for righteousness' sake. What evidence did you see that these Nephites were blessed for the persecution they faced? Read Alma 1:29–31 as a family, and make a list of the ways the Nephites prospered because they endured persecution in a righteous way.

Alma 1:25–33
How does our faith cause us to be different from others?

Have family members search Alma 1:25–33 and mark or list each place that describes the righteousness of members of the Church. After reading the verses, have your family share the things they marked. Now, as a family, read Alma 1:32 and mark how those who were not members of the Church were different. Ask, "Can that same contrast be seen today between faithful Church members and those who

do not believe? Are we becoming more like the world?" Share the following quotation from President Gordon B. Hinckley: "I lift a warning voice to our people. We have moved too far toward the mainstream." ("Look to the Future," *Ensign,* November 1997, p. 69.) Share with your family what that statement means to you. As a family, identify ways members of Christ's church should be different from the world.

ALMA 2: THE LORD SPARES THE RIGHTEOUS NEPHITES

Alma 2:1–7
Why is it important to let our voices be heard?

Read the following statement to your family:

"In this election year we urge Church members *to register to vote,* to study the issues and candidates carefully and prayerfully and then vote for those they believe will most nearly carry out their ideas of good government. Latter-day Saints are under special obligation to seek out and then uphold leaders who will act with integrity and are 'wise,' 'good,' and 'honest' (see Doctrine and Covenants 98:10)." (Gordon B. Hinckley, Thomas S. Monson, and James E. Faust, Priesthood Bulletin, 30 August 2002.)

Have a family member express in his or her own words what the First Presidency wants us to do about elections. How might following this counsel bless us as a people? As a family, read Alma 2:1–7. Ask:

- What kind of a man was Amlici?
- How did he want to change the government?
- What did he want to do to the Church?
- What was the outcome of the election?
- What might have happened if enough Nephites had chosen not to get involved?

Invite your family to mark footnote 7a in their

scriptures; then read Mosiah 29:25–27. Discuss why it is important that members of your family make sure their voices are heard.

Alma 2:7–11
Whom do you chose to follow?

 Divide your family into two groups and have them sit on opposite sides of the room. Tell one side that they love the color blue; tell the other they love red. Have them tell each other why their color is best. After some reasons are given, ask your family what could happen to the family if they each had serious feelings about their color. Can you think of any examples where something like this has happened?

Read together Alma 2:7–11 and ask someone to explain what this election was all about. Ask:

- How did the Nephites react when they won the election?
- What did the followers of Amlici do even though they lost the election?
- How were these people "distinguished" from each other?

Read together Mosiah 1:11; 5:7–9 and have someone tell what name King Benjamin wanted his people to be "distinguished" by. Discuss the following questions:

- Why would you rather be known as a follower of Jesus Christ than a follower of a man like Amlici?
- Are there people today who make the mistake of forsaking the Savior to follow those who are popular with the world?
- What is the difference between what the Savior wants for you and what worldly people want from you?
- What could we do as a family to avoid being deceived by worldly things?

Alma 2:15–31
Is war ever necessary?

 Ask your family if they think it is ever necessary to go to war. Invite them to describe situations where war might be justified. Share the following quotation from David O. McKay:

"There are . . . two conditions which may justify a truly Christian man to enter—mind you, I say *enter, not begin*—a war: (1) an attempt to dominate and to deprive another of his free agency, and (2) loyalty to his country. Possibly there is a third, . . . defense of a weaker nation that is being unjustly crushed by a strong, ruthless one." (David O McKay, *Gospel Ideals,* p. 287.)

Discuss with family members any wars that might fit President McKay's description. As a family read Alma 2:9–10, 15. Ask:

- Were the Nephites justified in going to war? Why?
- What principle given by President McKay were the Amlicites breaking?
- How might the innocence of the Nephites help them in their coming battle with the Amlicites?

As a family, take turns reading Alma 2:16–31. The following questions might be useful as you discuss each verse:

- Who was the leader of the Nephite Army? (Verse 16.)
- Why were there fewer Nephites killed than Amlicites? (Verse 18.)
- What did Alma do to keep track of the movement of the Amalicites? (Verse 21.)
- What did the Nephite spies discover about the Amlicites? (Verse 24.)
- Why were the Nephites victorious even though they were outnumbered? (Verses 28, 30.)
- Who fought with and slew Amlici? (See verses 29–31.)

Testify that we may face wars among men but every day we face wars with devils. Discuss the principles we learn from Alma and the Nephites that would apply to the battles we face each day.

ALMA 3: THE AMLICITES MARK THEMSELVES

Alma 3:4–19

Should we "mark" ourselves?

As a family, make a list of names of people you have studied in the Book of Mormon. After the list is made, have your family classify each individual listed as righteous or wicked. Mark the wicked ones with a red dot. An example is provided below:

Lehi	Sariah	Nephi	Jacob
Laman●	Lemuel●	Sam	Joseph
King Benjamin	Nehor●	Amulon●	Enos
King Noah●	Abinadi	Sherem●	Alma

As you read together Alma 3:4–19, tell your family to look for ways individuals or groups of people are marked or distinguished from each other. After reading the verses, discuss the following questions:

- What did the Amlicites do to distinguish themselves? (Verses 4, 13.)
- How were the Lamanites distinguished from Nephites? (Verses 5–6.)
- Why did the Lord set a mark upon Laman and Lemuel and those who associated with them? (Verses 6–8.)
- Why would God want to keep his people separate from unbelievers? (Verse 8.)
- What happened to those who "did mingle his seed with that of the Lamanites"? (Verse 9.)
- How were the markings of the Amlicites a fulfillment of prophecy? (Verses 14–19.)
- In what way did the Amlicites and the Lamanites "bring upon themselves the curse"? (Verse 19.)
- What are some of the ways individuals or groups "mark" themselves today? (Dress, language, entertainment, diet.)

Share with your family President Gordon B. Hinckley's remarks on the importance of keeping our bodies holy:

"Did you ever think that your body is holy? You are a child of God. Your body is His creation. Would you disfigure that creation with portrayals of people, animals, and words painted into your skin?

"I promise you that the time will come, if you have tattoos, that you will regret your actions. They cannot be washed off. They are permanent. Only by an expensive and painful process can they be removed. If you are tattooed, then probably for the remainder of your life you will carry it with you. I believe the time will come when it will be an embarrassment to you. Avoid it. We, as your Brethren who love you, plead with you not to become so disrespectful of the body which the Lord has given you.

"May I mention earrings and rings placed in other parts of the body. These are not manly. They are not attractive. You young men look better without them, and I believe you will feel better without them. As for the young women, you do not need to drape rings up and down your ears. One modest pair of earrings is sufficient.

"I mention these things because again they concern your bodies. How truly beautiful is a well-groomed young woman who is clean in body and mind. She is a daughter of God in whom her Eternal Father can take pride. How handsome is a young man who is well groomed. He is a son of God, deemed worthy of holding the holy priesthood of God. He does not need tattoos or earrings on or in his body. The First Presidency and the Quorum of the Twelve are all united in counseling against these things." ("A Prophet's Counsel and Prayer for Youth," *Ensign*, January 2001, pp. 7–8.)

Ask your family if we can mark ourselves *positively* as well as *negatively* in such areas as dress and appearance, language, entertainment, Sabbath observance, and so on. Have them share examples. (Now would be a good opportunity to refer to the *"For the Strength of Youth"* pamphlet and discuss the guidelines and standards the First Presidency has given in these areas.)

Alma 3:26–27
Who pays your wages?

 Make two checks, one from "The Heavenly Bank" and another from "The Other Place Bank." Leave them blank where they say "Pay to the order of," and instead of filling in the dollar amount, on "The Heavenly Bank" check, write "eternal happiness." On "The Other Place Bank," check write "eternal misery." Also leave the signature line blank. Show family members the two checks and ask which one they would like to have their name on. Have them read Alma 3:26–27 and find what determines which "wages" we will receive. Ask whose signature they think would be on each check, and have them list specific things they could do to help make sure they get the check they want.

ALMA 4: ALMA BEARS DOWN IN "PURE TESTIMONY"

Alma 4:2–5
Why do the people of Zarahemla mourn?

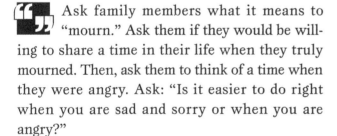 Ask family members what it means to "mourn." Ask them if they would be willing to share a time in their life when they truly mourned. Then, ask them to think of a time when they were angry. Ask: "Is it easier to do right when you are sad and sorry or when you are angry?"

To help answer that question have them read Alma 4:2–5 and ask:

- How did the Nephites feel about the terrible battles they had with the Lamanites?
- What reasons did the Nephites have to mourn?
- What did the Nephites believe was the cause of their afflictions?
- What did they do when they realized that their afflictions were caused by their own disobedience?

- How might they have behaved differently if they had gotten really angry and blamed the Lamanites for the war?

Share the following statement:

"When we are out for revenge we blame, accuse, and provoke others to wrath and then we blame them for it. Only when we quit seeing each other in such self-justifying ways can lasting, substantial changes take place. In other words, it is not until we quit looking to the other for change, begin to be honest about ourselves, and take responsibility for our own behavior that a change of heart can take place." (C. Richard Chidester, "A Change of Heart: Key to Harmonious Relationships," *Ensign,* February 1984, p. 9.)

Discuss how taking responsibility for our own behavior could increase peace and harmony at home.

Alma 4:6–9
Repetitive pride problems

 Place the following items (or pictures) on a table where your family can see them: money, a silk dress or tie, a garment made of linen, gold and silver jewelry, name brand shoes or clothing. Take turns reading Alma 6:6–9 and discuss the following questions:

- What do these items have to do with Alma 6:6?
- How did the Nephites obtain these things?
- How do we obtain these things?
- How did these Nephites change when they became wealthy?
- How did Alma and the other church leaders feel about those changes?
- What are some problems we have with pride in our society because of our possessions?

As a family, review Alma 1:27–30 and look for the right way to deal with prosperity. Have your family compare Alma 4:1 and Alma 4:6 and find how many years it took the Nephites to turn from humility to pride. What does this teach us about the dangers of wealth and pride?

Alma 4:10–11
How does wickedness within the Church affect those who are not members?

 Sing with your family "Do As I'm Doing" (*Children's Songbook,* p. 276). As one of the activities during the song, have family members follow you in stumbling over a concrete block, brick, or large rock that has been placed on the floor. When finished, read Alma 4:10 and ask family members what the activity had to do with the verse. Why is the "block" in Alma 4:10 referred to as a stumbling block?

Give each family member a small piece of paper and ask them to write on it what they think is the stumbling block in Alma 4:10. Tape correct answers to the item the family tripped over during the song. Ask your family how the bad example of Church members can have a negative influence on those who do not belong to the Church. What is the consequence of this iniquity? (See Alma 4:11.) Invite each family member to share ideas on what they can do to avoid being a stumbling block to neighbors and friends that are not of our faith.

Alma 4:12–14
How can we "retain a remission of our sins" and be "filled with great joy"?

 Pass out strips of paper to each family member. As you read Alma 4:12, have them underline all the Nephite behaviors they can find. Then ask them to select and write one of these behaviors on their strips of paper. Now review Alma 4:13 and compare the behavior listed on each strip of paper with those listed in verse 13. What can your family learn about the condition of Nephite society at this time?

Sing (or read) "Do What Is Right" (*Hymns,* no. 237). Following the hymn, search Alma 4:14 and list the "consequences" (or blessings) that come to those described in verse 13.

Discuss what you can do as a family to enjoy similar blessings. You might select a family service project to do this week for someone less fortunate.

Alma 4:15–20
What did Alma do to combat wickedness among his people?

 Carefully read Alma 4:15 with your family and invite someone to summarize how Alma felt about the conditions of his society. Despite Alma's strong feelings, what do we learn in Alma 4:15 that gives us confidence that Alma will be all right? ("The Spirit of the Lord did not fail him.") Read together Alma 4:16–20 and find a reason it was important for Alma to have the Spirit. Ask the following questions:

- What powerful position did Alma give up?
- What position would that be like in our government?
- What was the name of the man that Alma selected to take his place?
- What position did Alma retain?
- Why do you think he chose to be the high priest rather than the chief judge?
- Which position would you rather have?

Review Alma 4:19 and have your family mark the reasons why Alma chose to retain his position as high priest. Ask them why they think Alma was not going to try to save his people by implementing better government, better laws, or a stronger military. Read the following statement by Elder L. Tom Perry:

"Alma understood a basic fact of life. There is no way of caring for the problems of mankind unless the great majority of them have been taught and subscribed their lives to a code of conduct which will keep them from falling into sin. The Lord, in the very beginning established for our first earthly parents commandments and covenants which, if observed and obeyed, will keep us from the heartache and waste of unrighteous living. As we consider conditions in the world today, we should be asking the question: 'How can we more effectively prevent the loss resulting from an overwhelming increase in spiritual, emotional, and physical problems now afflicting mankind?' It seems as if we are spending too much of our time and energy in repairing the damage of sin and not enough time in teaching them the Lord's law as a foundation on which they can govern their lives." ("'But the Labourers Are Few,'" *Ensign,* May 1992, p. 23.)

If you have had experiences in "stirring people up to a remembrance of their duty" or "bearing down in pure testimony," share those experiences with your family or invite them to do so.

ALMA 5: A MIGHTY CHANGE OF HEART

Alma 5:1
Alma's model of powerful teaching

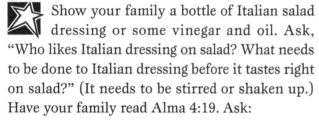 Show your family a bottle of Italian salad dressing or some vinegar and oil. Ask, "Who likes Italian dressing on salad? What needs to be done to Italian dressing before it tastes right on salad?" (It needs to be stirred or shaken up.) Have your family read Alma 4:19. Ask:

- What does Alma 4:19 have to do with the bottle of dressing?
- Besides stirring the people up to remembrance, what else did Alma want to do for the people in Zarahemla?
- What was the only way he could see to do this? (Bear down in pure testimony.)
- Why do you think pure testimony might help influence people?
- When are some times you have been stirred or shaken up spiritually because of the testimony of others? (Family home evening, seminary, girls camp, Especially for Youth, and so on.)

Read together Alma 5:1–2 and have your family find the words that show where Alma taught. Tell your family to look for ways that Alma used "pure testimony" in shaking up the people of Zarahemla to righteousness as they study Alma 5. Discuss what will happen to the Italian dress-

ing if it sits for a long time. Why is it important to continually shake people up spiritually? How often do you need to be reminded of your duties and responsibilities in the Church? Keep the Italian dressing out while reading Alma 5. Invite family members to shake the dressing bottle each time Alma asks a question or shares a teaching that could stir a person up to righteousness.

Alma 5:3–13
What is the value of studying history?

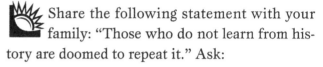 Share the following statement with your family: "Those who do not learn from history are doomed to repeat it." Ask:

- What do you think that statement means?
- What kinds of lessons can we learn from people who lived before us?
- Whose examples and experiences have been especially helpful for you?
- Do you think it is better to learn from your own experiences or from the experiences of those who have lived before you? Why?

Have your family read Alma 5:3–13 and look for what part of their history Alma wanted his people to remember. What lessons did he want them to learn from Alma, Noah, and Abinadi? How has reading about the experiences of these people helped you?

Alma 5:13–62
Why did Alma ask so many questions?

 Hold up the following objects or write these words on individual pieces of paper: Ruler, Thermometer, Scale, Barometer, Teaspoon, Clock, and Question Mark. As you show each object (or display each word), have your family tell what measurements can be taken with each item (for example, a clock measures time and a ruler measures length). When the question mark is displayed, your family may be puzzled. Explain that when priesthood leaders ask us questions, those questions can help us measure how strong we are spiritually. Temple recommend questions are an example.

Have your family scan Alma 5:13–20 and count how many question marks there are. Ask, "Why might Alma have asked the people so many questions? What is the value of thinking about spiritual questions? Do you think Alma wanted them to answer out loud? Why or why not?"

Take turns reading Alma 5:13–62 and pause briefly after every question. Have your family consider how they would answer each question. Invite them to talk about any of the questions they do not understand. When you have finished, discuss how these questions could help give an accurate measurement of our personal spirituality.

Alma 5:14
His image in your countenance

Have each family member look in a mirror while you read Alma 5:14 aloud. Discuss the following questions:

- What does it mean to have Christ's image in our countenances?
- What are some ways we can become more "Christlike"?
- Who are some people you think most remind you of Jesus Christ?
- Why would our countenances change as we become more holy?

Share the following quotations with your family:

"'Mormonism' keeps men and women young and handsome; and where they are full of the Spirit of God, there are none of them but will have a glow upon their countenances; and that is what makes you and me young; for the Spirit of God is with us, and within us." (Brigham Young, *Journal of Discourses,* 5:210.)

"Your body is God's sacred creation. Respect it as a gift from God, and do not defile it in any way. Through your dress and appearance, you can show the Lord that you know how precious your body is. You can show that you are a disciple of Christ." (*For the Strength of Youth,* p. 14.)

Alma 5:15–22
How do you look in white?

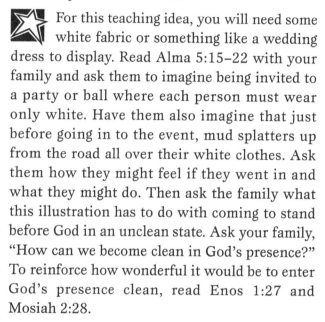 For this teaching idea, you will need some white fabric or something like a wedding dress to display. Read Alma 5:15–22 with your family and ask them to imagine being invited to a party or ball where each person must wear only white. Have them also imagine that just before going in to the event, mud splatters up from the road all over their white clothes. Ask them how they might feel if they went in and what they might do. Then ask the family what this illustration has to do with coming to stand before God in an unclean state. Ask your family, "How can we become clean in God's presence?" To reinforce how wonderful it would be to enter God's presence clean, read Enos 1:27 and Mosiah 2:28.

Alma 5:53–56
Have you ever trampled on the Lord?

Before reading Alma 5:53, place a picture of the Savior on the floor. Ask your family why they would never step on the picture. Invite each member of your family to read Alma 5:53–56 and mark every inappropriate action they can find. How would doing the things you marked be like trampling on the Lord? Why are these things considered wrong? Read 1 Nephi 19:7 and share your hopes that your family will choose to follow the Lord instead of neglecting his counsel.

Alma 5:1–62
Share What You Think

After studying Alma 5 with your family, review some of Alma's questions and ask family members to answer some of them in their journals. For example, your family could write about the following questions:

- "Have you been spiritually born of God?"

(See verse 14.) Write down a particular experience related to that.

- Do you feel the same now as you did when you had that "born of God" experience? (See verse 26.) What can you do to feel that way again?
- Can you imagine standing before God to be judged? How would you feel if you were standing there right now? How do you want to feel when you stand before God? (See verses 15–23.)

ALMA 6: ALMA SETS THE CHURCH IN ORDER IN ZARAHEMLA

Alma 6:1–8
What is the purpose of the Church?

Ask a family member to read aloud the heading to Alma 6. Ask your family what they think it means to "cleanse" and "set in order" the Church. To help answer that question, take turns reading Alma 6:1–6. As you do, ask the following questions:

- How are leaders chosen for the Lord's Church? (Verse 1; see also Articles of Faith 1:5.)
- What does the Church do for those who repent? (Verse 2.)
- What about those who are proud and refuse to repent? (Verse 3.)
- Who should be allowed to attend Church meetings? (Verse 5.)
- What is one thing we should do at Church meetings? (Verse 6.)

Share the following statement from President Ezra Taft Benson: "The mission of the Church is glorious—to invite all of us to come unto Christ through proclaiming the gospel, perfecting our lives, and redeeming our dead." ("Come unto Christ, and Be Perfected in Him," *Ensign,* May 1988, p. 85.) How did the things Alma did in Zarahemla help fulfill the mission of the Church?

ALMA 7: JESUS CHRIST SHALL OVERCOME DEATH AND BEAR THE SINS OF THE PEOPLE

Alma 7:1–7
Why was Alma's message in Gideon different from the one in Zarahemla?

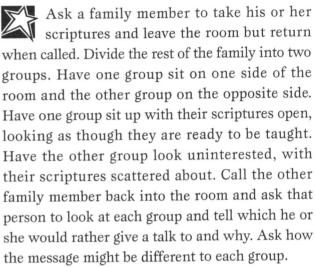 Ask a family member to take his or her scriptures and leave the room but return when called. Divide the rest of the family into two groups. Have one group sit on one side of the room and the other group on the opposite side. Have one group sit up with their scriptures open, looking as though they are ready to be taught. Have the other group look uninterested, with their scriptures scattered about. Call the other family member back into the room and ask that person to look at each group and tell which he or she would rather give a talk to and why. Ask how the message might be different to each group.

Remind your family of Alma's difficult mission in Zarahemla. Tell them he is now ready to teach the Saints in Gideon. Have your family scan Alma 7:1–6 and look for differences between the people of Zarahemla and the people of Gideon. Invite them to share what they find. Ask them which people they would rather teach. What did you learn about the people in Gideon that would explain why Alma's joy over them was different from his joy over the people in Zarahemla?

Read together Alma 7:7–10 and ask:

- What did Alma say was the most important event in their future?
- What did he say the people must do to prepare for that event?
- Why do you think Alma was able to spend more time teaching the people of Gideon about the Savior and less time teaching repentance?
- What can we do to make sure we can receive the most important messages the Lord can send to us through his servants?

Alma 7:11–13
Is the Atonement just for sinners?

Show a picture of Christ in Gethsemane (such as *Gospel Art Picture Kit*, no. 227) and ask your family what Jesus suffered for. (Most will answer that he suffered for our sins.) Read Alma 7:13 to your family and have them mark the phrases that show that truly the Atonement of Jesus Christ does have the power to cleanse us from sin. Then ask them if the Atonement does anything else? Have your family silently read Alma 7:11–12 and look for other things the Atonement has the power to help us with (tell your family to read each word "that" as "so that"). Ask the following:

- How can Jesus help you with your "pains and sicknesses"?
- What did Jesus do about the fact that you will someday die?
- What is the difference between "sicknesses" and "infirmities"? (Infirmities could be weaknesses we have that are not related to health, such as fear of speaking in public.)
- What can the Savior do about areas of your life where you feel weak and inadequate?
- Are there any trials, problems, or challenges you face that are not covered under the four categories of pains and sicknesses, death, infirmities, and sins?

Have your family mark the words and phrases in verses 11–13 that identify the four areas where the Atonement can help us. Share the following quotation from Elder Neal A. Maxwell:

"Can we, even in the depths of disease, tell [Jesus] anything at all about suffering? In ways we cannot comprehend, our sicknesses and infirmities were borne by Him even before they were borne by us. The very weight of our combined sins caused Him to descend below all. We have never been, nor will we be, in depths such as He has known. Thus His atonement made perfect His empathy and His mercy and His capacity to succor us, for which we can be everlastingly

grateful as He tutors us in our trials." (*Even As I Am*, p. 116.)

Bear your testimony of the Savior's enabling power and how he has strengthened your life.

Alma 7:14–18
How do I get the Atonement to work for me?

Provide a soft ball or beanbag to be passed around the room. Have your family silently read Alma 7:14–16 and mark the things we must do so Christ's atonement can have power in our lives. Invite a family member to share one thing he or she found and pass the beanbag (or ball) to another person. Have that person share one thing. Keep going until everyone has had a chance to share. Quickly review the verses again, but this time look for the blessings that come to us through the Atonement as we do our part. Ask your family if there is anything Satan has to offer that would be more wonderful and valuable than to live forever as God lives.

Alma 7:19–21
What is the path of the righteous?

Give each family member a sheet of paper and make available colored pencils, crayons, or markers. Tell your family to read Alma 7:19–21 and draw "the path of righteousness" according to the information given in the verses. Give them time to complete their drawing. Then invite them to show their pictures and explain why they drew them the way they did. (The path is straight, leads to the kingdom of God, doesn't vary, and so on.)

Discuss with your family some things you could do to better walk "the path of righteousness" each day.

Alma 7:21–25
How does it feel to be unclean?

Ask your family to recall a time when they were really covered in dirt or grime. Perhaps some might share their experience. How badly did they want to take a bath or shower and become clean? Share the following story by Elder Neil L. Anderson:

"I remember my father awakening me one cold night in early February when I was about sixteen. I remember feeling startled; I had only been asleep about an hour. He explained that a steer from our small farm had gotten through the fence, wandered onto the highway, and been hit by a truck. The animal was dead, and to save the meat we would have to act quickly. The task ahead would prove to be an experience I could never forget.

"After we dragged the steer from the road to an open shed with our old tractor, our next task was to hoist the animal up. We tied its hind feet together and then threw the rope over a beam. I remember struggling to get my arms under the animal's hindquarters and lift as my father pulled. To lift with any effect required wrapping my whole body around the slippery animal. By the time the body was hung, the mud and stench had become ingrained in my clothes. I felt miserable, but our work had only begun.

"Together my father and I cleaned the dead animal. We didn't finish until about three in the morning. The smell, the slime, the dirt, and the filth clung to me.

"I went back to the house. Although it has been twenty-five years, the events of the next hour are very vivid in my mind. I remember clearly the satisfaction of removing my shirt. Peeling off each layer of clothing brought relief. I began washing—first my hands, then my arms to the elbows. It was not the kind of dirt that would disappear quickly. Then I showered, first washing the ears, then the hair, back to the hands and fingernails, and to the hair again. It was some time before I felt satisfied that the cleansing was done.

"Slipping into a clean pair of pajamas, I lay awake in bed for a while reliving the experience. It was four in the morning. I was exhausted, but the feelings of tiredness did not approach the sensational satisfaction of being washed and clean.

"Yet as memorable as that experience was, there are wonderful feelings far surpassing the physical feelings I felt on that cold winter night. I speak of marvelous spiritual feelings that come through the gift of the Savior's atonement as the layers of sin are washed away and we come to feel spiritually clean." ("The Joy of Becoming Clean," *Ensign,* April 1995, p. 51.)

After reading the story, discuss the following questions:

- Have you ever had an experience like the one Elder Andersen related?
- How did he say his experience was like becoming spiritually clean?
- How can those who are unclean because of sin become spiritually clean again? (See Alma 7:13.)

Read to your family Alma 7:21 and ask why it is important to keep spiritually clean. Then read together Alma 7:23–25 and list those things we can do to keep ourselves spiritually clean. Bear testimony that our bodies are temples of God and that as we keep them clean we can enjoy God's blessings.

ALMA 8: AMULEK IS CALLED TO PREACH WITH ALMA

Alma 8:1–2
The need to rest

Have your family scan Alma 8:1 to find how many cities Alma had worked in so far as a missionary. Have them find why Alma returned to Zarahemla at this time. What benefits would resting bring to Alma?

Share the following story about the Prophet Joseph Smith: "[Joseph Smith] said it tried some of the pious folks to see him play ball with the boys. He then related a story of a certain prophet who was sitting under the shade of a tree amusing himself in some way, when a hunter came along with his bow and arrow, and reproved him. The prophet asked him if he kept his bow strung up all the time. The hunter answered that he did not. The prophet asked why, and he said it would loose its elasticity if he did. The prophet said it was just so with his mind, he did not want it strung up all the time." (Hyrum Andrus, *Joseph Smith: The Man and the Seer,* p. 16.)

As a family, plan some wholesome recreational activities that will help the whole family rest from their labors.

Alma 8:1–6
What were some of the cities Alma preached in?

Show your family a map of the world. Have them find places on the map where some of the missionaries they know are serving. Read together Mark 16:15–16 and talk about why the Lord sends missionaries to many different locations around the world. Explain that while missionaries are called to a particular mission, they may serve in many different cities and areas during their mission. (If you served a mission, tell your family about some of the areas you worked in as a missionary, and talk about some of the blessings that come from serving in different areas).

Have your family read Alma 8:1–6 and make a list of the places Alma worked as a missionary. Show your family the Map of the Nephite Lands. (See p. 122 in this book.) Identify each of these cities on the map.

Alma 8:7–27
How did the Lord bless Alma on his mission?

Divide Alma 8:7–27 between the members of the family and have each family member read the verses assigned to them. After they have finished reading, ask the following questions and have those who read that information answer the question:

- Why did the people of Ammonihah reject the message of Alma? (Verse 9.)
- How did Alma prepare himself to preach to the people of Ammonihah? (Verse 10.)

- What does it mean to wrestle with God? (Verse 10, see also Enos 1:2.)
- What was Alma struggling with? (Verse 10.)
- How was Alma's message received? (Verses 12–13.)
- How did the rejection of his message make Alma feel? (Verse 14.)
- What happened to Alma on his way to the city of Aaron? (Verse 15.)
- What was the message the angel gave Alma? (Verses 15–17.)
- How did Alma respond once the message was delivered to him? (Verse 18.)
- Upon Alma's return to Ammonihah, whom did he meet? (Verse 21.)
- Was it an accident that Alma met Amulek? (Verse 20.)
- What did Amulek do for Alma? (Verse 22.)
- Why was Alma so hungry? (Verse 26.)
- What did Alma do for Amulek and his family? (Verse 22.)

Have your family look again at Alma 7:12 and tell what the Lord will do about our infirmities or weaknesses. How is what the Lord did for Alma when he went back to Ammonihah (Alma 8:15–20) an example of what the Lord will do about our infirmities?

Alma 8:16–17, 29–32
When will the Lord destroy a people?

Review with your family the chapter headings to Mosiah 11 and ask them what King Noah and his people were doing wrong. Review the heading to Mosiah 12 and ask them who the Lord sent and what his message was. (Abinadi's message was that they must repent or be destroyed.)

Have your family search Alma 8:16–17 and find what Alma's message was to the people of Ammonihah. Have them compare Alma 8:17 with 2 Nephi 1:7 and tell why the people of Ammonihah were in danger of being destroyed.

Next read Alma 8:29–32 with your family and have them mark the things Alma and Amulek did that showed that the power of God was with them. Ask your family why they think the Lord showed those people such powerful signs through Alma and Amulek.

To show your family how this story applies to our day, have them read what Moroni prophesied about the Americas in Ether 2:9. Ask them what warning we have been given that is like Alma's warning to the people of Ammonihah. What signs of God's power has the Lord shown us in our day? Discuss with your family what we should do to be worthy of the Lord's blessings and be protected from the destructions that are prophesied upon the wicked.

ALMA 9: ALMA CALLS THE PEOPLE OF AMMONIHAH TO REPENT

Alma 9:1–7
The divine law of witnesses

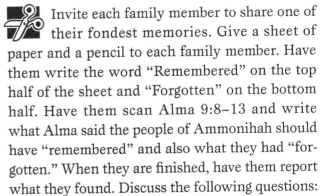 Announce a family contest that each member will compete in alone. However, have one team consist of two family members. Do a simple contest (such as putting together a puzzle the fastest or stacking blocks in a certain time limit). When the contest is over, the team with two players should have won. Ask your family why the team with two members had the advantage. Besides this particular contest, are there other times when being with a teammate or companion would provide an advantage?

Show a picture of missionaries and ask your family why they think the Church sends them out two by two. After discussing their ideas, explain that this is part of the Lord's law of witnesses. Read Deuteronomy 17:6, Matthew 18:16, and D&C 6:28 with your family. Ask them what other reason the Lord gives for sending his servants out in twos.

Tell your family that Alma and Amulek are an example of how this law of witnesses works. Have your family scan Alma 9:1–7 and find the reason

the people gave for rejecting Alma's testimony. According to the law of witnesses, was it acceptable to reject the testimony of just one witness? (Yes, it could be.)

Tell your family that in the next chapter Amulek will stand and testify to the same things that Alma said. Have someone read Alma 10:12 aloud and tell how the people's attitude changed when Amulek stood as a second witness. Ask your family what they think will happen if these people reject the testimony of two witnesses. Read together Alma 9:4–5 and ask what boast the people of Ammonihah made about their city. Invite your family to mark footnote a in Alma 9:4 and then read Alma 16:9–10. What does this teach us about the dangers of rejecting the Lord's servants?

Alma 9:8–13
"Do ye not remember?"

Invite each family member to share one of their fondest memories. Give a sheet of paper and a pencil to each family member. Have them write the word "Remembered" on the top half of the sheet and "Forgotten" on the bottom half. Have them scan Alma 9:8–13 and write what Alma said the people of Ammonihah should have "remembered" and also what they had "forgotten." When they are finished, have them report what they found. Discuss the following questions:

- Which of the events Alma reminded them of should have been fond memories to the people of Ammonihah?
- How might things have been different if they had remembered them better?
- What could be the price for their forgetfulness?
- What are some of the events our family should remember that will help us remain faithful?

Share the following statement by President Spencer W. Kimball:

"When you look in the dictionary for the most important word, do you know what it is? It could be 'remember.' . . . Our greatest need is to remember. That is why everyone goes to sacrament meeting every Sabbath day. . . . 'Remember' is the word. 'Remember' is the program." ("Circles of Exaltation," *Charge to Religious Educators,* 2d ed., 28 June 1968, p. 8.)

Alma 9:14–17
Are traditions good or bad?

Have your family name some family traditions. Discuss what might make a tradition good or bad. Read together Alma 9:8, 16 and identify the traditions of the Nephites and the Lamanites. Ask:

- What was the Nephite tradition? (Keep the commandments.)
- What had happened to the Lamanites because of their traditions? (They were ignorant of the things of God.)
- According to verse 17, what did Alma prophesy would happen to the Lamanites?

Ask your family to list which family traditions help bring them closer to Heavenly Father. What are some other activities you could make into family traditions to help with your eternal goals? Testify of the power of good traditions to help save the family.

Alma 9:18–23
Why would the Lord allow the Lamanites to destroy the Nephites?

Invite the youngest child to stand next to the oldest. Ask, "If both had committed the same mistake, how would you determine the punishment given to each? Would the punishment be the same? Why or Why not?" Read together Alma 9:18–19 and find the reason the Lord would allow the Nephites to be destroyed. Ask someone to read D&C 82:3 aloud and tell how that explains why the Lord was more strict with the Nephites.

Pair up the younger children with the older ones. Have them review Alma 9:20–22 and list the ways the Lord blessed the Nephites with

greater light. You might have family members mark each one in their scriptures as they find them. Have them share what they found. Read Alma 9:23 with your family and discuss how this warning also applies to members of the Church today.

Alma 9:25–28
What hope does Christ offer all of us?

Ask your family to imagine a situation where at work or at school there is someone they don't get along with. This person doesn't always keep the rules, and he doesn't like you because you try to be obedient. One day that person does something hurtful to you, and just as he does, he gets caught and punished for his bad behavior.

Ask your family how they would feel in that situation. Would they be angry? Glad? Sorry? Sad? Have a family member read aloud Ezekiel 33:11. Ask, "What does that verse teach about how the Lord feels about the punishments that come upon the wicked?"

Read Alma 9:25–30 together and discuss the following questions:

- What did the Lord do for the people of Ammonihah so they could escape punishment?
- What was the message of an angel sent to the people of Ammonihah?
- What did Alma teach about Jesus Christ?
- How was it a message of hope?
- What responsibility did he give to the people of Ammonihah?
- How did Alma feel about those people even though they had abused him?

Share the following statement by President James E. Faust:

"All of us have made wrong turns along the way. I believe the kind and merciful God, whose children we are, will judge us as lightly as He can for the wrongs that we have done and give us the maximum blessing for the good that we do. Alma's sublime utterance [in Alma 9:26] seems to me an affirmation of this." ("'Woman, Why Weepest Thou?'" *Ensign,* November 1996, p. 53.)

Discuss as a family the hope that comes to all of us because of the gospel of Jesus Christ.

ALMA 10: AMULEK TEACHES THE PEOPLE OF AMMONIHAH

Alma 10:1–3
What tribes were the Book of Mormon people from?

 Ask your family if they are aware that there are prophecies in the Bible about the coming forth of the Book of Mormon. Invite someone to read aloud Ezekiel 37:15–17. Then share the following statement:

"From the beginning of this dispensation, this scripture has been interpreted to apply to the Bible and the Book of Mormon. The prophet Joseph Smith in April 1830 identified the Book of Mormon as 'the stick of Joseph in the hands of Ephraim.' (*History of the Church,* 1:84.) And in August 1830, the book was again recognized as 'the record of the stick of Ephraim.' (D&C 27:5.)" (Edward J. Brandt, "Using the New LDS Editions of Scripture—As One Book," *Ensign,* October 1982, p. 42.)

Ask your family how we know that Lehi and his little colony are descended from the tribe of Joseph? Have someone read 1 Nephi 5:14 and tell what Lehi learned about his genealogy from the plates of brass. Then read Alma 10:1–3 together and mark what additional information Amulek tells us about Lehi. (He was from the tribe of Joseph through Joseph's son Manasseh.)

Ask, "If Lehi was from the tribe of Joseph through Manasseh, how can the Book of Mormon also be called the book or "stick of Ephraim"? Share the following quotation from Elder Erastus Snow:

"The Prophet Joseph informed us that . . . the first Book of Nephi, [is a] record of Nephi individ-ually, *he himself being of the lineage of Manasseh; but that Ishmael was of the lineage of Ephraim,* and that his sons married into Lehi's family, and Lehi's sons married Ishmael's daughters." (*Journal of Discourses,* 23:184; italics added.)

Alma 10:5–11
Describe Amulek

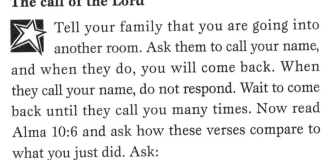 Have a family member stand. Ask the others in your family to imagine that the person is Amulek. Have everyone read Alma 10:5–11 and identify words or phrases describing Amulek. After everyone has done so, have the person being Amulek talk about what he or she thinks is the most impressive thing about this man.

Alma 10:6
The call of the Lord

Tell your family that you are going into another room. Ask them to call your name, and when they do, you will come back. When they call your name, do not respond. Wait to come back until they call you many times. Now read Alma 10:6 and ask how these verses compare to what you just did. Ask:

- What does it mean when Amulek said he was "called many times"?
- Who was calling him?
- In what manner had Amulek been called?
- What does it mean when he said, "I would not hear"?
- What does it mean to be "rebelling against God"? (See also Mosiah 2:36–37.)
- Why do you think some people ignore promptings from the Spirit?
- When have you failed to respond to spiritual promptings?

Invite family members to write in their journals, about a spiritual prompting they have received. Talk about things your family can do to better listen to and follow these promptings.

Alma 10:11
Before and After

 Have family members compare Alma 10:11 with Alma 15:16 and tell what changed in Amulek's life. Why do you think members of Amulek's family rejected him? What lessons can be learned from these two verses?

Ask your family if they can think of any experiences or people whose families rejected them because they accepted the gospel or chose to follow the Lord. When they have finished sharing, read Matthew 19:29 and discuss how the Lord can comfort those who sacrifice much for the sake of the gospel.

Alma 10:13–17
What do Amulek, Abinadi, and Jesus have in common?

Take turns reading Alma 10:13–17 with your family. Ask, "In these verses, what does Amulek have in common with Abinadi and with Jesus?" If they need help with the answer, compare Amulek with Abinadi by reading Mosiah 12:18–19 and compare Amulek with Jesus by reading Matthew 22:15–22.

Alma 10:17–27
What are the traps of the devil?

Collect and bring to scripture study any traps you can find that use bait, such as a mouse, rat, bug, or steel trap. If you do not have any of these, draw a picture of a mousetrap. Read Alma 10:17 to your family and point out the word "trap." Show your family a trap and ask:

• What are some baits used on traps to make them work?
• How could bait and traps be compared to Satan's temptations?
• What are some baits and traps Satan uses today?

Have your family search Alma 10:18, 25–27 and look for who was helping Satan set traps for Amulek. What were the lawyers and judges doing

that was wrong? What can we do to protect ourselves from the traps of Satan and his followers today?

Alma 10:22–23
Does prayer really make a difference?

Read Alma 10:22–23 with your family and ask the following questions:

• What difference did prayer make for this city?
• What do you think the righteous were praying for that protected the city?
• When was the last time you prayed for your city?

Share the following statement by Elder Gordon B. Hinckley: "I know of no better way to inculcate love for country than for parents to pray before their children for the land in which we live, invoking the blessings of the Almighty upon it that it may be preserved in liberty and in peace. I know of no better way to build within the hearts of our children a much-needed respect for authority than remembering in the daily supplications of the family the President and the Congress and others who carry the burdens of government." ("Except the Lord Build the House," *Improvement Era,* January 1964, pp. 33, 56.)

Encourage family members to pray for such things as your city, state, nation, branch, ward, stake, and schools.

ALMA 11: AMULEK WITHSTANDS ZEEZROM'S ATTACK

Alma 11:1–20
How did Nephite lawyers get paid?

 In preparation for a role-play, read Alma 11:1–3, 20. Cut some paper into dollar-size strips and label them as silver senum. Assign the following roles to family members: a judge, a court assistant, a farmer wrongly accused of taking a cow, a merchant, a man who owes the merchant money, and a wealthy landowner who was caught selling grain for too much money. Make adjustments according to the size of your family.

Sit the judge in a chair on one side of the room while the others stand on the opposite side. Have the court assistant bring the farmer to the judge. Have the farmer explain that he has been falsely accused. The judge rules that the farmer is not guilty. As a family, review Alma 11:3 and determine the farmer's bill, assuming he spent the day in court. The farmer pays a silver senum and goes back to his farm.

The judge calls, "Next case." The court assistant brings the merchant and the debtor to the judge. Have the merchant explain that the debtor owes him two silver senums. See Alma 11:2 to determine the punishment. (For example, the judge could order two senums taken from the man's pocket and given to the merchant.)

The judge exclaims, "Next case," and the wealthy landowner is brought before the court. The assistant announces the charge against him. He is found guilty. See Alma 11:20 to determine what the rich landowner knows about the judge. The landowner offers the judge ten silver senums and is set free. Ask your family the following:

- How much money did the judge get for each day's work? (Verse 3.)
- What was the main goal for the judge? (Verse 20.)
- What did the judges and lawyers do to get more work? (Verse 20.)
- How does this compare to today?

Explain to your family that the purpose of Alma 11:1–20 is to help us understand the Nephite legal system, and it shows why the judges and lawyers stirred the people up against Alma and Amulek. This becomes important when Amulek is offered money from Zeezrom in Alma 11:21–22.

Alma 11:21–22
Would you sell the gospel for money?

 Review with your family Alma 11:3, 11–13 and make a chart like the one below:

Silver Money		Day's Wage
1 senum	=	1 day's wage
1 amnor	=	2 days' wages
1 ezrom	=	4 days' wages
1 onti	=	7 days' wages

Read together Alma 11:21–22 and have your family look for the test Zeezrom gave Amulek. Ask:

- Where did Zeezrom learn how to deal with people?
- What was his intent?
- Looking at the chart, how many days' wages did Zeezrom bribe Amulek with?
- Why would he offer him so much money?
- What was Amulek willing to give up for the gospel? (See Alma 15:16.)
- Why do you think Zeezrom believed Amulek could be caught with a bribe?

Tell your family that "six onties" equaled forty-two days of pay for a judge. Explain that in our society, if a judge made $100,000 a year working five days a week, he would make $384 a day. A bribe equaling forty-two days of work would be $16,128. Discuss the following questions:

- Would you be tempted to deny God for that amount of money? Why or why not?
- Do you have a price for which you would deny the gospel?
- What can we learn from Amulek's answer in Alma 11:23?

Alma 11:23–41
Amulek contends with Zeezrom

 Prepare a "reader's theater," which is a dramatic reading that allows your family to put themselves in the place of the characters they are reading about. Assign family members to the following roles: Zeezrom, Amulek, and a narrator. If your family has more than three people, you may want to divide the verses into two parts, having two Zeezroms, two Amuleks, and two narrators so everyone can participate. Read Alma 11:21–41 as a family with everyone reading the verses that are spoken by his or her character. After the reader's theater, discuss the following questions:

- What name did Amulek call Zeezrom two different times? (See verses 23, 36.)
- Why did Zeezrom offer Amulek the money? (See verses 24–25.)
- What questions did Zeezrom ask to try to catch Amulek in a lie about doctrine?
- How did Amulek respond to Zeezrom's question in verse 38? (Jesus is the Eternal Father because He created the "heaven and . . . earth" [verse 39], and also because "he shall take upon him the transgressions of those who believe on his name" [verse 40].)
- How is Jesus Christ also your Eternal Father? (For more help, see the teaching idea for Mosiah 15:1–5 on p. 131.)

Alma 11:40–46
What doctrine made Zeezrom tremble with fear?

 Show your family a glove. Explain that it represents the physical body and that your hand represents the spirit body. Put your hand into the glove, wiggle your fingers, and ask how this is like the spirit in the body. Take the glove off your hand, lay it on the table, and ask what happens to the body when the spirit leaves. (The body dies.)

Read together Alma 11:40–42 as you put the glove back on. Have your family find answers to the following questions:

- What has the Lord promised to do about this temporal (physical) death?
- How is that like putting the glove back on?
- Who will receive the blessing of the resurrection? (Verse 42.)

- What is another blessing described in verse 40?
- Who will receive that blessing and who will not?
- Why might that doctrine make Zeezrom nervous?

Next take turns reading aloud Alma 11:43–46 and ask:

- What will a resurrected body be like? (Verses 43–44.)
- What will our memories be like in the resurrection?
- What happens to us right after the resurrection? (Verse 44.)
- How is a resurrected body different from a mortal one? (Verse 45.)
- What effect did this information have on Zeezrom? (Verse 46.)
- Why do you think this doctrine caused him and others to fear?

Ask the oldest member of your family or perhaps an elderly grandparent how he or she feels about the promise of a resurrection. Ask how the person's feelings have changed since he or she was young. Invite each family member to express how they feel about the Savior's gift of the resurrection and the chance to gain eternal life.

ALMA 12: ALMA TEACHES THE PLAN OF REDEMPTION

Alma 12:1–7
How secret are our thoughts?

 Have one family member think of two numbers between one and one thousand. Tell the person not to say what the two numbers are but to concentrate on them. Have the other family members see if they can guess the two numbers. Ask, "Is it possible to know what another person is thinking?" Read D&C 6:16 aloud and ask who does know what we are thinking. Have your family search Alma 12:1–7 and find who, besides God, knew what Zeezrom was thinking. How were Alma and Amulek able to know Zeezrom's thoughts? Share the following quotation from Elder Bruce R. McConkie:

"Men's thoughts are secret and cannot be pried into by other men, or for that matter by devils. . . . However, the Lord can and does on occasion reveal to his prophets the thoughts and intents of the hearts of men. [Jacob 2:5; Alma 10:17.] This revealing of the thoughts of another is one of the gifts of the Spirit; it is akin to the spirit of prophecy; it comes by the power of God and not of man. [Alma 12:3, 7; 18:16–20, 32; Helaman 9:41.] Our Lord during his ministry frequently exercised the power to read the thoughts of those among whom he labored." (*Mormon Doctrine,* p. 777.)

Alma 12:9–11
Who can know the mysteries of God?

Introduce these verses by explaining that "a mystery is a truth that cannot be known except through divine revelation—a sacred secret." (Hyrum M. Smith and Janne M. Sjodahl, *The Doctrine and Covenants Commentary,* p. 141.) Take turns reading Alma 12:9–11 and then ask the following questions:

- Who do you think is included in the "many" that "know the mysteries of God"? (Verse 9.)
- What determines how much of the mysteries the prophets are able to share with us? (Our "heed and diligence," verse 9.)
- What does it means to have a hard heart?
- How does having a hard heart affect our obedience?
- What blessings are promised to those who do not harden their hearts? (Verse 10.)
- What do the hard-hearted lose? (Verse 11.)

Invite your family to think about some questions they have about eternal things (such as pre-earth life, life after death, the Creation, or the nature of the universe). From what Alma just taught us, what is the best way to receive answers to our deepest questions?

Alma 12:12–15
How can I purify my thoughts?

Write the following words on three separate pieces of paper: "Words," "Works," "Thoughts." Ask your family to suggest an example of a word, an action, and a thought that would be good. Also decide on a word, action, and thought that would be bad. Write the good and bad examples on the three pieces of paper.

Have someone read aloud Alma 12:15 and identify who the "him" is that we will one day have to stand before. Why will we stand before the Lord? Have another family member read aloud Alma 12:14 and tell what we will be judged on. Ask how Heavenly Father might feel about the bad examples listed on the three pieces of paper. What would your judgment be like if your words, works, and thoughts matched the good examples you listed?

Read together Alma 12:12–14 and ask which of these three things (words, works, or thoughts) is the hardest to control. Why do you think it is so hard to control our thoughts? Share this counsel that Bishop H. Burke Peterson gave on purifying our thoughts and our lives:

"First, we must stop the flow into our minds of . . . vulgar stories, jokes, pictures, conversation, and a myriad of other satanic products. . . .

"Now, assuming we have cut off the flow—not cut it down, but cut it off—the second thing we must do is to develop a filtering system that will cleanse the great reservoir of our mind so that the life-giving thoughts coming from it may again be pure and fit for our use. . . .

"The secret to cleansing our spirit of whatever the impurity is not very complicated. It begins with prayer every morning and ends with prayer every night. This is the most important step I know in the cleansing process. . . .

"Secondly, an added refinement will come in the filtering process: An added measure of spiritual purity, if you please, can be found in a daily study of the scriptures—not long, perhaps, but *every day*. . . .

"Third, feed refreshment to your spirit that comes when you do something good for another that he or she doesn't expect. Keep it simple, but *do* it—daily. It may only be a cheery hello, a short visit to [someone who is] homebound, a phone call, or a note. . . .

"And finally, pick up a commandment you are still struggling with and give it an honest chance to bless your life." ("Purify Our Minds and Spirits," *Ensign*, November 1980, pp. 38–39.)

Alma 12:19–37
Understanding the plan of redemption

Take turns reading Alma 12:25–33 and have your family look for and mark the phrase that is repeated seven times. Ask your family to list other names they know of for this plan. Share the following statement: "In the scriptures we read of the many names of the plan: 'the great plan of happiness,' 'the plan of redemption,' 'the merciful plan of the great Creator,' 'the plan of salvation,' 'the plan of justice,' and 'the great plan of the Eternal God.'" (L. Aldin Porter, "Our Destiny," *Ensign*, November 1999, p. 65).

Explain to your family that you are going to play a game that will give them an opportunity to show their understanding of the plan. Divide your family into two teams. Tell them you are going to say a word or phrase that appears in Alma 12:19–37. The object of the game is to see which team can be the first to find the word or phrase in a verse. Have them raise their hands when they find it. Call on the first person to tell what verse it is in. Someone else on the same team must then tell how that word or phrase fits into the plan of redemption. Examples of words and phrases to be used are given below. Choose ones that you feel will be at the appropriate level for your family.

Fall (verse 22)
Tree of life (verses 21, 23, 26)
Probationary state (verse 24)
Resurrection (verses 24–25)
Temporal death (verse 24)
First parents (verse 26)
Judgment (verse 27)
Commandments (verses 31–32)
Repent (verses 33, 37)
Only Begotten Son (verses 33–34)
Rest (verses 34–37)

Explain to your family that entering into the "rest of God" means entering into "the fulness of his glory" (see D&C 84:24), or eternal life, which gift is the greatest of all the gifts of God (see D&C 14:7). Conclude by having your family read Alma's challenge in Alma 12:37. Bear testimony of the importance of accepting that challenge.

ALMA 13: THE DAY OF SALVATION

Alma 13:1–3
When were we called?

Read Alma 13:1–3 with your family and ask them to underline the phrase in verse 3 that tells when priests received their callings. Share the following statements:

"Faithful men held priesthood power and authority first in pre-existence and then again on earth. (Alma 13.) 'Every man who has a calling to minister to the inhabitants of the world was ordained to that very purpose in the Grand Council of heaven before this world was.' (*Teachings of the Prophet Joseph Smith*, p. 365.)." (Bruce R. McConkie, *Mormon Doctrine*, p. 477.)

Discuss with your family what this teaches about priesthood holders. Ask if it is possible that women were also called in the pre-existence to do certain things. This may be a good time to share patriarchal blessings and learn about callings other family members received before their birth. Encourage your family to make a journal entry about insights they have received from their patriarchal blessings and what they can do to achieve the promises they have been given.

Alma 13:3–13

What qualifications are needed to become a high priest?

Give each family member a pencil and a sheet of paper. Have them fold the paper in half, label the left side "Characteristics of high priests," and label the right side "Characteristics of those who reject the Spirit of God." Ask your family to read Alma 13:3–13 and list all the characteristics they can find under the appropriate title. Have older children help younger ones. When they are finished, discuss the following:

- What are the characteristics of faithful high priests?
- What are the characteristics of those who reject the Sprit of God?
- What can we do to be more like faithful high priests?
- What does it mean to "look upon sin . . . with abhorrence"? (Verse 12.)
- Can you share an experience when you successfully did so?
- What do you think it means to enter into the Savior's "rest"? (Verse 13; see also D&C 84:23–24.)

This would be a good time to discuss appropriate topics in *For the Strength of Youth* pamphlet (such as dress, media, music, language, and so on).

Alma 13:14–19

How did Melchizedek get his people to change their behavior?

Read Alma 13:19 out loud and ask your family what they learned about Melchizedek. Take turns reading Alma 13:14–18 and look for those things that explain why there were none greater than Melchizedek. Discuss the following questions:

- What priesthood did Melchizedek hold?
- Why do you think Abraham paid his tithing to him?

- What were the people like when Melchizedek became their king? (Verse 17.)
- What principles of the gospel did Melchizedek teach his people that caused them to change their behavior?
- Why was Melchizedek called the Prince of Peace?
- Who else do we know in scripture with the title Prince of Peace? (See Isaiah 9:6.)
- How can we use the principles of faith and repentance to have peace in our home?

Alma 13:20

What does it mean to wrest the scriptures?

After reading Alma 13:20 with your family, ask them if they know what "wrest" means. Have them write the following definition in the margin of their scriptures: To distort, twist, or pervert. (See Noah Webster, *An American Dictionary of the English Language,* "Wrest.")

- According to this definition, what is Alma suggesting that people are doing with the scriptures when they "wrest" them?
- Why would "wresting" the scriptures bring personal destruction?
- Have you ever been in a situation when someone was twisting the scriptures for their own purpose?
- What should we do when people interpret a scripture for their personal benefit?

Alma 13:21–26

What day is coming?

Have your family draw pictures of angels. If you have younger children, you might choose to make angels with suckers, gumdrops, and paper doilies. (The sucker is the angel's head; put the sucker stick in a gumdrop for its feet and wrap the doily around the sucker stick for the angel's robe.) Read Alma 13:21–26 together as a family and ask:

- What do you think "the day of salvation" refers to? (Verse 21.)

- How do you prepare for the Lord's coming?
- Who is telling all the nations about the "day of salvation"? (Verses 22, 24–26.)
- How can we help the angels "prepare the hearts of the children of men to receive his word"?
- Can you name some times when angels have declared "glad tidings" in the latter days? (See Joseph Smith—History 1:17–20, 30–47, 59, 68–70; D&C 128:20.)
- When would Alma like the "day of salvation" to be? (Verse 25.)
- What must we all do so that we will not be fearful but excited for the Lord's "day of salvation"?

Conclude by singing "Now Let Us Rejoice" (*Hymns,* no. 3). Note the reference to the "day of salvation" in verses 2 and 3.

Alma 13:27–30
Alma's admonitions

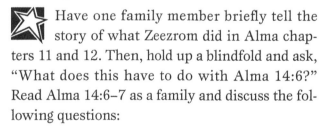 Have your family search Alma 13:27–28 and underline phrases that reveal Alma's deep feelings. What was Alma anxious for the people of Ammonihah to do? (Cast off their sins and repent.)

Invite a family member to read aloud 1 Corinthians 10:13 and tell what God will not suffer (allow) to happen to his children. (To be tempted above their strength to resist.) Now compare 1 Corinthians 10:13 with Alma 13:28. Ask your family what Alma says we should do to avoid being tempted beyond our ability to resist. How will the Spirit strengthen us if we do "watch and pray continually"?

Have your family read Alma 13:29–30 and underline the blessings that come from obedience and the consequences that follow from failure to be obedient to these principles. Conclude by singing "Do What Is Right" (*Hymns,* no. 237).

ALMA 14: THE WICKED PEOPLE IN AMMONIHAH DRIVE OUT AND SLAY THE BELIEVERS

Alma 14:1–4
What's your reaction?

Have family members read Alma 14:1–4 and tell what the two basic reactions were to Alma's and Amulek's preaching. Ask:

- Who had more people in their group, the believers or the destroyers?
- Why were the wicked angry with Alma and Amulek?
- Why are the wicked often angry when they hear the truth? (See 1 Nephi 16:2; 2 Nephi 33:5.)

Have your family members think of a time when they were chastised for doing something wrong. Do they remember how they reacted to the correction? Who are we listening to when we get angry when we are called to repentance? What can we do to accept correction more humbly?

Alma 14:6–7
Is guilt good or bad?

Have one family member briefly tell the story of what Zeezrom did in Alma chapters 11 and 12. Then, hold up a blindfold and ask, "What does this have to do with Alma 14:6?" Read Alma 14:6–7 as a family and discuss the following questions:

- How did Zeezrom feel when he realized his lies "blinded" the minds of the people?
- How did Zeezrom show he was sorry for what he did?
- How did the people treat him?
- Do you think Zeezrom felt better or worse after his efforts to correct his wrong?
- Did his actions please God or man? (See also Galatians 1:10.)
- Why do you think Zeezrom was so anxious to correct his lies?

• What does this teach us about how damaging our actions can be to others?

Alma 14:8–13
Why does the Lord sometimes allow innocent people to suffer?

As a family, study Alma 14:8–13 and look for what the wicked people in Ammonihah did to the people who believed in the word of God. Ask your family how they might have felt if they were forced to watch this awful destruction. What did Amulek suggest that he and Alma do? (verse 10). Why did Alma refuse to stop it?

Read together Alma 60:13 and D&C 98:13 and discuss why the Lord sometimes allows the righteous to suffer. Share the following statement from Elder Spencer W. Kimball:

"Could the Lord have prevented these tragedies? The answer is, Yes. The Lord is omnipotent, with all power to control our lives, save us pain, prevent all accidents, drive all planes and cars, feed us, protect us, save us from labor, effort, sickness, even from death, if he will. But he will not. . . .

"If we looked at mortality as the whole of existence, then pain, sorrow, failure, and short life would be calamity. But if we look upon life as an eternal thing stretching far into the premortal past and on into the eternal post-death future, then all happenings may be put in proper perspective. . . .

"If all the sick for whom we pray were healed, if all the righteous were protected and the wicked destroyed, the whole program of the Father would be annulled and the basic principle of the gospel, . . . agency, would be ended. . . .

"Should all prayers be immediately answered according to our selfish desires and our limited understanding, then there would be little or no suffering, sorrow, disappointment, or even death, and if these were not, there would also be no joy, success, resurrection, nor eternal life and godhood." (*Faith Precedes the Miracle*, pp. 96–97.)

Ask your family why Alma and Amulek were

spared (verse 13). To conclude, have your family summarize what they have learned about why the Lord allows innocent people to suffer at the hands of the wicked.

Alma 14:14–29
What is the moral of the story?

 Ask your family if anyone can explain what is meant by the "moral of the story"? For example, in the story "The Three Little Pigs," what would be the moral of the story? (That we are most safe when we are most prepared.) Briefly and quickly help your family understand this idea by having them identify some morals in the following true stories:

Noah and the ark.
David and Goliath.
Moses parting the Red Sea.

Tell your family you now want them to find the moral in an important story in the Book of Mormon. Divide your family into two groups. Give each group paper and markers or crayons. Assign one group Alma 14:14–22 and the other group Alma 14:23–29. Explain that they are to read their verses, draw pictures depicting what happened, and decide what is the most important lesson being taught. Each group will then share their pictures, storyline, and important lesson with the rest of the family. When everyone is finished sharing, have your family decide what the most important moral is in this true story.

ALMA 15: THE CONVERSION OF ZEEZROM

Alma 15:1–3
Can a person become physically sick because of sin?

Ask your family to suggest reasons why people get sick. Read together Alma 14:6–7 and Alma 15:1–3 and look for the reason Zeezrom felt physically sick. Ask:

- Can our sins cause us to feel sick?
- Why did Zeezrom feel guilty?
- What is the best way to overcome our feelings of guilt? (See Alma 15:8.)
- Was Zeezrom physically or spiritually ill?
- Which would be a greater miracle, to heal a sick body or to heal a sick soul?

Read the following quotation from President Harold B. Lee:

"The great call has come now in the sermons of the Brethren to aid those who are in need of aid, not just temporal aid, but spiritual aid. The greatest miracles I see today are not necessarily the healing of sick bodies, but the greatest miracles I see are the healing of sick souls, those who are sick in soul and spirit and are downhearted and distraught, on the verge of nervous breakdowns. We are reaching out to all such, because they are precious in the sight of the Lord, and we want no one to feel that they are forgotten." ("Stand Ye in Holy Places," *Ensign*, July 1973, p. 123.)

Ask your family what they can do to reach out to those who are suffering in the ward or neighborhood.

Alma 15:4–5
They went immediately

Ask a member of your family to go get something for you, such as a bookmark, a pencil, or something from another room for scripture study. Ask the rest of your family how quickly this family member responded to what was asked. Have your family turn to Alma 15:4–5 and look for answers to the following questions:

- What word describes how Zeezrom responded when he heard that Alma and Amulek were nearby?
- How quickly did Alma and Amulek respond when they were invited to come to Zeezrom?
- Why do you think they responded so quickly?
- How important is it to respond to the Lord immediately when he calls us?

- How should we respond when the bishop asks us to do something?
- How quickly should children respond when their parents ask them to do something?

Alma 15:5–12
The healing of Zeezrom

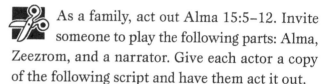 As a family, act out Alma 15:5–12. Invite someone to play the following parts: Alma, Zeezrom, and a narrator. Give each actor a copy of the following script and have them act it out.

Narrator: (Read Alma 15:5.)

Alma: Believest thou in the power of Christ unto Salvation? (Verse 6.)

Zeezrom: Yea, I believe all the words that thou hast taught. (Verse 7.)

Alma: If thou believest in the redemption of Christ thou canst be healed. (Verse 8.)

Zeezrom: Yea, I believe according to thy words. (Verse 9.)

Alma: O Lord our God, have mercy on this man and heal him according to his faith which is in Christ. (Verse 10.)

Narrator: (Read Alma 15:11–12.)

Ask your family by what power Zeezrom was healed. Share any examples from your family of the gift of healing. Bear your testimony of the importance of having faith in the Lord Jesus Christ and in the power of the priesthood.

Alma 15:13–15
What is the difference between hard and soft hearts?

Have your family compare the condition of Zeezrom's heart in Alma 15:4 with the hearts of the people in the land of Ammonihah in Alma 15:15. Have your family describe what a hard-hearted person does. How can we soften our hearts? (See 1 Nephi 2:16; Mosiah 21:15; Alma 24:8.) Have your family draw what they see in their minds when they think of a hard heart and a soft heart and then share what they drew.

Alma 15:16–19
Fortification against Satan, death, and destruction

 Ask your family what they would do to prepare if they knew that an enemy was coming to attack their home. Read together Alma 15:16–19 and look for answers to the following:

- Who is the enemy identified in these verses? (Satan.)
- What did it cost Amulek to follow Alma? (Verse 16.)
- What did the Church members do to protect themselves against Satan? (Verse 17.)
- How did Alma help Amulek? (Verse 18.)

ALMA 16: AMMONIHAH IS DESTROYED

Alma 16:1–11
Why was the city of Ammonihah destroyed?

 Ask your family what a "consequence" is. Have them identify the consequences for some of the following actions: touching a hot stove, turning on a light switch, doing their chores, paying their tithing. Have someone read aloud D&C 130:20–21 and summarize what the Lord tells us there about consequences.

Assign the following verses to different members of your family. Have each person report what happens in his or her verse.

- Alma 9:1. (Alma and Amulek preach to the people of Ammonihah.)
- Alma 9:18. (Amulek warns the people the Lamanites will utterly destroy them if they do not repent.)
- Alma 10:23. (Amulek warns the people that if they cast out the righteous they will be destroyed.)
- Alma 15:1. (The righteous are cast out of Ammonihah.)

Ask your family to guess what consequences would come to the people of Ammonihah because of their behavior. Read together Alma 16:1–3, 9–11 and see how your family's guesses compared to what actually happened.

Alma 16:4–9
What are the consequences of following the prophet?

 Sing or read the primary song "Follow the Prophet" (*Children's Songbook,* p. 110) and have your family pay close attention to the words. Ask:

- What do you think the phrase "he knows the way" means?
- How is a prophet able to know the future?

Read together Alma 16:4–9 and have your family look for evidences that the prophet Alma could foresee the future. Why would it be wise, then, to follow the prophet? Have your family list some of the things the prophet has counseled us recently to do or not do. What wisdom can you see in following his counsel?

Alma 16:12–21
Victory over Satan

 Have your family members think of a victory they have achieved in sports, school, or a favorite activity. Ask them to talk about their "favorite victory" of all time. Ask a family member to read Alma 16:21 and look for what victory is spoken of there. How would it feel to be victorious over Satan? What do we need to do to be victorious over Satan? Share the following statement by President George Q. Cannon:

"Satan will be bound by the power of God; but he will be bound also by the determination of the people of God not to listen to him, not to be governed by him. If Satan, therefore, has power with man, it is because man yields to his influence." (*Gospel Truth,* 1:86–87.)

Ask your family to summarize what would prevent our victory over Satan according to President Cannon.

Read together Alma 16:18–19 and have your

family list things we should not do and that we should do to be victorious over Satan. Discuss what each word in your list means.

Explain that in the war against Satan, the Lord and his servants can help us very much. Have your family members read through Alma 16:12–16. Make a list of the things the Lord does to help us and a list of what his servants do to help us in this battle. Invite your family members to identify one thing they could do to better fight in this battle against Satan. Have them write in their journals some goals they will work on.

ALMA 17: A JOYOUS REUNION WITH ALMA AND THE SONS OF MOSIAH

Alma 17:1–4
What makes a successful missionary?

Invite your family to recall a time when they were at an airport or home when a missionary returned from a mission. Ask them what their reaction or the reaction of the family was upon seeing the missionary. What do you think brings a family the greatest joy upon a child's return from a mission?

Read together Alma 17:1–4 and discuss the following questions:

- How long had Alma and the sons of Mosiah been on missions?
- What word shows how Alma felt about seeing the sons of Mosiah for the first time in fourteen years?
- What had the sons of Mosiah done to prepare themselves to be successful missionaries? (Verses 2–3.)

Discuss together what your family could do to improve their scripture study, prayers, or fasting that they might teach the gospel with greater power.

Alma 17:5–18
What can we expect as we serve our missions?

Invite a member of your family to share an experience from his or her mission that shows the trials missionaries encounter while serving the Lord. (If no one in your family has served, share an experience of a friend or other acquaintance.) Read as a family Alma 17:5, 14–15 and find some of the trials the sons of Mosiah encountered while serving their missions. Discuss as a family how missions are similar or how they are different from missions during Alma's time.

Read the following statements to your family:

"We must raise the bar on the worthiness and qualifications of those who go into the world as ambassadors of the Lord Jesus Christ." (Gordon B. Hinckley, "To Men of the Priesthood," *Ensign,* November 2002, p. 57.)

"What we need now is the greatest generation of missionaries in the history of the Church. . . . We don't need spiritually weak and semi-committed young men. . . . We cannot send you on a mission to be reactivated, reformed or to receive a testimony. . . . we need your whole heart and soul." (M. Russell Ballard, "The Greatest Generation of Missionaries," *Ensign,* November 2002, p. 47.)

Ask your family to share ideas on how they can "raise the bar." Invite your family to search Alma 17:9–13, 16 and list what the Lord told the sons of Mosiah that would help them be good missionaries. Discuss how believing in and practicing these principles might help people "raise the bar" as the prophet has asked.

Alma 17:19–39
How does the story of Ammon remind you of the life of Christ?

The story in Alma 17 of Ammon's defending the king's sheep and servants is such an interesting and powerful one that it would be good to read verses 19–39 together as a family before you stop to discuss them.

Then read Moses 6:63 to your family and explain that when the Lord said, "All things bear record of me," that is also true of the Lord's servants. Make a chart like the one below but leave off the descriptions. Assign the scripture references in Alma to different family members. Have them search their verses and report what happened there to Ammon. As they give their report, summarize each event on your chart as given at the bottom of the page.

Read together the references from the New Testament about Christ and discuss how similar they are to what happened to Ammon. Ask your family if they can see any other similarities between Ammon and the Savior. Do you think such similarities are an accident? Encourage your family to look for ways that the events and people in the scriptures and the world around them remind us of Jesus Christ.

Alma 17:26–39
The way we serve influences how others feel about the gospel

 Read the following statement by Elder Henry B. Eyring:

"Thousands of times every day, members of the Church are watched . . . by people curious to know something about our lives. Because we are under covenant to be witnesses, we will try to tell them how the gospel has brought us happiness. What they think of what we say may depend largely on how much they sense we care for them. Those we meet will feel the love. . . . It may not be in hours or days as it was for King Lamoni, but they will feel our love after testing our hearts. And when they find our concern sincere, the Holy Spirit can more easily touch them to allow us to teach and to testify, as it did for Ammon." ("Witnesses for God," *Ensign,* November 1996, p. 32.)

With your family, take turns reading Alma 17:26–39. Have them look for ways Ammon illustrates what Elder Eyring taught. Have someone summarize how Ammon was a servant to the king and his people while on his mission. Discuss ways your family can be of service to the Lord's children each day.

ALMA 18: AMMON TEACHES KING LAMONI

Alma 18:1–5
What did the Lamanites believe about God?

 Have a family member take one minute and tell what he or she knows about God. (For example they could tell about the powers he has, what blessings he gives us, or what he looks like.) Read D&C 130:22 together and compare what is taught there about God with what other Christian churches believe God is like.

Read Alma 18:1–5 together and ask the following questions:

- What did the Lamanites call God?
- Who did King Lamoni think Ammon was?
- Why did Lamoni feel that the Great Spirit was angry with him?

Ammon	Event	Christ
Alma 17:19–20	King's son goes on mission to his wayward brethren.	Matthew 3:16–17; 15:24
Alma 17:21–25	Offered the status of prince but chose to be a servant instead.	John 6:14–15; 13:12–16
Alma 17:25	Becomes a shepherd	John 10:11
Alma 17:26	Serves for three days and tries to bring the king's sheep to water.	John 7:37–38
Alma 17:33–36	The wicked were astonished at his power.	Mathew 13:54

- Where did Lamoni get his ideas about God?
- What false understanding did the Lamanites have about their own conduct? (Verse 5.)
- How can a false understanding about God lead to such incorrect ideas about ourselves?

Ask your family to imagine that God is not our Heavenly Father but just a great spirit that created us as a potter makes a clay pot. Would that change the way you feel about him? Imagine that you are not really his child and could never become like him. Would that change the way you live? Bear your testimony to your family of the power and purpose that come from a correct understanding of who God really is.

Alma 18:8–23

I'll listen to you when I know I can trust you

Ask the smallest member of your family to stand up and put on a blindfold. Have a bigger and stronger family member stand behind smallest one. Ask the blindfolded person to stretch out his or her arms to the side, fall backward, and trust that the other person will catch him or her. Then discuss some of these questions:

- Was it easy or hard to trust the person to catch you and why?
- What has that person done to earn your trust?
- Why is it easier to trust some people than others?
- What are some things we can do to build relationships of trust with others?

After this activity, have someone read Alma 18:23. Ask what he or she sees in that verse that shows that King Lamoni trusted Ammon. What did Ammon do to show the king he could be trusted? (See Alma 17:20–39.) How would gaining this kind of trust help a missionary be more effective?

Now have your family read Alma 18:8–22 and look for other ways Ammon earned the trust of the king. Ask your family to share what they dis-

covered. Talk about ways we can follow Ammon's example with our family, friends, and neighbors.

Alma 18:23–32

How to be a great missionary

Share the following statement from President Gordon B. Hinckley as he spoke to those not of our faith: "To these we say in a spirit of love, bring with you all that you have of good and truth which you have received from whatever source, and come and let us see if we may add to it." ("The Marvelous Foundation of Our Faith," *Ensign,* November 2002, p. 81.)

Discuss the following questions with your family:

- What do you think President Hinckley meant by that statement?
- What are some good and true beliefs those not of our faith have and follow?
- As a missionary, would it be important to build on those beliefs or disregard them? Why?
- Why is it also important to teach true doctrine where false ideas exist?

Read Alma 18:24–28 with your family and have them find one truth that Ammon and Lamoni had in common. (A belief in God.) Then have your family search Alma 17:29–39 to find answers to the following questions:

- What is the first thing Ammon taught about God? (Verses 28–32.)
- How did Ammon's teachings about the creation add to what the king already knew?
- After teaching that God is the creator of all things, what truths did Ammon teach next? (Verses 36–38.)
- What did Ammon teach to correct some false traditions the Lamanites had? (Verses 37–38.)
- After teaching about the Fall of Adam, what truth did Ammon teach next? (Verse 39.)
- Why do you think Ammon taught about the Fall of Adam before he taught about the plan of redemption?

Read Alma 18:40 and look for how Lamoni responded to Ammon's message. Testify of how important it is for missionaries to be outstanding teachers. Invite your family to think of some non-member friends with whom you could share the gospel. Encourage your family to watch for teaching moments when you can share your testimony with them.

ALMA 19: THE CHURCH IS ESTABLISHED AMONG THE LAMANITES

Alma 19:1–16

What role does faith play in true conversion?

One way to study Alma 19:1–16 is to do a role-play. You will need to portray the following characters: Ammon, the Queen, Servants, King Lamoni, and a narrator. Depending on the size of your family, some may need to play more than one role. As you read through Alma 19:1–16, have each family member read the part of his or her assigned character. When done, discuss some of the following questions:

- What replaced the dark veil of unbelief? (Verse 6.)
- What names does this light have? (Verse 6.)
- What effect did this light have on Lamoni? (Verse 6.)
- What other experience was Ammon familiar with where someone had fallen to the earth as if he were dead? (See Mosiah 27:8, 19.)
- What do we learn about the faith of the queen? (Verses 9–10.)
- How important is a soft heart and a willingness to believe in receiving a witness from the Spirit?
- After King Lamoni awoke, what was his testimony centered upon? (Verse 13.)
- Why did the king, the queen, and Ammon fall to the earth again?

Remind your family that Lamoni's experience

is unusual and that becoming converted is normally a slower process. See the teaching idea for Mosiah 27:11–14 for more information.

Alma 19:16–32

Abish, the woman servant, helps convert a nation

 Write the following names and titles on separate strips of paper: Queen, King, Missionary, Prophet, Soldier, and Servant. Show each strip of paper one by one. Have your family put the strips of paper in order of the most influential to the least influential. Ask why they placed them in the order they did.

Divide your family into groups. Assign the following scripture blocks to the groups: Alma 19:16–19, Alma 19:19–23, Alma 19:24–27, and Alma 19:28–32. When they are finished, have each group summarize what they read. The following questions will help in understanding:

- What was the name of the servant who didn't fall to the earth? (Verse 16.)
- What did Abish do when she saw that all the others had fallen to the earth? (Verse 17.)
- How did others react after they had gathered? (Verses 19, 20, and 25–27.)
- What happened to the man who raised his hand to kill Ammon and why? (Verse 22.)
- What happened when a hand raised the queen? (Verse 29.)
- How many people listened to the message of the king?
- How much influence did Abish, the woman servant, have on the Lamanites?
- What does this teach you about how important each person is in the Lord's plan?

Alma 19:33–36

The Lord poured out his Spirit on the Lamanites

Share the following story by Joseph Smith; it happened during the dedication of the Kirtland Temple:

"Brother George A. Smith arose and began to

prophesy, when a noise was heard like the sound of a rushing mighty wind, which filled the Temple, and all the congregation simultaneously arose, being moved upon by an invisible power; many began to speak in tongues and prophesy; others saw glorious visions; and I beheld the Temple was filled with angels, which fact I declared to the congregation. The people of the neighborhood came running together (hearing an unusual sound within, and seeing a bright light like a pillar of fire resting upon the Temple), and were astonished at what was taking place." (*History of the Church,* 2:428.)

Discuss with your family the power by which the Saints were able to enjoy these experiences in the Kirtland Temple (Holy Ghost). Ask what they think it might have been like to be there. What impact did it have on the nonmember "people of the neighborhood"?

Quickly review the chapter heading for Alma 19 to summarize the powerful spiritual experience of King Lamoni and the Lamanites. Then read together Alma 19:33–36 and ask:

- What similarities do you see between these two powerful stories?
- What evidence can you see that the Lord did "pour out his Spirit" upon the Lamanites?
- What influence did this experience have on nonmembers?
- According to verse 36, what are the requirements for receiving the Spirit of the Lord?

Bear your testimony to your family about the power of the Spirit to change our hearts and lives.

ALMA 20: AMMON MEETS LAMONI'S FATHER

Alma 20:1–7
How did Ammon know that his brethren were in prison?

 Have a family member read Alma 20:1–2 and tell where King Lamoni wanted

Ammon to go. Why didn't Ammon agree to go with the king?

Read Alma 20:2–7 together as a family. Ask:

- How did Ammon find out his brother Aaron and others were in prison?
- Why was it important for Ammon to hear "the voice of the Lord"?
- Did Lamoni hear the "voice" like Ammon?
- Have you heard the "voice of the Lord" in your life?
- What are some ways the Lord can speak to us?

Talk about some of the ways the Lord can speak to us and about what we can do to hear his voice more clearly. Also share these thoughts from Elder Francisco J. Vinas:

"I have carefully observed the effect that diligently and humbly listening to the voice of the Lord has had in the lives of people. . . . The voice of the Lord may be received by listening to the Lord's servants, studying the scriptures, and being prompted through the inspiration of the Holy Ghost. . . . I believe that our ability and our willingness to hear can be increased and that our ears can be opened to hear clearly the voice of the Lord." ("Listening to the Voice of the Lord," *Ensign,* November 1996, p. 78.)

Alma 20:8–16
How harmful is anger?

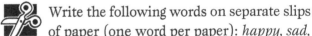 Write the following words on separate slips of paper (one word per paper): *happy, sad, scared, surprised, frustrated,* and *angry.* Divide the slips of paper among family members and have each one demonstrate the emotion on his or her paper. Have the other family members guess what emotion is being portrayed. Have anger be the last one demonstrated. After the family has guessed it, ask, "What are some reasons people become angry? What are some examples you have seen of people losing their temper? Does anger usually solve the difficulty or make matters worse?"

Read together Alma 20:8–16 and ask your family to identify:

- Who is angry and at whom.
- Why is he angry?
- What is his anger about to cause him to do?
- If he weren't angry, do you think killing his son would seem like a good idea to him?

Read 3 Nephi 11:29–30 together and ask what the Lord's attitude is about anger. Share these thoughts from President Gordon B. Hinckley about controlling our temper:

"A violent temper is such a terrible, corrosive thing. And the tragedy is that it accomplishes no good; it only feeds evil with resentment and rebellion and pain. . . . May I suggest that you watch your temper, now, in these formative years of your life. . . . This is the season to develop the power and capacity to discipline yourselves. . . . Anger is not an expression of strength. It is an indication of one's inability to control his thoughts, words, his emotions. Of course it is easy to get angry. When the weakness of anger takes over, the strength of reason leaves. Cultivate within yourselves the mighty power of self-discipline." ("Our Solemn Responsibilities," *Ensign,* November 1991, p. 49.)

Tell your family that sometimes a person will say, "I didn't mean to hurt you; I was just angry." Ask if they think being angry is ever an excuse for bad behavior. What should we do about angry feelings? Have your family share ideas about how to better control feelings of anger.

Alma 20:17–27
What brought about the change in Lamoni's father?

Have your family read Alma 20:17–27 and look for the changes in Lamoni's father. Ask the following questions:

- What did Lamoni's father want done to Ammon when they first met? (Verse 14.)
- What was Lamoni's father willing to give if Ammon would spare his life? (Verse 23.)
- What did Ammon ask for? (Verse 24.)
- What astonished Lamoni's father exceedingly? (Verse 26.)

- What did Lamoni's father grant to Lamoni and Ammon? (Verses 26–27.)
- What did Lamoni's father want to learn? (Verse 27.)
- What brought about this great change in Lamoni's father?

Have your family contrast the positive power of love with the destructive power of anger. (See Alma 20:8–16.) Also ask your family to watch for additional changes in Lamoni's father as they study Alma 22.

Alma 20:28–30
What may be our lot?

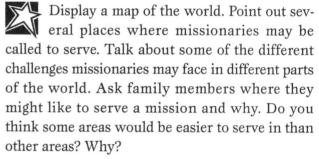 Display a map of the world. Point out several places where missionaries may be called to serve. Talk about some of the different challenges missionaries may face in different parts of the world. Ask family members where they might like to serve a mission and why. Do you think some areas would be easier to serve in than other areas? Why?

Read Alma 20:28–30 together and look for what kind of missionary experience the brethren of Ammon were having. Ask, "How does that compare to Ammon's experience? What can we learn from these missionary experiences that might help us as we serve the Lord?"

ALMA 21: AARON'S MISSION TO THE PEOPLE OF JERUSALEM

Alma 21:1–4
What is the advantage of having a missionary companion?

Ask one member of your family to read Alma 17:17 and identify a difference in the way the sons of Mosiah served their missions and the way missionaries serve today. Ask family members how they would feel about serving a mission to their mortal enemies without a companion. Read together Alma 21:1–4. Ask:

- To what city did Aaron go?
- Who were the Amalekites and Amulonites? (See Index, "Amalekites" and "Amulonites.")
- Why do you think these former Nephites had hearts that were "still harder" even than those of the Lamanites?
- What influence did they have on the Lamanites?
- How is this similar to those who leave the Church today?
- Why are they sometimes the worst enemies of the Church?
- What would you do to prepare for a mission among so many enemies of the Church?

Alma 21:5–10

What gospel would an Amalekite teach?

Tell your family that they are going to pretend to be Amalekites (former Nephites who lived among the Lamanites). Have them review Alma 21:5–8 and tell what Amalekites believed about the following questions: (1) who will be saved? (2) Are there really prophets? and (3) Is Jesus Christ the Son of God? Answers may include:

Who will be saved? "God will save all men."

Prophets: No man "knoweth of things to come."

Jesus Christ: Belief in Christ is a "foolish tradition."

Discuss with your family the intent of the Amalekite as he confronted Aaron. (He wanted to be contentious.) How did Aaron respond? Share the following statement by Elder Russell M. Nelson:

"As we dread any disease that undermines the health of the body, so should we deplore contention, which is a corroding canker of the spirit. I appreciate the counsel of Abraham Lincoln, who said: 'Quarrel not at all. No man resolved to make the most of himself can spare time for personal contention. . . . Better give your path to a dog than be bitten by him.' (Letter to J. M. Cutts, 26 October 1863, in *Concise Lincoln Dictionary of*

Thoughts and Statements, comp. and arr. Ralph B. Winn, New York: New York Philosophical Library, 1959, p. 107.)" ("The Canker of Contention," *Ensign,* May 1989, p. 68.)

Read together Alma 21:9–10. Ask:

- What did Aaron do instead of arguing with the Amalekite?
- What was Aaron able to teach from the scriptures?
- How did the people of Jerusalem respond to Aaron's teaching from the scriptures?
- What can we learn from his example?
- What can we do in our family to prepare to stand against the false doctrines taught by those who follow Satan?

Alma 21:11–23

What do we learn about missionary work?

Have your family name family or ward members who are now serving as missionaries. Ask if they think they are always happy. Why or why not? To help your family better understand how difficult a mission can be, give them the quiz below. Explain that most of the answers can be found in Alma 21:11–23.

- Why aren't missionaries always able to convince people to listen to them? (Verse 12.)
- What happened to the missionaries serving in the land of Middoni? (Verse 13.)
- What did they do as soon as they got out of prison? (Verse 15.)
- How did they know where to preach? (Verse 16.)
- What blessing finally came to these Nephite missionaries? (Verse 17.)
- How can government leaders sometimes make a difference for the missionaries? (Verses 20–22.)
- What kind of a missionary was Ammon, and how did that influence those he taught? (Verse 23.)
- What can we learn from Ammon and his brethren about missionary work?

Give each member of your family a piece of stationery and invite them to write a letter to one of the missionaries listed earlier. Have them write an encouraging letter using what they learned about missionary work from Alma 21. You might end by singing "I Hope They Call Me on a Mission" (*Children's Songbook,* p. 169).

ALMA 22: LAMONI'S FATHER AND HIS HOUSEHOLD ARE CONVERTED

Alma 22:1–5
What role does the Holy Ghost play in missionary work?

Ask your family, "On a scale of 1 to 10 (with 10 being highest), how important is the Spirit of the Lord in missionary work?" Talk about why they chose the number they did. Have someone read D&C 42:13–14 and tell what the Lord said there about teaching and the Spirit.

Ask your family to read Alma 22:1–5 and look for instances in these passages where the term "Spirit" is used. How did the Spirit help the missionaries in these verses? Read the following quotation from President Ezra Taft Benson:

"If there is one message I have repeated to my brethren of the Twelve it is that it's the Spirit that counts. It is the Spirit that matters. I do not know how often I have said this, but I never tire of saying it—it is the Spirit that matters most." (Address at mission presidents' seminar, 3 April 1985, cited in *Missionary Guide,* p. 73.)

Perhaps a family member can share an experience when the Spirit directed him or her to teach or help someone in need.

Alma 22:6–14
What tools did Aaron use to teach the king?

Show several tools to your family. As you show each tool, invite your family to suggest who might use that particular tool regularly (for example, a hammer would be used by a carpenter, a pencil might be used by an artist, a wrench would be used by a mechanic, and so on). Now show your family a set of scriptures and discuss ways that scriptures are tools. Who uses the scriptures as tools? (Missionaries, teachers, and so on.) What are some other tools missionaries use to help teach the gospel? (Missionary discussions, videos, flip charts, pamphlets, and so on.)

Ask your family to read Alma 22:6–14 and look for some tools Aaron used to help bring about the conversion of the king (for example, bearing testimony, verse 8; asking good questions, verse 10; teaching correct doctrine from the scriptures, verse 13; and teaching from the scriptures).

Why would these tools help a missionary be more effective? Discuss ways your family members can develop these tools to help them better prepare for missionary service.

Alma 22:15–18
"I will give away all of my sins to know thee"

Bring several miscellaneous items to family scripture study. Have your family guess the retail cost of the items. Talk about how items receive a "value." How does our willingness to give more money for something affect its value?

Now display a picture of the Savior. Ask, "How valuable is a testimony of the Savior. What would you be willing to give to know Him better?" Share the following statement from President Ezra Taft Benson:

"Each of us must surrender our sins if we are to really know Christ. For we do not know Him until we become like Him. There are some, like this king, who must pray until they, too, have 'a wicked spirit rooted' from them so they can find the same joy. Attaining a righteous and virtuous life is within the capability of any one of us if we will earnestly seek for it. If we do not have these character traits, the Lord has told us that we should 'ask, and ye shall receive; knock, and it shall be opened unto you.' (D&C 4:7.)." ("What

Manner of Men Ought We to Be?" *Ensign,* November 1983, p. 43.)

Have a family member review Alma 20:23 and remind the family what King Lamoni's father was willing to give to save his life when Ammon threatened to kill him. Then have the family compare Alma 22:15 with Alma 22:18. Ask:

- What was Lamoni's father willing to give up for eternal life?
- Is that what the Lord requires? (We may not be asked to give up everything, but we do have to be willing to. See JST, Mark 8:37–38.)
- What was he willing to give up to come to a knowledge of Jesus Christ?
- Do you think the price he was willing to pay was adequate? Why or why not?
- What does his offering tell you about the value he began to place on the Savior?
- What can we learn from the example of King Lamoni's father?

Perhaps family members could write in their journal what specific steps they want to take so that they can come to know the Savior better.

Alma 22:19–27

 Before reading Alma 22:19–27, explain to family members that they are going to be in a movie. Each person will need to volunteer for a part. The parts are as follows: (1) the King, (2) the Queen, (3) Aaron, (4) a Servant or two, and (5) a narrator

Have family members quickly read Alma 22:19–27 and study what their character does in this story. The narrator can then read the story while the family members act out their parts. If a video camera is available, consider having a family member record the play.

Alma 22:28–35
Book of Mormon geography

To help your family understand these verses better, use the following map.

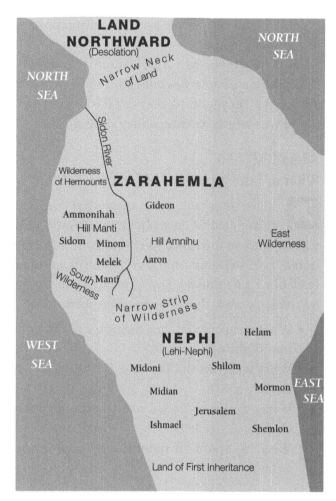

Book of Mormon Lands

ALMA 23: THE ANTI-NEPHI-LEHIS ARE FREED FROM THEIR CURSE

Alma 23:1–7
The conversion of the Lamanites

Divide your family into two groups and have them pretend they are television reporters. Have them read Alma 23:1–7 and look for two stories or events that they could report on a television broadcast for the Zarahemla News. Story ideas should include the Lamanite King's proclamation (see Alma 23:1–3) and the conversion of thousands of Lamanites (see Alma 23:4–7). Give each group several minutes to prepare their report. When the groups are ready, have them deliver their report as if they are reporting live on television.

After the reports, ask your family how they think these missionaries felt about their missionary efforts. Do you think they felt the success they found was worth hardships they suffered?

Alma 23:7–15

What are the "weapons of [your] rebellion"?

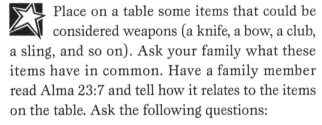 Place on a table some items that could be considered weapons (a knife, a bow, a club, a sling, and so on). Ask your family what these items have in common. Have a family member read Alma 23:7 and tell how it relates to the items on the table. Ask the following questions:

- What weapons did the Lamanites use to fight the Nephites?
- What weapons did they use to "fight against God"?
- What weapons do we use to rebel against God?
- What weapons of rebellion do people use today?

Quickly scan Alma 23:8–15 and find who was converted and who wasn't. Discuss why Mosiah's son's mission was so successful. Why wasn't it successful among the Amalekites and Amulonites? (See index, "Amalekites" and "Amulonites.")

Finally, cross-reference these verses with Mosiah 25:22–24. Read the Mosiah reference and list those things that led the Lamanites to lay down their weapons of rebellion and join the Lord's church. Discuss with your family how faith, repentance, taking the name of Christ, and having the Spirit can help them lay down their weapons of rebellion and become known as "the people of God."

Alma 23:16–18

Who were the Anti-Nephi-Lehies?

 Ask your family if they have ever wanted to change their first name? Why? Have them tell what name they would have chosen

instead. It might be interesting for the parents to explain how the children's names were chosen. Read together Alma 23:16–18. Ask:

- Why did the converted Lamanites want to be called by a new name?
- What was the name given to them?
- What words are used to describe the Anti-Nephi-Lehies after their conversion?
- Why do you think their conversion made them more industrious, friendly, and happy?

Ask your family if they can think of times when they take a new name. (Baptism, marriage, and in the temple.) Discuss the positive changes that occur when people take upon themselves each of these covenants.

ALMA 24: THE ANTI-NEPHI-LEHIES MAKE A COVENANT WITH GOD

Alma 24:1–10

What are the attributes of a person converted to the Lord?

Ask your family the following questions:

- What are some reasons people join the Church?
- How can you tell if a person is truly converted to the Lord?
- How might his or her behavior change?
- What are some ways you'll know if a person's conversion is sincere or not?
- What are some things members of the Church do that are different from what the world teaches?

Read together Alma 24:6–10, 23 and ask your family to find words and phrases that show the people of Ammon were truly converted. Have them search verses 1–2, 20–22 and find the trials they faced as a result of their conversion. Have a family member re-read Alma 24:7–10 aloud. Ask:

- How grateful were the people of Ammon, even in the midst of trials?
- How is this a sign of true conversion?
- What can you do to better show others you love the Lord?

Alma 24:11–19
Burying weapons of war

Make a pretend sword for each member of your family. (They could be drawn, or you might attach two Popsicle sticks together in the shape of a sword.) Ask your family to imagine how frightening it would be to actually have to go to battle against an enemy armed with just a sword. How frightening would it be to be in a battle like that and not have a sword? Explain to your family that these swords represent the swords belonging to the Anti-Nephi-Lehies. Read Alma 24:11–13 with your family and ask:

- What had the Anti-Nephi-Lehies done with their swords before their conversion?
- How did their misuse of their swords make them feel?
- What commitment were they willing to make? (To stain their swords with blood no more.)

Read Alma 24:14–17 and ask why the people of Ammon felt they should bury their weapons of war. Why was it significant that they buried their weapons rather than simply promising not to use them? (See also Matthew 5:29.) Have someone read Alma 24:18 and tell how the Anti-Nephi-Lehies' decision to bury their weapons showed their love for their fellowmen as well as for God.

Have your family members think of one habit, weakness, or sin that they know should not be a part of their lives. Have them privately write this on their sword. Talk to them about how important it would be to stop that particular sin or overcome that habit. Ask them if they would be willing to bury that sin or habit for the rest of their lives. Why or why not?

Take your family outside and dig a hole. Invite your family to bury their swords and the weak-

nesses or sins the swords represent. Encourage your family to follow the example of the Anti-Nephi-Lehies. Testify of the happiness that comes in our lives as we follow the Lord. Ask:

- In what ways does conversion increase a person's love for others?
- How did the unconverted Lamanites react when they saw that the Anti-Nephi-Lehies would not take up arms against them? (See Alma 24:20–27.)
- How many joined the people of God that day?

Alma 24:19–30
What is the moral of the story?

Ask your family, "Have you ever wanted to have someone pay close attention to something you were reading or saying? What did you do to get that person to pay attention to you?" Read Alma 24:19 and ask your family what phrase Mormon uses to get us to pay attention. ("And thus we see.") Tell your family that this phrase is used often by the prophet Mormon to help us see why he included a story in his record. He is summarizing the principles he wants us to learn. In effect he is saying, "This is the moral of the story." Invite your family to read Alma 24:19, 27, and 30 and tell what principles Mormon wants us to understand in these verses.

To better learn the principles Mormon taught, invite your family to share an experience when a person went through a severe trial. Read Alma 24:22 and ask what happened to the people of Ammon who made a covenant not to fight. Ask, "Why do you think the Lord didn't step in to save them from this disaster?" (See Alma 60:13.) Then read together Alma 24:23–26 and ask what happened to a group of Lamanites as a result of the death of the people of Ammon.

Testify that tragedies can sometimes actually turn into blessings. Share some examples of how you have grown spiritually through your personal trials and tragedies.

ALMA 25: ABINADI'S PROPHECY FULFILLED

Alma 25:1–3
What effect can anger have on our behavior?

Have your family members think of a time when they became angry over something that happened. Ask:

- Did you feel it was your fault or someone else's fault?
- When it happened, did you say something like: "He [or she] made me so angry!"?
- Can someone else really *make* you angry?
- Did you have a choice about how to respond to the situation?

Tell your family to think about those questions as you read together Alma 25:1–3. Ask:

- Why were the Lamanites angry? (See Alma 24:23–24.)
- Who did they believe was the cause of their feelings?
- How did they decide to respond to their feelings?
- Rather than repent or change, what did the Lamanites choose to do?

Invite family members to suggest other ways the Lamanites could have responded and how the consequences might have been different (note that the Lamanites did actually change later; see verses 13–16). Ask your family what they can learn from these Lamanites about what to do when we make mistakes in our lives.

Alma 25:4–12
A prophet's word fulfilled

Ask a family member to stand before the family and give a weather report as though he or she is on television. Have the person predict the weather for the next day or two. Then discuss the following questions:

- Why might you be reluctant to rely on your own weather predictions if you were planning an all-day picnic at the park?
- How does a meteorologist know what the weather will be in a day or two?
- How difficult would it be to predict the weather a week in advance? A month? A year?

Review with your family the prophecy Abinadi gave while being burned to death. (See Mosiah 17:14–19.) Tell your family that Abinadi was speaking to the priests of Noah, who were led by a man named Amulon. Now invite your family to search Alma 25:4–12 and mark the fulfillment of Abinadi's prophecy.

Invite family members to write "D&C 1:37–38" in the margin of their scriptures next to Alma 25:9–10. Have someone read D&C 1:37–38 and summarize what the Lord said about his prophets. Why is it so remarkable that a prophet can prophesy not just the weather but future events in our lives? Have your family name some prophecies of latter-day prophets that have been fulfilled. As an assignment for future discussion, have family members read a recent conference address and look for "things to come." Examples might include:

- What will happen if we live certain commandments?
- What will happen if we disobey certain commandments?
- What actions will bring the approval of God and the companionship of the Spirit?
- How should we prepare for the future?

Alma 25:13–17
What changes can the gospel make in a person's life?

Have your family bring their journals to scripture study. Ask them for examples of people in the scriptures or people they know who made changes for good in their lives. What do you think caused their change?

Read together with your family Alma 25:13–17 and discuss the following questions:

- Who made some major changes in these verses?
- Why did the Lamanites choose to make changes in their lives?
- How can you tell that their conversion was sincere?
- How did they feel about the Savior?
- How did the missionaries who taught them feel about this change?

Discuss with your family the changes the gospel can make in their lives. Invite them to list in their journals all the changes they can think of that the gospel has made in their lives.

ALMA 26: THE PSALM OF AMMON

Alma 26
Ammon's psalm of praise

Ask your family if they know what a psalm is. If no one does, have them look under the heading "Psalms" in the Bible Dictionary (p. 754) and read the definition. Explain that Alma 26 could be considered the Psalm of Ammon because of the praise Ammon expressed for his blessings from God. While studying Alma 26, have your family look for verses expressing praise. When you have concluded, have each family member write a psalm expressing praises for their blessings. Encourage your family to share their psalms with one another.

Alma 26:1–37
Select and share your favorite verses

As an alternative way to study Alma 26, ask each family member to read Alma 26:1–17 to themselves. Have them find two verses they like best and prepare to share why those verses are meaningful to them. After sharing some favorite verses, you could study Alma 26:18–37 in the same manner. (If you have children who cannot yet read, they can be paired with other family members who can.)

Alma 26:3–6
How can we help new converts?

Share with your family a missionary experience you have had and how it made you feel. Have someone read Alma 26:3–4 and tell who Ammon helped bring into the Church and how it made him feel. What do you think he meant when he said, "We have been made instruments in the hands of God"?

Read Alma 26:5 and ask:

- What do the sheaves of wheat represent? (Converts.)
- What does the sickle represent? (Missionary work.)

- Why was the wheat gathered into garners?
- How can we help new converts not be "wasted," meaning how can we help them not fall away from the truth once they have received it?

Read the following statement from President Gordon B. Hinckley about new converts: "Every one of them needs three things: a friend, a responsibility, and nurturing with 'the good word of God.'" ("Converts and Young Men," *Ensign,* May 1997, p. 47.) Ask your family what they are doing to help provide these three things for new converts. Also explain how this counsel is also helpful for families, children, and all members of the Church.

Alma 26:8–16
"I will not boast of myself, but . . . of my God"

Gather together objects that are used as instruments, such as scissors, a pencil, a flashlight, or a musical instrument. Show them to your family and ask:

- How useful are these instruments?
- How useful are they if there is no person to hold, use, or work them?

- Why is the person using the instrument more important than the instrument itself?
- Which should receive the most praise, the instrument or the user? Why?

Take turns reading Alma 26:8–16 together. As you do, have your family identify three things: (1) who would be considered the instrument (Ammon), (2) who is really doing the work (the Lord), and (3) what work is being done (conversion of Lamanites).

Have your family scan the verses one more time and mark every phrase they can find that shows Ammon gave proper credit to the Lord. Discuss the following questions:

- Why is it important to give credit to the Lord?
- What would be wrong with "boasting" in our own strength?
- What does that tell you about Ammon's humility?
- What are some specific ways you could apply Ammon's example in your own life?

Alma 26:17–21
Why did he do it?

Print the word "Justice" on one card, and the word "Mercy" on another. Show them to your family and talk about what these words mean. Ask which word best describes getting what you deserve. Which word best describes getting better than you deserve?

Read together Alma 26:17–21 and have someone identify who the "us" is in these verses. (Alma and the four sons of Mosiah.) Have family members vote which word (justice or mercy) best describes the treatment these five men received. What does this teach you about Heavenly Father's love for his children? What are some of the merciful blessings you have received from God? What do you think we can do to show God our gratitude for his mercy?

Alma 26:22
A formula for greatness

Explain to your family that the scriptures often have "formulas" of how to produce a desired result. Read together Alma 26:22 and have your family mark the four things we can do to help bring others to repentance. Talk about what those four things mean and why the Lord requires his servants to do those things.

Alma 26:30
How many converts did they expect?

Have your family imagine they are leaving today on a mission. Ask:

- What would be your main job as a missionary? (To teach and baptize.)
- How many people do you think you might teach?
- How many people would you like to baptize?
- Would it be worthwhile if you only baptized one person?

Have a family member read aloud Alma 26:30 and tell how many people Ammon and the sons of Mosiah hoped to convert. Read together Alma 26:22 and Alma 23:8–13 and ask your family how many people they actually did lead to the gospel?

Read D&C 18:10, 15–16 as a family and ask why the Lord gave these missionaries such great power and success in their missionary labors. Discuss ways your family could share in the joy those missionaries felt. Share the joy you have felt as you've helped bring others to the truth.

Alma 26:36
"It's my life!"

Ask your family if they have ever heard someone say, "It's my life!" Read Alma 26:36 together and ask if the intent of what Ammon said is the same or different from the statement "It's my life!" Why does someone usually say, "It's my life!"? What do you think Ammon wanted to do with the rest of his life?

Why do you think more people don't feel about doing God's work the way Ammon did?

ALMA 27: TAKING CARE OF NEW CONVERTS

Alma 27:1–14
What is the bond between missionaries and converts?

Summarize Alma 27:1–3 for your family, telling why the people of Anti-Nephi-Lehi were being violently attacked again. Discuss these questions:

- If you had been one of the missionaries who taught the Anti-Nephi-Lehies the gospel, what would you feel like doing for them?
- Why do missionaries feel so strongly toward those whom they have worked with?
- What feelings do you think converts have toward those who taught them?

Have family members take turns reading Alma 27:4–14 and look for things that show a bond between missionaries and converts. (For example, missionaries were "treated as though they were angels," missionaries were "moved with compassion" to do something for their converts, the king trusted Ammon's ability to obtain revelation for them, the people were willing to be obedient to the counsel Ammon received from the Lord.)

Discuss with your family how Ammon and his companions blessed the people of Anti-Nephi-Lehi. Ask how they helped save them physically. How did they help save them spiritually?

If you are a convert, share your own feelings about the missionaries who taught you. Or share feelings that you have for those you taught. Share the following excerpts from a letter to the missionary who first introduced the gospel to Elder Charles A. Didier and his family:

"We rapidly became good friends as your visits became more frequent. . . .

"We loved you. . . .

"You spoke to my heart by the power of the

Holy Ghost. I did not tell you how I felt that day. These are things we sometimes do not like to talk about because of the sacredness of our feelings, but it was the beginning of a new life for me, with new objectives, and a sure knowledge of the Church and of the truth. . . .

"We wanted to say: 'Thank you, Elder. Thank you for what has happened in our lives because of your testimony. You prepared the way of the Lord. You made his paths straight.'" ("Letter to a Returned Missionary," *Ensign*, November 1977, p. 66.)

Discuss with your family how they would feel if someone they had taught the gospel wrote them a letter like that.

Alma 27:16–19
What is the source of joy and happiness?

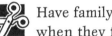 Have family members think about a time when they felt great joy and happiness. Invite them to tell what they were doing. Then have them think about a time when they felt really unhappy and angry. What were the circumstances that brought about such feelings?

Read Alma 27:16–19 with your family and have them underline the word "joy" each time it is used. Ask them what caused the great joy and happiness described in these verses. Have them compare the feelings of these missionaries with the feelings of the Lamanites and Amalakites in Alma 27:1–2. Ask what this teaches us about what leads to joy and what leads to bitterness and anger. Invite family members to share what they can do to feel like the men described in verses 16–19 more frequently.

Alma 27:20–24
How do covenants work for us?

Have your family read Alma 27:20–24 and look for key points of a covenant the Nephites extended to the Anti-Nephi-Lehies. Ask:

- What did the Nephites promise?
- What were the people of Anti-Nephi-Lehi to do?

• Do you think this was a fair covenant? Why?

• What does this teach about caring for new converts?

Ask your family to list the covenants they have entered into. Ask what kind of protection or safety our covenants with God provide today. Read and discuss the following statement:

"An important part of the plan for continued family relationships is to receive ordinances and covenants in the holy temples for ourselves and our ancestors. These ordinances and covenants are an anchor to safety for the family, both here and hereafter." (Joanne B. Doxey, "Strengthening the Family," *Ensign,* November 1987, pp. 91–92.)

Alma 27:25–30
What's in a name?

Invite your family to tell the different names they have been given (for example, the name they were given at birth and the name they took at baptism). Ask your family why we take upon ourselves a new name when we are baptized. How can taking upon ourselves the name of Christ make us different? Ask your family if they remember what the people of Anti-Nephi-Lehi were called before they took that new name. (Lamanites.) Read together Alma 27:25–30 and look for another new name the people of Anti-Nephi-Lehi were given. Ask:

• What was the new name they were given?

• What people were they numbered among?

• How would you describe their membership in Christ's church?

• How can you tell they understood there was life after death?

• Why would they be considered "a highly favored people of the Lord"?

• In what ways does this story show how new converts take part in the gospel of Jesus Christ?

ALMA 28: TENS OF THOUSANDS OF LAMANITES SLAIN

Alma 28:1–7
Fasting can help us deal with tragedy and pain

 Have your family silently read Alma 28:1–5. Ask them to ponder these events. Then discuss these questions together:

• Why would this war have been difficult to witness?

• How might it feel to lose a loved one during battle?

• What do you think you might have done to help deal with the sorrow and pain you would have felt if you were living then?

Have your family read Alma 28:6 and look for what the people did to help ease their pain. How would fasting and prayer bring relief? Have you ever fasted to gain help during times of great sorrow? Share these thoughts from Elder Joseph B. Wirthlin on the benefits of fasting and prayer:

"Fasting, coupled with mighty prayer, is powerful. It can fill our minds with the revelations of the Spirit. It can strengthen us against times of temptation.

"Fasting and prayer can help develop within us courage and confidence. It can strengthen our character and build self-restraint and discipline. Often when we fast, our righteous prayers and petitions have greater power. Testimonies grow. We mature spiritually and emotionally and sanctify our souls. Each time we fast, we gain a little more control over our worldly appetites and passions.

"Fasting and prayer can help us in our families and in our daily work. . . .

"Fasting in the proper spirit and in the Lord's way will energize us spiritually, strengthen our self-discipline, fill our homes with peace, lighten our hearts with joy, fortify us against temptation, prepare us for times of adversity, and open the windows of heaven." ("The Law of the Fast," *Ensign,* May 2001, pp. 73–75.)

Ask family members what they could do to make their fasts more meaningful. Encourage them to watch for more occasions when they would like to seek the added blessings of fasting.

Alma 28:10–12
Why do people view death differently?

Share with your family an experience you have had attending the funeral of a loved one or friend. Talk about the emotions you felt and how have you been able to cope with the loss of a loved one. Especially tell about others who may have had a difficult time handling their loss. Ask your family what other emotions those people might have had. Invite your family to share their feelings regarding death.

Have family members read Alma 28:11–12 and look for the reasons some people feared for those who died and for some reasons why other people rejoiced. Why do some mourners fear while others rejoice? Also read D&C 42:45. What does this teach us about death? What will determine whether we end up in "a state of endless wo" or "a state of never-ending happiness"?

Alma 28:13–14
What lessons should we learn from the phrase "and thus we see"?

Ask your family to find a phrase that is repeated three times in Alma 28:13–14. Explain that Book of Mormon writers often used this phrase to emphasize important lessons they wanted future readers to understand. (See 1 Nephi 16:29 for the first time this phrase is used.) Have family members read verses 13 and 14 carefully and then summarize in their own words the lessons Mormon intended us to learn from the story in this chapter.

ALMA 29: THE WISH OF ALMA'S HEART

Alma 29:1–3, 13
What was Alma's wish?

Give each family member an opportunity to answer these two questions: "If you could be anyone in the world, who would it be?" And "If you could do anything in the world, what would you do?"

After everyone has responded, read together Alma 29:1–2 and find who Alma wished to be and what he wished to do. Ask:

- How are Alma's wishes different from yours?
- Have you ever encouraged someone to repent? How did the experience go?
- How might Alma's desire have been influenced by his experience with an angel that helped him repent?
- What other reasons can you think of that might explain why he wished to declare repentance to the world?

Have someone read Alma 29:3 and find what Alma decided about his wishes. Discuss what it might mean to be "content with the things which the Lord hath allotted." Explain that another word for "allotted" is "assigned." Ask:

- According to Alma 29:13, what had Alma been "allotted" or assigned?
- What had the Lord blessed him with for his labors?
- What has the Lord "allotted" or assigned for you to do in life? (For an example, see your patriarchal blessing.)
- How might being discontent with our allotment in life be offensive to the Lord?

Share with your family this statement by Elder Neal A. Maxwell:

"True spirituality helps us to achieve balance between being too content with our present self and the equally dangerous human tendency we might have of wishing for more enlarged and impactful roles. Alma said, 'But behold, . . . I ought to be content with the things which the Lord hath allotted unto me.' . . . To develop that kind of justifiable contentment . . . is obviously one of our challenges. . . . We may feel underused, underwhelmed, and underappreciated even though we are ignoring unused opportunities for service all about us." (*Notwithstanding My Weakness,* pp. 115–16.)

Ask your family what they can do to render service, especially when they feel "underused, underwhelmed, and underappreciated."

Alma 29:4–5
Do we really get what we want?

Draw a line down the middle of a large sheet of paper or poster board. Have your family read Alma 29:4–5 and find the opposites contained in the verses. List one word on the left side of the board and its opposite on the right side of the board. When finished, the board might look something like the chart below:

Life	Death
Salvation	Destruction
Good	Evil
Joy	Remorse of conscience

Ask your family which list they would rather have and why. What would they be willing to do to enjoy those things?

Look again at Alma 29:4–5 and underline phrases showing that God allows us to have what we want (for example, "he granteth unto men according to their desire"; "he allotteth unto men . . . according to their wills"; "it is given according to his desires"). Ask:

- How might knowing that the Lord "granteth unto men according to their desire" in this life affect our decisions for the future?
- What can we do to show the Lord that we want life and salvation more than death and destruction?

Alma 29:9–17
What brought Alma joy?

Write the name of each family member on a separate slip of paper and put the papers in a basket. Have everyone draw a name and tell what would bring joy to the person named on the slip of paper. Take turns reading Alma 29:9–17 and make a list of the things that brought Alma joy. You could have the family underline each item in their scriptures as you find them. Discuss the following questions:

- Why do you think Alma found joy in these particular things?
- How are these similar to what brings the Savior joy? (See D&C 18:10–16.)
- What things bring you personal joy?
- How can you help bring joy to other members of the family?

Encourage family members to keep a daily journal of things they did to bring joy to others and to record how they felt being part of it.

ALMA 30: KORIHOR THE ANTICHRIST

Alma 30:6–29
Korihor's teachings are exposed

Ask your family to imagine they are playing in a championship athletic contest. Talk about what advantage it would be if your team had any of the following: the opposing team's playbook; a video of the opposing team's practice sessions; a microphone allowing you to hear every play the opposing team calls.

Have one family member read aloud Ephesians 6:12 and another Abraham 3:25–26. Discuss the following questions:

- How are our lives like a championship game?
- In what way is the contest of life much more serious than an athletic contest?
- Who is our adversary?
- What are the rewards for winning?

- What is the cost of defeat?
- How helpful would it be to know the adversary's strategies?
- Where and how can you find out about Satan's tactics?

Share the following statement from Elder Ezra Taft Benson:

"The Book of Mormon exposes the enemies of Christ. It confounds false doctrines and lays down contention (see 2 Ne. 3:12). It fortifies the humble followers of Christ against the evil designs, strategies, and doctrines of the devil in our day. The type of apostates in the Book of Mormon are similar to the type we have today. God, with his infinite foreknowledge, so molded the Book of Mormon that we might see the error and know how to combat false educational, political, religious, and philosophical concepts of our time." ("The Book of Mormon Is the Word of God," *Ensign*, May 1975, p. 64.)

Read together Alma 30:6–12 and find the name of the teacher of falsehood. Ask:

- What is an antichrist? (See also 1 John 4:3.)
- Was it legal for Korihor to express his beliefs?
- Is it legal for people to oppose the teachings of Jesus Christ today?
- What then, if anything, can we do to stop the work of wickedness in the world?

Have your family take turns reading Alma 30:12–29. As you read, highlight and identify each of Korihor's false teachings. Talk about why those teachings are false and what the truth is on each of these topics. Also think about different ways your family might combat each false idea.

Alma 30:37–44
The Power of Testimony

 Have a family member read aloud Alma 30:37–38 and explain what main doctrine Korihor struggled with. Ask your family how difficult it would be to believe in the plan of salvation, or any other true doctrine, if they did not believe in God.

Explain that in the *New Era* magazine there is a section where young people write in with a question and then other young people have a chance to help answer the question. One question posed there was, "I have a friend who claims to be an atheist. I want to try to convince her that there is a God. Nothing seems to get through to her. What can I do?" (*New Era*, August 1994, p. 17.) Allow family members time to answer the question in their journals and then to talk about their responses.

When you have finished, study Alma 30:39–44 and look for some of the things Alma did to help Korihor. (Alma bore testimony, shifted the burden of proof to Korihor, showed how all creation testifies of God, and used the scriptures.) Ask:

- What can you learn from Alma to help with your nonmember friends?
- Why was his approach a good one?
- What are at least five evidences Alma gave that there is a God?
- How strong is your testimony about those five things?

Explain to your family that it is not our responsibility as members of Christ's church to prove the truth of the gospel to other people. Our duty is to explain the gospel and bear testimony of the truth we have received. It is then their responsibility to find out for themselves that it is true. It is the responsibility of the Holy Ghost to answer their prayers and give them a testimony. (See Moroni 10:3–5.)

Alma 30:43–50
Is it appropriate to ask for a sign?

Ask your family if they have ever wished that the Lord would send some sort of a sign that would be concrete proof that the gospel is true. Explain that Alma 30 has the story of someone who demanded such a sign. Take turns reading Alma 30:43–50 together as a family. Ask what sort of sign Korihor might have been looking for. What sign did he get? Have someone read aloud Matthew 16:4 and tell what kind of people demand signs. Share the following statement from the Prophet Joseph Smith:

"When I was preaching in Philadelphia, a Quaker called out for a sign. I told him to be still. After the sermon, he again asked for a sign. I told the congregation the man was an adulterer; that a wicked and adulterous generation seeketh after a sign; and that the Lord had said to me in a revelation, that any man who wanted a sign was an adulterous person. 'It is true,' cried one, 'for I caught him in the very act,' which the man afterwards confessed when he was baptized." (*Teachings of the Prophet Joseph Smith*, p. 278; see also Alma 30:18.)

Alma 30:53
Can Satan give revelations?

Write the following question on a sheet of paper for your family to read: "Can Satan give people revelations?" Have your family read Alma 30:53 and look for an answer. Share the following statement from Elder Boyd K. Packer: "All inspiration does not come from God. (See D&C 46:7.) The evil one has the power to tap into those channels of revelation and send conflicting signals which can mislead and confuse us. There are promptings from evil sources which are so carefully counterfeited as to deceive even the very elect." ("Revelation in a Changing World," *Ensign*, November 1989, p. 14).

Ask your family how they can know if a revelation is from God or not. To help answer that question, read together D&C 50:17–25.

Alma 30:53–60
The devil will not support his followers

Ask your family to describe the characteristics of a true friend. After they have shared their ideas, ask:

- Would a true friend support you during difficult times? Why or why not?
- What are some characteristics of someone who was only pretending to be your friend?

- Would a false friend support you in difficult times? Why or why not?

Ask your family to read Alma 30:53–59 and look for the cursings that came upon Korihor. Ask them what Korihor did to be cursed by God. Who convinced him to teach such false doctrine and lead so many astray?

Read Alma 30:60 together and ask what we learn there about Satan. Ask:

- Why do you think that Satan will not support those who follow him?
- What does that teach you about the "rewards or blessings" that Satan promises?
- Why do people choose to believe Satan's lies rather than the Savior's truth?

ALMA 31: ALMA'S MISSION TO THE APOSTATE ZORAMITES

Alma 31:1–11
Which is more powerful, the scriptures or a sword?

Place a sword (or a picture of one) and some scriptures next to each other on a table. Ask your family which they would rather have in a battle. What if the battle is with evil ideas? Have a family member read aloud Alma 31:5 and tell which one Alma thought was more powerful. Discuss the differences between the sword and the scriptures in helping people "to do that which is just."

Read Alma 31:1–11 together as a family and look for reasons why Alma decided to "try the virtue of the word of God" instead of the sword. Ask:

- Who were the Zoramites? (Verse 8.)
- What were some of the things they were doing wrong? (Verses 2, 9–11.)
- How did the knowledge of their iniquity make Alma feel?

• What was another worry of the Nephites? (Verse 4.)

• What had happened to the Zoramites since they departed from the Nephites?

• How hard would a mission be among this kind of people?

Share the following statement from President Ezra Taft Benson:

"The word of God, as found in the scriptures, in the words of living prophets, and in personal revelation, has the power to fortify the Saints and arm them with the Spirit so they can resist evil, hold fast to the good, and find joy in this life." ("The Power of the Word," *Ensign*, May 1986, p. 80.)

Discuss as a family how the blessings President Benson listed might have helped help Alma and his brethren. How might they have blessed the lives of the Zoramites?

Alma 31:12–23
How did the Zoramites worship?

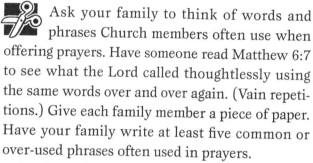 Ask your family if they think it is possible to offend Heavenly Father by praying. Have a family member stand on a chair and with a self-righteous voice read Alma 31:15–18. Ask your family to say what they think of such a prayer. Ask:

• What do the words of the prayer teach you about the Zoramites?

• What did they believe about themselves?

• What did they believe about everyone else?

• What did you learn about the god they worshiped?

• How would you like to have been a member of their ward?

Read together Alma 31:12–14, 19–23 and look for what else was wrong with the way the Zoramites worshiped. Discuss the following questions:

• How often did they worship? (Compare D&C 59:9–11.)

• What was the Rameumptom used for? (Verses 13–13, 21–22.)

• What problems do you see with what happened the rest of the week?

Write a family letter to a Mr. Zoramite that explains how we should worship Heavenly Father.

Alma 31:19–25
What is a selfsame prayer?

Ask your family to think of words and phrases Church members often use when offering prayers. Have someone read Matthew 6:7 to see what the Lord called thoughtlessly using the same words over and over again. (Vain repetitions.) Give each family member a piece of paper. Have your family write at least five common or over-used phrases often used in prayers.

Read together Alma 31:19–22 and explain how the Zoramites prayed. Then read together Alma 31:23–25 and discuss the following questions:

• How did Alma feel about the Zoramites' prayer? (Verse 19.)

• How did the Zoramites' prayer suffer from "vain repetitions." (Verses 20, 22.)

• How often did the Zoramites pray this way?

• What do you think is the problem with praying the same prayer over and over again?

• What were the Zoramites really interested in?

Post the "Top Five" list somewhere in the house where it will be most visible (a refrigerator, a bulletin board). Write on your list the five over-used phrases you identified above. Challenge family members to go one week without using any of these phrases in their personal and family prayers.

Alma 31:26–36
Compare Alma's prayer with the Zoramites' prayer

Divide your family into two groups (make sure younger children are teamed with someone older). Assign one group to find out how Alma described the Zoramite prayer in Alma

31:26–29 and the other group to find out how Alma prayed and what he prayed for in Alma 31:32–36. You might play some soft church music while the family reads. Ask:

- What are some of the differences between Alma's prayer and the Zoramite prayer?
- Who did Alma primarily pray for?
- What does this teach us about the Zoramites?
- What does this teach us about Alma?
- What does this teach us about prayer?

Sing "Sweet Hour of Prayer" (*Hymns,* no.142). After the song, have a family member share a personal experience of how one of his or her prayers was answered.

In a future family home evening, you might consider making prayer reminders for each member of the family. Some might want to make a prayer rock to be placed on a pillow as a reminder to pray each day. You can make a prayer rock by taking a rock and painting it or decorating it. You could also decorate a doormat or a carpet square to make a prayer rug that can be placed next to the bed as a reminder to pray.

ALMA 32: ALMA'S DISCOURSE ON FAITH

Alma 32:1–12
Why was Alma successful in preaching the gospel to the poor?

 Have your family search Alma 32:1–12 for answers to the following questions:

- What hill did Alma preach from?
- What group of people was most receptive to Alma's teachings?
- Why was Alma so happy about the poor people?
- Why do you think the poor were more willing to listen?

Read together Alma 32:6, 12; Luke 4:18; and D&C 136:32–33 and discuss what these verses teach about the relationship between humility and gaining gospel understanding and testimony.

Alma 32:13–16
God will have a humble people

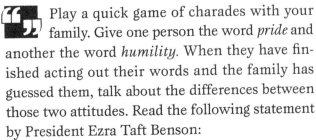 Play a quick game of charades with your family. Give one person the word *pride* and another the word *humility.* When they have finished acting out their words and the family has guessed them, talk about the differences between those two attitudes. Read the following statement by President Ezra Taft Benson:

"God will have a humble people. Either we can choose to be humble or we can be compelled to be humble." ("Beware of Pride," *Ensign,* May 1989, p. 6.)

Which of the two choices President Benson gave us seems preferable? Why? Read together Alma 32:13–16 and look for what Alma said about being humbled by force and being humble by choice. Why would it be better to choose to be humble?

Testify to your family that we can choose to be humble. Share some ideas from President Benson about how we can:

"We can choose to humble ourselves by conquering enmity toward our brothers and sisters, esteeming them as ourselves, and lifting them as high or higher than we are. (See D&C 38:24; D&C 81:5; D&C 84:106.)

"We can choose to humble ourselves by receiving counsel and chastisement. (See Jacob 4:10; Hel. 15:3; D&C 63:55; D&C 101:4–5; D&C 108:1; D&C 124:61, 84; D&C 136:31; Prov. 9:8.)

"We can choose to humble ourselves by forgiving those who have offended us. (See 3 Ne. 13:11, 14; D&C 64:10.)

"We can choose to humble ourselves by rendering selfless service. (See Mosiah 2:16–17.)

"We can choose to humble ourselves by going on missions and preaching the word that can humble others. (See Alma 4:19; Alma 31:5; Alma 48:20.)

"We can choose to humble ourselves by getting to the temple more frequently.

"We can choose to humble ourselves by

confessing and forsaking our sins and being born of God. (See D&C 58:43; Mosiah 27:25–26; Alma 5:7–14, 49.)

"We can choose to humble ourselves by loving God, submitting our will to His, and putting Him first in our lives. (See 3 Ne. 11:11; 3 Ne. 13:33; Moro. 10:32.)

"Let us choose to be humble. We can do it. I know we can." ("Beware of Pride," *Ensign,* May 1989, pp. 6–7.)

Alma 32:21
What is faith?

Have your family separate into two teams. Ask each team to read Alma 32:21 to learn about faith in the Lord Jesus Christ. Also ask them to read the Bible Dictionary's definition of faith. (See Bible Dictionary, "Faith," p. 669.)

When they are prepared, take turns having each team share one thing they know about faith. Have them share what they know from memory rather than reading again in the scriptures. See which team can share the most information. When all have finished, discuss their answers and talk about any questions they may have about faith.

Have your family write the following quotation in their scriptures next to Alma 32:21:

"Faith is a gift of God bestowed as a reward for personal righteousness. It is always given when righteousness is present, and the greater the measure of obedience to God's laws the greater will be the endowment of faith." (Bruce R. McConkie, *Mormon Doctrine,* p. 264.)

Share ideas you can use as a family to increase your faith. Set a goal for your family to become more obedient to a selected principle of the gospel or to a certain commandment you have been struggling with.

Alma 32:27–43
An experiment upon my words

Draw the following items on a poster: a seed, soil, a sprout, a tree, a piece of fruit. Take turns reading Alma 32:27–43 and look for a label

that could accompany each picture. Ask your family to share their ideas and write them under each picture. Their ideas may include the following:

Seed: Word of God. (See verse 28.)
Soil: Your heart (See verse 28.)
Sprout: Enlarging of your soul, enlightened understanding, and deliciousness. (See verse 28.)
Tree: Increased knowledge that the seed was good. (See verses 30–39.)
Fruit: Everlasting life. (See verses 41–43.)

Share your testimony of the importance of faith. Then discuss the following questions:

• What else you might compare to a seed to try the experiment to see if it is good and if you can exercise faith in it? (For example, you could experiment with the law of tithing, daily prayer, or regular fasting.)
• According to verse 28, you can know if the word of God is good if it begins to "enlarge your soul" and "enlighten your understanding" and is "delicious to you." What are some modern words you could use to describe these three experiences. (Perhaps something like: makes you a better person, helps you feel better about yourself, allows you to have a clearer perspective, is enjoyable.)
• Why would these three experiences increase your faith?
• Once you know that a gospel principle or doctrine is true, what can you do to continue to nourish your faith in that principle, as verse 37 suggests?
• What is one principle or doctrine of the gospel we as a family could experiment on?

Ask your family to select a goal you can try Alma's experiment with. Try "planting" and "nurturing" this principle or doctrine for a set period of time. When you have finished, talk as a family about how your lives have improved as a result. To help you with this project, you might also want to do one of the following activities:

Activity 1: Provide each family member with a seed of some kind, a small Styrofoam cup, and some potting soil. Ask, "How will you nurture this seed so that it will grow? How can you nurture your faith and cultivate your testimony?" Show your family a fully grown plant. Ask what will happen to this plant if it isn't given the light, water, and nutrients? How are our testimonies similar to this plant? What do our testimonies need to stay strong?

Activity 2: To teach the importance of planting the word of God in our hearts, assemble some gardening aids. You may want to have on hand a small bag of fertilizer, a trowel or small gardening shovel, a watering can, a picture of the sun, and a small plant. Place all these items in a box or bag. Invite family members to come up and choose one item. Once they have selected an item, have family members tell one thing that item suggests they can do to nurture the word of God by their faith in Jesus Christ.

Activity 3: Have your family read Alma 32:28. Ask them how the planting of the word of God in a person's heart makes him or her feel inside. Consider having them mark the words "swell," "enlarge," "enlighten," and "delicious." Invite family members to circle the first letter of each of those words. Ask, "If you put the first letters of each of those words together, what does it spell?" (SEED.)

ALMA 33: ALMA TEACHES THE ZORAMITES HOW TO WORSHIP

Alma 33:2–11, 23
What did Alma want the Zoramites to plant in their hearts?

Show your family a seed and remind them what Alma taught about the word of God, a seed, and developing faith. (See Alma 32:28–29.) Read together Alma 33:1 and list the questions asked by the Zoramites. (Should we believe in one God? How do we plant this seed in our heart? How do we exercise our faith?)

Discuss with your family how they would

answer these questions. Tell your family that Alma chose to answer by quoting three prophets: Zenos (verses 3–11), Zenock (verses 15–17), and Moses (verses 18–20). Invite family members to choose one of these prophets and search the verses, looking for answers to the questions asked by the Zoramites. As they share what they have learned, discuss the following:

- What did Zenos teach about where and when we should pray?
- Why is Heavenly Father able to have mercy on us and answer our prayers? (Verses 11, 16.)
- What did Jesus Christ do that made it possible for God to have mercy on us?
- What symbol of Christ did Moses raise in the wilderness to heal his people? (A brass serpent on a staff.)

Read together Alma 33:21–23 and talk about how the story of Moses and the brass serpent is like "planting" the word in our hearts and praying to know the truth. What blessings will come to those who plant this seed?

This might be a good time to tell your family that scripture study and prayer are more than just items on a checklist. Testify that they have the power to help us plant this seed, nourish it, and one day enjoy fruit from it. Share the following statement from President Spencer W. Kimball:

"I find that when I get casual in my relationships with divinity and when it seems that no divine ear is listening and no divine voice is speaking, that I am far, far away. If I immerse myself in the scriptures the distance narrows and the spirituality returns." (*Teachings of Spencer W. Kimball,* p. 135.)

Alma 33:18–22
What did the serpent on a pole symbolize?

Before scripture study, find or draw a picture of a snake. Put the picture in a backpack and set it on the floor. Tell your family to imagine that you are on a camping trip. While hiking in the nearby mountains, a family member is bitten by a poisonous snake. Ask your family what their first reaction would be.

Pick up the backpack and ask what they would hope to find in it to help treat the snakebite. Reach into the backpack and pull out the picture or drawing. Ask your family if they think this picture could actually heal someone.

Read Numbers 21:4–9 with your family and have them point out similarities to your story. Next have someone read Alma 33:19–22 and identify what Alma compared the brass serpent to. Ask:

- How was the brazen serpent a symbol of Jesus Christ?
- How could looking at the brass serpent heal a snake bite?
- Why did some people refuse to look at the serpent and be healed?
- Why do some people today refuse to try the teachings of Christ and see if those teachings will heal them?

Invite family members to share experiences where looking to the Savior helped them in a time of trouble or prevented them from doing things that spiritually destroy.

ALMA 34: AMULEK TESTIFIES OF CHRIST

Alma 34:8–14
The "what," "why," and "how" of sacrifice

Tell your family that Alma 34:8–14 teaches very important doctrine relating to the atonement of Jesus Christ and of his sacrifice for us. Read these verses with your family and have them look for answers to three questions:

- *What* is a "sacrifice?"
- *Why* did Jesus Christ need to be this sacrifice?
- *How* was the Atonement different from all other sacrifices?

Talk about what your family discovered in these verses. Then have family members take turns reading the following:

What: Have someone read the first paragraph under the entry "Sacrifice" in the Bible Dictionary, pp. 765–66.

Why: "There are several reasons why Jesus was the only person who could be our Savior. One reason is that Heavenly Father chose him to be the Savior. He was the Only Begotten Son of God and thus had power over death. . . . Jesus also qualified to be our Savior because he was the only person who ever lived on the earth who did not sin. This made him a worthy sacrifice to pay for the sins of others." (*Gospel Essentials,* p. 73.)

How: "No mortal being had the power or capability to redeem all other mortals from their lost and fallen condition, nor could any other voluntarily forfeit his life and thereby bring to pass a universal resurrection for all other mortals. Only Jesus Christ was able and willing to accomplish such a redeeming act of love. We may never understand nor comprehend in mortality how He accomplished what He did, but we must not fail to understand why He did what He did. Everything He did was prompted by His unselfish, infinite love for us." (Ezra Taft Benson, "Jesus Christ—Our Savior and Redeemer," *Ensign,* June 1990, p. 4.)

Alma 34:15–17
What principle of the gospel leads us to repentance?

Ask a family member to perform a task for you that is complicated enough that the instructions will need to be repeated several times. (For example, you could ask the person to draw a star or other figure for you but instead of calling it a star, give directions on what lines to draw). Talk about why repetition is helpful and why sometimes we are told the same thing over and over again.

Read Alma 34:15–17 together and have your family find the phrase that is repeated four times. Ask:

- What does "faith unto repentance" mean?
- Why does faith in Jesus Christ precede repentance?
- Why would it be important to emphasize this principle?

Alma 34:18–27
What are we supposed to pray for?

Take turns reading Alma 34:18–27 and after each verse have the person who read it explain in his or her own words what Amulek would have us pray for. Help your family discover modern applications for the things Amulek taught us to pray for. Give your family paper and coloring materials. Have them illustrate one thing they will begin to pray for more regularly, and challenge them to do so.

Alma 34:31–36
This life is the time to prepare to meet God

Show your family some of the obituary articles from today's newspaper. Ask them if most people know the day they are going to die. If tomorrow were your turn to die, what would be some of your concerns?

Read Alma 34:31–36 as a family and look for what Amulek said we ought to be concerned about. Ask:

- What is one of the main reasons we are here on earth?
- What will happen if we are unprepared to meet God when we die?
- What did Amulek say was our best preparation for the time when we will stand before God?
- What rewards will come to those who live each day prepared to meet God?
- Why is procrastination such a dangerous tendency?

Share the following from Elder Henry B. Eyring:

"Even the acceptance of personal responsibility may not overcome the temptation to believe that now is not the time to repent. 'Now' can seem so difficult, and 'later' appear so much easier. The truth is that today is always a better day to repent than any tomorrow. First, sin has its debilitating effects on us. The very faith we need to repent is weakened by delay. The choice to continue in sin diminishes our faith and lessens our right to claim the Holy Ghost as our companion and comforter." ("Do Not Delay," *Ensign,* November 1999, p. 34.)

Alma 34:37–41
A "to-do" list

Show your family a daily planner and ask, "What is a 'to-do' list? Why is it important to plan our daily activities? How can checking off those things we have accomplished help in our lives?"

Explain that Alma 34:37–41 could be compared to a "to-do" list from God. Have your family read these verses and put a checkmark by each commandment they find. Ask each family member to select one of those commandments they need to work on most and focus on doing better with it in the coming week.

ALMA 35: PREPARING THE LORD'S PEOPLE FOR DIFFICULT TIMES

Alma 35:1–11
Does the gospel unite or divide?

Ask your family to tell whether they think the gospel brings people together or divides them. Have them give examples. Then share the following story:

"Betty Powell was a student at the University of Tennessee when she first met some Latter-day Saint young people. Soon she was listening to the missionary discussions and feeling the Spirit's direction that the gospel she was being taught was true. She worried about how her family would react if she were baptized into another religion.

However, she could not deny the truth of the gospel and joined the Church. The day came for her to share the news with her family. Her worst fears were realized. Her family told her to renounce her new faith or be cut off both financially and socially. She would no longer be welcomed at home. She returned to school alone and unsupported.

"Months later, at a stake conference, Betty saw the missionary who had baptized her. She showed off her engagement ring and announced her wedding plans for the Swiss Temple. The missionary wept for joy that Betty once again had a family and a home in the gospel of Jesus Christ."

Ask your family how this story illustrates how the gospel both divides and unites.

Divide your family into two groups. Have one group review Alma 35:1–7 and the other Alma 35:8–11 and look for how the gospel either united or divided people. Invite them to share their insights. The following questions might be helpful in your discussion:

- Which Zoramites were angry? (Verse 3.)
- What was it about the gospel message that made them angry? (See also 1 Nephi 16:2.)
- What became of those who believed the words of Alma and his brethren? (Verses 6, 9.)
- How did the people of Ammon treat the outcast Zoramites? (Verses 8–9.)
- What did this division among the Zoramites eventually lead to? (Verses 10–11.)
- What do you learn from this story about who loves the gospel and who gets angry about it?
- How does this story show how the gospel can both divide and unite?

Alma 35:15–16
Why did Alma gather his sons to instruct them in the ways of the Lord?

 Display a picture of your family and ask each parent to share their greatest concerns about their family in the world in which they live. Discuss together the following questions:

- What is the best hope for the happiness of our family today? (Living the gospel.)
- Whose responsibility is it to teach the children the gospel? (See D&C 68:25–29.)
- How can children help parents fulfill their responsibility?

Explain that the welfare of the family has been the concern of parents in all ages. Read together Alma 35:15–16. Ask:

- What was the state of the world in which Alma's family lived?
- Why do you think Alma felt it necessary to teach his sons "concerning the things pertaining unto righteousness"?
- What would be the benefit of giving this charge to his sons separately?

Read the following quotation from President Ezra Taft Benson:

"The Book of Mormon, which is the most correct book on earth, demonstrates that the major responsibility for teaching our [children] the great plan of the Eternal Father—the Fall, rebirth, Atonement, Resurrection, Judgment, eternal life—rests with fathers. It should be done individually as well as in the family. It should be preached and discussed so our children will know the commandments. It should be done from their youth up—and often. May we teach our children as the exemplary Book of Mormon fathers taught their sons. And may they, like Nephi, listen and obey, knowing that because of those teachings they too were born of goodly parents." (*A Witness and a Warning,* pp. 71–72.)

Fathers or mothers might express gratitude for the opportunity to teach their family the gospel.

ALMA 36: ALMA TESTIFIES OF HIS CONVERSION

Alma 36:1–30
What is chiasmus?

 Draw an X on a paper, large enough so all family members can easily see it. Tell them that this is the letter X in the English language, but ask if anyone knows what it represents in the Greek language. (The twenty-second letter in the Greek alphabet—"chi"—pronounced "ki.") Tell your family there is a literary form called "chiasmus" (pronounced ki-Az-mus) in which the writer parallels the ideas and words used previously in reverse order. Ask if anyone can recite the first two lines of the nursery rhyme "Old King Cole." ("Old King Cole was a merry old soul, and a merry old soul was he".) Explain that this is a simple example of chiasmus that can be shown graphically as follows:

```
A       B
   X
B       A
```
(Add the A's and B's to the X on your paper).

Ask what the corresponding A and B parts would be from the nursery rhyme:

(A) *Old King Cole* was a (B) *merry old soul,*
And a (B) *merry old soul* was (A) *he.*

Ask your family to look at short examples of chiasmus from both the Old and New Testaments. Read Isaiah 55:8 and Matthew 10:39 out loud. As you do, have your family identify the related parts:

For (A) *my* thoughts are not (B) *your* thoughts,
Neither are (B) *your* ways (A) *my* ways, saith the Lord. (Isaiah 55:8.)

He that (A) *findeth* his life shall (B) *lose* it:
And he that (B) *loseth* his life for my sake shall (B) *find* it. (Matthew 10:39.)

Tell your family that instead of just two parts, often Chiasmi are expanded to include many parts. Each chiasmus, though, always has each element written in one order and then repeated in reverse order. This unique literary form is common in ancient Jewish writing. Chiasmus has also been discovered in the Book of Mormon. The entire chapter of Alma 36 is one complex chiasmus.

Write the following outline on a large piece of paper or chart. As you read the chapter as a family, write key words or phrases on the chart that indicate the message of the verse or verses.

```
A (v. 1)
   B (v. 2)
      C (v. 3)
         D (vv. 4–5)
            E (v. 6)
               F (v. 10)
                  G (v. 14)
                     H (v. 16)
                        I (v. 17)
                        I (v. 18)
                     H (vv. 19–21)
                  G (v. 22)
               F (v. 23)
            E (v. 24)
         D (v. 26)
      C (v. 27)
   B (vv. 28–29)
A (v. 30)
```

Explain to your family that another interesting characteristic of chiasmus is that the writer puts the point he wants to emphasize most at the center of the chiasmus. Ask, "What is the key point Alma is making in this chapter?"

Some other examples of chiasmus in the Book of Mormon are Mosiah 3:18–19, Mosiah 5:10–12, and Alma 41:13–14. Ask, "Why is it helpful to know there is chiasmus in the Book of Mormon? What does that teach you about the origin of the Book of Mormon?" (That it is a translation from Hebrew, and that Joseph Smith was the translator, not the author.)

(Adapted from John W. Welch, "Chiasmus in the Book of Mormon," in *Book of Mormon Authorship,* pp. 35–50.)

Alma 36:11–25
Can we be relieved of the burden of sin?

 Have a family member stand. Give the person several heavy items to hold, such as books or rocks. Have each item labeled with a particular sin appropriate to the age of your family.

Ask the person how he or she would like to carry this burden around all the time and explain why not. Begin to take away some of the heavy objects one at a time. Talk about the differences between the "heavy" load and the "light" load. In what way is sin a "heavy burden"? How can we take away the heavy burden of sin?

Tell your family you would like them to compare this to Alma's experience. Ask them to look for steps of repentance that Alma went through as they study Alma 36:11–25. Ask:

- How did Alma feel about the sins he had committed after the angel spoke to him and why?
- What particular thought came to mind as Alma remembered the teachings of his father?
- What did Alma do when he thought of Jesus?
- How did Alma feel after confessing his sins and pleading for mercy?
- What does that teach us about the power of the Atonement?
- How do you feel when you think of the Atonement?
- How did Alma try to make restitution for what he had done wrong?
- Why is it important for us to try to make up for things we have done wrong?

Ask a family member to summarize the steps of repentance. Bear testimony of the blessings of the Atonement in your life.

ALMA 37: ALMA COUNSELS HIS SON HELAMAN

Alma 37:1–4
To whom did Alma give the record?

Show your family the picture of Mormon with the Nephite records (if available, use *Gospel Art Picture Kit*, no. 306). Ask your family why they think the Nephites kept so many records. Read together Alma 37:1–4. Ask:

- Who was the next person to record Nephite history?
- What words did Alma use to describe these records?
- Why did they keep them? (One day they would "go forth" to all nations.)
- What are some records we should keep?

Have a family member share an inspiring story from a family record. Encourage family members to keep a record of their own history and invite them to share a future journal entry.

Alma 37:2–19
For what wise purpose was Helaman entrusted with the plates?

Ask a family member to read aloud Alma 37:2, 12, 14, 18 while the rest identify a common phrase in each verse. Ask why they think Alma repeated the phrase "wise purpose" four times. Then ask:

- What was Helaman to keep for a "wise purpose"?
- Why was it important to preserve them?
- According to verse 11, did Alma fully understand God's "wise purpose"?
- What generation would benefit from these sacred records?

Explain that we are part of the "future generation." Discuss with your family how God has shown forth his power by fulfilling his "wise purpose" in our day. It might be helpful to review the section headings for D&C 3, 10 and also D&C 1:17–30 for ideas.

Alma 37:6–10
What can result from "small and simple means"?

 Ask one of the children in your family to read the following poem:

Little drops of water, Little grains of sand,
    Make the mighty ocean and the beauteous

land. ("Little Things," *The Children Sing*, no. 92.)

Ask your family what the little drops of water and the little grains of sand turned into. How does this show that small things can lead to great things?

Tell your family that when Alma gave the Nephite records to his son Helaman, he testified why this calling was so important. Read together Alma 37:6–10. Ask:

- What did Alma teach about "small and simple things"? (Verse 6.)
- Why do you think the Lord uses "small means" to accomplish his work? (Verse 7.)
- What three blessings would come from the "small" act of preserving the records? (Verse 8.)
- What specific blessings did these records bring to "Ammon and his brethren"? (Verse 9.)
- What blessing did Alma hope the record would bring to future generations? (Verse 10.)

Alma 37:13–17
Why must we remember to keep the commandments of God?

 As you read Alma 37:13–14, have family members mark the things Alma told Helaman to remember. Suggest that family members circle the blessings for keeping the commandments and underline the consequences for not keeping the commandments. Ask your family why they think Alma seems so serious on this point.

Invite family members to share the most valuable thing they have ever lost and what it meant to them to lose it. Have you ever been able to replace it? Read together Alma 37:15–17 and ask:

- What would Helaman have lost for disobedience?
- Why would losing these sacred records change the world today?

- Why would it have been difficult to replace them?

Alma 37:21–25, 30
What were the Jaredite's sins?

 Have one family member read Alma 37:21–22, 30 to your family while another family member writes the Jaredites' sins on a piece of paper. Ask family members to identify Jaredite sins that can also be found in our society and have them give examples.

Ask your family to find words in Alma 37:25 that would fill in the following blanks:

People usually commit sin in _____ (darkness).

God will bring their dark works into the _____ (light).

To avoid destruction, people must _____ (repent).

Have someone read Alma 37:23–24 and tell what God will do to bring the Jaredites' dark works into the light. Share the following statement by Elder Bruce R. McConkie:

"With reference to the name Gazelam, it is interesting to note that Alma, in directing Helaman to preserve both the Urim and Thummim and the plates containing the Book of Ether, says that such record will be brought to light by the Lord's servant Gazelem, who will use 'a stone' in his translation work. (Alma 37:21–23.) It may be that Gazelem is a variant spelling of Gazelam and that Alma's reference is to the Prophet Joseph Smith who did in fact bring forth part at least of the Ether record. Or it could be that the name Gazelem (Gazelam) is a title having to do with power to translate ancient records and that Alma's reference was to some Nephite prophet who brought the Book of Ether to light in the golden era of Nephite history." (*Mormon Doctrine*, p. 307.)

Ask your family why they think God would go to the effort of preparing a stone for his prophets so that they could view the secret works and abominations of his children.

Alma 37:27–34

Why should we keep the secret things of darkness a secret?

If your children are old enough, ask them why they think prophets teach us never to view pornography. List their answers on a sheet of paper. Ask half of your family to search Alma 37:27–29 and make a list of those things Alma counseled Helaman not to reveal to his people. Have the other half of your family search Alma 37:32–34 and make a list of those things Alma told Helaman to preach to the people.

Compare the two lists and ask family members to share their feelings about why it would be unwise to teach the things in verses 27–29. Review the comments listed on why viewing pornography would be dangerous. Discuss the similarities between those answers and what is taught in Alma 37:27–29.

Now ask family members to tell why it would be helpful to teach the things in Alma 37:32–34. How might these principles fortify us and help us withstand temptation?

Alma 37:35–37

What should we learn in our youth?

Before family scripture study, ask the father of your family to be prepared to share his most heartfelt counsel to his children. When ready, invite him to share his counsel. Read Alma 37:35–37 aloud to your family. Ask if there are any similarities between Alma's counsel to Helaman and your father's counsel to them. Ask:

- What two gospel principles did Alma specifically admonish Helaman to keep? (Keep the commandments and pray.)
- Why do you think Alma encouraged Helaman to keep the commandments?
- What counsel did Alma give concerning prayer?

Prepare the following "prayer checklists" for each family member:

List 1:

I do not have personal prayer.
I only pray at mealtime.
I only pray with the family.
I only pray in the morning.
I only pray at bedtime.
I only pray in time of need.

List 2:

I pray out loud.
I pray silently.
I read scriptures before praying.
I ponder before praying.
I pray during the day.
I listen for answers.

Ask your family which list best represents the counsel Alma gave his son. Which list would bring you the greatest comfort or direction or help?

Encourage family members to keep the "prayer checklists" as a reminder to improve their prayers and gain the blessings that come with doing so. You might conclude by singing "Keep the Commandments" (*Hymns,* no. 303).

Alma 37:38–47

What do we have that is like a Liahona?

If you have a compass, show it to your family and teach them how it works. If you do not have a compass, show the picture of Lehi with the Liahona (if available, use *Gospel Art Picture Kit,* no. 302) or a drawing of a Liahona as a ball with some pointers or arrows. (See 1 Nephi 16:10 for a description.) Discuss what a compass or Liahona is used for.

Write the following quiz on a large sheet of paper or poster board and have your family look for the answers as they review Alma 37:38–47:

- Why was the Liahona given to Lehi's family? (Verse 39.)
- What made the Liahona work? (Verse 40.)
- When would the Liahona cease to work? (Verse 41.)

- What happened to Lehi's family when they failed to heed the Liahona? (Verses 42–43.)
- What did Alma compare to the Liahona? (Verse 44.)
- Where will the "word of Christ" point us? (Verses 44–45.)
- How can scripture study help us "look to God and live"?

Discuss as a family how often they look at and heed their personal Liahonas. Invite them to share an experience when the Spirit gave them direction as a result of scripture study.

ALMA 38: ALMA COUNSELS HIS SON SHIBLON

Alma 38:1–5

Can you be trusted?

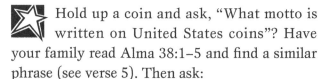 Hold up a coin and ask, "What motto is written on United States coins"? Have your family read Alma 38:1–5 and find a similar phrase (see verse 5). Then ask:

- What promises did Alma make to Shiblon if he would put his "trust" in God?
- How do we show our trust in God?
- How has putting your trust in God helped you during times of trial?

Have your family scan Alma 38:1–5 again and find another place where the word "trust" is used. (See verse 2.) Ask them who is expressing trust in whom. What qualities had Shiblon displayed that enabled Alma to trust him?

Tell your family that one of President David O. McKay's favorite sayings was, "To be trusted is a greater compliment than to be loved." (*True to the Faith*, p. 274.)

Share this story related by President N. Eldon Tanner. Explain that when he was fourteen years old, his father was serving as bishop and had gone to prepare for a funeral. He had asked Eldon and his brothers to do the chores while he was gone. President Tanner explained:

"We decided to ride some calves before we did what he had told us to do. We thought we would have plenty of time, but he came home while we were still riding those calves, and he called us over to him. . . . He pointed his finger at me and said, 'My boy, I thought I could depend on you.' That hurt me very much. I can still almost recall the exact feeling I had at that time. I made up my mind that he would never have a reason to say, 'I thought I could depend on you.' Right then I made up my mind that the Lord would never have reason to say, 'I thought I could depend on Eldon Tanner.'" ("In Memoriam: President N. Eldon Tanner," *New Era,* January–February 1983, p. 14.)

Ask family members to think of some ways they could earn the trust of parents, teachers, friends, and God. Have them share their ideas.

Alma 38:6–9

How can we gain a testimony?

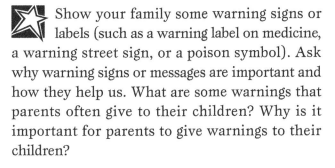 Ask a family member who you know has a strong testimony of the gospel to share what he or she did to receive it. Read together Alma 38:6–9 and discuss the following questions:

- What phrase did Alma use that sounds like a testimony? (I know these things of myself.)
- What are some things Alma did that helped him to know?
- What did Alma testify about Jesus Christ?
- What can we learn from Alma's example?

Alma 38:10–15

Why is it important to receive counsel and warning?

Show your family some warning signs or labels (such as a warning label on medicine, a warning street sign, or a poison symbol). Ask why warning signs or messages are important and how they help us. What are some warnings that parents often give to their children? Why is it important for parents to give warnings to their children?

Point out to your family that even though Shiblon had been faithful, Alma concluded his counsel to his son with some warnings. As you read Alma 38:10–15 together, have your family look for and list the warnings Alma gave Shiblon. Have family members take turns explaining what each of those warnings means, why it is important, and why it would be of value to follow today.

Alma 38:12
Bridle all your passions

 Show your family a picture of a bridle. Ask:

- Where on the horse is a bridle used?
- Is the purpose of the bridle to kill the horse?
- What is a bridle used for? (To control and direct a horse.)
- Is a bridle a good or a bad thing? Why?

Have someone read aloud Alma 38:12. Then discuss the following questions:

- What did Alma asked his son Shiblon to bridle?
- Did that mean he was to destroy his passions?
- Is controlling our passions a good thing or a bad thing? Why?
- What are some things we could do to control or direct our passions?

Share the following statement with your family:

"Is self-denial wise because there is something wrong with our passions, or because there is

something right with our passions? Alma taught his son: "See that ye bridle all your passions, *that ye may be filled with love.*" (Alma 38:12; emphasis added.) He did not say we should suppress or eliminate our passions but rather *bridle* them—harness, channel, and focus them. Why? Because disciplining our passions makes possible a richer, deeper love." (Bruce C. and Marie K. Hafen, "Bridle All Your Passions," *Ensign,* February 1994, p. 14.)

ALMA 39: ALMA TEACHES CORIANTON HOW TO REPENT OF HIS SINS

Alma 39:1–4
Why did Corianton fall into sin?

Read together Alma 39:1–4 and have your family identify the things Alma had against Corianton. (Boasting in his own strength and wisdom, leaving his mission, going after a harlot, and so on.) Ask your family how these things could lead to Corianton's mistakes. Have your family look again at verses 1–4 and look for what Corianton could have done to strengthen himself against temptation. For example, he could have followed the example of Helaman, his brother (verse 1); he could have given more heed (listened) to his fathers teachings (verse 2); and he could have "tended to the ministry" (focused on his mission, verse 4).

Discuss with your family how these things can strengthen us against temptation. Ask what else we can do to avoid falling into sin. Invite them to give examples.

Alma 39:5–6
What are the three most serious sins?

Write each of the following words or phrases on three separate strips of paper: murder, deny the Holy Ghost, sexual sin. Place a string across the floor in a straight line. Ask your family what they think are the most serious sins people can commit. Show your family the words and phrases on the strips of paper and ask where they would place them if one end of the string was the most serious and the other the least serious.

Once the family has agreed where each strip of paper goes, read together Alma 39:5–6 and look for the order in which the Lord placed these serious sins. If your placement of these sins differs from the Lord's, correct the order.

Ask your family why they think Alma taught these things to his son Corianton. What can we learn from Corianton's experience?

Alma 39:7–13
Corianton is counseled to repent

Have your family imagine that the bishop asked them to give a talk in sacrament meeting on the steps of repentance. Ask them what steps they would list. Give each family member a sheet of paper. Then have them read Alma 39:7–13 and list some steps to repentance given by Alma to his son Corianton. (The list might include: Cannot hide from God, Must confess sins, Forsake your sins, Turn to the Lord with all of your heart, might, mind, and strength.) Invite family members to highlight, mark, or number these steps to repentance as found in Alma 39:7–13.

Ask your family if they know what it might mean to "cross yourself." To help with that question, have them read Matthew 16:24 and then read the JST addition to that verse in footnote d. Ask them how self-mastery or self-control can prevent us from sinning. Why is it better not to sin than to sin and have to repent? Bear testimony that prevention is far better than repentance.

Alma 39:11
How does a person's example affect missionary work?

Have a family member read aloud Alma 39:11 and tell how Corianton's bad example affected the Zoramites. Ask them why it is important that we set a good example. Invite family members to share any examples they know of where the behavior of a Church member helped someone gain a testimony of the gospel. Ask how they think it would make them feel if someone rejected the gospel because of their bad example. How do you think you would feel if someone joined the Church because of your good example? Read together D&C 18:10–16 and then bear your testimony of the joy that comes from being a good example to others.

Alma 39:15–19
Does the atonement of Jesus Christ cover the sins of those who lived before it happened?

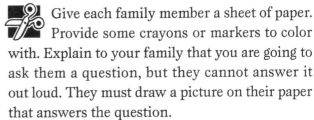 Give each family member a sheet of paper. Provide some crayons or markers to color with. Explain to your family that you are going to ask them a question, but they cannot answer it out loud. They must draw a picture on their paper that answers the question.

Ask your family the following questions: "Who can you think of in history that lived before the time of Jesus?" Have family members draw a picture of the person or persons who lived before the time of Jesus. After five minutes, invite family members to show their pictures and explain whom they chose to draw or color.

After discussing with your family each person they drew that lived before the time of Jesus, ask if they think the Atonement will cover their sins. To help answer that question, read together Alma 39:15–19 and discuss what Alma taught on this subject. Bear testimony that the Atonement covers the sins of all those who have lived and who will yet live on the earth. (See also D&C 20:25–28.)

ALMA 40: THE DOCTRINE OF RESURRECTION

Alma 40:1
Why was Corianton worried?

 Have your family read together Alma 12:3 and find an example of who, besides God, can know our thoughts. Have a parent read Alma 40:1 out loud and answer this question: "Why do you think Alma was able to perceive the mind of his son, Corianton?" Discuss with your family the following questions:

- Why might the idea of being resurrected to stand before God worry Corianton? (See Alma 39:8.)
- What would he have to do to be happier about the resurrection? (See Alma 39:13.)
- Why was it beneficial for Alma to perceive Corianton's thoughts? (So he could counsel his son.)

Share this statement with your family: "The Lord's plan has given us those who care and comfort us in times of failure and sin: our parents, bishops, quorum leaders, and advisers. I am grateful for a plan that provides these wonderful parents, leaders, and teachers who really care! I'm especially grateful for our Savior, whose Atonement makes repentance and forgiveness possible." (Duane B. Gerrard, "Flight Plan for Life," *New Era*, February 1999, p. 6).

Alma 40:2–26

Answering questions about the resurrection

Read Alma 40:2–26 one verse at a time. Before reading each verse, ask family members the accompanying true/false questions. Have them find the correct answers as they study the scriptures. Talk about any questions your family might have about the doctrine of resurrection.

- T F No resurrection took place until after Christ's first coming. (Verse 2.)
- T F Christ brings about the resurrection. (Verse 3.)
- T F Alma never prayed about the resurrection. (Verse 3.)
- T F A time is appointed for everyone to be resurrected. (Verse 4.)
- T F Priesthood holders know when their family members will be resurrected. (Verse 4.)

- T F As soon as we die, we will be resurrected. (Verse 6.)
- T F Mortals are more concerned about time than God is. (Verse 8.)
- T F Alma prayed to know what happens to us after death but before the resurrection. (Verse 9.)
- T F Righteous spirits will go to paradise, where they will be happy, peaceful, and at rest from their troubles, cares, and sorrows. (Verse 12.)
- T F Wicked spirits will also be in paradise, but they will weep, wail, and gnash their teeth because of their own iniquity. (Verse 13.)
- T F Wicked people choose to be evil. (Verse 13.)
- T F The devil takes possession of wicked people. (Verse 13.)
- T F Everyone will have to remain in paradise until the resurrection. (Verse 14.)
- T F The first resurrection began at the time of Christ's resurrection. (Verse 16.)
- T F Resurrection means the reuniting of the soul with the body. (Verse 18.)
- T F The souls and bodies of the righteous were reunited at the resurrection of Christ. (Verses 19–20.)

Share the following statement by Elder Joseph Fielding Smith to clarify verse 19:

"Verse 20, however, makes it plain that Alma did not intend to say that *all* the dead were to come forth at that time, and he therefore modified his first remark and said it was his 'opinion' that the souls and the bodies are reunited 'of the righteous,' at the resurrection of Christ and his ascension into heaven. It is evident Alma's understanding of the extent of the resurrection at the time the Savior came forth from the dead was limited, therefore he stated only his opinion." (*Answers to Gospel Questions,* 1:56.)

Read Mosiah 15:26 with your family. Ask what Abinadi teaches about the resurrection of those who perish in their sins. How does Abinadi's statement clarify what Alma said in verse 19?

T F Restoration involves our bodies and souls being reunited and all things being restored to their proper and perfect frame. (Verses 22–24.)

T F The righteous will shine forth in God's kingdom. (Verse 25.)

T F Unclean people cannot be where God is. (Verse 26.)

T F Wicked people will "drink the dregs of a bitter cup." (Verse 26.)

ALMA 41: WICKEDNESS NEVER WAS HAPPINESS

Alma 41:2–7
What is the plan of restoration?

Gather some blocks or other items with which you can build. Invite each family member to build or create something of his or her choice. Next, take turns rolling a ball at each others' creations in an attempt to destroy them. After each creation has been destroyed, have someone read Alma 41:2 and find the name of the plan that would put their creations back together again. (The plan of restoration.) Ask:

- What does the plan of restoration do? (Puts everything back in its "proper order.")
- What example of this plan does this verse give? (Resurrection.)

Read together Alma 41:3 and have your family look for another example of what the plan of restoration will bring about in our lives. Ask your family why they think those who do good things are "restored unto that which is good." Why won't those who do bad things enjoy the same blessing? To help you teach your family how the plan of restoration works, write the following words on a sheet of paper for them to see: Evil works, Mortality, Happiness, Misery. Have them read Alma 41:4–7, 13 and find the best words that match those in the list. (Evil, immortality, endless happiness, endless misery.)

Discuss with your family what they can do to enjoy the "endless happiness" instead of the "endless misery"? (Repent.) How does this plan show that we become our own judges? (See verse 7.)

Alma 41:8–10
Why can't I be happy when I'm bad?

Ask your family why sin or disobedience makes us feel guilty and scared. Why doesn't being bad ever make us feel happy and free the way being good does? Read together Alma 41:8–10 and ask:

- Why was Alma concerned about his son Corianton?
- What was the risk involved in his life?
- Why can't the "plan of restoration" restore us "from sin to happiness"? (See Alma 41:3–4.)

Share the following statement by President Gordon B. Hinckley:

"The way of the Lord is the way of happiness. 'Wickedness never was happiness' [Alma 41:10]. Transgression never was happiness. Sin never was happiness. Disobedience never was happiness. The way of happiness is following the way of the Lord. I believe this with all my heart. If there is any message that runs through all the Book of Mormon, it is this great, transcendent message—that when the people lived in righteousness, they were happy and they were prospered; and when they fell into wickedness, they were miserable, they were at war, they were in poverty, they were in trouble. That theme goes all the way through the Book of Mormon. As it was true then, so it is true now. The way of happiness for the people of this Church lies in following the ways of the Lord." (Oahu, Hawaii, regional conference, 18 February 1996.)

Have your family share some happy moments from their lives. Help them discover how they were keeping commandments when they were happy. Testify that this is how they can have endless happiness.

Alma 41:11–15

What does the plan of restoration teach us about how we should treat others?

 Show your family a seed and a fruit that comes from a different seed. Tell them that you are planning to plant the seed in one hand so you can eat a lot of the fruit in the other hand. Ask your family what they think of your plan. Ask one family member to read Galatians 6:7–8 and another to read Matthew 7:12. Ask:

- What does Paul teach us in Galatians about seeds and fruit? (You reap what you plant.)
- How is this like the "plan of restoration"? (See Alma 41:2.)
- What is the popular name for the truth taught in Matthew7:12?
- Why do you suppose it is called the "Golden Rule"?

Read together Alma 41:11–15 and invite your family to pick out what they think are the most important reasons for doing good to others. Invite each person to share what they chose.

Ask your family if they have ever wanted to do some good thing but circumstances prevented them from accomplishing their desire. Share the following insight from Elder Dallin H. Oaks:

"Just as we will be accountable for our evil desires, we will also be rewarded for our righteous ones. Our Father in Heaven will receive a truly righteous desire as a substitute for actions that are genuinely impossible. My father-in-law was fond of expressing his version of this principle. When someone wanted to do something for him but was prevented by circumstances, he would say: 'Thank you. I will take the good will for the deed.' . . .

"This principle means that when we have done all that we can, our desires will carry us the rest of the way. It also means that if our desires are right, we can be forgiven for the unintended errors or mistakes we will inevitably make as we try to carry those desires into effect. What a comfort for our feelings of inadequacy!" (*Pure in Heart*, p. 59.)

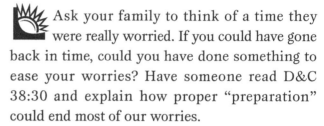

ALMA 42: CORIANTON LEARNS OF JUSTICE AND MERCY

Alma 42:1

Why was Corianton worried?

Ask your family to think of a time they were really worried. If you could have gone back in time, could you have done something to ease your worries? Have someone read D&C 38:30 and explain how proper "preparation" could end most of our worries.

Read together Alma 42:21 and look for what worried Corianton. Ask:

- Why do you think Corianton was worried about how God would deal with sinners? (See Alma 39:3–5.)
- Why do people sometimes make excuses for their sins instead of taking responsibility for them?
- How is Corianton like so many people today who, when punished for their sins, exclaim, "That's not fair!"?

Alma 42:2–13

Are you on probation?

Create a make-believe jail out of chairs in the middle of the room. Have a family member pretend that he or she has been put in jail. Ask the person how he or she might feel if this was a "life sentence." Would being put on probation be a better alternative? Why? (Explain that probation is when people are let out of jail but are watched carefully to see that they don't do anything wrong and to make sure they have reformed their bad behavior.)

Read Alma 42:2–13 as a family. Mark each time the word "probationary" is used. As you read, ask your family to think about what is being compared to a time of probation. Then ask:

- How is life on earth like a time of probation? (See also Abraham 3:25.)

- What two things would cause us to be lost forever? (Verses 6–9, death and sin.)
- How did Adam bring death into the world? (Because of the Fall, Adam became mortal.)
- How did the fall of Adam bring sin into the world? (It ensured that we would all live away from God's presence, have agency, and be accountable for our own choices.)
- In what way could death and sin be compared to jail? (They alienate us from God.)
- What power gives us the opportunity to be free from death and sin so that we can prove ourselves during this time of probation? (Verses 11–13, the plan of redemption through the Atonement of Jesus Christ.)

Talk about how each of your family is doing with his or her time of "probation." Also share your love for Jesus Christ for making it possible to someday return to our Heavenly Father.

Alma 42:14–15
Do we want justice or not?

 Ask your family to choose the sentence that best describes the word *justice:*

1. Getting more than you deserve.
2. Getting exactly what you deserve.
3. Getting less than you deserve.

Show your family a balanced scale or draw a simple picture of one.

 Explain why a balanced scale represents justice. Talk about some places (like school and work) where we are rewarded justly, according to what we actually deserve.

Read Alma 42:14 together. Ask:

- How will you like it if God is perfectly just with you on judgment day?
- What would happen if God gave us just what we had earned?
- Why can't we return to God's presence based on our obedience to his laws? (See Romans 3:23 and 1 Nephi 15:43.)

Put the scale out of balance (or draw one out of balance with the word "sins" on one side) and ask how our sins cause us to be unacceptable to God. What will be our fate if nothing is done to balance the scale?

Ask your family to read Alma 42:15 together and look for the only power that can put the scale back into balance. Place a picture of Jesus Christ on the scale and testify of your love for Him.

Alma 42:16–25
Can mercy rob justice?

 Take turns reading Alma 42:16–25 aloud and then discuss the following questions:

- In God's eyes, what must happen if a law is broken? (Verse 17, there must be a punishment.)
- Why has God given us laws? (Verses 19–21.)
- Why can't God just ignore it when we break the law and give us mercy anyway? (See verses 22–26.)

To illustrate this principle, read the following parable by Elder Boyd K. Packer about justice and mercy. (With a little advance preparation, you could role play or act out this story for your family.)

"There once was a man who wanted something very much. It seemed more important than anything else in his life. In order for him to have his desire, he incurred a great debt.

"He had been warned about going into that much debt, and particularly about his creditor. But it seemed so important for him to do what he wanted to do and to have what he wanted right now. He was sure he could pay for it later.

"So he signed a contract. He would pay it off some time along the way. He didn't worry too much about it, for the due date seemed such a long time away.

"As it always does, the day came, and the contract fell due. The debt had not been fully paid. His creditor appeared and demanded payment in full.

"'I cannot pay you, for I have not the power to do so,' he confessed.

"'Then,' said the creditor, 'we will exercise the contract, take your possessions, and you shall go to prison.'

"But the debtor begged, 'Will you not show mercy?'

"The creditor replied, 'Mercy cannot rob justice.'

"There they were: One meting out justice, the other pleading for mercy. Neither could prevail except at the expense of the other. . . .

"Both laws, it seemed, could not be served. They are two eternal ideals that appear to contradict one another. Is there no way for justice to be fully served, and mercy also?

"There is a way! . . . but it takes someone else. And so it happened this time.

"The debtor had a friend. He came to help. He knew the debtor well. . . . He wanted to help because he loved him. He stepped between them, faced the creditor, and made his offer: . . .

"'You demand justice. Though he cannot pay you, I will do so. You will have been justly dealt with and can ask no more. . . .'

"And so it was that the creditor was paid in full. . . . The debtor, in turn, had been extended mercy. Both laws stood fulfilled. Because there was a mediator, justice had claimed its full share, and mercy was fully satisfied." (Adapted from "The Mediator," *Ensign,* May 1977, pp. 54–56.)

Alma 42:31
Did Corianton repent and change his life?

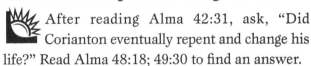 After reading Alma 42:31, ask, "Did Corianton eventually repent and change his life?" Read Alma 48:18; 49:30 to find an answer.

ALMA 43: COMPARING THE TWO SIDES OF THE BATTLE, GOOD AND EVIL

Alma 43:1–22
How can we prepare for battle?

Show a piece of protective gear (such as a bicycle helmet or pads used in athletic events). Discuss the role of this equipment and what can happen to those who participate in these activities without protection.

Make a chart like the one below and compare the Lamanite and Nephite armies by having each family member answer one of the questions from the chart using the references provided.

Contrast how the Lamanites and Nephites prepared for battle with our spiritual preparation for war with the powers of darkness. Do this by asking:

	Lamanites	Nephites
Who belonged to their group? (Verses 4, 6, 11, 13–14.)		
Who were their leaders? (Verses 15–16, 23.)		
What were their motivations? (Verses 7–9, 11–12, 30, 45–47.)		
How large was their army? (Verses 21, 51.)		
What physical preparations did they make for war? (Verses 18–20, 26, 31–33.)		

- Who are we fighting against for our spiritual lives?
- What can we learn from the comparisons in the chart that will help us overcome Satan and win our spiritual battles?

Read together Alma 43:23–24 and ask someone to explain what Moroni did to learn the position of their enemy. How do our modern prophets help us learn where our spiritual enemies will most likely attack us?

Share the following statement as an example of that kind of advanced warning from President Gordon B. Hinckley:

"We cannot be unclean and expect the help of the Almighty . . .

"You cannot afford to partake of things that will weaken your minds and your bodies. These include cocaine, 'crack,' alcohol, tobacco. You cannot be involved in immoral activity. You cannot do these things and be valiant as warriors in the cause of the Lord in the great, everlasting contest that goes on for the souls of our Father's children . . .

"We are engaged in a great eternal struggle that concerns the very souls of the sons and daughters of God. We are not losing. We are winning. We will continue to win if we will be faithful and true. We can do it. We must do it. We will do it." ("The War We Are Winning," *Ensign,* November 1986, p. 44.)

Invite family members to tell of other counsel given by modern prophets to help us win our spiritual battles. Remind family members that refusing to be obedient to the counsel of the prophets is not only to ignore the wisdom he has about the enemy's tactics, but it is also like going into battle—like the Lamanites—without protective covering.

Alma 43:8–9
When is war a choice God will allow?

Ask your family to list as many reasons as they can think of why nations go to war against each other. Discuss the following questions:

- Which of those reasons do you think are good and which are bad?
- How might God's reasons for justifying war be different from man's reasons?
- Under what circumstances might God allow his people to go to war?

Read together Alma 43:8–9 and look for reasons the Nephites went to war with the Lamanites. Ask:

- What was the intent of the Lamanites?
- What was the intent of the Nephites?
- Which of these reasons would be approved by God?

Read and discuss the following statement from President David O. McKay:

"There are . . . two conditions which may justify a truly Christian man to enter—mind you, I say enter, not begin—a war: (1) an attempt to dominate and to deprive another of his free agency, and (2) loyalty to his country. Possibly there is a third, . . . defense of a weak nation that is being unjustly crushed by a strong, ruthless one." (*Gospel Ideals,* p. 287.)

Alma 43:23–54
How can obedience assist us in our spiritual battle?

Stretch a piece of rope out on the floor and tell your family that the rope will represent the River Sidon. One end of the rope will be the headwaters of that river. Have your family stand near the headwaters of the River. Label three sheets of paper the "Land of Jershon," the "Land of Antionum," and the "Land of Manti." Place these papers on the floor around the river in the proper places relative to each other. (See the map of Book of Mormon lands on p. 187.) Take turns reading Alma 43:23–54 with your family and use the map on the floor to help explain what is happening and where the battles are taking place. Ask:

- Why were the outnumbered Nephites able to stop the much larger Lamanite army? (Verses 23, 38.)

- What role did obedience play in the Nephite victory?
- What role does obedience play in our war against Satan?

Read and discuss the following comment by Elder Boyd K. Packer: "Obedience is powerful spiritual medicine. It comes close to being a cure-all." ("Balm of Gilead," *Ensign,* November 1987, p. 18.)

Tell your family about a time in your life when obedience saved you a lot of trouble. Bear your testimony of the importance of being obedient to the council of our leaders.

ALMA 44: ZERAHEMNAH'S ARMY IS DEFEATED

Alma 44:1–7
Moroni's offer of peace

 Stand up. Have your family members also stand and circle around you. Read Alma 43:53 aloud and ask:

- Whom do I represent? (Zerahemnah's army.)
- Whom does the rest of the family represent? (Moroni's Army.)
- Why is it an advantage to have your enemy surrounded?
- If you were surrounding an enemy's army, what would you do?

Take turns reading Alma 44:1–7 and have your family look to see what Moroni did in this situation. Ask:

- What do Moroni's actions tell you about him and his desires?
- What reasons did Moroni give for the Nephites' success in battle?
- Why do you think those reasons helped Moroni's army succeed?
- What were the terms of Moroni's offer for peace?

Tell your family that they might not be involved right now in a military battle but

occasionally they do have arguments and quarrels with those around them. Discuss with your family how they could apply the Moroni's principles of dealing with an adversary to their own situations.

Alma 44:8–20
A covenant of peace

 Tell your family they are going to act out the story found in Alma 44:8–20. Use props if you can, and assign each member of your family one of the following parts: Zerahemnah, Moroni, Soldier of Moroni, Lamanite Soldiers, Nephite Soldiers, and a narrator.

As the narrator reads the story, have the assigned family members read the words and do the actions corresponding with their parts. When you have finished, discuss the following questions:

- Why wouldn't Zerahemnah make an oath of peace?
- What does that teach you about his feelings regarding oaths?
- How does that compare to how people today feel about oaths, promises, or covenants?
- Why is it important for us to keep promises or commitments we make?
- What are some promises you have made to the Lord?
- Why would it be important to keep those?

Share the following experience related by President N. Eldon Tanner, who served in the First Presidency. Talk about how it relates to the story of Zerahemnah and Moroni:

"A young man came to me not long ago and said, 'I made an agreement with a man that requires me to make certain payments each year. I am in arrears, and I can't make those payments, for if I do, it is going to cause me to lose my home. What shall I do?'

"I looked at him and said, 'Keep your agreement.'

"'Even if it costs me my home?'

"I said, 'I am not talking about your home. I am talking about your agreement; and I think your wife would rather have a husband who would keep his word, meet his obligations, keep his pledges or his covenants, and have to rent a home than to have a home with a husband who will not keep his covenants and his pledges.'" (Conference Report, October 1966, p. 99.)

Testify to your family that if we make and keep sacred covenants with the Lord, he will certainly bless us. (See D&C 82:10.) Express your hope that they will all, one day, go to the temple and there make sacred covenants with the Lord.

Alma 44:18

Have family members imagine being in a football game where they are the only players without a helmet or shoulder pads. Why would that be difficult or dangerous? Have a family member read Alma 44:18 and explain why the Lamanites were so vulnerable. Ask your family if Heavenly Father has provided them with any "armor" against the attacks of Satan. Read together D&C 27:15–18 and discuss how each element in the "whole armor of God" helps protect us in our battles with Satan. Why is it dangerous to go without the "armor of God"?

ALMA 45: ALMA GIVES BLESSINGS AND CURSINGS BEFORE HE LEAVES

Alma 45:1
How did the Nephites show their thanks to God?

Invite family members to relate a time when someone did something nice for them. Have them tell how they showed their gratitude for what was done. Then ask them to talk about the last time they felt deep gratitude for God. Invite them to share what they did to show their thanks for him.

Read Alma 45:1 and ask your family to tell why the Nephites were rejoicing. Have them number in their scriptures the four ways the Nephites

showed their gratitude. The list might include the following: "They gave thanks," "They did fast much," "They did pray much," "They did worship God with joy."

Discuss how each thing the Nephites did showed gratitude to God. Ask:

- Why is it sometimes hard to do these things with joy?
- How might doing these things improve your relationship with God?
- How could we as a family do these same things "with exceedingly great joy"?

Alma 45:2–14
How accurate is prophecy?

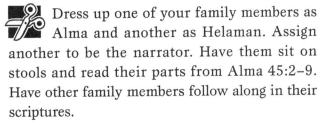 Dress up one of your family members as Alma and another as Helaman. Assign another to be the narrator. Have them sit on stools and read their parts from Alma 45:2–9. Have other family members follow along in their scriptures.

After the reading, discuss with your family the following questions:

- What will cause Helaman to be blessed and prosper? (Verses 6–8.)
- What blessing do you think we would be given if we were equally obedient?
- What secret does Alma want Helaman to keep? (A prophecy.)

Have the person who is playing Alma read Alma 45:10–14 aloud. After each verse, have your family mark in their scriptures the specific details of Alma's prophecy. The following questions will help you identify those details and discuss their meaning:

- What is the first sad thing Alma predicted would happen to the Nephites? (Verse 10.)
- When would this occur? (Verses 10–11.)
- What would happen next after they stopped believing? (Verse 11.)
- Why would the Nephites be punished so severely for becoming wicked when the Lamanites were also wicked? (Verse 12, the

Nephites sinned against "great light and knowledge." See also D&C 82:3.)

- What would happen to the wicked Nephites who were not killed? (Verses 13–14.)
- What would happen to those Nephites who remained "disciples of the Lord"? (Verse 14.)

Tell your family that the time for the fulfillment of Alma's prophecy has already passed. This gives us a perfect opportunity to see how accurate prophecy can be. Read together with your family Mormon 8:1–7 and have them compare what Moroni says has happened to his people with what Alma predicted in Alma 45:10–14. Ask your family what this teaches us about the Lord's ability to tell his prophets about the future. What advantage would there be in paying close attention to what modern prophets are saying about our future?

Alma 45:15–17
What does Alma bless, and what does the Lord curse?

Draw a line down the middle of a poster board or sheet of paper and label one column "Things Alma Blesses" and the other "Things the Lord Curses." Have your family read Alma 45:15–17 and list those things they find for each column. You might have them mark the curses and blessings differently. Discuss for whom Alma blessed the earth and also for whom the Lord cursed it. Ask:

- Why does the Lord bless the land for the righteous but curse it for the wicked?
- How might this lead the righteous to continue in obedience?
- How might it lead the wicked to change?

Ask your family to look again at Alma 45:16 to find how God feels about sin. Find footnote 16d and turn to and read the cross-reference found there (D&C 1:31). Ask your family how there can be any hope for us since we have all sinned. Have someone read aloud D&C 1:32 and identify the hope that God offers us there. Invite family mem-

bers to tell about a memorable blessing they received for obedience.

Alma 45:18–19
Were Alma and Moses translated?

Tell your family that Alma 45 gives us some information about an important event in the Bible that is missing from the Bible and not available anywhere else. Read with your family Deuteronomy 34:5–6 and ask them who "buried" Moses when he died? (The Lord.) Read together Alma 45:18–19 and ask:

- What happened to Alma in these verses?
- How was the experience of Alma similar to that of Moses?
- What "scriptures" would Alma be referring to in verse 19? (The Old Testament record from the plates of brass.)
- What do these verses say about Moses that is different from the account in Deuteronomy? ("The Lord took Moses unto himself.")
- What, then, is the real reason that the burial places of Moses and Alma are not known?
- What is another term for being "taken up by the Spirit"? (Being translated.)

Share the following statement from Elder Joseph Fielding Smith: "The scriptural inference is that Moses also was translated as was Alma." (*Answers to Gospel Questions,* 5:38.)

Alma 45:20–24
What effect did war have on the Nephite church?

Ask your family to imagine what it would be like if an invading army attacked your city. Ask:

- Who would have to fight?
- What effect would it have on the schools?
- How would it affect our family life?
- How would it change your Church activities?

Invite your family to think of these things while you read together Alma 45:20–24. Then ask these questions:

- What did Helaman do to help the people recover from their wars and dissensions?
- Why would it be helpful for the church to be established and the gospel preached again among them?
- What did Helaman do in verse 22 to re-establish or "regulate" the Church again?
- Why didn't some people respond to Helaman's call they way they should have?

Tell your family that today there are wars and dissensions going on all around us also. Ask them if they can think of any "regulations" our modern prophets have given us? (For example, the First Presidency letter of 2 November 1999 asking families to give their best effort to family home evening and gospel study to help combat the growing wickedness in the world, or "The Family: A Proclamation to the World.")

Discuss with your family what could be done to better hear "the word of God" in your family and cheerfully incorporate prophetic regulations into your lives.

ALMA 46: THE TITLE OF LIBERTY

Alma 46:1–10
"And thus we see"

 Remind your family that the phrase "and thus we see" is important in the Book of Mormon. That phrase identifies key messages and is often found at the end of a story. (See the teaching idea for Alma 24:19–30.)

Read the story of Alma 46:1–7 as a family. At the conclusion, ask each family member to write their own "and thus we see" statement, describing what they think is the main lesson learned from this story. Have each one share what he or she wrote.

Now read Alma 46:8–10 and find the three "and thus we see" lessons Mormon pointed out about this story. Compare what Mormon identi-

fied as main messages to the messages your family wrote.

Alma 46:11–24
What was the title of liberty?

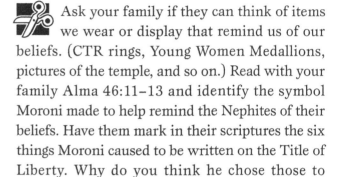 Ask your family if they can think of items we wear or display that remind us of our beliefs. (CTR rings, Young Women Medallions, pictures of the temple, and so on.) Read with your family Alma 46:11–13 and identify the symbol Moroni made to help remind the Nephites of their beliefs. Have them mark in their scriptures the six things Moroni caused to be written on the Title of Liberty. Why do you think he chose those to remind the Nephites of things?

Pass out paper, crayons, and markers to family members. Ask them to draw what they think the Title of Liberty looked like. Allow everyone to show his or her picture. Then take turns reading Alma 46:19–22. Discuss how the Nephite people reacted to the Title of Liberty and why it was so effective.

Take turns reading Alma 46:23–41 with your family. Ask:

- What ancient prophet did Moroni remind the Nephites they were descended from?
- What did Moroni teach the people about Joseph and his coat?
- How was the Title of Liberty like Joseph's coat of many colors?
- How did the people who followed feel about their cause compared to how the people of Amalickiah felt about their cause? (Verses 29–35.)
- Where did Moroni place the Title of Liberty, and what long-term effect did it have on the people? (Verses 36–41.)

To expand this activity, take ideas from the pictures everyone made and work together as a family to make a family banner or flag that could be displayed. Include on your family's banner a family motto or mission statement. Hang your own "Title of Liberty" somewhere in your home to remind your family of the standards, ideals, and motto that you wish to live by as a family.

Read the following statement by Elder Vaughn J. Featherstone:

"We, as Latter-day Saints, should resolve to hold high our modern-day "title of liberty" in memory of our God and our religion, our fathers and our mothers, our flag, and our country. (See Alma 46:12, 36.) We can honor through our lives the thousands who died crossing the plains and in the valleys and settlements. The spiritual values for which they died should ever be lodged in our hearts. We will carry the torch of faith which they bequeathed to us to light the way for those who follow." ("Following in their Footsteps,"*Ensign,* July 1997, p. 10.)

Alma 46:39–41
How can people leave this world rejoicing?

Ask your family to consider this question: "If you were to die today, would you have any regrets?" Read together Alma 46:39–41 and look for the way many of the Nephites handled death. Ask:

- What qualities did the people possess who "went out of the world rejoicing"?
- Why do you think living a faithful life, could cause rejoicing when we die?
- Why would it be important to you to have this same experience when you die?

Share your testimony that living the commandments brings joy in life and death. Invite your family to live in such a way that they will have no regrets when they leave this earth.

ALMA 47: AMALICKIAH–FROM REFUGEE TO ROYALTY

Alma 47:1–36
The lies and trickery of Amalickiah

 Ask your family how they think people usually become kings and queens. (They are born, or marry into, a royal family, take the position by force, and so on.) Tell your family that Alma 47:1–36 contains a story about a man named Amalickiah who had conspired (but failed) to become king of the Nephites but now sought to become the king of the Lamanites. As you study Alma 47, look for the way Amalickiah sought to achieve his desire.

Note that Amalickiah used a five-part plan to become king of the Lamanites. If possible, assign the following plans to family members, have them read the scripture reference accompanying their plan, and have them summarize their reading.

Part 1 (Alma 47:1–8). (Amalickiah stirred up the Lamanite king to go to battle against the Nephites. When a major portion of the Lamanite army refused to go to war, Amalickiah was given command of the remaining army and charged by the king to force the others into arms.)

Part 2 (Alma 47:9–15). (Amalickiah tricked Lehonti, the commander of the rebel Lamanite army, into combining their forces. Lehonti would have been in command if he agreed to put Amalickiah as second in command.)

Part 3 (Alma 47:16–19). (Amalickiah had Lehonti poisoned until he died, knowing that by Lamanite tradition the second in command would replace the commander.)

Part 4 (Alma 47:20–30). (Upon his return with the Lamanite army, Amalickiah had his men stab the Lamanite king to death as the king and his servants came to greet them. Amalickiah placed blame on the king's servants who had fled. He won the people's hearts by pretending to have cared deeply about the king.)

Part 5 (Alma 47:31–35). (Amalickiah used false witnesses to convince the queen of his innocence. He later sought her favor and took her as his wife.)

You might discuss the following questions:

- What do you think of how Amalickiah became king?
- How would you judge the intelligence or cunning of Amalickiah?

- What does that teach us about the ability of some of those who choose to follow Satan? (Just because people choose to follow evil does not mean they are stupid.)
- What similarities do you see between Amalickiah and Satan?

Discuss with your family some of the clever ways Satan tries to deceive us today. Read together D&C 10:43 and discuss what our best approach would be for avoiding Satan's deceptions.

Alma 47:36
Why do those who leave the Lord often entirely forget him?

Ask a family member to tell what it means to dissent. (To have a difference of opinion.) Have your family search for a similar word in Alma 47:35 and tell what they think "dissenters of the Nephites" were. Explain that many Nephites who were unhappy living the commandments among the Nephites often chose to live with the Lamanites.

Draw a line down the center of a sheet of paper. At the top of the first column write "What they had in common" and at the top of the other write "How they were different." Have your family carefully read Alma 47:36 and find what the Nephites and their dissenters had in common and then what made them different. Ask:

- What do we learn about those who chose to leave the Lord?
- Why is it such a tragedy when people become so hardened?
- What do you think leads them to "entirely [forget] the Lord their God"?

Share the following story:

"Daniel Tyler records a conversation that he and Isaac Behunnin had with the Prophet Joseph Smith about the trials and persecutions to which the Prophet had been subject. As they talked, the Prophet observed that his greatest difficulties came at the hands of those who had once tasted of the things of the Spirit and then turned against them. To this, Elder Behunnin remarked: 'If I should leave this Church, I would not do as those men have done; I would go to some remote place where Mormonism had never been heard of, settle down, and no one would ever learn that I knew anything about it.'

"Joseph Smith replied: 'Brother Behunnin, you don't know what you would do. No doubt these men once thought as you do. Before you joined this Church you stood on neutral ground. When the gospel was preached, good and evil were set before you. You could choose either or neither. There were two opposite masters inviting you to serve them. When you joined this Church you enlisted to serve God. When you did that you left the neutral ground, and you never can get back on to it. Should you forsake the Master you enlisted to serve, it will be by the instigation of the evil one, and you will follow his dictation and be his servant.'" (As cited in Joseph Fielding McConkie and Robert L. Millet, *Doctrinal Commentary on the Book of Mormon,* 3:172.)

ALMA 48: CAPTAIN MORONI, A MAN OF GOD, A MAN OF ACTION, A TRUE HERO

Alma 48:1–10
Preparation precedes performance

Show your family a picture of an athlete and ask them to give suggestions on what is necessary to become a great athlete in any sport. Continue the discussion by asking:

- In what sports would it be wise to learn about those you will compete against?
- What advantage do you gain by knowing your competitors' strengths and weaknesses?
- If you had a choice as a coach, would you prefer people of strength of body or strength of character to be on your team? Why?

Read with your family Alma 48:1–6 looking for

what Amalickiah did to persuade the Lamanites to attack their brethren the Nephites. What two words does Alma 48:7 use to describe Amalickiah's tactics? Who does that remind you of?

Read Alma 48:7–10 with your family and look for what Moroni did to prepare his people for war. Ask:

- What is the difference between the two preparations?
- Where did Moroni place the greatest number of soldiers?
- Why would other places require fewer soldiers?
- According to verse 10, what were Moroni's people fighting for?

Ask your family what similarities they see between the struggle Moroni and the Nephites were involved in and the battles we face today. Ask:

- How is Amalickiah like those who would destroy us and our family today?
- What similarities do you see between Amalickiah's tactics and the tactics of the wicked in our day?
- How could Moroni's strategy be applied to our battles?
- How can we fortify ourselves so that wicked people will not influence us to make wrong choices?
- The Nephites built walls to protect them. What kind of "walls" can we use to protect our family from evil influences?

Alma 48:11–18
How can I become more like Moroni?

Invite your family to make a list of the things they think make someone popular in the eyes of the world. Then read together Alma 48:11–13 and list the qualities in Moroni that made him popular in the eyes of our Father in Heaven. Ask:

- How did Moroni's qualities compare with Amalickiah's qualities?

- How can you develop some of Moroni's qualities in your life?
- Who were some other people who were listed as being men like Moroni?
- What would you need to do to become part of that list?

Read the following statement by President Howard W. Hunter:

"Not everyone at school is going to be the student body president or the Relief Society president, or the teacher of the elders quorum. Not all of you are going to be like Moroni, catching the acclaim of your colleagues all day every day. No, most will be quiet, relatively unknown folks who come and go and do their work without fanfare. To those of you who may find that lonely or frightening or just unspectacular, I say you are 'no less serviceable' than the most spectacular of your associates. You, too, are part of God's army." (In *Brigham Young University 1990–91 Devotional and Fireside Speeches,* p. 2.)

Tell your family that just as some people can lead in wickedness, like Amalickiah, so others can lead in righteousness, like Moroni. Read Alma 48:17 aloud and encourage your family to memorize that verse. Discuss the following questions:

- Who do you know in the Church that is like Moroni?
- What if each member of our family were like Moroni?
- How would you like to marry a person who had the qualities of Moroni?
- What kind of person would you need to be for a person like Moroni to want to marry you?

Alma 48:14–16; 21–25
What were the Nephites' attitudes toward war?

 Open a newspaper and read to your family any headlines dealing with war or rumors of war. Ask:

- What feelings do you have as you hear these headlines being read?
- Do you wonder if you'll ever have to defend the rights and freedoms that we enjoy?
- What is the Church's stand on war? (See D&C 98:32–36.)

Read Alma 48:14–16 with your family and have them mark what the Nephites were taught about war. Have them take turns reading Alma 48:21–25 and look for how the Nephites felt about going to war with their brethren the Lamanites. Ask them what the difference is between the Nephites' attitudes on war and the attitudes of those who followed Amalickiah. Read 3 Nephi 12:43–44 with your family to discover what the Lord said is most important in dealing with our enemies. Discuss with your family what makes loving our enemies so difficult. What could we do as a family to reduce the hatred, fear, and suspicion that exists between different people and nations?

ALMA 49: MORONI PREPARES THE NEPHITES FOR WAR

Alma 49:1–12
What was the difference between the two attacks on the city of Ammonihah?

Ask your family if they can think of or imagine a time in a sporting event when one team defeated the other team quite easily and yet on a rematch the defeated team easily won the second game. Discuss what might happen to make this possible.

Read Alma 16:2, 9–10 with your family and find how long it took the Lamanites to destroy the city of Ammonihah the first time. Then take turns reading Alma 49:1–12 and look for the difference between that earlier attack on Ammonihah and this second attack. Invite your family to list those differences as they find them. Then discuss the following questions:

- Why did the Lamanites choose to attack the city of Ammonihah first? (Verse 3.)
- Why were the Lamanites "astonished exceedingly" when they saw the city? (Verse 5.)
- Why did they decide not to attack the city? (Verses 8, 11.)

Remind your family that this was the second time Moroni surprised the Lamanites with the way he prepared his people for war. Ask if they remember what he did the previous time. (See Alma 43:19–21.) Where do you think Moroni kept getting these ideas about how to prepare for their enemies? What might the Lord know about the enemies, physical or spiritual, we will have to face?

Alma 49:10, 26–27
What difference does a righteous leader make?

Discuss as a family how much difference a great leader can make to a company, a sports team, a city, or a nation. Ask if they can think of a time when a company or team received a new leader and went from failure to success. What made the difference?

Make two columns on a sheet of paper. Label one "Captain Moroni" and the other "Amalickiah." Ask half of the family to read Alma 48:11–13, 17 and the other half to read Alma 49:10, 26–27. Have each group list in the appropriate column the words or phrases that describe the leader in their verses. Ask:

- What were the differences between these two leaders?
- Who would you rather be led by? Why?
- Why do you think the Nephites were blessed in their wars with the Lamanites at this time?
- Was Moroni the only righteous person among the Nephites? (Verse 30.)
- Who can you think of today that is a leader like Moroni?
- Can you think of any like Amalickiah?

Alma 49:1–28

Why were the Nephites so well prepared for war?

 On a piece of paper write "Preparation precedes performance." Show the paper to your family and ask what they think this means and how it applies to the following:

- Playing a piano.
- Running a business.
- Doing well in a sporting event.
- Qualifying for college.

Invite your family to silently read Alma 49:4, 23, 28. Then ask:

- What did the Nephites do that prepared them for war with the Lamanites?
- What do you think it means that the Nephites had "all power over their enemies"?
- To whom did the Nephites give credit for their victory over the Lamanites?
- How does this show that they prepared both physically and spiritually?

Discuss as a family how you can better prepare for spiritual battles and give thanks to Father in Heaven for life's victories.

ALMA 50: CAPTAIN MORONI FORTIFIES HIS LAND

Alma 50:1–11

Protecting cities and families

 Use pillows or books to make part of a "fort" that might be used for protection. Read Alma 50:1–5 with your family. Ask:

- How often did Moroni prepare for war?
- Why do you think it was important for him to continually prepare?
- How did Moroni construct the city walls? (Heaps of dirt topped with timbers, pickets, towers, and places of security.)
- What does that effort teach you about preparation?

Read together Alma 50:6–11 and have your family look for additional lessons we can learn from Moroni's preparations. Discuss the following questions:

- Why do you think Moroni fortified every city?
- How does that apply to our family?
- What are some weapons Satan uses to destroy a family? (Contention, selfishness, pride, outside interests and friends, inappropriate entertainment, and so on.)
- What "walls" could keep these influences out of our homes?
- What did Moroni do about the Lamanites who were getting too close to the Nephites in the "east wilderness"? (Verses 7–11.)
- How do evil influences get into our homes and our lives?
- How would Moroni's strategy apply to protecting each family member from the evils in the world?
- What could we do in our family that would be like stronger walls, banks of dirt, and timbers to keep evil out? (Curfews, monitoring television and Internet use, household rules, and so on).
- What things spiritually strengthen a family against evil? (Family prayer, family home evening, family scripture study, and so on.)

Invite your family to complete the fort by adding the additional fortifications they have suggested for your family. Ask them to suggest defenses they could use in their individual struggles against Satan that are like walls around a city. As a family, pick one fortification or boundary to help keep evil out of your home that your family can practice. Also pick one thing you can improve on to invite the Lord's Spirit into your home.

Alma 50:13–23

What brings happiness?

 Ask your family when they are usually more happy: when things are going well, or when they face difficult times. Have them explain why. Ask someone to review the chapter headings for Alma 48 and 49 and tell what has been happening to the Nephites. Then read Alma 50:23 and ask: "Why do you think the Nephites were so happy at this difficult time of conflict?"

Have your family read Alma 50:13–20 together and make a list of everything you find that would cause the Nephites to be happy. Your list may include such things as receiving divine guidance, being prepared, being delivered from their enemies, working hard, and keeping the commandments. Ask your family which of those things are available to us today? What would keep us from being happy even in difficult times?

Alma 50:20–22
What really causes war?

 Talk to your family about a war that has taken place recently. Ask their opinion about what causes war. After they have shared some opinions, have them search Alma 50:20–22 to find the Lord's teachings about the cause of war. Invite them to share what they found and have everyone mark those causes in their scriptures. Then have them suggest what would bring safety and strength to a nation. Share the following statement from President Gordon B. Hinckley:

"God our Eternal Father will watch over this nation and all of the civilized world who look to Him. He has declared, 'Blessed is the nation whose God is the Lord' (Ps. 33:12). Our safety lies in repentance. Our strength comes of obedience to the commandments of God." ("The Times in Which We Live," *Ensign*, November 2001, p. 74.)

Ask your family what many people consider essential to the strength of a nation that the prophet did not include (such as the economy or having the strongest military in the world).

Alma 50:25–36
A lesson in irony from Morianton

Share with your family the well-known fable of the dog who was carrying a bone in his mouth. When he passed over a bridge, he looked down and saw his reflection in the water. He thought it was another dog with a bone that looked larger than his own. He growled and barked at the other dog, hoping to get the larger bone, and in his greed he dropped his bone in the water and lost it.

Ask your family to keep that fable in mind as you read together Alma 50:25–36. Discuss the story of Morianton with the following questions:

- What did Morianton and his people want?
- What were they prepared to do to get more land?
- How would you describe Morianton from what he did in these verses?
- What did Morianton end up with in the end? (Just enough land to bury him in.)
- How is that like the dog in our fable?
- What happened to the people of Morianton who were not killed?
- How much better off would they have been if they had settled their difficulties with charity and kindness in the beginning?

Invite each family member to suggest ways he or she can apply the principles taught in this story.

ALMA 51: THE KING-MEN AND THE FREEMEN

Alma 51:1–21
How strong is a divided nation?

 Divide your family into two groups and have them stand on opposite sides of the room. Ask what would happen to the family if half of the family hated the other half. Make a list of the negative things that would come from such feelings. Ask if they can think of any positive results for the family.

Now assign one group the name "freemen" and the other group the name "king-men." Have each group sit down, study Alma 51:1–8, and be prepared to tell who they are and what they believe in. Invite each group to choose a leader who will share what they learned about their group of Nephites. Ask the following questions:

- What issues divided these groups of Nephites?
- Why do some people let such issues determine how they feel about each other?
- What happens to a nation that is so divided?
- What happens to a family that is so divided?

Have your family search Alma 51:9–12 and find what else was happening at this time. Why would this make it a particularly bad time for the Nephites to be fighting among themselves?

Read together as a family Alma 51:13–21 to see how Captain Moroni ended their civil war. Discuss the following questions:

- Why was Captain Moroni "exceedingly wroth" with the king-men? (Verses 13–14.)
- What did the "voice of the people" want Moroni to do?
- What had the people learned about the dangers of contention? (Verse 16.)
- What happened to the king-men? (Verses 17–19.)
- What does this teach us about how important freedom is?
- Why is freedom important enough to die for? (See 2 Nephi 2:25–27.)

Ask your family how contention is dangerous in a family as well. Discuss ways you can bring more unity to your family.

Alma 51:9–12, 22–32
Who is the enemy?

Show your family a broom and ask them what it is used for and how it works. What would happen to the broom's ability to do what it was created to do if every other straw were pulled out? Have a family member read the chapter heading for Alma 51 and tell how the situation with the Nephites is similar to the object lesson. (When the Nephites were divided, they couldn't do all that God had created them to do.) Read together Alma 51:9–12. Ask someone to explain why this was a dangerous time for an invasion by the Lamanites.

Read together Alma 51:22–32 and have your family underline the different cities and lands mentioned. Discuss the following questions as you read:

- Why were the Lamanites able to conquer many of the Nephite cities? (Verse 23).
- How do you think the civil war affected the Nephites' ability to stand against the Lamanites?
- How were the Nephites finally able to stop the Lamanites? (Verses 29–32).
- What does this story teach us about our own land?
- What lessons do we learn here that could help us preserve our own freedoms?

Alma 51:33–37
Is killing during war considered murder?

Have a family member read aloud Exodus 20:13. Ask your family to explain what the Lord's counsel is on taking life. Why do you think killing is such a serious sin?

Read together Alma 51:33–37 and ask:

- What did Teancum do to help end the war?
- Was that a good thing or a bad thing?
- How does the commandment against killing apply to what Teancum did?
- How does killing Amalickiah compare to murdering someone for money?

Read the following statement, dated April 6, 1942, from the First Presidency: "The Church is and must be against war. . . . It cannot regard war as a righteous means of settling international disputes; these should and could be settled—the nations agreeing—by peaceful negotiations and adjustments.

"But the Church membership are citizens or subjects of sovereignties over which the Church has no control. The Lord himself has told us to 'befriend that law which is the constitutional law of the land . . .'

"When, therefore, constitutional law, obedient to these principles, calls the manhood of the Church into the armed service of any country to which they owe allegiance, their highest civic duty requires that they meet that call. If, harkening to that call and obeying those in command over them, they shall take the lives of those who fight against them, that will not make of them murderers, nor subject them to the penalty that God has prescribed for those who kill." (Quoted by Elder Boyd K. Packer, Conference Report, April 1968, p. 34.)

ALMA 52: SUCCESS AMID "DANGEROUS CIRCUMSTANCES"

Alma 52:1–40
Why were the Nephites successful?

 Ask your family to imagine themselves as television news reporters on assignment to cover the war going on near the land Bountiful. Divide the verses in Alma chapter 52 into the following groupings (1–18 and 19–40). Have each family member read one of the groupings and name two people from their verses they would like to interview. For each individual named, have the family member choose two questions they would ask in the interview and then suggest the answers they might receive.

After reviewing the chapter with the activity above, ask your family what principles, attitudes, or actions they noticed in Alma 52 that could be applied to earthly conflicts. Ask, "What did you learn in that chapter that would help us defend ourselves and our families in the battle against Satan?" Allow time for thinking and have each individual report on his or her findings. Discuss those findings as a family.

Alma 52:6
Where can we turn for protection?

Read Alma 52:6 together as a family. Ask:

- How did Teancum have his men prepare to defend and protect themselves?
- What are "places of resort"? (Fortifications.)
- What "places of resort" do we have today to help us in the battle against evil?

Share these statements with your family:

"Our Heavenly Father has organized us into families for the purpose of helping us successfully meet the trials and challenges of life. . . . Our family is our safety place, our support network, our sanctuary, and our salvation." (Rex D. Pinegar, "Home First," *Ensign,* May 1990, p. 9.)

"Our homes should be the strong place to which children can come for the anchor they need in this day of trouble and turmoil." (Harold B. Lee, *His Servants Speak,* p. 154.)

Alma 52:12–14
What are Satan's tactics?

 Have family members read Alma 52:12–14. Ask:

- What strategy did Ammoron use to try to gain advantage over the Nephites? (He attacked in several places at once.)
- How is that similar to the tactics Satan uses? (He tempts us with many things at the same time.)
- How can knowledge of Satan's tactics help us withstand his temptations?
- What did the Nephites do to overcome this "dangerous circumstance"? (See verses 15–19.)
- How could we apply these ideas in overcoming spiritual challenges that face our family? (One suggestion follows below, but there are others.)

Alma 52:19
What are the values of councils?

Have a family member read Alma 52:19 aloud and identify how the Nephites decided what course of action to take against the Lamanites. Ask your family if they are familiar with any councils today. To help answer that question, share the following statement:

"The family council is the most basic council of the Church. Under the direction of the father and the mother, this council can meet to discuss family problems, work out finances, make plans, support and strengthen each other, and pray for one another and the family unit." (*Our Family,* pamphlet, 1980, p. 6.)

President Stephen L Richards said: "I have no hesitancy in giving you the assurance, if you will confer in council as you are expected to do, God will give you solutions to the problems that confront you." (Conference Report, October 1953, p. 86.)

Invite any family members who have seen the blessing of working in councils to share their experience and testimony. Ask your family if there are topics or problems they feel would be helpful to discuss in family council.

ALMA 53: THE POWER OF OATHS

Alma 53:1–7
How did Moroni fortify against the Lamanites?

 Study Alma 53:1–7 with your family and have them construct a model of how Mulek and Bountiful may have looked by using some of the following items: popsicle sticks, brown clay, chocolate pudding, or dirt. Different-colored gummy bears could be used as Lamanite prisoners and Nephite guards. If you don't have these items, your family could draw a picture of how Mulek and Bountiful may have looked. Ask:

- How did Lamanites become a tool to defeat a Lamanite army?
- What benefits came by keeping Lamanite prisoners busy building fortifications?
- How did these efforts make the cities of Mulek and Bountiful stronger?

Alma 53:2
What strengthens friendship?

 Have family members share the name of their best friend. Ask:

- Why is the person you have named your best friend?
- How is your friend like you?
- What common values do you and your friend share?

Read Alma 53:2 and ask:
- Why were Moroni and Lehi best friends?
- How long had they been friends?
- Why do you think they were "beloved by all the people of Nephi"?
- How can we be a friend like Moroni and have a friend like Lehi?

Alma 53:8–9
Who placed the Nephites in a most dangerous circumstance?

 Place a toy boat in a pan of water. Ask your family what would happen if the water was on the inside of the boat instead of outside. (It would sink.) As you read aloud Alma 53:8–9, have your family identify how water symbolically got inside of the Nephite boat. Ask:

- How were the Lamanites able to gain Nephite ground?
- How many cities did the Lamanites take from the Nephites?
- What three things caused the Nephites to be placed in this dangerous circumstance?

Ask your family how the following poem explains why the Nephites had these problems:

> All the water in the world,
>   However hard it tried,
> Could never sink the smallest ship
>   Unless it [gets] inside.
> And all the evil in the world,
>   The blackest kind of sin,
> Can never hurt you the least bit
>   Unless you let it in.

(Quoted by Elder Boyd K. Packer in "The Spirit of Revelation," *Ensign,* November 1999, p. 24.)

Discuss together what specific things your family needs to do to keep the sins of the world from sinking your family ship.

Alma 53:10–17
How important is it to keep promises, covenants, and oaths?

Ask your family to think about different promises they have made. Ask them how they felt when they kept their promises compared to how they felt when promises were broken. Read Alma 53:10–16 and ask the following questions:

- What promises had the people of Ammon made? (Verse 11.)
- Why did they want to break their oath? (Verse 13.)
- Why did Helaman persuade them not to break their oath? (Verses 14–15.)
- What promises were their sons able to make in their place? (Verses 16–17.)
- What does this teach you about the importance of oaths, promises, and covenants?
- Why were the sons of the people of Ammon free to go defend their families while their fathers were not? (See Alma 24:10–12.)
- What does this teach us about the freedom that comes from keeping the commandments?

Share the following statement from President David O. McKay with your family:

"Fellow members of the Priesthood, do you so esteem your word? In all sincerity I ask it, tonight. You and I have given our words, our covenants. Do we hold them as sacred as did the people of Ammon, the story of whom you find in the Book of Mormon, who made an oath that they would never shed blood, and the time came when their benefactors were being punished, persecuted, killed, and the people of Ammon thought they would break that oath, but Helaman said no. And so those good men and women preferred death, if necessary, rather than break their word, violate their oath." (Conference Report, October 1952, p. 89.)

It might be helpful to discuss some or all of the following questions:

- Have you ever been tempted to break a promise for a good reason?
- What promises have you made to Heavenly Father?
- What are some occasions when it would be important that you keep your word?
- Why is it important for us to keep our promises especially to God?
- Under what circumstances could our souls be in jeopardy for breaking our promises (covenants)?
- How rare a person would you be if you always kept your word?

Alma 53:20–23
What qualities do true heroes exhibit?

Ask family members who their hero is and then have them explain why they have chosen that individual. List their hero and reason on a poster board.

Read together Alma 53:20–23 and have family members identify the qualities of the 2,000 stripling soldiers. Add these qualities to the poster board. Put a star by those heroes who have qualities similar to the 2,000 stripling soldiers. Ask:

- What does it mean to be "exceedingly valiant"?
- What does it mean to be "true at all times"?
- What does it mean to be "men of truth and soberness"?
- How would these qualities make these young men successful in any time and any place?
- What qualities do you desire to develop in your life?

ALMA 54: MORONI AND AMMORON EXCHANGE EPISTLES

Alma 54:1–24
How does the Lord feel about taking life in wartime?

Display an American flag for your family. Express your feelings about your freedoms and how blessed you are to live in this country. Read or sing "My Country, 'Tis of Thee" (*Hymns,* no. 337). Ask:

- In the first verse it talks of our fathers who died so we could be free. How do you feel about those people?
- How would you feel about giving your life in defense of your country?
- How would you feel about having to take a life in defense of your country?
- What are some other difficult decisions that come in wartime?

Have someone read Alma 54:1 and tell what Ammoron wanted Moroni to do. Tell your family that in this chapter Moroni and Ammoron exchange letters about this proposal. Have half your family read Moroni's epistle (Alma 54:5–14) and the other half read Ammoron's epistle (Alma 54:15–24). When they have finished, have each group summarize what their letter contained. Discuss the differences between these two letters, including the differences between the two leaders and their motivations. Some of the following questions might be helpful in your discussion:

- What did Moroni want to teach Ammoron about? (Verses 5–7.)
- What did Moroni warn Ammoron about? (Verses 9–10, 12–13.)
- What was Moroni's opinion of Ammoron? (Verse 11.)
- What conditions did Moroni put on the proposed exchange of prisoners? (Verse 11.)
- What did Ammoron accuse Moroni and the Nephites of doing to his brother? (Verse 16.)

- Is the taking of life in wartime the same as murder?

Share the following statement from President Harold B. Lee:

"There are many who are troubled and their souls harrowed by the haunting question of the position of the soldier who in combat duty kills the enemy. Again, the First Presidency has commented:

"'When, therefore, constitutional law, obedient to those principles, calls the manhood of the Church into the armed service of any country to which they owe allegiance, their highest civic duty requires that they meet that call. If, hearkening to that call and obeying those in command over them, they shall take the lives of those who fight against them, that will not make of them murderers, nor subject them to the penalty that God has prescribed for those who kill, beyond the principles to be mentioned shortly: for it would be a cruel God that would punish his children as moral sinners for acts done by them as the innocent instrumentalities of a sovereign whom he had told them to obey and whose will they were powerless to resist.' God is at the helm." ("From the Valley of Despair to the Mountain Peaks of Hope," *New Era,* August 1971, p. 5.)

ALMA 55: NEPHITE PRISONERS ARE FREED

Alma 55:1–25
How were the Nephite prisoners delivered from the Lamanites?

Give each member of your family an old sock. Have family members put the sock on the hand that they do not write with. Explain to your family that they are going to perform a puppet show. Characters of the show include a narrator (who has the largest part), Moroni, Lamanite guard, and Laman, all of whom have speaking parts. The nonspeaking parts are Ammaron and soldiers in the Nephite army.

Assign family members a character to play. Pass

out markers so they can draw a face on the end of their sock. Once the faces are drawn, invite everyone to open their scriptures to Alma 55. Ask the narrator to read Alma 55:1 and have family members follow along, reading their parts as listed below:

Character and Verses:
Narrator 1, 4, 5, 6, 7, 8, 9, 13–25
Moroni 2, 3
Lamanite guards 9, 11
Laman 10, 12

Have family members act out their parts with their puppets as the narrator reads about them. After the puppet show, ask the following questions:

- Why do you suppose Moroni was unwilling to kill the Lamanite guards?
- What does that teach us about Moroni?
- How were the Nephites delivered from the Lamanites?
- How is that like what the Savior does for us? (The Savior delivers us from death and the bondage of sin.)

Bear testimony of the atonement of Jesus Christ and the power of his deliverance.

Alma 55:26–35
The value of remembering the Lord

Ask your family if they have ever been in a situation where they were about to make a bad decision, but at the last minute they remembered something that saved them from that bad choice. Take turns reading Alma 55:26–34 with your family and have them look for a similar situation among the Nephites. As you read, discuss the following questions:

- What strategies did the Lamanites use in their attempts to destroy the Nephites? (Verses 26–30.)
- What kept the Nephites from falling into the Lamanite traps? (Verse 31.)
- How can remembering the Lord keep us safe from Satan's traps today?

Read the following statement from President Joseph F. Smith:

"The more righteous and upright, pure and undefiled, the Latter-day Saints become, the less power will Satan have over them, for in proportion to your unity and uprightness, honesty, and fidelity to the cause in which you are engaged, in such proportion will the power of the adversary be weakened, and those who are seeking to entice your sons and daughters into haunts of shame, and dens of wickedness, that they might be defiled, corrupted, wicked and like the rest of them will have less power over you, if you will watch your children better, and live better lives yourselves." (Conference Report, October 1911, p. 11.)

Discuss what it means to be righteous, pure, and undefiled. Invite family members to accept a challenge to improve in at least one area of personal righteousness.

ALMA 56: THE SAVING INFLUENCE OF MOTHERS

Alma 56:1–29
Review game

 Have each member of your family read Alma 56:1–29 in preparation for a game. Tell them you will ask questions from those verses to see which family member can correctly answer the fastest. Make up questions from the verses, or use some of the following:

- How did the Nephite military leaders communicate with one another? (Epistles; see verse 1.)
- How many of the sons of Ammon were brought into battle? (Verse 3.)
- Were these sons Lamanites or Nephites? (Verse 3.)
- Because of the Nephites' afflictions, what were the people of Ammon ready to do? (Verse 7.)

- What army did Helaman and his 2000 striplings join? (Verse 9.)
- What were the cities and lands taken by the Lamanites? (Verse 14.)
- Why were the armies of Antipus depressed? (Verse 16.)
- What did the Nephites do to keep track of the Lamanites? (Verse 22.)
- How large did the army of the Nephites become? (Verse 28.)

Alma 56:30–56

How can we be preserved from the evils of the world?

Write the following word definition on a sheet of paper for your family to see: "A cunning plan to deceive an enemy." Ask your family to read Alma 56:30 and find the word that matches the definition they just read. ("Stratagem.") Explain that Alma 56:30–57 contains the plan or stratagem the Nephites used in their battle against the Lamanites.

To help visualize the stratagem used by the Nephites, draw the following on a sheet of paper:

```
                North

                2nd night campsite (v. 40)

                1st night campsite (verse 38)
Sea
                ◯ Antiparah

                        ◯ Judea
```

Divide your family into three groups and give each group a different-colored crayon or marker. Assign one group to be Helaman's army, another to be the Lamanite army, and the third group to be Antipus' army. Take turns reading Alma 56:30–57 and have each group draw their travels on the paper in their own color. After going through this exercise, ask your family the following questions:

- Why did the Lamanite army chase after Helaman and his 2,000 striplings?
- How long did the chase go on? (Verses 38–41.)
- What was unique about that Lamanite army? (Verse 36.)
- Why did Helaman and his 2,000 stripling warriors turn around and go back toward the Lamanite army? (Verses 42–48.)
- What reason did the 2,000 striplings give Helaman for their great courage? (Verses 47–48.)
- How is it possible that not one of the striplings was killed in this battle? (Verses 47, 56; see also 1 Samuel 17:37 for a similar situation.)

Share your testimony that if we will place our trust in our Father in Heaven, we too will be delivered, in the way the Lord chooses, from the evils of the world.

Alma 56:45–48

What difference can a righteous mother make?

Have your family read silently Alma 56:45–48. Then give each person an opportunity to describe the mothers of these young men in one sentence. Write their descriptions on a sheet of paper.

Next have your family take turns sharing favorite memories about their mother or grandmother. Have each person give a one-sentence description of his or her mother or grandmother and write these on another paper. Discuss the similarities between the two lists. What qualities do all good mothers share? How does a testimony of the gospel affect the qualities and the effectiveness of a mother?

Read the following statement from President David O. McKay:

"Motherhood is the greatest potential influence either for good or ill in human life. The mother's image is the first that stamps itself on the unwritten page of the young child's mind. It is her caress that first awakens a sense of security; her kiss, the first realization of affection; her sympathy and tenderness, the first assurance that there is love in the world. True, there comes a time when Father takes his place as exemplar and hero of the growing boy; and in the latter's budding ambition to develop manly traits, he outwardly seems to turn from the more gentle and tender virtues engendered by his mother. Yet that ever-directing and restraining influence implanted during the first years of his childhood linger with him and permeate his thoughts and memory as distinctively as perfume clings to each particular flower." (*Gospel Ideals,* p. 452.)

If you have daughters, ask, "What can we, as a family, do to help you be better mothers?" If you have sons, ask, "What can we do to help your sisters prepare to be good mothers?" Have the mother of the home share her testimony of the importance of her calling as mother. Have the father share his love for his wife and what a positive, powerful influence she is in the home. Consider allowing family members to do a special service for a mother or grandmother, like making dinner, making a special art project or card, or bringing her some flowers.

ALMA 57: TWO THOUSAND STRIPLING WARRIORS ARE REWARDED FOR THEIR FAITH

Alma 57:13–18, 28–35
How does the Lord deliver us from "the hands of our enemies"?

Invite your family to share a time when a great trial in their lives actually turned out to be a blessing. Ask:

- What would be the advantage of seeing the end from the beginning?
- Why do you think our Father in Heaven doesn't always allow us to see the end from the beginning?
- What principle of the gospel is strengthened

when we believe something that cannot be seen?

To help your family better understand how God strengthens us as we exercise faith in him, invite them to read the chapter heading for Alma 57. Ask what two Nephite cities had been retaken by the Nephites from the Lamanites. (Antiparah and Cumeni.) Have a family member read aloud Alma 57:13 and discover how many Lamanite prisoners were taken from those cities. Read together Alma 57:14–18. Ask:

- What dilemma faced the Nephites and what did they do about it? (Verses 14–16.)
- When they came under attack, how do you think the Nephite commander felt about having sent so many soldiers to guard the Lamanite prisoners?
- Who returned to help save the army? (Verse 17.)

Read Alma 57:28–35 together and discuss the following questions:

- What allowed these Nephite guards to return and save the army at Cumeni? (Verses 30–34.)
- How did the decision to take prisoners to Zarahemla turn out to bless the Nephite army?
- How did the Lord deliver the Nephites "out of the hands of [their] enemies"?
- How is that like how the Lord delivers us from the hands of our enemies today?

Invite family members to share examples of how the Lord has turned what we thought was a problem into a blessing.

Alma 57:19–27
How can we develop faith in Jesus Christ in time of war?

Ask your family how a person would prepare to run a marathon (a marathon is about twenty-six miles). Ask:

- How much time do you think it would take to prepare for such a race?

- Why wouldn't it be wise to run a marathon without training?
- Do you think there are some who begin a marathon that give up and never finish? Why?

Read aloud Alma 57:20 and ask your family who was about to "give way" (give up) during a battle with the Lamanites and who stepped up to save them. (The Nephite army was rescued by the stripling warriors.) Ask your family to search Alma 57:19–27 and mark key phrases that indicate how the stripling warriors prepared for their marathon battle with the Lamanites. Discuss the meaning of each phrase. The following are examples of phrases that could be marked:

- Firm and undaunted.
- They did obey every command with exactness.
- Everything was done according to their faith.
- They believed what their mothers had taught them.
- Not one of them was killed in battle.
- They were preserved according to their faith and trust in the power of God.

Discuss the following questions:

- Who had taught them how to live and increase in faith?
- How can we remain "firm and undaunted," even when friends, associates, and others are "about to give way"?
- What can we do to be more like these stripling warriors as we face our enemies?
- What would you say is the most important thing we can learn from these young men?

Share the following statement from the First Presidency:

"We counsel parents and children to give highest priority to family prayer, family home evening, gospel study and instruction, and wholesome family activities. However worthy and appropriate other demands or activities may be, they must not be permitted to displace the divinely-appointed duties that only parents and families can

adequately perform." (First Presidency letter, 11 February 1999.)

Discuss with your family how to better strengthen and defend your home today.

ALMA 58: HELAMAN'S WARRIORS TAKE THE CITY OF MANTI

Alma 58:1–41
The "guess how many" game

 To prepare for this lesson, you will need a small cup or jar filled with small candies. Breakfast cereal could also be used. Count the exact number of candies contained in the jar and write it down.

Explain to your family that they will play a game with Alma 58. Take turns reading Alma 58:1–41 with your family and ask them to study and mark the chapter carefully so they can answer the game questions. After the chapter is read, ask the questions below. To answer a question correctly, family members will need to give the answer and the verse containing the answer. When a question is answered correctly, the family member can then guess the number of candies in the jar or cup. The person in charge then says if the guess is too high or too low. Continue this process until one person is able to guess the exact amount. That person wins the candies, which can then be shared with the entire family. If you believe the amount of reading is too much for one day, the chapter and questions can be divided up. Another container of candy can be used for the second half.

First Half

- What city was Helaman's army trying to recapture? (Verse 1.)
- Which army was receiving great strength and provisions? (Verse 5.)
- Who brought the food to Helaman's army? (Verse 8.)

- When Helaman's army was "grieved" for not receiving more strength, what did they do? (Verse 10.)
- Helaman wrote that the Lord "did speak _____ to our souls." (Verse 11.)
- Why did the Lamanites think they could "easily destroy" Helaman's army? (Verse 15.)
- What did Helaman have his men do when the Lamanites came to attack? (Verse 18.)
- Why did Helaman have part of his army hide in the wilderness before the Lamanites came after them? (Verse 21.)

Second Half

- How many Lamanites went to destroy Helaman's army from the city? (Verse 22.)
- Why did the Lamanite army stop chasing Helaman's army? (Verse 24.)
- What did Helaman's army do in the night? (Verse 26.)
- How many Nephites were killed when taking the city of Manti? (Verse 28.)
- What did Helaman's army believe was the reason they were victorious? (Verse 33.)
- Give one of the two possibilities Helaman believed was the reason he had not received more support? (Verses 35–36.)
- Who were they "strict to remember . . . from day to day"? (Verse 40.)
- To whom was Helaman writing? (Verse 41.)

When the game is finished, ask your family what they think are the most important lessons taught in this chapter and how they apply in their lives. For example, you might discuss verses 10–12, verses 26–28, or verses 34–37.

Alma 58:39–41
How does a soldier in God's army act?

Have your family imagine they are going to coach a sports team. Have them list some of the qualities and abilities they would like members of their team to have. Now have them list some qualities they would like from those participating if they led a musical group, a large business, or a military organization.

Read Alma 58:39–41 together as a family. As you do, underline characteristics and actions that made these young soldiers great men of God. Now read Moroni 4:3 and ask:

- What promises do we make when we take the sacrament?
- How do those three promises compare with the characteristics and actions of the stripling warriors?
- Why would these three things be important for these warriors?
- How can you apply these things in your life, and how would they help you?

ALMA 59: APATHY, THE "CRISIS OF OUR TIME"

Alma 59:1–13
Why was Moroni angry?

Ask a family member to read the following statement from Elder Alexander B. Morrison:

"I believe that the real reason for the crisis of our time is . . . an exhaustion of the soul. This spiritual apathy is described by the word *acedia,* a word which comes from the Greek *a* ('not') plus *kedos* ('care')—hence, not caring, boredom, or apathy. . . .

"But *acedia* signifies more than just spiritual laziness or even indifference. It connotes misplaced priorities, a darkening of the soul, a hatred of the good, a death of the heart. It leads to spiritual paralysis, leaving its victims 'past feeling' (1 Ne. 17:45)." ("A Caring Community: Goodness in Action," *Ensign,* February 1999, p. 16)

Ask your family the following questions:

- What does Elder Morrison say is the "crisis of our time"?
- Why is apathy such a serious concern for us?
- What examples can you give of apathy in our society? In our Church?

Read together Alma 59:1–13 and look for reasons for Captain Moroni's anger. Ask:

- What request did Moroni make in his letter to the government? (Verse 3.)
- Why did the Nephites lose the city of Nephihah? (Verses 5–8.)
- Why did Moroni not send help to the Nephites in Nephihah? (Verses 9–10.)
- Why was Moroni sorrowful and full of doubt?
- What word in verse 13 indicates that apathy may have existed in the Nephite government? ("Indifference.")

Explain to your family that Moroni's feelings of anger, sorrow, and doubt were not based on fact. Tell them that they will learn in Alma 61 the real reason for the government's lack of help.

As a family, search the references for the word *apathy* in the Topical Guide. Discuss ways your family can resist apathy. Using the scriptures, create a family motto. Then put it on the refrigerator so that all may see it and remember to apply it.

ALMA 60: MORONI'S LETTER TO PAHORAN

Alma 60:1–11, 19–22
A call for help?

 Ask one parent or an older child to go into another room. Have the person pretend the room is dangerous, especially when the lights are turned off. Say that calling for help may be the only way he or she can be saved. Leave the person alone in the room, turn off the lights, and hold the door so he or she cannot get out. When the person calls out for help, open the door and gather again together as a family.

Perform this object lesson again. However, this time, choose not to help the person when he or she calls. After some time has passed, open the door and gather as a family.

Repeat this object lesson a third time. This time tell the person going into the room that only a certain member of your family can open the door. When he or she calls for help from that person, stop that person from helping. After a short time, open the door and gather as a family. Talk about some of these questions:

- What are some times when you have felt like you've needed help?
- Who have you called on for help?
- How did you feel in the first object lesson when help arrived quickly?
- How did you feel the second time, when no one came to help you?
- How did you feel the third time when the person you thought should help did not?

Now read Alma 60:1–11, 19–22 together. Have your family look for answers to the following questions. Then discuss them.

- Why did Moroni and his army need help?
- Who did Moroni think should have helped him?
- What did Moroni think the reasons were that help did not come?

Teach your family that we often need the help of others. Also, others often need our assistance. President Spencer W. Kimball taught:

"God does notice us, and he watches over us. But it is usually through another mortal that he meets our needs. Therefore, it is vital that we serve each other in the kingdom." (*The Teachings of Spencer W. Kimball*, p. 252.)

Have family members think of a person in need. Have them talk about ways they can help or serve that person in the coming week.

Explain that even though Moroni was angry at Pahoran for not sending help, we will learn in Alma 61 why Pahoran was unable to do so. This is similar to the third part of the object lesson you did previously. Tell the family member who called for help the third time that the person he or she called was detained and could not help. Discuss how that changes the person's feelings about the situation. Tell your family that as you study Alma 61, they will better understand Pahoran's situation and why he did not help his friend Moroni.

Encourage each family member to ask Heavenly Father in prayer each day to know how to help those he wants to bless and help.

Alma 60:12–13
Why does the Lord allow the righteous to be slain?

 Ask your family to ponder the following questions:

- Do only wicked people die in war?
- Why does the Lord permit righteous people to be killed?
- What happens to righteous people who are killed?

Ask them to read Alma 60:12–13 and tell how Moroni would answer those questions. What does that teach us about how the Lord views this life?

Alma 60:15–22
What weakens a nation?

 It will be helpful to have a bag of small treats for this activity. Divide the family members in pairs and have them sit at a table or lie on the floor where they can rest their elbows. Tell them to clasp hands in preparation for an arm wrestle. Explain that the object is to get the other person's hand to touch the table or floor as many times as possible in thirty seconds. They will get a treat for each time they are successful. Time them for thirty seconds and give treats accordingly.

Tell your family that in Alma 60:15–22, Moroni explained some of the reasons why the Nephites were not being successful in their battles against the Lamanites. Have them read Alma 60:16 and look for reasons Moroni gave for the Nephites' lack of success that would also relate to the arm wrestle. ("We were contending amongst ourselves.") Ask, "Do you think you could have been more successful in earning treats in the arm wrestle if you had been united and worked together instead of contending or working against each other?" (You could demonstrate with a partner how many times you could have the other person's hand touch the table or floor if you work together instead of resisting each other in an arm wrestle.) Ask:

- Why do you think it would be important for an army to be united?
- How might this relate to a family, a ward, a stake, or the Church?
- What are some things our family could do to be more united?
- What blessings would come to our family if we always helped and supported one another?

Alma 60:22–36
Cleansing the inner vessel

 Show your family two bowls, one that is dirty on the outside and one that is dirty on the inside. Ask them if they had to eat from one of the bowls, which would they choose and why?

Have someone read Alma 60:22–23 aloud and tell what Moroni was most concerned about that is like the two bowls and why. Read Alma 60:23–36 together as a family and look for what Moroni threatened to do if the government did not respond appropriately. Ask one family member to summarize what Moroni said he would do. How is this like what the Lord said he would do in the last days in D&C 112:23–26?

Hold up the two bowls again and ask, "How could we apply this in our lives?" Read together Mark 7:14–23 and invite the family to identify what Jesus said about why we should cleanse the inner vessel. Share this quotation from President Ezra Taft Benson:

"All is not well in Zion. As Moroni counseled, we must cleanse the inner vessel (see Alma 60:23), beginning first with ourselves, then with our families, and finally with the Church. . . .

"If we are to cleanse the inner vessel, we must forsake immorality and be clean. . . .

"My beloved brethren and sisters, as we cleanse the inner vessel, there will have to be changes made in our own personal lives, in our families, and in the Church. The proud do not change to improve, but defend their position by rationalizing. Repentance means change, and it takes a humble person to change. But we can do it" ("Cleansing the Inner Vessel," *Ensign,* May 1986, pp. 4–7)

Encourage family members to decide some things they can change in their lives to cleanse their inner vessel.

ALMA 61: PAHORAN'S RESPONSE TO MORONI'S ACCUSATIONS

Alma 6:1–21

A search for principles

You might consider dressing up like a detective (with a magnifying glass, hat, and so on). Ask your family to define the word *principle.* Share the following definition by Elder Richard G. Scott:

"Principles are concentrated truth, packaged for application to a wide variety of circumstances. A true principle makes decisions clear even under the most confusing and compelling circumstances. It is worth great effort to organize the truth we gather to simple statements of principle." ("Acquiring Spiritual Knowledge," *Ensign,* November 1993, p. 86.)

Tell your family that, simply put, a principle is a truth by which we can govern our behavior. Explain that we will be detectives in search of principles found in Alma 61. Review the setting of this chapter by reading the following quotation from Elder Neal A. Maxwell:

"We must always realize that in a perfect church filled with imperfect people, there are bound to be some miscommunications at times. A noteworthy example occurred in ancient American Israel. Moroni wrote two times to

Pahoran complaining of neglect because much-needed reinforcements did not arrive. Moroni used harsh language, accusing the governor of the land, Pahoran, of sitting on his throne in a state of 'thoughtless stupor.' (Alma 60:7.) Pahoran soon made a very patriotic reply, explaining why he could not do what Moroni wanted. Though censured, Pahoran was not angry; he even praised Moroni for 'the greatness of your heart.' (Alma 61:9.)." (*All These Things Shall Give Thee Experience,* p. 119.)

To help your family identify principles, read Alma 61:9 and share the following two principles found in this verse:

- We can choose not to be angry even when we are incorrectly censured.
- Rather than be angry, we can look for the greatness in others' hearts.

Give each family member a red pencil. Have them write a "P" in the margin next to a verse each time they find a principle. After family members have identified principles, have them share examples. Invite them to state how they will incorporate that principle into their lives.

Alma 61:9

How can we respond to those who falsely accuse us?

To help involve younger children, have three of your youngest dress up as Moroni, Pahoran, and a runner. Take a piece of paper, write on it the words of Alma 61:9, burn the edges so that it looks like an antique document, and roll it into a scroll around a stick.

Ask family members to share experiences when someone said things that were untrue about them. Find out how they felt about such experiences and how they resolved them. Then have the child playing Pahoran hand the scroll to the runner, who in turn delivers it to Moroni. Moroni should then read the verse written on the scroll. Ask the following questions:

- Why do you think Pahoran chose not to be angry at Moroni's accusations?
- Why would Pahoran look for the good in Moroni following Moroni's censure of him?
- How would our lives be better if we behaved like Pahoran?

Invite one member of your family to read the following story told by Elder Neal A. Maxwell:

"Parley P. Pratt recalled an episode when President Brigham Young chastened him and others for their management of the westward migration. In this instance also, there were two letters of a scolding nature, even alleging insubordination. Of this Elder Pratt wrote, 'I could not realize this at the time, and protested that in my own heart, so far as I was concerned, I had no such motive; that I had been actuated by the purest motives. . . .' Later it became clear to Elder Pratt that some of those scolded had motives that were not as pure as his. He commented further, ' . . . yet I thank God for this timely chastisement; I profited by it, and it caused me to be more watchful and careful ever after' (*Autobiography of Parley P. Pratt,* pp. 341–42).

"It is worth remembering that Elder Pratt protested in his heart, not publicly. He took it. Perhaps President Young, like Moroni, might have taken note of how Elder Pratt was even sick at the time—but, like Moroni, President Young did not know of the full conditions.

"The stuff out of which offense is made is all around us, if we wish to seize upon it. What we learn, however, from men like Pahoran and Elder Pratt should give us pause, especially when we may be inclined to take umbrage instead of following the Brethren." (*All These Things Shall Give Thee Experience,* pp. 119–20.)

Ask:
- How were Elder Pratt and Pahoran alike?
- What can we do to be like them?

ALMA 62: COURAGEOUS, RIGHTEOUS PEOPLE MAKE A DIFFERENCE

Alma 62:1–11
On to victory together

Ask family members to think of a letter, note, or phone call they received that evoked strong emotions, such as happiness, sadness, or anger. Invite them to share what they can about the situation and how it made them feel. Explain that Moroni received a letter from Pahoran that evoked two contrasting emotions "exceedingly." Read Alma 62:1–2 together to find what Moroni was feeling. Ask someone to summarize what caused Moroni "exceedingly great joy." Ask another to explain what caused Moroni to "mourn exceedingly."

Read with your family Alma 62:3–11 and find what Moroni and Pahoran did about the rebellion among their own people. Discuss the following questions:

- How was Moroni able to gather a sufficient army to battle against the dissenters? (Verses 3–6.)
- Who was the king of the dissenters and what happened to him? (Verses 6–8.)
- What law was "strictly observed for the safety of their country"? (Verses 9–11.)
- What does this story teach us about the importance of unity?
- What does this story teach about the value of freedom?

Alma 62:12–39
The power of national unity

Show your family a magnifying glass and a bright light. Hold the magnifying glass between the light and a white piece of paper. Then move the glass until the light on the paper is as small as possible. Ask someone to explain why the light is so much brighter after it goes through the magnifying glass. (All the light is concentrated or focused on a single spot.)

Tell your family that Captain Moroni and the Nephites are an example of a similar principle in Alma 62. Divide your family into two groups. Assign one group Alma 62:12–26 and the other Alma 62:27–39. Ask them to read their assigned verses, discuss what happened with their group, and then summarize their findings for the rest of the family. Ask the following questions to help with the discussion:

- What difference did it make that the Nephites were now united in the war effort? (Verses 12–14.)
- What was interesting about the way the Nephites treated the Lamanites that they took prisoner? (Verses 16–17, 27–29.)
- What part did the people of Ammon play in these wars? (Verses 17, 27–29.)
- What strategy did Moroni use to take the city of Nephihah?
- What happened in the "land of Lehi" that was different from the way the Nephites took the city of Nephihah? (Verses 31–32.)
- What is impressive about Teancum again? (Verses 35–36, compare Alma 51:34.)
- How is the power of the Nephites like the light through the magnifying glass? (Verses 31–32, 38. When the Nephites were united or focused, they were powerful enough to drive the Lamanites out.)

Share your feelings with your family about the power of family unity to provide protection against those forces that seek to destroy the family today.

Alma 62:40
How important are "the prayers of the righteous"?

Have one family member read Alma 62:40, another read Alma 10:22–23, and another read Helaman 13:12–14. Talk about the important principle taught in each of these verses and cross-reference them together. Invite a family

member to share their testimony of the power of prayer.

Alma 62:41
Why do people react differently to the same event?

Ask family members to think of times when they have seen people react differently to the same event. Have them share examples and tell why they think the people acted differently. Read Alma 62:41 together with your family. Ask:

- What had been going on between the Nephites and the Lamanites?
- How long had the Lamanites and Nephites been at war? (About thirteen years—see Alma 43:3 and Alma 62:39.)
- What different ways did the Nephites react to the long wars?
- Why do you think some were "hardened" and some were "softened"?

Share this explanation by C. Max Caldwell:

"These people all had basically the same experience. The war was the same length for all people; yet out of the same experience some were hardened and some were softened. What made the difference? It was what they thought of God and his Son." ("What Think Ye of Christ?" *Ensign,* February 1984, p. 18.)

Invite family members to ponder for a few moments what they think of God and his Son. How can this affect how we will react to different challenges we will face in our lives?

ALMA 63: PASSING DOWN THE NEPHITE RECORDS

Alma 63:1–17
Who were the people in this chapter?

Take turns reading aloud Alma 63 as a family. Choose one person to be a scribe to write down the names of every person mentioned in the chapter as you read. When you have finished, assign a family member to each name listed. Give each family member time to do the following for each person assigned to him or her:

1. Think of a symbol or picture that represents your person and draw it if possible.

2. If this person were to visit our family for a day, what valuable things do you think we could learn from him? (Tell the assigned family member to include things they know about this person from previous chapters in the Book of Mormon as well.)

3. Have family members share their pictures and ideas.

Alma 63:1–2

What kind of person was Shiblon?

Ask your family if they were to leave on an extended visit to a place far away, who would they trust to take care of their most precious possessions left behind. Why?

Read Alma 63:1–2 and ask your family the following questions:

- What possessions were being "left behind" and entrusted to Shiblon?
- What was Shiblon doing the last time we read about him? (See Alma 38:1–3).
- Why do you think Shiblon was entrusted with such sacred things?

Invite family members to name sacred and important things God has entrusted them with. Discuss things that God may yet entrust members of your family with if they live as Shiblon did. (Receiving temple endowments, serving a mission, a higher priesthood office, Church callings, parenthood, and so on.)

Alma 63:4–9

Why were Nephites migrating to the land northward?

 Divide the family into two groups. Give to each group a sheet of paper, some crayons,

and a pair of scissors. Assign each group to read Alma 63:4–9 and try to discover how many ships Hagoth built. With the materials provided, have family members draw a picture of what Hagoth's fleet of ships may have looked like. Ask:

- Why do you think so many people were traveling to the land northward?
- Why would people attempt to go into the unknown to make a new home?
- Would the events of the previous ten to fifteen chapters of Alma suggest any reasons for this exodus?
- How many ships do you think Hagoth built?
- How many ships came back for more passengers?

Discuss as a family what it might have been like to be the first settlers to come to America. How might this portion of the Nephite record be similar to how America began?

Alma 63:10–13

The importance of the sacred records

 Read together Alma 63:10–13 and ask:

- Who did Shiblon pass the sacred records to?
- How was this in keeping with Nephite tradition? (Verse 13.)
- What did Helaman send forth "among the children of men"?
- What do you think these sacred records became to those who received them? (Scriptures.)

Explain that these sacred records of the Nephites were much like our journals and family histories. Ask:

- What could your children, grandchildren, and so on learn about you from the journals and family histories you have completed to this point in your life?
- What would you want them to know?
- Are there some important events and experiences that have not yet been recorded?

Tell your family that some people believe they have nothing valuable or important to say in a journal or history. Share with your family the following from President Spencer W. Kimball:

"No one is commonplace, and I doubt if you can ever read a biography from which you cannot learn something from the difficulties overcome and the struggles made to succeed. These are the measuring rods for the progress of humanity. As we read the stories of great men, we discover that they did not become famous overnight nor were they born professionals or skilled craftsmen. The story of how they became what they are may be helpful to us all. Your own journal, like most others, will tell of problems as old as the world and how you dealt with them.

"Some of what you write may be humdrum dates and places, but there will also be rich passages that will be quoted by your posterity. Get a notebook, my young folks, a journal that will last through all time, and maybe the angels may quote from it for eternity. Begin today and write in it your goings and comings, your deepest thoughts, your achievements and your failures, your associations and your triumphs, your impressions and your testimonies. Remember, the Savior chastised those who failed to record important events." ("The Angels May Quote from It," *New Era,* October 1975, p. 5.)

Have family members write in their journals their testimonies of the Book of Mormon.

Alma 63:14–17
The exclamation point of the book of Alma

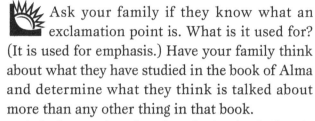 Ask your family if they know what an exclamation point is. What is it used for? (It is used for emphasis.) Have your family think about what they have studied in the book of Alma and determine what they think is talked about more than any other thing in that book.

Ask them to imagine that the book of Alma is one long sentence. Invite them to read Alma 63:14–17 and find what might be the exclamation point of the book of Alma. Ask:

- How might a war between the Lamanites and Nephites be considered an exclamation point for the book of Alma?
- What seems to be all too familiar about verse 14?
- Why is it fitting that it was Nephite dissenters that stirred the Lamanites up to war against the Nephites?
- How would you characterize the book of Alma?
- What would be the most important lesson you learned from that book?

HELAMAN

The Book of Helaman covers a period of history from about 52 B.C. to near the time of the Savior's birth. Its authors lived in a day of intense wickedness. Gadianton Robbers were rampant upon the land, desiring to gain power by murder, robbery, secrecy, and deception. They were led by Satan and administered secret oaths in his name. Mormon warned that these secret combinations would eventually "prove the overthrow, yea, almost the entire destruction of the people of Nephi." (Helaman 2:13.) During this time, the Lamanites became more righteous than the Nephites. Samuel, a Lamanite prophet, was sent to declare repentance to the Nephites.

HELAMAN 1: POLITICS AND WAR

Helaman 1:1–13
What are the results of contention?

Invite family members to write a definition for the words *cooperation* and *contention*. Have them share their definitions. Then ask:

- What is the difference between contention and cooperation?
- When is a time you have seen cooperation in our family?
- Can you think of a time when we have had contention?
- How do you feel when there is contention?
- How do you feel when there is cooperation.
- Which feeling do you like the best?

Take turns reading Helaman 1:1–13. As you read, have your family look for and mark the words "contend" or "contention" each time they occur. To help them find the principles in these verses, ask some of the following questions:

- Why was there contention among the Nephites? (Verse 2.)
- What was the result of their contention? (Verses 4, 8–9, see also verse 21.)

- How might things have been different if Pahoran's three sons had cooperated rather than contended?
- If they could go back and do it over again, which do you think they would choose?
- What do you think the Nephites should have learned from this experience?
- How does contention weaken nations, communities, stakes, wards, families, and individuals?
- Have you ever had an argument with someone and later wished you could go back and change the way you acted?
- What can we do in our family to foster unity and avoid contention?

You might like to share the following statements with your family:

"If Satan can succeed in creating in us the pastime of arguing, quarreling, and contention, it is easier for him to bind us with heavier sins which can destroy our eternal lives." (Marvin J. Ashton, Conference Report, October 1991, p. 99.)

"Beginning in the days of Cain and continuing through all generations, whenever there have been unrighteous and apostate peoples on earth, Satan has revealed unto them his oaths, vows, and secret combinations. Cain first took upon himself the secret oaths as they were administered by Satan; then he killed Abel. Murder, plunder, robbery, power, the destruction of freedom, and the persecution of the saints have been the objectives of these societies ever since." (Bruce R. McConkie, *Mormon Doctrine,* p. 698.)

Helaman 1:1–34
Play a guessing game

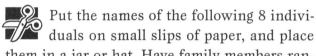 Put the names of the following 8 individuals on small slips of paper, and place them in a jar or hat. Have family members randomly select one or more of the papers.

> Pahoran II (Helaman 1:1–9)
> Paanchi (Helaman 1:1–8)
> Pacumeni (Helaman 1:1–3, 13, 21)
> Kishkumen (Helaman 1:9–12)
> Coriantumr (Helaman 1:14–32)
> Tubaloth (Helaman 1:14–17)
> Moronihah (Helaman 1:25–33)
> Lehi (Helaman 1:28–29)

Read together Helaman 1:1–34 and have family members pay particular attention to the verses that describe the people on the papers they selected. Then have each person take a turn describing the actions, evil works, sins, and so on of the individual they selected without divulging the name. Allow other family members to guess who is being described. You might choose to give a small reward to those who guess correctly.

HELAMAN 2: THE GADIANTON ROBBERS

Helaman 2:1–14
Why did Mormon tell us about Gadianton and his band?

If possible, show your family a bag of apples. Also hold an apple that is beginning to rot in your hand. Ask your family what would happen if you put this very ripe apple in the bag. Ask them if they have heard the phrase "One bad apple spoils the whole bushel." How many of them think this phrase is true? (The phrase is true. Ripened fruit excretes a chemical called ethylene that makes other fruit ripen faster than usual.) Discuss what you might do to save a bag of apples that has an overly ripe apple in it. (Take the bad apple out of the bag.)

As you read together Helaman 2:1–14, have your family look for things that are like the following items:

- Bad apples.
- Bushel of apples.
- Casting out bad apples.

After you have discussed the chapter, your family may have found the following comparisons:

- Bad apples = Kishkumen, Gadianton, and the secret combination of robbers.
- Bushel of apples = Helaman, his servant, and the Nephite people.
- Casting out bad apples = Killing of Kishkumen and hunting the Gadianton robbers.

The following questions might aid your discussion:

- What motives did Gadianton, Kishkumen, and their band of robbers have? (Verses 5, 8.)
- Why do you think "secret combination" is a good name for this band of robbers?
- How was their purpose thwarted? (Verse 9.)
- What was Mormon's warning about Gadianton and his secret combination? (Verse 13.)
- In what ways is this scriptural account similar to the object lesson?

Ask your family if they think secret combinations existed before Gadianton. (See Moses 5:28–32.) Are there secret combinations today? Read the following statement by Elder M. Russell Ballard:

"Among today's secret combinations are gangs, drug cartels, and organized crime families." (Conference Report, October 1997, p. 51.)

Discuss ways your family can help stamp out

secret combinations in your neighborhood or community.

HELAMAN 3: MIGRATION AND CHURCH GROWTH

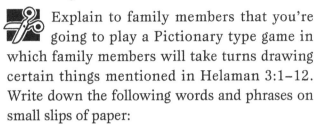

Helaman 3:1–12
Pictionary

 Explain to family members that you're going to play a Pictionary type game in which family members will take turns drawing certain things mentioned in Helaman 3:1–12. Write down the following words and phrases on small slips of paper:

- Contention. (Verse 3.)
- Many rivers. (Verse 4.)
- Houses of cement. (Verses 7, 9.)
- Temples. (Verse 9.)
- Shipping timber. (Verse 10.)

Have each person quickly read the verses. Then give a slip of paper with one of the clues on it and drawing materials to a family member. Have him or her draw what that verse describes and have the others guess what is being drawn and what verse it came from. Take turns drawing and guessing.

Helaman 3:13–15
"A hundredth part . . . cannot be contained in this work"

Read together Helaman 3:13–15. Ask:

- What portion of Nephite and Lamanite history is included in the Book of Mormon?
- Where is the rest of the Nephites' record?

Read the following account given by Brigham Young:

"When Joseph got the plates, the angel instructed him to carry them back to the hill Cumorah, which he did. Oliver says that when Joseph and Oliver went there, the hill opened, and they walked into a cave, in which there was a large and spacious room. He says he did not think, at the time, whether they had the light of the sun or artificial light; but that it was just as light as day. They laid the plates on a table; it was a large table that stood in the room. Under this table there was a pile of plates as much as two feet high, and there were altogether in this room more plates than probably many wagon loads; they were piled up in the corners and along the walls." (*Journal of Discourses,* 19:38.)

Helaman 3:24–36
An increase of pride

 Duplicate the chart below large enough for your family to write on:

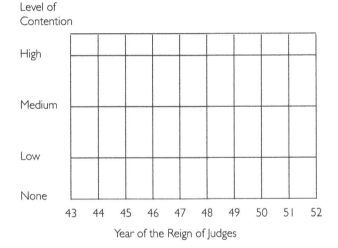

Have your family search Helaman 3:1–3, 17–19, 22–28, 32–37. As they do, ask them to chart the level of the Nephites' wickedness, pride, and contention over the space of ten years. Have them draw on this graph, showing how it changed from year to year.

When you have finished, discuss your findings by asking:

- What does righteousness lead to?
- Why did the people prosper?
- What challenges come with prosperity?
- Why did people want to join the church?
- Why do you think they went from righteousness to pride so quickly?

Ask a family member to read the following quotation from Brigham Young:

"The worst fear that I have about this people is that they will get rich in this country, forget God and His people, wax fat, and kick themselves out of the Church and go to hell. This people will stand mobbing, robbing, poverty, and all manner of persecution, and be true. But my greater fear for them is that they cannot stand wealth; and yet they have to be tried with riches, for they will become the richest people on this earth." (*Autobiography of James Brown,* pp. 119–23, cited in Preston Nibley, *Brigham Young, the Man and His Work,* pp. 127–28.)

Ask your family to reread Helaman 3:1, 33–34, 36 and look for different descriptions of the level of pride. Write the following on the paper with your chart and have your family fill in the blanks:

Helaman 3:1, "a _____ pride."
Helaman 3:33, "pride which _____ to enter."
Helaman 3:34, "_____ in pride."
Helaman 3:36, "_____ pride."

Discuss the following questions to emphasize the principles taught in these verses:

- Why pride was such a big problem for the Nephites in times of prosperity?
- Would you say we are more or less prosperous than the Nephites were?
- Are there people today for whom pride is a problem?
- What kind of bondage do the proud suffer today?
- What should we do as a family to avoid becoming proud and letting prosperity drag us into bondage?

Helaman 3:35
Wax and righteousness

Tie a small weight (like a bolt or washer) to a piece of string. Also find a long candle. Hold up the candle and the string and ask, "How could you make this string into a candle?" Explain that a candle maker would take a wick (like the string) and dip it in melted wax. It's then dipped in water to cool the wax. This dipping process is done back and forth until the desired thickness of the candle is achieved.

Read Helaman 3:35 and ask:

- What does the making of a wax candle have to do with the word "wax" in Helaman 3:35?
- How is becoming like the Savior a gradual process like making a candle?
- What will happen as we progress?
- What are the things that make a person progress?
- What specific things can we do to "yield our hearts to God"?

Share the following statement by President Ezra Taft Benson:

"We must be careful, as we seek to become more and more godlike, that we do not become discouraged and lose hope. Becoming Christ-like is a lifetime pursuit and very often involves growth and change that is slow, almost imperceptible." ("A Mighty Change of Heart," *Ensign,* October 1989, pp. 2–5.)

HELAMAN 4: BY THE SWORD THE NEPHITES REGAIN HALF OF WHAT THEY LOST BY WICKEDNESS

Helaman 4:1–10
The Nephites pay the price of contention—again!

Invite your family to recall a time when they had an argument with another family member. Ask them to describe the kinds of feelings they had. What effect can these feelings have on the family? Read together Helaman 4:1–10. Ask:

- What led the Nephite nation to lose half of their possessions? (Verse 1.)
- Why is it significant that there were "many dissensions in the church"?

- Why do people get angry and dissent from (leave) the Church? (See Alma 3:36.)
- How can living the gospel help strengthen individuals, families, and nations?

Cross-reference Helaman 4:1 to Mosiah 4:14–15 and D&C 68:28. Ask a family member to read those verses aloud. Then ask the following questions:

- What did King Benjamin say that parents should not "suffer their children" to do?
- Who are we serving when we "fight and quarrel"?
- How might it have helped strengthen the Nephites and kept them from losing half of their possessions?
- How might loving and serving one another help strengthen our family?

Read the following statement:

"By learning to avoid contention and to control our anger, we stop evil from being passed along and become more like the Savior, whose sacrifice of self made eternal life possible for all who come unto him and emulate his example." ("Charity Is Not Easily Provoked," *Ensign,* July 1988, p. 47.)

Ask your family to share ways they can avoid contention. Write their responses on a poster and place it where they can see it often.

Helaman 4:11–16
What can come from teaching repentance?

Ask your family to think of a time when they were physically ill. Discuss what it feels like to be sick and what was done to get well again. How is being physically ill similar to being spiritually ill? Read together Helaman 4:11–13 and have your family number each spiritual sickness suffered by the Nephites. Underline those things that came upon them as a result of their spiritual condition.

Ask your family to suggest what they would do, if they had lived at that time, to help the Nephites overcome their spiritual sickness. Read together Helaman 4:14–16. Ask:

- What did Moronihah, Nephi, and Lehi do to help the Nephites overcome spiritual sickness?
- What message did they preach?
- What happened when the Nephites began to obey their teachings?
- What is it about the teaching of the gospel that can bring such great changes in people's lives?

Read the following story from Elder Yoshihiko Kikuchi that illustrates the power and importance of the message that missionaries share:

"I met this gentleman at a special fireside. . . . With tears in his eyes, and as he was holding my hands, he said, 'Oh, Elder Kikuchi, I thank our Heavenly Father for this glorious gospel,' and then he related the following story:

"'One day eight years ago, on my way home from work, I was hit by a hit-and-run driver. For eleven days I was unconscious, and for two years I was in a hospital. When I was finally released from the hospital, my wife had left me and had taken the children with her. We had had a fine family life before the accident, but my life became a total wreck. I was lonesome and depressed, for I had lost my most precious possession—my family. I attempted suicide many times. My only living came from welfare. I was emotionally and physically exhausted; I had become a living vegetable. I couldn't walk, so I would transport myself by rolling over on the floor and crawling on all fours.

"'One evening I went to the hospital to see my doctor for the final results of a series of operations. He told me there was no hope for recovery. Though I had expected him to say so, it was still very shocking for me. All was lost. As I approached a railway bridge on my return from the doctor's, I wept to see my own face in the wet reflection on the pavement. It was a pitiful sight.'

"Brothers and sisters, just when he was about to jump in front of the oncoming train, he met one of your missionary sons. . . .

"Cottage meetings began immediately. In them, Mr. Sugiyama learned that the gospel is true, that

Jesus Christ is our Savior, Joseph Smith was a prophet of God, and the true church of God has been restored in this last dispensation.

"As usual, missionaries invited him to church; however, because he couldn't walk, he said he wouldn't be able to come. But on the morning of the Sabbath, he awoke early and bravely headed for the church. Though it was close, it took him nearly three hours to traverse the distance between his home and the closest station to the Yokohama chapel. The Yokohama chapel is situated high upon a hill. From the station to the church it took him almost an hour, although ordinarily it would take a person only five minutes. He would cling to the wall, then fall down, only to struggle again to his feet. He finally reached the chapel where the sacrament was in progress. The missionaries had never expected him to come to church. But Brother Sugiyama felt the pure love of God from the missionaries and members and felt himself drawn to it. . . .

"The morning following his baptism, he woke up bright and early. He stretched his legs out in preparation to roll over as usual. But this time, brothers and sisters, something was different. He felt strength in his legs, and his whole body surged with power. He sat up and gradually, eventually, stood on his feet. He hadn't stood in years without other supports. He walked away that morning! He found that his body had been made whole. . . .

"Brother Sugiyama said, 'Love hath made me whole, and I will go in peace in the Lord's way.'" ("Send Missionaries from Every Nation," *Ensign*, November 1979, pp. 29–30.)

Read together Mark 2:1–12 and ask your family how the story of Brother Sugiyama is like the story in Mark 2. Why do you think there is a relationship between our faith and receiving miraculous blessings from our Heavenly Father?

Invite your family to write in their personal journals, some specific changes they can make to increase their faith and receive the Lord's blessings.

Helaman 4:21–26
What do you lose through wickedness?

 Before scripture study, hide a small object like a ring or coin somewhere in the room. Have a contest to see who can find the "lost" item. When you have finished, ask your family if any of them have lost something valuable and then found it again. Ask them how they felt when they realized it was missing. What did it mean to them to find it again?

Have your family take turns reading Helaman 4:21–26 and look for the most valuable things the Nephites lost because of their wickedness. As they share what they found, discuss how each lost item might change a person's life. They may find some or all of the following:

- Blessings that come from keeping commandments. (Verse 21.)
- "Their laws had become corrupt." (Verse 22.)
- They lost "the spirit of prophecy and of revelation." (Verse 23.)
- The Holy Ghost had withdrawn from them. (Verse 24.)
- The Lord no longer "preserved them" from their enemies. (Verse 25.)
- They had lost their strength. (Verse 26.)

Invite the parents of the family to share how the world has changed since they were children by responding to the following questions:

- Is the world more or less righteous than when you were young?
- What are some of the things that have been lost because of wickedness in our day?
- What blessings of those days do you miss the most?
- Are there some blessings you have now that you didn't have when you were younger? Why?

Discuss with your family some of the warnings the prophets have given for our day and how you, as a family, can avoid losing the Lord's blessings.

HELAMAN 5: NEPHI AND LEHI ARE MIRACULOUSLY SAVED

Helaman 5:1–4
"Ripening for destruction"

Remind your family that King Mosiah gave the Nephites a warning when he proposed that the government be led by elected judges instead of a king (also note that this chapter takes place sixty-two years after that warning; see Helaman 5:18). Read Mosiah 29:25–27 together to find his warning. What did Mosiah say would happen if the majority of the people chose evil?

Now, have family members read Helaman 5:1–4 individually and ask:

- Why were the Nephites "ripening for destruction"? (Verses 2–3.)
- What did Nephi do to try to bring about change in the people? (Verse 4.)
- Who had done a similar thing about fifty-three years earlier? (See Alma 4:18–19.)
- Who joined with Nephi in an effort to change the people? (Verse 4.)
- Why do you think Nephi believed he could do more to help his people by "preaching the word of God" than by being the Chief Judge? (See Alma 31:5.)
- What would be the best thing we could do "the remainder of [our] days" to help further the Lord's work? (See D&C 15:4–6.)

Helaman 5:5–14
Will you remember?

Play the game Concentration with your family using UNO, Rook, or Old Maid cards. Lay the cards face down in even rows. The first player turns over any two cards. If the cards match, the player keeps them and takes another turn. If they do not match, the cards are returned to their original position and the second player takes his or her turn. Players must try to remember the position of all the cards they have seen.

The player with the most cards at the end of the game wins.

After quickly playing the game, ask what the key is to winning the game. (Remembering.) Have family members search Helaman 5:6–14 and find how many times the word "remember" or "remembered" is used, and to mark each one. As a family, make a list of things Helaman asked his sons to remember.

Share the following statements by Elder Spencer W. Kimball:

"When you look into the dictionary for the most important word, do you know what it is? It could be remember. Because all of you have made covenants—you know what to do and you know how to do it—our greatest need is to remember. . . . Remember is the word. Remember is the program." ("Circles of Exaltation," p. 8.)

"Remembering covenants prevents apostasy. . . . I suppose there would never be an apostate, there would never be a crime, if people remembered, really remembered, the things they had covenanted at the water's edge or at the sacrament table and in the temple. . . . I guess we as humans are prone to forget. It is easy to forget. Our sorrows, our joys, our concerns, our great problems seem to wane to some extent as time goes on, and there are many lessons that we learn which have a tendency to slip from us. The Nephites forgot." (*Teachings of Spencer W. Kimball,* pp. 112–13.)

Ask family members to find a verse showing that Nephi and Lehi remembered what they had been taught. (See verses 5, 14.) Encourage family members to ponder about and then share ideas of how they will better remember Jesus Christ.

Consider having your family sing "The Wise Man and the Foolish Man" (*Children's Songbook,* p. 281). Then show them a rock and ask:

- According to Helaman 5:12, who is the rock upon which we must build?
- How can we make Christ the foundation of our lives?

- What promises do we receive when we make Christ our foundation?
- What will be our fate if we try to build our lives on anything else?

Helaman 5:6–7
Remembering our names

Find a book of baby names and have each family member look up the meaning of his or her name. Have parents share why they chose each child's name. If you were named after an ancestor or other person in the past, what does that tell you about how the parents felt about that ancestor? What does the choice of the name tell you about how the parents felt about each child?

Read together Helaman 5:6–7 and ask your family what Helaman named his sons and why. (Verses 6–7.) What does that tell you about Helaman? What does that tell you about Helaman's feelings and his hopes for his sons?

Ask your family if they have ever wondered what Heavenly Father called them when they lived with him in heaven. What do you suppose he wants us to become? (See Moses 1:39.)

Helaman 5:14–19
The power of God's words

Give each family member a paper and pencil. Have them search Helaman 5:14–16 and race to see who can list in twenty seconds the most locations where Nephi and Lehi preached.

Read together Helaman 5:17–19. Ask the following questions:

- What effect did their preaching have among Nephite dissenters? (Verse 17.)
- How successful were they among the Lamanites? (Verse 19.)
- Why do you think they were able preach with such power? (Verse 18.)

Read Alma 17:2–3 together and discuss how a person can become a powerful teacher. Then read

D&C 18:15–16 and discuss why a person would want to be a great missionary.

Helaman 5:20–52
"Encircled by fire"

 Have a family member read Helaman 5:20 aloud and tell where Nephi and Lehi went after their great success in the land of Zarahemla. Tell your family that Helaman 5:21–52 relates some very interesting experiences that Nephi and Lehi had in the land of Nephi. To help your family better visualize this story, consider doing one of the following activities:

Reader's theater: Assign family members each of the parts in the story (Narrator, Nephi, Lehi, Heavenly Voice, Aminadab, Lamanite guards). Have the assigned persons read their parts as you study Helaman 5:21–52.

Family play: Let each family member be assigned a role from Helaman 5:21–52. Give each one time to quickly read, prepare, and act out the story. You could even videotape your production.

Art show: Have each family member silently read Helaman 5:21–52. Provide paper, pencils, and crayons and have each person draw a picture of what he or she read. Allow each person to display the picture and explain it.

When you have finished your activity, talk about the following questions with your family:

- What was your favorite part of this story?
- What do you think is the most important lesson we can learn from this experience?
- What does this story teach you about the power of God?
- How does this story testify to the truth of Alma 31:5? (Moronihah was able to regain only half of their lands by the sword. Nephi and Lehi were able to regain the rest of the Nephite lands and many converts as well. See Helaman 4:16–18.)
- What can we do as a family to qualify for and receive greater power from God?

HELAMAN 6: SATAN "GOT GREAT HOLD UPON THE HEARTS"

Helaman 6:1–6
Righteousness vs. wickedness

Change something in the room where you hold family scripture study so that it looks opposite of the way it normally looks. For example, turn a lamp upside down. When the family notices it, tell them it symbolizes a significant change recorded in the book of Helaman.

Draw a line down the middle of a piece of paper, creating two columns. Label the first column "Evidence that the _____ changed for the better." Label the second column "Evidence that the _____ changed for the worse."

As you read Helaman 6:1–6 with your family, have them first fill in the blanks and then suggest words and phrases for each column that provide evidence of change. Discuss why these changes were so significant in the Book of Mormon.

Tell your family that most of these words and phrases are also worth relating to our own experience. For example, verse 1 speaks of Lamanites who were "righteous, firm, and steadfast in the faith." Invite family members to think of times when they acted "righteous, firm, and steadfast in the faith." On the other hand, have them think of times when they acted "hardened," "impenitent," or even "wicked." Ask:

- Why did they choose to act in these ways?
- What leads to these different feelings and actions?
- What will you do to pursue a course that leads to being steadfast rather than hardened?

Helaman 6:7–13, 17
How does the Lord bless us?

Sing "Count Your Blessings" (*Hymns*, no. 241) with your family. Ask them how long they think it would take to name all the Lord's blessings "one by one."

Take turns reading aloud Helaman 6:7–13. Have each family member identify a way the Lord blessed the Nephites or Lamanites and how it is similar to a blessing the Lord has given that family member.

Read aloud verse 17 and ask:

- What happened when the Lord abundantly blessed the Nephites and Lamanites for a long time?
- Why do you think this happens so often?
- How could they have prevented such attitudes and actions?
- How is our family doing at staying close to the Lord rather than "setting [our] hearts upon [our] riches"?

Helaman 6:15–19
Keeping secrets

Ask your family why people keep secrets. Have them list some good reasons for keeping secrets and some bad reasons. Have them read Helaman 6:15–19 and find out who was murdered, who the murderer was, and the reason for the murder. Ask:

- What kinds of things did the Nephites begin to do in secret?
- Why did they turn to doing these things in secret?
- How can our family avoid being "lifted up one above another"?

Helaman 6:18, 20–24, 31–40
Actions, attitudes, and consequences

Place a stick on the ground with one end labeled "Actions" and the other end "Consequences." Ask a family member to pick up the stick. Ask, "Is it possible to pick up one end of the stick without the other end coming with it?" Explain that although we may not like the consequences, we "pick them up" when we chose our initial actions and attitudes.

Divide your family into two groups. Assign one group to look at the actions and attitudes of the

Lamanites and the other group to look at the actions and attitudes of the Nephites. Give each group a piece of paper, one providing the references for the Lamanites and the other for the Nephites like the example below.

Lamanites

Actions and attitudes:	Consequences:
Helaman 6:18, 20, 34, 37	Helaman 6:34, 36–37

Nephites

Actions and attitudes:	Consequences:
Helaman 6:20–24, 31, 33–34, 38	Helaman 6:34–35, 38–40

Have each group list the attitudes and actions they find and their consequences. Then have them share what they found.

Sing "Do What Is Right" (*Hymns,* no. 237) with your family and ask:

- What do you think it means to "do what is right, let the consequence follow"?
- What blessings do you think await us when we do what is right?
- What specific ways could we apply what we learned from the Nephites and Lamanites in this activity? (See Helaman 6:20, 37.)
- How could "preaching the word" destroy wickedness in our family?

Helaman 6:25–31

How does Satan get a hold on our hearts?

Set a timer for one minute and ask your family to recall as many evil influences as they can that Satan uses with Heavenly Father's children. One family member could list each example on a sheet of paper.

Assign the references below to family members. Have them read their verses and report the names or descriptions of individuals influenced by Satan.

1. Helaman 6:26, 29.
2. Helaman 6:27.
3. Helaman 6:28.
4. Helaman 6:31.
5. Helaman 6:25, 30.

Ask some of the following questions:

- What is the result of secret oaths and covenants? (Verse 25.)
- What can result when a nation follows Satan? (Verse 28.)
- Who is the author of sin? (Verse 30.)
- How do you think Satan gets hold of our hearts? (Verse 30.)
- What did the Nephites do that enabled Satan to get hold of their hearts? (Verse 31.)

Look up and read "Lucifer" in the Bible Dictionary (p. 726). Talk with your family about how a spirit with such potential could become the leading force for evil in our world. Share this statement by the Prophet Joseph Smith with your family:

"All beings who have bodies have power over those who have not. The devil has no power over us only as we permit him. The moment we revolt at anything which comes from God, the devil takes power." (*Teachings of the Prophet Joseph Smith,* p. 181.)

Ask your family what they can do to ensure that Satan does not get hold of their hearts.

Helaman 6:34–41

"Thus we see"

Tell your family that one of the most important things we can do as we study the scriptures is to find principles to help us learn and live the gospel better. Sometimes the principles are clearly identified by prophets. Have your family silently read Helaman 6:34–41 and look for a phrase that introduces important principles. Once they have discovered the "thus we see" phrases, have them rewrite each principle so they can apply it in their lives. For example, "When I sin and harden my heart, the Spirit leaves me." (See verse 35.)

HELAMAN 7: NEPHI PRAYS FOR HIS PEOPLE

Helaman 7:1–3, 21–29
What does it mean to prophesy?

Show your family a picture of our current prophet from the most recent conference issue of the *Ensign*. Have each family member tell one thing the prophet has counseled us to do. (Look up his talks, if necessary.) Ask them to look most closely at his talks for what he says will be the consequences of obeying his counsel. How about the consequences for disobeying?

Explain that when prophets tell us how to live and discuss the consequences of such actions, they are prophesying. One of the most common manifestations of the spirit of prophecy is when God's prophets tell us how our current actions affect our future lives—both now and in eternity.

Have a family member read Helaman 7:1–3 aloud. Ask:

- What two things did Nephi, son of Helaman, do in the land northward?
- What was the response?
- What was the consequence of that response?

Explain that although we do not know what the "many things" were that Nephi prophesied in the land northward (see verse 3), we do have other prophecies he made. Remind family members prophesying means speaking of things that will be—including future consequences of present actions. Then have family members read to themselves Helaman 7:16–29 and put a small x next to every verse that has a prophecy in it. Then have your family share what they learned.

You might then take the recent conference addresses of the current prophet and do the same thing as a family (mark and discuss the prophecies). Consider Helaman 7:1–3 again and ask:

- What two things does the current prophet do?
- What is our response?

- What might be the consequence of that response?

Helaman 7:4–9
How wicked had the Nephites become?

Ask your family, "If you could live at any time and any place in the history of the world, where and when would it be? Why?" Read together Helaman 7:4–6 and consider how wicked the Nephites had become. Discuss how this description compares to today's world. Read together Helaman 7:7–9 and look for the reasons why Nephi wanted to live in the "good old days." Read the following statement by Elder Neal A. Maxwell: "Wishing one had lived in another age, though sometimes understandable, is not usually helpful. One person in Book of Mormon times wrote, "Yea, if my days could have been in those days, then would my soul have had joy." (Hel. 7:8.) Yet that leader came to see how God's call to serve in a particular period of time is as much a part of His call as to perform certain duties during our days. Thus, youth of the Church, by Divine appointment, these are your days! You will live in a time of prophecy in fulfillment, of history converging, of special promises, of stark contrasts, and of blessed reassurances." ("These Are Your Days," *New Era,* January–February 1985, p. 4.)

Share with your family some reasons you believe this is such a great time to live.

Helaman 7:10–11
Nephi pours out his whole soul

Have the family read Helaman 7:10–11 and look for words that describe how Nephi prayed. Ask:

- What does it mean when it says that Nephi poured out his soul unto God in prayer?
- What would such a prayer be like? (Compare Enos 1:1–4.)
- How does Enos's prayer differ from some of the prayers our family offers from day to day?

• Can you share a time when you have participated in an especially powerful prayer?

Read the following statement by Elder James E. Talmage:

"Prayer is made up of heart throbs and the righteous yearnings of the soul, of supplication based on the realization of need, of contrition and pure desire. If there lives a man who has never really prayed, that man is a being apart from the order of the divine in human nature, a stranger in the family of God's children. Prayer is for the uplifting of the supplicant. God without our prayers would be God; but we without prayer cannot be admitted to the kingdom of God." (*Jesus the Christ*, p. 238; emphasis added.)

Helaman 7:10–21
Why did the people gather around Nephi's tower?

 Explain to the family that they are going to take part in a play. You will need the following parts: Nephi, a narrator, and some people in a crowd. Have the family member playing the part of Nephi stand on a chair or ladder. Have the rest of the family gather around the chair or the ladder as the crowd.

Ask the narrator to read Helaman 7:10–12 while Nephi and the crowd perform their parts according to the verses. Be sure Nephi reads Helaman 7:13–21 with passion. When you have finished, ask:

• What key points did Nephi share with his people?
• Why do you think Nephi asked so many questions?
• What question do you think would be hardest for them to answer? Why?
• Why did the people choose wickedness? (Verses 18, 21.)
• What did Nephi say that would also apply to people today?
• Would Nephi add anything if he were speaking today?

• What lessons can our family learn from Nephi's teachings?

HELAMAN 8: NEPHI TESTIFIES AS A PROPHET OF GOD

Helaman 8:1
Responses to correction

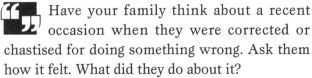 Have your family think about a recent occasion when they were corrected or chastised for doing something wrong. Ask them how it felt. What did they do about it?

Take turns reading Helaman 8:1–10 as a family and look for different ways people responded to Nephi's correction and chastisement. Ask:

• Why do you think some people became angry when chastised? (Verse 4.)
• What was their purpose in "[stirring] up the people to anger against Nephi"? (Verse 7.)
• Why did some believe Nephi was a prophet? (Verse 9.)

President Ezra Taft Benson taught:

"The scriptures testify that the proud are easily offended and hold grudges. (See 1 Nephi 16:1–3.) They withhold forgiveness to keep another in their debt and to justify their injured feelings.

"The proud do not receive counsel or correction easily. (See Prov. 15:10; Amos 5:10.) Defensiveness is used by them to justify and rationalize their frailties and failures. (See Matt. 3:9; John 6:30–59.)" ("Beware of Pride," *Ensign*, May 1989, p. 6.)

Cross-reference Helaman 8:4 with 1 Nephi 16:2 and ask why the guilty are afraid of the truth. Encourage your family to be more aware of how they accept and deal with correction and chastisement.

Helaman 8:6–24
What is the message of all the prophets?

 For this activity you will need a large piece of paper and a marker. Explain that

Helaman 8:6–24 talks about many Old Testament prophets and what they did. Assign family members the following prophets:

- Moses. (Helaman 8:11–16.)
- Abraham. (Helaman 8:17–19.)
- Zenos. (Helaman 8:19.)
- Zenock. (Helaman 8:19–20.)
- Ezias. (Helaman 8:19–20.)
- Isaiah. (Helaman 8:19–20.)
- Jeremiah. (Helaman 8:20–21.)

Invite family members to read about the prophet they were assigned and write down on the paper something this particular prophet did or testified of. Read together Helaman 8:22–23 and discuss what is the most important message that prophets share.

At the bottom of the page, write the name of the current prophet. Invite family members to write down what he has taught or prophesied. Refer to a recent Church magazine for help. Look especially for ways he testified of Christ.

Helaman 8:25–28
What is the role of a prophet?

 Have your family read Helaman 8:25–28. Ask:

- What did Nephi announce to the people?
- Who do you think told Nephi that the judge was murdered?
- How does the Lord speak to prophets?
- Why do you think Nephi was given this information?

Share the following story:

"[Shortly after the death of President David O. McKay,] one of the Church brethren approached Elder [Harold B.] Lee and asked, 'Is it correct what I have heard that they're going to make Joseph Fielding Smith the President of the Church?'

"That wasn't a very good question to ask of Elder Lee at that time. Elder Lee answered politely and confirmed that he thought that would be the case.

"But the man persisted and said, 'How can that be? I can't believe that. How can we sustain Joseph Fielding Smith? He's ninety-three years old. Why, he's so old I'm not sure he is really quite with it.' The man continued developing this point—how could a man at that age, his body weak and worn down, still direct this Church?

"President Lee listened for a while, but his sharp mind was spinning. He responded, 'My good brother, do you know what it takes to be a prophet of the Lord?'

"The man said, 'Well, I guess I really don't know exactly.'

"'Well,' said Elder Lee, 'what do you think it would take?'

"The fellow then said, 'Well, I suppose he'd have to know all about genealogy, the missionary program of the Church, and the missionaries and what they're doing and how to supervise them. He would need to know about the Primary and the Relief Society and the building and construction programs.' He named quite a few other major functions of the Church.

"When he finished Elder Lee said, 'That's all wrong.' He could sometimes say that quite pointedly. The man was taken back a bit. Then Elder Lee answered his question by stating, 'Shall I tell you what it takes to be a prophet? There's only one capacity; just one. And that is to be able to hear the voice of the Lord. That's all. He's got all the rest of us to do the work. He just has to do one function. Do you suppose that this great living Apostle, who has been sustained a prophet for six decades, longer than any other man on earth, might be able to do that?'

"The brother was feeling a little low by then, but Elder Lee continued, 'Do you suppose that Joseph Fielding Smith, who was a home teaching companion of President Wilford Woodruff, might know something about that?'

"By this time the man, in some humility, was on the retreat." (Gene R. Cook, as told in *He Changed*

My Life: Personal Experiences with Harold B. Lee, pp. 32–33.)

Ask a family member to summarize what it takes to be a prophet. Testify that not only do our modern prophets hear the Lord's voice but also that we can hear the Lord's voice by being attentive to the words of the prophets. (See D&C 68:4.)

HELAMAN 9: THE CHIEF JUDGE'S MURDERER IS FOUND

Helaman 9:1–3
How can you know that someone is a prophet?

Ask your family what the differences are between *predictions* (such as those in supermarket tabloids) and *prophecies* (made by the Lord's prophets)? Who are some people who *try* to predict the future? According to Deuteronomy 18:22, how can we tell that a prophecy is actually from God? Read Helaman 8:27–28 and ask:

- What did Nephi say had occurred?
- What did the Nephites do to see whether Nephi's prediction was true?
- What does Helaman 9:3 testify about Nephi?

Ask your family what other ways we have of knowing if a person is a true prophet.

Share the following testimony from Elder Boyd K. Packer:

"Some weeks before the meeting of last April, I left the office one Friday afternoon thinking of the weekend conference assignment. I waited for the elevator to come down from the fifth floor.

"As the elevator doors quietly opened, there stood President Joseph Fielding Smith. There was a moment of surprise in seeing him, since his office is on a lower floor.

"As I saw him framed in the doorway, there fell upon me a powerful witness of God. That sweet voice of Spirit that is akin to light, that has something to do with pure intelligence, affirmed to me that this was the prophet of God.

"I need not try to define that experience to Latter-day Saints. That kind of witness is characteristic of this Church. It is not something reserved to those in high office. It is a witness, not only available but vital, to every member." (*That All May Be Edified,* p. 311.)

Helaman 9:4–9, 39–41
People react differently toward prophets

Talk about different reactions people may have after attending general conference (some may say it was wonderful; another might have fallen asleep during the meeting; still another may be upset by what was said). Why do you think people react differently to the same experience?

Remind your family that Nephi prophesied the murder of the chief judge. (See Helaman 8:27–28; 9:1–3.) Tell them there were three different responses from those who learned the truth of Nephi's words. Read the following verses to learn about how each group responded and discuss the accompanying questions or quotes.

Group 1: Five Men. (Helaman 9:4–5.)
- Why did they begin to believe Nephi's words?
- According to verses 8–9, what did they face as a result?
- Have you ever been accused of doing something wrong just because you were "in the wrong place at the wrong time"?

Group 2: Some Nephites. (Helaman 9:39.)
- What caused this group to believe Nephi's words?
- Who do you know that has a strong testimony of the gospel of Jesus Christ?
- How can you hold on to their testimony until you receive your own?

President Harold B. Lee said, "You young Latter-day Saints here tonight, some of you may not have that testimony as firmly rooted as you would like to. May I ask you then, if you don't have, cling to my testimony tonight, until you can develop one for yourselves." (LDSSA Fireside, Utah State University, October 1971.)

Group 3: Some people. (Helaman 9:40–41.)

- What caused this group to believe?
- According to Helaman 10:1, what did they do even after realizing Nephi was a true prophet?
- Why would they do that?

President Ezra Taft Benson said, "The two groups who have the greatest difficulty in following the prophet are the proud who are learned and the proud who are rich. The learned may feel the prophet is only inspired when he agrees with them; otherwise, the prophet is just giving his opinion—speaking as a man. The rich may feel they have no need to take counsel of a lowly prophet." (*The Teachings of Ezra Taft Benson,* p. 138.)

Helaman 9:1–41
A murder mystery

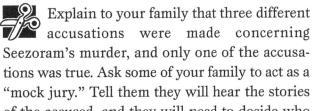 Explain to your family that three different accusations were made concerning Seezoram's murder, and only one of the accusations was true. Ask some of your family to act as a "mock jury." Tell them they will hear the stories of the accused, and they will need to decide who really murdered Seezoram.

Have three members of your family choose one of the following roles: group of five people, Nephi, Seantum. Have them study the verses listed below and prepare to act as if they are this person or group during a mock trial. Take turns letting each one stand before the jury and respond to the question "Did you murder Seezoram?" Have them tell their story as part of their response.

Group of five people: Helaman 9:3–15.

Nephi: Helaman 9:16–25.

Seantum: Helaman 9:26–35.

When you have finished, read together Helaman 9:36–38 to find the real outcome of the trial.

HELAMAN 10: PRIESTHOOD POWER IS REVEALED

Helaman 10:1–3
How does pondering help us receive answers to prayer?

Have a family member read Helaman 10:1–3 and find a word that indicates Nephi was thinking about what the Lord had just shown him. Ask your family how the word *pondering* is different from *thinking*. (*Pondering* means meditating or thinking deeply about something).

Ask each family member to silently read 1 Nephi 11:1 and 3 Nephi 17:2–3. According to these verses, what are some of the results of pondering the things of God? Share the following statement from Elder Bruce R. McConkie:

"I have spent many hours poring over and pondering the scriptures. In seeking to learn the doctrines of salvation I have studied, weighed, and compared what the various prophets have said about the same subjects. Time and again, after much praying and pondering about a given point, new and added concepts have burst upon me showing deep and hidden truths that I had never before known. It can be so with all of us if we will read, ponder, and pray about the holy word." ("Come: Hear the Voice of the Lord," *New Era,* December 1985, p. 13.)

To help your family see how the Lord speaks to us as we ponder, read together the following scriptural references: Helaman 10:3, Enos 1:10, and D&C 8:2–3. Ask:

- What value is there in pondering the things of God?
- What are some of the different ways the voice of the Lord comes to us?

- How does pondering help us communicate with God?

As a family, decide on a time when each member of your family could spend some time "pondering." The next Sunday could be a good time. Allow your family to briefly share their experiences with pondering during a scripture study time.

Helaman 10:4–10
What power was given to Nephi?

It might be interesting for your family to play a game of Red Rover. Divide your family into two teams and have them face each other about ten feet apart. Have each team stand in a straight line holding hands. One team calls a family member's name from the other team by saying: "Red Rover, Red Rover, send [family member's name] right over." The person whose name has been called runs toward the other team, trying to run through and break the handgrip of any two people. If successful, the person called takes one member of the opposing team back to the original team. If not successful in breaking apart the hands, the person called stays with the team whose hands he or she tried to separate. Continue to play this game for a few minutes. When finished, ask your family what gospel message they think can be learned from this experience. You might also ask:

- What is the value of having two strong people stand next to each other?
- Where would Satan try to run through? (Between two weak people.)
- What advantage would there be to having a strong person holding hands with those who were not so strong?
- What would happen if you tried to run through two pieces of steel welded together?

Have your family take turns reading Helaman 10:4–10. Ask:

- What great blessings were promised to Nephi. Why?

- According to verse 7, what power did Nephi receive from the Lord?

Assign someone to read aloud Matthew 16:19 and another to read aloud D&C 132:45–46 and tell who else has held this power. Then read the following statement by President Boyd K. Packer:

"Peter was to hold the sealing power, that authority which carried the power to bind or seal on earth or to loose on earth and it would be so in the heavens. Those keys belong to the President of the Church—to the prophet, seer, and revelator. That sacred sealing power is with the Church now. Nothing is regarded with more sacred contemplation by those who know the significance of this authority. Nothing is more closely held. There are relatively few men who have been delegated this sealing power upon the earth at any given time—in each temple are brethren who have been given the sealing power. No one can get it except from the prophet, seer, and revelator and President of The Church of Jesus Christ of Latter-day Saints." ("The Holy Temple," *Ensign*, February 1995, p. 36.)

Discuss as a family how this power blesses families today. How can the sealing power "weld families together" so that Satan can't "break through" and destroy them?

Helaman 10:11–19
How did Nephi use the sealing power?

Ask your family to imagine having great magical power. If you wanted to share that power with others, what kind of a person would you choose? Why? Read together Helaman 10:4–5 and ask:

- What kind of a person was Nephi?
- Why do you think he could be trusted to have God's power?
- What word would you mark in verses 4 and 5 that best describes Nephi's faithfulness? (Unwearyingness.)
- How do you think he would have used this power?

Take turns reading Helaman 10:11–19 and ask:

- What message did the Lord command Nephi to declare to the Nephites?
- How effective was he in fulfilling the Lord's command?
- What did he prophesy would happen if they refused to repent?
- In what way did this prophecy come to pass?

Share your testimony and express gratitude for the priesthood and its sealing powers.

HELAMAN 11: NEPHI USES PRIESTHOOD POWER

Helaman 11:1–17
Why would a prophet send a famine upon his people?

 Begin this idea by asking your family the following questions:

- If your parents gave you a car, would you always ask beforehand if you could use it? Why or why not?
- What power had Nephi been given in the previous chapter? (See Helaman 10:6–7.)
- Why was God willing to trust him with this sealing power? (See Helaman 10:5.)
- How is a parent's giving a child a car similar to Nephi's receiving the sealing power?

Read Helaman 11:1–17 together and have your family try to understand Nephi's relationship with God as he used this power. After you have finished the reading, ask:

- Why do you think Nephi always prayed before using the power God had given him?
- Why would Nephi use the phrase "wilt thou" (see verses 11–13) in prayer instead of just demanding that the famine begin or end?
- What does 2 Nephi 32:9 have to do with Nephi's attitude?
- What does Nephi's example teach about prophets of God?

Read D&C 121:41–42 and ask your family what attitudes help us unlock the powers of heaven.

Helaman 11:18–19
Why do we hear so little about Nephi's brother, Lehi?

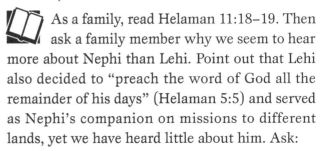 As a family, read Helaman 11:18–19. Then ask a family member why we seem to hear more about Nephi than Lehi. Point out that Lehi also decided to "preach the word of God all the remainder of his days" (Helaman 5:5) and served as Nephi's companion on missions to different lands, yet we have heard little about him. Ask:

- What kind of a man do you think Lehi must have been?
- Why don't we hear more about him?
- Can you think of any other brothers who have been in a similar supporting role? (For example, Sam to Nephi or Hyrum Smith to the Prophet Joseph.)

Read the following quotation from Elder Howard W. Hunter:

"Not all of us are going to be like [Captain] Moroni, catching the acclaim of our colleagues all day every day. Most of us will be quiet, relatively unknown folks who come and go and do our work without fanfare. To those of you who may find that lonely or frightening or just unspectacular, I say, you are 'no less serviceable' than the most spectacular of your associates. You, too, are part of God's army.

"Consider, for example, the profound service a mother or father gives in the quiet anonymity of a worthy Latter-day Saint home. Think of the Gospel Doctrine teachers and Primary choristers and Scoutmasters and Relief Society visiting teachers who serve and bless millions but whose names will never be publicly applauded or featured in the nation's media." ("No Less Serviceable," *Ensign,* April 1992, p. 64.)

Discuss as a family why you should be willing to serve, even if you don't get much attention for it. Ask whose attention we should seek. (See Matthew 6:1–4.)

Helaman 11:24–38
Waxing wicked

 For this object lesson, you will need a string and candle like those used in the teaching suggestion for Helaman 3:35. Before showing the candle, read Helaman 11:20–21 and ask your family to guess how many years they think it will take before the Nephites become wicked again. To see whose prediction is correct, compare Helaman 11:21 and Helaman 11:37 to see how many years passed before the Nephites were ripening in iniquity again.

Show the candle and string, read Helaman 11:36–37, and ask:

- Do you remember what the word *wax* means in the scriptures? (To grow or increase.)
- How were the Nephites "waxing" or growing differently in these verses than in Helaman 3:35?
- Why do you think some people slowly increase in righteousness and others slowly increase in wickedness?

Read Helaman 11:22–35 together and see how the Nephites' wickedness slowly waxed greater. Ask:

- Why do you think it is important for us to learn about this increased wickedness among the Nephites?
- How would learning about this help us deal with the problems of our day?
- Can you think of examples of people or society increasing in wickedness in our day?

Read the following statement by President Ezra Taft Benson:

"I testify that wickedness is rapidly expanding in every segment of our society. It is more highly organized, more cleverly disguised and more powerfully promoted than ever before." ("Prophet's Counsel Powerful, Timeless," *LDS Church News*, 4 June 1994.)

HELAMAN 12: LESSON'S LEARNED ABOUT OUR MORTAL NATURE

Helaman 12:1–6
Why are we so quick to forget the Lord?

 Have one member of your family stand on a chair. Ask how safe the person feels. Then ask how safe he or she would feel if two family members picked the chair up off the floor. Why wouldn't the person feel as safe then?

Read together Helaman 12:1–3. Ask:

- What phrase in verse 1 best describes this situation? ("Unsteadiness of the hearts of the children of men.")
- What evidence does Mormon give that suggests the unsteadiness of mortal men? (As soon as God blesses them, they forget him.)
- How can we show the Lord that he can trust us?
- Why does the Lord "chasten his people with many afflictions"?

Divide a sheet of paper into two columns, labeling one "Quick" and the other "Slow." Read as a family Helaman 12:4–6 and find what mortals are *quick* to do and also what they are *slow* to do. List responses in the appropriate column.

Have someone read aloud D&C 101:8. Ask:

- Why do some people turn to God only during times of affliction?
- To whom do people tend to give credit for their success?
- What does pride have to do with this cycle of behavior?
- What would happen if we would remember God when we have success?

Invite your family to write the reference D&C 101:8 in the margin of their scriptures next to Helaman 12:4–6. As a family, plan ways you can receive the Lord's blessings and at the same time remember him. (See Alma 34:37–39; D&C 59:21.)

Helaman 12:7–22
The elements obey

Place the following items on a table: dirt, water, a rock, and a coin. Invite a member of your family to move any of these items just by speaking. Ask, "Why wouldn't the items move when you told them to?"

Read as a family Helaman 12:7–19. Have your family circle the following words: "dust," "earth," "waters," "mountain," and "treasure." Ask:

- What happens when the Lord speaks to the dust, the earth, the water, a mountain, or the treasures of the earth?
- In contrast, what happens when the Lord commands man?
- Unlike the elements, why can man refuse to obey the Lord? (See 2 Nephi 2:27.)

Read to your family the Lord's warning in Helaman 12:20–24. Ask:

- In what sense is man "less than the dust of the earth"?
- Why will the disobedient be "accursed forever"?
- What is the only way we can be saved?
- According to verse 26, what will happen to those who repent and those who refuse to repent?

As a family sing "Master, the Tempest Is Raging" (*Hymns,* no. 105). Pay particular attention to the chorus. Discuss what you can do as a family to be more obedient to the Lord.

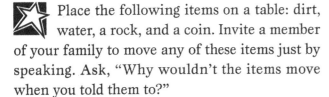

HELAMAN 13: THE PROPHECIES OF SAMUEL THE LAMANITE

Helaman 13:1–11
What is Samuel's message to the Nephites?

Have a family member stand on a chair or table and with a loud voice read Helaman 13:6, 9–11. Ask the other family members whom they think the reader is portraying and what his message was. To help answer that question, ask your family to carefully study Helaman 13:1–11. When they are finished, discuss the following questions:

- Why was Samuel preaching from a wall? (Verse 4.)
- Was this the first time Samuel had preached to the people? (Verse 2.)
- How long had he preached before and what was his message? (Verse 2.)
- How did Samuel know what to say? (Verses 3–5, 7.)
- How long would it be before the sword of justice would fall upon the Nephites? (Verse 5.)
- What was the only thing that could save them? (Verse 6.)
- What is the only thing that can save us?
- What two other things did the Lord say he would take away from them unless they repented? (Verse 8.)
- What withdraws from us if we harden our hearts?
- Who would behold the "utter destruction" of the Nephites? (Verse 10.)
- What does the Lord promise those who repent and turn to him? (Verse 11.)
- Is it possible to repent without turning to the Lord?

Share this statement from President Ezra Taft Benson on what constitutes true repentance:

"Repentance means more than simply a reformation of behavior. Many men and women in the world demonstrate great will-power and self-discipline in overcoming bad habits and the weaknesses of the flesh. Yet at the same time they give no thought to the Master, sometimes even openly rejecting Him. Such changes of behavior, even if in a positive direction, do not constitute true repentance.

"Faith in the Lord Jesus Christ is the foundation upon which sincere and meaningful repentance must be built. If we truly seek to put away sin, we must first look to Him who is the Author of our salvation.

"... repentance involves not just a change of actions, but a change of heart." ("A Mighty Change of Heart," *Ensign*, October 1989, p. 2.)

Helaman 13:12–16
When are a people "ripe for destruction"?

 Show your family a basket of fruit. Talk about what they would do under the following conditions:

- One of the pieces of fruit is rotten.
- Most of the pieces of fruit are rotten.
- All but one piece of fruit is rotten.
- All the fruit is rotten.

Hold up a piece of fruit and ask family members what definition comes to mind when they hear the word *ripe*. Have your family read Helaman 5:12–16 and underline the phrase containing that word. Ask:

- What makes a people "ripe for destruction"?
- Why was the great city Zarahemla spared at that time?
- How do the righteous in Zarahemla compare to the fruit that was not rotten in the earlier object lesson?
- How do you think the wickedness of some of our cities today compares with the wickedness of the Nephite cities of Zarahemla, Gideon, and others?
- What effect can a few righteous people have on a nation? On a city? On other people? (See also Alma 10:22–23; 62:40; and Genesis 18:24–33.)

Share your hope that members of your family are among the righteous in the world. Testify that your family will bring great blessings into the lives of others as they continue faithful.

Helaman 13:20–22
Upon what is your heart set?

 Ask someone to explain what a "priority" is. Invite family members to share some of their top priorities. Ask them how you can tell when something is a top priority in a person's life. Ask, "Do your day-to-day actions and time commitments match your top priorities?"

Read Helaman 13:20–22 together as a family and find what the Nephites had set their hearts upon. Ask:

- How can someone tell what his or her heart is set upon?
- Who had the Nephites forgotten?
- According to D&C 59:21, how can we offend God?

Have a family member share the following statement from President Ezra Taft Benson:

"The Prophet Joseph is reported to have said at one time that one of the greatest sins for which the Latter-day Saints would be guilty would be the sin of ingratitude. I presume most of us have not thought of that as a serious sin. There's a great tendency for us in our prayers—in our pleadings with the Lord—to ask for additional blessings. Sometimes I feel we need to devote more of our prayers to expressions of gratitude and thanksgiving for blessings already received. Of course we need the daily blessings of the Lord. But if we sin in the matter of prayer, I think it is in our lack of the expressions of thanksgiving for daily blessings." ("Receive All Things with Thankfulness," *New Era*, November 1976, p. 4.)

Discuss with your family the following questions:

- In what ways can we show gratitude to the Lord?
- What was a suggestion made by President Benson about our prayers?
- What can you do to improve your prayers?

Encourage your family to make a list of the blessings they are most grateful for and remember them in their prayers.

Helaman 13:24–29

Do we cast out true prophets in support of false ones?

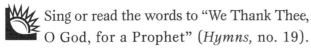 Sing or read the words to "We Thank Thee, O God, for a Prophet" (*Hymns,* no. 19). Ask your family their feelings about living when we have true prophets to guide us.

Have a family member read Helaman 13:24–29 aloud. Ask the following questions:

- What were the Nephites doing to the prophets of their day? (Verse 24.)
- What did the Nephites say they would not have done if they had lived in the days of their fathers? (Verse 24.)
- Why did Samuel say the Nephites were worse than their fathers? (Verses 26–27.)
- Why do people sometimes praise past prophets but reject living ones?
- By what kind of "guides" were the people being led? (Verse 29.)
- What can we do to keep ourselves from being led astray?

Explain that prophets tell us what we *need* to hear, not necessarily what we *want* to hear. Share the following statement with your family from President Spencer W. Kimball:

"Prophets have a way of jarring the carnal mind. Too often the holy prophets are wrongly perceived as harsh and as anxious to make a record in order to say, 'I told you so.' Those prophets I have known are the most loving of men. It is because of their love and integrity that they cannot modify the Lord's message merely to make people feel comfortable. They are too kind to be so cruel. I am so grateful that prophets do not crave popularity." ("Listen to the Prophets," *Ensign,* May 1978, p. 77.)

Share your feelings about our living prophet today and the importance of following his counsel to us.

Helaman 13:38

What brings happiness?

Ask family members what makes them happy. Let each person respond. Read Helaman 13:38 as a family and discuss how the Nephites had been seeking happiness. Ask a family member to read aloud Alma 41:10–11 and tell how those verses relate to Helaman 13:38. Discuss why a person cannot do wrong and feel right. Have your family write the reference Alma 41:10 at the end of Helaman 13:38.

Share the following statement from Joseph Smith:

"Happiness is the object and design of our existence; and will be the end thereof, if we pursue the path that leads to it; and this path is virtue, uprightness, faithfulness, holiness, and keeping all the commandments of God " (*Teachings of the Prophet Joseph Smith,* pp. 255–56).

Ask family members to raise their hands if they want to be happy. According to what we have read, what is the only way to be happy?

HELAMAN 14: SAMUEL CONTINUES TO WARN THE NEPHITES

Helaman 14:1–8, 20–27

Signs of the Savior's birth and death

Invite your family to name some common road signs and their meanings. Ask what they think the purpose is for road signs. How are they helpful to us? Tell them that we will be looking for some "road signs" of a different sort in Helaman 14.

Divide your family into three groups. Give each group the following things in paper bags:

Group 1: white or yellow paper, scissors, glue sticks, and glitter. Write "Helaman 14:1–8" on the paper bag.

Group 2: black paper and scissors. Write "Helaman 14:20, 27" on the bag.

Group 3: brown paper (to make mountains, cities, highways). Also white paper (to make lightning) and scissors. Write "Helaman 14:21–26" on the bag.

Have each group read the verses of scripture written on their bag and then make representations of the signs mentioned in the verses with the items they find in their bags. When each group has finished, have them show their sign and ask the rest of the family to guess whether it is a sign of the Savior's birth or death. Attach string to the signs and hang them from your ceiling.

Discuss some or all of the following questions:

- In how many years did Samuel prophesy that the Son of God would be born? (Verse 2.)
- What would it be like to have "a day and a night and a day" with no darkness?
- Would such a sign cause you to believe that the Son of God was to be born?
- What do you think it would have been like to have seen all these amazing events?
- How convincing would three days of darkness be that the Savior was crucified?
- How would you prepare yourself if our prophet gave such a warning?
- What warnings have the prophets given about Christ's second coming?
- What can we do to prepare? (See D&C 45:35–75 and JS—Matthew 1:22–55.)

Helaman 14:9–19, 29–31
Samuel follows the instructions of an angel

Show your family the picture of Samuel testifying from the walls of Zarahemla. (See "Samuel the Lamanite on the Wall," *Gospel Art Picture Kit,* no. 314; see also a similar picture in paperback copies of the Book of Mormon.) Ask your family to describe what is happening in this picture. Why was Samuel testifying under such dangerous circumstances? (See Helaman 13:7.)

Have your family take turns reading Helaman 14:9–19, 29–31 and find the things the angel commanded Samuel to proclaim to the Nephites. List

these things on a sheet of paper. Encourage your family to ponder the things on this list by discussing the following questions:

- How did the Nephites receive Samuel's message? (Verse 10.)
- How do the things on this list make you feel about repentance?
- What do you learn about the Savior's death? (Verse 15.)
- How would you describe the two deaths that Christ can save us from? (Verses 16–19.)
- What on the list gives you feelings of gratitude for the Savior?
- What can we learn from Samuel about what to do when people reject us when we deliver God's message?

HELAMAN 15: THE LAMANITES ARE BLESSED BECAUSE THEY ARE CONVERTED

Helaman 15:1–3
Who's telling the truth?

 Write the following definitions on three separate pieces of paper and hand them out to three members of your family:

Chastened: To have been pursued or chased after.

Chastened: To have kept one's self morally pure.

Chastened: To have been corrected through punishment or suffering.

Have those with papers read aloud their definitions. Ask the rest of the family to guess which of the three definitions is correct. Read Helaman 15:1–3 together to find the correct definition. Explain that other synonyms of the word *chasten* are *chastise, reprove, reprimand,* and *discipline.* Ask:

- According to these verses, who chastens whom?
- What motivates the Lord to punish and reprimand people? (Verse 3.)

- Why would you put a leash on a pet that otherwise runs into a busy street?
- Would the dog like being tied up?
- What does love have to do with discipline?
- Why do parents discipline their children?

Read and discuss D&C 95:1 together. The following questions might be useful:

- What does chastisement do for us?
- How can we respond to parents who chasten us?
- How will responding to parents appropriately help us in responding properly to the Lord's chastisement.
- What can we do to remember we are loved when someone is chastening us?

Helaman 15:4
Did God hate the Lamanites?

Ask your family if they think God hates any of his children. Read together Helaman 15:4 and discuss what they think Samuel might have meant by the phrase "the Lamanites hath [God] hated." Contrast this verse with 1 Nephi 17:35 and ask, "In what ways were the Nephites favored or preferred over the Lamanites? For the most part, why did God bless and favor the Nephites?"

If needed, share the following statement:

"*The Lamanites hath he hated.*' This is strong language. One would assume that Samuel did not mean to convey the thought that God actually hated the Lamanites, at least not in the sense that mortal men hate one another. Rather, because of their rebellion, because they rejected the light and spurned the association with God through the Spirit that they might have enjoyed, they alienated themselves from the love of the Father. It is not that God does not love them, but that he simply is unable to bless them as he would those who choose the right. 'If you keep not my commandments,' a modern revelation attests, 'the love of the Father shall not continue with you, therefore you shall walk in darkness' (D&C 95:12)." (Joseph Fielding McConkie and Robert L. Millet,

Doctrinal Commentary on the Book of Mormon, 3:418.)

Helaman 15:4–10
What changed the Lamanites?

 Show an old photo of a family member alongside a recent photo of the same person. Ask your family what changes they can see in this person. What sort of changes might have happened to this person that do not show up in a photo? (For example changes in wisdom or spirituality.)

Divide your family into pairs and have each pair study Helaman 15:4–10. As they study, ask them to mark each word or phrase describing something that helped the Lamanites change and remain changed. Have each pair share their discoveries. Then discuss what they learned by using the following questions:

- Which of the things you marked do you think is most important? Why?
- Which of those items do you think our family needs to work on the most?
- What could we do to improve in that area?

Helaman 15:10–16
What blessings are promised to the Lamanites?

Have family members think of a kind deed they would be willing to do today for another family member. Ask them to write the deed and the person they would do it for on a slip of paper. Put the papers in a jar and let each person draw one out. Challenge each person to do the kind deed for the person listed on the paper drawn from the jar. Explain that sometimes the Lord makes wonderful promises to his children. These promises, like the kind deeds of service, are wonderful blessings and can help us feel happy and blessed.

Have each person silently read Helaman 15:10–16 and mark the blessings the Lord promised to give to the Lamanites. Have each person share what he or she marked. Talk about why each of those things is a great blessing to the Lamanites today. What can we do to help these promises be fulfilled among Lehi's descendants? (Missionary work, sharing the Book of Mormon, contributing to the Perpetual Education Fund, and so on.)

Share the following statements:

"God gave us the Book of Mormon and the chief reason, as set forth in one of the revelations, is that it shall be the means of bringing to the descendants of Father Lehi the knowledge of the Redeemer of the world, and to establish them in the faith of their fathers. I bear witness to you that nothing on earth shall ever bring them out of their thralldom save the gospel of the Lord Jesus Christ. I rejoice, therefore, that the day dawn is breaking, the night is dispelling, and the day of their redemption cometh." (Heber J. Grant, Conference Report, October 1926, p. 40.)

"They must have the enlightening gospel. It will break their fetters, stir their ambition, increase their vision and open new worlds of opportunity to them. Their captivity will be at an end—captivity from misconceptions, illiteracy, superstition, fear. The brighter day has dawned. The scattering has been accomplished, the gathering is in process. May the Lord bless us all as we become nursing fathers and mothers (see Isa. 49:23 and Nephi 21:23) unto our Lamanite brethren and hasten the fulfillment of the great promises made to them." (Spencer W. Kimball, Conference Report, October 1965, p. 72.)

HELAMAN 16: SAMUEL THE LAMANITE IS PROTECTED ON THE WALL

Helaman 16:1–8
Why did some Nephites believe Samuel while others did not?

Ask your family if after a talk at Church they have ever heard one person say, "That was a great talk," and another person say, "That was totally boring." How could two people have such opposing views after hearing the same talk? Explain that there are probably many answers to this question. To see one possible explanation, read together Helaman 16:1–8 and discuss the following:

- What are the two different ways that people responded to Samuel's message?
- Why do you suppose some believed his words and sought to be baptized?
- Why were others angry enough to try to kill him? (See Proverbs 29:10.)
- What did the Lord do to protect Samuel?
- How can knowing about Samuel help when you suffer persecution?

Invite a family member to play the part of Samuel the Lamanite and stand on a chair or table as if high on the city wall. Have other family members gather large cookie sheets, plates, or pans and stand around Samuel as his "armor." Then have another family member try to throw marshmallows past the protective armor and slay Samuel.

After the activity, ask family members what the armor might represent. (See Helaman 16:2.) Discuss with your family some ways the Spirit can protect us.

Helaman 16:9–23
What was the spiritual condition of the Nephites?

Draw a warning sign (such as STOP or YIELD) and a direction sign (such as a right turn arrow) and show them to your family.

Ask what the purpose would be for each sign. (One shows the way to go, the other the way not to go.) Read together Helaman 16:9–14. Ask:

- How many years passed between verse 9 and verse 13?
- How did the spiritual condition of the Nephites change from the 86th year to the 90th year?
- What signs and wonders were given at this time? ("Great signs" and "angels.")

- Who saw the "great signs" and "wonders." (Everybody, verse 13.)
- Who saw the "angels"? (Wise men, the righteous, verse 14.)
- Which of the signs above do you think the "great signs and wonders" are most like? (Warning.)
- Which sign would seeing an angel be most like?
- What would be the consequences to the wicked if they ignored the warning signs?
- Why do you think angels were sent to the righteous?

To see how most of the Nephites responded to the "great signs . . . and wonders," take turns reading Helaman 16:15–23. Then discuss the following questions:

- What signs or wonders do we see today?
- What signs would your friends believe?
- What signs do you think the world would believe?
- What similarities do you see in our world today when compared to the world the Nephites lived in just a year before the Savior's birth? (See bottom of page 406 for the date.)

Helaman 16:22–25
What are some tactics Satan used to harden the hearts of the Nephites?

Ask your family if they were at war how valuable it would be to find out the enemys' tactics. Read Helaman 16:22–23 and look for and underline some of the tactics Satan uses. Ask your family if they knew that spreading rumors and being involved in contention are tactics of Satan.

How can we protect ourselves against Satan's influence? Read the following statements from latter-day prophets:

"I have little or no fear for the boy or girl, the young man or the young woman, who honestly and conscientiously supplicate God twice a day for the guidance of His spirit. I am sure that when temptation comes they will have the strength to overcome it by the inspiration that shall be given to them. Supplicating the Lord for the guidance of His spirit places around us a safeguard, and if we earnestly and honestly seek the guidance of the Spirit of the Lord, I can assure you that we will receive it." (Heber J. Grant, *Gospel Standards,* p. 26.)

"There is a power in the [Book of Mormon] which will begin to flow into your lives the moment you begin a serious study of the book. You will find greater power to resist temptation. You will find the power to avoid deception." (Ezra Taft Benson, *The Teachings of Ezra Taft Benson,* p. 54.)

Bear testimony that the words of these latter-day prophets are true. Promise family members that if they pray sincerely each day and ask for the Lord's protection, and if they seriously study the Book of Mormon, they can avoid Satan's tactics and deceptions and the heartache that comes to those who fall for his ploys.

3 NEPHI

The book of 3 Nephi is sometimes referred to as the "fifth Gospel" because it gives an account of the ministry of the resurrected Christ to the people in the land of Bountiful. These American Christians were the "other sheep" Jesus told his Jewish apostles about. (See John 10:16; 3 Nephi 15:21.) Because of their great faith, the Savior was able to teach even greater gospel truths, in greater simplicity, than he was able to teach in Jerusalem. The time period covered by this book is about A.D. 1 to A.D. 35.

3 NEPHI 1: A SIGN OF THE SAVIOR'S BIRTH

3 Nephi 1:1–23

Will you be true no matter the cost?

Have your family tell of different times in history when people have been killed for what they believed. Ask, "Why would one group of people kill another group for what they believe?"

Take turns reading 3 Nephi 1:4–9. Ask:

- What were the wicked people going to do to the righteous? Why?
- Why do you think the truth makes some people so angry? (See Helaman 13:25–28.)
- If your life was threatened by a wicked group of people because of what you believed, what would you do?

An example of tremendous courage in the face of certain death is the story of Rafael Monroy and Vicente Morales, two brethren from Mexico who lived during the Mexican civil war. The rebels who fought against the government in hopes of gaining power were called Zapatistas; they were followers of Emiliano Zapata. The civil war caused much bigotry, cruelty, anarchy, and bloodshed, reaching into the most isolated villages. Amid the violence, personal, political, and religious scores were often settled. In 1912 while this terrible civil war was in full swing, the Monroy family was contacted by LDS missionaries. They eventually accepted the gospel and were baptized.

"They were accused of having abandoned the faith of their fathers, consorting with foreigners, and selling poisoned food in their store. Even local religious leaders ridiculed them. Some townspeople began painting graffiti on the walls of their home, while others boycotted their store. Despite these trials, the family stood firm with an increased commitment to the Church.

"Rafael had been a member only three months when the civil war forced the evacuation of all foreign missionaries from Mexico. Before leaving Mexico, President Pratt ordained Brother Monroy to the Melchizedek Priesthood and set him apart as president of the San Marcos branch. . . .

"The Zapatistas eventually arrested President Monroy and his three sisters for associating with North Americans and for allegedly being in league with the Constitutionalists. The Zapatistas also arrested Vicente Morales, who had married into the Monroy family and served with Rafael in the San Marcos branch presidency.

"Acting on erroneous reports that the Morales family was hiding guns and ammunition, the Zapatistas ransacked the family store. Finding no weapons, they demanded that the men 'give up their arms.' Brothers Monroy and Morales were beaten after they presented their scriptures in reply. Later, they were told their lives would be spared if they would denounce their faith. When they refused, they were executed. One author wrote of the family's loss:

"'It had rained most of the night, and the air was damp. Jesucita Monroy had not slept and was out on the street early, pleading with the officers of the Zapatista army. . . . Her early morning appeal was successful, and the Zapatistas released her three daughters from army custody. After getting two of her daughters home, Jesucita and her oldest, Guadalupe, went to the place where the two executions had taken place the evening before. Already burdened with emotion and grief, these two women began the task of moving the . . . bodies of their son and brother, Rafael, and their nephew-in-law and cousin-in-law, Vicente Morales, home to prepare for the funeral and burial. Victims of the brutality of a civil war in Mexico, these two men had lost their lives in the violence they had deplored. For many members of the family and for many friends, Rafael and Vicente became examples of faith and dedication to The Church of Jesus Christ of Latter-day Saints.'" (F. LaMond Tullis, "Los Primeros: Mexico's Pioneer Saints," *Ensign*, July 1997, pp. 49–51.)

As a family, read 3 Nephi 1:10–23 and look for what happened to the righteous Nephites who were condemned to die because of what they believed. Ask:

- What most impresses you about this group of Nephites?
- Even though they were spared, how was their faith tried?
- How do you think they felt when "at the going down of the sun there was no darkness"? (Verse 15.)

- Do you think you would have remained faithful in this circumstance? Why or why not?
- Even though we may not face the threat of death, what lessons can we learn from 3 Nephi 1 about preparing for the Second Coming?

3 Nephi 1:27–30
How can the disease that infected the Gadianton robbers be stopped?

Ask your family how a disease like cancer spreads. What will happen if the disease is not stopped? As a family read 3 Nephi 1:27–30. Ask:

- What sort of "disease" was infecting the land? (Verse 27, the Gadianton robbers.)
- How quickly was this infection spreading? (Verse 28.)
- Which group of people was being most affected? (Verse 28.)
- What group among the righteous Lamanites were being infected? (Verses 29–30.)
- What was causing the infection to spread so fast?

Read the following statement from Elder Bruce R. McConkie:

"Flattery is the act of ingratiating oneself into another's confidence by excessive praise, or by insincere speech and acts. It includes the raising of false and unfounded hopes; there is always an element of dishonesty attending it." (*Mormon Doctrine*, p. 287.)

Discuss the following questions with your family:

- How flattery can be compared to cancer?
- What was flattery destroying?
- Why do you think Satan directs so many of his attacks on the "rising generation"?
- What can we do in our family to protect ourselves against Satan's flattering lies?

3 NEPHI 2: THE NEPHITES ARE THREATENED WITH UTTER DESTRUCTION

3 Nephi 2:1–10
What caused the Nephites to lose their faith?

Trace a large star on a sheet of paper and select a family member to cut it out while you tell the following story:

Kaitlyn sat in her seminary class and listened to the lesson. As her teacher testified about the importance of repentance in our lives, Kaitlyn felt an impression from the Spirit. She was filled with an urgent desire to rush home to pray and commune with her Father in Heaven. After seminary was over, the feeling continued with her for some of the day. But when she got home from school, what was once a powerful spiritual feeling was now nearly exhausted.

Discuss as a family the kinds of things that can cause us to lose strong spiritual feelings. What can we do to make those spiritual feelings last longer?

Have the family member who cut out the star display it. Ask your family to recall what a star had to do with the Savior's birth. Read together 3 Nephi 1:17 and discuss the impact the signs of the Savior's birth had on the Nephites. Why do you think this would be an experience you would not soon forget?

Take turns reading 3 Nephi 2:1–5, 10. Ask:

• Why does the passing of time often cause us to forget spiritual events in our lives?
• What was the attitude of some of the Nephites toward the signs and wonders they had previously seen?
• What influence did Satan have in this situation?
• According to verse 10 what did the Lord do to help them remember spiritual things?

3 Nephi 2:11–19
Why did the Nephites and Lamanites unite as one people?

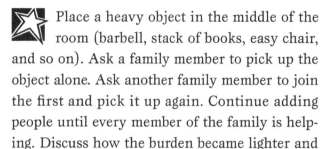 Place a heavy object in the middle of the room (barbell, stack of books, easy chair, and so on). Ask a family member to pick up the object alone. Ask another family member to join the first and pick it up again. Continue adding people until every member of the family is helping. Discuss how the burden became lighter and easier to handle as more hands were added.

Invite a family member to read 3 Nephi 2:11–12 and ask the family to identify an event that might be similar to the object lesson. Ask:

• Why did the Nephites and converted Lamanites unite as one?
• What were they forced to do to save themselves from the Gadianton robbers?
• What did they hope to maintain? (Their rights, religion, and freedom.)

Now take turns reading 3 Nephi 2:13–19, discussing the following questions as you go:

• As a result of their unity, what miraculously happened to the Lamanites? (Verse 15.)
• How can uniting with those who share our beliefs help us grow stronger?
• Why weren't the Nephites able to "gain some advantage" over the Gadianton robbers? (Verses 18–19.)
• What do you think Mormon meant when he said, "The sword of destruction did hang over them"?

Tell your family that these events occurred just before the coming of Christ to the Americas. Discuss how the world will be in a similar condition at the second coming of Jesus Christ. What can we do to strengthen the Church against latter-day Gadianton robbers? (See D&C 115:5–6.) Testify of the importance of always being ready for the Lord's coming.

3 NEPHI 3–4: A SHOWDOWN AGAINST THE GADIANTON ROBBERS

3 Nephi 3:1–26
How do you respond to negative peer pressure?

 Ask your family if they have ever had an experience where others have mocked them for doing what is right and perhaps also have tried to pressure them into doing something wrong. Ask those who feel comfortable sharing their experiences to do so and tell how they handled that pressure.

Tell your family that a similar situation is found in 3 Nephi. Have your family take turns reading 3 Nephi 3:1–10. When you have finished, discuss the following questions:

- Who is Lachoneus and who is Giddianhi?
- What did Giddianhi say that was flattering to Lachoneus, and why do you think he said that? (Verses 2, 5.)
- What did Giddianhi say that was mocking? (Verse 3.)
- What did he say that was just plain lies? (Verses 4, 9–10.)
- What was he pressuring Lachoneus to do that was wrong?
- How was Giddianhi's letter like some of the negative influences and pressures you have faced?

Explain to your family that the rest of chapter 3 includes some tactics Lachoneus used to deal with the negative pressure he faced. Make a chart like the one below but leave the modern application column blank. Read together 3 Nephi 3:11–26 and find and mark the phrases listed. After marking each phrase, invite your family to think of modern applications that could be drawn from Lachoneus' tactics. Have each person share his or her ideas and insights. Use the suggestions in the modern application column if needed.

Ask your family to think again of situations they have faced (or might face in the future) where they were pressured to do wrong. Discuss how Lachoneus' example could help them make right choices in specific situations.

Phrase	Verses	Possible Modern Application
"He was exceedingly astonished"	11	We should watch for and recognize negative peer pressure.
"a just man, and could not be frightened"	12	The closer we are to the Lord, the less the wicked will frighten us or influence us.
"he did not hearken to the epistle of Giddianhi"	12	Do not give in to negative peer pressure.
"cause that his people should cry unto the Lord"	12	Turn to the Lord for help when others entice you toward evil.
"gather together"	13	Unite with friends who are good and make good choices.
"caused that fortifications should be built round about them"	14	Participate in other wholesome and uplifting activities in harmony with "For the Strength of Youth."
"appoint for their chief captains . . . some one that had the spirit of revelation" (Gidgiddoni)"	17–20	Look to the leadership of the Lord's prophet, who has the spirit of revelation.

3 Nephi 4:1–33
Tic-Tac-Toe

 Explain to your family that you will be playing a tic-tac-toe game with chapter 4. Get a piece of paper and make a large tic-tac-toe grid. Have family members take turns reading 3 Nephi 4:1–33. Divide the family into two groups with one person acting as the game host to read the statements and mark the tic-tac-toe paper. Flip a coin to see which group goes first. If the team answers the statement correctly, they get their symbol in the square. If the team is wrong, the square goes to the other team. Turns are taken back and forth regardless of whether the last question was answered correctly or not. After an answer is given, look back at the indicated verse to see if the statement was false or true, and why. If one team is not able to get three in a row, then the team with five squares wins. During the game, pause and discuss the things you want your family to learn from the verses.

The following are the true/false statements for the game.

- The Gadianton Robbers were able to live in the lands the Nephites deserted. (Verses 1–3.)
- The people gathered a year's supply just as we are commanded to. (Verse 4.)
- The Nephites did not fear the robbers when they attacked. (Verse 10.)
- This battle was the bloodiest in 600 years. (Verse 11.)
- After the first battle, the Nephites did not spare any robbers that fell into their hands. (Verse 13.)
- The robbers thought they could surround the Nephites, cut them off from supplies, and starve them out. (Verses 16, 18.)
- The Gadianton Robbers enjoyed a healthy diet of foods found in the four food groups. (Verse 19.)
- The Gadianton Robbers were going to retreat into the land northward. (Verse 24.)
- The second Gadianton Robbers leader was beheaded. (Verse 28.)

- The Nephites praised their wise military leaders for their victory. (Verses 30–33.)
- God delivered the Nephites because of their repentance and humility. (Verse 33; see also 3 Nephi 3:15.)

Ask each family member in turn to tell what they thought was the most meaningful lesson they learned from this chapter.

3 NEPHI 5: MORMON, A DISCIPLE OF JESUS CHRIST, WRITES THE HISTORY OF HIS PEOPLE

3 Nephi 5:1–6
How powerful is the word of God?

Ask your family if any of them have ever seen the inside of a prison. Have them describe what they saw. If no one has seen a prison, perhaps they could imagine what it's like or recall a picture or movie that shows one. Ask the following questions:

- What do you think it would be like inside a prison?
- What would be the biggest difference from life outside of prison?
- Why are people there?
- What do people hope inmates will do before being released?
- Why would it be important to you for inmates to "change their lives."

Read 3 Nephi 5:1–6 as a family and ask the following questions:

- What do verses 1–3 tell you about Nephite society at this time?
- What caused the Nephites to believe the prophets?
- According to verses 4–6, how did the Nephites bring an end to secret combinations?
- How were many robbers led to change their lives?
- With this story in mind and if you had

control over the prisons in your community, what could you do to help reform inmates?

3 Nephi 5:10–20
How did Mormon get his name and what does it mean?

Ask your family to give the full name of the Church. (The Church of Jesus Christ of Latter-day Saints.) Discuss why some people call members of the Church "Mormons." Read 3 Nephi 5:12 and find where Mormon, who abridged the Book of Mormon, got his name. Ask your family what they think the name Mormon means. Explain that the Prophet Joseph Smith said that the name *Mormon* "means, literally, 'more good.'" (*Teachings of the Prophet Joseph Smith,* p. 300.)

As a family, read 3 Nephi 5:10–20 and make a list that describes the kind of person Mormon was and what he accomplished. You might discuss the following questions:

- What contributions did Mormon make? (Verses 10–11.)
- What did Mormon consider himself to be? (Verse 13.)
- What do we know about Mormon's genealogy? (Verse 20.)

Read the following statement from President Gordon B. Hinckley:

"Anyone who comes to know the man Mormon, through the reading and pondering of his words, anyone who reads this precious trove of history which was assembled and preserved in large measure by him, will come to know that Mormon is not a word of disrepute, but that it represents the greatest good—that good which is of God. ("Mormon Should Mean 'More Good,'" *Ensign,* November 1990, p. 53).

3 Nephi 5:24–26
What is the purpose of the gathering?

Scatter on the floor or table some toothpicks, stick matches, or other items that can be easily picked up. Set a container in the midst of the scattered items. Invite your family to gather the scattered items and put them into the container. Ask, "If the scattered items represent the children of Israel, what gospel principle does picking up the items and placing them in the container represent?" When your family has guessed the "gathering," read together 3 Nephi 5:24–26. Ask:

- From what locations will the Lord gather his people? (Verse 24.)
- Who will be gathered? (Verse 24.)
- What does the "house of Jacob" have to do with the gathering? (Verse 25.)
- What will the scattered house of Jacob come to know when they are gathered? (Verse 26.)

Share with your family the following insights from Orson Hyde and Parley P. Pratt, members of the first Quorum of the Twelve Apostles in this dispensation:

"Let them come [the Jews] like clouds and like doves to their windows. Let the large ships of the nations bring them from the distant isles; and let kings become their nursing fathers, and queens with motherly fondness wipe the tear of sorrow from their eye. . . . Let them know that it is Thy good pleasure to restore the kingdom unto Israel." (From the dedicatory prayer given by Orson Hyde in Jerusalem and recorded in *History of the Church,* 4:456–57.)

"And we further testify that the Jews among all nations are hereby commanded, in the name of the Messiah to prepare to return to Jerusalem in Palestine, and to rebuild that city and temple unto the Lord." (*Writings of Parley P. Pratt,* p. 3.)

Share with your family the following facts:

- In 1845, when elders Hyde and Pratt made the statements above, there were an estimated 5,000 to 10,000 Jews living in Israel. (See LaMar C. Barrett, *Discovering the world of the Bible,* p. 268.)
- According to the *CIA World Fact Book 2002,* as of July 2002 Israel's population was 6,029,529.

Ask your family what these two facts suggest

about the gathering of Israel. What can we do to assist in gathering scattered Israel?

3 NEPHI 6: FROM PEACE AND PROSPERITY TO A STATE OF AWFUL WICKEDNESS

3 Nephi 6:1–17
What brings about change?

Ask your family to describe what life was like one year ago (leave the question general and open-ended, allowing for greater variety in responses). How do you think life will change during the next year? Have your family open their scriptures to 3 Nephi 6. Ask a family member to read aloud the last ten words of verse 3 and all of verses 4, 5, and 9. Ask, "What were the conditions among the Nephites from the 26th through the 28th year?"

Have another family member read aloud 3 Nephi 6:16–17. Ask, "What were conditions like in the commencement of the thirtieth year?" How could the Nephites go from peace and prosperity to a state of awful wickedness in just one year?

Explain to your family that 3 Nephi 6:10–16 describes steps the Nephites followed to reach such an awful state. Read 3 Nephi 6:10–16 as a family and make a list of the points that led the Nephites to a state of wickedness.

Share this statement from President Ezra Taft Benson:

"The record of the Nephite history just before the Savior's visit reveals many parallels to our own day as we anticipate the Savior's second coming." ("The Savior's Visit to America," *Ensign*, May 1987, p. 4.)

Ask:

• What evidences of pride and boastings are in our society today?
• What are some examples of class distinctions you have seen? (Social status based on clothing styles, neighborhoods in which we live,

the types of cars we drive, or grade-point averages in school.)

Share the following statement from President N. Eldon Tanner:

"We also learn that among the causes of iniquity are pride, wealth, unrighteous dominion, class distinctions, selfishness, lusts for power, and the like. It is demonstrated to us that the righteous remain so by faith, by constant communication with God, by devotion to their leaders, by being humble and submissive to the mind and will of the Lord." ("The Inevitable Choice," *Ensign*, September 1977, p. 2.)

Discuss what specific changes you can make as a family to avoid the iniquity he described.

3 Nephi 6:18
Does knowledge make sin more serious?

Assign one family member to imagine being a Protestant living in Europe. Assign another member to imagine being a new convert to the Church. Assign a third family member to represent a lifelong member of the Church. Ask:

• Is each of these people equally responsible for the sins they commit? Why or why not?
• Is something like breaking the word of wisdom considered a sin for all three of these people? Why or why not?
• Do you think wickedness is more serious if you have been taught the truth and still choose to sin? Why or why not?

Read 3 Nephi 6:18 together as a family. Also read Mosiah 3:11–12 and D&C 82:3. Talk about what it means to "not sin ignorantly" and why more is required of those who have "greater light."

3 Nephi 6:20–30
How do you react when you are told you are doing wrong?

Ask family members to recall a time when someone told them they were doing something wrong. Have several in your family share their experience and talk about how they reacted when it happened. Have your family read 3 Nephi 6:20–24 and ask:

- How did many of the Nephites reacted to the preaching?
- Why do you think people sometimes get angry when told they are doing wrong?
- What happened to many of those who testified boldly of the redemption of Christ?
- How do you think these people should have reacted to correction?
- What would Jesus want us to do when we are told our actions are wrong?

Read verses 3 Nephi 6:25–30 together as a family and see if the people ever changed their attitudes and repented. Ask:

- What did their anger lead the people to do?
- What effect do you think this will have on the country?
- What does this teach us about sin and anger?

3 NEPHI 7: THE GOVERNMENT IS DESTROYED AND THE PEOPLE DIVIDE INTO TRIBES

3 Nephi 7:1–7
What led to the downfall of the government?

Talk with your family about their feelings about local, state, and national government. Ask them to think of things that benefit or complicate their lives because of government. It may be interesting to discuss a current political issue. Then read together 3 Nephi 7:1–7 and ask:

- What happened to the Nephite government? (Verses 1–2.)
- What did the people turn to when their government failed? (Verse 2.)
- What were the specific causes of the breakdown of their government? (Verses 5–6.)
- What do you think would happen if our government collapsed?

- Where would you go for safety if that happened?

Have someone in your family read the following definition for the word *tribe:* "A social organization or division comprising several local villages, bands, lineages, or other groups and sharing a common ancestry, language, culture, and name." (*Webster's New Dictionary.*) Compare this definition with what is written in verses 2–4 and talk about the similarities.

Ask your family to imagine that the government collapsed. From what we've read in 3 Nephi 7, if we separated into a tribe, what name would we use to identify us? Use a poster board or a large sheet of paper to make a poster or sign that gives the name of the tribe and an object or image that symbolizes the tribe's name.

- How would the dividing of our country into tribes change the world in which we live?
- What kinds of things are happening in our country today that are similar to those recorded in 3 Nephi 7? (Verses 5–7.)
- Why is it important to help the people around us turn to righteousness? (Verse 7.)

Invite your family to share their ideas on what our Heavenly Father thinks about government. You might invite a Primary-age child to recite or sing "The Twelfth Article of Faith" (*Children's Songbook,* p. 131). Discuss what you can do as a family to help strengthen your government.

3 Nephi 7:9–13
How did secret combinations once again become a dangerous power?

Ask your family what it means to flatter someone ("To compliment excessively and often insincerely; to please or gratify the vanity of; insincere praise" [*Webster's New Dictionary,* "Flatter," "Flattery"]). Discuss how it feels to be flattered or to hear someone else being flattered. What can flattery lead a person to do?

Empty a bag of candy (such as gummy bears) onto a table. Have a family member read 3 Nephi

7:9–10 and find out who was made king of the "wicked band" of robbers. Select one of the gummy bears, put a toothpick in its paw, roll a small piece of aluminum foil into a ball, and place it on the end of the toothpick to represent King Jacob's scepter.

Invite another family member to read 3 Nephi 7:11 and discuss what King Jacob and his "wicked band" decided to do and why. Have family members help move King Jacob and some of the other gummie bears northward until they reach the edge of the table.

Finally, read 3 Nephi 7:12 and discuss King Jacob's plan to build his "wicked band." What key word indicates how he was going to get others to join him? Did it work? Have family members move the rest of the gummie bears to join those "northward" at the edge of the table. Ask some of the following questions:

- Why did Jacob move his tribesmen to the "northernmost part of the land"? (Verses 11–12.)
- What did Jacob do to attract dissenters to his kingdom? (Verse 12.)
- What is the danger of listening to or speaking flattery?

Consider sharing the following statement from Elder Neal A. Maxwell:

"We should, . . . without being artificial, regularly give deserved, specific praise. . . . We are so certain, sometimes, we do not really have a particular skill or attribute that we severely discount praise. One of the reasons we need regular praise from 'outside auditors' is to offset the low level of self-acknowledgment most of us have. Flattery is a form of hypocrisy to be avoided, but in overreacting to it, some close the door to commendation." (*All These Things Shall Give Thee Experience,* p. 78.)

3 Nephi 7:14
Have you ever "stoned" a prophet?

 Show your family a picture of the current prophet. Ask how they would feel if they saw someone throwing rocks at him. Read together 3 Nephi 7:14. Ask:

- Though these people seemed to have political peace in their land, what caused them to stone the prophets and cast them out?
- How might that have led to the collapse of their government and dividing into tribes?
- Do people today throw rocks at the prophet?
- Is it possible to throw rocks symbolically without using real rocks?

Share this statement with your family:

"If any of you have found fault with the Bishop of your ward, or with the president of your stake, or with the presiding authorities of the Church, go home and repent of your sins, and put your households in order. . . . I tell you the seed that you sow in the hearts of your children will be hard to uproot. I bear testimony unto you that no man speaking by the Spirit of the Lord will ever criticize the authorities of the Priesthood which God has placed over him, after he has had the privilege of lifting up his hand either to support or not support that man." (John W. Taylor, *Collected Discourses,* 5 April 1895.)

Discuss ways your family can avoid "stoning" living prophets.

3 Nephi 7:15–26
Nephi—an instrument in God's Hands

 Hold up a musical instrument or a picture of one and ask your family what it takes for an instrument to become useful in someone's hands. Ask how they would like to be an instrument in the hands of God.

Divide your family into three groups and assign each to study one of the following: Nephi, the People, Converts. Give each group paper and pencils. Have them read 3 Nephi 7:15–26 and learn about their assigned person or group by answering the questions provided below.

Questions about Nephi:

- What were Nephi's qualities that enabled him to be an instrument in God's hands?

- What miracles did Nephi perform? (Verse 19.)
- What made it possible for Nephi to perform miracles? (Verse 19.)
- What will you do to keep your life worthy to be able to be an instrument in the Lord's hands?

Questions about the People:

- Why do you think the Nephites turned so quickly from righteousness to wickedness? (Verse 15.)
- How might a blindfold and a rock represent what grieved Nephi? (Verse 16.)
- What caused the people to be angry with him? (Verses 18, 20.)
- How can you emulate Nephi and be an instrument in God's hands when people are angry at you?

Questions about Converts:

- How would you describe the conversion of the few who were converted unto the Lord? (Verses 21–22.)
- How did they show "a witness and a testimony before God" that they had repented of their sins? (Verses 24–25.)
- What gifts of the Spirit have you recognized in your life since being converted?
- How can you use your gifts to be an instrument in God's hands?

When the groups have finished their study, have each one report what they learned. Encourage your family to record their answers in their journals.

3 NEPHI 8: GREAT DESTRUCTION AND DARKNESS

3 Nephi 8:1–22
Samuel the Lamanite's prophecies are fulfilled

 Ask family members to think about the worst storm they have ever been in. Have them describe what happened, the problems it caused, and how they felt. Also discuss news articles or reports of some recent natural disasters and talk about how they compare.

Have someone read aloud 3 Nephi 8:5. Ask how the storm described in that verse compares to the ones your family has experienced. When did this great storm take place?

Read together 3 Nephi 8:1–4 and have your family look for what was happening just before the storm began. Ask what the people were looking for "with great earnestness" and why. Remind your family that Samuel the Lamanite had prophesied of terrible destructions that would take place when Jesus was crucified.

To show the fulfillment of Samuel's prophecies, have family members alternate reading the following verses. Have someone read the prophecy first, followed by a reading of its fulfillment.

Prophecy	Fulfillment
Helaman 14:21, 23	3 Nephi 8:5–7, 17–18
Helaman 14:24	3 Nephi 8:8–10, 14–15

Have a family member read Helaman 14:20, 27. Then ask a family member to read 3 Nephi 8:20–22. However, before the person reads, ask other family members to close their eyes and try to picture in their minds the destruction that had taken place. Ask what interesting phrase is used in verse 20 to describe the darkness. (They "could feel the vapor of darkness.") Ask your family what they can conclude about true prophets and their prophecies. Bear testimony about our living prophet.

Read 3 Nephi 8:19 as a family. Ask your family why destruction and total darkness are appropriate signs for the death of the Savior. Share this statement from Elder Spencer W. Kimball:

"These earth spasms [were] a revolt by the created earth against the crucifixion of its Creator." (Conference Report, April 1963, pp. 64–65.)

3 Nephi 8:19–25
Three days of darkness!

 Before scripture study, completely darken one room in your home. Invite your family into that room and have them listen silently as you read 3 Nephi 8:19–25 aloud on the other side of the door. When you have finished reading, turn the lights back on, join your family, and discuss the following questions:

- What did it feel like with the lights out?
- If you had been there, what might you have been thinking about during the three days?
- What might have been your greatest concerns?
- What would you do about your house?
- What would you do for food and shelter?
- What about missing family members?
- What might you have done to find comfort or peace?
- Why do you think three days of darkness is a fitting sign of the death of the Savior?
- How is that darkness like not knowing about the gospel or not living the gospel when you know it?

3 Nephi 8:23–25

Read together with your family 3 Nephi 8:23–25. Ask what the reaction was of those who survived the destruction. What did the people wish they had done to prevent the tragedy?

Remind your family of this statement by President Ezra Taft Benson: "The record of the Nephite history just prior to the Savior's visit reveals many parallels to our own day as we anticipate the Savior's second coming." ("The Savior's Visit to America," *Ensign,* May 1987, p. 4.)

Read Joseph Smith—Matthew 1:28–33 together as a family and compare what is prophesied there about what will take place before the Lord's second coming with what occurred in 3 Nephi 8. Ask, "What can we learn from the experiences of the Nephites that will help us

prepare for the Second Coming?" (See also D&C 1:12–14.)

3 NEPHI 9: CHRIST IS A LIGHT IN THE DARKNESS

3 Nephi 9:1–12
How were Nephite cities destroyed?

 Ask the children in your family to recall a time when they heard an announcement over the intercom at school. Ask how they felt about hearing a voice without seeing the person speaking. Did they listen as well as they would have if the person had been present in person? Read together 3 Nephi 9:1–2 and ask family members to imagine being in the dark, having survived the destruction, and hearing the voice of the Savior. Ask:

- Why do you think the devil was laughing and his angels rejoicing?
- Why had the "fair sons and daughters" been slain?
- What are "iniquities and abominations"?

Divide your family into two groups and have them complete the following matching quiz by reviewing 3 Nephi 9:3–12. The group who has the most correct answers after five minutes could be served breakfast by the other group.

____ 1. Zarahemla	A. Covered with earth.
____ 2. Moroni	B. Sunk with hills and
____ 3. Moronihah	valleys in its place.
____ 4. Gilgal	C. Covered by water.
____ 5. Mocum	D. Burned with fire.
____ 6. Gimgimno	E. Sunk into the depths
____ 7. Jacobugath	of the sea.
____ 8. Gad	F. Burned with fire.
	G. Sunk into the earth.
	H. Burned with fire.

Answers: 1:D, 2:E, 3:A, 4:G, 5:C, 6:B, 7:F, 8:H.

Discuss what it might have been like to see

such destruction. What would you be thinking and feeling if you were there?

3 Nephi 9:13–14
Can a person be righteous and still need to repent?

 Ask your family if they were to make a list of those who needed to repent, how long it would be. Read together 3 Nephi 9:13–14. Ask:

- Why were some Nephites spared from the destruction?
- Why did those who were spared still need to repent?
- What did the Savior promise he would do for them if they "return[ed] unto [him]"?

Have a family member read 3 Nephi 18:32 to learn what else we can do to be "healed" by the Savior. Invite family members to share an experience when they have turned to the Savior and been healed.

3 Nephi 9:15–18
What are some of the roles of Jesus Christ?

Have each family member give a name or title for Jesus Christ. Go around as many times as needed until no one can think of any more names.

Divide your family into two groups and give each a blank sheet of paper and a pen. Invite them to read 3 Nephi 9:15–18 and write down as many names and titles of the Savior as they can. The group who comes up with the most names and titles first could win a prize. After they have completed their lists, ask:

- What are some of the important roles Jesus Christ plays in Heavenly Father's plan?
- Are there any of the names or titles that you do not understand?
- If we combined our lists and then added the important roles, how many names, titles, or roles would we come up with?

Turn to page 633 of the Bible Dictionary and show the family the section titled "Christ, names

of." Have your family guess how many actual names, titles, and roles of the Savior are listed there. (Nearly 200.)

Have your family look back at 3 Nephi 9:2–12 and find another role the Savior played in the destruction of the wicked. (Twelve times it is recorded that Jesus personally destroyed those cities.) What does that teach us about Jesus Christ?

Ask your family to share which role of the Savior means the most to them and why. Invite family members to share their feelings about the Savior.

3 Nephi 9:19–22
The law of Moses is fulfilled

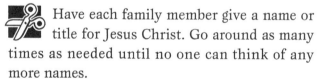 Ask your family to tell the difference between the following two laws:

- Thou shalt not kill.
- Thou shalt not be angry with thy brother.

Have them share which law they think was part of the old law of Moses and which the new law of Christ. (See 3 Nephi 12:21–22.) Why do you think things changed when Jesus came into the world?

Read together 3 Nephi 9:19–22. Ask:

- When Jesus appeared to the Nephites, what did he say was no longer required? (The offering of sheep, goats, and other animals for sacrifice.)
- What did he require instead? (A broken heart and a contrite or humble spirit.)
- What would the Savior give back in return for the broken hearts and contrite spirits? (Verse 20.)
- Who will be saved because of the Savior's sacrifice? (Verse 22.)

Ask a family member to read the following quotation from President J. Reuben Clark:

"Under the new covenant that came in with Christ, the sinner must offer the sacrifice out of his own life, not by offering the blood of some other creature; he must give up his sins, he must repent, he himself must make the sacrifice." (*Behold the Lamb of God,* pp. 107–9.)

Discuss the changes that your family might need to make to be worthy of the blessings that the Savior offers. (See 3 Nephi 9:22.) How might these changes be considered a sacrifice?

3 NEPHI 10: THE "MORE RIGHTEOUS" PEOPLE ARE SPARED FOR THE COMING OF THE SAVIOR

3 Nephi 10:1–8
What did Christ promise those who were spared destruction?

 Turn off all the lights in the house. Invite your family to be totally quiet for three minutes and imagine that they have been in darkness for three days. Quietly tell them that they are alone, their family is lost, and they hear weeping and howling everywhere. Ask:

- How would you feel if your entire town was destroyed?
- What feelings would you have if your family was lost?
- Why do you think people were howling?
- Have you ever been so miserable that you wept and howled?

Either turn the lights on or read by candlelight if you prefer. Read together 3 Nephi 10:1–8. Discuss some or all of the following questions:

- Why did silence finally come "for the space of many hours"? (Verse 2.)
- What finally broke the silence? (Verse 3.)
- How would you describe the message of this voice? (Verses 4–5.)
- What did the Savior promise the Nephites who were spared? (Verse 6.)
- When would the Savior fulfill this promise?

3 Nephi 10:9–17
What would it be like to see the Savior?

 Make a list of the following words on a sheet of paper:

Darkness
Trembling and loud noises of the earth
Weeping and wailing
Mourning
Lamentations

Show your family your list and ask them to review 3 Nephi 10:9–10 and look for those things that replaced the descriptions on the list. Discuss how Jesus Christ was the center of all these changes. Ask them what kind of changes Jesus might be able to make in our lives.

Invite family members to take a close look at 3 Nephi 10:12–13 and make another list of reasons why these particular people were spared and would ultimately be invited to meet the Savior in 3 Nephi 11. Why do you think following the Lord's prophets is so important to our preparation for the Savior's return?

Invite your family to scan 3 Nephi 10:14–17, circling the names of those prophets who had prophesied and testified of the destruction that had just taken place. What are some important things that our current prophet has warned us about?

Read the following story to your family:

"I was talking to a priesthood leader just last weekend. We had finished our Saturday night leadership meeting, which was on missionary work, and he said to me, 'You know, you are really a missionary General Authority.' And I said, 'No, I don't consider myself a missionary General Authority. If I can be remembered for anything (and I hope that somehow, somewhere I can), I would settle for that which my father taught me and for which I feel he was known, and that is *one who is willing to give allegiance to and follow a prophet of God. And if that can be my lot, then I feel I will have accomplished the thing the Lord has sent me to do.*'" (Loren C. Dunn, "Receiving a Prophet," *Ensign,* May 1983, p. 30; emphasis added.)

Discuss what you can do as a family to better follow the prophet. Read 3 Nephi 10:18–19 and testify that as your family follows the living prophets that one day you might receive the same blessing given to the righteous Nephites and

Lamanites at this time. Give your family time to make a journal entry about what it would be like to see the Savior.

3 NEPHI 11: THE APPEARANCE OF JESUS CHRIST IN THE AMERICAS

3 Nephi 11:1–2
Stand in holy places

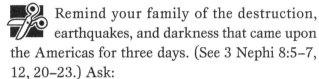 Remind your family of the destruction, earthquakes, and darkness that came upon the Americas for three days. (See 3 Nephi 8:5–7, 12, 20–23.) Ask:

- If you survived this destruction, where might you have gone as soon as the light returned?
- Who would you look for first?
- Who would you worry most about?
- What kinds of conversations do you think the people had once they could see the destruction?

Show your family a picture of the temple as you read 3 Nephi 11:1–2. Ask:

- Why do you think they would gather around about the temple?
- What are some of the feelings you have when you visit the temple?
- Do you think they were able to experience some of those same feelings then?

Divide your family into three groups. Give each of them one of the following scripture passages to look up. Have them find answers to the questions listed below their scripture.

Group 1: D&C 45:32
Who will stand in holy places? What will the wicked be doing?

Group 2: D&C 87:8
How long should we stand in holy places?

Group 3: D&C 101:22
Who should stand in holy places?

Discuss what these verses teach about how we can prepare for the coming of the Savior in these last days.

3 Nephi 11:3–7
The Savior appears at the temple in Bountiful

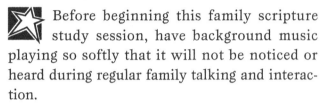 Before beginning this family scripture study session, have background music playing so softly that it will not be noticed or heard during regular family talking and interaction.

Begin by visiting, interacting, and just talking with your family about today's events. Stop and ask them to make as long a list as possible of everything they can hear right now. Have family members report what they heard. Then ask:

- How long have the sounds you listed been taking place?
- When was the first time you noticed the sounds?
- Can you think of a situation where it might be important for us to pay attention to hear and understand some quiet sounds?

Read 3 Nephi 11:3–7 together and discuss the following questions:

- What do you think these people were "conversing" about?
- What may have been one reason they didn't understand the voice the first two times? (They may not have been paying attention to it.)
- What did they finally do so they could understand the voice? (Verse 5.)
- What do you think it means to "open" your ears?
- Whose voice did they hear? (Verse 7, Heavenly Father's.)
- What can we learn from this experience about hearing spiritual things?
- How does the Lord speak to us today?
- What can we do as a family to be more sensitive to the voice of the Lord?

3 Nephi 11:7

What would it be like to hear the voice of God?

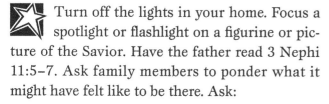 Turn off the lights in your home. Focus a spotlight or flashlight on a figurine or picture of the Savior. Have the father read 3 Nephi 11:5–7. Ask family members to ponder what it might have felt like to be there. Ask:

- Who was speaking, and what was his message?
- According to footnote 7a, what are other times in history when God the Father has spoken?
- What words does Heavenly Father use to tell how he feels about his Son?

Invite the parents in your family to share what pleases them about each of their children. Ask each family member to read 3 Nephi 11:8 silently as they think of Jesus. Have them write in their journals their feelings toward and their testimony of the Savior.

3 Nephi 11:9

A most important event

Ask your family to guess how many verses there are in the Book of Mormon (6,522). Ask each family member which of all those verses they think might be the most significant and why. Read the following statement from Elder Jeffrey R. Holland:

"As the people gazed into heaven, a man clothed in a white robe descended, emanating the very essence of light and life. His glory was a splendid and sharp contrast to the three days of death and darkness experienced earlier by these people.

"Then the Son spoke, with a voice that penetrated to the marrow, saying simply, 'I am Jesus Christ, whom the prophets testified shall come into the world.'

"That appearance and that declaration constituted the focal point, the supreme moment, in the entire history of the Book of Mormon. It was the manifestation and the decree that informed and inspired every Nephite prophet for the previous six hundred years, to say nothing of their Israelite and Jaredite forefathers for thousands of years before that.

"Everyone had talked of him, sung of him, dreamed of him, and prayed for his appearance—but here he actually was. The day of days! The God who turned every dark night into morning light had arrived." (*Christ and the New Covenant,* pp. 250–51.)

3 Nephi 11:9–10

What was the Savior's initial message when he appeared to the Nephites?

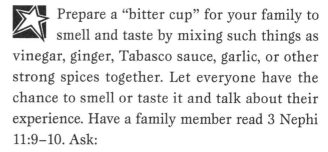 Prepare a "bitter cup" for your family to smell and taste by mixing such things as vinegar, ginger, Tabasco sauce, garlic, or other strong spices together. Let everyone have the chance to smell or taste it and talk about their experience. Have a family member read 3 Nephi 11:9–10. Ask:

- Why would the Savior say he had drunk from the bitter cup?
- What made the cup bitter?
- Why, then, was he willing to drink it? (See D&C 19:16.)
- Why do you think the first thing the Savior wanted the Nephites to know was that he had been completely obedient to the Father?

Testify of the Savior's love for us and share the following statement from Elder Jeffrey R. Holland:

"Of all the messages that could come from the scroll of eternity, what was the declaration he brought? . . . Fifty-six words. The essence of his earthly mission. Obedience and loyalty to the will of the Father, however bitter the cup or painful the price. This is a lesson he would teach these Nephites again and again during the three days he would be with them." (*Christ and the New Covenant,* p. 251.)

3 Nephi 11:12–17
"Thrust your hands into my side"

Ask your family to imagine standing before the resurrected Jesus Christ. Ask them how they might feel and what they would do. Have someone read 3 Nephi 11:12 and tell what the Nephites did. Why do you think the people fell to the earth?

Read together 3 Nephi 11:13–17. Ask:

- Why do you think the Savior invited the Nephites to feel the wounds in his side, hands, and feet? (Verse 14.)
- What would they know for sure after seeing, hearing, and touching?
- If you were invited to do so, would you touch the Savior's wounds?
- How many people were there that day? (About 2,500; 3 Nephi 17:25.)
- How long do you think it would have taken for every person to come forward "one by one" to touch his wounds?
- What does that tell you about how the Savior feels about individuals?
- How will knowing this help us as we minister to his children?

Share this experience of Elder Melvin J. Ballard with your family:

"I found myself one evening in the dreams of the night in that sacred building, the temple. After a season of prayer and rejoicing I was informed that I should have the privilege of entering into one of those rooms, to meet a glorious Personage, and, as I entered the door, I saw, seated on a raised platform, the most glorious Being my eyes have ever beheld or that I ever conceived existed in all the eternal worlds. As I approached to be introduced, he arose and stepped towards me with extended arms, and he smiled as he softly spoke my name. If I shall live to be a million years old, I shall never forget that smile. He took me into his arms and kissed me, pressed me to his bosom, and blessed me, until the marrow of my bones seemed to melt! When

he had finished, I knelt at his feet, and, as I bathed them with my tears and kisses, I saw the prints of the nails in the feet of the Redeemer of the world. The feeling that I had in the presence of him who hath all things in his hands, to have his love, his affection, and his blessing was such that if I ever can receive that of which I had but a foretaste, I would give all that I am, all that I ever hope to be to feel what I then felt." (Bryant S. Hinckley, *Sermons and Missionary Service of Melvin J. Ballard,* pp. 155–56.)

Invite your family to share their testimony of the Savior and of his love for them personally.

3 Nephi 11:18–27, 33–34, 37–41
The ordinance of baptism

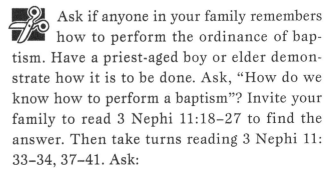

Ask if anyone in your family remembers how to perform the ordinance of baptism. Have a priest-aged boy or elder demonstrate how it is to be done. Ask, "How do we know how to perform a baptism"? Invite your family to read 3 Nephi 11:18–27 to find the answer. Then take turns reading 3 Nephi 11: 33–34, 37–41. Ask:

- Why do you think baptism is the second principle of the gospel the Savior taught?
- Why is baptism so important? (Verse 33.)
- What will happen to those who are not baptized? (Verse 34.)
- What do you remember about the feelings you had during your own baptism?
- What principle of the gospel did the Savior teach after his instruction on baptism? (Verses 37–38.)
- What is the promise to those who repent and are baptized? (Verse 39.)
- Now that Nephi and others had been taught these gospel principles, what did the Savior ask them to do? (Verse 41.)
- What can we do to help others understand the Savior's message about repentance and baptism?

3 Nephi 11:28–31
The Savior commands the Nephites not to contend

Ask family members how they feel when everyone is getting along and they are enjoying a family activity. How is that different from how they feel when there is fighting and quarreling? Have everyone read silently to themselves and then mark how the Savior feels about contention in 3 Nephi 11:28–30. Ask these questions:

- Why do you think the Nephites had been contending over doctrinal issues? (They were in a state of apostasy before the Savior's visit.)
- When we have the "spirit of contention," whom do we follow? (Verse 29.)
- What is the Savior's doctrine regarding contention? (Verses 30–31.)
- According to the Savior's instruction, is it acceptable to argue if you are right?

Share the following statement by Hugh Nibley with your family:

"The family is also Satan's primary target. He is waging war on the family. One of his schemes is the subtle and cunning way he has of sneaking behind enemy lines and entering our very homes and lives.

"He damages and often destroys families within the walls of their own homes. His strategy is to stir up anger between family members. Satan is the 'father of contention, and he stirreth up the hearts of men to contend with anger, one with another.' (3 Ne. 11:29; emphasis added.) The verb stir sounds like a recipe for disaster: Put tempers on medium heat, stir in a few choice words, and bring to a boil; continue stirring until thick; cool off; let feelings chill for several days; serve cold; lots of leftovers." (Lynn G. Robbins, "Agency and Anger," Ensign, May 1998, p. 80.)

Talk about ways your family can avoid contention. Have each family member make a list of specific things they will do in the coming week to lessen any contention in your home.

3 NEPHI 12: SERMON AT THE TEMPLE, PART 1

3 Nephi 12:1–12
How is this sermon similar to the Sermon on the Mount?

If possible, display several pictures of Christ around the room. Ask your family to choose one of the pictures and tell why they chose it. Have each one share how they might use the picture they chose to describe an aspect of Jesus' character to another.

Explain to your family that in 3 Nephi 12 the Savior began a sermon at the temple in Bountiful among the Nephites that was very similar to the Sermon on the Mount given to the Jews. (See Matthew 5–7.) Read the following statement by President Harold B. Lee:

"In His Sermon on the Mount the Master has given us somewhat of a revelation of His own character, which was perfect, or what might be said to be 'an autobiography, every syllable of which He had written down in deeds,' and in so doing has given us a blueprint for our own lives." (Stand Ye in Holy Places, p. 342.)

Begin studying the Sermon at the Temple by learning about the Beatitudes. The following references and questions might help your discussion:

3 Nephi 12:1–2
- What kind of people was the Savior teaching?
- What promises does he make to those who follow him and listen to his servants?
- According to Matthew 5:3 footnote a, what other words could be used besides "blessed"?

3 Nephi 12:3
- What do you think it means to come unto Christ? (See 3 Nephi 9:14; Ether 12:27.)
- How could being "poor in spirit" (humble) help us come unto Christ?

3 Nephi 12:4
- What do you think it means to mourn? (Sorrow or grieve.)

- In what ways can we be blessed because we mourn, and in what ways does God comfort us? (See Mosiah 18:9; James 4:8–10; Moses 7:45.)

3 Nephi 12:5

- What does it mean to be meek? (To be gentle and forgiving.)
- How does the following insight from President Gordon B. Hinckley help you understand meekness?

"Meekness implies a spirit of gratitude . . . , an acknowledgment of a greater power beyond oneself, a recognition of God, and an acceptance of his commandments." ("With All Thy Getting Get Understanding," *Ensign,* August 1988, pp. 3–4.)

3 Nephi 12:6

- Can you describe a time when you were truly hungry or thirsty?
- What quenched the Nephites' thirst or satisfied their hunger?
- What should we "hunger and thirst" after?
- What is it that fills our spiritual thirst and hunger?

3 Nephi 12:7

- According to D&C 64:4, 9–10, what does God require of us before we can obtain his mercy?

3 Nephi 12:8

- How can we become pure in heart? (See D&C 93:1.)
- What blessing is given to those who purify their hearts?

3 Nephi 12:9

- Who are the people in this Church that proclaim peace to the world? (Leaders, missionaries, parents, and so on.)
- How can we be peacemakers in our homes, schools, and communities?

3 Nephi 12:10–12

- Why does the world frequently persecute those who do what is right?

- How should we respond to persecution? (See 3 Nephi 12:44.)

Testify that as we study and apply the Beatitudes and other teachings of this sermon, we will learn more about the Savior's character and also how we can pattern our lives after his.

Note that the Beatitudes seem to chart our progress following our baptism into Christ's church. We humble ourselves, feel sorrow for our sins, seek forgiveness, desire to know truth, are forgiven of our sins, desire to share the gospel with others, suffer persecution for our beliefs, and receive a fullness of joy for our faithfulness. You may want to share this idea with your family

3 Nephi 12:13–16
What does it mean to be the salt of the earth and the light of the world?

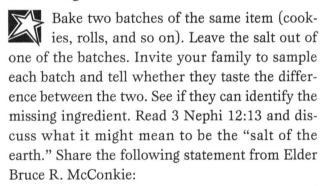 Bake two batches of the same item (cookies, rolls, and so on). Leave the salt out of one of the batches. Invite your family to sample each batch and tell whether they taste the difference between the two. See if they can identify the missing ingredient. Read 3 Nephi 12:13 and discuss what it might mean to be the "salt of the earth." Share the following statement from Elder Bruce R. McConkie:

"Among the ancient Hebrews *salt* . . . was used as a preservative, in seasoning food, and in all animal sacrifices. (Lev. 2:13; Ezek. 43:24; Mark 9:49–50.) So essential was it to the sacrificial ordinance that it was the symbol of the covenant made between God and His people. . . .

"Accordingly, our Lord's statement, made first to the Jews and then to that other great body of Hebrews, the Nephites, that they had power 'to be the *salt of the earth,*' takes on great significance. . . . They had power, in other words, to be the seasoning, savoring, preserving influence in the world, the influence which would bring peace and blessings to all others." (*Mormon Doctrine,* pp. 667–68.)

Read aloud D&C 101:39–40 and discuss ways your family can become "the salt of the earth."

Invite a family member to read 3 Nephi 12:14–16 and find what else the Savior expects of us. (To be a light unto the world.) Prepare a room with obstacles that would make it hard to walk through in the dark. Shut out all light and allow a volunteer to walk through it. Then give another family member a flashlight and let him or her lead the way. Ask:

- How is this like the Savior's teaching about being a light unto the world?
- According to 3 Nephi 18:24, what is the light that we are to hold up? (Christ.)
- How do we do that? (The Savior did not say that *we* are the light of the world but that it is *given* to us—like an assignment. We let our light shine by doing the things Jesus would do.)

3 Nephi 12:17–47
How was the law of Moses fulfilled in Christ?

Read together 3 Nephi 12:17–19 and ask what Jesus told the Nephites about the law of Moses (He fulfilled the law of Moses). Have a family member read Alma 34:13–16 and ask how Christ fulfilled the law. Compare and discuss the following sets of scriptures to see how the law of Christ fulfilled the law of Moses:

    3 Nephi 12:21
    3 Nephi 12:22–24
    3 Nephi 12:27
    3 Nephi 12:28–30
    3 Nephi 12:31
    3 Nephi 12:32
    3 Nephi 12:33
    3 Nephi 12:34–37
    3 Nephi 12:38
    3 Nephi 12:39–42
    3 Nephi 12:43
    3 Nephi 12:44–45

Discuss what seems to be the difference between the law of Moses, and the higher law of Christ. You might make the following points:

- Our righteousness is inward and genuine.
- We live the higher law to become like the Savior in every thought and action.

3 Nephi 12:48
What does it mean to be perfect?

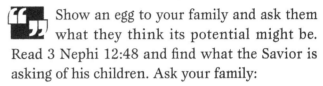 Show an egg to your family and ask them what they think its potential might be. Read 3 Nephi 12:48 and find what the Savior is asking of his children. Ask your family:

- What does the word *perfect* mean to you?
- How do you feel when you hear that it is the Savior's desire for us to become perfect?
- Do you think perfection is really possible?

Read the following quotation from Elder Joseph B. Wirthlin:

"In both His Old and New World ministries, the Savior commanded, 'Be ye therefore perfect.' A footnote explains that the Greek word translated as perfect means 'complete, finished, fully developed.' Our Heavenly Father wants us to use this mortal probation to 'fully develop' ourselves, to make the most of our talents and abilities. If we do so, when final judgment comes we will experience the joy of standing before our Father in Heaven as 'complete' and 'finished' sons and daughters, polished by obedience and worthy of the inheritance that He has promised to the faithful." ("The Time to Prepare," *Ensign,* May 1998, pp. 14–15.)

Show the egg again and ask:

- When will the egg reach its full potential or become whole and be like the parents that gave it life?
- When do you think each of us will reach our full potential to become like our Father in Heaven?

To further help us understand this principle and give us hope of becoming perfect, read the following statement from Elder Bruce R. McConkie:

"Everyone in the Church who is on the straight and narrow path, who is striving and struggling and desiring to do what is right, though he is far from perfect in this life; if he passes out of this life while he's on the straight and narrow, he's going to go on to eternal reward in his Father's kingdom. . . . If you're on that path and pressing forward, and you die, you'll never get off the path. There is no such thing as falling off the straight and narrow path in the life to come." ("The Probationary Test of Mortality," Address at U of U Institute, 10 January 1982, p. 12.)

Read with your family Moroni 10:32–33 and discuss how it is possible for us to eventually become perfect.

3 NEPHI 13: HYPOCRISY AND SEEKING GOD'S WILL

3 Nephi 13:1–6, 16–18
What is a hypocrite?

 Have a family member read aloud 3 Nephi 13:1–2 and ask what a hypocrite is. Show the accompanying figure and explain that in ancient Greece, the figures were called "The Hypocrites."

Ask, "How are actors similar to hypocrites?" (They both play a part or act in a certain way to receive approval from others.) Read together verses 1–2 again and look for words that suggest this meaning.

Explain to your family that they will get to be actors while learning about some of the verses in this chapter. Write the following references on small pieces of paper:

3 Nephi 13:2–4

3 Nephi 13:5

3 Nephi 13:6

3 Nephi 13:7–8

3 Nephi 13:16

3 Nephi 13:17–18

Read 3 Nephi 13:1–6 and 16–18 together and then have family members take turns drawing one of the papers from a jar. When it is a family member's turn, he or she should pantomime (no words or sounds) the actions described in the verses. The actor can stop pantomiming when someone identifies what verse the pantomime describes. After the activity, ask why people sometimes pretend to be righteous and why that is wrong.

3 Nephi 13:7–13
What is the right way to pray?

 Ask family members to write in a journal or on a piece of paper as many common prayer phrases as they can think of. (An example could be "that it might nourish and strengthen our bodies and do us the good we need.") Have each person share what he or she wrote.

Read 3 Nephi 13:7 and ask what Jesus meant when he said not to use "vain repetitions." You may need to explain to younger children that *repetition* means to repeat and *vain* mean worthless or of no value. Ask:

- What is wrong with saying the same phrases all the time when praying?
- How might vain repetitions make a prayer of no value?
- How would our friends feel if we said the same sentences to them day after day?
- How might vain repetitions make our Heavenly Father feel?
- How might changing the ways you say things add more meaning to your prayers?

Challenge your family to make their prayers more meaningful by not using the same phrases each time they pray.

As a family, list the things you think should be a part of every prayer. Then read together 3 Nephi

13:8–13 and ask family members to look for elements of prayer that Jesus suggested. These could include:

- We are to pray to our Father in Heaven (not to Jesus or anyone else, verse 9).
- We should give our will over to God. (Verse 10.)
- We should ask for help with earthly things.
- We should ask for forgiveness and help to forgive others.
- We should ask for help with temptation.

Invite your family to add these elements to their prayers. Share the following statement from President Ezra Taft Benson:

"Our prayers should be meaningful and pertinent. Do not use the same phrases at each prayer. Each of us would become disturbed if a friend said the same words to us each day, treated the conversation as a chore, and could hardly wait to finish in order to turn on the TV and forget us." (*God, Family, and Country*, pp. 121–22.)

3 Nephi 13:19–21
What is your treasure?

Read together 3 Nephi 13:19–21. Then give everyone a magazine and have each person find three pictures:

- A picture of something a moth could corrupt.
- A picture of something that could be destroyed by rust.
- An item someone might want to steal.

Have everyone show the others what pictures he or she selected. Ask the following questions:

- Does this mean that Jesus doesn't want us to have nice clothes, cars, or other things?
- What does it mean to make something our treasure?
- What does it mean to have our hearts set on our treasure?

Now have your family list things that moths, rust, and thieves can't hurt (such as family ties, faith, love of God, knowledge). Ask:

- Why are these things safe from thieves or rust?
- How long will these things last compared to new clothes?
- Why is it better to set our hearts on these eternal things than on earthly things?
- Why is a happy family more joyful than any earthly possession?
- How do we invest in this kind of treasure?

3 Nephi 13:24
Is it possible to serve two masters?

To prepare for this object lesson, get two straws and two cups. Fill one of the cups with water. Give a family member a straw and the empty cup and ask him or her to breathe through it. Then give the same person the other straw and the cup with water in it and ask him or her to take a drink through the straw. Next, have that person hold both cups and put both straws into his or her mouth and try to drink and breathe through the straws at the same time.

After the person has discovered that this is impossible, have another person read aloud 3 Nephi 13:24 and tell what the object lesson has to do with the scripture. Ask:

- What two masters do people often try to serve at the same time?
- What masters compete with God for attention?
- What does "Mammon" mean? (To find the answer, look up "Mammon" in the Bible Dictionary and have family members write the answer in their scriptures.)
- Why is trying to serve God and riches more dangerous than trying to breathe and drink at the same time?

3 Nephi 13:25–32
The privileges of being a servant

Have a family member read the chapter summary at the beginning of 3 Nephi 13 and remind everyone where else we can read the teachings Jesus gave in this chapter. (Matthew 6.)

Explain that although Matthew 6 and 3 Nephi 13 are similar, there are differences that help us understand Jesus' words better. Read together Matthew 6:25 and 3 Nephi 13:25 and ask what additional information is given in 3 Nephi 13:25 that is not in Matthew 6:25. Explain that many people misunderstand what Jesus said in Matthew because it is not clear that he is speaking to those he has called to "minister unto this people."

Take turns reading 3 Nephi 13:25–32 and discuss how the advice Jesus gives there would apply to those who serve the Lord full time but not to everyone. What would happen if all Church members did not bother to go to work to buy groceries but just depended on the Lord to supply their needs? Why do you think full-time missionaries are not to worry about these things?

3 Nephi 13:33–34
Putting first things first

To prepare for this object lesson, get a clear jar that will fit five or six golf balls in it but no more. Put the balls in the jar first and then fill the rest of the jar with rice or wheat. When the jar is full, dump its contents into a large bowl and you're ready for the lesson.

Read 3 Nephi 13:33–34 together and ask the family to name things we are asked to do each day that have to do with the kingdom of God. (Prayer, family scripture study, fulfilling Church callings, and so on.) Explain that those things are like the golf balls. Then ask the family what other things they need to do that do not relate directly to the kingdom of God. (Eating, homework, sleep, television, and so on.) Explain that the grain represents all the other things we do.

Invite a family member to pour the grain into the jar first and then try to get the golf balls to fit. When that doesn't work, invite him or her to start over again, put the golf balls in the jar first, and then fill the jar with the grain. Ask:

- What does this object lesson have to do with the verses?

- What does this teach us about our priorities?
- Do you think Heavenly Father wants us to have some of the nice things in life?
- Why do you think the kingdom of God should come first in our lives?
- What are some ways you can put God first?
- What could our family do better to make the kingdom of God our first priority?

Share the following statements:

"If you have not chosen the Kingdom of God first, it will in the end make no difference what you have chosen instead." (William Law, cited in James E. Faust, "A Message to My Granddaughters: Becoming 'Great Women,'" *Ensign*, September 1986, p. 20.)

"Someday, when we look back on mortality, we will see that so many of the things that seemed to matter so much at the moment will be seen not to have mattered at all. And the eternal things will be seen to have mattered even more than the most faithful of the Saints imagined." (Neal A. Maxwell, *Even As I Am*, p. 104.)

3 NEPHI 14: THE SERMON AT THE TEMPLE CONCLUDES

Tell your family that 3 Nephi 14 is made up of eight mini-lessons that Christ taught in the sermon at the temple in Bountiful. The following outline shows how they are divided:

1–5	Judging others.
6	Telling sacred things to those who can't appreciate them.
7–11	Prayer.
12	The Golden Rule.
13–14	The only way into Christ's kingdom is through the "strait gate" of baptism.
15–20	Beware of false prophets.
21–23	Works are an important part of the plan.
24–27	We must build on the sure foundation of Christ.

Divide your family into groups and have each group take one or more of the mini-lessons outlined above. Have them do the following for each one:

1. Read the verses.
2. Find the message.
3. Decide how the message applies to us.
4. Share what they have learned with the rest of the family

Below are some quotations, cross-references, stories, and questions that might aid your family as they study their assigned mini-lessons.

3 Nephi 14:1–5
What is the effect of a beam?

If possible, show your family a large piece of wood like a 2x4 and a very small sliver. Then read together 3 Nephi 14:1–5 and ask them how Jesus' disciples were being hypocritical. The following explanation from the *Ensign* may be helpful:

"Jesus was a carpenter. For him, a beam was a large piece of wood and a mote was a small speck of sawdust. . . . He was asking his disciples . . . why they were so skilled in perceiving the small inadequacies in others and yet were oblivious or nearly blinded to their own larger imperfections." (Brent A. Barlow, "To Build a Better Marriage," *Ensign,* September 1992, p. 15.)

Share the following example with your family. Thomas B. Marsh was president of the Quorum of the Twelve Apostles in Joseph Smith's day. He fell away from the Church and years later humbly realized his mistake. Upon his return to the Church he said:

"I became jealous of the Prophet . . . and overlooked everything that was right, and spent all my time in looking for the evil. . . .

"I thought I saw a beam in Brother Joseph's eye, but it was nothing but a mote, and my own eye was filled with the beam. . . . I got mad and I wanted everybody else to be mad. I talked with Brother Brigham Young and Brother Heber C. Kimball, and I wanted them to be mad like myself; and I saw they were not mad, and I got madder still because they were not." (Quoted by Elder Neal A. Maxwell in "Murmur Not," *Ensign,* November 1989, pp. 83–84.)

Discuss the following questions:

• What does the idea of a "beam in our eye" represent?
• Why do we choose to minimize our own faults and mistakes but openly criticize the faults of others?
• How can we recognize the "beam" in our own eyes and keep it from clouding our vision?
• How would daily prayer help us be more humble and forgiving?

3 Nephi 14:6
Why would someone cast pearls before swine?

Ask your family members to think of a time when they have made a decision or expressed an opinion and someone has mocked or ridiculed them for it. Ask, "How did that make you feel? How does that help explain why we do not open our temples and make the ordinances available to anyone who is curious?"

Remind your family that Jesus gave this same sermon to the Jews in the New Testament. Have them turn to the Joseph Smith Translation of Matthew 7:9–11 in the appendix of your LDS edition of the Bible (p. 803) and discuss the following questions:

• Why is a pearl of no interest to a swine (pig)?
• What does Jesus say there that helps us understand what our "pearls" are?
• What kind of people is Jesus describing as "swine"?
• With whom, then, should we share those things that are sacred to us?

Take some time to discuss with your family how they can tell who is sincerely interested and respectful and who is not.

3 Nephi 14:7–11

What is one way we can allow Christ in our lives?

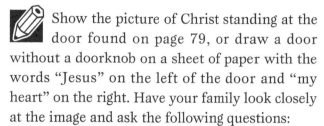 Show the picture of Christ standing at the door found on page 79, or draw a door without a doorknob on a sheet of paper with the words "Jesus" on the left of the door and "my heart" on the right. Have your family look closely at the image and ask the following questions:

- What is unusual about the door?
- Who is on the inside of the door? (Us.)
- Why is there no handle on the door to our heart? (We have to open the door from the inside.)
- What must we do if we want the Lord to be a part of our lives? (We must invite him in.)

Read 3 Nephi 14:7–11 and have each family member pick out a phrase that encourages us to pray.

Here are two possible scripture chains that you may want to do with your family. The first gives some of the reasons why we pray; the second helps us understand the process we must go through to get answers to prayer. A scripture chain is made by writing references next to verses of scripture that link them to each other. In this case, go to 3 Nephi 14:7–8 and write D&C 10:5 in the margin. Then go to D&C 10:5 and write D&C 19:38 in the margin. Continue this process until you have cross-referenced all the scriptures in the chain.

Why we should pray: 3 Nephi 14:7–8, D&C 10:5; 19:38; 31:12; 32:4; 90:24; 93:49; 3 Nephi 14:7–8.

How to get answers: 3 Nephi 14:7–8; 18:19–20; D&C 9:7–9; 88:64–65; Bible Dictionary, "Prayer," last paragraph on page 752 and the paragraph that follows; 3 Nephi 14:7–8.

3 Nephi 14:12

How can we apply the Golden Rule today?

 Ask your family if they have ever heard of the Golden Rule. Tell them that it comes from this sermon by the Savior. Invite someone to read aloud 3 Nephi 14:12 and explain in his or her own words what it is and why we call it the Golden Rule.

Share the following story as an example of how living the Golden Rule is a blessing:

"As a boy, I called my German grandpa, Eugen, by our nickname for him, Opi—but I didn't really know him. . . .

"Opi died while I was still too young for his death to mean anything to me. But he left behind written notes and talks, a journal with an entry for each day of his life, and a family history. . . .

"Before World War II, Eugen and his wife, Martha, joined The Church of Jesus Christ of Latter-day Saints. . . .

"When war came, Opi received his draft papers. I learned from his journals that many Germans, including Opi, did not support the Nazis. He disliked the war, but whenever possible, he tried to live the Golden Rule. . . . Following is a translation of one of his journal entries:

"'In World War II, I was a soldier for my country for five years. For a time, I was in charge of guarding Russian prisoners. These prisoners had to work very hard. I remember one man in particular—a teacher who was able to speak a little German. I tried to help him as much as possible in my position. I remembered the words of the Savior that we should love our enemies. The teacher and others I had command over showed me their thankfulness by trusting in me and by calling me their father. A short time later, I was transferred to the Russian front where a few of us were captured and put into a Soviet prison. We were sentenced to be shot the next day.

"'A soldier came to bring us out of prison and take us to a bunker, where we were to be guarded until our execution. To my surprise, the soldier was the teacher—the same man I had befriended a short time before when we were in quite the opposite position. Now I was the prisoner. He recognized me and said, 'You, good man, helped us—now I will help you, too!'

"'He came to us in the night and let us out of the bunker. He took us to an area close to a German encampment and let us go free. My life was spared, I believe, because I had tried to follow the words of the Savior.'" (Bruce Crandall, "Glimpses of My Grandpa," *Ensign,* March 1994, p. 28.)

3 Nephi 14:13–14
What is the "strait gate"?

 On some poster paper, draw a path that leads to a gate that has a blank sign on the front of it. Invite someone to read 3 Nephi 14:13–14 aloud. Ask your family what the "strait gate" is and what it leads to. What is the difference between a *strait* gate and a *straight* gate? (Have someone use a dictionary for help, if necessary.)

Read together 2 Nephi 31:17–18 and discuss the following questions:

- What do you think should be written on the sign? (Baptism.)
- How would you label the path on the other side of the sign? (The path to eternal life.)
- Why is a gate a good symbol for baptism?
- Why do you think the Lord called the gate "strait" (restricted or narrow)?

3 Nephi 14:15–20
How can we detect false prophets?

Show your family a piece of fruit and ask what they can tell about where this fruit came from. What can they tell about the tree?

Read 3 Nephi 14:15–20 with your family and have them find what comparison Jesus was making when he talked about fruit and trees. Ask them what "evil fruit" comes from those who pretend to be prophets or teachers sent from God but really are not. Invite your family to talk about the quality of the fruit that has resulted from their obedience to the counsel of the living prophet. Share your own testimony of the good that has come to your life from following true prophets.

3 Nephi 14:21–23
Are you a "doer" or just a "hearer"?

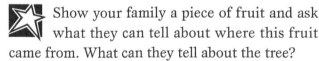 Have your family imagine that they are just getting on an airplane to fly across the country. As they enter, the pilot greets them. As part of their conversation with him, someone asks, "So how long have you been flying planes?"

He responds, "Well, I've never actually flown a plane. But I really like planes; I always have! And I've read tons of books on flying planes, so I'm excited to try it. I'm sure I'll do just fine."

Ask your family how that response would make them feel. Why would his lack of experience concern you? Read the following statements:

"David O. McKay said, 'The rich rewards come only to the strenuous strugglers.' In other words, to those who not only have faith but are willing to work and sacrifice in order to achieve their goals." (O. Leslie Stone, "The Constant Exercise of Our Faith," *Ensign,* July 1973, pp. 60.)

"Brethren, it is in doing—not just dreaming—that lives are blessed, others are guided, and souls are saved. 'Be ye doers of the word, and not hearers only, deceiving your own selves,' added James (James 1:22)." (Thomas S. Monson, "Priesthood Power," *Ensign,* November 1999, p. 51.)

Ask your family why a person who hears the gospel but doesn't actually live it is deceiving himself.

Read 3 Nephi 14:24–27 together with your family. Have them draw a picture of the two houses described in those verses and what would happen to them in a great storm. While they are drawing, share with them the following story:

"[An] example from Church history portrays the spiritual power that attends one who follows the counsel of prophets. Ephraim Hanks had known Brigham Young since the Nauvoo days. Eph's loyalty to the Brethren and his willingness to obey strictly the counsel of the prophet on any matter caused him to be much beloved and trusted by President Young, by whom Eph had been tested on more than one occasion.

"On a fall morning in 1848, President Young

drove to where Eph was building an adobe house inside the Old Fort. Looking over the completed foundation, he inquired as to the thickness of the rock wall. "Eight inches," replied Eph. "Tear it down and build it twice that thick," suggested Brigham, who then promptly drove away before Eph could answer. To rebuild meant hauling more rock and doing twice the work they thought was necessary. . . . Nevertheless, they widened the foundation to sixteen inches according to the leader's instruction. Eph was fitting the rafters on the house a month later when a heavy rain began falling, ultimately causing widespread flooding and considerable damage in parts of the valley. Eph's reinforced walls stood firm against the resulting deluge, however, thus preventing a possible collapse of the entire structure. Others were not so fortunate. From then on when Brigham talked, Eph listened." (Richard K. Hanks, *Eph Hanks, Pioneer Scout,* unpublished master's thesis, BYU, 1973, pp. 26–27; cited in Brent L. Top, Larry E. Dahl, and Walter D. Bowen, *Follow the Living Prophets,* p. 157.)

3 NEPHI 15–16: THE LAW OF MOSES AND "OTHER SHEEP"

3 Nephi 15:1
Doing what the Savior teaches us to do

Ask family members to read 3 Nephi 15:1 and identify what they think is the most important word in the verse. Have different family members tell what word they chose and why. (There is no one right answer, and you may get varied responses. Hopefully someone will choose the word "doeth.") Ask your family what is promised to those who *do* what Jesus taught and not just *hear* him. Have family members mark footnote 1b in 3 Nephi 15:1 and mark James 1:22 in the footnotes at the bottom of the page in their scriptures. Read James 1:22 together and then share the following story:

"Let me tell you of a young man who really understood these scriptures. He lives in Seoul, Korea. One day, when this young man was 15, his father received a call from a close friend who asked him if he were having financial difficulty. Being in affluent circumstances, he indicated 'No, everything is fine.' He then wanted to know why his friend would ask such a question. The man replied that he had seen his son selling newspapers on a street corner in Seoul.

"The father couldn't believe it because his son received quite a liberal allowance and would have no need to work for additional money. When asked if there couldn't have been a mistake, the friend said, 'No, I stopped and talked with him on the corner.'

"When the son returned from school that evening his father asked him about the incident. The son said, 'Yes, I was selling newspapers.'

"'Isn't your allowance sufficient to take care of your needs?' the father wanted to know.

"'Yes,' he said, 'but we had a lesson in seminary on the Good Samaritan, and I wanted to experience what it meant to be a Good Samaritan, not just learn about it. So I have taken my allowance and bought newspapers and asked some of my friends to join with me in selling them. We want to raise enough money to help one of our classmates, who is very poor, remain in school. Without the help, he would have to drop out.'

"In addition to this, sometime earlier, this young man had asked his mother to double his lunch. She had done so without questioning him, thinking that as a growing teenager he was just extra hungry. He told his father that this other student would have to go hungry each day if he did not share half of his lunch with him.

"This is what the Lord means when he encourages us to be doers of the word." (Victor L. Brown, "Do It. 'Be Ye Doers of the Word,'" *New Era,* March 1985, p. 4.)

Encourage family members to choose one of Jesus' teachings they will really try to "do" this week.

3 Nephi 15:2–10
Who fulfilled the law of Moses?

Before studying this section with your family, read the Bible Dictionary entry for "Law of Moses," pp. 722–23, and select those parts that will help your family better understand what the law of Moses was.

Read 3 Nephi 15:2–10 together and ask your family what law Jesus said was now fulfilled. Read together those parts of the Bible Dictionary explanation that you have chosen to use. Read together Alma 34:13–14 and 3 Nephi 15:5, 8 and ask someone to explain how Alma helps us understand what the Savior meant when he said the law was fulfilled in him. Make sure your family understands that the whole purpose of the law of Moses was to point to the infinite and eternal sacrifice that the Savior had now fulfilled.

Read 3 Nephi 15:5 again together and ask:

- Who gave the law of Moses to the Israelites?
- Who would then have the authority to end it?
- Does that mean the law of Moses was wrong?

Explain that the law of Moses had served its purpose and Jesus was replacing it with the higher law of the gospel. Ask your family to quickly review 3 Nephi 12 and find some examples of how Jesus replaced the law of Moses with a higher standard. (See 3 Nephi 12:21–48.)

3 Nephi 15:11–16:3
Who are the "other sheep"?

Designate one family member as the reader. Divide the rest of the family into three groups and have them move to three different areas in the room. Tell them they represent three different groups of people in the scriptures, and they will need to discover which particular group they represent and who the reader represents.

Have the reader go to the first group and read aloud 3 Nephi 15:17. Then have the reader go to the next group and read 3 Nephi 15:21. Ask your family who the reader represents. (Jesus.) Ask the

first two groups who they represent. (The Jews.) Ask the second group who they represent. (The Nephites.)

Have family members take turns reading 3 Nephi 15:11–24. Discuss the following questions to help them analyze what they read:

- Why didn't the Jews in Jerusalem understand who Jesus was referring to when he talked of his "other sheep"? (Because of stiffneckedness, unbelief, and iniquity.)
- Who did the Jews think Jesus was referring to as his "other sheep"? (The Gentiles.)
- How does unbelief prevent us from understanding the word of God?

Next have someone read aloud 3 Nephi 16:1–3. Ask your family if they know who this third group represents. Share this thought from Elder Bruce R. McConkie:

"Leaving his Nephite kinsmen, our Lord, risen and glorified, went to minister unto the lost tribes of Israel. (3 Ne. 16:1–5; 17:4.) Where he went and what he did we do not know. Did he visit one group or many? Did twenty-five hundred or thirty thousand more Israelites see his face? Someday we shall know. As of now we know in principle that these other Israelites were prepared and worthy, as all men must be who stand in the divine presence." (*The Promised Messiah,* p. 610.)

Discuss the following questions:

- What did the Savior prophesy concerning these lost tribes?
- What do we need to do to become part of his fold?
- What responsibilities do we have to find other sheep and bring them into the fold?

3 Nephi 16:4–20
How will scattered Israel be gathered?

Explain to your family that to better understand 3 Nephi 16 you have an activity for them to do and they will need to define a couple of terms that sometimes have multiple meanings. Begin by asking your family:

- What is "the house of Israel"? (Descendants of Jacob, from the Old Testament, whose name was changed to Israel.) The Nephites were of the house of Israel, as descendants of Jacob's son Joseph. (1 Nephi 5:14.) It also refers to all who repent and are baptized and become part of the Lord's covenant people. (2 Nephi 30:2.)
- Who are "the Gentiles"? ("As used throughout the scriptures it has a dual meaning, sometimes to designate people of non-Israelite lineage, and other times to designate nations that are without the gospel, even though there may be some Israelite blood therein. This latter usage is especially characteristic of the word as used in the Book of Mormon." (Bible Dictionary, p. 679.)

For the activity, prepare some figures or pictures of people. Label some of the figures "Israelites" and the rest "Gentiles." Place the Gentiles around the room but keep the Israelites together. Then read 3 Nephi 16:4–20 together as a family and ask:

- Who will be scattered forth upon the face of the earth? (Verses 4, 7–9.)
- Why will the Israelites be scattered? (Verses 4, 6–7. At this point scatter the Israelite figures around the room.)
- Which group will get the gospel first in the last days? (Verses 6–7.)
- What do the Gentiles have to do with the scattering and gathering of Israel? (Verses 4, 8–9.)
- When will the gospel again be taken to scattered Israel? (Verses 10–12.)
- What will happen to scattered Israel in the last days? (Verse 5. Have your family gather scattered Israel.)
- What will happen to the Gentiles who believe and repent? (Verse 13. At this point have your family gather in the Gentiles.)
- What will happen to the Gentiles who refuse to repent? (Verse 15.)

- What can we do individually and as a family to help with the gathering?

3 NEPHI 17: JESUS AND ANGELS MINISTER TO THE PEOPLE

3 Nephi 17:1–3
Ponder and pray

Have your family think of a time when they were sitting in a classroom and could not understand what was being taught. Ask members of your family:

- How did you feel about your lack of understanding?
- Was the problem with the teacher or with you?
- What did you finally do to be able to understand?

Invite a family member to read aloud 3 Nephi 17:1–2. Ask:

- Why were the Nephites unable to understand Jesus' words?
- Was the problem with the teacher or the learners?
- What do you think Heavenly Father wanted them to know "at this time"?

Ask family members to share what they do when they really want an answer to their prayers. Read together 3 Nephi 17:3 and have your family mark the things Jesus told them to do to be ready to learn more the next day. To help them analyze what Jesus taught, ask the following questions:

- Where did Jesus tell them to go to get ready for the next day? (Home, a quiet place where you can be alone and undisturbed.)
- What does it mean to "ponder"? (Meditate or think deeply about.)
- What were they supposed to ponder?
- How would that help them understand and be prepared for the next visit?

- Why do you think pondering is such an important part of prayer?
- Who should they turn to for help? (Plead with the Lord to enlighten your mind.)
- What do you think your Heavenly Father will do if you plead with him to help you understand something he wants you to understand?
- What did Jesus mean by "prepare your minds"? (Be ready to receive any instructions from the Spirit.)
- What kinds of preparation could we make to better understand what the Lord wants to teach us?

3 Nephi 17:4
How lost are the lost tribes?

Ask family members to recall something they have lost and have never been able to find. Ask how they felt about losing this item. Why haven't they forgotten about it?

Read 3 Nephi 17:4 and ask:

- What two destinations did Jesus say he was going to?
- How lost are the lost tribes of Israel?
- Since the lost tribes are not lost to our Father in Heaven, what does that say about his awareness of each one of us?

Since we know little about the lost tribes, it might be fun to have your family imagine being part of the lost tribes when Jesus appeared and explore the following questions:

- When the Savior visited the lost tribes, do you think he asked them to keep a record? (See 3 Nephi 16:4.)
- If they have kept records, what would be a great name for their book?
- Why might it be an interesting book to read?

3 Nephi 17:5–10
Why did Jesus heal the sick?

 Ask your family if they have ever had an experience when they really wanted some-thing from another person but were afraid to ask. Invite some family members to share what happened. Then read together 3 Nephi 17:5–6 and ask your family to tell what the people wanted from Jesus but didn't ask for out loud. How did Jesus respond to their unspoken desires? What does that teach you about the Savior?

Hand each family member a sheet of paper and a pencil. Give them two minutes (you might set a timer) to search 3 Nephi 17:7–10 and write those things that show the Savior's compassion. After the lists are complete, ask family members these questions:

- What quality did the Nephites possess that enabled the Savior to perform miracles among them? (Verse 8.)
- How did the Nephites show their gratitude for the Savior's blessings? (Verse 10.)
- What do you think the Savior would say to you if you approached him with the same kind of faith?

3 Nephi 17:11–25
Jesus blesses the little children

 Provide sheets of paper or poster board and drawing materials for your family. Assign different family members to draw the Savior praying, someone smiling, an eye, an ear, a tongue or mouth, and a heart. Then ask them to search 3 Nephi 17:11–21 and find out how their pictures relate to the verses being read. After they have reported, ask:

- How many children were gathered around Jesus?
- Why did Jesus groan? (Verse 14.)
- How would you describe Jesus' prayer and who do you think he prayed for?
- What do you think it meant to the children for Jesus to bless them "one by one"? What might it have meant to their parents?
- How does it make you feel to know that the Savior recognizes each individual?

3 Nephi 17:23–25
Angels minister in circles of fire

Help your family make angels using suckers, tissue paper, and gumdrops. Stick suckers in gumdrops so the angels will stand on their own and then tape tissue paper (robe) just below the sucker head. Place some baby dolls in the center of your table and stand the angels around the baby dolls. If you like, place birthday candles on jar lids around the angels and allow older children to light the candles. Turn out the lights in your home and have the father read 3 Nephi 17:23–25. Ask:

- How do you think it may have felt to be one of the children encircled with fire?
- What do you think it would be like to have an angel minister to you?
- Who does the Lord provide to minister to his children today?

Share this statement by President Hugh B. Brown with your family:

"Angels in heaven are your associates in teaching [children] the gospel. You parents, remember that home is the nearest thing to heaven, or should be, and that parenthood is next to Godhood. When any person, Primary teacher, officer, or anyone else helps the parents to improve the home they are helping to accomplish His avowed purpose 'to bring to pass the immortality and eternal life of man.'" (*The Abundant Life*, p. 205.)

It might be helpful to discuss ways your family can be angels and "minister" to each other. Ask family members what they think it means to minister to another. Share the following statement:

"[Angels] came down and encircled those little ones about, and they were encircled about with fire . . . ; and the angels did minister unto them. What do you mean by minister? . . . When angels come and minister, what they do is bring the word. That's what their ministry is, to bring the word, so they come and talk with us. . . . That's what ministry is—to take care of you, to explain things to you, to satisfy you." (Hugh Nibley, *Teachings of the Book of Mormon*, Semester 3, pp. 351–52.)

Invite your family to share experiences when they have enjoyed being ministered to by others. Encourage your family to choose someone to minister to and then report back during your next family scripture study.

3 NEPHI 18: THE SACRAMENT IS INTRODUCED TO THE NEPHITES

3 Nephi 18:1–10
What is the proper way to administer the sacrament?

Show your family a piece of bread and glass of water. Ask them what they think about when they see these emblems. Take turns reading 3 Nephi 18:1–10 with your family and then discuss the following questions:

- What are you usually thinking and feeling when the sacrament is administered each week?
- How might your thoughts and feelings change if the sacrament were administered by the Savior himself?
- What are some of the things that make it easier or harder to think about the Savior during the sacrament in your ward or branch?
- What are some things the Aaronic priesthood could do to make it a more spiritual experience?
- What are some things you could do to focus more on the Savior?

Share the following instruction to the young men of the Church from Elder Jeffrey R. Holland:

"Deacons, teachers, and priests should always be clean in appearance and reverent in the manner in which they perform their solemn and sacred responsibilities. . . . Teachers should always remember that the emblems they are preparing represent the body and blood of our Lord.

"To avoid distracting from the sacred occasion, priests should speak the sacrament prayers clearly and distinctly. Prayers that are rattled off swiftly or mumbled inaudibly will not do. . . . All should be helped to focus on those sacred words as they renew their covenants by partaking.

" . . . Brethren, remember the significance of those sacred prayers. You are praying as a servant of the Lord in behalf of the entire congregation. Speak to be heard and understood, and say it like you mean it.

"Deacons should pass the sacrament in a reverent and orderly manner, with no needless motions or expressions that call attention to themselves. In all their actions they should avoid distracting any member of the congregation from worship and covenant making.

"All who officiate in the sacrament—in preparing, administering, or passing—should be well groomed and modestly dressed, with nothing about their personal appearance that calls special attention to themselves. In appearance as well as actions, they should avoid distracting anyone present from full attention to the worship and covenant making that are the purpose of this sacred ordinance.

"This principle of nondistraction applies to things unseen as well as seen. If someone officiating in this sacred ordinance is unworthy to participate, and this is known to anyone present, their participation is a serious distraction to that person. Young men, if any of you is unworthy, talk to your bishop without delay.

" . . . I have a final suggestion. With the single exception of those priests occupied breaking the bread, all who hold the Aaronic Priesthood should join in singing the sacrament hymn by which we worship and prepare to partake." ("The Aaronic Priesthood and the Sacrament," *Ensign,* November 1998, pp. 39–40.)

3 Nephi 18:7, 11–14
Why must we remember the Savior while partaking of the sacrament?

Ask your family to think of a time when they felt the Spirit touch their hearts. (It may have been a family home evening lesson, a Church meeting, or during scripture study or personal prayer. Many young people do not understand that the warm feeling of peace and happiness that comes when we seek to get closer to God is the Spirit touching our hearts. Help your family identify those times and testify that those good feelings come from the Spirit.)

Have a family member read 3 Nephi 18:7 and find something we can do to have the Spirit with us more often. Suggest that they write the following sentence in their journals (help them fill in the missing word): "If we always remember him, we will have his _____ to be with us."

Share the following statements with your family:

"It is said of President Wilford Woodruff that while the sacrament was being passed, his lips could be observed in silent motion as he repeated to himself over and over again, 'I do remember thee, I do remember thee.'" (Marion G. Romney, "Reverence," *Ensign,* October 1976, p. 3.)

President David O. McKay called the sacrament "one of the most sacred ordinances of the Church of Jesus Christ of Latter-day Saints." ("The Most Important Meeting of the Church," *Improvement Era,* 64:214.)

Share with your family how important it is to you to have the Spirit with you daily. Discuss how partaking of the sacrament more worthily and reverently can help bring the Spirit into our lives.

3 Nephi 18:15–23
Jesus teaches the Nephites how to pray

Draw a line down the middle of a piece of paper. Label one side "What we usually pray for and when." Ask your family to tell when they usually pray and suggest things that are usually mentioned in their prayers. Have one person write them in the first column.

Next, label the other side "What Jesus taught the Nephites to pray for." As a family read 3 Nephi 18:15–23 and look for the principles that Jesus taught about prayer. Help your family discuss what Jesus taught by asking the following questions. Write what they learned in the second column on your paper.

- When did Jesus say we should pray? (Verses 15, 18–19, 21, 23.)
- What kinds of things should we pray for that would help us overcome the devil's temptations?
- Whose example should we follow when we pray? (Verse 16.)
- Why do you think the Lord told us three times to "pray always"?
- What can we do to make certain we get what we pray for? (Verse 20.)
- Besides our personal prayers, where else should we pray? (Verses 21–23.)
- How can family prayers and Church prayers be an important source of strength?

Have your family turn to pages 752 and 753 of the Bible Dictionary and find the entry on "Prayer." Read together the seventh paragraph, which begins, "As soon as we learn the true relationship. . . ." Ask your family what more they learn from this paragraph about getting the most out of our prayers.

3 Nephi 18:22–25
How should we treat those who are new to our Church?

Ask your family, "Do you know anyone who is a new Church member or a new neighbor?" Discuss the names of those who are new to your area. How do you think they might feel when they come to Church for the first time? If you recently moved, talk about how you and your family felt going to Church for the first time? Invite a family member to act out the feelings a newcomer might have and have your family guess what he or she is trying to portray. Have another family member act out the feelings those members who are not new might have toward newcomers and have your family guess what feelings he or she is acting out.

As a family, read 3 Nephi 18:22–25 and look for the instructions Jesus gave the Nephites about how to treat visitors at Church. Discuss how Jesus' suggestions would make the newcomer feel better and more welcomed. Ask, "How would Jesus' suggestions help the people who are not new? How can our family do a better job of holding up the light of Jesus Christ to those around us?"

3 Nephi 18:27–34
Why should we partake of the sacrament worthily?

Ask your family if they suppose that there has ever been a person in one of our meetings who has taken the sacrament but had no intentions of remembering the Lord or keeping his commandments? How do you think the Lord feels about that sort of thing? After they have had a chance to respond, have someone read 3 Nephi 18:27–29 and summarize what the Lord said. Then read to your family the following statement by President George Albert Smith:

"Before partaking of this sacrament, our hearts should be pure; our hands should be clean; we should be divested of all enmity toward our associates; we should be at peace with our fellow men; and we should have in our hearts a desire to do the will of our Father and to keep all of His commandments. If we do this, partaking of the sacrament will be a blessing to us and will renew our spiritual strength." (Conference Report, April 1908, p. 35.)

Remind your family that it is the bishop's responsibility to say whether or not a person can partake of the sacrament. Read together 3 Nephi 18:30–34 and discuss how we should treat those who are not worthy to partake of the sacrament.

3 NEPHI 19: JESUS BLESSES THE NEPHITES

3 Nephi 19:1–3
Who would you invite to meet the Savior?

Ask family members to ponder this question: "If you knew that Jesus was coming tomorrow, what would you do today?" Have family members write down their responses on a sheet of paper. Invite someone to read them aloud and ask family members to guess who wrote which paper.

Explain to your family that 3 Nephi 11–18 records the first day of the Savior's visit to America. 3 Nephi 19 records the beginning of day two. Since the Nephites knew that Jesus was coming back for a second visit, read together 3 Nephi 19:1–3 and look for what the Nephites did to prepare for the Savior's second visit. Ask:

- What did the Nephites do that was similar to what we said we would do if we knew Jesus was coming tomorrow?
- What are some specific things we can do to best prepare for Jesus' second coming today?
- What kinds of things would you not bother doing today that you normally think are important?
- What kinds of things would you make sure you did today that you normally think are not very important?

3 Nephi 19:4–14
Who were the Nephite apostles?

Get a recent November or May issue of an *Ensign* magazine and show your family the picture of the First Presidency and the Quorum of the Twelve Apostles. Cover their names so family members cannot see them. Invite family members to come forward and identify as many of the First Presidency and Quorum of the Twelve as they can.

If you do not have access to a general conference issue of the *Ensign*, invite family members to write down or name as many members of the

First Presidency and Quorum of the Twelve Apostles as they can.

Another option for teenagers would be to invite them to list as many things about the current apostles as they can (for example, what profession they were employed in, where they went to college, their home town, and so on).

Discuss as a family some of the ways in which the First Presidency and Quorum of the Twelve Apostles bless the members of the Church today.

Have family members scan 3 Nephi 19:4 and list the names of the Nephite apostles. Then take turns reading 3 Nephi 19:5–14 while looking for ways that the Nephite Twelve blessed their people. It might be helpful to ask some or all of the following questions:

- What did the Nephite apostles desire the most?
- Why do you think the Nephite apostles wanted the Spirit more than anything else?
- Who was the first Nephite apostle that was baptized and what did he do afterward?
- What happened after all the apostles were baptized?

3 Nephi 19:15–35
What did Jesus teach the Nephites about prayer?

Show a picture of a child in prayer (you could also use the picture of Joseph Smith praying in the Sacred Grove). Ask for a volunteer to teach the family the basic parts of a prayer. Tell your family that when the Savior appeared to the Nephites on the second day, the first thing he asked them to do was pray. (See 3 Nephi 19:16–17.) If possible, divide your family into four groups and assign each to study one of the groups of references and answer the questions below. When they're finished, have each group tell what they learned from the Savior about having more effective prayers.

3 Nephi 19:18–22
- Where did Jesus go to pray? (Verse 19.)

- What can we learn from the Savior about where to pray?
- What did Jesus ask the Father to give to the multitude? (Verse 21.)
- What role does faith play in receiving the Spirit?
- Why should we pray for the Spirit to be with us continually?

3 Nephi 19:23–26

- What are some things Jesus prayed for?
- How did the multitude know what to pray for? (Verse 24; see also 2 Nephi 32:8–9.)
- What did Jesus do as he watched the multitude pray? (Verse 25.)
- Why do you think Heavenly Father may smile as he watches us pray?
- Are there things you say in your prayers that would make Heavenly Father smile?

3 Nephi 19:27–30

- As Jesus resumed his prayer, what did he plead for this time?
- How did the multitude become purified like Jesus? (See 3 Nephi 19:20–21.)
- How does the Holy Ghost purify us and cleanse us?
- Why did Jesus smile upon the multitude again? (Verse 30.)

3 Nephi 19:31–36

- How did the multitude understand the words of the Savior's prayer?
- Why was his prayer not recorded? (Verse 34.)
- What compliment did Jesus pay to the multitude? (Verse 35.)
- Because of their faith, what was this group of people allowed to see that others haven't been privileged to see?

3 Nephi 19:35–36

What blessings can come to us as a result of sincere, faithful prayer?

 Have a family member read aloud 3 Nephi 19:35–36. Ask the rest of your family what

blessings came to those people because they prayed in sincerity and faith. What were the "great things" that the Nephites saw and heard because of their faith? (See 3 Nephi chapters 17 and 19.) Read the following statement to your family:

"If we would advance in holiness—increase in favor with God—nothing can take the place of prayer. . . . Give prayer—daily prayer, secret prayer—a foremost place in your lives. Let no day pass without it. Communion with the Almighty has been a source of strength, inspiration, and enlightenment through the world's history to men and women who have shaped the destinies of individuals and nations for good." (Ezra Taft Benson, *God, Family, Country,* p. 8.)

Invite family members to evaluate their prayers and to seek the Lord through prayer. You might conclude by singing "Secret Prayer" (*Hymns,* no. 144).

3 NEPHI 20: THE LORD MAKES A COVENANT WITH THE HOUSE OF ISRAEL

3 Nephi 20:1–9
Blessings of partaking of the sacrament

 Come to scripture study with a plate of treats and begin to eat them all by yourself. Tell your family how good they taste. Without giving them anything, ask, "Don't you think these are great treats?" Then set the treats aside and ask someone to explain why he or she would rather actually eat the food rather than just having someone talk about how enjoyable it is.

Invite your family to read 2 Nephi 32:3. Ask:

- What word in this verse indicates how we are to study the Lord's word?
- When referring to a meal, what does the word "feast" mean?
- What does the same word mean when referring to scripture study?
- As a family, do you think we feast or nibble upon the word of the Lord? Why?

Read together 3 Nephi 20:3–9 and discuss as many of the following questions as you think will be helpful:

- What sort of "nourishment" did the Savior offer the Nephites?
- What does the sacrament remind us of?
- How does the sacrament allow us to feast upon the word of the Lord?
- As you think about or read the sacrament prayers, what can you feast upon?
- What miracle occurred at this time and how would that affect how the people viewed the sacrament? (Verse 6.)
- What does your soul "hunger and thirst" after? (Verse 8; see 3 Nephi 12:6.)
- How can a hunger for righteousness be filled? (Verse 9.)
- How does being filled with the Holy Ghost satisfy our hunger and thirst for righteousness?

Read the following statement by Elder Dallin H. Oaks:

"Any who may have thought it a small thing to partake of the sacrament should remember the Lord's declaration that the foundation of a great work is laid by small things, for 'out of small things proceedeth that which is great' (D&C 64:33). Out of the seemingly small act of consciously and reverently renewing our baptismal covenants comes a renewal of the blessings of baptism by water and by the Spirit, that we may always have His Spirit to be with us. In this way all of us will be guided, and in this way all of us can be cleansed." ("Always Have His Spirit," *Ensign,* November 1996, p. 61.)

3 Nephi 20:10–46
What does it mean to be of the house of Israel?

Ask your family to think of a time when they or a friend made a promise and then broke it. Ask:

- How do you feel when you have broken a promise?
- How do you feel when someone breaks a promise made to you?
- Why are some people careful about keeping a promise while others seem unconcerned about it?
- In today's world, would you accept a person's word or would you prefer a written contract on a purchase agreement? Why?
- What do we call the promises we make with Heavenly Father? (See Genesis 6:18.)

Tell your family that 3 Nephi 20:10–46 lists covenants the Lord made with the children of Israel. Have your family quickly scan these verses and make a list of the covenants they find. Have them share their findings. To help them see how these covenants apply to your family, discuss some of the following questions:

- What has God promised to do for scattered Israel? (Verses 10–13.)
- How is our Heavenly Father gathering his children both spiritually and physically today?
- How can people not of the house of Israel receive these same promises? (See D&C 20:37.)

Read the following statement from President Joseph Fielding Smith:

"Every person who embraces the gospel becomes of the House of Israel. In other words, they become members of the chosen lineage, or Abraham's children through Isaac and Jacob unto whom the promises were made. The great majority of those who become members of the Church are literal descendants of Abraham through Ephraim, son of Joseph. Those who are not literal descendants of Abraham and Israel must become such, and when they are baptized and confirmed they are grafted into the tree and are entitled to all the rights and privileges as heirs." (*Doctrines of Salvation,* 3:244–46.)

Ask, "With this in mind, why does the Lord

send missionaries into the world? [See 3 Nephi 20:18.] What is our responsibility even if we are not full-time missionaries? [See D&C 88:81.]"

3 NEPHI 21: THE GENTILES HELP GATHER SCATTERED ISRAEL

3 Nephi 21:1–10
What do the Gentiles have to do with the scattering and gathering of Israel?

 Hold up a picture of a stop sign, a railroad crossing, a bass or treble clef, and some other signs. Have your family explain what each sign means or stands for. Then ask them how they know that is the proper meaning. (Someone has taught them correctly.)

Read 3 Nephi 21:1 out loud with your family. Ask them what the Lord says will let us know that the gathering of Israel is near. (A sign.) Ask your family to read 3 Nephi 21:2–10 and D&C 1:29 and look for the sign the Lord referred to. Ask:

- Who will bring the gospel to the house of Israel? (Gentiles; see 3 Nephi 21:6.)
- What is the marvelous work referred to in these verses? (The restoration of the gospel.)
- Who is the young servant who aided the restoration? (Joseph Smith.)

Read together the first paragraph from the Bible Dictionary definition of "Gentile" (p. 679). Discuss how the Gentiles helped establish the Untied States and how the founding of this nation was critical to the establishment of the Church.

3 Nephi 21:14–29
What will happen to the Gentiles?

Divide your family into two groups. Ask one group to read 3 Nephi 21:14–21 and make a list of prophecies about unrepentant Gentiles. Have the other group read 3 Nephi 21:22–29 and list what would happen to Gentiles

who repent. Ask each group to have a spokesman report what they found. Ask if they believe that the Lord will fulfill these prophecies.

After the reports are given, ask the first group which of the punishments listed in verses 14–21 seem the most distasteful and why. Ask the second group which of the blessings found in verses 22–29 they would desire and why. Ask them how we can obtain these blessings.

Ask the group that had verses 22–29 to tell other family members what the city would be called that would be built on this land in the last days (verse 23). You may want to point out that the original city of Jerusalem will also be restored. (See 3 Nephi 20:29–34.) Tell your family that the Jews will be given the land of Jerusalem as an inheritance.

Turn back to 3 Nephi 21:1 and ask your family what the Lord would establish among his people. (Zion) Turn to the Bible Dictionary and look up the word "Zion" (p. 792). Ask your family to list some of the things Zion refers to. Ask, "What do you think it would be like to live in Zion? Would it be worth the effort to be worthy to live there? How can our family begin to build Zion in their home, ward, or community today?"

3 NEPHI 22: THE STAKES OF ZION SHALL BE ENLARGED

3 Nephi 22:1–3
How are the stakes of Zion a "refuge from the storm"?

 Bring the following items with you to scripture study: a pole, a blanket or sheet, some string or twine, and a few tent stakes. Stand in the middle of the room and hold up the pole. Invite a family member to throw the blanket or sheet over the pole. Ask your family, "How many people can get under the blanket the way it is set up now"? What could we do with the blanket so more people could crowd under it for protection?

After the family gives their answers, illustrate what they have suggested by having individual family members taking hold of the corners of the blanket and pull it outward. Ask how we could fix the blanket to stay this way if we were outdoors. (With string and tent stakes driven into the ground.) How many people can we get under the tent now?

Read with your family 3 Nephi 22:1–3 and ask what the Lord is comparing to a tent like the one we just made. (Zion, see chapter heading.) Why do the cords need to be lengthened and the stakes strengthened? (Because of Zion's growth in the last days.)

To help your family understand how the Church is like a tent, read the following statement by President Ezra Taft Benson:

"The prophets likened latter-day Zion to a great tent encompassing the earth. That tent was supported by cords fastened to stakes. Those stakes, of course, are various geographical organizations spread out over the earth. Presently, Israel is being gathered to the various stakes of Zion. . . .

" . . . Stakes are a defense for the Saints from enemies both seen and unseen. The defense is direction provided through priesthood channels that strengthens testimony and promotes family solidarity and individual righteousness." ("Strengthen Thy Stakes," *Ensign,* January 1991, pp. 2, 4.)

Invite a family member to read D&C 115:5–6. Ask:

- What is the purpose of stakes today?
- What is a place of "defense"?
- Why do we need spiritual defense?
- What is a place of refuge?
- Why do we need spiritual refuge?
- What are some of the "storms that surround us"?
- How can we as a family help make our stakes a place of safety and a refuge from the storms that surround us?

3 Nephi 22:4–17
Why is the Savior referred to as a husband in these verses?

Invite the children in your family to describe traits they would like a future husband or wife to possess. Hold up a picture of the family's parents on the day thay were married and have them tell what it was that attracted them to each other and why they decided to get married. Read 3 Nephi 22:4–6 and ask how the Lord describes the relationship between him and the house of Israel. (The Lord is the husband and Israel the wife or bride.) Ask your family why they think the Lord chose this comparison. What does it tell us about his devotion to the house of Israel?

Read the following statement by Elder Jeffrey R. Holland:

"The imagery of Jehovah as bridegroom [husband] and Israel as bride is among the most commonly used metaphors in scripture, being used by the Lord and his prophets to describe the relationship between Deity and the children of the covenant. . . . Christ has, on occasion, been rightfully angry with backsliding Israel, but that has always been brief and temporary—'a small moment.' Compassion and mercy always return and prevail in a most reassuring way. The mountains and the hills may disappear. The water of the great seas may dry up. . . . But the Lord's kindness and peace will never be taken from his covenant people. He has sworn with a heavenly oath that he will not be wroth with them forever." (*Christ and the New Covenant,* p. 290.)

Read 3 Nephi 22:9–12. Invite your family to list phrases from those verses that indicate how much the Lord loves his people. Ask:

- What promises are made to those who live in Zion? (Verses 13–17.)
- Why might you enjoy living in Zion?
- Why do you think many people will flee to Zion in the last days? (See Isaiah 35:10 and D&C 45:68).

- What will we have to do to be worthy to live in Zion?

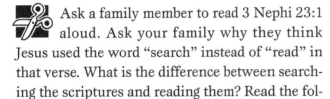

3 NEPHI 23: SEARCH THE SCRIPTURES DILIGENTLY

3 Nephi 23:1–14
How do Isaiah's words help us today?

Ask a family member to read 3 Nephi 23:1 aloud. Ask your family why they think Jesus used the word "search" instead of "read" in that verse. What is the difference between searching the scriptures and reading them? Read the following statement from Elder Henry B. Eyring to your family:

"We treasure the word of God not only by reading the words of the scriptures but by studying them. We may be nourished more by pondering a few words, allowing the Holy Ghost to make them treasures to us, than by passing quickly and superficially over whole chapters of scripture." ("Feed My Lambs," *Ensign,* November 1997, p. 84.)

Ask:

- According to Elder Eyring, what is one key to studying the scriptures? (Pondering them.)
- What part should we allow the Spirit to have in our scripture study or searching?
- What is the difference between "reading" a book and "treasuring" it?
- How would we be different if we came to "treasure the word"?

Divide your family into groups and assign each group one or more of the following verses. Have them study their verses looking for key words or phrases that give ideas on how to search the scriptures: Joshua 1:8; 2 Timothy 2:15; 1 Nephi 15:25; 1 Nephi 19:24; 2 Nephi 4:15; Joseph Smith—Matthew 1:37. Have each group report what they found.

Read together 3 Nephi 23:1–5. Ask:

- What did the Savior ask the people to search?

- Why did he want them to search the words of Isaiah?
- What does it mean to "heed" and "hearken" to the Lord's words? (Verses 4–5.)
- What blessing comes to those who hearken?

Invite your family to share some experiences where a particular scripture provided an insight into a problem or concern they were having. Discuss the following question: Since the scriptures give us such good insight into life's questions or problems, what might be a good goal for us in reading them? Conclude by singing or reading "As I Search the Holy Scriptures" (*Hymns,* no. 277).

3 Nephi 23:6–14
Why is it important to keep an accurate record?

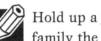

Hold up a journal and discuss with your family the value a journal has to an individual or family. Ask:

- Have there ever been times you wanted to recall the details of an event that happened in the past but you couldn't remember them?
- Have you ever wished that you had written the whole thing down?
- How could a journal entry of that event be helpful?

If appropriate, you could ask a family member to read an entry from his or her journal that helped or inspired the person.

Read as a family 3 Nephi 23:6–14. Ask:

- What did the Savior say was missing from their scriptures? (Verse 9.)
- Why would the account of others being resurrected after Christ be especially important? (Verse 11.)
- What did he ask them to do about the omitted account of Samuel the Lamanite? (Verse 13.)
- What does this teach us about the value of keeping accurate records and journals?
- After Jesus told the people to write Samuel's

prophecy, what did he command them to do? (Verse 14.)

Now would be a good time for family members to write something in their journals that inspired or impressed them during the past week. Encourage your family to continue keeping accurate and inspiring journals.

3 NEPHI 24-25: THE SAVIOR QUOTES MALACHI 3-4

3 Nephi 24:1-3
"Who shall stand when he appeareth?"

Ask a family member to read 3 Nephi 24:1 out loud and tell what event was being prophesied. (See the chapter heading for help if needed.) Have someone else read 3 Nephi 24:2-3 and find the two questions asked there about the Lord's second coming. Ask what the Second Coming is compared to that would make it difficult for people to "abide the day" or "stand when he appeareth"?

To help explain what a "refiner's fire" and "fuller's soap" are like, show your family a piece of gold or silver jewelry. Explain that when silver and gold are mined, they look very different from the precious metal in the piece of jewelry. To purify precious metals, extreme heat is used to separate the precious metals from the rock in which they are found. This process is called "refining." Have someone read the entry for "Fullers" in the Bible Dictionary (p. 676) and explain what fuller's soap does to clothes.

Discuss the following questions:

- What will happen at the Second Coming that is like a refiner's fire? (See D&C 64:23–24.)
- What will the Savior do for the faithful that is like fuller's soap? (See Alma 5:21.)
- Who are the "sons of Levi" that the Lord will purify in that day? (See D&C 13:1; 84:33–34; 128:24.)

Share the following statement by Elder James E. Faust:

"In the pain, the agony, and the heroic endeavors of life, we pass through a refiner's fire, and the insignificant and the unimportant in our lives can melt away like dross and make our faith bright, intact, and strong. In this way the divine image can be mirrored from the soul. It is part of the purging toll exacted of some to become acquainted with God. In the agonies of life, we seem to listen better to the faint, godly whisperings of the Divine Shepherd.

"Into every life there come the painful, despairing days of adversity and buffeting. There seems to be a full measure of anguish, sorrow, and often heartbreak for everyone, including those who earnestly seek to do right and be faithful. The thorns that prick, that stick in the flesh, that hurt, often change lives which seem robbed of significance and hope. This change comes about through a refining process which often seems cruel and hard. In this way the soul can become like soft clay in the hands of the Master in building lives of faith, usefulness, beauty, and strength. For some, the refiner's fire causes a loss of belief and faith in God, but those with eternal perspective understand that such refining is part of the perfection process" ("The Refiner's Fire," *Ensign*, May 1979, p. 53)

Share your testimony of how the Lord has refined you through the experiences and trials of life and how wonderful it will be to stand clean before the Lord at the last day.

3 Nephi 24:8-12
The blessings of tithing

For this object lesson, you will need ten pieces of candy. Before family scripture study, confide with a family member and explain that at some point during scripture study you will give him or her ten candies as a gift but then ask for one back. Tell the person to resist and refuse to give one back.

As your family gathers together, find some

reason to give the candy to the particular family member as explained above. When the person refuses to give one candy back, ask your family to silently read 3 Nephi 24:8-12. Have them look for how these verses relate to the experience they just witnessed. Read these verses again, aloud as a family, and ask:

- Why do some people not pay tithing?
- What blessings will the Lord pour out upon a person who pays tithing?
- What are some blessings that are specifically mentioned in verses 11-12 and how can they be applied to our modern situations?

This is also a good time to explain how tithing is calculated (see D&C 119:4) and to testify of the law of tithing.

3 Nephi 24:13-18
"I will make up my jewels"

Ask family members to read 3 Nephi 24:13-17 and try to paraphrase what is being said in their own words. After a few have put the verses in their own words, ask:

- Have you ever been a little bothered when you see people who do not serve God prospering and getting wealthy, while people living righteously are suffering and struggle just to get by?
- Have you ever felt you have not been blessed enough for doing what is right?
- What would happen if every time someone did something right, he or she were immediately and outwardly blessed?
- What would happen if every time someone did something wrong, he or she was immediately and outwardly punished?
- What blessings that are often not seen come from doing what is right?
- What did the Lord say about those who serve him faithfully? (Verses 16-17.)
- Why can't we always "discern between the righteous and the wicked, between him that serveth God and him that serveth him not"?

Share the following statement:

"The Lord promises that 'secret' acts of righteousness, seen only by him, will be rewarded openly. (See 3 Ne. 13:4, 6, 18.) This open rewarding, however, may not always be obvious in mortality. . . . In the meantime, as it continues to rain on both the just and the unjust (see Matt. 5:45), the properly motivated—and truly righteous—disciple is content with the inner peace he enjoys in service to and communion with God." (Danel W. Bachman, "Sermon of Sermons," *Ensign,* March 1991, p. 39.)

3 Nephi 25:1
Do I have roots and branches?

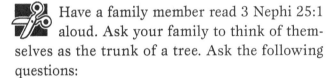

Have a family member read 3 Nephi 25:1 aloud. Ask your family to think of themselves as the trunk of a tree. Ask the following questions:

- If you were a trunk, what would your branches represent?
- What would your roots represent?
- What do these verses teach may happen to some people's "roots" and "branches"?
- Why will they be cut off from their ancestors and their posterity?
- Why is it important to you to be with your family forever?
- What do you think will protect and allow your family to be sealed forever?

Share the following statement from Elder Theodore M. Burton:

"In order to understand this passage of scripture, for root read 'progenitors' or 'ancestors' and for branch read 'posterity' or 'children.' Unless, then, through obedience to the laws of God you can qualify yourself to go to the temple and have your family sealed to you, you will live forever separately and singly in an unmarried state. It seems to me that would be a very lonesome type of existence—to live without the warming influence of family life among those you love, who in turn love you." ("Salvation and Exaltation," *Ensign,* July 1972, p. 79)

Invite family members to mark "Ancestors" in their scriptures by the word "root" and "Posterity" by the word "branch." Talk about the blessings of the temple and share your testimony of this important work.

Ask members of your family to draw a family tree. Have them list as many names of ancestors (parents, grandparents, great-grandparents, and so on) as they can think of. Ask them to put a check mark by each family member they know who has received the ordinances of the temple. Talk about ways your family can discover additional ancestors and how you can do temple work in their behalf.

3 Nephi 25:5–6
When will Elijah come?

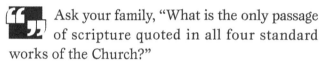 Ask your family, "What is the only passage of scripture quoted in all four standard works of the Church?"

Write the following scripture passages on four slips of paper and give them to four different family members: 3 Nephi 25:5–6; Malachi 4:5–6; D&C 2:2 and 110:15; Joseph Smith—History 1:38–39. Have each one read aloud his or her verses. Then discuss the following questions:

- When did the Lord promise to send Elijah?
- Why must Elijah come?
- What happens if he doesn't come?
- Has Elijah come, or are we still waiting for him?

Have your family mark footnote 5a in 3 Nephi 25:5 and the cross-reference D&C 110. Read D&C 110:13–16 together. Then share the following:

"Precisely on that day in 1836 when Elijah's appearance took place, Jews throughout the world were engaged in the celebration of the Passover. Since the time of Malachi, four centuries before Christ's mortal birth, Jews worldwide have awaited Elijah's coming at Passover with anxious anticipation. Elijah came, but not to Jewish homes; he came rather to a temple of the Saints

and to his legal administrator on earth, a descendant of Joseph and Ephraim. There Elijah bestowed keys of inestimable worth." (Robert L. Millet, "The Ancient Covenant Restored," *Ensign*, March 1998, p. 42.)

Read D&C 128:17–18 with your family and discuss what power Elijah brought and why it is of "inestimable worth." What things can we do so that the Second Coming will be a "great" day instead of a "dreadful" day?

Share the following statement from President Ezra Taft Benson:

"Elijah brought the keys of sealing powers—that power which seals a man to a woman and seals their posterity to them endlessly, that which seals their forefathers to them all the way back to Adam. This is the power and order that Elijah revealed—that same order of priesthood which God gave to Adam and to all the ancient patriarchs which followed after him." ("What I Hope You Will Teach Your Children about the Temple," *Ensign,* August 1985, pp. 9–10.)

Ask your family if they can see why this promise of Elijah's return might be found in every book of scripture.

3 NEPHI 26: JESUS REVEALS ALL THINGS FROM THE BEGINNING TO THE END

3 Nephi 26:1–5
All things are made known to the people

Choose one of the children in your family to focus on. Have a parent tell the following:

You were once a spirit child of our Heavenly Father in the premortal existence. You were a wonderful person there and had a strong desire to come to earth, receive a body, and gain experience. You were one of the valiant ones who stepped up and chose to follow God's plan. Then you were born on earth, and what a thrill it was to welcome your spirit into our home. (Briefly share some positive highlights from the person's life and what you see in his or her future, especially the possibilities for eternity.)

Ask your family what would it be like to see the past and look into the future and know what will happen to them. Take turns reading 3 Nephi 26:1–5 and ask your family to point out the things the Savior taught those in the ancient Americas about the future. Ask:

- How might this information about the future have affected the Nephites and Lamanites who heard it?
- What can you gain from it that will help you prepare for your future?

3 Nephi 26:6–12
How much of the revealed scripture do we have?

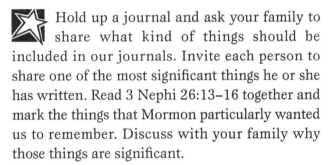 On a table or floor spread out 100 items (buttons, pennies, M&M candies, and so on). Tell your family that these 100 items represent all the things the Lord taught the Nephites. Place a copy of the Book of Mormon next to the items and ask your family to guess how much of what the Lord taught is found in our Book of Mormon.

Have someone read 3 Nephi 26:6 aloud. As the reading is going on, separate one of the items from the others. Explain that this one object represents the hundredth part that we presently have.

Take turns reading 3 Nephi 26:7–12 and discuss the following questions:

- Why was Mormon not allowed to write more of the things Jesus taught?
- What did Mormon want to have happen to the things he has written? (Verse 8.)
- When will we get the "greater things" Mormon was not allowed to write? (Verse 9.)

Share the following statement:

"Until we as Latter-day Saints live up to what is here in the Book of Mormon the Lord will give us no more. When we are willing to keep the commandments herein as the Nephites did for this short period of time, then the Lord is willing to bring forth the other records and give it to us." (Joseph Fielding Smith, Conference Report, October 1961, p. 20.)

3 Nephi 26:13–16
What Mormon wants us to remember

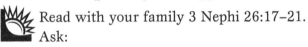 Hold up a journal and ask your family to share what kind of things should be included in our journals. Invite each person to share one of the most significant things he or she has written. Read 3 Nephi 26:13–16 together and mark the things that Mormon particularly wanted us to remember. Discuss with your family why those things are significant.

3 Nephi 26:17–21
What are disciples of Jesus supposed to do?

Read with your family 3 Nephi 26:17–21. Ask:

- What blessings came to those who believed and were baptized through the teaching of the disciples? (Verses 17–18.)
- What effect did the teachings of Jesus have on all the people? (Verse 19.)
- How do you think you would like to live in a place where everyone keeps the commandments, loves each other, and shares with one another?
- What do you think would be the best things about living with people like that?
- What do we call a people who live like that? (See Moses 7:18.)
- What can we do as a family and individually to be worthy to live in Zion?

3 NEPHI 27: "THIS IS MY GOSPEL"

3 Nephi 27:1–8
What shall the Church be called?

 Get a phone book and as a family look in the yellow pages under "Churches." Have your family count how many pages of churches there are and identify some different churches in your area. Ask how they think these churches received their names.

Have your family read 3 Nephi 27:1–3 together and ask them to find the question that was troubling the disciples. What was happening in the church that caused them to be concerned about that question? (Disputations.) Read 3 Nephi 27:4–8 together to find Christ's response. Why did he say it was important to name the church after Jesus Christ? Have a family member read D&C 115:4. Then ask what Jesus taught about the name of his Church in the latter-days.

Tell your family that Elder LeGrand Richards made an interesting observation about the Christian churches at the time of the restoration. He said, "The name of the Church was not obtained through study or research, but by revelation direct from the Lord. Does it not seem incredible that of all the churches in the world, there was not one that bore his name when the Lord restored his church in this dispensation?" (*A Marvelous Work and a Wonder,* p. 136.) What do you think the Lord wants us to remember by giving the Church his name?

Have a family member reread the first two lines of 3 Nephi 27:7 aloud. Ask your family to list some of the things we do in the name of Jesus Christ. Share the following statement from Elder Boyd K. Packer:

"Every prayer we offer is in His name. Every ordinance performed is in His name. Every baptism, confirmation, blessing, ordination, every sermon, every testimony is concluded with the invocation of His sacred name. It is in His name that we heal the sick and perform other miracles of which we do not, cannot, speak.

"In the sacrament we take upon ourselves the name of Christ. We covenant to remember Him and keep His commandments. He is present in all that we believe ("The Peaceable Followers of Christ," *Ensign,* April 1998, p. 64).

Share your feelings about our Savior Jesus

Christ and what it means to you to belong to his church.

3 Nephi 27:8–22
What is the gospel?

To prepare this object lesson, you will need two eggs. Empty the contents of one egg by poking a small hole in both ends of it. Blow into one of the holes, and the yoke will come out of the other hole. Show your family both eggs (being sure to cover the holes in the empty egg with your fingers). Tell them that one egg is good and one is bad. Ask:

• Which egg do you think is good and which is bad? Why?
• How would you be able to tell for sure? (Crack it open and look at the contents.)
• Why is it hard to tell from the shell alone?

Explain that in 3 Nephi 27 the Savior gave us two ways to determine if a church was truly his church and if it was good or true. Read 3 Nephi 27:8–11 together and have your family find and mark those signs of the true Church. (It would be called in his name and would be built on his gospel.)

Have your family mark the word "gospel" in 3 Nephi 27:13, 21. Explain that between these two verses Jesus gave a wonderful description of the elements of his gospel. You might want to explain that the word *gospel* means "good news." (See Bible Dictionary, "Gospels" p. 682.)

Take turns reading 3 Nephi 27:13–22 and have your family make a list the different aspects of the gospel mentioned in these verses. Here are some of the things you might want on your list:

Jesus came to do the will of the Father (verse 13)
The Atonement (verse 14)
The Resurrection (verses 14–15)
The Judgment (verses 14–15)
Faith in Jesus Christ (verse 19)
Repentance (verses 16, 19–20)
Baptism (verses 16, 20)

The gift of the Holy Ghost (verse 20)

Enduring to the end (verses 16–17, 19, 22)

Following the Savior's example (verse 21)

Ask your family how many times the word "do" occurs in 3 Nephi 27:21–22. Why did the Savior emphasize doing rather than merely knowing?

Share the following statement from Elder Bruce R. McConkie:

"Viewed from our mortal position, the gospel is all that is required to take us back to the Eternal Presence, there to be crowned with glory and honor, immortality and eternal life. To gain these greatest of all rewards, two things are required. The first is the atonement by which all men are raised in immortality, with those who believe and obey ascending also unto eternal life. This atoning sacrifice was the work of our Blessed Lord, and he has done his work. The second requisite is obedience on our part to the laws and ordinances of the gospel. Thus, the gospel is, in effect, the atonement. But the gospel is also all of the laws, principles, doctrines, rites, ordinances, acts, powers, authorities, and keys needed to save and exalt fallen man in the highest heaven hereafter." (*A New Witness for the Articles of Faith,* p. 134.)

Share your feelings about the hope you have for the future because of the gospel of Jesus Christ. Ask family members to explain how the gospel is "good news" to them.

3 Nephi 27:23–27
"What manner of men ought ye to be?"

 Ask your family to think about this question: "If you could become like any person in the world, who would you choose and why?" Have family members share who they chose and tell their reasons why. As a family, sing or read the first verse of "Do What Is Right" (*Hymns,* no. 237) and "I'm Trying to Be Like Jesus" (*Children's Songbook,* p. 78). Ask your family to think about those songs as you read together 3 Nephi 27:23–27. Then discuss the following questions:

- How do the messages of these songs relate to what is recorded in these verses?
- Where will our works be recorded?
- How will we be judged?
- What question did Jesus ask in verse 27?
- How did Jesus answer his own question in the same verse?

Share this statement from President Ezra Taft Benson on making Christ our example:

"Christ . . . has set us the example of what we should be like and what we should do. While many men have admirable qualities, there is only one man who ever walked the earth who was without sin. . . . Christ is God the Son and possesses every virtue in its perfection. Therefore, the only measure of true greatness is how close a man can become like Jesus. That man is greatest who is most like Christ, and those who love him most will be most like him. ("Listen to a Prophet's Voice," *Ensign,* January 1973, p. 57.)

Invite family members to silently consider what they can do to be more like the Savior. Encourage them to choose one specific thing they will work on during the next week.

3 NEPHI 28: THREE NEPHITE DISCIPLES BECOME TRANSLATED BEINGS

3 Nephi 28:1–7
What were the desires of Christ's twelve disciples?

 Ask family members if they have ever been able to talk alone to a person who was very important to them. Encourage them to share how they felt about that interview. If none has had that opportunity, have them imagine what it would be like and how they might feel. Ask them how they enjoy their interviews with their bishop or father.

Read together 3 Nephi 28:1 and ask your family why they think Jesus interviewed his disciples one by one rather than as a group. Ask if they can recall other times when the Savior visited with people one by one.

Ask your family if they could have one wish what it would be. What if the Savior asked the question? Have someone look again at 3 Nephi 28:1 and tell what the Savior asked his disciples. Have your family guess what they think Jesus' disciples desired most.

Divide your family into two groups. Give each group a reading assignment as listed below and have them find answers to their questions.

Nine Disciples— 3 Nephi 28:2–3	Three Disciples— 3 Nephi 28:4–7
What did nine disciples desire?	What did three disciples desire?
	How did Jesus know what they wanted?
	How does it make you feel knowing that the Savior knows our thoughts?
What did Jesus think of their desire?	What did Jesus think of their desire?
	In what way would those chosen to tarry be "more blessed" than those who chose to go to be with Jesus? (Verse 7.)
What would they be given?	What would they be given?

When the groups have finished, have each one share what they learned about the disciples. Then discuss the following questions:

• How was what the disciples asked for different from what many people would ask for if they had a chance to ask God for whatever they wanted?

• Why do you think all the disciples asked for a chance to continue serving, either on earth or with Jesus, instead of wealth or long life or other earthly things?

• Why would some people rather serve the Lord than have earthly wealth?

3 Nephi 28:7–10, 13–16, 18–22, 25–32, 36–40
What are translated beings?

 Ask your family to share with each other what they know about translated beings. List their answers on the left side of a poster board. Encourage them to name some individuals in scripture who have been translated. Turn to "Translated Beings" in the Topical Guide (p. 534) and take turns naming the individuals you find there.

Print the following verse numbers from 3 Nephi 28 on separate strips of paper: 7, 8, 9, 10, 13, 14, 15, 16, 18, 19, 20, 21, 22, 25, 26, 27, 28, 29, 30, 31, 32, 36–37, 38, 39, 40. Put the strips in a box. Have family members take turns drawing a paper strip out of the box until they are all gone. As they draw each strip of paper, have them look up the verse and write some brief information about translated beings on the strip of paper. After all the strips of paper have been read and written on, tape them to the right side of the poster board. You could ask family members if they have any questions about translated beings and then perhaps share this statement by Elder Bruce R. McConkie:

"Some mortals have been translated. In this state they are not subject to sorrow or to disease or to death. No longer does blood (the life-giving element of our present mortality) flow in their veins. . . . They have power to move and live in both a mortal and an unseen sphere. All translated beings undergo another change in their bodies when they gain full immortality. This change is the equivalent of a resurrection." (*The Millennial Messiah*, p. 644.)

Talk with your family about why someone would knowingly choose to remain on the earth for centuries (like the Three Nephites) rather than going to the spirit world.

3 Nephi 28:34–35
How do we offend God?

Bring to scripture study a very clean cloth (one you can risk damaging), a shoe that is smaller than the cloth, and a pan of dirt. Add water to the dirt to make mud. Place the bottom of the shoe in the mud and stamp it on the cloth. Ask your family how they would feel it someone deliberately did that to their favorite shirt or coat?

Read together 3 Nephi 28:34–35 and then discuss the following questions:

- According to verse 35, what have people done to God that is like our object lesson?
- According to verse 34, what two things do people do that is like trampling God under their feet? To help answer that question, share the following quotation from Elder Bruce R. McConkie: "Jesus and his servants are one; to believe in those whom He hath sent is to believe in Him, and to reject His messengers is to reject Him." (*The Mortal Messiah,* 4:396.)
- What will happen "at the last day" to those who refuse to believe Christ or his servants? (Verse 34.)
- What did Jesus say would have been a better fate for them than to be rejected by God? (Not to have been born, verse 35.)

Ask your family to think again about the object lesson and how they felt. How are God's reasons for being angry at those who reject him similar to or different from your reasons for being angry at those who mistreat you? After some discussion, share the following insight from Elder Neal A. Maxwell:

"We should think of God in terms of His divine attributes, for He is perfect in His love, mercy, and compassion—as well as in His justice. Only then can we begin to understand why His anger is kindled and to appreciate the loving concern which underlies His wrath. God's love for us is perfect, and His desire for our happiness is so deep that when His anger is kindled this signals much more

than we realize. Our God is not preoccupied with other concerns, nor is His ego offended, as are ours. Such narrow views of Him do an injustice to God who is perfect in His justice." (*Sermons Not Spoken,* p. 84.)

Ask your family how the wrath of God's justice might be a demonstration of his "loving concern." When they have had a chance to express their ideas, tell them that Elder Maxwell went on to say:

"While God's love is pure and perfect, Henry Fairlie has written that our mortal anger is often perverted love, for instance, 'the love of justice perverted into the desire for revenge' (*The Seven Deadly Sins Today,* p. 108). God's indignation is quite a different matter.

"God's anger is kindled not because we have harmed Him but because we have harmed ourselves. We are His children and He is a perfect Father. He does not want us, for instance, to take His name in vain, but this is because of what happens to us when we do. Our profanity cannot diminish from His Godhood, His love, His omnipotence, or His omniscience. But our profanity does damage us and can damage us profoundly." (*Sermons Not Spoken,* p. 84.)

Ask a family member to summarize what Elder Maxwell taught us by explaining how not hearkening to the Lord or his servants harms us rather than him. Ask your family what we can do to avoid being harmed by our own sins.

3 Nephi 28:37–40
We should inquire of the Lord

 Ask your family what they do when:

1. They make a mistake on a sheet of paper.
2. They make a mistake on a computer.
3. They lack insight into a principle of the gospel.

Explain that when the Book of Mormon prophets wrote on the gold plates, there was no way to correct their errors or lack of insight. Have your family read 3 Nephi 28:37–40 and find out what Mormon did when he gained a new insight about translated beings and could not alter the things already written earlier. Ask your family:

- How did he gain this new insight?
- What can we do when we lack understanding about gospel principles?

Share the following insights from Spencer W. Kimball about how to gain understanding:

"Understanding requires desire and patience. One's faith can be strengthened by . . . reading the scriptures with a happy frame of mind and desire to absorb additional truth. . . . As one reads something which does not for the moment seem to have meaning he can put that item on the shelf and move forward with the reading. In most instances the additional information gained and faith developed seem to provide the background so that the un-understandable item falls naturally into place. If anything seems to counter previous concepts, one can read and study and ponder and pray and wait and usually a clarification comes." (*The Teachings of Spencer W. Kimball,* p. 136.)

Ask your family what Mormon did in 3 Nephi 28:37 that seems to testify of President Kimball's instructions. What can we do when we need further understanding?

3 NEPHI 29–30: CHRIST'S WORDS TO THE GENTILES

3 Nephi 29:1–3
When will the Jews be gathered home?

In preparation to read 3 Nephi 29:1–3, tell your family that the phrase "these sayings" refers to the writings of the Book of Mormon. Ask someone to read those three verses and have the rest of the family look for what we should know after we see the Book of Mormon come forth. Ask someone to summarize what the Lord said about his covenant with the children of Israel and the words of the prophets.

Read together D&C 109:62–67 and discuss how those verses are like the prophecy in 3 Nephi 29:1–3. Share the following statement that demonstrates the ongoing fulfillment of one aspect of this prophecy:

"At the conference of the Church, held on the 6th of April, 1840, . . . Orson Hyde, a member of the Council of the Twelve, and John E. Page were called to go on a special mission to Jerusalem, for the purpose of dedicating the Holy Land for the latter-day gathering of the remnant of Judah. John E. Page failed in the accomplishment of the mission which was assigned him, but Orson Hyde, after surmounting many difficulties, a year and a half later knelt upon the Mount of Olives, and dedicated Palestine as the gathering place of the scattered remnant of Judah, and this servant of the Lord, moved upon by the spirit of prophecy, declared that inasmuch as it was by political power and influence that the Jews were scattered, it would be by political power and influence that they would be gathered, and that England was destined to be the nation which would take the leading part in the work of restoration." (Daniel H. Ludlow, *A Companion to Your Study of the Old Testament,* p. 77.)

Ask your family how the creation of the nation of Israel in 1948 helped fulfill this prophecy. What is happening today to fulfill this prophecy?

3 Nephi 29:4–9
What does "spurn" mean?

 Hand out the following definitions of "spurn" on small pieces of paper to family members.

Spurn: A type of saddle sore a horse gets when it has been ridden a long time.

Spurn: To reject or treat with extreme dislike.

Spurn: To finish something quickly.

Have them read each definition in turn and have other family members vote for the one they think is correct. Tell them that some clues about which definition is correct can be found in the Book of Mormon. Read 3 Nephi 29:4–9 together and have them pick out phrases that help explain the meaning of "spurn." Have someone summarize what you have learned.

Show some riding spurs or draw a spur for your family. Explain that riding spurs come from the same word "spurn" as it is found here in the Book of Mormon. Explain that "spurn" not only means to reject or to treat with contempt but also to kick or drive back with the foot.

Ask your family to look again at 3 Nephi 29:4–9 for answers to the following questions:

- What are the things the people would spurn? (Things from the Lord [such as revelations and other spiritual gifts], the Jews, and all the house of Israel.)
- What do most people today think of revelation or miracles?
- What are the consequences of spurning these things?

3 Nephi 30:1–2
Do you have any questions?

Break your family into groups of two or three. In groups, have your family write as many interesting questions as they can ask based on the information in 3 Nephi 30:1–2. Explain that they do not need to be able to answer the questions, only come up with the questions.

After they have written for two or three minutes, have them share the questions they wrote down and discuss the answers to the questions. For example, "What is the difference between 'lyings' and 'deceivings'?" Parents may need to explain some of the difficult words. After discussing the questions, ask your family to think of modern examples of the sins mentioned in verse 2. What blessings does the Lord promise those who turn away from these "evil doings"?

4 NEPHI

4 Nephi begins as 3 Nephi ended; both Nephites and Lamanites were converted to the gospel of Jesus Christ. They were living the Law of consecration and enjoying great prosperity. But after many generations had passed, wickedness, false churches, pride, and persecutions began to increase. As 4 Nephi ends, great wickedness had gripped the land as the Gadianton Robbers once again built up their secret combinations. This short book covers almost 300 years.

4 NEPHI 1: THE RISE AND FALL OF ZION

4 Nephi 1:1–3
The Nephites had all things in common

Invite your family to sit in a circle on the floor and close their eyes. Place a bag of grocery items (canned goods, produce, frozen foods, boxed items, and so on) in the middle of the family and tell them to open their eyes. Instruct family members to take as much food as possible. Once all the food is gone, ask family members to count how much they have. Ask the following questions:

- How many of you would be willing to share your food with other family members so that everyone in the family could have the same amount?
- How many of you would rather not share your food?
- Which of these attitudes would help to build Zion?
- Do you think the Nephites who lived just after the time of Christ were the type of people who would share all that they had with each other, or would they hoard their goods so that no one else could have them?

Read 4 Nephi 1:1–3 together as a family and discover what happened to the Nephites. Ask:

- How many of the Nephites were converted?
- Why were there no contentions or arguments among all the people?
- Why were there no poor people among them?
- Why did they have all things in common?
- How did they treat each other? (Verse 2.)
- How do you think you would have liked to live among them?
- What can we learn from their experience?

4 Nephi 1:4–18
How did the Nephites create a Zion society?

Ask your family to describe what they would consider to be a perfect society. Discuss things in the world that they would keep, those they would change, and those they would do without. Invite them to search 4 Nephi 1:4–18 and find things they think would help make an ideal society. The following questions might help you discuss these verses:

- Why were these people so happy?
- What blessings did they enjoy because they were all converted to the Lord?
- What was the key to their success? (Verse 15.)
- Where did they learn to love like Jesus

Christ? (These people knew the Savior personally and associated with him; they were able to model his love to those around them. See verses 11–17.)

- How can we learn to love others as the Savior loved others? (See Mosiah 5:1–2.)

4 Nephi 1:20–28
What led to the loss of Zion?

Ask your family if they have ever lost anything that they really treasured. Ask how they lost it. Did they ever think back on what happened and say something like, "If only I had done this or that, I would not have lost it"?

Read 4 Nephi 1:20–28 together and have your family look for the things that led the Nephites to lose their ideal society. Ask:

- What happened to the unity they once enjoyed? (Verse 20.)
- What was one of the first signs of wickedness among them? (Verses 24–25.)
- What happened to the Church? (Verses 26–27.)
- How long did this take? (Compare 4 Nephi 1:1 and 27.)

Read the following statement from Elder George Q. Cannon to your family:

"When the principles of the Gospel were practised among the . . . [Nephites] they were equal to a very great extent; but when they began to violate the principles of the Gospel, their inequality manifested itself. Some were lifted up in pride, some looked with scorn upon their poor brethren and sisters. Classifications arose in society which had their origin not in virtue, not in holiness, not in purity, not in any superiority arising from intelligence, but because some were richer than others, some could dress better than others, some could have better surroundings than others, doubtless dwell in finer houses, better furnished, and they were better clad, and had probably finer and nicer food. Distinctions of this kind grew up not out of the Gospel, but out of the violation of the principles of the Gospel. Wherever the Gospel of the Lord Jesus Christ is taught, ... it makes the man who may know and understand the things of God feel that he is not better than his fellow man, and the woman who understands the things of God feel that she is not better than her sister. . . . There is something in the human heart of that character that when human beings are prospering they are apt to be lifted up in pride and to forget the cause or the source of their prosperity; they are apt to forget God, who is the fountain of all their blessings, and to give glory to themselves. . . . God has sent us here and given unto us a mission on the earth not to accumulate riches, not to become worldly-minded, not to pile up the things of this world. . . . The happiness of a people does not consist in the abundance of worldly things." (*Journal of Discourses*, 22:99–101.)

Ask how can we protect ourselves so the pride and riches do not overtake us.

4 Nephi 1:35–39
What was the great division among the people?

Invite two family members to be "royalty for a day." During scripture study, make a real fuss over these two "kings" or "queens" (rub their feet or their shoulders, say nice things about them during family scripture study, and so on). During the lesson you might serve them their favorite breakfast while everyone else looks on.

When the other family members seem to be fed up with this show of favoritism, ask them how they felt about this "royal" class. Ask:

- Why did you begin to have bad feelings?
- Where do you think these feelings come from?
- Did any of you feel like "teaming up" against the royalty?

Explain that the Nephites began to experience similar feelings toward one another as some considered themselves to be "upper-class." Read as a family 4 Nephi 1:35–39 and look for divisions among the Nephites. Discuss the following:

- What were some of the characteristics of the Nephites?
- What were some "subdivisions" of the Nephites?
- Who were those that rejected the gospel?
- What did these rebels teach their families?
- Who does hatred originate from?

Reread 4 Nephi 1:15 and remind your family that *love* is what created unity and Zion among the Nephites. Discuss what happened to them because of *hate*.

4 Nephi 1:40–46

How do you build a Zion society?

 Read together 4 Nephi 1:40–46 and discuss the following questions:

- What new evil began again during these years? (Verse 42.)
- What changed about the Nephites during this time? (Verse 43.)
- What does it mean that there were "none that were righteous"?
- If you were to predict the future of the Nephites from these verses, what would you say?

As you read the following statement from President Spencer W. Kimball, have your family listen for counsel that might have been important for the Nephites to hear at that time:

"May I suggest three fundamental things we must do if we are to 'bring again Zion,' three things for which we who labor for Zion must commit ourselves.

"First, we must eliminate the individual tendency to selfishness that snares the soul, shrinks the heart, and darkens the mind. . . .

"Second, we must cooperate completely and work in harmony one with the other. There must be unanimity in our decisions and unity in our actions. . . .

"Third, we must lay on the altar and sacrifice whatever is required by the Lord. We begin by offering a 'broken heart and a contrite spirit.' We follow this by giving our best effort in our assigned fields of labor and callings. We learn our duty and execute it fully.

"Finally we consecrate our time, talents and means as called upon by our file leaders and as prompted by the whisperings of the Spirit." ("Becoming the Pure in Heart," *Ensign,* May 1978, p. 81.)

Discuss ways your family can help build a Zion atmosphere in your home and in your ward.

MORMON

Besides compiling and abridging the many records that now make up the Book of Mormon, the prophet Mormon recorded his own account of the things that took place in his day. It, too, is called the book of Mormon. The book of Mormon describes the events that occurred between approximately A.D. 322 and A.D. 385. After a futile attempt at calling his people to repentance, General Mormon saw and recorded their destruction. Before he was killed, Mormon also delivered the record he worked on and protected to his son Moroni. It was Moroni who eventually finished the sacred record and hid it up in the Hill Cumorah.

MORMON 1: A LIFETIME OF SERVICE

Mormon 1:1–19
People of all ages can serve

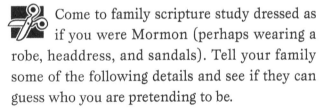 Come to family scripture study dressed as if you were Mormon (perhaps wearing a robe, headdress, and sandals). Tell your family some of the following details and see if they can guess who you are pretending to be.

1. I was named after my father.

2. When I was ten years old I was told I was a sober child and quick to observe.

3. When I was eleven I traveled to a new land with my father.

4. When I was fifteen the Lord visited me.

5. When I was twenty-four I received a sacred record, on metal plates, that I was to abridge and care for.

When your family guesses that you are Mormon, invite them to read Mormon 1:1–15 and mark the verses that record the information you gave. Ask:

- What other details can you find about Mormon's life that interest you?

- What kind of world did Mormon grow up in? (Verses 7–8, 11, 13–14.)

- What most impresses you about him?

- How does he compare to most ten-, eleven-, fifteen-, and twenty-four-year-old people you know?

- What other people can you think of in history who were given great responsibilities from the Lord at a young age? (Samuel, Joseph Smith, Nephi, and so on).

- What can you learn from the examples of these young men?

Share your testimony of the importance of being prepared though obedience, at any age, to do the will of God.

MORMON 2: MORMON LEADS THE NEPHITE ARMIES

Mormon 2:1–15
Why is suffering an important part of repentance?

 Take a small branch from a tree or bush and show your family how flexible it is. Place a bowl filled with mud near the branch.

Bend the branch so the leaves touch the mud and become filthy. Ask your family what they would do to clean the leaves. Remind your family that when this little branch is planted outside in the elements, a strong wind could bend it to the ground causing its leaves to become filthy again. Ask:

- If all we do is spray the mud off the leaves each time the wind blows, do we solve the problem?
- What might help keep this branch from bending so much in the wind? (Stake the tree in several places to provide support).
- In what ways is your life similar to this branch, and in what ways have you been given support?
- Who are some of the people that have supported and strengthened you?

To get a feeling of what the Nephites were like at this time, read together Mormon 2:1–8. Ask:

- How would you describe conditions at this time?
- Why do you think Mormon accepted the call to lead the Nephites at a time like this?
- How old was he when he accepted? (Verse 2.)
- How does verse 8 help explain why the Nephites were being driven by the Lamanites?

Read together Mormon 2:12–15. Ask:

- Why do you think Mormon was thrilled that his people were lamenting and mourning?
- How can a tragedy sometimes result in positive growth for some people?
- Can you share any experiences that testify of this truth?
- Why was Mormon's joy turned to sorrow? (Verses 13–14.)
- According to verse 15, what had the Nephites lost a chance to do? (Repent; see Alma 34:32–34).

Read the following statement by President Spencer W. Kimball:

"Very frequently people think they have repented and are worthy of forgiveness when all they have done is to express sorrow or regret at the unfortunate happening, but their repentance is barely started. Until they have begun to make changes in their lives, transformation in their habits, and to add new thoughts to their minds, to be sorry is only a bare beginning." ("What Is True Repentance?" *New Era,* January 1996, p. 6.)

Ask your family to compare Mormon 2:13–14 and Alma 36:12–13 and discuss the following questions:

- What differences do you see between the sorrow the Nephites felt and the sorrow Alma the Younger felt?
- What specifically was Alma sorry for?
- What were the Nephites sorry for?
- How does that help explain why the Nephites did not repent and Alma did?
- What did Mormon call the sorrow the Nephites felt? (Verse 13.)

Read the following statement by Elder Dallin H. Oaks:

"Alma the Younger certainly understood that easy and painless sorrow was not a sufficient basis for repentance. His experience, related in detail in the Book of Mormon, is our best scriptural illustration of the fact that the process of repentance is filled with personal suffering for sin.

"Alma said that after he was stopped in his wicked course, he was 'in the darkest abyss' (Mosiah 27:29), 'racked with eternal torment, for my soul was harrowed up to the greatest degree and racked with all my sins' (Alma 36:12).

"All of our personal experience confirms the fact that we must endure personal suffering in the process of repentance—and for serious transgressions, that suffering can be severe and prolonged." ("Sin and Suffering," *Ensign,* July 1992, p. 73.)

Ask your family to describe how Alma's experience is like the flexible branch or tree mentioned at the beginning of the lesson. Ask:

- Why would it be better to provide a way to

keep the leaves out of the mud than to continually clean the leaves?

• How does this apply to each of us as we battle to refrain from sin?

Mormon 2:17–29
Imagine being the prophet Mormon

 Ask your family if they consider twenty-four years to be a long time or a short time and why. What are some types of things that could transpire in a person's life in twenty-four years? Tell your family that Mormon 2 records the events in Mormon's life from age sixteen to age forty. (Compare verse 2 and verse 28.) Quickly review Mormon 2:2, 4, 10, 16, 20, 28–29 and create a mental picture of Mormon's life. Ask:

• How many of you would trade places with Mormon?
• What do you think was the most difficult part of his life?
• What would you do to try to change that world?

Read together Mormon 2:23–26 and discuss how Mormon tried to inspire his people. (Like Captain Moroni, he tried to get them to fight for the right things.) Also discuss with your family why his efforts didn't work.

Invite your family to put themselves in Mormon's place and write a journal entry. Then compare what they wrote with Mormon 2:17–19. Note what Mormon had hope in. How can this same hope give us strength as we face difficult times in our lives?

MORMON 3: MORMON'S INVITATION: REPENT, AND BELIEVE THE GOSPEL OF JESUS CHRIST

Mormon 3:1–16
Different ways of looking at things

 Show your family the following picture and discuss the questions below:

• What do you see first in the picture?
• What else can be seen in this picture?
• How long did it take for you to see the other perspective?
• What causes some people to see things differently from others?
• How does our perspective change our vision or understanding of things?

Divide a piece of paper into three columns. Put the following headings at the top of each column: The Righteous Believer (Mormon), The Wicked Believer (The Nephites), The Unbeliever (The Lamanites). Explain to your family that people often interpret events based on their understanding about God.

As you read Mormon 3:1–16, have part of your family pay close attention to the attitudes and perspectives of Mormon. Have another part of your family pay close attention to the attitudes and perspectives of the Nephites. Have a final part of your family pay close attention to the attitudes and perspectives of the Lamanites.

When you have finished reading, ask each group to answer the following questions according to the attitudes and perspective of their respective group:

• Why were the Nephites originally driven from their lands?
• Why was Mormon commanded to call them to repentance?
• Why were the Nephites twice able to beat the Lamanites?
• Why did Mormon lead the Nephite armies for so long?

- Why did Mormon refuse to lead the Nephites in verse 11?
- Why would the Nephites eventually be destroyed?
- How do our beliefs affect the way we see events and the decisions we make?

After the questions, you may want to show that the wicked often attribute success to themselves and failures to God while the righteous attribute success to God's blessings and failure to their own mistakes.

Mormon 3:11–13
What caused Mormon to love the wicked Nephites?

 Discuss the following questions:

- Why do you think it is easier to love people who like and respect you over those who disagree with and hate you?
- Can you think of someone who has been difficult for you to love? Why is that so?

Read Moroni 7:45–46, 2 Nephi 31:20, Mosiah 23:15, and Matthew 5:43–48 and talk about the Savior's teachings about loving other people. Also read Mormon 3:11–13 and ask:

- How did Mormon feel about the Nephites?
- Did the Nephites deserve Mormon's love?
- Why do you think he continued to love them?
- How did he, and how can we, gain such great love for all people? (See also Moroni 7:48; Mormon 1:15.)

Challenge your family to love and serve others as Mormon did. Encourage them to think about another person whom they can show greater love toward and to plan ways of doing so.

Mormon 3:17–22
The day of judgment

 Dress up like a judge and carry some kind of a gavel. You might also arrange the room to look like a courtroom. Ask a family member to imagine that he or she is a defendant and to

describe the role a judge would take in a court case regarding him or her. Now ask your family to imagine standing before the judgment bar of God. Do you know who will be your judge on that day?

Read Mormon 3:17–22 and ask:

- Who is the chief judge of all individuals? (Verse 20.)
- Who also will judge the twelve tribes of Israel who lived in the area of Jerusalem? (Verse 18.)
- Who will judge those who have been led away to the Americas? (Verse 19.)
- Who will judge the twelve disciples Jesus chose in the Americas? (Verse 19.)
- On what basis will we be judged? (Verses 20–22.)
- What should we do today to prepare for the day of judgment?

MORMON 4: THE WICKED PUNISH THE WICKED

Mormon 4:1–23
War and carnage continue among the Nephites and Lamanites

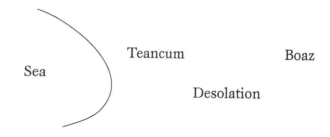 It might be helpful to establish a setting for this chapter. On a sheet of paper, draw a map that looks something like the one below.

Sea Teancum Boaz Desolation

As you read the sad tale recorded in Mormon 4:1–23, use two colored pens or pencils, one color for the Lamanites and the other for the Nephites. Trace the path each army followed to the Nephite cities of Desolation, Teancum, and Boaz. Also put a colored dot next to the city if the army was successful in conquering it. By the end of the chapter you will know how many times either army possessed a city. Note at the end of the chapter that the Lamanites had taken possession of both Desolation and Teancum and the Nephites had fled to Boaz.

Mormon 4:1–8
The Lord allows the wicked to punish the wicked

Read as a family 1 Nephi 2:20–24 and find the prophecy given there. (If the Nephites were disobedient, the Lamanites would scourge them.) Take turns reading Mormon 4:1–5 and then discuss the following questions:

- How was the prophecy in 1 Nephi 2 fulfilled in Mormon 4?
- Why do you think the Lord uses the wicked to punish the wicked?
- What does the fulfillment of this prophecy suggest about prophecies regarding our day?
- What examples can you see of the wicked punishing the wicked today?
- Where can we go to get protection from the wicked today? (See Alma 44:3–4.)

Have a family member read aloud Mormon 4:8 and tell how boasting had led the Nephites into disaster before. (See Mormon 3:9–11 and 4:4.) Have other family members read aloud James 3:5–6 and D&C 59:21 and discuss the following questions:

- To what did James compare boasting? (Small fire.)
- In what ways is fire and boasting similar? (They can destroy others, they can spread quickly, and so on.)
- How does God feel about those who don't acknowledge his hand in all their blessings?

Read the following statement from Elder Marvin J. Ashton:

"One of the most common of all sins among worldly people is relying on and then boasting in the arm of flesh. This is a most serious evil. It is a sin born of pride, a sin that creates a frame of mind which keeps men from turning to the Lord and accepting his saving grace. When a man knowingly or unknowingly engages in self-exultation because of his riches, his political power, his worldly learning, his physical prowess, his business ability, or even his works of righteousness, he is not in tune with the Spirit of the Lord." ("Neither Boast of Faith Nor of Mighty Works," *Ensign*, May 1990, p. 67.)

Mormon 4:11–14
Satan, the great counterfeiter

Read Moses 5:4–7 with your family and ask them what the purpose was for the sacrifices Adam was commanded to offer. (They were to teach him of the coming sacrifice of the Son). Explain to your family that Satan is a great counterfeiter. He will take something good and twist it into something evil. Read Mormon 4:11–14 with your family and have them find how Satan twisted the principle of sacrifice into an evil practice. Ask your family what other scriptural examples of this terrible practice they can think of (for example, Abraham 1:8–11). What other examples do you see of good things Satan is twisting into evil things in our day?

Mormon 4:23
How much time has passed?

Read Mormon 4:23 and ask your family how old they think Mormon was when he got the plates from the hill Shim. Have your family answer the following questions to find out:

- How old was Mormon in Mormon 1:2? (10 years).
- What was the date when Mormon was ten years old? (See the bottom of the page—about A.D. 322.)
- What is the date at the end of Mormon 4? (A.D. 375–380.)
- What do you get when you subtract A.D. 322 from A.D. 375? (53.)

- What do you get when you subtract A.D. 322 from A.D. 380? (58.)

Tell your family that when you add the ten years from Mormon 1:2, Mormon was between sixty-three and sixty-eight years old at the end of Mormon 4. Ask:

- How might that be considered a long life when you think of the number of battles he fought?
- Why do you think the Lord preserved his life?
- Of all the incredible things Mormon did in his lifetime, how important do you think abridging the Book of Mormon was?

Share your gratitude that the Lord preserved Mormon to abridge the Book of Mormon and bear testimony concerning the role the Book of Mormon has played in your life.

MORMON 5: THE PURPOSE OF MORMON'S WRITINGS

Mormon 5:1–7
Mormon relents and again leads the Nephite armies

Ask family members to each share an experience when they decided to not do something but later changed their minds. What eventually made them change your minds? Read Mormon 5:1–2 together. Ask:

- What had Mormon refused to do for a period of time? (See Mormon 3:11.)
- Why do you think he changed his mind?
- Why did the Nephites want Mormon to lead their armies?
- Why did Mormon think it was a hopeless battle?
- What could have made a Nephite victory possible?

Read Mormon 5:3–7 together and have your family look for what happened to the Nephites when the Lord was not with them. Ask your fam-

ily how this story could be applied to their lives. Ask, "Who do you rely on to help you win life's battles?"

Mormon 5:8–24
Why did Mormon write?

 Have three family members stand. Ask each one to point to one of the following parts of their body: eyes, ears, mouth. Ask other family members to think of inappropriate things for us to see, hear, or eat. (Some examples might be R-rated movies, bad music, or alcohol.) Ask your family what our modern prophets have counseled us about these things.

Read Mormon 5:8 to your family and ask:

- What did Mormon not want to include in his record?
- Why do you think he felt the way he did?
- What would be the danger of sharing too many explicit details?

Explain to your family that there was much, however, that Mormon did want to share with us. Ask your family the six questions listed below. Have them look for answers as they study Mormon 5:9–24. After they have read the verses, ask the questions again and see who can provide the answers.

- To whom was Mormon writing? (Verses 9, 11, 14.)
- When would his writings come forth? (Verses 12–13.)
- What was the intent of his writings? (Verse 14.)
- What would happen to the Lamanites? (Verse 15.)
- Who would receive the blessings the Lamanites could have had? (Verse 19.)
- What warning did Mormon give the Gentiles? (Verses 22–24.)

Ask a family member to summarize what he or she has learned from this chapter in the Book of Mormon.

Mormon 5:16–18
"Without Sail or Anchor"

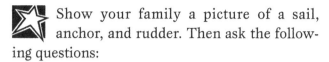 Show your family a picture of a sail, anchor, and rudder. Then ask the following questions:

- What does a sail do for a boat? (It harnesses the power and helps to steer the vessel.)
- What function does an anchor provide? (It keeps a boat in place).
- How does a rudder help a boat? (It is the steering mechanism).

Have one family member read aloud Mormon 5:16–18. Ask:

- How is this scripture like our discussion about the boat?
- How are the Lamanites like a boat without sail, anchor, or "anything wherewith to steer her"?
- How does the Savior's help in our lives compare to the help that a sail, anchor, or rudder give to a boat?
- How has the Savior helped stabilize, guide, and empower your life?

Mormon 5:19–24
A message from Mormon to us!

Ask a family member to read aloud 1 Nephi 2:20 and tell in his or her own words what the Lord promised Nephi. (A choice land of promise.) Have someone else read Mormon 5:19 and tell who Mormon said would get those blessings instead of the Nephites. (Gentiles.)

Tell your family that the last part of Mormon 5 contains a message from the prophet Mormon directly to us. Read together Mormon 5:20–24 and discuss the following questions:

- What would happen to the Lamanites when the Gentiles came to possess the land? (Verse 20, they would be driven and scattered.)
- Who were the Gentiles who scattered the remnants of Lehi descendants? (Some of them were our ancestors. Remind your fam-

ily that even though we are of the house of Israel, in the Book of Mormon we are called Gentiles because our ancestors came from Gentile countries.)
- What did the Lord promise to do after the Lamanites were driven and scattered? (Verse 20.)
- What testimony to the power of prayer do you find in verse 21?
- What warning did Mormon give us? (Verses 22–24.)
- Why do you think Mormon cared what happens to us?

MORMON 6: THE FINAL BATTLE

Mormon 6:1 Nephite destruction

Have family members read Mormon 6:1. Ask them to express how they might feel if they had a task like the one Mormon had. Ask how they think Heavenly Father feels when his children choose to suffer rather than repent.

Mormon 6:2–6
Why would an enemy grant a wish?

 Ask your family if they have ever had an enemy give them the things they wanted. Read together Mormon 6:2–6 and ask:

- What did Mormon want from the Lamanite king? (Verse 2.)
- Why do you think Mormon chose the Land of Cumorah? (Verse 4.)
- How many Nephites gathered there? (Verse 5.)
- Why do you think the Lamanite king agreed to Mormon's request?
- What did Mormon know and what did he do to prepare for it? (Verse 6.)
- Why do you think Mormon didn't just give up?

You might share this statement by Hugh Nibley: "The Nephites finally decided to call a halt by requesting for the last time the ancient courtesy of stipulating the time and place for a final showdown on a fair field. This was granted them." (*Collected Works of Hugh Nibley,* 7:333.)

Mormon 6:7–8
"That awful fear of death"

Ask the men in your family to imagine they were facing a battle. Would they take their wives and children into battle? Read aloud Mormon 6:7–8 and ask:

- Why do you think the women and children were gathered with their husbands for the final Nephite battle?
- How would you feel if you were with the Nephite men, women, and children?
- Why were they filled "with that awful fear" of death?
- Why do you think Mormon didn't seem to be afraid of dying?

Share the following statements with your family:

"In the last scene the Nephites are allowed the melancholy and terrifying privilege of enjoying one last tremendous spectacle—the full-dress approach of their executioners." (*Collected Works of Hugh Nibley,* 7:333.)

"When the forces of the Nephites, plus their women and children, saw the Lamanites approaching, they were filled with terror, a sort of intense or violent dread, that filled their hearts. The wicked fear and tremble when brought face to face with death. The awful fear of which Mormon writes, is the opposite of the fear of God, which means that reverence for Him that leads to obedience because of one's realization of His power, as well as of His love toward man. The Psalmist wrote of evil men and their works; his words may apply not only to the Lamanites, but also to the Nephites: ' . . . They are corrupt, they have done abominable works, there is none that doeth good. The Lord looked down from Heaven upon the children of men, to see if there were any that did understand, and seek God. They are all gone

aside, they are all together become filthy: there is none that doeth good, no, not one . . . ' (Psalm 14:1–5). A better description of both peoples cannot be had than this." (Reynolds and Sjodahl, *Commentary on the Book of Mormon,* 7:279–80.)

Have your family turn to Alma 27:28 and compare the attitude of the Anti-Nephi-Lehies with that of the Nephites. Ask:

- What makes the difference in our attitudes as we approach death?
- What can we do so that we will not look upon death with fear and terror?

Mormon 6:9–15
Nephite casualties

Write the names of the following Nephite captains on large name tags. Hand them out equally to family members.

Mormon	Moroni	Gidgiddonah
Lamah	Gilgal	Limnah
Jeneum	Cumenihah	Moronihah
Antionum	Shiblom	Shem
Josh	10 More	

Give everyone crayons and encourage them to design a battle banner on their name tags. Then have your family review Mormon 6:9–15 and write on the back of their name tags the number of casualties (deaths) their captain's armies suffered.

Pretend you are doing a news broadcast and interview the captains, asking for a report of their casualties. Keep a running total on a sheet of paper (230,000). Include in your broadcast a tally of Nephites who were still alive with Mormon, those who "escaped into the south countries," and those "who had deserted over unto the Lamanites."

As you interview Mormon, ask how many other casualties there might have been considering the women, children, and Lamanites. Ask Moroni how he feels about all the dead bodies strewn over Cumorah. Talk about the large number of deaths with your family and ask them to share what feelings they might have had if they had been Mormon or Moroni.

Mormon 6:16–22
Mormon's lamentation

Ask the father in your family to dress up as Mormon and read Mormon 6:17–22 to the family (or you might check out the Gospel Doctrine Book of Mormon Video from your ward library and show the clip "O Ye Fair Ones"). Discuss the following questions:

- How did Mormon refer to his slain people? (Fair ones.)
- What questions did he ask of them? (Verses 17, 19.)
- By whom will these Nephites be judged? (Verse 21.)
- What can we do to avoid departing "from the ways of the Lord" and rejecting the Savior who stands "with open arms to receive" us?

Read to your family Mormon 6:22 and find what would have been needed to reverse the horrible destruction they suffered. How can we apply the gift of repentance in our lives so that we do not destroy ourselves spiritually?

MORMON 7: MORMON'S FINAL TESTIMONY

Mormon 7:1–10
Mormon's farewell testimony

Ask family members to imagine that today is their last day on earth. Allow each member to write one paragraph expressing their last words to their family. Let everyone read his or her paragraph.

Explain to your family that, as far as we know, this chapter represents Mormon's final counsel to his readers because Moroni takes over the record keeping in Mormon 8 and informs the reader that Mormon has been killed. Although short, his final message is important and very powerful.

Mormon 7:1–10
Believe in Christ

Have a family member read aloud Mormon 7:1 and tell to whom Mormon was speaking. Divide your family into two groups. Have both groups read Mormon 7:2–10. Have one group look for what Mormon wants the people to *know* and the other group look for what Mormon wants the people to *do*. Have both groups share what they find and tell why they think it would be important to *know* or *do* those things.

Tell your family that Elder Bruce R. McConkie of the Quorum of the Twelve Apostles, in his last public appearance, which was less than two weeks before his death, spoke in general conference and bore his testimony. Share with your family this part of Elder McConkie's final remarks:

"And now, as pertaining to this perfect atonement, wrought by the shedding of the blood of God—I testify that it took place in Gethsemane and at Golgotha, and as pertaining to Jesus Christ, I testify that he is the Son of the Living God and was crucified for the sins of the world. He is our Lord, our God, and our King. This I know of myself independent of any other person.

"I am one of his witnesses, and in a coming day I shall feel the nail marks in his hands and in his feet and shall wet his feet with my tears.

"But I shall not know any better then than I know now that he is God's Almighty Son, that he is our Savior and Redeemer, and that salvation comes in and through his atoning blood and in no other way.

"God grant that all of us may walk in the light as God our Father is in the light so that, according to the promises, the blood of Jesus Christ his Son will cleanse us from all sin." ("The Purifying Power of Gethsemane," *Ensign*, May 1985, p. 9.)

Have family members take turns reading aloud Mormon 7:5–7. Ask your family to compare Mormon's testimony with Elder McConkie's testimony. What truths and doctrines did they both emphasize?

Remind your family that verse 10 consists of Mormon's last words. Ask:

- Why do you think he chose "it shall be well with you in the day of judgment" as his final words?
- What can we do to make sure that our final judgment is positive?
- What does D&C 38:30 help us to understand about this idea?
- Why is preparation so important?
- What are you doing to follow Mormon's counsel and prepare to meet the Lord?

Allow time for family members to ponder their feelings concerning the Savior. You may want to have a brief testimony meeting and allow all family members to share their testimony of Jesus Christ if they want to do so.

MORMON 8: MORONI SPEAKS TO THE PEOPLE OF OUR DAY

Mormon 8:1–12
"I even remain alone"

 Invite your family to imagine that they are in a remote place with no one around—no people, no noise, no phones, no friends, and no connection with other people whatsoever. Ask:

- How would you feel if you were that isolated and alone?
- How would you get along all by yourself?
- What would you miss the most the first week alone?
- What would you miss the most after a month alone?
- What would you miss the most if you had to stay there a year?
- What comfort would you find in knowing that sooner or later you would get to go home?

Tell your family that Moroni was in a situation a little like this. Read Mormon 8:1–12 and have your family pick out words that describe how Moroni felt at this time. Ask family members to share some of the words they found. Then discuss the following questions:

- How was Moroni's isolation different from the situation we imagined above?
- How would you feel if, instead of being away from your family and friends, they were all killed?
- How would your isolation be different if, instead of being alone, you were constantly being hunted by your enemies?
- What source of strength had the Lord sent Mormon and Moroni? (Verses 10–11.)

Ask your family to share experiences they have had when they had to stand alone in doing the right thing. Ask, "How has the Lord strengthened you during these times?"

Mormon 8:13–22
Moroni prophesies about our day

Tell your family they are going to play detective. Either as individuals or as a family, study Mormon 8:13–22 and look for clues to what Moroni is prophesying about for his future. When all have had a chance to search the verses, ask the following questions:

- What did Moroni say he was going to do with the "record"? (Verse 14.)
- What did Moroni mean when he said the plates were of "no worth" and yet the "record" was of great worth?
- What is the only motive the person must have before he can bring the record to light? (Verse 15.)
- Where will the record come from? (Verse 16.)
- What record or book fits the clues? (The Book of Mormon.)
- Who is the person that brought the record to light? (Joseph Smith.)
- What did Moroni predict for those who would condemn the book? (Verses 17–20.)

- What warning did Moroni give to those who would try to "destroy the work of the Lord"?
- Can you think of any person or people who have condemned the book or tried to destroy the Lord's work?

Mormon 8:24–40
The conditions on the earth when the Book of Mormon comes forth

 Get a clear glass of water and some food coloring and tell your family that you have a pure glass of water. Invite your family to look at Mormon 8:31, 38 and find two words that are the same in each verse. Discuss what is so bad about pollution. Drop a single drop of food coloring into the water and ask your family to describe the effect a little pollution has on its environment.

Assign family members the following scripture references:

Mormon 8:24–25
Mormon 8:26
Mormon 8:27–28
Mormon 8:29–30
Mormon 8:31–32
Mormon 8:33–34
Mormon 8:35–36
Mormon 8:37–38
Mormon 8:39–40

Assign family members to read their references and find at least two conditions that would be prevalent at the time of the coming forth of Book of Mormon. As each person shares what he or she learned, make a list of the conditions discovered. Discuss the following questions:

- How many of those conditions existed at the time of Joseph Smith? (All.)
- How many are still prevalent today?
- How are these conditions similar to the events that will transpire before the Savior comes again?
- Compared to the chemical pollutions the world is so concerned about today, what kind

of "pollutions" was Moroni warning us about? (Verses 31, 36–38.)
- How many of these pollutions seem prevalent in our world today?
- How can avoiding these conditions help prepare us for the Savior's second coming?

Mormon 8:34–41
For whom was the Book of Mormon written?

Ask your family if they have ever wondered how the prophets Mormon and Moroni decided what stories to include in this abridgment when they had so many records to choose from. Ask your family to read Mormon 8:34–35 and see if that helps answer that question.

Read the following statement by President Ezra Taft Benson:

"The Book of Mormon 'was written for our day.' The Nephites never had the book; neither did the Lamanites of ancient times. It was meant for us. . . . If they saw our day, and chose those things which would be of greatest worth to us, is not that how we should study the Book of Mormon? We should constantly ask ourselves, 'Why did the Lord inspire Mormon (or Moroni or Alma) to include that in his record? What lesson can I learn from that to help me live in this day and age?'" (*A Witness and a Warning,* pp. 19–20.)

Tell your family that since Moroni saw our day, maybe we can learn from his observations and warnings. As you take turns reading Mormon 8:36–41, look for things that concerned Moroni. Discuss the following questions:

- What would you list as the most serious concerns expressed by Moroni?
- What common theme is found in these verses?
- How can we fortify ourselves against the sins of this generation?
- What can we do to overcome pride, selfishness, and greed?

MORMON 9: MORONI CRIES REPENTANCE TO UNBELIEVERS

Mormon 9:1–29
Moroni speaks to unbelievers, those who deny revelations, and those who believe God can do no miracles

 Ask your family the following two questions:

- Why do you believe in Jesus Christ?
- Why do you think some people in the world do not believe in him?

After hearing their responses, have them search Mormon 9:1, 6, 7, 15, 26 and look for answers to the following questions:

- Was Moroni speaking to believers or unbelievers?
- Why do you think Moroni would address unbelievers?
- What are the chances of them reading the message?
- How can we get his message to them?

Write the numbers 1 through 26 each on separate slips of paper and scatter them on one half of a table. Then find an object or a picture for each of the words below (or just write the word on a strip of paper). Scatter these on the other half of the table. Have family members take turns reading Mormon 9:1–29. When a person has finished reading a verse, have him or her select an object, picture, or word strip that matches the verse. Have the person explain why he or she made that choice. Then answer any questions the person may have about that verse. The verses should match as follows:

Verse	Word Strip (ws)
1	unbelievers
2	scroll
3	commandments
4	something filthy
5	Christ
6	spotless white fabric
7	gifts
8	scriptures
9	shadow
10	God of miracles
11	earth
12	Adam
13	redemption
14	judgment
15	miracles
16	eyes
17	his word
18	apostles
19	unchangeable
20	know not God
21	doubting nothing
22	preach
23	baptism
24	a sign
25	believe
26	despise

After family members have matched all the objects with the correct verses, ask them to share things they learned from their verses. Talk about what Moroni's main message was to the unbelievers and why he might have given them that message.

Mormon 9:27–30
Moroni writes to us

 Give each member of your family a sheet of stationery and an envelope. Ask your family to write a brief letter to their future spouse or child. Tell them they can choose what they think would be important to say. When all have finished, briefly discuss the topics each one chose to write about and why. Tell them that, if they would like, you will seal the note and keep it until their wedding day, or until their first child's baptism. Then discuss the following questions:

- What does it feel like to write to someone you have never met, or who may not even have been born yet?

- Do you care for these people, even though you haven't met them yet? Why?
- How does this activity compare to the messages that Mormon or Moroni wrote for us?

Have a member of your family read Mormon 9:30 and 8:35 while the others follow along. Ask:

- Who did Moroni write to?
- How does it make you feel to know that his message was intended for you?

Ask your family members to silently read Mormon 9:27–29 and look for some of Moroni's teachings. Discuss the following:

- How applicable are those teachings for our day?
- Why do you think Mormon would mention those things specifically?
- Which one do you need to work on most?

Mormon 9:31
What does Moroni request of us?

 Read Mormon 9:31 aloud for your family and ask:

- What impression do you get of Moroni from that verse alone?
- Why do you think Moroni wrote on the gold plates if he was not perfect at it?
- What could we learn from his example concerning the things we are not perfect at?
- Why do you think his teachings about not condemning his writings are important?
- Why is it important not to condemn others or ourselves?

You might like to share Elder Neal A. Maxwell's statements with your family:

"A wise leader will be aware that his imperfections are noticed, but he will also humbly hope that when others see his imperfections, this will provide them with a chance to learn to be more

wise than he has been. Good parents, as well as good prophets, always so hope, too." (*All These Things Shall Give Thee Experience,* p. 112.)

"These concerns are noted not because of any array of imperfections in the Book of Mormon, but rather to show the conscientiousness of the dedicated writers and editors who with blood, sweat, and tears bequeathed the Book of Mormon to all mankind." (*Plain and Precious Things,* p. 4.)

Discuss how family members can show appreciation for the sacrifices of those who took part in providing the Book of Mormon for us. Encourage each member of your family to share his or her favorite thing about the Book of Mormon. You might like to sing "Count Your Blessings" (*Hymns,* no. 241) and talk about how that hymn relates to the message of Mormon 9:31.

Mormon 9:32–34
What are some significant facts about the Book of Mormon?

Show your family a picture of some of the characters Joseph Smith translated from the gold plates (see picture on p. 12). Ask if any family members know what language the characters are from. Read Mormon 9:32–34 together to find the correct answer. Ask:

- Why was that language chosen for the gold plates?
- What advantages did it have?
- What were disadvantages of using reformed Egyptian?
- According to Mosiah 8:19, what did the Lord provide so that the reformed Egyptian could be interpreted?
- Some people claim that Joseph Smith just made up the whole book. Do you think an uneducated young country boy could have invented this book?

ETHER

The Book of Ether is the record of the Jaredites, who came to the American continent at the time of the tower of Babel. (See Genesis 11.) It is named for the last Jaredite prophet, Ether, who witnessed and recorded the destruction of his people. Records left by Ether written on twenty-four gold plates were found by the people of Limhi and later translated by King Mosiah II. (See Mosiah 8:7–9; 28:10–19.) Moroni abridged this record and, after inserting a few of his own comments, placed it at the end of his father's book.

ETHER 1: THE JAREDITES ARE LED TO A PROMISED LAND

Ether 1:1–6
Where did the book of Ether come from?

Draw a line down the center of a large piece of paper. In a column on the left side write the following words: Limhi, Jaredites, twenty-four plates, Mosiah, Moroni, Tower, Ether. In a column on the right side, write the following references:

- "A Brief Explanation about the Book or Mormon," paragraph 1, number 3 in the front of the Book or Mormon.
- Mosiah 8:6–12.
- Mosiah 28:10–19.
- Ether 1:1–6.
- Genesis 11:1–9.

Assign family members one or more of the references. Have them search their reference and find which of the words the reference tells about. Have them report what they learned and write it next to the appropriate word on the paper. When all have reported, have someone summarize what your family has learned about where the book of Ether came from.

Ether 1:6–32
The importance of family histories

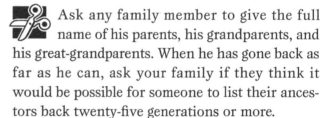 Ask any family member to give the full name of his parents, his grandparents, and his great-grandparents. When he has gone back as far as he can, ask your family if they think it would be possible for someone to list their ancestors back twenty-five generations or more.

Have your family review Ether 1:6–32 and ask:

- How many generations back could Ether list his ancestors?
- What does this list tell you about how the Jaredites felt about their families and genealogies?
- Why is keeping a family history important?

Fill in the names, dates, and places on a family group sheet for you and some of your ancestors. Ask your family how they would like to get to know some of their ancestors better. Discuss as a family what goals you might have for gathering family history information in the coming year.

Ether 1:33–43
What happened to Jared, his brother, and their families and friends at the tower?

Ask your family to think about a person that they really enjoy visiting with when they need spiritual guidance and help. Ask them why they chose that person. Read Ether 1:33–43 together and have your family look for who the people continued to call upon to help secure the blessings of God upon their friends and family. Ask:

- Why do you think they asked him?
- What could we do to help others feel this kind of respect and confidence regarding our relationship with the Lord and our spirituality?
- What are some of the ways the Jaredites were blessed because they sought the Lord throughout this time?
- What reason did the Lord give for blessing the Jaredites this way? (Verse 43.)

Encourage your family to rely on and pray for each other in the way this family did.

Ether 1:34–35
Who was the brother of Jared?

 Invite your family to read Ether 1:34–35 and look for the person that Jared turned to for direction. Ask them why they think the brother of Jared was asked to talk to the Lord for solutions to their problems.

Explain that Jared's brother is never named in the Book of Mormon. However, we do learn his name from an interesting story from the history of the Church. Share the following story:

"While residing in Kirtland Elder Reynolds Cahoon had a son born to him. One day when President Joseph Smith was passing his door he called the Prophet in and asked him to bless and name the baby. Joseph did so and gave the boy the name of Mahonri Moriancumer. When he had finished the blessing he laid the child on the bed, and turning to Elder Cahoon he said, the name I have given your son is the name of the brother of Jared; the Lord has just shown [or revealed] it to me. Elder William F. Cahoon, who was standing near heard the Prophet make this statement to his father; and this was the first time the name of the brother of Jared was known in the Church in this

dispensation." (George Reynolds, "The Jaredites," *Juvenile Instructor,* 1 May 1892, p. 282.)

Discuss possible reasons why his name is never listed in the scriptures. (Note that Ether 2:13 gives a possible clue to his name.) Testify that more important than his name might be the things that he accomplished. Encourage family members to watch for some of those accomplishments as they study the book of Ether.

Ether 1:40–43
What was the land "choice above all the lands of the earth"?

 Ask your family to say a place where they have always wanted to go and explain why. Discuss whether they would want others to go with them and who. Read together Ether 1:40–43 and ask:

- Where did the Lord want Jared to go?
- Who was to go with him?
- What land do you think is "choice above all the lands of the earth"?

Share the following explanation by Joseph Fielding Smith:

"The Book of Mormon informs us that the whole of America, both North and South, is a choice land above all other lands, in other words—Zion. The Lord told the Jaredites that he would lead them to a land 'which is choice above all the lands of the earth.' [Ether 1:42.] We understand that they landed in Central America where their kingdom existed the greater part of their residence in America." (*Doctrines of Salvation,* 3:73.)

ETHER 2: PREPARING TO TRAVEL TO THE PROMISED LAND

Ether 2:1–7
Master of the verses

Play "Master of the Verses" by handing out a piece of paper to each family member and explain that after they have studied Ether 2:1–7 they will be given a quiz to see who has "mastered" the information in the verses. Anyone who answers all questions correctly could receive a prize:

1. What families were included in the group we call the Jaredites? (Verse 1.)

2. Which verse talks about what may be the first fish tank? (Verse 2.)

3. How do you say "honey bee" in the language of the Jaredites? (Verse 3.)

4. How did the Jaredites know where they were supposed to go? (Verses 5–6.)

5. What was unique about the land they were taken to? (Verses 5, 7.)

6. Where was the Lord when he spoke to the brother of Jared? (Verse 5.)

7. What kind of watercraft did they use to cross the many waters? (Verse 6.)

Ask your family in what ways the journey of the Jaredites reminds them of the journey of Lehi's colony? (For example, they were both led to a promised land by the hand of the Lord.)

Ether 2:7–12
Could we be "swept off"?

Place a world map on the floor and place some small objects (candy, coins, game pieces, and so on) on it to represent people. Have a broom ready to use. Invite a family member to read Ether 2:7–12 aloud. Sweep off a few of the small objects each time the word "swept" is used. "Swept" could also be marked in everyone's scriptures. Ask:

• What does the Lord mean when he says people will be "swept off"?

• When did he say the sweeping would occur? (When they were ripe in iniquity.)

• What can we do to prevent being swept from the land of promise? (Verse 8.)

• What blessings come to those who righteously possess the land of promise? (Verse 12.)

• What can our family do to help strengthen our nation and its people?

Share the following statement by President Ezra Taft Benson and ask how it applies to your family:

"Too often we bask in our comfortable complacency and rationalize that the ravages of war, economic disaster, famine, and earthquake cannot happen here. Those who believe this are either not acquainted with the revelations of the Lord, or they do not believe them. Those who smugly think these calamities will not happen, that they somehow will be set aside because of the righteousness of the Saints, are deceived and will rue the day they harbored such a delusion. The Lord has warned and forewarned us against a day of great tribulation and given us counsel, through His servants, on how we can be prepared for these difficult times. Have we heeded His counsel?" (*The Teachings of Ezra Taft Benson,* p. 706.)

Ether 2:14–15
"Call upon the name of the Lord"

Ask your family to share their most memorable experience being corrected, chastised, or reprimanded. Have them tell how long it took and who did it. Invite a family member to read Ether 2:14–15 and ask:

• How did the brother of Jared's chastisement compare to yours?

• Why was he chastened?

• How did the chastening affect him?

Explain to your family that the brother of Jared had changed his pattern of personal prayer. To see his previous pattern, have family members scan through Ether 1:34–42 and note each occurrence of the phrase "cry unto the Lord." Also note the promise that came to the brother of Jared because of his prayers in Ether 1:43.

Next have someone read aloud Ether 2:13 and tell how long the Jaredites had remained in Moriancumer. Ask:

• Do you think there is any relationship

between being in Moriancumer four years and the brother of Jared's lack of prayer?

- What could that teach us about our personal prayers?
- What are some ways you could improve your personal prayers?

Ether 2:16–25
Barge-building contest

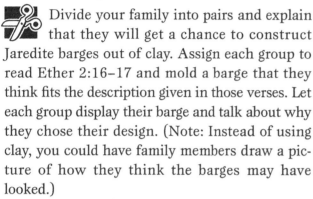 Divide your family into pairs and explain that they will get a chance to construct Jaredite barges out of clay. Assign each group to read Ether 2:16–17 and mold a barge that they think fits the description given in those verses. Let each group display their barge and talk about why they chose their design. (Note: Instead of using clay, you could have family members draw a picture of how they think the barges may have looked.)

After they have displayed their boats, ask the following questions:

- Even though we do not know precisely what the Jaredite barges looked like, how are they different from the kind of boats we see in our day?
- Would you like to sail across the ocean in boats built like your models?
- What problems do you see with them?

Read Ether 2:18–21 with your family and find the concerns the brother of Jared had with the barges. Ask your family what the Lord told him to do about the problem of getting air. Have them make their boats fit the changes the brother of Jared made in the Jaredite barges. Explain that the problem of getting light in the barges will be discussed in the next teaching idea.

Ether 2:23—3:28
The Lord's pattern of helping us solve problems

Ask a parent to share how he or she handles the situation when a child comes to talk about a problem. Have the parent talk about the pros and cons of the following approaches:

- Solve the problem yourself.
- Refuse to help and let the child work out a solution.
- Guide the child to find a solution.

Explain that Ether 2–3 contains a pattern the Lord used to help the brother of Jared with his problem. Share the pattern with your family and talk about the advantages of working through problems accordingly:

1. The Lord gives us personal responsibility and offers assistance for our problems. (2:23.)

2. The Lord helped clarify the problem for the brother of Jared. (2:23.)

3. The Lord clarified the objective. (2:25.)

4. The Lord helped the brother of Jared focus on realities and identify alternatives. (2:23–25.)

5. The Lord gave full responsibility to the brother of Jared. (2:25.)

6. The brother of Jared worked out a solution to his problem. (3:1–6.)

7. The Lord blessed and commended the brother of Jared. (3:6–28.)

ETHER 3: THE BROTHER OF JARED SEES THE PREMORTAL CHRIST

Ether 3:1–16
How can we get answers to our prayers?

Show sixteen marbles to your family. Ask them to name a story in the Book of Mormon that these sixteen marbles might represent.

Invite a family member to tell the story in Ether 2:18–25 in his or her own words. Make sure the person identifies the last problem mentioned by the brother of Jared and what the Lord said about it. Ask:

- How do you feel when you have a problem, go to the Lord for answers, and then don't feel like the Lord really gives a solution?
- What do you do about it?

As a family read Ether 3:1–5 to see what the brother of Jared did. (Point out that the marbles represent the sixteen stones the brother of Jared took to the mountain to be lighted by the Lord.) Discuss with your family what we might learn about personal revelation or getting answers to our prayers from the brother of Jared's example. Share the following quotation from Elder Henry B. Eyring:

"If you want to get revelation, do your homework. . . . The good works that really matter require the help of heaven. And the help of heaven requires working past the point of fatigue so far that only the meek and lowly will keep going long enough. The Lord doesn't put us through this test just to give us a grade; he does it because the process will change us." (*To Draw Closer to God,* pp. 94–95.)

Have family members identify things from the prayer in Ether 3:2–5 that show the brother of Jared was "meek and lowly."

Read also Ether 3:6–16 to show how the process changed the brother of Jared. It might be meaningful to have three family members read as one of the speakers in these verses: have one read the words of the brother of Jared, one read the words of the Lord, and one be the narrator. After reading these verses, ask:

- Do you think the brother of Jared would have had this experience if the Lord had simply handed him sixteen illuminated stones when he first asked in Ether 2? Why not?
- What does this experience teach about how we, too, might be "redeemed from the fall." (Verse 13.)

Share the following statement from President Brigham Young in which he identified the key element in this process:

"But if you had faith to go out to the graveyard and raise up scores of the dead, that alone would not make you Latter-day Saints, neither if the visions of your minds were opened so as to see the finger of God. What will? Keeping the commandments of the Lord, to walk humbly before your God, and before one another, to cease to do evil and learn to do well, and to live by every word that proceeds from the mouth of God; then you are a Latter-day Saint, whether you have visions or not." (*Journal of Discourses,* 3:211.)

Give each family member one of the marbles. Invite your family to put the marbles near their bed, not only to remind them to pray (a lesson learned by the brother of Jared in Ether 2) but also to remind them *how* to pray and what we must do to receive the help of the Lord.

Ether 3:17–28
What can we learn about the Urim and Thummim?

Have a family member read Ether 3:17. Then ask how much of what the brother of Jared saw is written in the Book of Mormon. Take turns reading Ether 3:21–28 to find out what happened to the record of the things the brother of Jared saw and learned. After reading these verses, ask:

- What did the brother of Jared see and learn? (Verse 25.)
- What instructions did the brother of Jared receive concerning what he saw and learned? (Verses 22–24, 27–28.)
- What are the "two stones" the Lord spoke about? (See Joseph Smith—History 1:33–35.)

Tell your family that the Prophet Joseph Smith's mother said that "this Urim and Thummim [he received from Moroni] was the same that was given to the brother of Jared upon the mount." (*The Revised and Enhanced History of Joseph Smith by His Mother Lucy Mack Smith,* p. 107.)

Have your family read the first paragraph of the entry for "Urim and Thummim" in the LDS Bible Dictionary (p. 786). Ask:

- What does the name *Urim and Thummim* mean?
- What is the purpose of the Urim and Thummim?

339

Share with your family the following statement by Elder Joseph Fielding Smith:

"The Lord has placed us on probation as members of the Church. He has given us the Book of Mormon, which is the lesser part, to building up our faith through our obedience to the counsels which it contains, and when we ourselves, members of the Church, are willing to keep the commandments as they have been given to us and show our faith as the Nephites did for a short period of time, then the Lord is ready to bring forth the other record and give it to us, but we are not ready now to receive it. Why? Because we have not lived up to the requirements in this probationary state in the reading of the record which had been given to us and in following its counsels." (Conference Report, October 1961, p. 20.)

ETHER 4: MORONI SEALS UP THE WRITINGS OF THE BROTHER OF JARED

Ether 4:1–2
Why keep a journal?

Ask your family to read Ether 4:1–2 and look for what the Lord commanded the brother of Jared to do. Ask if we have been given a similar commandment today. Share this statement from President Spencer W. Kimball:

"Every person should keep a journal and every person can keep a journal." ("Let Us Move Forward and Upward," *Ensign*, May 1979, p. 84.)

Ask:

- Who keeps a journal?
- How often do you write in it?
- What kind of things might be included in a journal?

If you have a journal, you may want to show it to your family and share an experience from it or have a family member share an experience he or she has written. You could share this example:

"My mother had a serious heart condition. She was told if she ever had a baby, she would probably die. But mother felt strongly she should have a baby. When I was only nine weeks old, my mother died. She loved me enough to willingly give her life for me. Those who knew mother best found it painful to talk about her, so I never learned much about her. When I was seventeen, my father gave me one of my dearest possessions. It was a journal my mother had written. She had kept it each day for one short year of her life. I had in my hands one year of my mother's life! She had been a school teacher in Wyoming that year, and through her own words she became for me a real person at last. She cried, she struggled, she laughed, she grumbled, she learned of her heart condition, she met and fell in love with my father, and I shared it all with her! That record, that precious, loved record—it seemed to me at that time that it was all I had of her." (See "For Your Remembrance: A Presentation on Record Keeping" [audiovisual presentation, 1975 MIA June Conference].)" (*Family Home Evening Resource Book*, p. 199.)

Have family members refer back to Ether 4:1–2 and discuss the following questions:

- Why do you think the Lord commanded the brother of Jared to record his experiences?
- Why do you think the Lord wants us to record our experiences?
- What event was to occur before the writings were made known?

Ether 4:3–7
Sealing up the writings

Ask your family if they have ever heard of the "sealed portion" of the Book of Mormon. Allow them to tell what they know about it. Then read together Ether 4:3–7 and discuss the following questions:

- Who does "I" refer to in verses 3–6? (Moroni).
- How did Moroni describe the vision of the brother of Jared? (Verse 4.)

- According to Ether 3:26, what did the brother of Jared see?
- What did the Lord command Moroni to do with the brother of Jared's record and the interpreters? (Verses 3, 5.)
- When will we be able to receive these records? (Verses 6–7.)
- What do you think is recorded on the "sealed portion"? (See 2 Nephi 27:7–10.)

Share the following statement from Elder Jeffrey R. Holland:

"Those sealed plates constitute the sealed portion of the Book of Mormon, which Joseph Smith did not translate. Furthermore, they will remain sealed, literally as well as figuratively, until future generations 'shall exercise faith in me, saith the Lord, even as the brother of Jared did . . .'

"The full measure of this unprecedented and unexcelled vision . . . are yet to be made known." (*Christ and the New Covenant,* p. 25.)

Ether 4:12–19
"Come unto me"

Hold up a picture of Jesus Christ. Ask your family to stand across the room from you with their scriptures. Have one family member read Ether 4:12–13 aloud and tell what Jesus asks us to do in those verses. (Come unto him.) Ask your family how we can know what choices lead to him. (Things that persuade us to do good.)

Invite family members to search Ether 4:14–19. Tell them that every time they find something good we can do, something that leads to Jesus Christ, to say it out loud. Have them also tell which verse it comes from. For every correct answer a family member gives, allow that person to take one step toward you. Continue this activity until someone reaches the picture of Jesus Christ.

You may also wish to have family members talk about choices they made in the past week that led to Jesus Christ, and choices they made that took them further away from him. Share ideas of how your family can draw closer to the Savior and what blessings come as we do.

ETHER 5: THREE WITNESSES

Ether 5:1
Do not touch

 Share with your family the following story about Emma Smith:

"When asked if she had seen the plates, Emma said she had not, but then gave this interesting description of her own experience with them: 'The Plates often lay on the table without any attempt at concealment, wrapped in a small linen tablecloth which I had given him to fold them in. I once felt the plates as they thus lay on the table, tracing their outline and shape. They seemed to be pliable like thick paper, and would rustle with a metallic sound when the edges were moved by the thumb, as one does sometimes thumb the edges of a book.'" (As cited in Gracia N. Jones, *Emma and Joseph, Their Divine Mission,* p. 37.)

Ask your family why Emma did not simply remove the cloth and handle and examine the gold plates. Have someone read Ether 5:1 for an answer. (Not even the Prophet Joseph was to touch them and seek to translate them—they were forbidden until the Lord gave permission. Emma was obedient to this command as well.)

Remind your family that occasionally there are things that the Lord forbids us to do. We show our faith in Heavenly Father and Jesus Christ—that they know how to best bless us—when we are obedient to their counsel.

Ether 5:2–6
Witnesses of the Book of Mormon

To demonstrate the principle of witnesses, ask your family to imagine that one morning you go to school as usual. After class has been going about fifteen minutes, one of your classmates comes in late. The teacher asks him why he is late, and he explains that some people are setting up a circus in the school parking lot and he couldn't help but stop and watch. He is known as a prankster and a goof-off. Ask your family if they believe the story about the circus and explain why or why not.

Tell your family to suppose that one minute later another student comes into the room. He has been sent to deliver some papers to your teacher from the school office. This student, though not known as a prankster himself, is a friend to the prankster in your class. You ask him if he saw anything in the school parking lot, and he says, "Yeah, they're setting up a circus out there." Ask your family if they believe the circus story now and explain why or why not.

Next, tell your family to suppose that a teacher comes into your class. He is also a coach, and the two previous boys are on his team. As he opens the door to enter, you hear the unmistakable sounds of a circus calliope. He speaks to your teacher and says, "Hey, did you know they were setting up a circus in the school parking lot?" Ask your family if they believe the circus story now and explain why or why not.

Finally, tell your family to suppose that your mother comes into the room and brings you a book that you forgot. You ask her if she saw anything unusual in the school parking lot. She replies, "I was wondering about that. It looks like they're setting up a circus out there." Discuss with your family the following questions:

- Now would you believe that there is a circus out there?
- How might your belief in the story change with the additional witnesses?
- How does physical evidence make the story more believable?
- Would it make a difference who the witnesses were?
- Why would the testimony of your mother make the most difference?

Explain that although no one was to open the sealed portion of the Book of Mormon plates, we do have witnesses that they exist. Read Ether 5:2–4 with your family and ask them the following questions:

- Who would be shown the plates?
- How would they see them?
- For what purpose would they be shown these things?

Have your family turn to Doctrine and Covenants 17 and read the section heading and verses 1–8. Here you learn some of the history behind the fulfillment of the promise in Ether 5, along with the instruction of the Lord to those who would be the witnesses. Share the following story with your family about the fulfillment of this promise:

"David Whitmer explained: 'We went out into the woods, near by, and sat down on a log and talked awhile. We then kneeled down and prayed. Joseph prayed. We then got up and sat down on the log and were talking, when all at once a light came down from above us and encircled us for quite a little distance around; and the angel stood before us.' This angel was Moroni. David said that he 'was dressed in white, and spoke and called me by name and said "Blessed is he that keepeth His commandments."' A table was set before us and on it the records were placed. The Records of the Nephites, from which the Book of Mormon was translated, the brass plates, the Ball of Directors, the sword of Laban and other plates.' While the men were viewing these things, they heard a voice that said: 'These plates have been revealed by the power of God, and they have been translated by the power of God. The translation of them which you have seen is correct, and I command you to bear record of what you now see and hear.'" (*Our Heritage: A Brief History of The Church of Jesus Christ of Latter-day Saints,* p. 10.)

Show your family the testimony of these three men in the front pages of the Book of Mormon. Ask them why they think the Lord showed only these men the plates. Why does he not have the whole world see them? Share the following statement by Elder Joseph Fielding Smith as part of an answer to that question:

"Personal visitations might become dim as time goes on, but this guidance of the Holy Ghost is renewed and continued, day after day, year after year, if we live to be worthy of it." (*Doctrines of Salvation*, 1:44.)

Read Ether 5:5 and ask:

- What does the Lord want the witness of the Book of Mormon to lead to?
- How can repenting and coming unto the Father and the Son save us?
- How is this different from, and yet more powerful than, having a spectacular witness?

Testify that the Holy Ghost is a more powerful witness than actually seeing the plates. The Holy Ghost can lead people to Christ through faith and repentance. Each of the Three Witnesses fell away from the Church at one time or another (although two of them came back). Their spectacular manifestation did not make them stronger than others who received the witness of the Holy Ghost, conformed their lives to the teachings of Christ, and stayed true to the end.

Ether 5:6
Who will stand by God?

 Discuss with your family the following questions:

- What do you imagine "the judgment bar of God" will be like?
- Who do you think will be there?
- What would be the purpose of someone else being there besides you and God?
- If you could choose an apostle or prophet to stand by you on judgment day, who would you choose and why?

Read Ether 5:6 and then ask:

- Who will "stand before God at the last day"?
- Why do you think Moroni will be there?
- What do you think it will be like to stand next to him and also be in the presence of God?
- What question do you think Moroni might ask us?
- What would you want to be able to say to him?

ETHER 6: BY FAITH THE JAREDITES REACH THE PROMISED LAND

Ether 6:1–4
Who is the rock?

 Show your family a rock with the reference Ether 6:1–4 written on it. Read those verses together and mark each time the word "stone" or "stones" appears. Ask:

- What did the stones do for the Jaredites?
- Why would the journey have been impossible without them?

Have a family member read 2 Samuel 22:2 and Helaman 5:12 to find what person is often referred to as the "stone." (See also Topical Guide, "Jesus Christ, Rock," p. 254.) Discuss who could be compared with the stones in the Jaredite barges. Re-read Ether 6:2–3 and replace the word "stone" with "Jesus Christ." Ask your family the following:

- How is Jesus our light?
- What can his light do for us?
- If the "great waters" represent our journey toward the celestial kingdom, how can Jesus Christ help us along the path?

Ether 6:4
What would you bring on the journey?

 Show your family a suitcase. Tell them to imagine going on a journey across the ocean that might take a year or more. Talk about what items they would pack for the journey. List the items your family mentions on a piece of paper and place it in the suitcase.

Read Ether 6:4 and look for some of the items the Jaredites brought on their journey. Discuss as a family how long they think they could live with only these necessities.

Ether 6:5–12
Faith is the moving cause of all action

 Tell your family a personal experience about following the Lord, especially under difficult circumstances or tremendous cost. Focus your experience on the faith you exercised to accomplish the Lord's commandment. Also share why that experience caused you to feel gratitude and reverence for the Lord. (An example might be serving a mission, accepting a difficult Church calling, or keeping a commandment that was particularly difficult for you.)

When you have finished sharing your story, ask:

- Why does the Lord call on us to do difficult things?
- What role does our faith play in accomplishing the Lord's commandments?
- Why is showing gratitude for the Lord so important?

Have family members read Ether 6:5–12 and look for verses that demonstrate the following:

- The Jaredites' journey would be especially difficult.
- The Jaredites exercised great faith under difficult circumstances.
- The Jaredites recognized the importance of gratitude at all times.

Have family members share what they discovered. Talk about the lessons your family can learn from the Jaredite example.

Ether 6:13–17
What does it mean to be "taught from on high"?

Ask your family to imagine moving to a new world where no one had ever lived before. There would be no roads, no cities, and no stores. How do you think you would get along?

Read together Ether 6:13–17 and discuss the following questions:

- What do you think it means that the Jaredites were "taught from on high"? (Verse 17.)
- Why would it be important for the Jaredites to receive revelation at this time?
- What determines whether or not we receive revelation?

Tell your family that Elder Bruce R. McConkie taught there are three ways to receive personal revelation: search the scriptures, keep the commandments, and ask in faith. He said, "Any person who will do this will get his heart so in tune with the infinite that there will come into his being, from the 'still small voice,' the eternal realities of religion. As he progresses and advances and comes nearer to God, there will be a day when he will entertain angels, when he will see visions, and the final end is to view the face of God." (*BYU Speeches of the Year, 1967*, p. 8.)

Ether 6:18–30
Why did the Jaredites prosper?

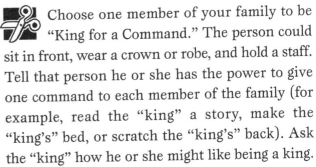 Choose one member of your family to be "King for a Command." The person could sit in front, wear a crown or robe, and hold a staff. Tell that person he or she has the power to give one command to each member of the family (for example, read the "king" a story, make the "king's" bed, or scratch the "king's" back). Ask the "king" how he or she might like being a king.

When you have finished, have your family scan Ether 6:18–30 to find who became king of the Jaredites. Ask:

- Why do you think Pagag refused to be king?
- According to verse 30, how good of a king do you think Oriah was?
- What did the brother of Jared say could go wrong when one person receives the power of being king? (Verse 23.)
- Why would being ruled by kings be dangerous?
- How did you feel when our family had a king ruling for just a short time? Why?

Divide your family into two groups. Have one group study 1 Samuel 8:10–18 and the other study Mosiah 29:16–23. Ask each group to look for teachings about kings and how each account compares with Ether 6:18–30. Have a member of each group share what they learned.

ETHER 7: MANY KINGS AND MUCH STRIFE

Ether 7:1–27
Actions and their consequences

 Begin your scripture study by singing or reading "Do What is Right" (*Hymns,* no. 237). Going along with the chorus of that hymn, share with your family the following observation of Elder Neal A. Maxwell:

"Another mistake we make is that we foolishly think we are free to choose, without wanting the consequences of those choices! (See Alma 29:4.) Bainville, the French philosopher, said, 'One must want the consequences of what one wants.'" ("The Holy Ghost: Glorifying Christ," *Ensign,* July 2002, p. 59.)

There are many people mentioned in Ether 7. Make a chart that has three columns on a large sheet of paper or poster board with the following headings: Who?, Righteous or Wicked?, Consequences of Their Actions on Themselves and Others.

Have someone serve as a scribe while the family reads aloud the chapter. Stop after each verse and record the names of any new people mentioned in the verse. Determine (if you can) whether they were righteous or wicked and what consequences came to them or others based on their actions. Sometimes you will have to "read between the lines" and visualize how the things described may have affected other people involved—like parents, other family members, citizens of the community and so forth.

After completing this for the whole chapter, ask family members to suggest lessons that can be learned from this chapter. Some of them might include:

- The words of the prophets will be fulfilled (such as Ether 6:22–23).
- "Wickedness never was happiness." (Alma 41:10.)
- Repentance leads to the blessings of heaven. (See Ether 7:25–27.)

- One of the reasons Heavenly Father wants us to keep the commandments is because breaking them usually causes bad things for others (as well as ourselves).

Invite family members to consider what kind of consequences they want in life and to more fully live in a way that will bring about those consequences.

ETHER 8: SECRET COMBINATIONS ARE OF THE DEVIL

Ether 8:2–26
What is the cure for secret combinations?

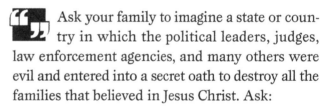 Ask your family to imagine a state or country in which the political leaders, judges, law enforcement agencies, and many others were evil and entered into a secret oath to destroy all the families that believed in Jesus Christ. Ask:

- What might conditions be like in such a place?
- Why would it be difficult to trust anyone?
- How would you know if a person loved God more than Satan?

Read the following statement from Elder M. Russell Ballard:

"The Book of Mormon teaches that secret combinations engaged in crime present a serious challenge, not just to individuals and families but to entire civilizations. Among today's secret combinations are gangs, drug cartels, and organized crime families. . . . They have secret signs and code words. They participate in secret rites and initiation ceremonies. Among their purposes are to 'murder, and plunder, and steal, and commit whoredoms and all manner of wickedness, contrary to the laws of their country and also the laws of their God' [Helaman 6:23]." ("Standing for Truth and Right," *Ensign,* November 1997, p .38.)

Remind your family that after the death of Jared and his brother, the Jaredites were ruled by a succession of kings. Have one family member read aloud D&C 121:39 and tell what that verse means to him or her.

Read Ether 8:2–3 aloud, and ask:

- What is happening here to indicate there is contention for the chance to become king?
- What did Jared do to his father?
- What do you imagine family life would be like in a home where a son would go to war against his father and put him into captivity?
- Which son in the premortal existence warred against his Father and led many astray?
- What are some ways Satan has continued that rebellion on earth?

Remind your family that the man named Jared in this chapter was a descendant of the Jared referred to in Ether 1–6. Read Ether 8:9–12 and ask your family what plan Jared's daughter created to make her father the king. According to Ether 8:13–18, how did this plan introduce secret combinations in the land?

Take turns reading Ether 8:21–26 and ask:

- What did Moroni say were the dangers of secret combinations?
- What do verses 23 and 26 teach us about why Moroni included these things in his record?
- What do verses 23–25 teach us about how to recognize secret combinations and protect ourselves from them?

Have a family member read aloud Helaman 6:37 and Alma 37:31. Talk about some of the cures we can implement to help overcome secret combinations today. (See also Alma 37:33–37.)

ETHER 9: SECRET COMBINATIONS THREATEN THE JAREDITES

Ether 9:1–1–35
What does the desire for power and gain lead people to do?

 Write the following phrase on a sheet of paper and show it to your family: "Power

tends to corrupt, and absolute power corrupts absolutely." (Lord Acton, in a letter to Bishop Mandell Creighton, 1887.) Discuss what that phrase might mean and ask your family to think of scriptural examples of its truth (King Saul, King Noah, and so on). Do you think power always corrupts? Think of examples where it didn't. (King Mosiah, King Benjamin, Jesus Christ, and so on.)

List the following names in a column on sheet of paper: Omer, Jared, Akish, Emer, Coriantum, Com, Heth. Have your family scan Ether 9 (and Ether 10:1) looking for the listed names. As they find each name, have them determine whether power corrupted that person or not. Then discuss each name and discover why some were corrupted and some were not. What can we learn from this exercise that might help us remain faithful as we are given opportunities for power in our lives.

Ether 9:1–14
The Jaredites suffer because of wickedness

Show a picture of your family. Invite family members to share different ways that families are under attack today. Ask:

- What influences exist in the world today that tend to harm families?
- What do you think is ultimately behind these influences?
- Why do you think Satan desires to destroy the family?

Tell your family that they are going to look at a snapshot of a Jaredite family. Have them silently read Ether 9:1–14 and be prepared to share the good and bad they noticed that influenced this family. Ask:

- Why do you think Omer was warned to depart? (Verses 2–3.)
- What do you think influenced his family not to love one another? (Verses 1, 4–6.)
- How would you describe the family life of

these people as a result of their wickedness? (Verses 5, 7–10.)

- Why do secrets and the desire for gain and power have such an evil influence on people? (Verses 1, 6, 11.)
- Why do you think Omer was placed back upon the throne as king? (Verse 13.)
- How might love keep Satan from being able to destroy a family?

Discuss what each family member can do to increase the feelings of love in your family.

Ether 9:15–35
The pride cycle

Tell your family that often in the Book of Mormon we see the people repeat a pattern of righteousness to wickedness that has been called "the pride cycle." It has been described in the following statement:

"In the Book of Mormon's pride cycle, the righteous tend to become rich because they are industrious, honest, living in harmony with God's laws, peaceable. But then they tend to become caught up in their possessions: pride, expensive buildings and clothes, stark social divisions, spiritual and governmental disintegration follow." (Todd M. Compton, "The Spirituality of the Outcast in the Book of Mormon," *Journal of Book of Mormon Studies,* Spring 1993, p. 157.)

Explain that Ether 9:15–35 is a good place to see an example of this cycle. Make a chart similar to the one below and review the elements in "the pride cycle":

Divide the verses in the left column among family members. Invite them to read their assigned

verses looking for evidence that the Jaredites were living according to the associated element of "the pride cycle." (See elements listed in the center column.) Write in the right column the evidence shared by your family. Some of the following questions might help your family see the events that fulfill "the pride cycle":

- What was prosperity like during the reigns of Emer and Coriantum? (Verses 15–25.)
- What did the people begin to do during the reign of Heth that showed their wickedness? (Verses 26–27.)
- What did the Lord do to warn the people of impending judgments from God? (Verses 28–29.)
- What judgments did the Lord send upon the people to humble them? (Verses 30–33.)
- What effect did God's judgments have upon the people? (Verses 34–35.)

Following the completion of the chart, discuss with your family why this is called "the pride cycle." Have your family imagine what it might be like to be wealthy, righteous, and living in peace and prosperity. Ask:

- Can people be wealthy and still remain righteous?
- How would our family, schools, and communities be different?
- Where do you think we stand as a country on "the pride cycle"?
- What can we do to remain humble amid our great prosperity?

Verses	"The pride cycle"	What occurred among the Jaredites
15–25	Prosperity and blessings	
26–27	Pride and sin	
28–29	Chastening	
30–33	God's judgments	
34–35	Humility and Repentance	

ETHER 10: GOOD AND BAD KINGS

Ether 10:1–34
What difference does a king make?

 Make a chart like the one below on a separate piece of paper. As your family reads Ether 10, ask them to help fill in the missing information. They should write the name of the king in the blank space next to the verses. Also ask them to put a smiley face in the circle if the king is righteous and a frowny face if the king is wicked. In the space to the right, ask family members to list a principle or teaching they learned from that king.

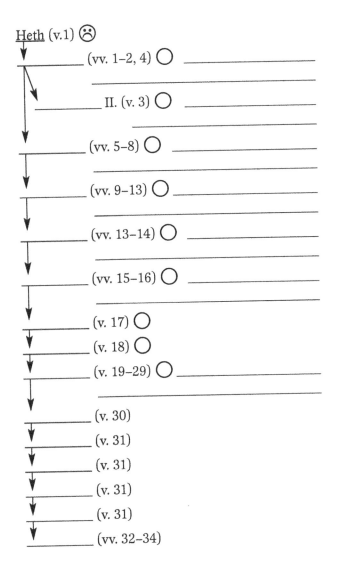

ETHER 11: PROPHETS, PEACE, AND PROSPERITY

Ether 11:1–23
The relationship of prophets to wickedness and righteousness

Read Ether 11 aloud as a family. As you read, have someone keep track of the kings by writing on a sheet of paper a royal pedigree chart like the following:

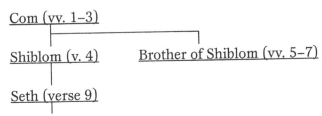

And so forth.

After going through the chapter and naming all the kings, identify which ones were described as wicked or righteous. Ask your family why they think so many were wicked. What did the people do repeatedly that indicated wickedness and trouble ahead? (Rejected the prophets; see verses 1–3, 5–7, 12–13, 20–22.)

Read to your family the following statement by Elder Henry B. Eyring:

"Because the Lord is kind, He calls servants to warn people of danger. That call to warn is made harder and more important by the fact that the warnings of most worth are about dangers that people don't yet think are real. . . .

"Those of us who have been parents have felt the anxiety of sensing danger our children cannot yet see. Few prayers are so fervent as those of a parent asking to know how to touch a child to move away from danger. Most of us have felt the blessing of hearing and heeding the warning voice of a parent.

"I can still remember my mother speaking softly to me one Saturday afternoon when, as a little boy, I asked her for permission to do something I thought was perfectly reasonable and which she knew was dangerous. I still am amazed at the power she was granted, I believe from the Lord, to turn me around with so few words. As I remember them, they were: "Oh, I suppose you could do that. But the choice is yours." The only warning was in the emphasis she put on the words could and choice. Yet that was enough for me." ("A Voice of Warning," *Ensign,* November 1998, p. 32.)

Tell your family of your love and concern for them and your desire for them to avoid the consequences of wickedness. Share an example of how heeding the word of the prophets has blessed you and your family. Discuss some of the warnings prophets have given in our day and invite them to evaluate how the family has responded to these warnings. Bear testimony that following the counsel of the prophets will, in large measure, determine the success and happiness of the family.

ETHER 12: THE IMPORTANCE OF FAITH AND COMING UNTO CHRIST

Ether 12:1–4
What can be an "anchor" in your life?

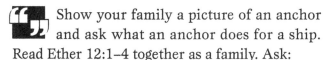 Show your family a picture of an anchor and ask what an anchor does for a ship. Read Ether 12:1–4 together as a family. Ask:

- What did the prophet Ether say acts "as an anchor to the souls"?
- How can our faith be like an anchor during "storms" in our lives?

Share this message from Elder M. Russell Ballard:

"Just as ships need anchors to keep them from drifting away on the open seas, people need spiritual anchors in their lives if they are to remain steadfast and not drift into the sea of temptation and sin. Faith in God and His Son, the Lord Jesus Christ, is the main anchor we must have in our lives to hold us fast during times of social turbulence and wickedness that seem to be everywhere today." ("Steadfast in Christ," *Ensign,* December 1993, p. 50.)

Discuss as a family the blessings that can come if Christ is our anchor.

Ether 12:5–6
How faith blesses lives

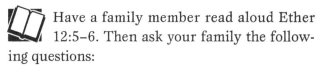 Have a family member read aloud Ether 12:5–6. Then ask your family the following questions:

- Why didn't the people believe the "great and marvelous things" Ether prophesied?
- How did Moroni define faith? (See also Hebrews 11:1 and Alma 32:21.)
- What do you think it means that we "receive no witness until after the trial of [our] faith"? (See also D&C 58:2–4.)

Share the following story told by Elder Boyd K. Packer:

"Shortly after I was called as a General Authority, I went to Elder Harold B. Lee for counsel. He listened very carefully to my problem and suggested that I see President David O. McKay. President McKay counseled me as to the direction I should go. I was very willing to be obedient but saw no way possible for me to do as he counseled me to do.

"I returned to Elder Lee and told him that I saw no way to move in the direction I was counseled to go. He said, 'The trouble with you is you want to see the end from the beginning.' I replied that I would like to see at least a step or two ahead. Then came the lesson of a lifetime: 'You must learn to walk to the edge of the light, and then a few steps into the darkness; then the light will appear and show the way before you.' Then he quoted these 18 words from the Book of Mormon:

"'Dispute not because ye see not, for ye receive no witness until after the trial of your faith.'

"Those 18 words from Moroni have been like a beacon light to me." ("The Edge of the Light," *BYU Today,* March 1991, pp. 22–23.)

Ask your family to think about some of the big questions or concerns they have in their lives. Discuss how Elder Packer's example of walking by faith could be applied to their problems.

Ether 12:7–22

The blessings of faith

Tell your family that in Ether 12:7–22, Moroni cites various miracles or wonders as examples of faith (a similar list is found in Hebrews 11). Invite family members to read Ether 12:7–22 and mark each time the word "faith" appears. Also have each family member choose a favorite example of the power of faith (either one of the examples Moroni cites or another example from the scriptures) and share why that example is powerful. Tell your family that they can find more information by using the footnotes in their scriptures. After everyone has shared an example, discuss some of the blessings your family has received because of faith.

Ether 12:23–27

How can we turn weaknesses into strengths?

Ask your family, "If you had important news to share with somebody else, would you prefer to do it in writing or by speaking to that person. Why?" Read together Ether 12:23–26. Ask:

- What was Moroni's concern about how the Gentiles would receive his record?
- What was the Lord's response?
- Why is meekness important in reading the scriptures?

Have family members think of a weakness they have that they would like to overcome. Ask what they would be willing to give or do to overcome this weakness. Have a family member read aloud Ether 12:27; have the others identify the source of our weakness. Share the following ideas from Elder Hartman Rector, Jr.:

"Where do you suppose we get these weaknesses? If you pose this question to a group of Saints, it will astound you how many different answers you get to this particular question. Some will say that they are responsible for their own weaknesses; well, if you keep your weaknesses, that's true, but that is not where they come from.

Another will say weaknesses come from heredity or environment; in either instance, we are passing the responsibility to someone else, either our parents or our neighborhood. Both of these sources have great influence upon us, but they do not give us our weaknesses. Still another may blame Lucifer, the devil, for their weaknesses; surely he is always on the job, but this is not where we get our weaknesses, either. Where do they really come from? The Lord tells us the answer to this question very plainly in the Book of Mormon. (Ether 12:27). So where do we get our weaknesses? We get them from the Lord; the Lord gives us weakness so we will be humble. This makes us teachable. Now don't misunderstand me—the Lord is not responsible for the sin; he is only responsible for the weakness. It seems that all men have weaknesses in one form or another, character traits that make one more subject to a particular temptation than another. . . . Giving us weakness, however, is one of the Lord's ways of getting our attention. He says that this is the means he uses to make us humble, but he also says that if we will come unto him and have faith in him, he will make us strong wherein we are weak. I know this is the truth." (Conference Report, April 1970, pp. 139–40.)

Discuss with your family the following questions:

- What can we do to help us recognize weaknesses we have? (Come unto Christ.)
- Why do you think the Lord gives us weaknesses?
- How can we overcome weaknesses and become strong in the areas where we were weak?

To help in personal application, read the scripture below and have family members fill in the blanks with their own names:

And if _____ comes unto me, I will show unto _____ his or her weakness. I give unto _____ weakness that _____ may be humble; and my grace is sufficient for all men that humble themselves before me; for if _____ humbles himself or herself before me, and has faith in me, then will I make weak things become strong unto _____.

Invite family members to share examples of the fulfillment of this promise in the scriptures, their own lives, or the lives of others.

Ether 12:28–41
Faith, hope, and charity

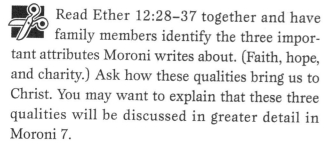 Read Ether 12:28–37 together and have family members identify the three important attributes Moroni writes about. (Faith, hope, and charity.) Ask how these qualities bring us to Christ. You may want to explain that these three qualities will be discussed in greater detail in Moroni 7.

Tell your family you are going to play a game called "Seek." Tell them that the object of the game is to be able to find a picture of Jesus within a certain time, and if they do they will get a treat. Ask for a volunteer to leave the room momentarily. While the family member is out of the room, hide a picture of the Savior. Invite the family member back into the room and let him or her begin searching. If the person has difficulty finding the picture, the rest of the family can help by saying "warmer" when the one seeking the picture is moving closer to it and by saying "colder" when the person is moving farther away from the picture. When the person has found the picture, give him or her a treat or reward. You could have several family members take a turn being the one trying to find the picture.

After the game, have a family member read aloud Ether 12:38–41. Ask:

- What does Moroni commend us to do?
- How can we "liken" the game we just played to what Moroni and all prophets ask us to do?
- In what ways can you "seek Jesus" in your life?
- What are some things we could do to bring us closer to him?

- How can we know if we are getting closer to him or moving farther away?
- What does the Lord promise those who seek him?
- Why do you think it would be worth the effort?

ETHER 13: ETHER RECORDS THE DESTRUCTION OF THE JAREDITES

Ether 13:1–2, 13–14
Why did the Jaredites reject their prophet, Ether?

Ask your family if they have ever been present when something was being destroyed (an old building, an ant pile, a friend's toy, a student's homework assignment, and so on). What kinds of feelings did you or others have? After family members have had a chance to share their experiences, share the following statement from Elder Sterling W. Sill:

"The Jaredites became a great nation and flourished upon this land for approximately nineteen hundred years, or almost the exact length of time that has elapsed since the birth of Jesus to our own day. . . . The Jaredites loved this land and enjoyed its blessings, as we have done. The Lord promised them that there should be no greater nation on the earth than the one which he should raise up for them upon this land." (Conference Report, April 1958, p. 11.)

Ask:

- Why do you think the Jaredites lasted so long as a great nation?
- What would it be like to see a great nation destroyed?
- What would bring such a great nation to an end?

Have your family read Ether 13:1–2, 13–14 and look for clues to help answer the questions listed above. Ask your family:

• How did the Jaredites in Ether's day respond to his teachings?

• In what ways did rejecting Ether as a prophet lead to the Jaredite's destruction?

• What did Ether have in common with Moroni and what feelings might they have shared?

• What do you think Moroni wanted us to learn by including the Jaredite record in the Book of Mormon?

Discuss how your family can help preserve this land as a choice and chosen place. Focus on the importance of following the Lord's prophets.

Ether 13:1–12
What did Ether see?

Tell your family that Moroni shared a glimpse into the great prophecies of the Jaredite prophet Ether. Have family members scan Ether 13:1–12 and see if they can find verses that refer to three different Jerusalems. Invite them to share answers as they find them. Since the answers may not be easily found, help your family discover and mark them by studying the following outline:

Jerusalem #1

Ether 13:3: This New Jerusalem will "come down out of heaven," and its people will be arrayed in white garments, washed by the blood of the Lamb. According to Elder Bruce R. McConkie, this Jerusalem is "Enoch's city—the City of Holiness that was taken up into heaven (see Moses 7:13–21) [which] will come down from heaven and be united with the earthly New Jerusalem." (*Doctrinal New Testament Commentary,* 3:581.) This uniting with the earthly New Jerusalem (see Jerusalem #2) is described in Ether 13:10 and in Moses 7:62–64.

Jerusalem #2

Ether 13:4, 6, 8: This New Jerusalem will be built by faithful Saints, "remnant[s] of the seed of Joseph" (verse 6), on the American continent (which Ether knew as "a choice land above all

others" [verse 2]). Revelation through the prophet Joseph Smith indicates that this city will also be known as the city of Zion and will be built in Missouri. (See D&C 57:1–2.) At the Second Coming it will be joined by the City of Enoch (see Moses 7:62–64), and the two cities will become one New Jerusalem.

Jerusalem #3

Ether 13:5, 11: This Jerusalem is the one we read about in the Old and New Testaments. It still exists today in Israel. Lehi lived there, and Jesus ended his mortal ministry there. It will also be rebuilt and inhabited by gathered Israel. At the Second Coming, it too will be "a holy city unto the Lord" (verse 5).

Ether 13:15–31
Fight to the death

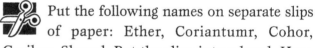
Put the following names on separate slips of paper: Ether, Coriantumr, Cohor, Corihor, Shared. Put the slips into a bowl. Have each family member draw one or more slips out of the bowl without letting anyone else see the name they drew. Have your family read Ether 13:15–31 to themselves, paying special attention to the name they drew. After a minute or two of preparation, have them stand and speak as the person they were assigned without giving the name. Ask them to describe the events in Ether 13 from that person's point of view. Invite other family members to guess which person in Ether 13 is being acted out.

As a summary, you might ask some of the following questions:

• How did the people attempt to destroy Coriantumr? (Verse 15.)

• Why was Coriantumr able to withstand their attacks? (Verse 16.)

• What did Ether observe? (Verse 18.)

• What would Coriantumr and his family and people suffer if they failed to repent? (Verse 21.)

- Why do you think the Jaredites wanted to kill Ether? (Verse 22.)
- How would you describe the struggle between Coriantumr and Shared? (Verses 23–28.)
- After he slew Shared, why didn't Coriantumr do battle for two years? (Verse 31.)
- What were the other Jaredite people doing during those two years? (Verse 31.)

Discuss with your family what it might have been like to live during these years and what might lead a people to resort to such senseless destruction. Ask, "What does this example teach you about the consequences of seeking for power and gain, and the effects of letting anger and revenge grow in our hearts?"

ETHER 14: THE AWFUL CONSEQUENCES OF WICKEDNESS

Ether 14:1–31
What are the consequences of war?

 Have a family discussion about the following questions:

- How many movies, television programs, or news reports are there that have war as a topic or theme?
- How is war glorified in today's movies?
- Why do you think people sometimes glorify war?
- Can you see any problems in war, especially glorifying war?

Write the following in a column down the left side of a piece of paper:

Carnage
Cruelty
Distrust
Death
Fear
Revenge
Sorrow
Lust for power

Invite your family to look for these concepts while you read Ether 14:1–31 together. Have them point out each time one of the concepts is found in a verse. Tally the number for each word and write the total of how often each concept is used. At the end of the chapter, go back and ask if war sounds glorious according to what they just learned.

Share the following statement made by President David O. McKay:

"When I think or read of the horrors of the most wicked of wars now going on in Europe, when I picture young men who have been forced to carry the gun and slay their fellow men . . . when I read of these men lying heaped in trenches, and in fancy hear their groans as they turn their ghastly faces to heaven, when I think of the devastated towns and see fleeing from those towns husbandless women, dragging fatherless children, when I think of the thousands of human beings who are going to die of starvation and disease . . . I try to find out the cause of it all.

"Each nation is calling its people to 'Come to the defense of the nation, because the war is forced upon us.' It seems to have such right on its side that it is fighting for its life, for its country, its God. But the real causes are not evident; however, you will discover that one cause of the disastrous war lies deeply rooted in the fact that those highly so-called Christian nations have never applied the gospel of Jesus Christ." (*Gospel Ideals*, pp. 271–72.)

Ether 14:24–25
"And thus we see"

 Read Ether 14:24–25 together with your family and discuss the following questions:

- What do you think Shiz would say if you could ask him why he wanted to kill Coriantumr?
- Do you think Shiz felt he was justified in seeking Coriantumr's life?
- Do you think Coriantumr would feel justified in killing Shiz if he had the chance?
- What, then, do you think they would say is the cause of the war between them?

Show your family a simple example of cause and effect (for example, you might show them that when you flip a light switch the light goes on or off, or you might explain that if you touch a hot stove you will be burned). Then have your family look again at Ether 14:25 and find the phrase that teaches about the real cause and effect. ("And thus we see.") Ask:

- Why does "and thus we see" show cause and effect?
- Why is this an important phrase in the Book of Mormon?
- According to Ether 14:24–25, what was the real cause or reason for the wars and destruction among the Jaredites?
- What do Ether 8:18–22 and Mormon 4:5 teach us about this cause and effect?

ETHER 15: THE JAREDITE NATION IS UTTERLY DESTROYED

Ether 15:1–3
The words of Ether were fulfilled

Place on a table the following items or pictures: a horoscope, a fortune cookie, and a crystal ball. Ask your family what these items have in common. Discuss how valuable these things would be if they actually predicted the future. What might be a better source for predicting or prophesying about the future?

As a family, read and compare Ether 13:20–21 with Ether 15:1–3 and discuss the following questions:

- What did Ether prophecy about Corantumr and his people?
- How did Corianumr feel when he realized that all of Ether's prophecies were coming true?
- How do you feel when you follow the prophet?

- What specific blessings have you received in your life from following a prophet?

Bear testimony that following the prophets brings peace and happiness. Rejecting the prophets leads to misery.

Ether 15:4–34
The final battles of the Jaredite nation

Ask your family to choose a favorite war they have learned about in school, at church, or in their personal study. Discuss why it is possible to have a favorite war. Tell your family that all wars bring pain and sorrow because of the loss of lives and homes and communities. Ask them in what situations might a war make sense or be good for a people in the end.

Divide the following references and questions among family members and have them find the answers. When they have finished, have them report what they learned in the order that follows:

- Ether 15:4–6. What did Coriantumr and Shiz write to each other in their letters?
- Ether 15:7–8. Where did the armies of Coriantumr and Shiz camp?
- Ether 15:9–10. Who won this battle and where did the armies of Shiz retreat?
- Ether 15:11–14. What did the people do for the space of four years?
- Ether 15:15–17. What did women and children do during these battles?
- Ether 15:18–19. Why did Shiz refuse to accept Coriantumr's offer? (See also Mormon 5:16.)
- Ether 15:20–23. How many people were left on both sides after this battle?
- Ether 15:24–25. How many people were left on both sides after this battle?
- Ether 15:26–33. Who were the last two survivors of the war and how did they die?
- Ether 15:34. Who was the lone survivor of the Jaredite nation and what was his only wish?

Ask your family to think back over what they have read in the Book of Ether and discuss whether the Jaredite war made any sense to them. Discuss some of the following questions:

- Did the war accomplish a worthy purpose?
- What do you think was the root cause of the complete destruction of the Jaredite nation?
- How did the loss of the influence of the Holy Ghost lead to their tragic end?

- What evidence can you list that the Jaredite nation for the most part had lost the influence of the Spirit?
- What are some things we can do as a family and as individuals to keep the Holy Spirit with us?

Invite family members to write in their journal what they will do this week to keep the Spirit with them.

MORONI

Moroni was the last Nephite prophet. He wrote this final book in the Book of Mormon. He included some important instructions about the Church, some of which were given by the Savior during his visit to the Americas. He also included some letters from his father Mormon and gave his final testimony to those who would receive this record in our day. He wrote this record on the gold plates before burying them in the Hill Cumorah in about A.D. 421.

MORONI 1: "I . . . WILL NOT DENY THE CHRIST"

Moroni 1:1–4
A disciple in word and deed

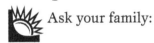 Ask your family:

- What's the worst thing someone has done to you because of your beliefs?
- How did you feel about their actions and words?
- What did you do in response?

Have family members read Moroni 1:1–3 and look for what the Lamanites wanted to do to Moroni and why they wanted to do it. Review other details of how difficult life was for Moroni by reading Mormon 7:1–5. What feelings would you expect Moroni to have had about the Lamanites?

Have someone read aloud Moroni 1:4 and ask:

- Why did Moroni continue to write? (For the benefit of the very people who sought his life.)
- What does that teach us about Moroni?
- What does this teach us about what the gospel can do about our feelings for our enemies?

Read with your family the teachings of Jesus in 3 Nephi 12:43–45 and ask how Moroni demonstrated the kinds of attitudes and actions Jesus taught us to have.

Discuss some of the following questions:

- Who are some people you might consider as your "enemy"?
- What would Moroni's example teach you about how to treat them?
- What do you think could give you strength to love all people, including enemies?
- According to Moroni 1:3, what seemed to be the source of Moroni's strength? (He would not deny the Christ—he was true and faithful always.)

Testify that the more faithful we are to Christ, the more power we will have to become like him.

MORONI 2–3: ORDINANCES IN THE EARLY CHURCH

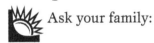 Show a picture of a family member on the day of his or her baptism, confirmation, ordination, or other sacred day. Invite family members to tell about a spiritual experience they have had in association with a priesthood ordinance or priesthood blessing.

Ask someone to explain what it means when a priesthood holder says in an ordinance or blessing that he does these things "in the name of Jesus Christ." To help answer that question, have your family turn to the entry for "Prayer" on pages 752–53 in the Bible Dictionary. Have someone read the first full paragraph on page 753 and discuss what it teaches about praying "in the name of Jesus Christ." You may want to remind them that the priesthood is the authority to act in the name of Christ.

Have family members read Moroni 2 and 3 and look for the phrase "in the name of Christ" and "in my name." They may want to mark these phrases in their scriptures. Ask:

- In both chapters, what were priesthood holders to do before they performed an ordinance or gave a blessing? (Pray in the name of Christ).
- Why do you think they were told to do that?
- Who, then, does the priesthood holder represent when he performs an ordinance or gives a blessing?
- When we receive a priesthood blessing, who, in effect, are we receiving that blessing from? (Jesus Christ.)

Invite each member of your family to express how that makes them feel about receiving or performing priesthood ordinances.

MORONI 4–5: THE SACRAMENT PRAYERS

Moroni 4:1–3–5:1–2
"To have his Spirit to be with us"

Set before the family a piece of bread and a cup of water and ask what bread and water do for our bodies. (Food and water nourish, strengthen, and renew our bodies and literally give us power to do all we do.) What kinds of things nourish and strengthen our spirits?

Have your family silently read Moroni 4 and 5. Ask the following questions:

- What does the priesthood holder do to the bread and wine? (Bless and sanctify it for our souls.)
- Why do we now use water instead of wine? (See D&C 27:1–4.)
- Once the bread and water are blessed and sanctified, we partake of them in remembrance of what? (The body and blood of Jesus—the physical symbols of his atoning sacrifice.)
- What blessing is promised at the end of each sacrament prayer?
- In what ways do the bread and water of the sacrament nourish our spirits?
- How is this similar to what food and water do for our physical bodies?

Write on one line of a sheet of paper the word "If" and on a second line the word "Then." Tell your family to read 3 Nephi 18:7, 11 and look for the "if-then" statements in those verses. As they find the statements, write the if-then statement on the sheet of paper as a principle. It may look like the following:

"If we always remember Jesus, then we will have his Spirit to be with us."

Discuss as a family how taking the sacrament each week helps us to "always remember" Jesus. Give family members a minute to think about what they will do to prepare for their next opportunity to partake of the sacrament so it will be a more meaningful event. Have each person share his or her ideas with the rest of the family.

Moroni 4:1–3–5:1–2
The sacrament prayers

 Have a priest, elder, or high priest share his feelings with the rest of your family about administering the sacrament. Ask him to briefly share ideas about the following:

- What do you do to prepare yourself to administer and bless the sacrament?
- What part of the sacrament prayers have you pondered about most and why?

- What are some of your duties when blessing, preparing, or passing the sacrament?
- What helps you focus on the Savior during this ordinance?

Share the following thoughts from Elder John H. Groberg:

"I love the Savior. I feel that as he hung upon the cross and looked out over the dark scene, he saw more than mocking soldiers and cruel taunters. He saw more than crying women and fearful friends. He remembered and saw even more than women at wells or crowds on hills or throngs by seashores. He saw more, much more. He, who knows all and has all power, saw through the stream of time. His huge, magnanimous, loving soul encompassed all eternity and took in all people and all times and all sins and all forgiveness and all everything. Yes, he saw down to you and to me and provided us an all-encompassing opportunity to escape the terrible consequences of death and sin.

"And even as he suffered for all of us, he voiced that most beautiful of all requests, 'Father, forgive them' (Luke 23:34).

"We must do our part and cry with full fervor of soul, 'Father, forgive me through the merits of thy Beloved Son as I partake of these emblems of his broken body and spilt blood for me. Please, Father, through him, forgive me! Help me to do better.'" ("The Beauty and Importance of the Sacrament," *Ensign,* May 1989, p. 40.)

Invite the priesthood holder to read the sacrament prayer aloud to family members from Moroni 4:3 and 5:2 and share his testimony of the importance of this ordinance in his life.

MORONI 6: MEMBERSHIP IN THE CHURCH

Moroni 6:1–9
Teaching and assisting new members

 Explain to your family that full-time missionaries have responsibilities to teach people the gospel, prepare them for baptism, interview them to be sure they are ready for baptism, and help them make the transition into Church membership. Moroni 6 provides important teachings to guide these efforts.

To study Moroni 6, divide your family into missionary companionships. Each set of "missionaries" is to do the following:

1. Using Moroni 6:1–3 as a guideline, make a list of questions that could be a part of an interview to see if someone is ready for baptism.

2. Using Moroni 6:1–3, make a list of principles you would be sure to teach investigators to help them desire and be prepared for baptism.

3. Using Moroni 6:4 for help, list what you will make sure happens for your investigators after they are baptized.

4. With the information found in Moroni 6:4–9, list things you will discuss with baptismal candidates to help them know what to expect as they become new members of the Lord's true church.

Have each "missionary companionship" share and compare the results of their efforts.

Concerning some of the principles in Moroni 6, President Gordon B. Hinckley has said:

"It is not an easy thing to become a member of this Church. In most cases it involves setting aside old habits, leaving old friends and associations, and stepping into a new society which is different and somewhat demanding.

"With the ever-increasing number of converts, we must make an increasingly substantial effort to assist them as they find their way. Every one of them needs three things: a friend, a responsibility, and nurturing with 'the good word of God' (Moro. 6:4.) It is our duty and opportunity to provide these things." ("Converts and Young Men," *Ensign,* May 1997, p. 47.)

As a family, discuss whom you might be able to help, and what you could do to help, as they make the transition into Christ's true church.

MORONI 7: MORMON SPEAKS OF FAITH, HOPE, AND CHARITY

Moroni 7:1–4
What is the setting and background of this chapter?

In preparation for scripture study, assign one or two family members to look at Moroni 7:1–4 and come up with five questions that can be answered in these verses. Have them focus on what they think is the most important information. Have them put their questions on a paper or poster labeled "Moroni 7" that can be displayed when the whole family is together.

When the family gathers for scripture study, show the paper or poster with the questions and invite other family members to try answering the questions. Read the verses together to find the correct answers.

Ask your family to name someone they know who they think is a "peaceable follower of Christ" and explain why they think so. Ask:

- Do you think Mormon would judge our family to be "peaceable followers of Christ"?
- Why or why not?
- What kinds of things could we do to leave no doubt as to whether we are?

Moroni 7:5–11
What is good?

Have a family member read aloud the first part of Moroni 7:6 (ending with the word "good"). Ask your family if they agree with the statement. (An evil man "*cannot* do that which is good.") Point out that this discussion depends on how we define "good." Ask someone to read aloud the rest of verse 6 and verse 7 and explain what Mormon meant. ("Good" refers to things that are "righteous" and that "profit" us in our eternal progression.)

Read together Moroni 7:8–10 and discuss the following questions:

- What two examples does Moroni give of what he meant by "good"?
- What phrase describes what could make this gift-giving and praying "good" and "profitable"? (Verse 9, "real intent of heart.")
- What distinction did Moroni make in these verses between *being* and *doing?* (Verse 10, "a man *being* evil cannot *do* that which is good.")

Share the following thoughts from Elder Dallin H. Oaks about the long-term difference between *doing* and *being:*

"Final Judgment is not just an evaluation of a sum total of good and evil acts—what we have *done.* It is an acknowledgment of the final effects of our acts and thoughts—what we have *become.* . . .

"We are challenged to move through a process of conversion toward that status and condition called eternal life. This is achieved not just by doing what is right, but by doing it for the right reason—for the pure love of Christ." ("The Challenge to Become," *Ensign,* November 2000, pp. 32, 34.)

Ask your family if they have ever tried to pretend they were somebody else or tried to act in a way that is not really the way they normally are. Consider the following questions:

- What eventually happens? (It becomes very hard to stay "in character.")
- How does Moroni 7:11 represent this idea? (Over time, who we really are—or desire to be—shows up in our actions.)
- Although this is bad news for those who live hypocritically, why is it a comforting doctrine to those who sincerely seek to follow Christ?
- If we find ourselves doing "good things" but not with "real intent of heart," what should we do?

Share the following statement from Elder Neal A. Maxwell as one answer to that question:

"What we insistently desire, over time, is what we will eventually become and what we will receive in eternity. . . .

"'Do you,' President Young asked, 'think that people will obey the truth because it is true, unless they love it? No, they will not' (in Journal of Discourses, 7:55). Thus knowing gospel truths and doctrines is profoundly important, but we must also come to love them. When we love them, they will move us and help our desires and outward works to become more holy.

"Each assertion of a righteous desire, each act of service, and each act of worship, however small and incremental, adds to our spiritual momentum. . . .

" . . . Therefore, declared President Joseph F. Smith, 'the education then of our desires is one of far-reaching importance to our happiness in life' (*Gospel Doctrine,* 5th ed. [1939], 297)." ("'According to the Desires of [Our] Hearts,'" *Ensign,* November 1996, pp. 21–22.)

Discuss with your family how the things Elder Oaks and Elder Maxwell taught can help us become good.

Moroni 7:12–19
How can we know and judge good from evil?

Turn off all the lights in the place where your family studies the scriptures, or go to some darker place in the house. Then turn on the lights again. Ask your family if they could tell the difference between the time it was dark and the time it was light. Invite someone to read Moroni 7:15 and talk about how this teaching compares to the object lesson. How easy did Mormon say it can be to judge good from evil?

Read together Moroni 7:16–17 and ask your family:

• What special gift has been given to all people to help them judge between things that draw us nearer to Christ and things that take us farther from him?

• What is the significance of the name of this gift? (The more we heed his Spirit, the closer we draw to Christ and the more we become like him).

Have someone read aloud Moroni 7:19. Ask:

• What are we to do with this light of Christ?

• Once we discern what is right, then what is our obligation? (To choose the good.)

• What will we become if we do? (Children of Christ.)

Invite family members to share experiences of how the light of Christ has operated in their lives to help them make judgments about events and experiences—such as in judging entertainment and situations they have had with friends, at work, or by themselves. Remind them that while the light of Christ shows us the way to judge, it does not force us to act. As President Thomas S. Monson has said, "Conscience always warns us as a friend before punishing us as a judge." ("Peace, Be Still," *Ensign,* November 2002, p. 54.) We must choose to have faith in the light we are given and act upon it to gain the full blessings of the light of Christ.

Moroni 7:20–39
How do we obtain faith? What are the blessings of faith?

Blindfold a member of your family. After you are sure the person cannot see, put a treat in some part of the house. Between the place where you have the treat and the place where the blindfolded person is, make sure there are several obstacles, turns, and so forth that will make the "journey" challenging. Tell the blindfolded person that two people will be giving directions. Assign one family member to give true instructions and another false instructions. Encourage the two who are giving instructions to compete for the attention of the blindfolded person. The one giving false instructions should deceive the blindfolded person, if possible, to eventually get him or her to run into walls or other obstacles.

After the activity, discuss what happened. Ask the blindfolded person how he or she finally determined which voice to listen to. Discuss how following the light of Christ is like this activity.

Have your family read Alma 32:21 and Ether

12:6, looking for an explanation of faith. How did following the voices in the activity require faith?

Have someone read Mormon's question in Moroni 7:20. Then have someone else read his answer in verse 21. Ask:

- Why does it require faith to follow the light of Christ?
- Like the example of the blindfolded person, what can happen if we exercise our faith by obeying the help we receive from the light of Christ? (We develop more confidence and attain greater faith. See also D&C 93:27–28.)

Read as a family Moroni 7:22–39 and make a list of what Mormon taught. Your list may include the following:

- The various ways we obtain faith.
- What happens when we exercise our faith.
- What happens when we don't have faith.

Invite family members to tell about things that have strengthened their faith—such as people or experiences that led them to have more faith. Invite them also to tell about a time when they had to exercise faith to "lay hold" on a "good thing."

Moroni 7:40–43
The gift of hope

Ask family members to tell about something they hoped for. Did it happen? Explain that while we normally use the word *hope* to mean something like the word *wish,* the doctrine of hope as found in the scriptures has a much more specific meaning. Have someone read the question Mormon asked at the beginning of Moroni 7:41 and then pause before reading the answer. According to Mormon, what is hope? (To have an assurance that Christ will save you if you continue to exercise faith in him.)

Have your family look at an example of someone in the scriptures obtaining this hope. Read Alma 22:15–18. As you read these verses ask:

- What did Lamoni's father want according to verse 15?

- In verse 16, what did Aaron call the thing Lamoni's father desired? (Hope.)
- According to verses 17–18, what did Lamoni's father do to obtain this hope? (Exercise his faith by calling upon God in humility and be willing to give up all his sins and live according to the ways of Christ.)

Read Moroni 7:42–43. According to Mormon, what must we do to obtain hope?

Ask your family why and how the gift of hope can be such a great blessing to the "peaceable followers of Christ" in times of great wickedness.

Moroni 7:44–48
Charity

Tell your family to think of a person who attends Church every week, is a full tithe-payer, graduated from seminary, and does his home teaching every month. Could that person be considered "nothing"? Why or why not? Invite your family to read 1 Corinthians 13:1–3 and Moroni 7:43–44 and then discuss their answers again.

At the top of a page of paper or poster board, write, "To have charity is to . . ." Have family members take turns listing one thing under the title from what they read in Moroni 7:45. As you make this list, give examples of people who are examples of that particular aspect of charity.

Next, give family members some paper and access to many different kinds of pencils, pens, crayons, markers, magazines to cut up, and so forth, and have them each draw at least one picture or make a design of some kind that represents charity or some aspect of charity. After everyone is finished, have each explain his or her picture. Figure out places to hang the pictures around the house to remind and inspire the whole family to seek for this greatest of all spiritual gifts.

Have your family read Moroni 7:47 and mark how Mormon summarized charity.

Share the following commentary from Elder Jeffrey R. Holland:

"The greater definition of 'the pure love of

Christ' . . . is not what we as Christians try but largely fail to demonstrate toward others but rather what Christ totally succeeded in demonstrating toward us. *True* charity has been known only once. It is shown perfectly and purely in Christ's unfailing, ultimate, and atoning love for us. It is Christ's love for us that 'suffereth long, and is kind, and envieth not.' It is his love for us that is not 'puffed up . . . , not easily provoked, thinketh no evil.' It is Christ's love for us that 'beareth all things, believeth all things, hopeth all things, endureth all things.' It is as demonstrated in Christ that 'charity never faileth.' It is that charity—his pure love for us—without which we would be nothing, hopeless, of all men and women most miserable. Truly, those found possessed of the blessings of his love at the last day— the Atonement, the Resurrection, eternal life, eternal promise—surely it shall be well with them." (*Christ and the New Covenant*, p. 336.)

According to Moroni 7:48, how do we obtain charity, and what will it help us become? Encourage family members to pray for charity in both personal and family prayers.

MORONI 8: MORMON EXPLAINS THAT LITTLE CHILDREN DO NOT NEED BAPTISM

Moroni 8:1–3
The concern of parents for children

Read Moroni 8:1–3 with your family and have them look for words and phrases that help us know how Mormon felt about his son, Moroni. Give each family member an opportunity to choose a word or phrase and explain what it teaches us about the father's feelings for his son.

Discuss the following questions:

- Who else was "mindful" of Moroni besides Mormon? (Jesus Christ.) How do you think Mormon knew this? (You may want a parent to tell about a time when the Spirit helped

him or her know how much the Lord loves his or her children.)
- How often did Mormon think and pray about Moroni?
- How do you think that made Moroni feel? (Have a parent tell about a time when he or she gained strength from knowing that someone was thinking about and praying for a child. Assure your family that you pray for them often and encourage all family members to remember each other in their prayers.)
- What did Mormon especially pray would happen in Moroni's life? (You may want to tell about some of the things you especially pray for in the lives of your family members.)

Moroni 8:5–28
Little children and baptism

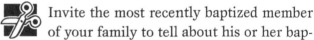 Invite the most recently baptized member of your family to tell about his or her baptism. Make sure the person discusses why he or she was baptized, what the requirements were for being baptized, who did it, how the person felt about the experience, and what difference it has made in his or her life. Name a family member who is an infant or small child, or name a small child your family knows. Ask your family why he or she is not baptized.

Have someone read Moroni 8:5 aloud and identify the problem Mormon heard about among the Nephites. Then take turns reading Moroni 8:6–26, pausing with each verse to record on a paper or poster anything that verse teaches about the following:

- Why little children *do not* need baptism.
- Why all accountable people *do* need baptism.

Note: As you list and discuss together these verses, you may want to read D&C 68:25–28 to find the age at which we begin to become accountable and need baptism and the things parents are required to teach their children to help prepare them for baptism.

After looking at the two lists you made from Moroni 8:6–26, ask:

- What do these verses teach us about the power of the Atonement?
- How should these things affect the way we deal with little children?
- What impact should these teachings have on those of us who have been baptized?

Have your family look again at the blessings promised in Moroni 8:26 to those who will sincerely receive baptism and the Holy Ghost. Ask them to share the difference it would make in our homes and communities if we continually possessed these gifts.

Tell your family that instead of the "meekness" and "hope" and "love" promised above, the Nephites were experiencing a very different condition. Read together Moroni 8:27–29 and answer the following questions:

- How would you describe the condition of the Nephites at this time?
- What reason did Mormon give for why the Nephites were on the verge of destruction? (Verses 27–28.)
- What do you think is the most striking difference between the life the Nephites had and the promises they could have had in verses 25–26.
- Why do you think the Nephites chose to "reject so great knowledge" as they once had?

Have family members offer suggestions about how our baptismal covenants can be a bigger influence in our lives from day to day. The following statement from Elder Robert D. Hales may help in your discussion:

"When we understand our baptismal covenant and the gift of the Holy Ghost, it will change our lives and will establish our total allegiance to the kingdom of God. When temptations come our way, if we will listen, the Holy Ghost will remind us that we have promised to remember our Savior and obey the commandments of God. . . .

"By choosing to be in His kingdom, we separate—not isolate—ourselves from the world. Our dress will be modest, our thoughts pure, our language clean. The movies and television we watch, the music we listen to, the books, magazines, and newspapers we read will be uplifting. We will choose friends who encourage our eternal goals, and we will treat others with kindness. We will shun the vices of immorality, gambling, tobacco, liquor, and illicit drugs. Our Sunday activities will reflect the commandment of God to remember the Sabbath day and keep it holy. We will follow the example of Jesus Christ in the way we treat others. We will live to be worthy to enter the house of the Lord.

"We will be examples 'of the believers, in word, in conversation, in charity, in spirit, in faith, in purity' (1 Tim. 4:12).

"We will receive 'a mighty change . . . in our hearts, that we have no more disposition to do evil, but to do good continually.' We will keep our 'covenant with our God to do his will, and to be obedient to his commandments in all things . . . all the remainder of our days.' (Mosiah 5:2, 5.)

"We will demonstrate that we 'are desirous to . . . be called his people, and are willing to bear one another's burdens, that they may be light;

"'Yea, and are willing to mourn with those that mourn; yea, and comfort those that stand in need of comfort.' (Mosiah 18:8–9.)" ("The Covenant of Baptism: To Be in the Kingdom and of the Kingdom," *Ensign,* November 2000, pp. 7–8.)

MORONI 9: MORMON WRITES ABOUT WICKEDNESS IN THE LAND

Moroni 9:1
What does this letter contain?

Invite your family to find the word Mormon used in Moroni 9:1 to describe the contents of this letter ("grievous"). Have someone look up this word in a dictionary and share the meaning with the rest of the family. Explain to your family that Mormon wrote this at the time when the Nephite civilization was nearly destroyed because of wickedness (as described in Mormon 1–6).

Be aware that this chapter gives a more detailed description of the wickedness of the Nephites and Lamanites than any other part of the Book of Mormon. You may want to prepare ahead of time how to approach the more graphic descriptions—especially for the less-mature members of your family.

Moroni 9:4–26
How do we deal with those who are very wicked?

Have your family put together a list of phrases that describe the society Mormon and Moroni lived in by looking at Moroni 9:5, 8–13, 18–20. Discuss how a follower of Christ might respond to such a society. Then read together Moroni 9:4, 6, 21 and have family members select phrases that describe what Mormon did amid such wickedness, and why he did it.

Share the following comment from Bishop Glenn L. Pace:

"The great prophet Mormon set another example worthy of emulation. He lived at a time that was hopeless. Imagine this: 'There were no gifts from the Lord, and the Holy Ghost did not come upon any, because of their wickedness and unbelief.' (Morm. 1:14)

"In spite of this hopeless situation Mormon led their armies, for, in his words, 'Notwithstanding their wickedness I . . . loved them, according to the love of God which was in me, with all my heart; and my soul had been poured out in prayer unto my God all the day long for them.' (Morm. 3:12.)

"This prophet had Christlike love for a fallen people. Can we be content with loving less? . . .

"When we get emotionally and spiritually involved in helping a person who is in pain, a compassion enters our heart. It hurts, but the process lifts some of the pain from another. We get from the experience a finite look into the Savior's pain as He performed the infinite

Atonement. Through the power of the Holy Ghost, a sanctification takes place within our souls and we become more like our Savior. We gain a better understanding of what was meant when He said, 'Inasmuch as ye have done it unto one of the least of these my brethren, ye have done it unto me.' (Matt. 25:40.)

"As the last days unfold, we will see all the prophecies fulfilled. We will see today's problems compounded, and we will see new challenges scarcely imaginable at this time. We must reach out to those who are suffering from these events. We must not become fatalistic or judgmental—even if we warn the people in the world something a thousand times and they heed us not." ("A Thousand Times," *Ensign,* November 1990, pp. 8, 10.)

Ask your family how they think we can maintain such attitudes. What counsel did Mormon give his son in Moroni 9:25–26 that could help us?

MORONI 10: MORONI'S FINAL TESTIMONY AND PROMISE

Moroni 10:1–33
Moroni's exhortations

Have a family member look up the word *exhort* in a dictionary and read the definition to the rest of the family. Have someone else read Moroni 10:1–2 and find what Moroni said he wanted to do in this last chapter of the Book of Mormon. (Speak a few words "by way of exhortation.") Help your family find and highlight the word *exhort* in verses 3, 4, 7, 8, 18, 19, 27, 30.

On a poster or large paper write, "I exhort you to . . ." Use this poster or paper to make a list that summarizes Moroni's exhortations in this final chapter of the Book of Mormon. As you identify each thing Moroni exhorted us to do, discuss it as a family. Use the ideas below to help in your discussion.

Verse 3—Remember God's mercy and ponder it

Since Moroni exhorted us to do this as we read the Book of Mormon, invite your family to give examples from the Book of Mormon that testify of God's mercy. Ask which one most impresses them and why.

Verse 4—Ask God if these things are true

Have your family find the phrases in verse 4 that describe how we should ask God (sincere heart, real intent, having faith in Christ). Discuss each of these phrases. Explain that each phrase seems to mean that we must be genuine and willing to live according to whatever God would reveal to us. Faith implies that we try to live what we've learned before asking for this special manifestation. Read also verse 5 and ask what Moroni said about how we will know. Ask your family what we must do to be worthy for the Holy Ghost to give us this witness.

This would be an excellent time to have family members tell about times when they have felt the Holy Ghost as they have studied the Book of Mormon as a family. Tell them that this is a witness that the things in the book are true. You may also want to invite your family to make special efforts to ask God in private prayer for the witness of the Holy Ghost regarding the truthfulness of the things they have read in the Book of Mormon.

Verse 7—Deny not the power of God

Ask your family to think of ways people deny the power of God. (See also D&C 58:31–33.) When we choose to disobey counsel that comes from God, what are we saying to God about his wisdom and our wisdom? (That we know better than he does.)

Verse 8—Deny not the gifts of God

Ask your family to search verse 8 for the reason God gives us spiritual gifts. Read verses 9–17 with your family and have them mark all the spiritual gifts mentioned there. Explain that this is a

just a small sampling of the many gifts of the Spirit.

Share the following list of some "less-conspicuous" gifts that Elder Marvin J. Ashton compiled:

"The gift of asking; the gift of listening; the gift of hearing and using a still, small voice; the gift of being able to weep; the gift of avoiding contention; the gift of being agreeable; the gift of avoiding vain repetition; the gift of seeking that which is righteous; the gift of not passing judgment; the gift of looking to God for guidance; the gift of being a disciple; the gift of caring for others; the gift of being able to ponder; the gift of offering prayer; the gift of bearing a mighty testimony; and the gift of receiving the Holy Ghost." ("There Are Many Gifts," *Ensign,* November 1987, p. 20.)

Elder Dallin H. Oaks said that "spiritual gifts come to those who have received the gift of the Holy Ghost," but that they "do not come visibly, automatically, and immediately to all. . . .

"The scriptures tell us that we should desire and zealously seek spiritual gifts. (See D&C 46:8; 1 Cor. 12:31; 14:1, 11.) . . . In every case, the receipt of spiritual gifts is predicated upon faith, obedience, and personal righteousness. . . .

"We should seek after spiritual gifts. They can lead us to God. They can shield us from the power of the adversary. They can compensate for our inadequacies and repair our imperfections." ("Spiritual Gifts," *Ensign,* September 1986, pp. 68–69, 72.)

Verse 18—Remember that every good gift comes from Christ

Ask your family what the Lord is telling us when he gives us spiritual gifts. (That he loves us and is helping us to become like him—now, and in eternity).

Verses 19 and 24—Remember that as long as we believe in Christ we will have the gifts of the Spirit

Have your family read verses 19 and 24 and tell what Moroni says is the only reason spiritual gifts would be taken away from us. Ask how we can show that we believe in Christ and desire to be more like him through the gifts he bestows. President George Q. Cannon suggested a way in the following statement you could share with your family:

"If any of us are imperfect, it is our duty to pray for the gift that will make us perfect. . . . No man ought to say, 'Oh, I cannot help this; it is my nature.' He is not justified in it, for the reason that God has promised to give strength to correct these things, and to give gifts that will eradicate them. If a man lacks wisdom, it is his duty to ask God for wisdom. The same with everything else. That is the design of God concerning His Church. He wants His Saints to be perfected in the truth. For this purpose He gives these gifts, and bestows them upon those who seek after them, in order that they may be a perfect people upon the face of the earth." (*Millennial Star,* April 1894, p. 260.)

Remind your family that when we quit desiring to become like the Savior, that is when we lose the gifts of the Spirit.

Verses 30–33—Come unto Christ

Have your family search verses 30–33 and find phrases that describe how we come unto Christ. (Touch not the unclean thing; arise from the dust; deny ourselves of all ungodliness; love God with all our might, mind, and strength; deny not his power.) Ask your family to explain what they think each of those things means (for example, how do we know what is godly or not? What is symbolized by "might, mind, and strength"? How are we tempted to deny God's power?)

Ask your family if they have ever worried about attaining the level of perfection required to live as God lives. Tell them that Moroni teaches us some truths that can help with that concern. Ask:

- What does Moroni say will occur when we come unto Christ? (Verses 32–33, by his grace we will become perfect in Christ—sanctified, clean, and like him.)
- What things have we read in the Book of Mormon that demonstrate this power in people's lives?
- How have you seen it work in your own life?
- How have the things we have read in the Book of Mormon brought you closer to Christ?

Moroni 10:34
A final testimony

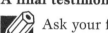 Ask your family whom they would like to see and talk to when they die. Read as a family 2 Nephi 33:10–15, Ether 12:38–41, and Moroni 10:27, 34. Ask:

- Whom will we see after we die? (Nephi and Moroni—the first and last writers of the Book of Mormon.)
- Why will we stand before them?
- What will they have to say to us?
- How do you imagine you will feel when you meet them?
- What would you like to say to them?

Invite members of your family to share their testimony of the Book of Mormon. You may want to take the time and formally write them out (as did Nephi and Moroni and others) and keep these written testimonies in a special place in your family history.

BIBLIOGRAPHY

Andrus, Hyrum. *Joseph Smith: The Man and the Seer.* Salt Lake City: Deseret Book, 1960.

Asay, Carlos A. *Family Pecan Trees: Planting a Legacy of Faith at Home.* Salt Lake City: Deseret Book, 1992.

Ballard, M. Russell. *Counseling with Our Councils: Learning to Minister Together in the Church and in the Family.* Salt Lake City: Deseret Book, 1997.

Ballard, Melvin J. *Melvin J. Ballard: Crusader for Righteousness.* Salt Lake City: Bookcraft, 1966.

Barrett, LaMar C. *Discovering the World of the Bible.* Provo, Utah: Brigham Young University Press, 1974.

Benson, Ezra Taft. Address at Mission Presidents' Seminar, 3 April 1985. Cited in *Missionary Guide: Training for Missionaries.* Salt Lake City: The Church of Jesus Christ of Latter-day Saints, 1988.

———. *God, Family, Country: Our Three Great Loyalties.* Salt Lake City: Deseret Book, 1974.

———. *The Teachings of Ezra Taft Benson.* Salt Lake City: Bookcraft, 1988.

———. *A Witness and a Warning: A Modern-day Prophet Testifies of the Book of Mormon.* Salt Lake City: Deseret Book, 1988.

The Book of Mormon for Latter-day Saint Families. Ed. Thomas R. Valletta et al. Salt Lake City: Bookcraft, 1999.

Brewster, Hoyt W., Jr. *Isaiah Plain and Simple: The Message of Isaiah in the Book of Mormon.* Salt Lake City: Deseret Book, 1995.

Brigham Young University 1988–89 Devotional and Fireside Speeches. Provo: Brigham Young University Press, 1989.

Brigham Young University 1990–91 Devotional and Fireside Speeches. Provo, Utah: Brigham Young University, 1991.

Brown, Hugh B. *The Abundant Life.* Salt Lake City: Bookcraft, 1965.

Brown, James. *Autobiography of James Brown.* Salt Lake City, 1941.

BYU Speeches of the Year, 1967. Provo, Utah: Brigham Young University, 1968.

Cannon, George Q. *Gospel Truth: Discourses and Writings of President George Q. Cannon.* 2 vols. Ed. Jerreld L. Newquist. Salt Lake City: Deseret Book, 1974.

The Children Sing. Salt Lake City: Deseret News Press, 1951.

Children's Songbook. Salt Lake City: The Church of Jesus Christ of Latter-day Saints, 1989.

Clark, J. Reuben. *Behold the Lamb of God.* Salt Lake City: Deseret Book, 1991.

Collected Discourses, Delivered by President Wilford Woodruff, His Two Counselors, the Twelve Apostles, and Others. 5 vols. Comp. Brian H. Stuy. Burbank, Calif.: B.H.S. Publishing, 1987–92.

Concise Lincoln Dictionary of Thoughts and Statements. Comp. Ralph B. Winn. New York: New York Philosophical Library, 1959.

Cook, Gene R. *Raising Up a Family to the Lord.* Salt Lake City: Deseret Book, 1993.

Doctrines of the Book of Mormon: The 1991 Sperry Symposium. Ed. Bruce A. Van Orden and Brent L. Top. Salt Lake City: Deseret Book, 1991.

Dyer, William G., and Phillip R. Kunz. *Effective Mormon Families: How They See Themselves.* Salt Lake City: Deseret Book, 1986.

Eyring, Henry B. *To Draw Closer to God: A Collection of Discourses.* Salt Lake City: Deseret Book, 1997.

Family Home Evening Resource Book. Salt Lake City: The Church of Jesus Christ of Latter-day Saints, 1984.

Farlie, Henry. *The Seven Deadly Sins Today.* Washington: New Republic Books, 1978.

Featherstone, Vaughn J. *A Generation of Excellence.* Salt Lake City: Bookcraft, 1975.

For the Strength of Youth. Salt Lake City: The Church of Jesus Christ of Latter-day Saints, 2000.

Gospel Principles. Salt Lake City: The Church of Jesus Christ of Latter-day Saints, 1997.

Grant, Heber J. *Gospel Standards.* Comp. G. Homer Durham. Salt Lake City: Deseret Book, 1981.

Hanks, Richard K. "Eph Hanks, Pioneer Scout." Master's thesis, Brigham Young University, 1973.

Harris, Franklin S., Jr. *The Book of Mormon: Message and Evidences.* Salt Lake City: Deseret News Press, 1961.

Hinckley, Bryant S. *Sermons and Missionary Service of Melvin J. Ballard.* Salt Lake City: Deseret Book, 1949.

Hinckley, Gordon B. *Be Thou an Example.* Salt Lake City: Deseret Book, 1981.

———. *Teachings of Gordon B. Hinckley.* Salt Lake City: Deseret Book, 1997.

———. *Way to Be!* New York: Simon & Schuster, 2002.

His Servants Speak. Comp. R. Clayton Brough. Bountiful, Utah: Horizon, 1975.

Holland, Jeffrey R. *Christ and the New Covenant: The Messianic Message of the Book of Mormon.* Salt Lake City: Deseret Book, 1997.

Hunter, Howard W. *That We Might Have Joy.* Salt Lake City: Deseret Book, 1994.

Hymns of The Church of Jesus Christ of Latter-day Saints. Salt Lake City: The Church of Jesus Christ of Latter-day Saints, 1985.

International Dictionary of Thoughts. Chicago: J. G. Ferguson Publishing, 1969.

Jones, Gracia N. *Emma and Joseph, Their Divine Mission.* American Fork, Utah: Covenant Communications, 1999.

Journal of Discourses. 26 vols. London: Latter-day Saints' Book Depot, 1854–86.

Kimball, Spencer W. "Circles of Exaltation." Brigham Young University devotional address, 28 June 1968.

———. *Faith Precedes the Miracle.* Salt Lake City: Deseret Book, 1972.

———. *The Miracle of Forgiveness.* Salt Lake City: Bookcraft, 1969.

———. *The Teachings of Spencer W. Kimball.* Ed. Edward L. Kimball. Salt Lake City: Bookcraft, 1982.

Latourette, Kenneth Scott. *A History of the Expansion of Christianity.* Grand Rapids, Mich.: Zondervan, 1970.

Lee, Harold B. *Stand Ye in Holy Places.* Salt Lake City: Deseret Book, 1974.

———. *The Teachings of Harold B. Lee.* Ed. Clyde J. Williams. Salt Lake City: Bookcraft, 1996.

———. *Youth and the Church.* Salt Lake City: Deseret News Press, 1945.

Lewis, C. S. *Mere Christianity.* New York: Collier Books, 1960.

Love. Salt Lake City: Deseret Book, 1986.

Ludlow, Daniel H. *A Companion to Your Study of the Old Testament.* Salt Lake City: Deseret Book, 1981.

———, ed. *Encyclopedia of Mormonism.* New York: Macmillan, 1992.

Maxwell, Neal A. *All These Things Shall Give Thee Experience.* Salt Lake City: Deseret Book, 1980.

———. *Even As I Am.* Salt Lake City: Deseret Book, 1982.

———. *Notwithstanding My Weakness.* Salt Lake City: Deseret Book, 1981.

———. *Plain and Precious Things.* Salt Lake City: Deseret Book, 1983.

———. *Sermons Not Spoken.* Salt Lake City: Bookcraft, 1985.

———. *Things As They Really Are.* Salt Lake City: Deseret Book, 1978.

McConkie, Bruce R. *Doctrinal New Testament Commentary.* 3 vols. Salt Lake City: Bookcraft, 1973.

———. *Doctrines of the Restoration: Sermons and Writings of Bruce R. McConkie.* Ed. Mark L. McConkie. Salt Lake City: Bookcraft, 1989.

———. *Mormon Doctrine.* 2d ed. rev. Salt Lake City: Bookcraft, 1966.

———. *The Millennial Messiah.* Salt Lake City: Deseret Book, 1982.

———. *The Mortal Messiah.* 4 vols. Salt Lake City: Deseret Book, 1979–81.

———. *A New Witness for the Articles of Faith.* Salt Lake City: Deseret Book, 1985.

———. *The Promised Messiah.* Salt Lake City: Deseret Book, 1978.

McConkie, Joseph Fielding, and Donald W. Parry. *A Guide to Scriptural Symbols.* Salt Lake City: Bookcraft, 1990.

McConkie, Joseph Fielding, and Robert L. Millet. *Doctrinal Commentary on the Book of Mormon.* 4 vols. Salt Lake City: Bookcraft, 1987–92.

McKay, David O. *Gospel Ideals: Selections from the Discourses of David O. McKay.* Salt Lake City: Improvement Era, 1953.

———. *Home Memories of President David O. McKay.* Comp. Llewelyn R. McKay. Salt Lake City: Deseret Book, 1956.

———. *True to the Faith.* Comp. Llewelyn R. McKay. Salt Lake City: Bookcraft, 1966.

Nibley, Hugh. *Collected Works of Hugh Nibley.* 14 vols. Salt Lake City: Deseret Book and Provo, Utah: Foundation for Ancient Research and Mormon Studies, 1986–2000.

———. *Teachings of the Book of Mormon, Semester 3.* Provo, Utah: Foundation for Ancient Research and Mormon Studies, 1993.

Nibley, Preston. *Brigham Young, the Man and His Work.* Salt Lake City: Deseret News Press, 1936.

Nyman, Monte S. *Great Are the Words of Isaiah.* Salt Lake City: Bookcraft, 1980.

Nyman, Monte S., and Robert L. Millet. *The Joseph Smith Translation—The Restoration of Plain and Precious Things.* Provo, Utah: BYU Religious Studies Center, 1985.

Oaks, Dallin H. *Pure in Heart.* Salt Lake City: Bookcraft, 1988.

Our Family. Salt Lake City: The Church of Jesus Christ of Latter-day Saints, 1980.

Our Heritage: A Brief History of The Church of Jesus Christ of Latter-day Saints. Salt Lake City: The Church of Jesus Christ of Latter-day Saints, 1996.

Packer, Boyd K. "Teach the Scriptures." Address to Religious Educators, 14 October 1977.

———. *Teach Ye Diligently.* Salt Lake City: Deseret Book, 1975.

———. *That All May Be Edified.* Salt Lake City: Bookcraft, 1982.

Parry, Donald W., Jay A. Parry, and Tina M. Peterson. *Understanding Isaiah.* Salt Lake City: Deseret Book, 1998.

Petersen, Mark E. *The Great Prologue.* Salt Lake City: Deseret Book, 1975.

Pratt, Parley P. *Autobiography of Parley P. Pratt.* Salt Lake City: Deseret Book, 1961.

———. *Writings of Parley Parker Pratt.* Salt Lake City, 1952.

Rasmussen, Ellis T. *A Latter-day Saint Commentary on the Old Testament.* Salt Lake City: Deseret Book, 1993.

Reynolds, George, and Janne M. Sjodahl. *Commentary on the Book of Mormon.* 7 vols. Salt Lake City: Deseret Book, 1955–61.

Richards, LeGrand. *A Marvelous Work and a Wonder.* Salt Lake City: Deseret Book, 1976.

Smith, Hyrum M., and Janne M. Sjodahl. *The Doctrine and Covenants Commentary.* Salt Lake City: Deseret Book, 1978.

Smith, Joseph. *History of The Church of Jesus Christ of Latter-day Saints.* 7 vols. Ed. B. H. Roberts. Salt Lake City: The Church of Jesus Christ of Latter-day Saints, 1932–51.

———. *Lectures on Faith.* Salt Lake City: Deseret Book, 1985.

———. *Teachings of the Prophet Joseph Smith.* Sel. Joseph Fielding Smith. Salt Lake City: Deseret Book, 1938.

Smith, Joseph F. *Gospel Doctrine.* Salt Lake City: Deseret Book, 1939.

Smith, Joseph Fielding. *Answers to Gospel Questions.* 5 vols. Salt Lake City: Deseret Book, 1957–66.

———. *Church History and Modern Revelation.* 4 vols. Salt Lake City: Deseret Book, 1947–49.

———. *Doctrines of Salvation.* 3 vols. Comp. Bruce R. McConkie. Salt Lake City, Deseret Book, 1954–56.

———. *Man, His Origin and Destiny.* Salt Lake City: Deseret Book, 1954.

Smith, Lucy Mack. *History of Joseph Smith by His Mother.* Salt Lake City: Stevens and Wallis, 1945.

———. *The Revised and Enhanced History of Joseph Smith by His Mother Lucy Mack Smith.* Ed. Scot Facer Proctor and Maurine Jensen Proctor. Salt Lake City: Bookcraft, 1996.

Sperry, Sidney B. *Book of Mormon Compendium.* Salt Lake City: Bookcraft, 1968.

Talmage, James E. *The Articles of Faith.* Salt Lake City: Deseret Book, 1984.

Top, Brent L., Larry E. Dahl, and Walter D. Bowen. *Follow the Living Prophets.* Salt Lake City: Bookcraft, 1993.

Wassermann, Jacob. *Columbus, Don Quixote of the Seas.* Boston: Little, Brown, and Co., 1930.

Welch, John W. "Chiasmus in the Book of Mormon." *Book of Mormon Authorship.* Ed. Noel B. Reynolds. Salt Lake City: Bookcraft, 1982.

Whitney, Orson F. *Life of Heber C. Kimball.* Salt Lake City: Bookcraft, 1945.

Widtsoe, John A. *Evidences and Reconciliations.* Salt Lake City: Bookcraft, 1960.

Young, Brigham. *Discourses of Brigham Young.* Comp. John A. Widtsoe. Salt Lake City: Deseret Book, 1954.

TOPICAL INDEX

Note: Some scripture entries include more than one lesson or activity. For example, the index entry for Alma 43:1–22 also includes the activity for Alma 43:8–9.

Accountability: Alma 9:18–23
Activities. *See* Games
Adoption: Mosiah 25:12
Adversity: 1 Nephi 1:1; 16:18–25, 31; 2 Nephi 2:1–4
Agency: 2 Nephi 2:11–12, 15–16, 27–29; 24:12–23; Alma 29:4–5
Ancestors: 3 Nephi 25:1, 5–6
Angels: Mosiah 3:1–4; 3 Nephi 17:23–25
Anger: Alma 20:8–16; 25:1–3
Antichrist: Alma 30:6–29
Apathy: Alma 59:1–13
Apostasy: Alma 47:36
Apostles, Nephite: 3 Nephi 19:4–14
Arguing: Helaman 1:1–13
Armor of God: Alma 44:18
Atonement: 1 Nephi 10:4–6; 2 Nephi 2:3–27; 9; Mosiah 3:5–18; 4:1–3; 13:27–35; 16:6–8; Alma 7:11–18; 33:18–22; 34:8–14; 36:11–25; 39:15–19; 42:16–25; 55:1–25; 3 Nephi 27:14; Moroni 8:5–28
Attitude: 1 Nephi 3:1–7; 7:5–12; 16:18–25, 31; 17:1–6; Jacob 7:26; Mosiah 4:24–25

Baptism: Mosiah 15:6–13; 18:1–11, 13–14; 3 Nephi 11:18–27, 33–34, 37–41; 14:13–14; 27:16, 20; Moroni 8:5–28
Beatitudes: 3 Nephi 12:1–12
Blessings: Mosiah 10:1–10, 19–21; 26:15–20; Alma 3:22–26; 26:17–21; Helaman 4:21–26; 6:7–13; 15:10–16
Boasting: Mormon 4:1–8
Bodies as temples: Alma 3:4–19
Borrowing: Mosiah 4:28

Charity: Alma 50:25–36; Ether 12:28–41; Moroni 7:44–48

Chastening: 1 Nephi 16:1–5, 37–39; Helaman 8:1; 5:1–3; 3 Nephi 6:20–30
Chiasmus: Alma 36:1–30
Children: Moroni 8:5–28
Choices: Mosiah 19:1–8; Alma 2:7–11
Church, mission of: Alma 6:1–8; 3 Nephi 27:1–22
Commandments: Alma 37:13–17
Commitment: Alma 24:11–19; 3 Nephi 1:1–23
Condemnation: Mormon 9:31
Condescension: 1 Nephi 8:1–36; 11:16, 26; 2 Nephi 7:6
Consecration: 4 Nephi 1:1–3
Consequences: Alma 16:1–3, 9–11; 37:6–10; Helaman 6:18, 20–24, 31–40; 7:1–3, 21–29; Ether 7:1–27
Contention: Alma 11:23–41; 21:5–10; 51:1–21; 60:15–22; Helaman 1:1–13; 4:1–10; 3 Nephi 11:28–31
Conversion: Enos 1:5–8; Mosiah 5:1–2; Alma 20:17–27; 23:1–7, 16–18; 24:1–10; 25:13–17; 3 Nephi 18:22–25; Moroni 6:1–9
Councils: Mosiah 22:1–16; 29:25–27; Alma 38:10–15; 52:19
Counterfeit: Mormon 4:11–14
Courage: Mosiah 13:1–10
Covenants: 1 Nephi 22:1–12; 2 Nephi 30:1–8; Mosiah 5:5–12; 18:1–11; 21:1–4; Alma 24:11–19; 27:20–24; 44:8–20; 46:11–24; 53:10–17
Criticism: 1 Nephi 5:4–6; 3 Nephi 7:14

Death: Alma 28:10–12; 46:39–41; 60:12–13; Mormon 6:7–8
Desires: Alma 29:1–5, 13; 3 Nephi 28:1–7
Diligence: Mosiah 4:27
Discipleship: Mosiah 26:21–24; Alma 5:13–62; 7:1–7; 10:11, 13–17; 13:3–13; 3 Nephi 15:11–16
Dishonesty: Alma 47:1–36
Disobedience: 2 Nephi 7:10–11; 9:27–39; Mosiah 9:1–18; 12:1–8; Alma 41:8–10; 50:20–22

Education: 2 Nephi 9:28–29
Elijah: 3 Nephi 25:5–6
Endurance: 3 Nephi 27:16–17, 19, 22
Enemies: Moroni 1:1–4